WORKING CAPITAL MANAGEMENT
Strategies and Techniques

SECOND EDITION

HRISHIKES BHATTACHARYA

Formerly, Professor of Finance and Control
Indian Institute of Management Calcutta

PHI Learning Private Limited

New Delhi-110001
2009

Rs. 375.00

WORKING CAPITAL MANAGEMENT—Strategies and Techniques, 2nd ed.
Hrishikes Bhattacharya

ISBN-978-81-203-3636-0

The export rights of this book are vested solely with the publisher.

Twelfth Printing (Second Edition) ... ... **September, 2009**

Published by Asoke K. Ghosh, PHI Learning Private Limited, M-97, Connaught Circus, New Delhi-110001 and Printed by Baba Barkha Nath Printers, New Delhi-110015.

Dedicated to

Dr. Mohit Kumar Sarkar

— the Good Samaritan

Contents

Preface

The first edition of this book was published in 2001. Since then, it has seen nine reprints, which I must admit, indicate the growing popularity of the book. This has encouraged me to improve the quality of the book by updating it with the recent researches on the subject.

Working capital management continues to hold the central position (a source of constant headache to corporate and functional managers!) in the fast changing business environment. This is true for a very small enterprise as well as a large corporation. In the former case the problem is more acute (and perhaps, the only problem) due first to the inadequate knowledge on the subject and second to the comparative inaccessibility of institutional finance. In this revised edition, I have specially addressed the problems of small and medium enterprises (SMEs).

I have been receiving suggestions from academics and students that I should incorporate my work on the theories of trade credit, as without this a book on working capital management remains incomplete. In Chapter 2, I have critically reviewed major works on the subject and indicated their usefulness and limitation in practical applications. During the recent years, Logistics and Supply Chain Management has enlarged the domain of working capital management. Although substantial work has been done on the technical and operational aspects of this emerging discipline, not much attention is paid to the financial side of the problem. A new chapter is added in this edition where both the operational and financial aspects of logistics and supply chain management are discussed (Chapter 8). All other chapters are updated as far as possible, though one cannot claim completeness in this ever-changing world of management.

Over the last six years I have received numerous suggestions from my colleagues and students towards improvement of this book. I thank all of them for being so kind to me. I avoid any particular mention, because I fear that it may leave out many. I must, however, express my gratitude to Biswajit Saha and Subal Mukherjee of Indian Institute of Management Calcutta and Maharathi Basu of the Centre for Monitoring Indian Economy who helped me in updating the book by providing literature and necessary data.

I must thank Ms. Pushpita Ghosh, Managing Editor and Marketing Director of PHI Learning, New Delhi, and her editorial and production staff for being very helpful and patient to me in all stages of preparing the manuscript for the second edition of this book.

My daughter, Orphi and son, Saraswat, have now become busy in their own vocations. But their growing knowledge in commerce and computing has cleared many of my doubts. My wife, Gouri, continues to be as tolerant as ever.

Hrishikes Bhattacharya

Preface to the First Edition

Working Capital is so much in use in common parlance and is so much misunderstood. Even among the professional managers the controversy and confusion persist. While an accountant will regard working capital as current assets minus current liabilities and call it the net working capital, a finance manager will consider gross current assets as the working capital. Both may be true, but their concerns differ. The former's concern is arithmetical accuracy, trained as he is to tally the two sides of the balance sheet. But the finance manager's concern is to find the fund for each item of current assets at such costs and risks that the evolving financial structure remains balanced between the two.

Suppose one asks a production controller: what is working capital? His answer is very simple and straightforward. To him working capital is the fund needed to meet the day-to-day working expenses, i.e. to pay for materials, wages and other operating expenses. Is there any difference between the statements of the accountant, the finance manager, and the production controller? In the ultimate analysis, the latter may be true, but according to the accountant or the finance manager it is the very working expenses that get blocked in current assets along the productive-distributive line of an enterprise, and the net working capital is that liquidity which takes care of the working expenses if the line gets extended due to any reason.

But the notion of liquidity itself has undergone considerable changes with the advances in financial management during the recent years. Liquidity has so far been defined as a pyramid of current assets in descending order of realisability with cash holding the top position and inventory, the last. This notion has given rise to liquidity ratios such as current ratio or quick ratio, and later to the concept of *net working capital*. The pyramid is now upside down with inventory at the top. When we examine the pipeline theory of working capital (Chapter 1), we will find that the pipeline of the productive-distributive system of an enterprise consists of only inventories which, at different stages, take on different names like work-in-process, finished goods, accounts receivable, cash balance, etc. Working capital structure is being so designed today in efficient organisations as to take care of this fundamental liquidity of an enterprise with zero or even negative net working capital. In Chapter 6 we will analyse this evolving working capital structure.[1]

---

[1] Chapter 7 in the present edition

With the development of financial markets the concept of liquidity has undergone further transformation. It is no longer liquidity **per se** but access to liquidity that has taken the centre-stage of liquidity management. The beginning was made with the emergence of credit cards. Access to liquidity frees the resources for profitable investments. A number of direct financial instruments like commercial paper, or indirect (off-balance sheet) instruments like forward rate agreement, have emerged to provide a market for accessing quick liquidity. The market is also getting ready to provide such access not only to firms with high creditworthiness but also to those who do not have such a good standing in the market, by the mechanism of credit enhancement. Some of these emerging market instruments are discussed in the later part of Chapter 6.[2]

Accounts receivable capture a major share of working fund of an enterprise. Hence the trade credit policy should be such as to increase the value of the business, without endangering it. Marketing people in their bid to sell, often forget that the profit margin of the sale might be more than offset by extending uneconomic line of credit. The same happens with improper credit selection. The probability of bad-debt increases with the length of credit, but at the same time trade credit is a means of increasing sales, particularly when a firm desires to increase its market share. Credit policy problems should, therefore, be jointly addressed by the finance and marketing functions.

While trade credit blocks the working fund, cash discount releases it at one stroke. This is not to be construed as a distress policy for firms in difficulty. The discount policy worked out within a present value framework can result in quickening of cash flows on a continuous basis and at the same time in lowering down the incidence of bad-debts. Cash discount acts as a great incentive for the buyers to pay up early because it effectively reduces the cost of materials. These issues are discussed in Chapters 2, 3 and 5.[3]

In Chapter 3, we will see that inventory management has come to major focus in the working capital management of an enterprise.[4] While the risk of being out of stock is very high both on the production floor and in the marketing outlets, overstocking eats into the profitability of an enterprise both in terms of cost of fund and wastage of materials. It has been found that some items of inventories are held for more than a year's requirement. Discretionary purchase of small value inventories, the allurement of quantity discounts and also the availability of longer credit lines at the times of glut in supply, contribute to overstocking. Anxiety of the finance manager is to find fund for carrying such inventories and to protect the firm against overtrading in the latter case. Of all the various models developed so far to enable an enterprise to decide on an appropriate quantity purchases and, therefore, the level of inventory, economic order quantity (EOQ) model, invented as early as 1915, has stood the test of

---

[2] *Ibid*
[3] Chapter 3, 4 and 6 in the present edition
[4] Chapter 4 in the present edition

time because of its amenability to evolving complexities of inventory management. The EOQ model and its variations are dealt with extensively in Chapter 3.[5]

It is often claimed that all the order-point models, derived from EOQ specifications, are good for the control of inventories, but they do not work so well in manufacturing situations where the management controls production as well as inventories of components. A more effective solution can be found in material requirement planning (MRP) which takes a total view of the manufacturing operations of a business. The bill of materials, linked to master production schedule, gives out data on each type of material in hand and lead time available to procure additional units so that the production runs without hiccups.

Besides MRP, Chapter 3 also introduces just-in-time inventory management, Kanban System and other advancements in the discipline.[6]

During the past one and a half decade, cash flow approach to liquidity management has been gaining ground over the funds flow approach and has come to be firmly established in the discipline of financial management. Although in the ultimate analysis the funds gap shall always be equal to cash gap, an incorrect understanding of profit and cash can cause severe liquidity problem simply because all the profit may not contain cash and, it is by cash alone that one pays the bills.

Within the cash flow framework, day-to-day management of liquidity can be done with the help of certain well-established models. Most important among them are those developed by Baumol, Miller and Orr, and Stone. These models are discussed in Chapter 4 with their applicability and limitations in real-life situations.

Cash collection is integral to both accounts receivable and cash management. Despite the emergence of the electronic payment system, cheque continues to be the dominant mode of payment and post office as the delivery agent. As discussed in Chapter 5, the payer enjoys the float from the date he mails the cheque to the date of its actual encashment through bank clearing (which also provides him additional float).[7] Faced with such a situation the Accounts receivable manager sets up collection centres with or without the aid of a banking system. Concentration banking and Lockbox system are two such popular methods widely used in the United States and across European countries. In India, concentration banking has been in practice for a long time but Lockbox system is yet to gain popularity.

Management of current assets is different from management of current liabilities. The latter include accounts payable, bank loan and other short-term sources of finance. Accounts payable being the opposite face of accounts receivable, the trade credit policy of the supplier, to a large extent, influences the accounts payable policy of the debtors.

---

[5] *Ibid*
[6] *Ibid*
[7] Chapter 6 in the present edition

The major source of financing the working capital requirement is commercial bank. In India, security-oriented lending was replaced by need-based financing with the adoption of the Tandon Committee's recommendations by the Reserve Bank of India in 1975. The Chore Group followed it up in 1979 and streamlined the cast credit system of financing. What emerged ultimately came to be known as MPBF system in which bank finance is made available under a given current ratio and norms for holding different current assets as prescribed by the Reserve Bank of India from time to time. In spite of adequate flexibility provided for in the system, it acquired rigidity over a period of time, and thus became unable to meet the demand of the industry and trade during the post-liberalisation period. A study of the credit policy documents of various banks reveals that the MPBF system continues to hold the basic structure of their lending systems, except the incorporation of the cash flow based appraisal methodology. In Chapter 6 we will discuss the existing appraisal system of commercial banks with the help of a case study.[8] We will also study some alternative short-term instruments which can aid financing a part of working capital requirements of a firm.

This book is an outgrowth of my one and a half decade of tenure with a commercial bank and a similar period of teaching, training and consultancy experience at the Indian Institute of Management Calcutta. Numerous examples, illustrations and case studies are presented to explain every concept introduced in this book. All the mathematical models are explained arithmetically for ease of understanding and application.

Primarily addressed to postgraduate students of management institutes and universities, who are majoring in finance, the book would be equally useful to students of professional bodies like Institute of Chartered Accountants of India, Institute of Costs and Works Accountants of India, and Institute of Company Secretaries. The book will also be of immense help to practising finance managers who are engaged in working capital management and control, and to purchase managers, materials controllers and inventory managers who have the unenviable task of keeping a balance between the demands of production and costs of procurement.

January 2001   **Hrishikes Bhattacharya**

---

[8] Chapter 7 in the present edition

Acknowledgments

The contributions made by many of my PGP students who have reviewed and prepared the summary for each chapter, have enriched the book. Special mention must be made of Mahesh Subramaniam and Niraj Gupta who have not only reviewed the chapters allotted to them but also corrected several mistakes which escaped my attention.

The well-drawn illustrations, produced by Debabrata Pathak out of my free hand sketches, were of immense help. Subal Mukherjee and Asit Manna together brought out excellent copies from the PC, which were then xeroxed by a team comprising Patras Singh, Md. Illias and Sudhakar Khan. I am extremely thankful to all of them.

As always, my family bears the major brunt of my writing a book of this volume. They simply do not get me. My wife Gouri has become used to it for long. My daughter Orphi and son Saraswat, having grown up in this environment, have by now become tolerant. But all of them love to see my books in print.

I am pleased to express my sincere appreciation to the publishers, PHI Learning for their support and assistance throughout the production of this book.

Hrishikes Bhattacharya

CHAPTER 1

Working Capital: A Techno-Financial Analysis

Never cross the border
Wisdom says
There's fire beyond the border

INTRODUCTION

In economics, capital is often used to refer to capital goods consisting of a great variety of things, namely machines of various kinds, plants, houses, tools, raw materials and goods-in-process[1]. A finance manager of a firm looks for these things on the assets side of the balance sheet. For capital, he turns his attention to the other side of the balance sheet and never commits the mistake—as warned by the economists—of adding the two together while taking the census of total capital of the business[2]. His purpose is to balance the two sides in such a way that the net worth of the firm increases without increasing the riskiness of the business. This balancing may be called financing, i.e. financing the assets of the firm by generating streams of liabilities continuously to match with the dynamism of the former.

The term 'liability' implies a promise to be fulfilled. By making promises to various parties, including the shareholders, the firm obtains funds to install plant and machinery which, in the process of operation, generate various kinds of operating assets wherein further funds get blocked. The balance sheet of a firm on a particular date reveals this blockage phenomenon while profit and loss account narrates simply the operations of the business; the latter, to a great extent, is independent of the balance sheet except affecting the net worth by a profit or loss. It may be noted here that two similar profit and loss accounts of two firms may not have similar balance sheets because financing of the operations and also the blockage pattern peculiar to these two firms might give rise to two different pictures.

NATURE OF CURRENT ASSETS

Although assets denote wealth. an entrepreneur may not like to hold many of the assets appearing on the balance sheet. While he may like to hold fixed

---

1. Samuelson, P.A. and W.D. Nordhaus, *Economics,* 18th ed., McGraw-Hill, Kogakusha, Tokyo, 2005.
2. *Ibid.*

assets like plant and machinery which generate goods and services (the sale of which gives him a profit), he would hate to hold 'current assets' like debtors, stock or even cash. He would like to imagine himself in a situation where his production process takes very little time to convert the input to finished product which gets sold immediately in cash the moment it rolls out of the process; and the input market is so perfect that any amount of raw material is available at any time at a fixed price. But the entrepreneur's dream is hardly realised. He finds, instead, that his production process takes quite some time; the finished products are not sold so quickly which means a quantity of stocks remains in the godown. Moreover, the sales are not always in cash—some amount of credit has to be given and the input market is so uncertain that he has to keep a certain amount of safety stock all the time. The 'non-ideal' technology and market thus generate certain assets which are called current assets. The entrepreneur does not like them because, in effect, these current assets block his funds which should have been otherwise available to him for meeting working expenses. Each and every current asset of a firm is, therefore, nothing but congealed fund for working expenses. And because business is a continuous process, every cycle of operation generates these current assets which need to be funded for immediate financing of working expenses. This funding for working expenses is done by, what we popularly call, *working capital.*

THE CONTROVERSY

The concept of working capital was, perhaps, first evolved by Karl Marx, though in a somewhat different form. Marx used the term 'variable capital' meaning outlays for payrolls advanced to workers before the goods they worked on were complete. He contrasted this with 'constant capital' which according to him, is nothing but 'dead labour', i.e. outlays for raw materials and other instruments of production produced by labour in earlier stages which are now needed for live labour to work with in the present stage[3]. This 'variable capital' is nothing but wage fund which remains blocked—in terms of financial management—in work-in-process along with other operating expenses until it is released through sale of finished goods. Although Marx did not mention that workers also gave credit to the firm by accepting periodical payment of wages which funded a portion of work-in-process, the concept of working capital, as we understand today, was embedded in his 'variable capital'.

But with the evolution of the concept came the controversy about the definition of working capital. Guthmann and Dougall[4] defined working capital as excess of current assets over current liabilities. This view was elaborated by Park and Gladson[5] when they defined working capital as the excess of current assets of a business (cash, accounts receivables, inventories, for example) over

---

3. Luxemburg, Rosa, *The Accumulation of Capital,* Modern Reader Paperbacks, Monthly Review Press, New York, 1968.
4. Guthman, H.G. and H.E. Dougall, *Corporate Financial Policy,* 2nd ed., Prentice-Hall, Inc., New York, 1948.
5. Park, C. and J.W. Gladson, *Working Capital,* Macmillan, New York, 1963.

current items owed to employees and others (such as salaries and wages payable, accounts payable, taxes owed to government). Gole[6] also held more or less the same view. This concept of working capital, as has been commonly understood by the accountants, is more particularly understood as net working capital to distinguish it from gross working capital (to which we are coming later). Walker[7] held that this concept is useful to groups interested in determining the amount and nature of assets that may be used to pay current liabilities. These interested groups, as suggested by Walker, mostly composed of creditors, particularly the supply creditors who may be concerned to know the 'margin of safety' available to them should the realisation of current assets be delayed for some reasons. But it is doubtful whether supply creditors do pay so much attention to this margin of safety which is commonly indicated by current ratio or more precisely by quick ratio. The falling current ratio and quick ratio of UK manufacturing companies, during the recent decades, well below the standard 2 and 1 respectively[8] are indicators of the diminishing reliance on this net concept. It has also been found that these two ratios based on net working capital have not been found to be very good predictors of bankruptcy, possibly because they are *static* indicators.[9]

This accountant's view of working capital, i.e. *net working capital* is based on 'gone concern approach' and, therefore, does not appeal much to modern finance managers who take on a 'going concern approach' where both the current assets and current liabilities have a dynamic stability. To them, the primary objective of working capital management is to maintain and/or improve upon this dynamic stability. When a business is a going concern, market practices evolve a pattern by which a portion of sales as also of supplies are never paid for and a minimum level of inventory never leaves the system because, although there are continuous payment and issues of inventory, fresh liabilities and assets are also contracted continuously according to the established pattern. The job of a modern finance manager has, therefore, been enlarged from only finding finance for the business as in olden days to the management of all current assets and current liabilities so as to ensure an intra-dynamic stability among them and inter-dynamic relationship between them. This leads us to the gross concept of working capital.

GROSS WORKING CAPITAL vs GROSS CURRENT ASSETS

Gross working capital and gross current assets are often referred to as synonymous or interchangeable terms.[10] Although, arithmetically speaking, the

6. Gole, V.L., "The Management of Working Capital", *Australian Accountant*, June 1959, pp. 229–250.
7. Walker, E.W., *Essential of Financial Management*, 2nd ed., Prentice-Hall of India, New Delhi, 1974.
8. Kirkman, P., "Working Capital Management", *in: Issues in Finance*, M. Firth and S.M. Keane (Eds.), Philip Allen Publishers, Oxford, 1986.
9. *Ibid.*
10. Bogen, J.I., *Financial Handbook*, Ronald Press, New York, 1948.

two, culled from a balance sheet, will always be equal but some conceptual elaboration is necessary to make it operational.

Although economists regard fixed capital as what is represented by long-term assets, a finance manager defines fixed capital as that having long-term maturity. It is not essential for a finance manager to restrict utilisation of the fixed capital to finance fixed assets only; rather, as a good finance manager, he would like the fixed capital to finance a part of current assets also in addition to financing fixed assets. There may also be a situation where all his fixed and current assets are financed from fixed capital only. In the latter case, he will have current assets but no current liability, but we cannot say that the firm does not have any need for working capital. The firm might not desire to contract current liability, but its operations would have generated current assets which have to be funded to ensure continuity of production. Capital needed to fund these current assets is called gross working capital. This fund is, in fact, an additional fund over and above the fund required to meet working expenses of the firm. For example, if total cost of sales of, say ten units of output is Rs. 100, a single venture firm producing only ten units and selling in cash would at best require Rs. 100 as working capital. If the firm has sold on credit, say for three months, then because it is a single venture firm, it would still require no more than Rs. 100 as working capital plus, perhaps the interest cost. If, however, it is a going concern, then its first dose of working capital would be blocked in work-in-process and then in debtors, and hence it would need additional fund equal to the amount of these two assets so that its fund for working expenses of successive batches of production is released. Similarly all other current assets, so generated, block the current fund of the business almost perpetually, and here, the distinction between fixed assets and current assets is virtually blurred from the point of view of funds analysis. The production manager manages each piece of plant and machinery to keep it optimally productive— the asset itself being not a constraint for him though the capacity may be—the finance manager has to treat each item of current assets as a constraint for the ultimate productivity of the plant and machinery and hence the firm. Management of current assets is, therefore, distinct from the management of fixed assets. But more important than this tautology is that because of the dynamism of the current assets the finance manager has to be constantly on guard to ensure that their dynamic stability is not impaired to affect the net worth of the firm negatively. Gross current assets should, therefore, be understood by their own meaning, connotation and effect on the firm and should not be mechanically equated with gross working capital just because arithmetically the two may appear to be same in a balance sheet.

Besides, the funding operations of the current assets are quite distinct from the management of current assets. A modern day finance manager first projects the level of current assets of the firm under a projected sales and then tries to find out sources to finance these current assets in such a way that cost of capital is optimised. Management of gross current assets and gross working capital or simply working capital, as some writers prefer to call it, are not one and the same. The total of projected current assets is an aggregate figure for which capital has to be raised and the two may not have any bearing on each other. The profiles of the types of capital so raised in regard to the risk, opportunity for gain or loss and also the cost are different from that of current assets.

LIMITATIONS OF OPERATING CYCLE THEORY: CURRENTNESS CONCEPT

The second controversy relates to the currentness of assets and liabilities that enter into the domain of working capital management. For many years the most popular definition of current assets has been 'cash, bank balances and other resources that are reasonably expected to be realised or consumed within one year from the date of the balance sheet' and that of current liabilities has been 'those obligations of the enterprise that are reasonably expected to be liquidated within one year from the date of the balance sheet, either through the use of resources classified as current assets or through the creation of other current liabilities.'[11] These two definitions were under attack immediately after the publication of IASC monograph because in case of both current liabilities and current assets, there may be firms where maturity period of any of the items may be more than a year. Most glaring example, besides trade liabilities, is the bank finance for working capital under cash credit system. Many such bank overdrafts are, in reality, medium-term finance, although, in theory, they are repayable on demand. Bankers would raise serious objections to any firm's attempt to delete this item from current liabilities, but in reality, cash-credit liability of a firm has lost its currentness long time back. This is one of the reasons why in the Western world and also in Japan cash credit system has long been replaced by loan system. In India, its acceptability is rather slow, though it was recommended by Chore Committee as early as 1979.[12]

Park and Gladson[13] held that the one year temporal standard to determine the currentness was arbitrary and not universally valid. What was current or non-current depended on the nature of core business activity marked by technological requirements and trading practices. He used the term *natural business year* within which an activity cycle is completed. The yardstick for judging currentness of an item, both of assets and liabilities, would be this 'natural business year'. It could be three months for a fruit-processing unit or two to three years for a ship-building firm. This 'natural business year' concept was developed later into operating cycle (OC) theory of working capital. Accounting Principles Board of the American Institute of Certified Public Accountants while defining working capital used this operating cycle concept. Numerous attempts have later been made to find more satisfactory definition of

---

11. International Accounting Standards Committee, *Current Assets and Current Liabilities*, IAS–13, 1978.
12. Reserve Bank of India, Report of the Working Group to Review the System of Cash Credit, headed by K.B. Chore, Bombay, August, 1979. See also Chapter 7 for further discussion.
13. Park, C. and J.W. Gladson, *ibid.*

working capital, usually linked to the length of the operational cycle of the business, but none of these has come to be generally acceptable.[14]

In India, perhaps the first attempt to capture the essence of 'natural business year' and translating it to operating cycle was made by Chakraborty.[15] He defined 'currentness' on the basis of operating cycle and stated that any item liquidating itself or getting converted into cash within the OC period is a 'current' item, the rest are 'non-current'. It is necessary to go, at length, into the calculation of operating cycle proposed by him to understand its meaning and limitation.

Chakraborty identified four current assets, viz. raw materials in store, work-in-progress, finished goods in store and receivables, and only one item of current liabilities, i.e. trade creditors, to calculate operating cycle of a business. The operating cycle of Union Carbide India was calculated by him from published accounts as shown in Table 1.1.

Table 1.1 Operating Cycle of Union Carbide India

Item	Formula used	No. of days for Union Carbide
1. Raw materials in store	$\dfrac{365 \times \text{Average stock of raw materials}}{\text{Annual consumption of raw materials}}$	105
2. Work-in-progress (conversion process)	$\dfrac{365 \times \text{Average stock of work-in-progress}}{\text{Cost of finished goods produced}}$	14
3. Finished goods in store	$\dfrac{365 \times \text{Average stock of finished goods}}{\text{Cost of goods sold}}$	23
4. Receivables	$\dfrac{365 \times \text{Average receivables}}{\text{Sales during the year}}$	16
	Total	158

Chakraborty assumed that the company was able to secure 55 days credit from suppliers of raw materials (although it is not clear why he made this assumption and also whether these 55 days represent consumption days or purchase days of raw materials) and deducting this from the days of raw materials in store he finally calculated operating cycle of Union Carbide as 103 days (50 + 14 + 23 + 16).

The methodology adopted by Chakraborty in calculating operating cycle contradicts the conceptual frame work presented by him. The 103 days operating cycle for Union Carbide India is, in fact, net operating cycle of the

14. Kirkman, P., *ibid.*
15. Chakraborty, S.K., "Management of Working Capital and the Operating Cycle Concept", *Economic and Political Weekly*, August 25, 1973.

company which is more or less equivalent to net working capital. This cannot be equated with 'natural business year' of the company within which all the current items mature. Suppose, for example, the company could manage to obtain credit from its suppliers equal to or more than 158 days,[16] then according to the methodology adopted, the company would have zero or negative operating cycle. A situation like this, though very probable, betrays the concept of operating cycle because in such cases, all the current items would either mature on zero days or on 'negative days'. In fact, Ramamurthy found it odd enough to have negative operating cycle for rubber plantation industry. He could not explain it theoretically except saying that this was due to suppliers' credit being nearly for a year.[17] Chakraborty, perhaps, mixed up the operating cycle of a business with the financing of it and finally landed with the net working capital. If we conform to the definition of operating cycle as emanated from the concept of 'natural business year', then for Union Carbide the operating cycle should be 158 days and not 103 days or if the credit available from the market is more than 158 days, say 160 days, then the operating cycle should be 160 days and neither 158 days nor (–)2 days. If, therefore, we follow the logic of 'natural business year', then the true operating cycle of a business should be either the days of current assets or current liabilities (trade creditors under this concept) whichever is higher. Only in such an operating cycle all current items, as considered by Chakraborty, will mature.

LIMITATIONS OF OPERATING CYCLE THEORY: PROJECTION OF WORKING CAPITAL

While there could be some justification in following operating cycle theory for judging the currentness of assets and liabilities, but Chakraborty went a little further. He calculated working capital (net) turnover of Union Carbide India as 3.5 (365/103) and projected working capital (net) requirement of the company for a projected sale of Rs. 5280 lakh as Rs. 1310 lakh by dividing the projected operating expenses (treated with inflationary price rise of 6 percent) with the working capital turnover (3.5). The implicit assumption here is that projected operating expenses and the working capital turnover, as derived from operating cycle, are divisible. That they are not can be proved by the following analysis.

Let us first put the operating cycle proposed by Chakraborty in algebraic form as some writers have done:[18]

$$OC = (R_t - C_t) + W_t + F_t + D_t$$

where R_t, C_t, W_t, F_t and D_t are days of holding of raw materials inventory,

16. Such a situation need not be imaginary particularly in India, where many firms manage to obtain such long credit by exploiting numerous small suppliers. It may also happen when a unit has become financially sick and is unable to pay the creditors.
17. Ramamoorthy, V.E., *Working Capital Management*, Institute for Financial Management and Research, Madras, 1976.
18. Sen, P.K., "An Alternative Approach to Operating Cycle Concept for Estimating Working Capital Needs," *Mimeo*, Indian Institute of Management Calcutta, 1985.

supply credits, work-in-progress inventory, finished goods inventory and debtors respectively.

This form of presentation (which is correct in terms of operating cycle concept laid down by Chakraborty) may lead us to a mathematical fallacy because we are led to assume that all the ts representing days are similar, universal and comparable. If we refer back to the calculations of OC days shown earlier, we will find that R_t of 105 refers to raw material consumption days, W_t of 14 refers to days of cost of production, F_t of 23 means days of cost of goods sold and D_t of 16 represents days of sales. All these 'days' are not similar because these are not derived from a common numerator or denominator. These are distinct 'days'. Since the variables come successively as in a chain, we may know at best the blockage of fund at each stage in terms of number of days of operating expenses of that stage (but that too is incorrect as we shall see later). The exercise on operating cycle theory with all its shortcomings should have stopped here. Extending it to the forecasting of working capital requirement of a firm creates all the more problems.

Reversibility Test

The 3.5 times turnover of operating cycle or net working capital of Union Carbide India means simply that the fund blocked in net current assets got released 3.5 times in a year. While agreeing that working capital is needed to meet all operating expenses of a firm, dividing the projected operating expenses with the turnover of the operating cycle will be wrong because each component of the operating cycle had been derived with different numerators and denominators and none of them was the *operating expenses* of the firm. If the numerator was common all through, then it could be so divisible because only in such a case the model would have satisfied the reversibility condition. But as this condition was violated we could not go back to the net working capital level prevalent in Union Carbide during the year 1970. Let us prove this point from the following analysis.

Total operating expenses of the company in 1970 were Rs. 3935.30 lakh; dividing it with 3.5 turnover rate, the net working capital of the company in 1970 should have been Rs. 1124.37 lakh. Let us now calculate the actual net working capital for the same period on the same basis.

	(Rs. in lakh)
Average stock of raw materials	545.80
Average work-in-progress	140.00
Average stock of finished goods	262.40
Average receivables	210.00
Average gross current assets	1158.20
Less: Average sundry creditors	
(converting 55 days credit to consumption	
of raw materials as in the example)	285.70
Average net current assets or net working capital	
level for 1970	872.50

All the above current assets and liabilities are taken as average of opening and closing balances because operating cycle has been calculated on this basis only.

Now if the given methodology was correct, we should get back to the above figure of net working capital but, instead, we have got an entirely different figure. This is because different numerators were used for calculating all the above variables to obtain days of holding. If the same numerator, i.e. operating expenses was used throughout, then we should have obtained the same figure in both forward and backward calculations. The turnover of net working capital so derived from operating cycle cannot, therefore, be used to project the net working capital requirement of a firm.

While elaborating on the concept, it was stated that the meaning of the operating cycle was that each rupee put into the business on the first day of the year would start again in the cycle of operations immediately after the passage of operating cycle days. As pointed out earlier, each component of operating cycle represents funds blocked into it in terms of a particular expense item. This may not have anything to do with actual days for which the fund is blocked. Particular problem is created here by the work-in-progress, the holding of which has been derived in terms of days of cost of production. These 'days' may be totally different from the actual days taken by a particular process. A certain number of days of cost of production may be held in the process for a different number of actual days and the fund will be released from the process only after these technical days. Hence, a rupee put to the process gets released not after the cost of production days but after the process or technical days. Any calculation of operating cycle or 'natural business year' of a firm should, therefore, be based on actual days of holding of the current assets and not on their financial days.

Cash Concept of Operating Cycle

Chakraborty did not shift basically from his proposition in his subsequent writings.[19] Only, possibly in his last work on this subject, he drew special attention to each component of operating cycle rather than on the cycle itself claiming that component-wise computation of forecasted cash funds was better than applying one single operating cycle duration and deriving working capital needs from its turnover.[20] However, there had not been any fundamental shift from his basic theory on this issue. In fact, he said the same thing in a different way.

Richards and Laughlin[21] proposed a weighted cash conversion cycle (WCCC). It measures the weighted number of days funds are tied up in

19. Chakraborty, S.K., "Cash Working Capital vs Balance Sheet Working Capital", *Economic and Political Weekly*, March 9, 1974.

20. Chakraborty, S.K., et al., *New Perspectives in Management Accounting*, Macmillan, New Delhi, 1979, pp. 110–125. This view was also upheld by V.E. Ramamoorthy, *Ibid.*

21. Richards, V.D. and E.J. Laughlin, "A Cash Conversion Cycle Approach to Liquidity Analysis", *Financial Management*, Spring 1980, pp. 32–38.

inventories and receivables less the weighted number of days cash payments are deferred to suppliers. The weights used to perform the adjustment are determined by dividing the amount of cash tied in each component by the final value of the product (sales). WCCC is developed in two stages. In the first stage, the weighted number of days that funds are tied up in raw materials inventory, working-in-process inventory, finished goods inventory and accounts receivable are calculated, which when added up gives rise to weighted operating cycle (WOC). In the second stage, weighted number of days funds provided by accounts payable are calculated. These days are then deducted from WOC to derive WCCC. The model looks like the following.

$$WOC = w\ (RMI_D + WIPI_D + FGI_D + AR_D) + x\ (WIPI_D + FGI_D + AR_D)$$
$$+ y\ (FGI_D + AR_D) + z\ (AR_D)$$

and

$$WCCC = WOC - p\ (AP_D)$$

where

RMI_D = Raw materials inventory in days of consumption of raw materials
$WIPI_D$ = Work-in-process inventory in days of cost of production
FGI_D = Finished goods inventory in days of cost of goods sold
AR_D = Accounts receivable in days of (credit) sales
AP_D = Accounts payable in days of purchases

w, x, y, z and p are weights assigned to the above variables in terms of sales in the following manner:

  (a) Weight for RMI_D = w = Raw materials consumption during the period/Sales
  (b) Weight for WIP_D = x = (Cost of production – Raw materials consumption)/Sales
  (c) Weight for FGI_D = y = (Cost of goods sold – Cost of production)/ Sales
  (d) Weight for AR_D = z = (Sales – Cost of goods sold)/Sales
  (e) Weight for AP_D = p = Accounts payable/Sales

Note that the sum of w, x, y and z will be equal to zero.

The model prescribed by Richards and Laughlin is definitely an improvement over unadjusted operating cycle theory of Chakraborty and others. But the additive nature of the model implicitly assumes that all the variable-days are similar, while in fact they are not: consumption days of materials inventory are not similar to cost of production days of work-in-process inventory.

Pandey adopted this method in his book, "Financial Management".[22] But in the example worked out there he excluded depreciation while calculating cash cost of production and cash cost of goods sold but did not deduct proportionate depreciation amount from work-in-process inventory and finished goods inventory. Similarly, the same adjustment for depreciation was made in

---

22. Pandey, I.M., *Financial Management,* 8th ed., Vikas Publishing House, New Delhi, pp. 809–814, 1999.

arriving at cash cost of goods sold but neither the depreciation element nor the profit element was adjusted against debtors, which was taken as face value. All these contaminated the result further.

Operating cycle theorists claim that money is blocked first in raw materials; labour and other conversion costs come later; selling and distribution costs come in the end. Thus all items do not need cash support for the entire operating cycle days. Hence, the need for aggregate working capital could be more accurately derived by considering each component of working capital. It is doubtful whether in an ongoing business, expenses are incurred in such a sequential manner. However, going back to Chakraborty we find that probably he did not mean it because in calculating turnover rates for each phase of operating cycle he adopted a going concern approach. He first calculated the total length of operating cycle in terms of days as usual and then calculated turnover rates for each phase of operating cycle taking into account only the expense items particular to a component and its total blockage period in the cycle. That is, cash blocked in raw materials would last for the whole of operating cycle while manufacturing expenses (exclusive of raw materials) blocked in work-in-progress stage, selling and distribution costs blocked in finished goods storage and the sales blocked in debtors would last from their sequential commitment to the remaining period of the operating cycle. Under this method Chakraborty came to a net working capital which is different from the one he derived by dividing the projected operating expenses with the turnover of net working capital and claimed that the former was a more correct estimate. Arithmetically, the resultant figures under both the two methods must be the same. The difference was due to taking debtors on sales value, where besides operating expenses, an element of profit was also included. Under his first method the total operating expenses were divided by the net working capital turnover to arrive at the projected level of net working capital.

TOWARDS AN ALTERNATIVE THEORY OF WORKING CAPITAL

In earlier sections, we have argued that 'natural business year' or operating cycle theory has only limited use to judge the currentness of some of the balance sheet items, provided we take into account the *actual* days of blockage of fund in a current asset and not the financial days. Further, we cannot use this concept in its present form for projection and management of working capital of a firm.

In business operations, a firm generates quite a few 'other' assets besides what have been taken into consideration in calculating the operating cycle. Some of these assets are, advances made to suppliers and employees (not of long-term nature), security deposits with suppliers or with various statutory authorities, current account balances with customs, port trust, excise department, etc. advance received against sales, advance income tax, minimum cash balances, etc. Operating cycle theory does not capture these items. Any of these assets and liabilities may fall outside the operating cycle days and hence, should be taken out of the 'current' list according to that theory. If these items are not current items, then how do we term and manage them? Sometime back, Reserve Bank of India invented a term *non-current asset* which, however, was not defined by them clearly except by way of examples in the prescribed credit appraisal format that included some of the items mentioned above, though not all. From an analysis of the examples given by Reserve Bank of India, we are led to believe that non-current assets are half-way between fixed assets and current assets as we understand normally. Their convertibility into cash is restricted (as in the case of encumbered fixed deposits) or doubtful due to passage of time (as in the case of debtors more than six months' old). Banks have been asked not to take these items into account while calculating working capital requirement of a firm. Obviously Reserve Bank of India wanted the firm to finance these non-current assets from its long-term resources. This was more in the nature of a policy decision of Reserve Bank of India to gradually reduce the level of short-term lending to commercial sector than making an attempt to properly define the nature of these assets.

Total Systems View

The items mentioned above are almost compulsorily generated out of operations of the business. Whatever name one can ascribe to them, there is no denying that current funds of the firm get blocked in these assets. And like all other 'current liabilities or assets' these groups of items also have a dynamic stability. And hence, a finance manager's worry is not solved by simply taking them out of the *current list*. In fact, finance managers are increasingly disillusioned with the traditional division of assets and liabilities into current and non-current headings. A research monograph of American Institute of Certified Public Accountants suggested that we should now begin to move away from the current/non-current classification.[23]

Whatever new classifications may emerge from these exercises, a finance manager needs a theory and tools by which he can estimate true working capital requirement of the firm and manage various assets and liabilities generated out of operations of the business in such a way that their dynamic stability is maintained and/or improved. In this section we shall lay down the foundation for developing an alternative theory and tool of working capital management, which can take care of these requirements.

We start with the basic premise put forward earlier that once a firm has installed plant and machinery, it needs capital to finance working expenses required to generate sales. This capital, which is needed to pay for working expenses, is what we call *working capital*. Instead of making disputable distinction between 'current and non-current' assets (and hence liabilities) we shall simply concentrate on items which are generated out of operations where funds, otherwise available for meeting working expenses, get blocked (in liabilities where it gets released).

---

23. American Institute of Certified Public Accountants, "Financial Reporting and Evaluation of Solvency", *Accounting Research Monograph*, No. 3, 1978.

SYSTEMS APPROACH: PIPELINE INVENTORIES

We shall first adopt a systems approach in analysing the production and distribution process of a manufacturing firm and then examine their financial implications to evolve a theory of working capital. This theory will then be applied to forecast working capital requirement of a firm and to indicate a methodology for its control and management.

A productive system can be defined as the means by which resource-inputs are transformed into utility products or services. A distributive system is defined as the means by which such utility products are distributed to consumers. The process by which inputs are transformed into outputs is popularly called conversion process. This is determined by the technology adopted by a particular firm. It is central to the productive-distributive system of a manufacturing business. By linking it backwardly to the input market and forwardly to the output market we can determine levels of holding of assets at various stages of the system. A finance manager has to take an integrated view of the whole system for proper management of working capital. In the present study we shall take up each sub-system individually and then link them together to an integrated system.

Productive System

Let us assume that the conversion process of a productive system has three sequential stages, S_1, S_2 and S_3, taking 6 hours, 4 hours and 8 hours respectively. The technology being given, the operations manager will find that there will be idle time and consequent overheads between stages. He will, therefore, have to balance the line in such a way that there is minimum idle time. Although sophisticated computerised procedures are available to solve complex line balancing problems, a straightforward way to solve a somewhat simple problem like this is to take the lowest common multiple of designated hours of each stage and increase the number of work places under each stage accordingly.[24] In the present case the LCM being 2, S_1 will have three workplaces and S_2 and S_3 will have two and four workplaces respectively. Assuming that there is sufficient demand in the market and the process is continuous, the balanced conversion line will generate 12 units every day—the determining factor being the highest hourly time amongst the three stages—and the cycle time will be 2 hours. We can present this balanced conversion process in the form of a flow chart as shown in Figure 1.1.

---

24. Buffa, E.S., *Modern Production Operations Management*, 7th ed., Wiley Eastern, New Delhi, 1984.

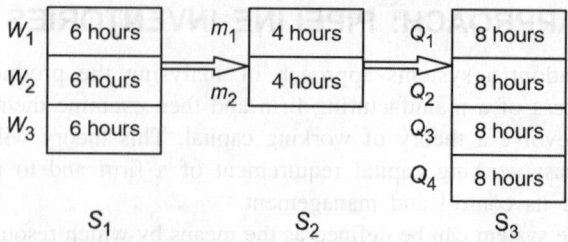

Note: W_1, m_1 and Q_1 are workplaces for stages S_1, S_2 and S_3 respectively.

Figure 1.1 Flow chart of conversion process.

Excepting the first operation of the conversion process given in Figure 1.1 the line will run continuously with no stage remaining idle any time, and produce one unit every two-hour. But an examination of the conversion process will reveal that in order to enable the process to produce one unit every two-hour all workplaces of each stage must always be full. That is, in all, 9 units of inputs will always be in the pipeline.

Distributive System

Let us now design an elaborate distribution system of the outputs produced in this firm. As the process is continuous, flow of finished goods from the conversion process is 12 units per day. This finished goods inventory passes through various stages of the distribution system before it reaches the final consumer. With this passage of goods there is always some passage of time which holds up some amount of inventory all the time along the pipeline. Let us make the following reasonable assumptions to devise a distribution system.

(a) Goods produced from the process are immediately transferred to the factory storage and then the day's productions are transferred to warehouse everyday. It takes one day to transfer the goods from factory to warehouse.

(b) Warehouse takes five days to handle the goods and process orders from the distributor, and it takes five days to transport goods from warehouse to distributor.

(c) Distributor takes two days for handling and processing of orders. Transport time from distributor to retailer is three days.

(d) Retailer takes one day for handling and processing, and transports the goods to the final consumers in one day on thirty days credit.

On the basis of the above assumption average holding along the distribution pipeline is given in Table 1.2.

Table 1.2 Pipeline Inventory of Finished Goods
(Average Flow of Goods—12 Units per Day)

Sequences		Average time in days	Average pipeline inventory (12 × no. of days)
1.	Factory storage	1	12
2.	Factory to warehouse	1	12
3.	Handling and processing delay at warehouse	5	60
4.	Warehouse to distributor	5	60
5.	Handling and processing delay with distributor	2	24
6.	Distributor to retailer	3	36
7.	Handling and processing at the retailer	1	12
8.	Retailer to consumer	1	12
	Total	19	228

Pipeline Inventories

We can now present a flow chart in Figure 1.2 for the entire distribution system of the firm with the help of Table 1.2 after adding to it the selling sub-system assuming that a day's production of 12 units get sold every day on 30 days credit.

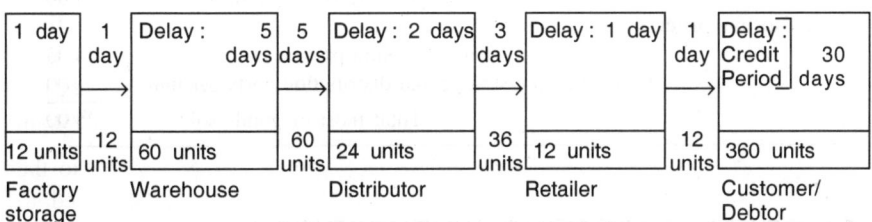

Figure 1.2 Flow chart of distribution process.

It may be seen from Figure 1.2 that pipeline inventory of the distribution system as a whole is 588 units of which finished goods inventory is 228 units and debtors, 360 units. Assuming now that one unit of input is producing one unit of output, the entire pipeline of the productive-distributive system will contain 588 + 9 = 597 units. In order to enable the system to produce one unit of output every two-hour and sell twelve units a day under the given technology and distributive practices, the pipeline inventory of 597 units cannot be reduced. It may also be observed that pipeline inventory is proportional to the system's flow rate and physical flow time. If the system's flow rate increases, inventory in the pipeline will also increase proportionately and vice versa. It also holds true for physical flow time. Once every stage of the pipeline is full and the system is operating continuously, every day it will not only produce 12 units but will also give back the value of 12 units to the production process. This makes the system self-sustaining. No additional inventory of raw materials or other inputs should normally be necessary.

Before we proceed further on the subject let us combine all the three segments of the pipeline in both physical and financial terms for easy understanding of the system. For this purpose monetary values (shown in Table 1.3) are assigned to units at different transformation stages. We have not added profit to the cost of goods sold because our purpose is to find out the quantum of operating fund blocked in the system. We have also excluded depreciation and interest cost from our calculation because the former is not a cash expense and the latter is a finance cost. Flow chart of the entire productive-distributive system is given in Figure 1.3.

Table 1.3 Assigning Monetary Values to the Units held in Productive-Distributive System

Conversion process			(Rs.)
Stage one (S_1)	Raw materials		10.00
	Other manufacturing expenses		2.00
		Total	12.00
Stage two (S_2)	Value received from S_1		12.00
	Other manufacturing expenses		4.00
		Total	16.00
Stage three (S_3)	Value received from S_2		16.00
	Other manufacturing expenses		8.00
		Total (cost of goods sold)	24.00
Distribution process			
	Value received from conversion process		24.00
	Average administrative and distribution costs per unit		1.00
		Total (cost of goods sold)	25.00

DISCRETE OPERATING INVENTORIES

It may be clear from Figure 1.3 that the productive-distributive process becomes self-sustaining once the pipeline is full. But independent of this pipeline, inventories are also built up or funds are blocked in some other forms in response to

(a) broader corporate objectives of optimising cost and usage of fund, ensuring a reasonable liquidity, maintaining customers' goodwill and shareholders' confidence and

(b) the demand and regulation of public authorities and customs of the trade.

Two types of inventories that get built up due to above are discussed below.

Cycle Inventories

Each of the operators in the productive-distributive process like the factory, warehouse, distributor, etc. does not order for inventory as and when necessary

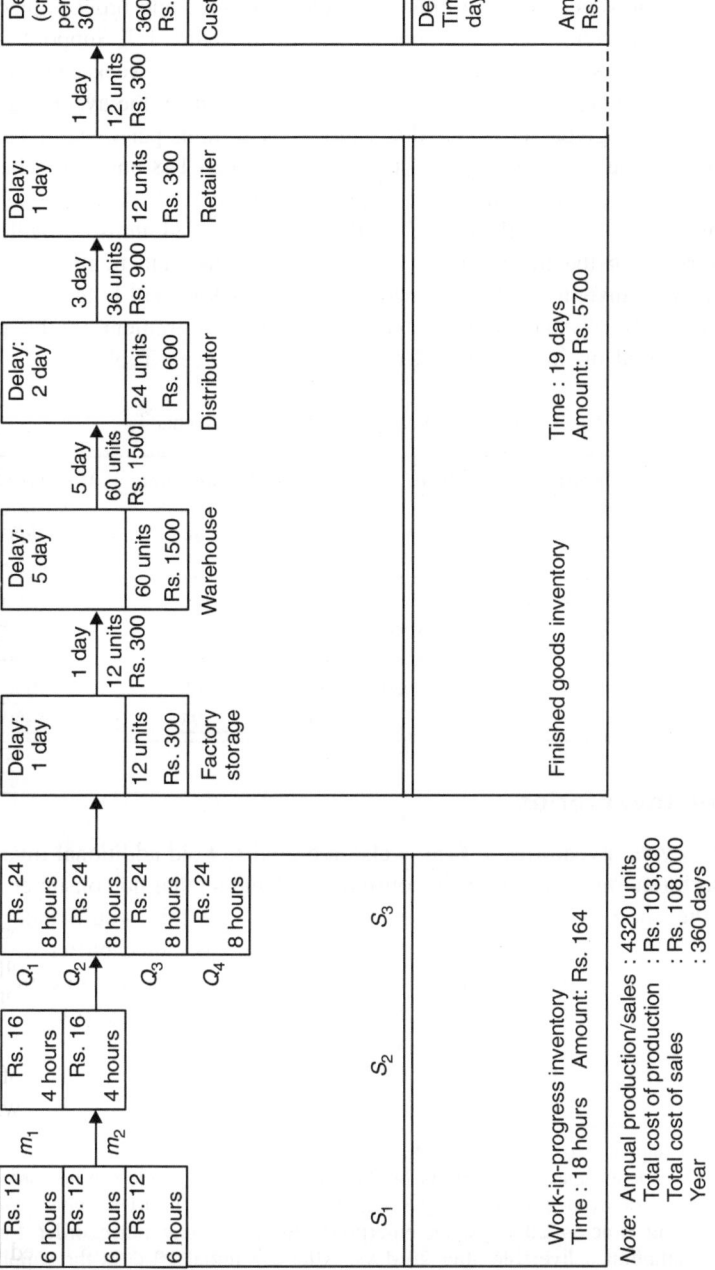

Figure 1.3 Flow chart of the entire production and distribution process and the pipeline inventory.

but follows a cyclical replenishment method based on review of demand and inventory status, transmission time, regulatory requirements for controlled items, etc. However, once an ordering cycle is decided and order is placed the physical flow cycle follows the one as shown in Figure 1.3. Suppose that the distributor has decided to have an ordering cycle of two weeks, i.e. when he places an order, it must be for a two-week supply to meet the average demand. In the example given above, the distributor sells 84 units per week or 168 units during two-week ordering cycle. That is, no less than 168 units must be in his hand to service sales during the replenishment period. Average inventory holding in this case will be half of this figure, i.e. 84 units.[25] While other operators along the integrated process like warehouse and retailers will have similar cycle inventories for finished goods, the factory will hold the same for raw materials. A statement of cycle inventory requirement in the present example based on imaginary ordering cycle is given in Table 1.4.

Table 1.4 Cycle Inventory Requirements[26]

Operator	Ordering cycle (in weeks)	Type	Average cycle inventory (in units)	Monetary value of average holding (in Rs.)
Factory	3	Raw materials	126	1260
Warehouse	1	Finished goods	42	1050
Distributor	2	Finished goods	84	2100
Retailer	1	Finished goods	42	1050
		Total	294	5460

Buffer Inventories

Besides cycle inventories, a firm is also required to hold additional inventories to absorb random fluctuations in consumer demand so that no consumer returns from the shop for want of the product, otherwise this would hamper the goodwill of the firm in the market. This inventory is called buffer inventory. Several models based on probabilistic distribution are available to estimate the buffer stock necessary to cushion the effects of greater than expected demand

25. See Chapter 4 for the method of calculation of average inventory.
26. In an efficient market, inventory holding due to ordering cycle can be considerably reduced or even eliminated by staggering placement of orders. For example, if ordering time is 20 days, an enterprise can every day place order for day's consumption deliverable after 20 days. After the initial 20 days the supply cycle operates continuously to deliver day's consumption to the delivery point as if, on a conveyer belt. One of the objectives of just-in-time inventory management (discussed in Chapter 4), is to eliminate the cycle inventory altogether. A logistically integrated supply chain also eliminates the requirement of ordering cycle inventory. This is discussed in Chapter 8.

and the average demand during the supply lead time.[27] Let us assume that on the basis of one such model the firm has decided to hold buffer stock as given in Table 1.5.

Table 1.5 Buffer Inventory Requirements

Operator	Type	Average buffer inventory (in units)	Monetary value of average holding (in Rs.)
Factory	Raw materials	90	900
Warehouse	Finished goods	14	350
Distributor	Finished goods	80	2000
Retailer	Finished goods	86	2150
	Total	270	5400

A summary of the total inventories blocked up in the system as a whole is given in Table 1.6.

Table 1.6 Total System's Inventories

Type	Units	Amount (Rs.)	Remarks
Pipeline inventories	597	14,864	Refer Figure 1.3
Cycle inventories	294	5460	Refer Table 1.2
Buffer inventories	270	5400	Refer Table 1.3
Total	1161	25,724	

It will be clear from Table 1.6 that the productive-distributive system of the firm as a whole would demand 1161 units of inputs/outputs and hence, block a fund of Rs. 25,724 all the time under the assumed structure of the system, ordering rules and the service levels used. This is the minimum possible amount necessary to operate the system. Inventories might be larger than this minimum if controls were not effective or if seasonal inventories got accumulated in the system.

A finance manager must have clear idea of the physical and financial implications of the system dynamics discussed above. A small rise or fall of demand at the tail end of the pipeline may have severe impact on the system as a whole, making it totally unbalanced and creating strain on the firm's resources. However, it may not be necessary that he has to fund the entire system unless the firm owns the system as a whole like Bata India Ltd. If the firm sells all its products to the distributor, the firm system ends at warehouse stage, but the inventory will include the goods-in-transit to the distributor. In such a case the distributor will not be satisfied with 30 days' credit. He will

---

27. Buffer stock is also called safety stock. Some of the models to determine safety (buffer) stock are discussed in Chapter 4.

calculate the system's flow in days/units commencing from his stage to the end of the pipeline. Instead of 30 days' credit, he may demand a minimum of 37 days' credit from the manufacturer. The same rule will apply in case the firm-system stops short of retailer-stage. In our subsequent analysis, however, we shall take the entire productive-distributive system as given in Figure 1.3.

Other Discrete Assets

We have indicated earlier that besides funds blocked in physical inventories, the productive-distributive system of the firm may generate other discrete assets, independent of the pipeline where funds also get blocked. The first example is cash *per se*. A firm may have to hold a certain level of liquid cash, like buffer inventory, as a cushion against sudden lengthening of the pipeline or a rise in its intensity caused by a demand push. Some other examples are security deposit with statutory authorities like excise and customs departments and/or, in some cases, with the suppliers of raw materials; advance payment of income tax or even advance paid to suppliers and employees, etc. These assets, for some firms, capture a sizeable amount of fund. But the operating cycle theory, is unable to capture these important items excepting, perhaps to some extent, the cash, by days of working expenses.[28]

All the current assets and current liabilities that we have discussed here are generated out of or due to operations. Our analysis excludes financial current assets (like bank deposits, short-term investments in securities etc.) and financial current liabilities (like bank loans, bills discounted, dividend payable etc.). This is consistent with Fleuriet's[29] approach of differentiating operating current assets and current liabilities from financial current assets and current liabilities.

We shall now propose an alternative theory of working capital by incorporating all the assets generated from operations into the integrated operational system of the firm. For this purpose a summary of the pipeline, cycle, buffer inventory and other discrete assets (value assumed) is presented in Figure 1.4.

TECHNO-FINANCIAL APPROACH

Figure 1.4 gives an analytical presentation of the generation of various assets due to operation of the business. While the amounts shown in bottom row are aggregate of these assets that we see in a balance sheet under the head *current assets*, columns under each head show how these have been generated and their distinct nature.

---

28. Sen, P.K., *ibid.*
29. Fleuriet, M., R. Khedy, and G. Blanc, *Fleuriet's Model: The Financial Dynamics of Brazilian Firms: A New Method for Analysis, Budgeting and Financial Planning*, Campus, Rio De Janeiro, 2003.

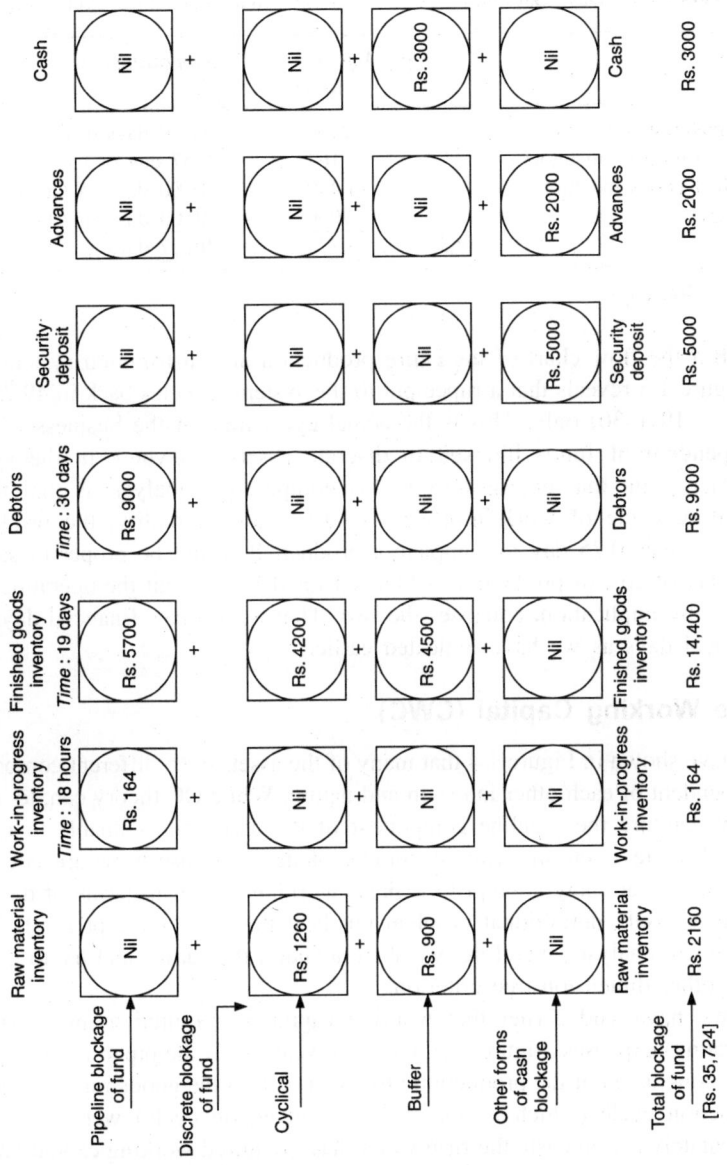

Figure 1.4 Summary of pipeline and discrete blockage of fund.

Under operating cycle method—which stops at the block of debtors—a rupee put into the system will recycle back in 96.57 days as calculated in Table 1.7.

Table 1.7 Days' Holding of Current Assets under Operating Cycle Theory

Assets		Amount (Rs.)	Operating cycle
Raw materials inventory		2160	18.00 days of consumption
Work-in-process inventory		164	0.57 day of CP
Finished goods inventory		14,400	48.00 days of COS
Debtors		9000	30.00 days of COS
	Total	25,724	96.57 days

Year = 360 days

But the flow chart of the entire production and distribution system given in Figure 1.3 reveals that a rupee put to the system recycles back in 49.75 days (0.75 + 19 + 30) only. This is the actual cycle time of the business which is independent of funds blocked in discrete assets elsewhere in the system. Another point that emerges from this comparative analysis is that though operating cycle of work-in-process is 0.57 day, in reality, the production process takes 0.75 day to complete a product. It would be proper to say that 0.57 day of cost of production is blocked for 0.75 day, but the operating cycle theory, by implication, equalises the two. That is, it mixes financial days with technical days as we have indicated earlier.

Core Working Capital (CWC)

We have shown in Figure 1.4 that many of the assets have different components independent of each other in origin and nature. While OC theory can, to a great extent, capture the pipeline component of the assets, it is unable to capture other discrete assets in terms of number of days because these are not in the pipeline. In fact, any attempt to express working capital in terms of days will create not only definitional problem but beat the cycle concept itself. In our subsequent analysis, therefore, we shall abandon the 'days' and try to develop some other dimension-free criterion.

We have said earlier that working capital is required to meet working (operating) expenses. Figures 1.1 and 1.3 reveal that if the pipeline were to stop at the conclusion of the production process, i.e. if all the goods released by each production cycle (which is not same as conversion cycle) were to get sold immediately and in cash, the firm would have required working capital only for meeting the first dose of all operating expenses which get blocked in the conversion process. We may call this as *core working capital* (CWC). All other assets can then be expressed in terms of this CWC, implying thereby, as we have already said, that all such assets block an amount of fund which is otherwise available for meeting operating expenses of a firm.

In the example given in Figure 1.3, the firm has produced 4320 units in a year (360 days), the cost of production and cost of sales of which are Rs. 103,680 and Rs. 108,000 respectively, the distribution and administrative overheads being Rs. 4320. The conversion cycle of the firm takes off every time from the entry of inputs into stage S_1 of the process and ends at the point of rolling out of finished product from stage S_3. Operating expenses are incurred on these cycles.

As is generally understood, operating expenses are broadly divided under two heads, viz. variable and fixed expenses. The former is proportional to the volume under conversion in the process, while the latter is a period cost presumed to be incurred uniformly throughout the period. Extending this presumption, it can be argued that every conversion cycle uniformly absorbs overheads. That is, every finished product coming out of the process per conversion cycle not only absorbs variable input costs but also proportional fixed overheads. If a portion of the selling cost is found to be variable with volume of sales, there is no harm in allocating this cost also to conversion cycle and thence to the finished products coming out of it because, if the system is continuous it can be presumed that the sales are also continuous and uniform and hence, selling costs are also being incurred continuously and uniformly.

Allocation of Overheads

We have seen in Figure 1.1 that actual (physical) conversion cycle of the firm is 18 hours. An attempt can be made to allocate overheads and selling costs in terms of hours spent in the conversion process. Although it is possible for a finance manager to do this job product- and process-wise if the firm is producing only a few products, when it has multiple products he may face difficulty in calculating and allocating these costs. An outside analyst will face bigger problem because he may not be aware of different processes and time spent on them. A solution to these problems can be found if we abandon the time cycle concept altogether and instead, turn our attention to the fund cycle of the production process. A firm may have a single or multiple products, but it is not difficult to calculate funds blocked in the processes in terms of expenses which are variable to the volume under conversion in the process. In fact, the coefficients of the inputs are almost pre-determined at the installation stage of the project. An outside analyst will also not face much difficulty because published balance sheet of companies reveal both the opening and closing balances of work-in-process.

The amount of variable working expenses fund engaged in a conversion process is thus nothing but the value of the work-in-process, as we commonly understand in accounting terminology. The conversion fund cycle can now be determined by dividing the aggregate cost of production with the value of the work-in-process at any point of time. In our present example, cost of production is Rs. 103,680 whereas fund engaged in work-in-process is Rs. 164. Dividing the former with the latter we obtain 632.20 conversion fund cycle in a year. In other words, velocity of conversion fund is 632.20 times a year. We now take the reciprocal of this figure and obtain the unit velocity (UV) of the conversion fund which is dimensionless. (It can also be calculated straightaway by dividing the work-in-process fund with the cost of production.) The unit velocity of the conversion fund so calculated is 0.00158179. (It is always preferable to take five decimal points because of the sensitivity of the unit velocity.)

The overheads for the firm are Rs. 4320 (presently allocated at Re. 1 per unit). Multiplying this with the unit velocity we obtain Rs. 6.83 which is allocated to each cycle of conversion fund. Total fund blocked in the conversion cycle is, therefore, Rs. 164 + 6.83 = Rs. 170.83. This is the minimum amount of fund the firm requires under ideal condition which we have termed as core working capital (CWC).

PROJECTION OF WORKING CAPITAL

As CWC is the aggregate of conversion expenses, variable selling expenses and fixed overheads per conversion fund cycle, its unit velocity will obviously be the same as that of conversion fund cycle. Suppose, in the given example (Figure 1.3) the volume is doubled from 4320 units to 8640 units; the cost of production and the fund in conversion process being composed of variable expenses, will also be doubled to Rs. 207,360 and Rs. 328 respectively. Assuming now that fixed overheads remain fixed at Rs. 4320, the cost of sales for increased volume will be Rs. 211,680. Multiplying appropriate figures with the pre-determined unit velocity we get the following value:

	(Rs.)
Conversion fund cycle (0.00158179 × 207,360)	328.00
Overheads per cycle (0.00158179 × 4320)	6.83
Core working capital	334.83

The CWC figure thus calculated will be same as that derived by multiplying new cost of sales with the same unit velocity: (0.00158179 × 211,680) = Rs. 334.83. It may be observed that fixed overheads per cycle remain at Rs. 6.83 irrespective of an increase in the volume. This is in conformity with the principles of cost accounting because when volume increases per fund cycle, the full cost per unit is reduced because the same amount of overheads get distributed over a larger quantity of outputs.

We have already said that assets (both pipeline and discrete), generated out of operations, block funds for operating expenses. In other words, if these assets were not generated, conversion cycle would have proceeded smoothly with the first dose of fund equivalent to the operating expenses engaged in the process. It can, therefore, be said, that each of such assets blocks a certain number of fund cycles, or in our terminology, CWC cycles. All such assets can, therefore, be expressed in terms of number of cycles they block. In Table 1.8 we have transformed all such assets, generated from operations of our imaginary firm, into CWC cycles.

Table 1.8 Blockage of Core Working Capital Cycles in Various Operating Assets

Assets	Amount (Rs.)	No. of CWC cycles/ multipliers	Remarks
Work-in-process inventory	164	0.96	1. Core working capital
Raw materials inventory	2160	12.64	= Rs. 170.83
Finished goods inventory	14,400	84.29	
Debtors	9000	52.68	2. No. of CWC
Security deposit	5000	29.27	cycles/multipliers
Advances, etc.	2000	11.72	= Operating asset / CWC
Cash	3000	17.56	
Total	35,724	209.12	

It can now be said that the entire productive-distributive system of the firm requires 209.12 CWC cycles or multipliers divided between various operating assets to keep it continually operating. Gross operating assets of the firm is thus represented by the aggregate of these CWC cycles.

Current Liabilities

The way the CWC cycles are blocked in various operating assets, some of these also get released by operating (current) liabilities like trade and expense creditors, advances and deposits from customers, etc. That is, these liabilities supply some of the CWC cycles of the firm. Current trade liabilities are dependent primarily upon the volume of production, ordering cycle and risk-taking capacity of the firm (buffer stock) for a given period and hence, they also enjoy the dynamic stability similar to operating assets. Assuming now that trade and expense creditors of the firm in the present example aggregate to Rs. 10,000 and the total of other operating liabilities is Rs. 5000, it is clear that they must have supplied 58.54 and 29.27 CWC cycles respectively or in aggregate, 88 cycles approximately. Deducting these cycles from the total CWC cycles of operating assets we obtain 121 net CWC cycles which can be said to be equivalent to *net working capital* of the firm assuming that the firm has not taken any short-term finance from banks.

Let us assume now that the firm has projected a 50 percent rise in sales in the next year. While variable input coefficients will remain the same, the firm expects a rise in fixed overheads to Rs. 5500. We can project the working capital level of the firm through the following few steps. Final projections are tabulated in Table 1.9.

(a) Projected cost of production (50 percent rise) — 155,520

(b) Projected cost of sales (Rs. 155,520 + 5500) — 161,020

(c) Projected conversion fund cycle
   $(0.00158179 \times 155,520)$ — 246.00

(d) Projected fixed overheads per CF cycle
   (0.00158179×5500) — 8.70

(e) Projected core working capital
   $[0.00158179 \times 161,020$ or (c) + (d)] — 254.70

Table 1.9 Projected Working Capital

Operating assets/liabilities	CWC multiplier	Level (Rs.) (col 2 × 254.70)
Work-in-process inventory	0.96	244.51
Raw materials inventory	12.64	3219.41
Finished goods inventory	84.29	21,468.66
Debtors	52.68	13,417.60
Security deposit	29.27	7455.07
Advances, etc.	11.72	2985.08
Cash	17.56	4472.53
Sub-total (A)	209.12	53,262.86
Less: Trade and expense creditors	58.54	14,910.14
Other operating liabilities	29.27	7455.07
Sub-total (B)	87.81	22,365.21
Net CWC cycles net working capital (A − B)	121.31	30,897.65

Projected net working capital of Rs. 30,897.65, as calculated in Table 1.9, is in fact the working capital gap. If the entire requirement is financed by the firm from its own long-term sources, the gap will continue to be termed as net working capital. However, if a part of this gap is financed from bank loan (which normally is the case), the remaining part, as financed from long-term sources, will be treated as net working capital.

CHARACTERISTICS OF CORE WORKING CAPITAL

The unit velocity of CWC is dependent upon given technology and operating condition. Hence, it should remain stable for a reasonably long period of time. When there is a change in technology or operating condition the unit velocity should be calculated afresh. This new unit velocity will then be valid for another technology-period.

The CWC multipliers are homogeneous quantities which describe the operating-financial structure of a firm in one unit of measurement. These multipliers for various operating assets of a firm were also found to be more or less fixed for about three years.[30] But that does not mean that, in general, these multipliers shall have to be compulsorily fixed for any operating asset even within that period excepting, perhaps, for work-in-process inventory. It only indicates that the firms for which these multipliers were found to be stable for three years, were unable to reduce the CWC multipliers for operating assets. While it may not be possible to do much about the work-in-process, there is scope for a finance manager to reduce the number of multipliers along the distribution pipeline of the firm by reducing the delays at various stages. This is also applicable to discrete component of the operating assets even under the

---

30. Bhattacharya, Hrishikes, *Comprehensive Credit Appraisal*, Economic Publishers, Calcutta, 1985.

same head by realigning the ordering cycle and making fresh risk-adjustments for buffer holding of a particular asset. It must be remembered that reducing one multiplier means release of one cycle fund or a unit of CWC.

The unit velocity of CWC, which is nothing but the unit velocity of conversion fund, is independent of capacity utilisation. It can be calculated under any given level of capacity utilisation. Increased capacity utilisation increases operating expenses which, when multiplied by the calculated unit velocity, will indicate the level of CWC for the increased volume of business.

Unit velocity of CWC is also independent of changes in price level. Suppose price level is expected to increase by a certain percentage in the projected year, the unit velocity will capture this inflationary expectation via increased level of operating expenses and indicate an appropriate level of core working capital for the projected year.

The assumption behind the theory of working capital presented here is that production is continuous and uniform in regard to volume throughout the year. Hence, fund held in the conversion process will also be uniform at any point of time throughout the year. The year-end value of work-in-process as appears in the balance sheet of a firm as on a particular date, can therefore be regarded as being held at any point of time during the previous year in regard to that year's volume of production, and hence, be taken as the basis for calculating unit velocity of conversion fund (or CWC). However, in real business situation when this uniformity could not have been maintained because volume of production per conversion cycle could be stepped up only gradually or there had been some other bottlenecks, then it is preferable to take weekly or monthly averages of work-in-process fund. However, an outside analyst may not have access to this inside information. In that case, it is advisable for him to take average of opening and closing balances of work-in-process from published balance sheets. Unless the previous year had been very unusual, the unit velocity of CWC calculated by the outside financial analyst will not be much different from that calculated by the finance manager of the firm. The same rule applies to the calculation of CWC multipliers for other operating assets and liabilities. However, whatever method is adopted it must be uniform for calculation of both the unit velocity of CWC and its multipliers for operating assets and liabilities.

CONTROL MECHANISMS

The techno-financial theory of working capital presented here has the unique advantage of enabling a finance manager to view and control the entire operating system of the business in terms of a single unit of measurement—the CWC multiplier. Even for calculation of projected working capital, he need not have to use different criteria for different types of operating assets as in operating cycle theory.

The CWC multiplier can also be used for control of working capital. Any reduction or increase of cost or of delay (which includes credit period allowed to debtors) along the productive-distributive pipeline or among the discrete components of the system presented in Figure 1.4 will be reflected in an item-wise and/or aggregate variance analyses done in terms of CWC multipliers.

Unit velocity of CWC determines the inter-firm technical efficiency within an industry. A highly efficient firm both in respect of modern technology and operating condition will have smaller unit velocity than a less efficient firm. It will also enable an investor to determine the techno-financial viability of competing projects.[31]

SUMMARY

The 'non-ideal' production technology and imperfect market and distribution systems are responsible for the generation of current assets which block the funds of an enterprise. Working capital is needed to release such blockage of funds.

But there are controversies about the definition of working capital. Karl Marx defined it as variable capital consisting of wage fund, others defined it as excess of current assets over current liabilities. These net concepts are based on 'gone concern' approach. A 'going concern' approach takes a total view of the business and considers *gross current assets* as the *gross working capital* requirement of a business, and management of working capital as management of current assets and current liabilities to ensure dynamic stability between generation of current assets and their funding operations.

The other controversy relates to the meaning of currentness as embedded in current assets. One view is that all assets and liabilities which mature within one year are treated as current. The other view takes into consideration the "natural business year" of an enterprise, which is not restricted to any temporal period. The OC theory of working capital is based on this concept. The weakness of OC theory is its implicit assumption that operating expenses and the working capital turnover are divisible. That they are not, is proved by the fact that turnover of various current assets and current liabilities are calculated using different denominators, not working expenses, as the uniform base. Hence, the OC theory could not stand the reversibility test.

As against the aforementioned theory, the pipeline theory of working capital holds that funds are blocked along the productive-distributive line of a business in terms of actual days, not the financial days, as embedded in the OC theory. Besides, the pipeline theory takes into account all current assets and current liabilities generated out of the operations of business, while the OC theory restricts itself to certain manufacturing and sales assets (and liabilities) only. The pipeline theory is based on the techno-financial framework of a business. By adopting a systems approach, it shows that the first dose of working capital is blocked in the conversion process which is technology given. This is the *core working capital* (CWC). All other current assets, which are generated along the distribution channel of a business, are divided by the

---

31. Original version of this chapter first appeared in an article form in *Economic and Political Weekly*, August 29, 1987.

CWC to arrive at CWC cycles of individual current assets. Similar exercise is done for current liabilities as well. This theory recognises that besides the pipeline current assets, there are discrete operating assets which get generated independent of the pipeline in order to conform to the broader corporate objectives of optimising cost and usage of funds, maintenance of customers' goodwill and shareholders' confidence, and also due to the demand and regulation of public authorities (for example, cash, various deposits with public authorities, advance payments, etc.). These assets also have a dynamic stability and hence, are divisible by CWC to arrive at the CWC cycles embedded in them. Having thus calculated CWC cycles for all current assets and current liabilities, the working capital structure of an enterprise is defined in terms of CWC cycles, more precisely by CWC multipliers, the CWC acting as the denominator throughout. The structure so defined in terms of CWC cycles will remain fixed under a given technology of production and distributive practices. Projection of working capital for a given rise in sales is done easily by first determining the CWC for the projected increase in sales and then multiplying it with the CWC multipliers already determined for each group of current assets and liabilities.

Unit velocity of CWC (calculated by taking the reciprocal of CWC) can be used for distributing overheads along the productive–distributive chain of a business; it can also act as a standard of comparison among different firms to judge the efficiency of working capital management. The same goes with the CWC multipliers of individual current assets and current liabilities.

CHAPTER 2
Theories of Trade Credit

I have come here to narrate a story
A story not written by me
A story never to be told
A story known to all

INTRODUCTION

Substantial work has been done during the past three decades to determine the theories of trade credit. But as observed by Frank and Maksimovic[1], though the theories apply in specific circumstances, they are unable to explain the widespread use of trade credit and the empirical patterns of its use. Long, Malitz and Ravid[2] also held that although trade credit is a very useful source of finance for different firms, its explanation, as yet, is not very clear. In this chapter we shall present a critical evaluation of each of these theories, highlighting the problems associated with it and indicating specific areas of its application. This chapter will form the basis of our discussion on Receivables Management (Chapter 3) and Payables Management (Chapter 6).

FINANCING THEORY

The oldest view of trade credit is that it is a type of financing made available by the seller to the buyer[3]. It may be through a formal agreement similar to a loan document or by informal arrangement through exchange invoices evidencing exchange of goods or services and terms of credit. Thus, trade credit can be viewed as a substitute for institutional financing. According to this theory, suppliers have several advantages over financing institutions in offering trade credit to buyers. One such advantage is that the suppliers being in close contact with the buyers are in a superior position not only to evaluate credit worthiness of their customers but also to monitor them almost on a day-to-day basis. Such an advantage is not available with a financial institution. The second advantage is that supplies have more effective and quicker ways of liquidating assets of defaulting buyer-firms than institutional financiers. If the

---

1. Frank, M. and V. Maksimovic, *Trade Credit, Collateral, and Adverse Selection*, Working Paper, University of Maryland, 1998.
2. Long, M.S., I.B. Malitz and A. Ravid, "Trade Credit, Quality Guarantees and Product Marketability", *Financial Management*, Winter, pp. 117–127, 1993.
3. Emery, G.W., "An Optimal Financial Response to Variable Demand", *Journal of Financial and Quantitative Analysis*, Vol. 22, pp. 209–225, 1987.

goods supplied are durables in nature, it is easier for the supplier to repossess them through their network and sell the repossessed goods quickly with or without additional processing. It has been observed that if the goods have more value as collateral to sellers than the financial institution, the seller considers this as reduction of credit risk and, therefore, can offer better credit terms than the financial institutions.[4] Suppliers can also threaten the buyers to stop supplies if the payment is delayed. Such an opportunity is not available with a bank or financial institution.

The financing theory does explain why the sellers would offer trade credit but it does not explain why the buyers will accept the trade credit vis-à-vis institutional finance. Several empirical investigations are made to answer this question. The theoretical foundation of such investigations is that trade credit exists because of inefficiency of financial market. All firms do not have equal access to institutional finance because perceived risks of some firms (may be, due to asymmetry of information) might be greater than the risk-tolerance limit of the financial institutions. Hence, these firms (which are mostly small businesses) would resort to trade credit. For this reason they are also prepared to bear high cost of trade credit[5]. Wilner[6] found that firms with greater probability of default prefer trade credit to a loan from financial institution and consequently, trade credit interest rates exceed the credit market rate. Earlier, Petersen and Rajan[7] found that a creditor reduces the rates it charges more rapidly as a customer's likelihood of default decreases.

Firms that have better access to cheaper institutional finance would act as second level intermediaries for those firms, which do not have such access. That is, there is a transmission of institutional credit via credible firms to those whose perceived risks are not of acceptable standards. The credible firms now assume this risk. They can do it because information opacity of the buyer-firms is considerably reduced through day-to-day association. In fact, this 'secondary financial market' reflects the risk of such firms more accurately. Bias and Gollier[8] had also observed that granting of trade credit to a supplier by a credible seller gives a positive signal to banks, which alleviates credit rationing faced by a supplier. But this does not explain why large corporate organisations, which have access to institutional finance, are also found to

---

4. Ng, C.K., J.K. Smith and R.L. Smith, "Evidence on the Determinants of Trade Credit Terms Used in Inter-firm Trade", *Journal of Finance*, Vol. 54, pp. 1109–1129, 1999. See also, Mian, S. and C.W. Smith, "Accounts Receivable Management Policy: Theory and Evidence", *Journal of Finance*, Vol. 47, pp. 169–201, 1992.
5. For example, a 2/10 net 30 credit terms allows a customer to enjoy a 10 percent discount if he pays within 10 days. If, however, he pays immediately after the expiry of 30 days period (credit period 20 days) the implicit interest rate comes to be 36.7 percent p.a.
6. Wilner, B.S., "The Explanation of Relationships in Financial Distress: The Case of Trade Credit", *Journal of Finance*, Vol. 55, pp. 153–178, 2000.
7. Petersen, M.A. and R.G. Rajan, "The Effect of Credit Market Competition on Lending Relationships", *Quarterly Journal of Economics*, Vol. 110, pp. 407–444, 1995.
8. Bias, B. and C. Gollier, "Trade Credit and Credit Rationing", *Review of Financial Studies*, Vol. 10, pp. 903–937, 1997.

make use of trade credit. Perhaps, this could be explained by the Market Power theory of trade credit discussed later.

LIQUIDITY THEORY

This theory is an extension of Financing theory discussed above. It holds that credit-constrained firms are likely to use more trade credit than those having access to institutional finance. As large firms are more liquid and/or have lower cost of holding liquidity, they do not have the same incentive to use trade credit as others. It follows therefore, that liquid firms are more likely to be providers of trade credit (which may not be applicable in developing countries as we shall see later). This is more pronounced during a period of monetary restrictions when institutional credit is rationed. Nielson[9] using a sample of small firms found that such credit-rationed firms typically demand more trade credit from large corporates. That is, they make up for the financing gap created by credit rationing by resorting to more trade credit. When a customer has bargaining advantage with the supplier he can exploit it to obtain better credit terms during a financial restriction[10]. Petersen and Rajan[11] also found that firms increase trade credit when they suffer from negative cash flows and lose sales. According to them, this happens because of their inability to realize their own accounts receivable in time. These firms being small cannot credibly threaten to cut off supplies to ensure in-time payment. It has also been observed that when a firm has higher level of inventories, whether of raw materials or finished products, it would use less trade credit because they also buy less and wait for the inventories to move out. Ferris[12] observed that firms could ease their problems by maturity adjustments between payables and receivables. That is, they may separate the payment cycle from delivery cycle.

Liquidity theory does explain why credit-constrained firms and those having negative cash flows or high-level of inventories use trade credit but it does not explain, as in case of Financing theory, why even large firms not suffering from any of these constraints do use trade credit.

FINANCIAL DISTRESS THEORY

This theory is based on 'buyer opportunism' which was first noted by Petersen and Rajan[13] and further evidenced by Wilner[14]. When a supplier cannot credibly threat to stop supplies, e.g. when he is in financial distress, the buyer

9. Nielson, J., "Trade Credit and the Bank Lending Channel", *Journal of Money, Credit and Banking*, Vol. 34, pp. 226–253, 2002.
10. Petersen, M.A. and R.G. Rajan, "Trade Credit: Theories and Evidence", *Review of Financial Studies*, Vol. 10. pp. 661–691, 1997.
11. *Ibid.*
12. Ferris, J.S., "A Transaction Theory of Trade Credit Use", *Quarterly Journal of Economics*, Vol. 96, pp. 243–270, 1981.
13. Petersen and Rajan (1997), *ibid.*
14. Wilner, (2000), *ibid.*

is found to pay less promptly. This opportunistic behaviour is more manifest when the buyer is one of the principal customers; the supplier simply cannot afford to make such threats. Indeed, as Wilner observed, majority of suppliers cannot even charge late payment penalty and even those firms which invoice the penalty half of them could not collect it. This is true across countries belonging to both the developed and developing world. Besides delaying payment, buyers also extract several other concessions, e.g. larger discounts from the suppliers in financial distress.

Evans[15] found that suppliers (trade creditors) desiring to maintain enduring product market relationships are found to grant more concessions to a customer in financial distress, as compared to similarly-positioned lending institutions. Wilner[16] also found that if the degree of dependence of the supplier on the customer is high, the customer in financial distress obtains larger concessions in renegotiation of credit terms.

On the other side of the market there also exists 'seller opportunism' the major source of which is the monopoly supplier power. The supplier firm has an incentive to keep the buyers (debtors) dependent on it in order to hold and expand the market share and, also to later squeeze them when they are brought to fold. Petersen and Rajan[17] showed that such suppliers initially 'aid' small businesses by offering 'teaser rates' (competitively relaxed credit terms) to lure them to their fold and subsequently earn larger profits by charging higher rates. At that time it would be difficult for the buyers to switch over to other suppliers.

However, if the suppliers are small there exists the 'free-rider problem' which aggravates financial distress of the suppliers, particularly those that sells to many customers. Each debtor being small would feel that prompt payment of the small amount of debt would not have much effect on the firm in financial distress. Rather, if he delays the payment and, in the meantime the firm goes bankrupt, he can avoid the payment altogether.

Although 'buyer opportunism' generally holds, Petersen and Rajan[18] found evidence of principal customers mitigating financial distress of their suppliers by paying more promptly, especially when they have a long-term stake in the relationship.

QUALITY GUARANTEE THEORY

This theory is based on asymmetry of information between buyer and seller. The buyer does not know the quality of the product he is buying. If he pays cash on delivery and the product turns out to be of poor quality, he ceases to have effective control over an errant supplier. He loses the cash and the product as well. In other words, if the buyer cannot insure himself against malfunctioning

---

15. Evans, J.D., *Are Lending Relationships Valuable to Equity Holders in* Chapter 11, *Bankruptcy?* Working Paper, Georgia State University, 1998.
16. Wilner (2000), *ibid.*
17. Petersen and Rajan (1995), *ibid.*
18. Petersen and Rajan (1997), *ibid.*

of the product, he will discount the value he expects to gain from the purchase with his estimation of the risk factor. Hence the more risky the product, the lower is the expected value of the purchase[19].

Firms do offer warranties or even money-back guarantees. But enforcement of such warranties or even money-back guarantees often takes a long time during which period the buyer is deprived of the service of the product while his money is blocked. The seller may also be out of business by the time the defect in the product gets ascertained. If the buyer is a reseller, he may not get payment against such sale; most likely goods will be returned to him. When the product is an important input for a manufacturer the entire production process may stop or low quality finished products may come out from the process. Hence normal desire of buyers of products whose quality is uncertain is to pay only after the quality is ascertained. Trade credit is an effective tool to take care of such anxiety. If the product does not perform the buyer simply does not pay. Smith[20] also found that it is often the sellers who offer trade credit to enable the buyers to verify product quality before making payment. Long, Malitz and Ravid[21] also held that if the quality of the product cannot be easily verified, trade credit offers an opportunity to do so before making final payment. They also found that manufacturers, whose products take longer time to produce and/or where it takes longer time to verify the quality of the product, may offer trade credit to enable the buyer to check the quality of the product. However, supplier's willingness to offer trade credit for quality guarantee will be higher if both the importance and credit quality of the customer is higher. On the other hand, the buyer's ability to extract this guarantee will be higher if he has more hold over the supplier.

Guarantee theory is valid for some types of manufacturers, for some category of products and for some time only. When the manufacturer is supplying for the first time, the demand for quality verification from the buyer's side or proving the quality of the product from the seller's side through trade credit holds, but once the quality of the product is established from a few supplies such a necessity does not exist so also the trade credit. But in real-life situation it is found that the original credit term continues, which ultimately becomes the new norm. In case of perishable commodities, time required for quality determination is very insignificant but payment period is found to be much longer; the two are, therefore, unconnected.

There may be cases where seller may try to pass off low quality products. But as the market gets to know about it, the buyers will demand extended line of credit, the cost of which will soon become prohibitive to profit from such practices[22]. Moreover, sellers cannot afford to supply low quality goods while

19. Horen Van, N., *Customer Market Power and the Provision of Trade Credit: Evidence from Eastern Europe and Central Asia,* Policy Research Working Paper No. 4284, The World Bank, Development Prospects Group, July 2007.
20. Smith, J.K., "Trade Credit and Informational Asymmetry", *Journal of Finance,* Vol. 42, pp. 1–19, 1987.
21. Long, Malitz and Ravid (1993), *ibid.*
22. Wei, P. and S.M.L. Zee, "Trade Credit as Quality Signal: An International Comparison", *Managerial Finance,* Vol. 23, pp. 63–72, 1997.

executing bulk orders from principal customers for fear of losing substantial business. For the same reason, it is unlikely for principal customers to demand trade credit for quality guarantee. It is also found that firms with capacity constraints would sell only to high quality customers who may not want the subsidy of trade credit nor the supplier could afford to sell low quality goods to this category of customers.

TRANSACTION COSTS THEORY

This theory holds that when transactions between sellers and buyers are frequent both parties may reduce transaction costs by agreeing to a periodical payment schedule. The purpose here is not financing but reducing transaction costs. This work so long as saving in transaction costs remains more than the cost of holding receivables.

Mian and Smith[23] found that when supply of goods and credit are made from one point there is an overall reduction in costs and increase in efficiency as both the monitoring of supplies and the credit could be done from the same point. Sellers in general, but more particularly those having large inventory, can save on warehousing and related costs by effecting sales with attractive credit terms. This is possible when marginal cost of holding inventory is greater than the cost of holding receivables.

Firms whose product suffers from high demand fluctuations may resort to trade credit, which is found to be the least cost solution, the others being adjustment of production schedule or effecting price reduction. The seller could relax credit terms when the demand is slackening and tighten them when demand shows an upswing. This hypothesis of Emery[24] found support in the empirical findings of Long, Malitz and Ravid[25] who concluded that firms with high variable demand extend more credit than firms enjoying demand stability.

Some writers suggest that by offering trade credit suppliers can defer tax payment or benefit from tax shields in the short run[26]. When buyers and sellers are in different tax brackets, cost of financing is also different, other things remaining constant. A firm in high tax bracket has lower net interest cost than a firm in low tax bracket. Hence, the former has an incentive to offer trade credit to save on marginal tax[27].

Different dimensions of Costs theory suggest that trade credit is an operational tool to reduce various costs.

One of the main criticisms of Costs theory relates to the incentive of settling payments periodically to reduce transaction costs. It might have been valid till 1980s but with the revolutionary improvement in information and

23. Mian, S. and C.W. Smith, "Accounts Receivable Management Policy: Theory and Evidence", *Journal of Finance*, Vol. 47. pp. 169–201, 1992.
24. Emery (1987), *ibid.*
25. Long, Malitz and Ravid (1993), *ibid.*
26. See for example, Mian and Smith (1992), *ibid.*
27. Brick, L.E. and W.K.H. Fung, "Taxes and the Theory of Trade Debt", *Journal of Finance*, Vol. 39, pp. 1169–1175, 1984.

payment technology during the past two decades transaction cost has come down so much that this incentive is withered away. When such is the case, the level of trade credit should have come down during this period but in reality this has not happened.

The advantage of saving on warehousing costs by effecting credit sales may not be available when there is a general fall in the demand of the product; the buyers would not be too willing to pick up goods which may remain unsold.

The other criticism is that it is difficult to practise variable credit policy in tune with variable demand. Market may react strongly against such a policy, as it generally prefers a uniform policy.

The problem with tax incentive is that it has a very restricted application. Firms belonging to a given industry with tax bracket below the industry average cannot benefit from this. Moreover, it does not explain why trade credit exists between firms belonging to the same tax bracket.

PRICE DISCRIMINATION THEORY

This theory is based on the assumption that when market is highly competitive sellers have to resort to non-price competition strategy to increase sales[28]. As buyers are heterogeneous, it calls for charging different prices to different customers. But there are both market and regulatory restrictions to practise such price discrimination. Besides, management of discretionary price-cuts is costly. Trade credit can overcome these restrictions while successfully discriminating prices. Market power of firms can be enhanced considerably by practicing price discrimination through offering of trade credit. This becomes evident when an aggressive manufacturer attempts to occupy shelf-space of the traders in a bid to capture more market share. Mostly, firms enjoying high price-cost margin are found to resort to price discrimination through trade credit offerings.

The difficulty with Price Discrimination theory is that trade credit terms typically follow industry practice. Any attempt to alter an established practice is not viewed kindly by the market. Hence, trade credit as an alternative mode of price discrimination can be used selectively and for limited purpose only. Besides, customers who have low default risk and, therefore, can obtain institutional finance at better terms may not be willing to accept trade credit so offered because implicit cost of trade credit is considerably higher than institutional finance. Hence, the offer is attractive only to high-risk marginal customers whose access to institutional finance is prohibitively costly. This raises the incidence of bad debts.

Existence of higher price-cost margin as an incentive to provide trade credit for price discrimination has not been found to have any effect on firms with credible principal customers. The logic behind this is that as firms direct a significant portion of their supplies to large principal customers, quality of

---

28. Soufani, K., "On the Determinants of Factoring as a Financing Choice: Demand Analysis," *Journal of Economics and Business*, Vol. 54, pp. 239–252, 2002.

the remaining pool also improves. As a result, the incentive to price discrimination wanes away. The focus is shifted to matching of short-term liabilities with short-term assets for both the suppliers and buyers[29].

PRODUCT DIFFERENTIATION THEORY

The basis of this theory is that trade credit is similar to other sales promotion tools like advertising, to differentiate a product from competition. Trade credit is considered here as long-term investment like advertising, to help maintain long-term relationship with customers, and again like advertising, it generates income over time.

Nadiri[30] was the first to use this concept. He showed that like advertising, trade credit is a non-price variable that influences product demand through differentiation. He found that optimal ratio of trade credit to sales is directly proportional to the elasticity of demand for the product with respect to trade credit and inversely proportional to price elasticity of the product. As optimal profit margin is inversely related to price elasticity, the trade credit to sales ratio is positively related to profit margin. This is consistent with the findings of Bernan et al.[31] that accounts receivable is positively related to the supplier's price-cost margin.

Blazenko and Vandezande[32] extended the work of Nadiri to examine the interplay of profit and trade credit. In their model they hypothesised that when price elasticity of a product is constant elasticity of trade credit may influence demand. Depending on the economic environment profit margin may either fall or rise when marginal cost rises. For example, a firm may increase product price when marginal cost rises but as a consequence sales might fall because of constant price elasticity of the product. But the firm may arrest such decline in sales by increasing trade credit. They also observed that when elasticity of demand of the product with respect to trade credit is high more lenient trade credit policy greatly increases the product demand.

Product differentiation strategy through advertising and provision of trade credit are not quite similar because their focus is not similar. While advertisement generally focuses on the entire market or a market segment with the aim to motivate the ultimate consumers, trade credit is mostly restricted to dealers. Although during recent times manufacturers of durable articles and implements do offer buyer's credit through their financing arms or allied financing companies, the very separation of financing activity makes it different

29. Banerjee, S., S. Dasgupta, and Y. Kim, *Buyer-Supplier Relationships and Trade Credit,* Working Paper, SSRN, September 2004.
30. Nadiri, M.I., "The Determinants of Trade Credit in U.S. Total Manufacturing Sector", *Econometrica,* Vol. 37, pp. 408–423, 1969.
31. Bernan, M.J., V. Maksimovic, and J. Zechner, "Vendor Financing", *Journal of Finance,* Vol. 43, pp. 1127–1141, 1988.
32. Blazenko, G.W. and K. Vandezande, "The Product Differentiation Hypothesis for Corporate Trade Credit", *Managerial and Decision Economics,* Vol. 24, pp. 457–469, 2003.

from offering trade credit, which is a single point disposal of both materials and credit. The terms of financing agencies and that of trade credit are quite different. For example, a '2/10 Net 30' credit term may not find place in loan terms of financing companies, rather there may be a penalty for early payment.

Moreover, when product differentiation is practiced through trade credit there is a likelihood of increasing both the customer-base and volume of credit, which may increase the transaction costs, and administrative costs of managing trade credit. On the face of such rising costs, the product differentiation strategy may not be an optimal policy.

MARKET POWER THEORY

One common theme that runs through all the theories discussed above is that the purpose of trade credit is to increase sales. A manufacturer is not in financing business; he provides finance only when there is a possibility of increased sales. As the name suggests, trade credit is meant for traders or intermediaries in the distribution channel. It is intended to motivate traders to push products of one manufacturer over the others. In fact, trade credit is associated with the 'Push' strategy of sales promotion. It is oldest sales strategy, so is the trade credit as an instrument of implementing such strategy. A 'Push' strategy aims at inducing intermediaries to carry, promote, and sell the product to the end users[33]. It is most appropriate for products having low consumer loyalty for the brands or the brands are not well known. To a large extent, these types of products are trader-dependent. Hence, the traders should be adequately motivated through various incentives to push products to consumer. The provision of trade credit is, perhaps, the strongest of such incentives.

On the other hand, under 'Pull' strategy, which is of recent origin, the focus is directly on the end consumers. It involves using advertisements and other consumer promotions to induce consumers to ask intermediaries to order for it. This strategy is especially appropriate for products with high brand loyalty: the consumers are aware of the differences between brands, and they choose a brand before they go to the store[34]. Thus, manufacturer's reliance on traders is much reduced.

The prerequisite of a 'Pull' strategy is brand loyalty. The American Marketing Association defines brand as a name, sign, symbol or design, or a combination of them, intended to identify the goods or services of one setter or group of sellers and to differentiate them from those of competitors. Developing a brand requires substantial investments in advertisement and promotion. These investments are considered to be long-term in nature as brands take time to acquire value, which we call brand equity. It is a combination of recognition or recall of brand name, perceived brand quality and strong emotional association with the brand such that a consumer

---

33. Kotler, P., *Marketing Management: The Millennium Edition*, 10th ed., Prentice-Hall of India, New Delhi, 2002.
34. *Ibid.*

pre-decides the purchase, which compels the traders to stock the product. Internally, firms do value their brand equity (though not published in the balance sheet) like any other assets, from marketing point of view a brand represents a set of loyal customers. It is, in fact, customer equity.

Investments in trade credit and brand equity are both long-term in nature. Manufacturers though have a choice between 'Push' strategy (trade credit) and 'Pull' strategy (brand equity)[35], every firm whether big or small moves towards creating its own brand; it may be in a niche market or among the few buyers the firms have. Examples are rife for large wholesalers and retailers developing their own brands. International trading organisations like Kenmore appliances, Marks & Spencer and The Body Shop of United States, and Sainsbury and Tesco of the United Kingdom make substantial selling of their own branded products. Even a small grocer operating within a small area attempts to create his own brand name as an 'honest trader', as in Jeffrey Archer's novel[36].

One of the objectives of creating such brands is to lessen the dependence on often-exploitative manufactures (for trading organisations) and traders (for manufacturing organisations) and usurpation of market power unto themselves. In the ultimate analysis, market power comes from the brand equity.

There are various advantages that accrue to a brand builder vis-à-vis trade credit:

(a) A firm having brand equity enjoys higher trade leverage in barraging with the dealers because consumers want the latter to stock the products. This translates into offering of lower discounts and minimum trade credit.

(b) On the supply side, firms with strong brand equity command larger discounts and longer credit period from the suppliers.

It follows, therefore, that firms having high brand equity should have lesser receivables and higher payables. This is in contrast with the findings of the studies on firms in United States where large firms are found to be net suppliers of trade credit, i.e. receivables are larger than payables. Banerjee, Dasgupta and Kim[37] who studied large U.S. manufacturing firms also found that trade credit and market power are negatively related. But Horen Van[38] who studied a large sample of firms located in twenty countries of Eastern Europe and Central Asia found a strong positive relationship with customer power and trade credit. He found the relationship to be stronger when the suppliers are small and more risky and located in countries with limited financial development. His study shows that in these countries when a supplier faces a customer with strong market power would have to submit to the demand of trade credit by the

---

35. It is not that manufactures always choose between two extremes. They may follow a combination of both the strategies depending upon the nature of the target market. A firm may also follow 'Push' strategy in one market and 'Pull' strategy in another market.

36. Archer, Jeffrey, *As The Crow Flies*, Harper and Collins Publishers, London, 1997.

37. Banerjee, Dasgupta and Kim (2004), *ibid.*

38. Horen Van. (2007), *ibid.*

customers. In an earlier study of small firms, Wilson and Summers[39] also found a similar positive relationship with customer power and trade credit. These two contrasting findings indicate that in matured economies large firms are net suppliers of credit and in developing economies they are net takers of credit.

As value of brand equity is not published, except in case of acquisition, we may use advertising and sales promotion expenditure as proxy for brand equity or market power. We intend to show, by way of two examples, that in a developing country like India, higher the advertisement and sales promotion expenditure, lower the receivables and higher the payables.

Hindustan Lever Limited (now, Hindustan Unilever Limited) and ITC Limited have over a period of time built up strong brand equity both for the company and also a range of their products. The two companies are household names in India. In Table 2.1 we have calculated relevant ratios from their published Annual Reports to discern their market power and approach towards trade credit.

Table 2.1 Market Power Ratios of Hindustan Lever Limited and ITC Limited

Hindustan Lever Limited

Ratios	2001	2002	2003	2004	2005	2006
Advertising and sales promotional expenditure sales(%)	7.51	8.46	7.49	8.25	8.97	10.38
Sales/trade debtors (days)	14	13	17	20	18	14
Sales/trade creditors (days)	78	88	88	86	93	94
Trade creditors/trade debtors	5.53	6.51	5.18	4.41	5.11	6.72
Trade creditors/materials inventory	3.93	3.67	3.60	2.83	3.66	3.61
Trade creditors/total inventories	1.92	1.90	1.75	1.60	2.11	1.99

ITC Limited

Ratios	2001	2002	2003	2004	2005	2006
Advertising and sales promotion expenditure sales(%)	4.35	3.56	3.74	4.12	2.89	2.30
Sales/trade debtors (days)	91	66	14	14	26	21
Sales/trade creditors (days)	105	114	128	158	91	80
Trade creditors/trade debtors	1.16	1.73	9.39	11.59	3.52	3.85
Trade creditors/materials inventory	1.32	1.98	2.32	2.21	1.43	1.18
Trade creditors/total inventories	1.06	1.34	1.64	1.34	0.95	0.82

Notes:

1. Materials inventory includes stores and spares, and packing materials.
2. Total inventories comprise materials inventory, work-in-process inventory and finished goods inventory.
3. Debtors turnover ratios and creditors turnover ratios are both calculated on net sales, though normally the former is taken on total sales and the latter on purchases. However, this departure from standard method will not affect our analysis.

---

39. Wilson, N. and B. Summers, "Trade Credit Terms Offered by Small Firms: Survey Evidence and Empirical Analysis", *Journal of Business Finance and Accounting*, Vol. 29, pp. 317–351, 2002.

The advertising and promotional expenditure of Hindustan Lever Limited (HLL) is highest in corporate India; it is also growing continuously. Presently, it is more than 10 percent of net sales. In comparison, the ratio is rather low for ITC Limited but it should be qualified by the fact that in India, advertising for cigarettes and tobacco products, which constitute more than 85 percent of ITC's sales, is prohibited. If this ratio is normalised by factoring in the segment percentage of sales, it may be found that it is more than 15 percent in 2006 (2.30 * 100/15).

Both the companies are leader in their market, enjoy tremendous brand equity and hence, market power at both ends of the market. They provide least credit to their buyers and extract most credit from their suppliers. HLL provides about three weeks' credit to its buyers and obtains nearly twelve weeks' credit from the suppliers. Market command ratio (trade creditors/trade debtors) for HLL is 5.58 on an average. That is, the company takes 5.58 times the credit it provides to the market. The striking feature is that supply creditors cover materials inventory by 3.55 times and that of total inventories by 1.88 times.

The picture is more or less similar for ITC. This company also provides about three weeks' credit to its buyers and takes about twelve weeks' credit from its suppliers. Average market command ratio of ITC is 5.20. However, the inventory coverage ratios of ITC are not as high as HLL, though on an average these are more than 1.

The *prima facie* conclusion that can be reached from the above analysis is that in contrast to the United States, in India brand equity or market power enables companies to extract more credit than they provide. That is, they are net takers of credit, which is consistent with the findings of Horen Van[40].

SUMMARY

In this chapter we have categorised theories of trade credit developed so far. There are eight such categories, namely financing theory, liquidity theory, financial distress theory, transactions costs theory, quality guarantee theory, price discrimination theory, product differentiation theory and market power theory.

Oldest among these theories is the financing theory, which views trade credit as a substitute for institutional finance, particularly for those firms, which do not have access to it owing to substandard credit worthiness. Liquidity theory holds that firms suffering from negative cash flows or which are losing sales demand use more trade credit. The reason lies in their inability to collect sales in time. Financial distress theory is based on 'buyer opportunism'. When a supplier is in financial distress the buyers pay less promptly, which aggravates the crisis further. Transaction costs theory shows that when there are frequent transactions between buyers and sellers, trade credit can be used to reduce transaction costs for both the parties by opting for periodic payment terms. Quality guarantee theory explains that when quality of a product cannot be

---

40. Horen Van (2007), *ibid.*

ascertained immediately buyers demand trade credit, which provides them time to check the quality of the product before making payment. Price discrimination theory is based on the assumption that when market is highly competitive sellers resort to non-price competition like, trade credit to effectively discriminate price, which is otherwise not permitted by regulatory restrictions. Product differentiation theory claims that trade credit is similar to various trade promotion tools like advertisement to differentiate a product from competition. Market power theory explains why in contrast to matured economies, in developing economies like India, large corporates with market power are net users of credit. They provide much less credit to the buyers and extract more trade credit from the suppliers.

In conclusion, we must emphasise that each of these theories is applicable in specific circumstances only. A general theory of trade credit is yet to emerge.

CHAPTER 3

Management of Accounts Receivable

I was light inside out when I was a child
As I age, I see darkness with borrowed light

INTRODUCTION

Accounts receivable do not feature in the national accounts of a country; similar is the case with accounts payable because the two get cancelled out at the macro-economic level. What we find is the inventory—the real physical stocks—around which these debit-credit transactions take place. A credit flow normally runs parallel to the productive-distributive line of a firm which meets finally at the terminal point of consumer credit. This flow of credit is akin to credit creation by the banking system, though for a limited span of time, but considering the volume of credit-backed inventory flow through an economy, its impact often makes all calculations of monetary authorities topsy-turvy. The longer is the productive-distributive line and the more complex it is, as in Japan, higher the impact of this quasi-credit creation on the monetary targets of an economy. At some points, bank finance does enter into this process to smoothen the flow of inventory through the economy, but it also energises the process of credit creation by providing 'reserve money'. In this chapter we shall discuss various techniques of receivables management. Wherever necessary, relevant theories of trade credit, as discussed in Chapter 2, will be further elaborated to provide background support.

CREATION OF ACCOUNTS RECEIVABLE

Accounts receivable of a firm are created on both sides of the productive system. On one side of this system, the firm may make advance payments to the suppliers of inventories (raw materials) to ensure timely supply, particularly when the suppliers hold monopolistic position in the market place, or when materials are in short supply, or simply to develop a captive supply base. A firm may also be motivated to make advance payments for pure short-term financial and profitability considerations. Any one or a combination of them will create accounts receivable on the left side of the productive system (see Chapter 1 under para "Other Discrete Inventories" and Figure 1.4) which may replace the box for supply creditors or hinge parallel to it.

On the other side of the productive system, accounts receivables are created by a firm when it sells its outputs on credit. These are popularly termed as *sundry debtors* by the English to distinguish it from other forms of accounts receivables. Sundry debtors constitute nearly 60 percent of accounts receivables of an enterprise. Many of the considerations that weigh in the minds of a seller are similar to that of making advance payment for supply of materials, though often on the opposite direction. But there are more to it than this, which will be discussed later.

SIZE OF ACCOUNTS RECEIVABLE

Although accounts receivable does not find much place in economics literature because of its non-existence in national accounting framework and the assumption of perfect financial market, its enormity as a financial variable cannot be ignored at the firm level when we find that even in an advanced economy like the United States, it constitutes more than 20 percent of the total assets of manufacturing firms[1]. In India, it is about 26 percent. In Table 3.1 we have presented data to capture the quantum and movement of receivables in Indian corporate sector during 1997–1998 to 2005–2006.

Table 3.1 Movement of Accounts Receivable in Indian Industry

(Rs. in crore)

Particulars/Year	1997-98	1998-99	1999-00	2000-01	2001-02	2002-03	2003-04	2004-05	2005-06
Total Assets	2,069,727	2,391,400	2,692,958	3,092,698	3,424,782	3,838,149	4,266,467	5,002,309	5,752,392
All receivables	373,203	406,830	452,737	520,100	589,289	685,166	706,402	753,847	838,634
	(18.03)	(17.01)	(16.82)	(16.82)	(17.21)	(17.85)	(16.56)	(15.07)	(14.58)
Sundry debtors	139,116	144,490	158,914	179,365	193,500	204,989	199,901	229,502	240,323
	(6.72)	(6.04)	(5.90)	(5.80)	(5.65)	(5.34)	(4.69)	(4.59)	(4.18)
Gross sales	836,704	935,823	1,092,820	1,307,434	1,355,512	15,44,957	1,754,862	2,081,082	2,335,645
Net sales	763,450	857,777	1,004,988	1,216,176	1,255,006	1,434,209	1,628,712	1,940,727	2,171,478
Turnover ratio of Debtors (Days of gross sales)	61	56	53	50	52	48	42	40	38

Basic data source: Industry: Financial Aggregates and Ratios, Centre For Monitoring Indian Economy (CMIE). The turnover ratio is calculated from the basic data.

Notes: 1. Figures in bracket indicate percentage of total assets.
2. Average daily sales is calculated by dividing gross sales by 365 days.

GENERAL TREND IN ACCOUNTS RECEIVABLE

We may observe from Table 3.1 that share of aggregate accounts receivable, and sundry debtors in the total assets of Indian industrial sector has slowly come down from 18.03 percent in 1997–98 to 14.58 percent in 2005–06 in case of former and from 6.72 percent to 4.18 percent in case of latter for the same period. This is in tune with advanced economies where this share has also gradually declined with the expansion of financial system both in breadth and depth. In India, the movement is rather slow due primarily to the prevalent cash credit system of working capital finance and absence of alternative financial instruments. It is expected that in India, with the liberalisation of financial market and gradual replacement of cash credit by loan system of financing, the situation will improve further.

1. Mian, S.L. and Clifford W. Smith, Jr., "Accounts Receivable Management Policy: Theory and Evidence", *The Journal of Finance,* March 1992, pp. 169–200.

Table 3.1 also reveals that in Indian industrial sector number of days of sales locked in accounts receivable has also come down over time. That is, sales are being realised faster than before. This may be partly ascribed to recent changes in the financial market where every firm has to compete for fund, which forces it to give lesser credit to its customers. In India, days of easy availability of bank finance to corporate sector are over. With expanding breadth of financial market banks also have multiple avenues for investment; they are no longer so much dependent on the industrial sector for deployment of fund. As long as the burden could be passed over to the market, corporate sector did not bother much about strengthening itself internally for better management of its current assets. But with the competition the market has ushered in new norms for allocation of financial resources based on the economic principles of marginal productivity of capital. It is, therefore, imperative for firms to look internally and gear up its machinery for working capital management with particular attention to receivables management where major part of current funds gets blocked.

TRADE CREDIT: MARKETING-FINANCE TRADE OFF

Whatever way we look at it, accounts receivables imply trade credit, and the decision to grant trade credit may either be part of marketing strategy or pure finance strategy, but mostly it is a trade-off between marketing and finance strategies of a business.

An important goal of marketing is matching of the demand of a market segment with adequate and timely supplies. Choice of a correct distribution system or channel is, therefore, key to achieving such a goal. The decision to pick up a particular channel has a long-term effect on the business. Once a channel is chosen it is difficult to alter it in short-term because of commitments made to a large number of people and to independent firms whose principal business is distribution. It often takes years to develop a distribution channel which may remain external to the enterprise, but gets integrated so much with it that it takes up the character of a total business system. Any attempt to snap even a small part of this chain may have the effect of ultimately blocking the inventory flow through the system. In this sense it is akin to the productive system chosen by an enterprise; the only difference is that a productive system is technology-driven while a distribution system is market-driven.

DISTRIBUTION CHANNELS

Choice of a particular distribution channel has a direct impact on inventory holding and level of receivables. In Chapter 1, while presenting a generic framework of the distribution channel of an enterprise, we have shown that even when an enterprise does not desire to own the entire channel, working capital requirement does not change, except marginally. Such is the importance of correct choice of a distribution channel.

Direct marketing or owning a marketing channel (which is also called *zero-level channel*) is best from the point of view of receivables management. As the manufacturer has direct control over the distribution system, receivables are closely monitored resulting into lower level of receivables holding. There is also less distortion in marketing and credit information flow to the business. While marketing research information enables the firm to understand quickly the changing consumer needs and product behaviour, the credit information helps it understand credit behaviour of customers, which forms the basic input to decide whom to grant trade credit and the degree of monitoring required for a particular customer or a group of customers owing to any change in their creditworthiness.

There are several ways by which direct marketing is being performed in India, e.g. manufacturer's own selling outlets, viz. mail order, door-to-door sales, telemarketing and TV selling, of which the last two are just being introduced. Direct marketing is most prevalent in India for products like shoes (Bata), sewing machines (Singer), certain electrical items like gensets, steel furniture, automobiles and also cosmetics.

Direct marketing entails combining two functions, viz. manufacturing and retailing. The latter must give sufficient return—at least equal to that of manufacturing—to justify its existence. This return, however, need not be an absolute ROI. It shoud be weighted by taking into account the opportunity cost of marketing and credit information, the latter resulting into a lower level of receivables and/or bad-debt.

Example A company having investments in manufacturing assets of Rs. 20,000 produces 360 units a year at a cost of Rs. 100 per unit. Market price of the product is Rs. 150 per unit.

The company can sell its entire output to distributors at a 10 percent trade discount on the listed price with a credit period of two months.

Should the company go for direct marketing, capital investments in marketing assets would be Rs. 4000. In addition to that Marketing Department's overheads will claim Rs. 3000 per year. But holding of receivables will come down to one month.

Option I: The company chooses external distribution channel

	Rs.
Market price per unit	150
Less: 10% trade discount	15
Net sale price	135
Less: Cost per unit	100
Operating profit per unit	35
Operating profit from sale of 360 units at Rs. 35 per unit = Rs. 12,600	
Investment in manufacturing assets	20,000
Add: Investments in receivables, $\dfrac{(360 \times 135 \times 2)}{12}$	8100
Total investments	28,100

Hence, return on investments $= \dfrac{12,600}{28,100} \times 100 = 44.84$ percent
(ignoring investment in inventories)

Option II: The company decides to go for direct marketing

The marketing department receives from the manufacturing department 360 units at Rs. 135 per unit (the net price at which goods are sold to distributors).

	Rs.
Price per unit	150
Less: Cost per unit	135
Return per unit	15
Gross return (360 × 15)	5400
Less: Overhead costs	3000
Operating profit	2400
Capital investment in marketing assets	4000
Receivables for one month, $\dfrac{(150 \times 360)}{12}$	4500
Total investments in marketing assets	8500

Return on investments in marketing assets $= \dfrac{2400}{8500} \times 100 = 28.24$ percent (ignoring investment in inventories)

It appears, on the face of it, that option II is infeasible because of a much lower return on investment as compared to the manufacturing function. But if we now add a further information that under option I, the company is presently required to spend an amount of Rs. 1800 per annum for continuous market research and credit information through external agencies (formal credit reporting firms are yet to develop fully in India) which will be reduced to Rs. 300 per annum under option II, then the decision might as well turn in favour of option II as the following calculation will reveal.

	Rs.
Operating profit	2400
Add: Opportunity savings in information cost (Rs. 1800 – 300)	1500
Total return	3900

Notional return on investment in marketing assets will, therefore, be: $\dfrac{3900}{8500} \times 100 = 45.88$ percent which is more than that under option I where ROI now stands reduced to 38.43 percent owing to incidence of information cost[2].

CREDIT INFORMATION

In direct marketing where a firm uses its own sales force, market and credit information are more likely to be generated as a by-product so much so that it can virtually replace external agencies normally engaged for these purposes.

---

2. For further discussion on other marketing ratios see, Bhattacharya, Hrishikes, *Total Management by Ratios*, 2nd. ed., Sage Publications, New Delhi, 2007.

As the firm's own sales people are directly in contact with the buyers they must be adequately motivated to obtain credit information. One way of doing it is to decentralise trade credit decisions. In such a structure the sales people, who have the most direct knowledge of the buyers, make credit extension decisions. This acts as a direct motivation for them and enhances the competitive advantage of the firm in the market place. But it also increases the monitoring costs and the probability of bad-debt losses. This negative impact can be minimised if sales commissions are adjusted against uncollected receivables. But such adjustment should not be done at one stroke. It should be spread over a period of time, otherwise it might act as a disincentive which will kill the very purpose of decentralisation.

FROM SELLERS' MARKET TO BUYERS' MARKET

As the number of players in a product market increases, the comparative advantage of direct marketing declines. One of the main reasons behind this is that customers would always prefer to visit a store which displays products of different manufacturers. They are no longer willing to dispense with their newly acquired 'right to choose'. There is an inherent conflict between a manufacturer who typically produces a large quantity of a limited variety of goods and the consumers who usually desire to buy only a limited quantity of a wide variety of goods.[3] Secondly, the investment required for setting up a direct marketing organisation has become very high these days owing to rising cost of office space and increase in the cost of direct communication network. Economies of scale now tends to favour specialised distribution agencies external to the manufacturing organisation.

When a firm moves from sellers' market to buyers' market, consequent movement from a dedicated marketing and distribution system to external agencies is one of the most crucial strategic decision that it has to take. The adjustment process is often agonising. The manufacturer appears to be almost placing the firm's destiny in the hands of intermediaries. The immediate consequences would be a rise in receivables holding and reduction in the speed and accuracy of information flow. Some firms attempt a middle-of-the-road policy, i.e. they retain a part of the distribution system. The advantage is that the firm learns about managing retail outlets. It can rapidly and flexibly test new products and ideas and provide a model for operator-owned outlets, and user-owned outlets to benchmark the performance of operator-owned outlets. The disadvantage is that operator-owners may resent the competition coming from company-owned outlets for fear that the company will eventually buy out the operators. Dual distribution often creates channel conflict.[4] This conflict is more pronounced in receivables management because the firm is compelled to follow a uniform trade credit policy which often is disadvantageous for the firm-

---

3. Louis W. Stern and Abel I. El-Ansary, *Marketing Channels*, Prentice-Hall, Englewood Cliffs, N.J., 1992.
4. Kotler, Philip and K.L. Keller, *Marketing Management,* 12th ed., Prentice-Hall of India, New Delhi, 2006.

owned outlets. The power of trade credit as a differentiating instrument is virtually lost in such a dual distribution system.

Direct marketing tends to be inefficient in a competitive economy and this inefficiency is passed on to the consumers in the form of higher prices for the product. As mentioned above, this inefficiency is the result of diseconomies of scale embedded in direct marketing. For example, if there are four manufacturers and four customers in a market, as many as $4 \times 4 = 16$ contacts will be required by all the manufacturers to reach all the customers. As against this, if all the manufacturers send their goods to one distributor number of contacts get reduced to $4 + 4 = 8$. That is, the aggregate cost of contacts is reduced by half, a part of which, net of distributor's commission can be passed on to consumers. Besides this, the market also enjoys other economies of scale when a distributor deals with a number of manufacturers. Distributor's overheads are then distributed amongst a wide range of manufacturers.

MOTIVES FOR EXTENDING TRADE CREDIT

Theoretically speaking, a distributor is expected to be neutral amongst various manufacturers of a product under uniform terms and conditions of distribution, e.g. commission, discount, cost reimbursement, etc. This leaves the products of individual manufacturer to compete among themselves in terms of their attributes like price, quality, etc. But in practice, such a perfection does not exist. Various other factors beyond the basic attributes of the product itself influence not only the buying decision of a customer, but also the distributor's preference to push the products of a particular manufacturer. One such attribute is trade credit which exercises tremendous influence in altering preferences of both the distributor and the consumers, and is almost similar to price. In fact, trade credit often acts as a valuable price discrimination tool at the hands of a manufacturer who has financial power. However, when trade credit is granted by a manufacturer to wholesalers or retailers (rather than to customers directly) in an effort to create price discrimination, it may lead to successive monopoly problem[5]. From customers' point of view, trade credit for any period of time against cash purchase effectively reduces the price of the product because of the time value of money. For the manufacturer, motives for extending trade credit are operating, marketing and financial.

Operating Motive

This motive flows primarily from the anxiety of the producer to keep its manufacturing function insulated from the 'vagaries of the market'. Every firm suffers from irregularity of demand due to seasonality or uncertainty of the market. One way to resolve the problem is by temporary modification of operations, i.e. by varying the rate of production. Except for highly

---

5. Hirshleifer, Jack, "Internal Pricing and Decentralised Decisions", *in*: C.P. Bonini, R.K. Jaedicke, and R. Wagner (Eds.), *Management Controls*, McGraw Hill, New York, 1964.

synchronised just-in-time manufacturing where production is triggered only on receipt of an order, changes in operations are often costly. It may also create problem for absorption of overheads. Ultimately, such charges may turn out to be costly to the buyers also through both price mechanism and quality of products[6].

Another way to respond to the problem is by varying price of the product in response to the demand situation. That is, by lowering the price when the demand is low and increasing the price when the demand is high. Even ignoring the price war that may follow (which may eat into the bottom line of a producer) such variation in prices may not always make the prospective customers responsive to lift the production. Price-elasticity plays a crucial role in such a situation, besides the availability of spendable resources at the hands of the consumers.

The third alternative to absorb the shocks of varying demand is formation of customer queues (when demand is high) or product queues, i.e. inventories (when demand is low). In the former case customers' loyalty may suffer, and in the latter case holding costs of inventories may simply be prohibitive.

The best alternative, according to Emery[7], is to allow receivables to absorb the shocks of fluctuation in demand. A firm may meet a temporary deficit (excess) in demand with temporary relaxation (tightening) of credit terms or credit standards. Receivables are thus allowed to fluctuate in response to deviations in demand keeping the manufacturing function undisturbed. While this method of response is not costless, it can be implemented quickly and has the advantage of confining the disturbance to the financial structure of the firm. Although this method is the best amongst all the alternatives discussed so far, in the final analysis it rests on the financial power of the firm because, in effect, a part of such power is transferred to the customers who may not have it at a time of recession. The cost aspect of this method will be discussed under *Financial Motive*.

Marketing Motive

This motive emanates from the desire of a firm to break into a new market, or increase market share in the existing market. Trade credit extension as an effective tool for price discrimination can be used in a market whose competitive structure cannot otherwise be altered. This instrument can be used either singly or with other instruments, e.g. occupying of shelf or display space of distribution outlets. When this method is employed consequent upon the rise in receivables, monitoring costs will also increase besides the carrying costs of receivables. All these costs should preferably be bracketed under promotional costs, no matter how these are ultimately treated in financial accounting.

---

6. Alchain, A., "Information Cost, Pricing and Resource Unemployment", *in:* E.S. Phelps (Ed.), *Microeconomic Foundations of Employment and Inflation Theory*, W.W. Norton & Co., New York, 1970.

7. Emery, G.W., "A Pure Financial Explanation for Trade Credit", *Journal of Financial and Quantitative Analysis*, September 1984, pp. 271–285.

Financial Motive

Schwartz[8] while discussing the impact of trade credit on monetary policy and price control observed, *inter alia*, that a seller having a better access to capital than its customers would profit by giving trade credit to the latter. This inherently presupposes an imperfect financial market. Lewellen et al.[9] pointed out that trade credit cannot be used to increase firm's value when financial markets are perfect, because in such situations all credit terms that are acceptable to both the seller and the buyer are the present value equivalents of cash terms. Hence, searches for an optimal credit policy need to be focussed explicitly on the existence of financial market imperfections. In fact, exploitation of opportunities thrown up by market imperfections is the source of financial motive for extending trade credit.

At the firm level, these imperfections are manifested in liquidity crisis requiring ad hoc borrowings (if available readily) and the risk of insolvency as a consequence of payment failures. Sudden lengthening of productive-distributive pipeline for operational reasons may also contribute to this crisis. We have already shown in Chapter 1 that in order to withstand this crisis, firms normally maintain a cash stock as liquid reserve. On the other hand, the productive-distributive line can unpredictably be shortened throwing up sudden additional cash which cannot just be invested in production or other physical assets immediately, or it may not be desirable to do so. Hitherto, a firm could keep all these cash in its cash credit account which, by freeing the limit to the extent of cash deposit, would not only provide adequate liquidity, but also would enable the firm to earn (save) interest on cash credit account which offered (charged) one of the best (worst) rates available in the economy. But with the gradual replacement of cash credit system of lending by term loans, firms would be deprived of this arrangement. In fact, they would now be forced to install a proper cash management system within their organisations so that all these idle or contingent cash are invested properly. The cash can be kept in the current account with a bank which will fully satisfy the liquidity need of the firm but would not earn any income. Other strategy could be to hold the whole or a greater part of this cash in highly liquid marketable securities—preferably gilt-edged instruments either directly or through units of Money Market Mutual Funds—which will enable the firm to earn the benchmark rate of return of the money market. At the same time, it will also provide a quick access to liquidity.

A part of this fund can also flow to commercial paper or inter-corporate deposit market. This is a short-term market which is operated on risk-return trade-off. In effect, this market provides a lending opportunity to firms having investible cash for short period.

8. Schwartz, R., "An Economic Model of Trade Credit", *Journal of Financial and Quantitative Analysis*, September 1974, pp. 643–657.
9. Lewellen, W., J. McConnell, and J. Scott, "Capital Market Influences on Trade Credit Policies," *Journal of Financial Research*, Fall 1980, pp. 105–113.

An alternative lending opportunity is also available to firms beyond the money market, which is, lending through receivables. Firms can loan a part of their liquid resources directly to their customers as trade credit for a definite period. The extension of trade credit for this purpose is analogous to the purchase of directly placed commercial paper or inter-corporate deposit and is preferable to market lending if the seller can charge an implicit interest rate, that is greater than the market lending rate of return.[10] The liquid reserve, which is now converted into receivables, is still available to the seller as and when necessary by discounting it with a bank or other lenders in the *bill market.*

Financial Market Tariff

When a firm operates in the financial market to find investment opportunities for its liquid reserve, its treasury function ultimately takes on the role of a financial intermediary. This role is more pronounced when it engages itself in financing its customers through receivables. When the financial market is imperfect due primarily to asymmetry of information, market borrowing rate and lending rate are different (which should be uniform in a perfect financial market). If the market borrowing rate of interest exceeds the market lending rate, a seller with a liquid reserve would be additionally motivated to extend trade credit, because the transaction costs due to asymmetry of information is considerably less to him than a regular finanacial intermediary, like bank. This is so due to the fact that unlike a bank, a seller's customers are homogenous people whose closeness to the seller is much more than that to a bank which reduces the information asymmetry to a large extent and hence, lowers down the transaction costs. Besides, in case of default, a seller can repossess the goods, rework it if necessary and then sell them once again, often at normal price. For a bank, it is only distress sale which ultimately increases the collection costs.

The pure financial motivation of trade credit discussed above can be further explained with the help of the following example.

Example   Suppose, a buyer purchases goods worth Rs. 10,000 from a seller. Buyer does not give immediate cash to make payment but he borrows the amount at a borrowing rate of 20 percent p.a. He expects to repay the loan in 3 months. Borrowing cost of the buyer would, therefore, be

Rs. $\dfrac{10,000 \times 0.20 \times 3}{12}$ = Rs. 500.

When the buyer pays to the seller, the latter receives Rs. 10,000 immediately. Assuming now that presently he does not have the opportunity to invest the cash in real assets of the firm like inventories, the amount will be taken to liquid reserve which is now available for short-term lending in the market. If the market lending rate available to the seller is 18 percent p.a., he

would receive Rs. $\dfrac{10,000 \times 0.18 \times 3}{12}$ = Rs. 450 at the end of three months. It

---

10. Emery, G.W., *ibid.*

would appear that the cost paid by the borrower (buyer) and the income received by the lender (seller) are different by Rs. 50 which is not available to any one of them. It is simply lost to the market. This is akin to a tax imposed on the market players due to financial market imperfections.

It is possible for both the buyer and the seller to recover the financial market tariff through trade credit transactions. Suppose the seller can wait to be paid at 3 months, he may extend trade credit for this period, but he must, at the same time, compensate himself for the time value of money. He should therefore charge a price greater than the base price of Rs. 10,000. There are three ways to do it:

1. He can put in a maximum load of Rs. 500 or 20 percent p.a. (which is the borrowing rate of the customer) and recapture the financial market tariff entirely unto himself.

2. He can also add Rs. 450 or 18 percent p.a. for three months to the base price (which is the maximum lending rate available to the seller) and allow the customer to recover the tariff entirely.

3. He can choose any rate between these two maximums which will allow the tariff to be recovered both to himself and the buyer, though not necessarily, in exact proportions. For example, if the seller loads the receivables at 19 percent p.a. the buyer ends up paying Rs. 475 as interest cost, thereby saving Rs. 25. The seller also receives Rs. 475 as interest income at the end of three months, thereby gaining Rs. 25 over and above what he is getting at present from the financial market. In reality, however, the recovery of the financial market tariff cannot be made in full because transaction costs (information and collection costs) will eat some portion of it. But as discussed before, transaction costs for a seller of merchandise is much lower than a direct intermediary, like bank. This is an added incentive for a seller to circumvent the financial market and deal in receivables for profitable investment of his surplu cash.

Existence of financial market tariff and the opportunity available to a merchandise seller to recover a larger part of this tariff through trade credit in the manner described above enables a firm to take diferent strategic positions in marketing its goods and services. These are discussed in the following sections.

Price Discrimination

In a highly competitive product market, where prices of the base goods are determined at the market place, perhaps the only effective method available to a seller to discriminate prices is through varying credit terms. The assumption here—which is quite valid in real life situation—is that although the product market is perfect, the financial market suffers from several imperfections giving rise to different finance cost to different persons or groups of persons. Since price discrimination is a very effective tool to increase market share it can be administered through a trade credit policy which effectively lowers down gross price of the product to a customer. This is done by allowing him to share the whole or a larger part of the recovery of the financial market tariff through receivables financing. In the example given above, gross price of the product to the customer including borrowing cost comes to be Rs. 10,500. Trade credit can reduce the price effectively to Rs. 10,450 without making the seller any loser in the bargain. Larger the financial market tariff between the buyer and the seller, higher is the opportunity to effectively practise price discrimination for capturing larger market share in a competitive product market. This is more true for customers in lower-income segment. Emery's observation in this respect is worth noting:

> "Since the value of the interest subsidy depends on the amount financed, offering below-market interest rates provides lower effective prices to lower-income customers. And if these customers have more elastic demands, a policy of lowering credit terms rather than lowering prices of the product, more effectively discriminates price, and thus increases firm value."[11]

Pushing the Product

If the demand for the product is inelastic or there is inventory piling up due to recession in the product market, availability of fund for buyer's purchase often acts as 'add-on' which effectively differentiates the product in the market place and energises the buying motive of the customer. This may not always increase immediate consumption of the product very substantially, but may cause the inventories to be transferred from the manufacturers' godown to consumer-households or warehouses for future consumption. But the combined cost of the product and credit must be sufficiently low to enable the customer to overcome the inelasticity barrier. Lowering down the product price coupled with transferring the recovery of entire financial market tariff to the customer is a good strategy in such situations.

This strategy is also equally applicable to a firm with significant seasonality in sales. It can motivate the retailers to hold larger inventories during lean periods by changing trade credit policies over time. By lowering the price of credit during slack season the firm can raise the off-peak demand from the retailers and thus lower the inventory carrying cost and reduce the costs of varying production over the cycle as discussed earlier.

Trade credit is also used as an effective tool to expand the total market of a product. A market leader normally gains the most when the total market expands. It is, therefore, his duty to see tnat whenever the market for the product is reaching a saturation point steps are taken to break the stagnancy by adopting appropriate strategies in the circumstances. One such measure is new-market strategy whereby newer and hitherto unexplored segments are developed to increase the total size of the market. Another strategy could be market-penetration strategy whereby non-users in a market segment are encouraged to use the product. If the targeted market segment belongs to low-income category, then trade credit is a useful tool to develop this segment. The

---

11. Paraphrased from Mian, S.L., et al., *ibid*, p. 173.

form of trade credit in such circumstances may be installment plan. When colour television or personal computer markets were saturating, this strategy helped enlarging the market to a great extent.

Motivating Distribution Channel Members

Truly speaking, middlemen in the distribution channel do not act as the selling agents of the manufacturers they represent, but as purchasing agents of their customers unless they have special motivation to alter the role. Since any alteration of this basic role is, in a way, a disservice to his customers there must be sufficient incentives to overcome the 'ethical' barrier. Such incentives may come in various forms, viz. larger commission/discount, reimbursement of expenses, rentals of shelf-space, performance rewards/gifts, etc. Competition in providing such incentives is very high among manufacturers to woo the middlemen to alter their original role in preference to the product of a particular manufacturer. Unfortunately, competition itself often standardizes many of these incentive-offerings in a product market making them less effective as differentiating mechanisms. Besides, cash incentives which, though, is often very attractive for the ultimate consumer, is not so for a middleman, particularly when it is coupled with early payment, because a middleman is used to deal in volume and hence, he is more interested in aggregate profit than a larger commission on a particular product. In order to make such volume, he needs fund to carry an assortment of goods in his store because the demand for these goods depends more on the marketing activity of the manufacturer than his selling activity. This fund requirement of a market intermediary is a crucial factor in India where, culturally banks and financial institutions tend to favour a manufacturer than a trader. Major sources of fund for these middlemen are non-banking financial institutions and unorganised financial market. Cost of fund in this market is very high. Even when banks do provide them loans, rate of interest charged on such loans is often higher than what is charged to a manufacturer. In such a situation trade credit acts as a tremendous incentive for a middleman. Between a larger discount/commission and a longer trade credit, an Indian trader often tends to favour the latter. It is found that a typical Indian trader would sell faster (often at a lower margin) the products of a manufacturer who offers longer trade credit, because with the money so available, he is in a position to increase his total turnover. As the financial market tariff faced by the trader is very high, trade credit can act as a very effective tool at the hands of a market planner to induce the middleman to shift his preference.

LIMITATIONS

Marginal Cost Consideration

From a theoretical point of view, trade credit can be extended for an infinite length of time. The trade credit model developed by Emery[12] assumes a

---

12. Emery, G.W., *ibid.*

monotone increasing in 't'. But in real-life situation we find firms not offering extremely long periods of credit. One of the reasons behind this, is embedded in marginal cost considerations. If the seller is pursuing pure financial motive in extending trade credit, i.e. to earn an excess rate of return by lending to customers, then he would continue to extend trade credit to customers until the marginal cost of offering trade credit becomes equal to the market borrowing rate of interest. As marginal cost of fund for a seller rises both with time and size of the fund, at some point of time, it will equal the market borrowing rate of his customers. Beyond that point, the customers would not be motivated to obtain trade credit. The time period at which marginal cost of fund of a seller equals the market borrowing rate of the customer, is the maximum period for which trade credit can be extended.

Tax Considerations

Tax has both positive and negative impact on the firm's value depending upon the types of accounts receivables that a firm contracts. When receivables are installment-loans (e.g. financial lease) the seller books profit over the loan life rather than at the point of sale, and hence pay taxes also by installments over a period of time. As a result, present value of taxes will always be lower than when it is paid at the point of sale. The firm may not have any cash flow problem to pay taxes if installment-repayment by the customer is timed appropriately to take care of advance tax payment obligation, which is quarterly under Indian Income Tax Act.

In case of ordinary accounts receivable, full profit is booked at the time of sale under accrual system of accounting and quarterly advance tax is paid on it. If the tax is paid before the realisation of receivables, the firm ends up paying more taxes in terms of present value. Besides, tax is payable on full operating profit which includes interest recovery for delayed payment also. That is, the firm is required to pay tax on its opportunity cost and the amount of this tax increases with the length of the credit period and at some point of time, the present value of the after-tax profit falls resulting into a negative *net present value* (NPV). The illustration given in Table 3.2 will clarify the position.

It may be seen from Table 3.2 that as the credit period is lengthened, net present value of the receivable starts falling and at 12 months it becomes negative. It is true that as the credit period is increased the net present value is bound to fall and at some point it becomes negative, but the impact of taxation at the point of sale makes the fall faster. For example, if the tax is levied on realisation of sales (cash basis) the NPV would remain positive even at 12 months as the following calculation will prove:

Table 3.2 Trade Credit—Period

(Amount in rupees)

	3 *months*	6 *months*	9 *months*	12 *months*
1. Base price of the product(s)	10,000	10,000	10,000	10,000
2. Loading @ 24% p.a. (or 2% p.m.) (opportunity cost)	600	1200	1800	2400
3. Final price	10,600	11,200	11,800	12,400
4. Cost of sales	8000	8000	8000	8000
5. Net profit	2600	3200	3800	4400
6. Income tax @ 45%	1170	1440	1710	1980
7. Profit after tax	1430	1760	2090	2420
8. Amount payable at the point of sale (item no. 4 + 6)	9170	9440	9710	9980
9. Amount receivable after the credit period (item no. 3)	10,600	11,200	11,800	12,400
10. Discount factor @ 2% p.m. (opportunity cost)	0.9423	0.8880	0.8368	0.7885
11. Present value of amount receivables after the credit period (item no. 9 × 10)	9988	9946	9874	9777
12. Net present value (item no. 11 – 8)	818	506	164	– (203)

Note: Discount factors in item no. 10 are calculated at an opportunity cost of 2 percent per month as the practice is to load the receivable in terms of month(s) of credit period allowed.

	(Rs.)
Gross realisation after 12 months	12,400
Less: Income tax	1980
Net realisation	10,420
Discounted value (Rs. 10,420 × 0.7885)	8216
Cost of sales	8000
Net present value	216

The problem is compounded further because the firm has to pay taxes on its own opportunity cost. Beyond a certain period the firm ends up paying out more in terms of taxes than it intends to realise. This happens in the present case at the credit period of 12 months as the following calculation will reveal.

Opportunity cost for 12 months' receivables is Rs. 2400 of which income tax @ 45 percent or Rs. 1080 is payable at the point of sale leaving only Rs. 2400 – 1080 = Rs. 1320 as the net realisation, the discounted value of which is Rs. 1320 × 0.7885 = Rs. 1040. Net present value of this opportunity cost, therefore, comes to be Rs. 1040 – 1080 = Rs. (–) 40.

Determining Maximum Length of Trade Credit

The constraints discussed above, limit the maximum length of credit period that a firm can allow on its receivables. In the present example (Table 3.2), the period must lie somewhere between 9 months where the NPV is positive and 12 months where it becomes negative. Maximum length of the credit period should, therefore, be such where NPV is close to zero. With the help of the following formula we can arrive at the maximum credit period for the example given in Table 3.2.

$$M = m + \frac{N}{N - W} \times (n - m)$$

where

M = maximum length of the credit period

m = credit period immediately before the NPV becomes negative, which in the present case is 9 months (refer Table 3.2)

N = NPV at the credit period m, which in the present case is Rs. 164

n = credit period immediately after m at which NPV becomes negative, which in the present case is 12 months

W = NPV at the credit period n, which in the present case is Rs. $(-)203$

For the example presented in Table 3.2 maximum length of the credit period should be

$$M = 9 + \frac{164}{[164 - (-203)]} \times (12 - 9)$$

$$= 9 + \frac{164}{367} \times 3$$

$$= 10.34 \text{ months, at which credit period the NPV will be close to zero.}$$

Check

1. Base price of the product	10,000
2. Loading at @ 2% p.m. opportunity cost for 10.34 months	2068
3. Final price	12,068
4. Cost of sales	8000
5. Net profit	4068
6. Income tax @ 45%	1830
7. Profit after tax	2238
8. Amount payable at the point of sale (item no. 4 + 6)	9830
9. Amount receivable after the credit period (item no. 3)	12,068
10. Discount factor @ 2% p.m.	0.8147
11. Present value of amount receivable after the credit period (item no. 9 × 10)	9831
12. Net present value (item no. 11 – 8)	1, (say '0')

Note: Discount factor is calculated as follows:

$$D_f = \frac{1}{\left(1 + \dfrac{i}{12}\right)^n} = \frac{1}{\left(1 + \dfrac{0.24}{12}\right)^{10.34}} = \frac{1}{(1.02)^{10.34}} = 0.8147$$

This is how the discount factors for other credit periods are calculated in Table 3.2.

We should point out that the above formula enables the trade credit manager to determine the maximum length of the credit period with close approximation to what can be arrived at with mathematical precision by using a sophisticated numerical model. Such a precision is not required for taking managerial decision to grant trade credit. Even in the present case, a trade credit manager would convert the 10.34 months to approximately 10 months and 10 days as the maximum length of credit that he may extend.

ELEMENTS OF TRADE CREDIT POLICY

Importance of Written Trade Credit Policy Document

Although accounts receivables are short-term in nature, the policy decisions that create accounts receivables often have a long-term impact on the organisation and its financial structure, because once a receivables policy is determined, it is difficult to come out of it except at the cost of adverse market reactions. Besides, as we have mentioned before, credit policy decisions are part of an integrated approach, which interface actively with production, marketing and finance functions of an enterprise. Hence, frequent alternation of credit policies may create severe imbalances in the functional structure of the organisation.

In view of long-term commitment of both financial and organisational resources in receivables management, trade credit policies of an enterprise must be decided by the top management preferably at the board level. It is always desirable that credit policies form part of written policy documents and communicated at all appropriate levels of management. In the absence of written credit policy document credit decisions suffer from short-term considerations and ad-hocism which may often cause a severe liquidity crisis. If it is found that an organisation is suffering intermittently from cash crises, the reason may well be found in the absence of a written credit policy document.

The efficacy of a credit policy lies in its easy understanding and implementation by even the last decision-making line of the marketing organisation, namely sales people at the grass-root level. This is possible only when decision variables and their parameters are standardised. It is often claimed that the major deterrent to standardisation is the subjectivity that creeps into any trade credit decision. It is true that it is difficult, rather impossible to eliminate subjectivity. (It is also not always desirable because that takes away the very charm of decision making.) But the negative aspect of subjectivity can be minimised to a large extent by standardising the subjective elements also in a scientific manner. Even the high priest of statistical inferences—the probabilistic estimation—has emerged from out of attempts made by both pure and social scientists to standardise the subjectives and judgementals. While discussing elements of trade credit policy we shall try to adopt this approach. But before we do so, we should analyse the impact of a trade credit decision on an organisation in order to develop a framework within which credit policies should evolve and operate.

To begin with, we can use the original framework prescribed by Smith[13] with some modifications. The framework is illustrated with the help of the following example.

Sales	Rs. 100
Return on sales	10%
Additional collection expenses	
for delayed payment (ignore costs of fund)	Re. 1

Alternative outcomes of a credit decision are presented in Table 3.3.

Table 3.3   Alternative Outcomes of a Credit Decision

	Customer pays promptly	Customers delays payment	Customer never pays
Grant credit	Sales and profitability increased	Increased collection expense	Increased collection expense + bad-debt
Amount	10	10 − 1 = 9	−(1 + 90) = (−)91
Probability	0.60	0.35	0.05
Weighted value	6.0	3.15	(−) 4.55
Reject credit	Lost sales and profitability	Lost sales and profitability − collection expenses	Collection and bad-debt expenses avoided
Amount	(−) 10	−(10 − 1) = (−) 9	1 + 90 = 91
Probability	0.60	0.35	0.05
Weighted value	(−) 6.0	(−) 3.15	4.55

The six alternative outcomes of a credit decision shown in Table 3.3 are not exhaustive. There may be some other outcomes which we are not able to capture in the above framework. For example, question may be raised about the behaviour of some customers who have been good pay-masters for many years but suddenly start defaulting particularly when large orders are placed. Besides, erratic payment behaviour of certain customers may often be due to volatility of their own sales or that of the industry to which they belong.

The example illustrated in Table 3.3 explains the working of the credit decision framework. It may be seen that the final values of corresponding outcomes are same under 'Accept' or 'Reject' decision with plus and minus signs respectively. However, it is only the 'Accept' decisions that are reflected in the financial accounting reports. 'Reject' decisions never feature in the body of accounts. It can only be captured within this framework as opportunity lost. Only a well-established management audit system can highlight the impact of negative decisions on firm's value.

The probabilities attached to different outcomes enable a credit manager to use the framework for day-to-day decision-making by evolving suitable standards. In the example given above, the aggregate weighted value of the

13. Smith, Keith, V., *Guide to Working Capital Management,* McGraw-Hill, New York, 1978.

outcomes under 'Accept' or 'Reject' decision is 4.60. A firm may decide that it will reject the trade credit proposal of a customer if the aggregated weighted value of the outcomes is less than 4.50. This benchmarking depends on the risk-profile of an enterprise which, in turn, depends *inter alia*, on its fund position and cost thereof, market share objective, culture and attitude of the organisational personnel—conservative, progressive or aggressive—and general state of the industry—cyclical up or down turn. As the risk-profile of the enterprise changes, the benchmark value will also change during periodical reviews. This makes the system dynamic. Attaching probabilities to different outcomes is a function of both subjective and objective analysis of a customer's credit proposal which we shall discuss at the appropriate place. However, at this stage it is necessary to provide a framework for setting up credit limit for individual buyer. This is necessary to prevent ad-hocism and arbitrary decisions by the credit managers.

CREDIT LIMIT

Credit limit can be defined as the maximum amount of outstanding receivables and/or a maximum order size for a particular buyer. When such limit exceeds it triggers appropriate actions. The question is whether there should be only one type of omnibus credit limit, as is the general practice. Scherr[14] addressed this question and suggested that instead of one there should be two credit limits. He observed that risk, in terms of uncertainty about the expected payment and default characteristics of customers calls for one set of triggers and actions, and risk, in terms of changes in payment probability or costs associated with order size requires another. He proposed the following two types of credit limits.

Information Credit Limit

This is defined as the internal control mechanism that alerts the credit manager of the need for credit investigation. According to Scherr, this limit is necessary because the cost of such investigation is fixed, while the other costs and revenues associated with the credit granting decision increases with the order size. For example, if the current ratio of a buyer-firm has fallen below the standard requirement, it triggers a credit manager to enquire into the reasons behind such a fall and if necessary, to revise the credit limit, as we shall see later.

Risk Credit Limit

This is defined as the point at which the marginal present value of granting further trade credit to a customer becomes negative owing to increase in risk or unit costs. In fact, this credit limit addresses changes in the risk, default probability and other factors that are affected by the amount of credit granted. For example, for some buyers probability of default increases with the order size.

---

14. Scherr, F.C., "Optimal Trade Credit Limits", *Financial Management*, Vol. 25, pp. 71–85, Spring, 1996.

Information credit limit and risk credit limit are not mutually exclusive. Rather, they are interdependent because risk and order size for a particular buyer depends on the credit investigation triggered by the information credit limit.

The operational aspect of this policy is that when a customer's order size increases, the lower of these two limits governs the actions to be taken. If the information credit limit is lower than the risk credit limit, further investigation is triggered before the risk credit limit is reached. On the other hand, when the risk credit limit is less than the information credit limit, the customer's order size is restricted until order sizes are large enough to trigger additional credit investigation. Based on such investigation, the risk and/or information credit limits are revised.

GOAL AND FUNCTIONS OF ACCOUNTS RECEIVABLE MANAGEMENT

Functions of accounts receivable management emanate from its goal which is stated simply as setting out credit terms, selecting the customers, installing appropriate collection and monitoring system and financing the receivables for maximising the firm's value.

Credit Terms

As indicated before, trade credit policy choice is not an isolated function of the credit administration department alone; rather it must be so as to subserve the goals of production, marketing and finance functions of a business in an integrated manner. We have shown that the goal of credit policy should be such that production function is insulated from the vagaries of market; marketing is able to increase or consolidate the market share and finance function can lower down the costs and increase profitability of the business. These functional goals are often in conflict with each other. An appropriate credit policy should aim at resolving this conflict.

Although funds invested in accounts receivable is considered in project formulation as one of the components of current assets, it is hardly given any serious consideration as compared to investments in plant and machinery and other fixed assets. Generally, market norms of holding accounts receivable and inventories are incorporated in the project as initial investment, and their rise with sales over a period of time are taken as incremental funds outflow. Consideration of alternative credit policies generally comes only after the business is on the way, though it is always desirable to evaluate the impact of alternative credit policies on the value of the project as we shall see later.

Normally, acceptance or rejection of an alternative credit policy is dependent upon whether marginal profit is equal to, more than or less than the marginal cost of projected new sales. Costs include, cost of goods sold, collection and administration costs, bad-debt losses and cost of fund invested in carrying additional receivables. Certain issues must be settled before we embark on evaluating alternative credit policy.

Opportunity Cost

The first such issue is what should constitute cost of fund. Some finance managers are found to take the borrowing cost of working capital as the cost of fund. This rate is easily available and is straightforward in the sense that the finance manager feels the pinch of borrowing cost in day-to-day management of working capital. Another section would go for average cost of capital which includes all the debts and equity of the enterprise. While the latter is a better estimate than the former, it focuses only on the external cost of fund and thus ignores the (required) rate of return or opportunity cost of rupees invested in the business. For example, if return on funds invested in the current assets of a firm is 30 percent before interest and taxes, any amount released from current assets, say by sale of inventories, is expected to be reinvested in the current assets at the same rate notwithstanding the external cost at which these funds have been raised. In fact, this rate of return is often used as the basis for deciding a particular liability structure of a business by its proper allocation among different claimants like government (taxes), equity (earning per share) and debt holders (interest).

Looking at it from another angle, fund invested in accounts receivable is nothing but an input which is as scarce as any other inputs engaged in the business. This scarce resource (fund) of the enterprise can be invested in a variety of areas—the determining factor being the most favourable alternative use. For example, if the rate of return on funds invested in current assets is lower than the market rate of return on gilt-edged securities the firm can as well invest the available (released) fund in these securities rather than reinvesting it in current assets. Hence, the opportunity cost of fund in this case would be return on gilt-edged securities. In other words, opportunity cost of fund is nothing but the best value of scarce funds of the business which, ultimately is the true cost of fund.

Receivables at Cost or Sale Price

The second issue is whether receivables and bad-debt losses should be taken at full value or at cost for the purpose of evaluating an alternative credit policy. Generally, analysts are found to take the receivables at cost of various inputs incurred to manufacture and sale of a product (i.e. excluding the element of profit). Sometime, Reserve Bank of India also took this stand while laying down norms for receivables holding, though later on, it revised its stand and allowed banks to take receivables at full sale value for the purpose of determining permissible bank finance. Without going into the background of RBI's policy reversal we can say that the argument for taking receivables at *cost of sales* is that fund invested originally in inventories gets transferred to receivables when the inventories are sold on credit. Hence, like inventories, accounts receivable should also be taken at cost of goods sold.

But this proposition wrongly asserts that the out-of-pocket expenses are the only relevant costs to consider while evaluating the profitability of alternative credit policies, and retained earning (in the form of profit elements in credit sales) is simply a source of financial capital which does not have a cost[15]. This also beats the very concept of opportunity cost, which as we have already said, is the value of cash flow invested in accounts receivable. The reason behind this is that when a sale is made, it is at full value including the profit. If the firm chooses to sell it in cash, the full amount is immediately available for alternative usage. One such usage could be investment in further accounts receivable itself, but it does not necessarily so happen. As one of the objectives of credit policy analysis is to examine whether investment in additional receivables satisfies the value criteria (opportunity cost) of the business, it is desirable to take receivables at full value.

Treatment of accounts receivable—at cost or at selling price—in the decision framework may sometime have serious implication on 'Accept' or 'Reject' decision of alternative credit policies. The following example will make it clear.

Example The existing sale of an enterprise is Rs. 800 crore with an average collection period of 30 days and bad-debt losses of 1 percent. Variable costs of goods sold is 80 percent of selling price.

If the present credit policy is relaxed, the firm is expected to increase its sales by Rs. 200 crore. But the average collection period of sales and bad-debt losses will increase to 90 days and 2 percent respectively. Cost of capital of the business is 20 percent.

In Table 3.4 we have presented the results under alternative methods of valuation of receivables.

Table 3.4 Marginal Profitability and Cost Calculations for Alternative Valuationof Accounts Receivable

(Rs. in crore)

Particulars (1)	Receivables valued at cost (2)	Receivables valued at selling price (3)
1. Marginal profitability of sales (operating) $200(1-0.80)$	40	40
2. Additional investments in accounts receivable valued at cost $\left(\dfrac{1000\times0.80\times90}{365}\right)-\left(\dfrac{800\times0.80\times30}{365}\right)$	144.66	—
3. Additional investments in accounts receivable valued at selling price $\left(\dfrac{1000\times90}{365}\right)-\left(\dfrac{800\times30}{365}\right)$	—	180.82
4. Marginal cost at (2) above $(0.20\times144.66)+$ $(1000\times0.02-800\times0.01)\,0.80$	38.53	—
5. Marginal cost at (3) above $(0.20\times180.82)+(1000\times0.02-800\times0.01)$	—	48.16

15. Dyl, E.A., "Another Look at the Evaluation of Investment in Accounts Receivable", *Financial Management*, Winter 1977.

It would appear from Table 3.4 that while column 2—where receivables are valued at cost—is signalling an 'Accept' decision (because marginal profitability is larger than marginal cost), column 3—where receivables are valued at selling price—is signalling a 'Reject' decision (because marginal profitability is lower than marginal cost). However, such conflicting signals will appear in situations like this only. But when the receivables valued at cost gives a signal for rejection, the valuation at selling price will also indicate the same signal. If a tighter credit policy were considered, evaluating the change in receivables valued at cost would understate the marginal opportunity saving. Thus conflicting signals might arise only in the decision to reject the tighter credit policy. If the marginal opportunity saving from cash flow, released through a reduction in receivables, were greater than or equal to the marginal cost of reduced sales, an understatement of the savings would bias toward a rejection of the proposal[16].

Short-Term Credit Policy Changes

Credit policy choices have a distinct temporal bearing. Criteria for decision making in short-term are often different from that in the long-term. For example, an easier credit policy may be the appropriate choice in short-term to move piled up inventory or to park additional cash flows in receivables rather than in marketable securities. A firm can also make the same policy choice when it intends to increase the market share or break into a new market. In the following example, we shall first take a short-term view. The same example will then be modified to explain a long-term strategic choice of a business:

Example Company A, which is facing the problem of slow-moving inventories, gathers information from its market intelligence that it can make additional sales of Rs. 375 crore if it relaxes the credit period to 90 days. Fraction of new sales expected to be bad-debt is 2 percent.

Cost of goods sold (variable, including collection expenses) is 80 percent of selling price. Opportunity cost of capital of the company is 20 percent.

This kind of problem is generally faced by firms which are subjected to seasonal fluctuation in sales or when the industry to which they or their customers belong, is in the grip of cyclical downturn. (In fact, concerted action by firms to extend trade credit often acts as a tremendous fillip to pull up an industry from cyclical downturn.) When the problem is short-term in nature, behaviour of major variables analysed for taking a 'yes' or 'no' decision should also be considered on short-term basis. For example, in the above case only variable cost of the product is considered; Overheads are assumed to be unchangeable during short-term. Besides, as the objective is to run down the piled-up finished goods inventory, there shall not be any additional build-up of inventories along the productive-distributive line of the enterprise (which will happen when credit policy changes are considered for the long term, as we shall see later).

---

16. Oh, John, S., "Opportunity Cost in the Evaluation of Investment in Accounts Receivable", *Financial Management,* Summer 1976, pp. 32–36.

The following model enables us to evaluate the above proposal.

$$p = s(1 - v) - \left(sb + ivc \, \frac{s}{365} \right) \qquad (3.1)$$

where

p = incremental profit

s = additional sales expected due to a change in credit policy

v = variable cost of sales in percentage

b = expected bad-debt losses as percent of additional sales

i = opportunity cost of capital in percentage

c = credit period

In the present case, incremental profit from the proposed change in credit policy will be as follows:

$$p = 375 \, (1 - 0.80) - \left(375 \times 0.02 + 0.20 \times 0.80 \times 90 \, \frac{375}{365} \right)$$

$$= 75 - (7.5 + 14.80)$$

$$= Rs. \ 52.70 \ crore$$

On the face of it, the proposal is acceptable because p is a positive value. (We have not considered here time value of money which we shall discuss later.)

The above is a case of transferance of fund invested in inventory to accounts receivable. Hence, opportunity cost of fund has been considered only for the receivable period. But besides the fund cost, there are also other costs associated with the holding of inventories which are eliminated once the goods move out from manufacturer's godown. This can be incorporated in the above model as below:

$$p = s(1 - v) - \left(sb + ivc \, \frac{s}{365} \right) + gsv \qquad (3.2)$$

where g is physical carrying cost of inventory as percentage of cost of goods sold. Assuming this to be 0.5 percent, resultant p will be

$$= Rs. \ 52.70 + 0.005 \times 375 \times 0.80$$

$$= Rs. \ 54.20 \ crore$$

Long-Term Credit Policy Changes

We can now consider long-term credit policy change by modifying the above example suitably.

Example Present market size of company A's product is Rs. 5000 crore which is growing at 10 percent p.a. Existing market share of the company is 20 percent or Rs. 1000 crore. It desires to increase its market share by 5 percent.

As a part of various strategy formulations, the company is also considering an alternative receivable policy. Marketing department is of the opinion that the company can increase its market share to 25 percent if its present credit policy is relaxed. But as a consequence of it, the average collection period is likely to be increased from 60 days at present to 90 days.

The company believes that relaxation of credit policy would not have any major impact on its existing customer both in respect of collection efforts and bad-debt losses. Cost of the collection department is presently Rs. 5 crore which is likely to be increased by 20 percent due to rise in sales. Relaxation of credit policy may cause bad-debt losses to rise more for new customers. Overall impact is expected to be 1.30 percent as against the present level of 1 percent. Cost of sales, which is presently 80 percent of sales, is likely to be reduced to 78 percent due to economies of scale within the existing capacity.

Core working capital of the company is presently Rs. 16.34 crore which is estimated to be Rs. 22.56 crore for the projected sales. Current assets (excluding debtors) and current liabilities comprise the following CWC cycles:

(a) Work-in-process inventory   0.96 CWC cycles
(b) Raw materials inventory   3.52 CWC cycles
(c) Finished goods inventory   4.30 CWC cycles
(d) Other current assets   5.36 CWC cycles
(e) Trade and expense liabilities   3.87 CWC cycles

Physical carrying cost of inventories is 0.5 percent p.a.
Opportunity cost of capital of the company is 20 percent p.a.

As compared to the earlier example, the credit policy changes proposed here have a long-term bearing on the company's future, because if the company finally decides to relax its credit standards, it would commit itself generally to the market, i.e. both to its existing and future customers. Although we have assumed in the above example that the new credit policy would not have much impact on the behaviour of existing customers, this may not always be the case. For example, a relaxed credit policy often makes a good pay master go relaxed.

In the earlier example, the relaxation in credit standards was necessitated to clear the accumulated inventory and as a consequence, there was some savings in the physical carrying cost of inventories. But in the present case, there shall be additional build-up of inventories along the productive-distributive chain of the business. However, generation of additional inventories need not be the direct result of credit policy changes; it is rather due to increase in sales which can as well occur by adoption of any other marketing strategy, for example, special publicity campaign followed by occupation of shelf-space, etc. But whatever strategy is employed (including credit policy changes) financial evaluation of such strategy must cover every impact level including inventories. From this perspective, the alternative strategy proposed in the above example is evaluated.

Projected Sales

Present market of the company's product is Rs. 5000 crore which is growing at 10 percent per annum. The company desires to capture 25 percent of the market. Hence projected sales will be:

Rs. 5000 × (1.10) × 0.25, or Rs. 1375 crore as against present sales of Rs. 1000 crore.

Net current assets formation (excluding accounts receivable) for the existing and projected sales is given in Table 3.5.

Table 3.5 Net Current Assets Formation under Alternative Credit Policies (excluding Accounts Receivable)

(Rs. in crore)

Item (1)	CWC multipliers (2)	Existing amount (Rs. 16.34 × col. 2) (3)	Projected amount (Rs. 22.56 × col. 2) (4)
Work-in-process inventory	0.96	15.69	21.66
Raw materials inventory	3.52	57.52	79.41
Finished goods	4.30	70.26	97.00
Other current assets	5.36	87.58	120.92
Subtotal	14.14	231.05	318.99
Less: Trade and expense liabilities	3.87	63.24	87.31
Net current assets (excluding accounts receivable)	10.27	167.81	231.68

Investments in accounts receivable are calculated in Table 3.6 both at full sale price and at cost of sales for existing as well as projected sales. Finally, profitability of alternative credit policies is examined in Table 3.7.

Table 3.6 Calculation of Investments in Accounts Receivable

(Rs. in crore)

	At sale price	At cost of sales
Existing	(Rs. 1000 × 60)/365 = Rs. 164.38	(Rs. 1000 × 0.80 × 60)/365 = Rs. 131.50
Projected	(Rs. 1375 × 90)/365 = Rs. 339.04	(Rs. 1375 × 0.78 × 90)/365 = Rs. 264.45

Table 3.7 reveals that marginal profitability of sales is larger than marginal cost under both types of receivables valuation. Hence, the new credit policy appears to be acceptable.

Table 3.7 Profitability Statement of Alternative Credit Policies

(Rs. in crore)

Particulars	Receivables valued at cost	Receivables valued at sale price
1. Marginal profitability of sales [1375 (1 − 0.78)] − [1000 (1 − 0.80)]	102.50	102.50
2. Additional investments in net current assets (receivables valued at cost) (231.68 + 264.45) − (167.81 + 131.50)	196.82	—
3. Additional investments in net current assets (receivables valued at sale price) (231.68 + 339.04) − (167.81 + 164.38)	—	238.53
4. Marginal cost at (2) above (196.82 × 0.20) + [(5 × 1.20) − 5] + [(0.013 × 1375) 0.78 − (0.01 × 1000) 0.80]	46.30	—
5. Marginal cost at (3) above (238.53 × 0.20) + [(5 × 1.20) − 5] + [(0.013 × 1375) − (0.01 × 1000)]	—	56.58

CAPITAL BUDGETING APPROACH

In so far as 'Accept' or 'Reject' decision of a new credit policy, the framework presented above may be considered sufficient (though further precision is possible by disaggregating the components of a credit policy as we shall discuss later), but it does not tell us the effect of credit policy changes on firm's value. In order to understand this impact, we have to consider time value of money within a capital budgeting framework. This framework integrates the accounts receivable decision within the overall corporate goal via opportunity cost of capital. In simple terms, the evaluation of investment in accounts receivable and other related current assets should be same as in any other capital asset. In fact, while evaluating proposed investment in a project, any increase/decrease in net current assets is considered as cash outflows/inflows for the current period. What we propose to do presently is to take out this component of project evaluation for indepth analysis of a proposed change in credit policy.

We have seen in Chapter 1 that sales made daily for a definite credit period generates a continuous cash flow stream which helps maintain the continuity in the productive-distributive chain of a business. This is similar to cash flow stream of a project which when discounted at the opportunity cost of capital gives the present value of cash inflows. For purpose of credit policy decisions cash outflows will be cost of sales, collection and bad-debt costs. However, when long-term policy change is considered, cost of carrying additional inventories has also to be considered for reasons mentioned earlier. One way of looking at investment in the inventories is to treat them similar to an investment in plant and machinery. From the point of view of funds analysis there is no difference between the two types of investments. But problem arises in their treatment within the net present value (NPV) framework. In case of evaluation of ordinary capital expenditure, investment in plant and machinery is regarded as the major cash outlay in the '0' year against which present value of future cash flows is compared. At the end of the life of the project, the salvage value of the plant and machinery is discounted back along with the net current assets which are presumed to have been liquidated at current market prices. Theoretically speaking, the same treatment can be meted out to inventories for evaluating alternative credit policies, but it may create serious practical problems because exercises for changing credit policies are often made within the given life of a project in response to various strategic options. In credit policy decisions, unlike receivables which periodically mature for payment, the inventories do not so mature for payment though there may be continuous *inter-se* movement of inventories. The funds blocked in inventories do not get realised except at the end of the project. It is preferable, therefore, to treat the cost of holding and carrying the inventories as cash outlay for the purpose of evaluating alternative credit policies.

The capital budgeting approach discussed above is explained further with the help of the last illustration.

To bring the credit policy decisions within capital budgeting framework we may assume, as we have done in Chapter 1, that all sales are made and all costs are incurred uniformly throughout the year on a daily basis. For example, in the illustration given above, the company makes Rs. 1000 crore/365 = Rs. 2.74 crore sales daily on two months credit. That is, this sum is realised less of bad-debts every day after the initial take-off period of two months. Costs are also similarly calculated on a daily basis. The NPV approach in a capital budgeting framework now requires calculation of daily discount rate for a cost of capital (opportunity cost) of 20 percent p.a. This is done in the following manner:

$$(1 + r)^{365} = (1 + i)$$

where r is the required daily discount rate, i is the opportunity cost of capital. In the given case r is calculated as

$$(1 + r)^{365} = (1 + 0.20)$$

or $\qquad 365 \log (1 + r) = \log 1.20$

or $\qquad \log (1 + r) = 0.0791812/365$

or $\qquad 1 + r = $ antilog 0.000216934

$\qquad\qquad\qquad\quad = 1.0004996$

or $\qquad\qquad\qquad r = 0.0004996$

In Table 3.8 comparative analysis of existing and proposed credit policies are made.

As indicated before, in the matter of 'Accept' or 'Reject' decision the NPV approach gives signal similar to earlier methodology explained in Table 3.7 but, in addition to that, which is more important from the point of view of overall corporate objectives is that it tells us by what amount firm's value will increase or decrease due to a new credit policy. In the present case, the firm's value will increase daily by the incremental NPV of Rs. 47.04 lakh – Rs. 33.27 lakh = Rs. 13.77 lakh.

Table 3.8 Evaluation of Alternative Credit Policy

(Rs. in crore)

	Existing	Proposed
1. Daily sales realisation Less of bad-debt		
(a) $\dfrac{\text{Sales }(1 - \text{bad-debt \%})}{365}$	$\dfrac{1000\,(1 - 0.01)}{365} = 2.7123$	$\dfrac{1375\,(1 - 0.013)}{365} = 3.7182$
(b) Present value of (a) above	$2.7123 \times \dfrac{1}{(1 + 0.0004996)^{60}} = 2.6322$	$3.7182 \times \dfrac{1}{(1 + 0.0004996)^{90}} = 3.5548$
2. Daily cost		
(a) $\dfrac{\text{Cost of sales}}{365} + \dfrac{\text{Collection cost}}{365}$	$\dfrac{1000 \times 0.80 + 5}{365} = 2.2055$	$\dfrac{1375 \times 0.78 + 6}{365} = 2.9548$
(b) Holding cost of current assets + carrying cost of inventories $\dfrac{\text{Net current assets}}{365} \times \text{Opportunity cost}$ $+ \dfrac{\text{Inventories}}{365} \times \text{Carrying cost}$	$\dfrac{167.81 \times 0.20}{365} + \dfrac{143.47 \times 0.005}{365} = 0.0940$	$\dfrac{231.68 \times 0.20}{365} + \dfrac{198.07 \times 0.005}{365} = 0.1296$
(c) Total daily cost (a + b)	2.2995	3.0844
3. Net present value [1(b) – 2(c)]	0.3327	0.4704

CHANGING CREDIT STANDARDS

We have so far considered aggregate credit policy changes without making any distinction between two components of a credit policy, namely, change in credit standards and change in credit period. This distinction was first brought forth by Dyl[17]. He argued that the analysis for a change in credit standards and for a change in credit period offered are not the same because their objectives and impact on the customers are different.

Credit standards may either be relaxed to attract new customers or tightened to eliminate unprofitable customers. However, in both the cases the dominant consideration are the change in firm's investments in accounts receivable and consequent profit or loss.

Relaxation of credit standards implies that the firm is now willing to extend credit to customers of higher risk categories. Customers belonging to these categories may either have a cash flow problem or a capital adequacy problem, or both. If the firm decides to relax the standard of integrity demanded of its customers, the problem is compounded further. All these may ultimately have the effect of delay in payment and increased percentage of bad-debt losses among the new customers who come to the fold. The assumption here is that the existing customers would not dilute their own standard of payment performance except under circumstances beyond their control. This assumption is valid to a large extent provided the firm does not lax in collecting debts.

Example Let us assume that a firm is considering loosening its existing credit standards upto a point which will enable it to increase its sales from the present level of Rs. 1000 crore to Rs. 1400 crore. It is estimated that the average collection period of new customers would rise to 90 days as against 60 days for the existing customers, and bad-debt losses will be 3 percent for the new customers while presently it is 1 percent. Cost of sales is 75 percent of sale price and the opportunity cost of capital of the firm is 20 percent per annum. Assume further that the collection cost will be 1 percent of new sales; presently, it is 0.5 percent.

Ignoring cost/savings of carrying additional inventory and assuming that the firm has enough capacity to generate new sales, incremental profit/loss due to lowering down of credit standards will be given by the following formulas:

$$p = s(1 - v) - \left(svb + sq + ivc \, \frac{s}{365} \right)$$

if receivables and bad-debts are reckoned at cost, and

$$p' = s(1 - v) - \left[s(b + q) + ic \, \frac{s}{365} \right]$$

---

17. Dyl, E.A., *ibid.*

if receivables are carried at full sale price

where

p = incremental profit

s = additional sales

v = cost of sales as a percentage of sale price

b = bad-debt losses as a percentage of additional sales

q = collection cost as a percentage of additional sales

i = opportunity cost of capital

c = average collection period for additional sales

Hence, in the present example, incremental profit (p or p') is given by

$$p = 400\,(1 - 0.75) - \left[(400 \times 0.75 \times 0.03 + 400 \times 0.01) \right.$$

$$\left. + \left(0.20 \times 0.75 \times 90\,\frac{400}{365} \right) \right]$$

$$= 100 - (13 + 14.80)$$

$$= \text{Rs. } 72.20 \text{ crore, and}$$

if the receivables are considered at full value, then

$$p' = 400\,(1 - 0.75) - \left[400\,(0.03 + 0.01) + 0.20 \times 90\,\frac{400}{365} \right]$$

$$= 100 - (16 + 19.73)$$

$$= \text{Rs. } 64.27 \text{ crore}$$

As incremental profit (p or p') is positive, the marginal customers are clearly profitable, and hence the dilution of credit standards is acceptable.

In conclusion, it may be noted that the rise in average collection period for new customers is not the result of official extension of credit period which generally remains unchanged, but due to mobility of these customers to adhere to the credit period officially granted. The firm tacitly tolerates the delay without making it official lest it might influence the existing customers.

CHANGING THE CREDIT PERIOD

While a change in credit standards does not ordinarily change the payment behaviour of existing customers, official announcement of a change in credit period does. The impact of such a change is a rise in average collection period of receivables and consequently a larger investment in accounts receivable.

When a new credit period is announced without a dilution in credit standards, bad-debt losses are not expected to rise, but sales are, whether it is used as a tool to beat the competition or to clear the godowns of slow moving inventories, or simply, to satisfy the pure financial motive discussed earlier. It is not that all the existing and future customers will take the enhanced credit period. Some may continue to pay as before (which may be earlier than the existing credit period) while some may enjoy the benefit of the extended credit period. Field sales persons are able to provide enough market intelligence in regard to change in payment behaviour of existing and prospective customers (the latters are of course likely to take the new credit period fully). Assume now that a firm announces the extension of credit period from existing 60 days to 90 days with the expectation of rise in sales from Rs. 1000 crore to Rs. 1400 crore, analysis of market intelligence report may reveal the following payment behaviour of the customers (Table 3.9).

Table 3.9 Existing and Altered Payment Behaviour of Customers with Change in Credit Period

(Rs. in crore)

	Payment pattern (1)	Percent of customers (2)	Sale value (Rs.) (3)	Weighted average (col. 1 × col. 2) (4)
Existing				
	30 days	15	150	450
Sales: Rs. 1000 crore	60 days	60	600	3600
	75 days	25	250	1875
		100	1000	5925
Average collection period: 5925/100 = 59.25 or say, 60 days.				
Proposed				
	30 days	10	140	300
Sales: Rs. 1400 crore	60 days	20	280	1200
	90 days	70	980	6300
		100	1400	7800
Average collection period 7800/100 = 78 or say, 80 days.				

We may observe from Table 3.9 that a large part of customers who were already paying in less than 60 days would continue to do so even when the credit period is extended to 90 days. While new customers are expected to avail themselves of full credit period, their rank will be swelled up by customers who were hitherto enjoying fully the existing credit period and sometimes an extended credit period also (75 days).

As a result of the announcement of the new credit period, average collection period of the entire (projected) sales will stand increased to 90 days. This will call for additional investment in accounts receivable which is likely to be more than what we had, when credit standards were diluted. Evaluation of a policy change in credit period can be made with the help of the following formula:

$$P = S_N(1-V) - \left[VB_N S_N + Q_N S_N + i\left((C_N - C)\frac{S}{365} + V\left(C_N \frac{S_N}{365}\right)\right) \right]$$

where

P = incremental profit due to credit period extension

S = existing sales

S_N = expected incremental sales due to credit period extension
V = cost of sales as percentage of sales
B_N = expected bad-debt losses as percentage of new sales
Q_N = cost of collection as percentage of new sales
  i = opportunity cost of capital
C_N = new average collection period due to credit period change

Example Using the same data as in the last example (except that on receivables) we can evaluate the proposed policy change on credit period extension.

$$P = 400\,(1 - 0.75) - \Big[0.75 \times 0.03 \times 400 + 0.01 \times 400$$

$$+\,0.20\Big((90 - 60)\frac{1000}{365} + 0.75\Big(90\,\frac{400}{365}\Big)\Big)\Big]$$

$$= 100 - [9 + 4 + 0.20\,(82.19 + 73.97)]$$

$$= \text{Rs. } 55.77 \text{ crore}$$

Although the proposed policy of extending credit period appears to be viable because incremental profit is positive at Rs. 55.77 crore, the latter is lower than that under changed credit standards for the simple reason, that as the existing customers change their payment habits to avail themselves of the more generous credit period, the accounts receivable attributable to these customers increase.

It may be seen that throughout the above equation, the accounts receivable are valued at cost except in the fourth term of the right-hand side of the equation where the current sales are valued at sale price. The reason behind this is that due to $(C_N - C)$ days delay in receiving the proceeds from current sales the firm loses the opportunity to earn its required rate of return (opportunity cost) on both profit and the investment in cost of sales for these days. Hence, both profit and 'cost' are treated as foregone earning opportunity which is the real cost of extending credit period.

When the receivables are treated at full sales value, there is no need to make the above distinction. All the profit elements in all receivable terms of the above equation are treated as opportunity foregone and hence the cost of alternative credit period policy, as already discussed before. The incremental profit would necessarily be less in such a situation which can be calculated by simply deleting 'V's from the right-hand side of the above equation (given on p. 74) except the first term. In the present case it will be

$$P' = 100 - [12 + 4 + 0.20(82.19 + 98.63)]$$

$$= 100 - (16 + 36.16)$$

$$= \text{Rs. } 47.84 \text{ crore}$$

Shortening the Credit Period

Credit period changes need not necessarily be always for extension only, it can as well be shortening of credit period. A firm may adopt this policy as a part of credit rationing strategy necessitated by tight financial condition including high rate of interest or high demand outstripping the supply. Unless the firm enjoys a monopolistic position in the market or its product is price inelastic, shortening of credit period will ordinarily lower down sales. However, investment in accounts receivable will go down when there is a reduction in sales. If the market share is not a major consideration, shortening of credit period may often be beneficial to the firm from the profitability angle. Evaluation of such a policy can be made by modifying the earlier equation as given here

$$P = S_N(1-V) - \left[VBS_N + QS_N + i(C_N - C)\frac{S + S_N}{365} + V\left(C\frac{S_N}{365}\right)\right]$$

Example We can use the same example on the reverse to explain the above equation. S is now Rs. 1400 crore and S_N is (–) Rs. 400 crore whereas $C = 90$ days and $C_N = 60$ days; B and Q are bad-debt losses and collection costs that are associated with S_N. Other things remaining same, incremental profit (P) or loss (–P) is calculated as:

$$P = -400(1-0.75) - \left[0.75 \times 0.03(-400) + 0.01(-400) \right.$$

$$+ 0.20\left((60-90)\frac{1400-400}{365} + 0.75\left(90\frac{-400}{365}\right)\right) \Bigg]$$

$$= -100 - \left[-9 - 4 + 0.20\left(\frac{-30 \times 1000}{365} - 73.97\right)\right]$$

$$= -100 - [-13 + 0.20(-82.19 - 73.97)]$$

$$= -100 + 44.23$$

$$= \text{Rs. } -55.77 \text{ crore}$$

When accounts receivable are valued at sale price, incremental profit/loss position (P') will be

$$P' = -100 - [-12 - 4 + 0.20(-82.19 - 98.63)]$$

$$= -100 + 52.16$$

$$= \text{Rs. } -47.84 \text{ crore}$$

As both P and P' are negative, the shortening of credit period is not feasible. This is because the loss of profit due to reduction in sales is not made good by savings in costs of carrying receivables and other expenses.

DISCOUNT POLICY

There are two types of discounts that a firm offers to its customers: trade discount and cash discount. The former is generally offered to intermediaries as a percentage cut on the list price which takes into account their expenses and profit margin. This is often used as a price discriminating tool to motivate the intermediaries to alter their preference in favour of the firm's products. But as the product market becomes competitive, trade discount loses its competitive teeth. The market eventually evolves product-wise standard rate of discount which a firm can ill-afford to alter. It finally gets reduced to remuneration given to an intermediary for services offered. Trade discounts are not generally reckoned in the books of accounts of an enterprise. Sales net of discounts are deemed to be price obtained by a firm and recorded as such in its books of accounts.

Cash discount has a completely different purpose, though, at times, there is an element of price-effect in such offerings (to be discussed later). The principal objective of offering cash discount is to induce buyers to pay up early. This may be used as a very effective instrument in short-term to tide over a temporary cash flow problem, or this may form part of overall credit policy of a business. The impact of cash discount offer, when accepted by the customers or a group of customers, is immediately felt by the quickening of cash inflows and reduction in accounts receivable. Profitability of a discount policy will depend to a large extent by the ability of the enterprise to invest the additional cash flows at its opportunity cost. If a firm lacks in such opportunities and/or it already has excess liquidity, it is preferable to extend credit and take on the role of financial intermediary as discussed earlier.

Impact on Bad-Debt Losses

It is often claimed that the by-product of cash discount offerings may be a reduction in bad-debt losses because of the quickening of collection process. But it depends upon the risk categories of customers who accept the discount offer. It is likely that marginal customers who are more risk-prone may not accept the cash discount while those in better risk-category are likely to accept the discount. This may solve the cash flow problem but may not reduce the bad-debt losses. If the discount policy is such as to motivate the marginal customers to pay up faster, it will have a beneficial impact upon the level of bad-debts. For example, if a credit term of 2/10 net 60 (2 percent discount if paid within 10 days' or 60 days' credit for full price) is offered, it is likely that marginal customers who suffer from cash flow problems would rather enjoy the long credit period of 60 days than taking the discount. In such a case, the impact on bad-debt losses may just be nil. But if the credit term is 2/10 net 30, motivation for a marginal customer to take the discount is great because it effectively reduces his cost. As a result, bad-debt losses will be reduced.

The discount offer may have a price-effect because it effectively reduces the cost as mentioned above. While a large section of marginal customers may accept the discount offer, motivation for good pay masters would be larger and hence, there may be a rise in general demand for the product due to this price-effect. But the size of this demand will depend upon the elasticity of demand for the product. Unless the demand is highly elastic the effect will not be large because the range of cash discount changes is quite small.

Preamble to Policy Formulation

Before a cash discount policy is formulated, it is necessary to make an estimate of the number of customers who are likely to accept the discount offer. A study of the payment behaviour of the existing customers during the past would certainly be highly indicative of their reactions to a discount offer.

Besides, a confidential information about payment behaviour of the customers with other firms in the industry would be of much help, particularly about the real behaviour of firms towards a discount offer.

Between good pay masters and bad pay masters, larger number of customers accepting the discount offer would come from the former category because they do not ordinarily suffer from cash flow problem and, therefore, would like to avail themselves of the effective price reduction through discount offer. As indicated above, for the better category of customers, discount offer must be such as to motivate them against credit enjoyment. But still, many of them would not be able to accept the discount and pay up early because either they have cash flow problem or their access to borrowed fund is limited both in terms of quantum and cost.

When cash discount is offered as a part of credit policy it is often found that discount is just taken as a matter of course whether payment is made within the due time or not. Thus the unearned discount virtually causes reduction in selling price without any incremental cash flows or reduction in receivables holding. A study made by Agrawal[18] revealed that in Indian private sector about 25 percent of firms offer cash discounts, but most of them felt that it was difficult to administer discount policy due to unearned discount. Firms market their products through established dealers. If sometimes, payment is not received within the credit period, it is just not possible to deny discount as it would spoil business relations!

In India, till recently, cash discount as a tool for receivables or cash management has not found much favour. The reason behind this is not embedded so much in unearned discount but in cash credit system of working capital finance by banks which virtually withered away the necessity of effective cash management. But with the gradual replacement of cash credit system by loan system, the stiff competition for funds in a shortage economy and its rising cost, firms are now forced to 'unearth internal sources' of fund through effective cash management, and towards this endeavour, cash discount comes in as a handy tool.

---

18. Agrawal, N.K., *Management of Working Capital*, Sterling Publishers, New Delhi, 1983.

DETERMINATION OF MAXIMUM RATE OF CASH DISCOUNT

Determination of a cash discount policy essentially boils down to a trade-off between the cost of giving up a part of invoice price on the one hand, and the benefits of quickening of cash inflows, increase in sales, reduction in receivables and a possible decrease in bad-debt losses on the other.

In what follows, we shall be structuring cash discount decisions in terms of trade-off between costs and benefits discussed above.

Cash Discount that Alters the Timing of Cash Flows

When a cash discount is offered, it changes the existing timing of cash flows resulting finally into a change in receivables holding. The decision criteria is ultimately the present value of cash flows before and after the introduction of cash discount. Let us explain this with the help of the following example.

Example Present annual sales of a firm is Rs. 1000 crore. Although all sales are made on 60 days' credit (net 60), analysis of the collection registers reveals that 50 percent of the customers pay in 60 days while the rest pay in 120 days. As a result of this payment pattern the firm is facing cash flow problems. Among other alternatives like, factoring and bills discounting the firm is also considering offering a cash discount of 2 percent if payment is made within 10 days (2/10 net 60). The firm expects that the customers who are presently sticking to the credit terms, i.e. paying in 60 days would accept the cash discount while the others will not. Cost of capital (opportunity cost) of the firm is 20 percent p.a.

Presently, the average collection period of sales is $0.50 \times 60 + 0.50 \times 120$ = 90 days and hence, average accounts receivable is

$$\frac{1000 \times 90}{365} = \text{Rs. } 246.58 \text{ crore}$$

It is expected that 50 percent of the customers would accept the discount offer and pay in 10 days while the remaining 50 percent customers would continue to pay in 120 days. Average collection period is, therefore, reduced to $0.50 \times 10 + 0.50 \times 120 = 65$ days. The average receivables holding will be

$$\frac{1000 \times 65}{365} = \text{Rs. } 178.08 \text{ crore}.$$

Opportunity cost of discount offer will be

$$1000 \times 0.50 \times 0.02 = \text{Rs. } 10 \text{ crore annually}$$

There is a fund release of Rs. $246.58 - 178.08 = $ Rs. 68.50 crore from accelerated collections due to cash discount offer. At 20 percent p.a. the opportunity savings will be $68.50 \times 0.20 = $ Rs. 13.70 crore. As the opportunity savings is greater than the opportunity cost of discount offer, the proposal is acceptable.

Break-Even Point

The next obvious question an accounts receivable manager would normally ask is, what could be the maximum cash discount that this firm could offer under the circumstances given above, or in other words, what is the break-even point of cash discount where costs and benefits would just equalise each other.

A close examination of the problem would reveal that break-even discount does not depend upon the volume of sales but on the proportion of customers accepting the discount, change in the timing of payment and opportunity cost of the firm. For example, in the above case, present average collection of sales is 90 days which we designate as N; proportion of customers (rupee value of sales) who are likely to accept the discount is 50 percent which we designate as $p = 0.50$; average payment days of the remaining customers $(1 - p)$ is 120 days which is denoted by Q; average payment days of the customers who accept the discounts is 10 days (2/10) which is designated as M and the daily opportunity cost of capital which is denoted by i is calculated as $0.20/365 = 0.00055$.

The break-even point of cash discount is given by

$$D_{B-E} = 1 - (1+i)^{M-Q}\left[1 - \frac{1}{p} + \frac{(1+i)^{Q-N}}{p}\right]$$

Incorporating the relevant figures in the above equation, D_{B-E} of the firm will be

$$D_{B-E} = 1 - (1 + 0.00055)^{10-120}\left[1 - \frac{1}{0.50} + \frac{(1 + 0.00055)^{120-90}}{0.50}\right]$$

$$= 1 - \frac{1}{(1.00055)^{110}}\left[1 - 2 + \frac{(1.00055)^{30}}{0.50}\right]$$

$$= 1 - 0.9413\,[1 - 2 + 2.0333]$$

$$= 1 - 0.9413 \times 1.0333$$

$$= 0.0274$$

Thus, the firm can offer a maximum cash discount of 2.74 percent. Let us check this from the above example.

Check
   (a) Opportunity cost of discount offer = $1000 \times 0.5 \times 0.0274$ = Rs. 13.70 crore.
   (b) Opportunity savings on reduction of receivables = 68.5×0.20 = Rs. 13.70 crore.

Cash Discount Affecting both Timing of Payment and Sales Volume

We have already indicated that offering of cash discount can have a price-effect resulting into additional sales because cash discount effectively reduces buyer's cost. The volume however, depends upon the elasticity of demand of the product.

With the change in sales volume, cost of sales also changes resulting in additional cash outflow.

In the above example, let us assume that as a result of 2/10 net 60 discount offer, sales of the firm is expected to rise by 25 percent. Cost of sales is 80 percent of sales, all other things remaining the same.

Increase in sales will be $1000 \times 0.25 =$ Rs. 250 crore. As these additional customers (sales) are motivated primarily by the discount offer, it is expected that they will take the full discount and pay in 10 days. Proportion of total sales accepting 2/10 offer will, therefore, be $\dfrac{1000 \times 0.5 + 250}{1250} \times 100 = 60\%$.
Remaining 40 percent will continue to take 120 days' credit.

Average collection period under the proposed change in policy will, therefore, be $0.60 \times 10 + 0.40 \times 120 = 54$ days. We can now calculate the change in accounts receivable as below:

Existing accounts receivable $= \dfrac{1000 \times 90}{365} =$ Rs. 246.58 crore

Receivables under the proposed policy $= \dfrac{1250 \times 54}{365} =$ Rs. 184.93 crore

Funds released = Rs. 61.65 crore

Profit from additional sales $= 250 \,(1 - 0.80) =$ Rs. 50.00 crore

Opportunity savings in accounts receivable $= 61.65 \times 0.20 =$ Rs. 12.33 crore

Total Rs. 62.33 crore

Less: Opportunity cost of discount offer $= 750 \times 0.02 =$ Rs. 15.00 crore

Surplus Rs. 47.33 crore

As the aggregate of profit from additional sales and opportunity savings in accounts receivables is larger than the opportunity cost of discount offer, the change in discount policy is acceptable.

The problem can also be solved under NPV framework by the following formula:

$$P = \left[Sp(1-d)\frac{1}{(1+i)^M} + S(1-p)\frac{1}{(1+i)^Q} - VGS_0\,(1+i)^C \right] - S_0\,\frac{1}{(1+i)^N}$$

where

P = incremental surplus

S_0 = existing sales

S = proposed sales

C = average payment day of cost of sales which in the present case is assumed to be zero

d = discount offer

p = proportion of sales accepting the discount
V = cost of sales
G = growth rate in sales
M = average payment day for discount offer
Q = average payment days of remaining customers
N = present average collection days of sales

Putting figures in the above equation, incremental surplus will be

$$P = \left[1250 \times 0.60 \ (1 - 0.02) \ \frac{1}{(1.00055)^{10}} + 1250 \ (1 - 0.60) \ \frac{1}{(1.00055)^{120}} \right.$$

$$\left. - \ 0.8 \times 0.25 \times 1000 \ (1.00055)^0 \right] - 1000 \ \frac{1}{(1.00055)^{90}}$$

$$= [735 \times 0.9945 + 500 \times 0.9361 - 200] - 1000 \times 0.95171$$

$$= (730.97 + 468.07 - 200) - 951.71$$

$$= \text{Rs. } 47.33 \text{ crore}$$

Maximum rate of cash discount that can be offered under the given circumstances of rising sales is estimated by the following equation:

$$D_{Max} = 1 - (1 + i)^{M-Q} \left[1 - \frac{1}{p} + \frac{(1 + i)^{Q-M} + VG(1 + i)^{Q-C}}{p(1 + G)} \right]$$

Incorporating the figures in the above equation, maximum rate of cash discount offer is calculated as

$$D_{Max} = 1 - (1.00055)^{10 - 120} \left[1 - \frac{1}{0.60} \right.$$

$$\left. + \frac{(1.00055)^{120-90} + 0.80 \times 0.25 (1.00055)^{120-0}}{0.60 (1.25)} \right]$$

$$= 1 - \frac{1}{(1.00055)^{110}} \left[1 - 1.6666 + \frac{1.0166 + 0.2136}{0.75} \right]$$

$$= 1 - 0.9413 \ (1 - 1.6666 + 1.6403)$$

$$= 0.0834; \text{ i.e. } 8.34\%$$

Check
Aggregate of profit from additional sales and opportunity
savings in accounts receivable (as calculated before)   Rs. 62.33 crore
Less: Opportunity cost of maximum discount offer
(750 × 0.0834)   Rs. 62.55 crore

[*Note*: The difference is due to approximation of decimal figures.]

Example A petrol pump in a metropolitan city is presently selling petrol and diesel and other petroleum products on cash basis. As the credit card has gained currency in India, the proprietor feels that if customers are allowed to pay by credit card, sales are likely to be increased by 20 percent. It is expected that 30 percent of the customers will avail themselves of this opportunity. A commission of 2.5 percent is payable to the credit card issuing bank on all billings which are paid in 30 days through credit card. Average cost of sales of all the products sold is 90 percent. The question is whether the petrol pump proprietor would be better off by offering payment by credit cards. Assume opportunity cost of fund is 20 percent.

The problem essentially boils down to finding the internal rate of the proposal (which is nothing but the maximum discount offerable under the circumstances) and, comparing it with the commission payable to the bank issuing credit cards. We can use the same equation in solving the problem. Here $N = Q = 0$ because presently, all sales are made on cash basis. $M = 30$ days; $C = 0$; $p = 0.30$; $G = 0.20$; $V = 0.90$ and $i = 0.00055$.

$$D_{Max} = 1 - (1.00055)^{30-0} \left[1 - \frac{1}{0.30} + \frac{(1.00055)^0 + 0.9 \times 0.2 (1.00055)^0}{0.30 (1.20)} \right]$$

$$= 1 - 1.0166 \left[1 - 3.3333 + \frac{1 + 0.18}{0.36} \right]$$

$$= 1 - 1.0166 \times 0.9445$$

$$= 0.0398; \text{ i.e. } 3.98\%$$

As the maximum internal discount rate is 3.98 percent which is larger than the 2.5 percent commission payable on credit card sales, the petrol pump should offer payments by credit cards to its customers.

OPTIMAL DISCOUNT RATE

So far we have been engaged in determining the maximum discount rate that a firm could offer under different circumstances. Within this maximum what should be the rate that a firm should actually offer is a practical question faced by an accounts receivable manager. Answer to this question lies in resolving an optimisation problem, i.e. at which discount rate present value of cash flows is maximised.

Generally speaking, higher the discount offer, the higher is the number of customers taking the discount. By studying the payment behaviour of existing customers and the experience of other firms offering various ranges of discount it is possible to evolve a pattern of customers' response to various discount offers. Once this is specified, it is possible to pick up the discount rate at which present value of cashflows is the highest.

In Table 3.10 we have presented customer-response pattern of the annual credit sales of Rs. 1000 crore (S) against various discount offers (d). Proportion of customers accepting each discount offer (p) are expected to pay up in 10 days

Table 3.10   Present Value of Sales under Various Cash Discount Offers

Discount rate (%)	Percent of sales accepting discount offer	Sales under discount	Amount receivable net of discount	Days of sales outstanding (M)	Remaining sales (1 − p)	Days of sales outstanding (N)	PV of col. 4	PV of col. 6	Total PV (col. 8 + col. 9)
(1)	(2)	(3)	(4)	(5)	(6)	(7)	(8)	(9)	(10)
0.5	10	100	99.5	10	900	90	98.95	856.55	955.50
1.0	20	200	198.0	10	800	90	196.91	761.37	958.28
1.5	30	300	295.5	10	700	90	293.88	666.20	960.08
2.0	40	400	392.0	10	600	90	389.85	571.03	960.88
2.5	50	500	487.5	10	500	90	484.83	475.86	960.69
3.0	60	600	582.0	10	400	90	578.81	380.69	959.50
3.5	70	700	675.5	10	300	90	671.80	285.52	957.32
4.0	80	800	768.0	10	200	90	763.79	190.34	954.13
4.5	90	900	859.5	10	100	90	854.79	95.17	949.96
5.0	100	1000	950.0	10	—	—	944.80	—	944.80

time (M). Remaining customers (1 − p) are expected to pay on an average of 90 days (N) as before. Opportunity cost of capital is 20 percent p.a. or 0.20/365 = 0.00055 per day (i).

A study of columns (1) and (2) of Table 3.10 suggests that the relationship between discount offer (d) and percent of acceptance (p) is given by p = 20d; e.g. if the discount offer is 1.5 percent, 20 × 1.5 = 30 percent of customers will accept the offer.

Present values of cash flows for sales under discount are calculated by the formula, $Sp\,(1-d)\,\dfrac{1}{(1+i)^{M}}$ and that of remaining sales by the formula, $S\,(1-p)\,\dfrac{1}{(1+i)^{M}}$. These figures are given in columns 8 and 9 respectively and their totals are shown in column 10.

We observe from column 10 of Table 3.10 that present value (PV) of cash flows is highest under 2 percent discount offer. Immediately thereafter it starts falling with the rise in discount offers. On the face of it one may be tempted to pick up 2 percent discount as the optimal discount offer by the firm. But since figures appearing in column 1 (discount offers) are not continuous variables but discreet in nature with an interval of 0.5 percent, it is just possible that the maximum cash flows may lie between 2.0–2.5 percent discount offers. This optimal rate of discount (D_L) can be determined by the following equation:

$$D_L = \frac{[1-(1+i)^{M-N}]}{2}$$

Putting respective figures in the above equation we can find the optimal discount rate as follows:

$$D_L = \frac{[1-(1.00055)^{10-90}]}{2}$$

$$= \frac{\left[1 - \dfrac{1}{(1.00055)^{80}} \right]}{2}$$

$$= 0.0215, \text{ i.e. } 2.15\%$$

Check

	Discount offer (*d*)	Percent accepting the discount (*p*)	Present value calculations	PV of cash flows
(a)	2.15%	43%	$1000 \times 0.43\,(1 - 0.0215)$	
			$\times \dfrac{1}{(1.00055)^{10}} + 1000 \times 0.57$	
			$\times \dfrac{1}{(1.00055)^{90}}$	$= 960.927$
(b)	2.20%	44%	$1000 \times 0.44\,(1 - 0.0220)$	
			$\times \dfrac{1}{(1.00055)^{10}} + 1000 \times 0.56$	
			$\times \dfrac{1}{(1.00055)^{90}}$	$= 960.922$

It appears from the above calculations that present value of cash flows at 2.15 percent discount is larger than at 2 percent that we have seen earlier in Table 3.10. Once the discount rate is raised to 2.20 percent the PV of cash flows immediately falls. We may, therefore, conclude that optimal discount rate for the firm is 2.15 percent. Although more precise estimate of optimal discount rate can be made with the help of a computer, such an accuracy is not required for managerial decision-making. However, for determination of the optimal discount rate when volume of sales also changes in response to various discount offers, we have to make use of a computer.[19]

Cash Discount and Bad-debt Losses

We have indicated earlier that impact of cash discount offer on bad-debt losses cannot be directly prescribed. Only when the discount rate is such that it can motivate the marginal customers to pay up early, then it may have some beneficial effect upon bad-debt losses. We must mention, however, that for these reasons the relationship between cash discount and bad-debt losses cannot often be easily established. It requires a thorough empirical investigation to discern whether and to what extent such a relationship exists for a firm's clientele. In the example worked out below we have assumed that such a relationship exists for the illustrative firm.

---

19. For the mathematical presentation of such a model and precise derivation of other mathematical models used in this section, see, N.C. Hill and K.D. Riener, "Determining the cash discount in the firm's credit policy", *Financial Management,* Spring 1979, pp. 68–73.

Example Presently, with no discount offer, bad-debt losses of the firm is around 1 percent of annual sales of Rs. 1000 crore. If the firm offers a cash discount of 2/10 net 30, not only the sales will rise by 25 percent, but bad-debt losses will also come down to 0.5 percent of total sales. At present, 50 percent of customers pay in 30 days and the remaining, in 60 days making the average collection period to be $0.5 \times 30 + 0.5 \times 60 = 45$ days. It is estimated that 70 percent of the customers will accept the cash discount and pay up in 10 days while the remaining customers will continue to pay in 60 days. This will change the average collection period to $0.7 \times 10 + 0.3 \times 60 = 25$ days. Cost of sales is 80 percent of sales and the opportunity cost of capital is 20 percent p.a. The feasibility of the proposal is examined as follows:

(Rs. in crore)

Existing accounts receivable $= \dfrac{1000 \times 45}{365}$ = 123.29

Receivables under new policy $= \dfrac{1250 \times 25}{365}$ = 85.62

Funds released	= 37.67
Profit from additional sales = 250 (1 − 0.8)	= 50.00
Opportunity savings in accounts receivable = 37.67 × 0.2	= 7.53
Savings on bad-debt losses = (0.01 × 1000) − (0.005 × 1250)	= 3.75
	= 61.28
Less: Opportunity cost of discount = 0.02 × 1250 × 0.7	= 17.50
Surplus	= 43.78

As the available surplus under the proposed policy is positive at Rs. 43.78 crore, the proposal is acceptable. We can now calculate the maximum discount rate that can be offered by the firm under the given circumstances by using the following equation:

$$D_{\text{Max}} = 1 - (1+i)^{M-Q}\left[1 - \frac{1}{p} + \frac{(1-b)(1+i)^{Q-M} + VG(1+i)^{Q-C}}{p(1+G)(1-b+k)}\right]$$

where

b = existing proportion of bad-debt losses, which in the present case is 1% or 0.01

k = bad-debt loss reduced as a percentage of total sales due to change in policy, which in the present case is 1% − 0.5% = 0.5% or 0.005

C = average days of cash outflows due to cost of sales, which in the present case is assumed to be paid on 'zero date'

All other notations are as before.

Putting figures in the above equation we now calculate the maximum discount rate that can be paid by the firm.

$$D_{\text{Max}} = 1 - (1.00055)^{10-60}\left[1 - \frac{1}{0.7} + \frac{(1-0.01)(1.00055)^{60-45} + 0.8 \times 0.25(1.00055)^{60-0}}{0.7(1.25)(1-0.01+0.005)}\right]$$

$= 1 - 0.9729\,(1 - 1.4284 + 1.3844)$

$= 1 - 0.9729 \times 0.956$

$= 0.07$; i.e. 7%

The firm can, therefore, offer a maximum discount rate of 7 percent under the given conditions.

Check

Profit from additional sales (as calculated before)	= Rs. 50.00 crore
Opportunity savings in receivables (as calculated before)	= Rs. 7.53 crore
Savings on bad-debt losses (as calculated before)	= Rs. 3.75 crore
	= Rs. 61.28 crore
Less: Opportunity cost of maximum discount offer	
(1250 × 0.7 × 0.07)	= Rs. 61.25 crore
Surplus	= Rs. 0.03 crore or nil

SELECTING THE CUSTOMERS

When we talk of selection of customers under *receivables management,* we are, in fact, talking about selection of credit risk because pure cash sales do not entail any risk, but every credit sale involves some risk.[20] The problem essentially boils down to 'whom to sell and for what amount?' In the final analysis, efficient administration of a credit policy in all its ramifications must aim at maximising sales with minimum collection costs and bad-debt losses.

In the absence of independent credit rating agencies, as in the United States and other developed nations, assessment of credit risk in India is essentially a firm level operation. This calls for a more rigorous structuring of credit information system in a business. But unfortunately, our experience with Indian companies—both large and small—shows that not many companies have well-structured information gathering and analysis system in their credit department. A credit manager should always remember that quality of a credit decision depends on the quality of information that goes into evaluation of a prospective customer. In this section we shall try to present a step-by-step procedure for credit selection.

Information-gathering begins with an application for credit limit. The application form should be standardised and not left to the discretion of the applicant. A well-structured application form itself communicates a message to the prospective customer how serious is the seller in his credit administration. Information sought for in an application, forms the basis for gathering further information and doing the checking. Hence, the firm must be clear about what kind of information is required for taking a credit decision as, otherwise, it might either be too sketchy or too cumbersome. Later, we have suggested a model application form, the important elements of which are discussed below.

---

20. A variation of cash sales is *cash on delivery* (COD), but it entails some risk and associated costs. A customer to whom goods have already been despatched under COD may refuse to honour the contract either because he does not have fund at that time or he has become bankrupt by the time goods reached the destination or in-between the price might have fallen. Costs of repossessing the goods and other adjustment costs are often substantial, particularly for export sales.

Types of Customer

The applicant should ordinarily be a sole proprietory firm, a partnership or a limited company. Each has its own peculiarity in terms of risk and its management.

Individual or Sole Proprietory Firm

Sole proprietory firm though is of unlimited liability, both in respect of the business and the individual owner, it is characterised by limited management base and suffers from continuity risk. Generally, these are small firms with limited ambition which, however, does not apply to quite a few large business houses of India which had a humble proprietory beginning. The old adage that 'customers are by and large honest' apply largely to this class of customers provided they are cultivated properly and credit limits are increased only gradually. It has often been found that a hitherto good pay master belonging to this class suddenly turns defaulter immediately after a sizable jump in the credit limit. The fault lies not so much in the sole proprietory firm but in the credit granting organisation.

A large section of these firms are retailers who form the bottom line of the distributive chain of any manufacturing firm. Being directly in touch with the market they provide the customer-face. These firms are highly competitive among themselves but together they are a cognizable force which no manufacturer would dare tinker with. But these people are highly secretive in sharing financial information with the suppliers. A profit and loss account and balance sheet are hardly to come by. In view of these difficulties many manufacturing firms avoid this last part of distributive chain and stops at the wholesalers or the distributor who are generally more broad-based. These are either partnership firms or private limited companies which are discussed in the following sections.

Partnership Firms

Although in India, law does not prevent constitution of oral partnership, the predominant pattern in real-life business is the written and registered partnership firms because of several advantages they enjoy over the oral partnership.

As mentioned before, a partnership firm is more broad-based than a proprietory firm in the sense that it takes at least two to make a partnership. Partnership provides a good 'deep-pocket' security because not only the business (assets) of the partnership firm is liable for the debt, all the partners (except the sleeping or 'minor' partners) are jointly and severally liable for the same. Taken together—liability of the firm and its partners—they virtually offer an unlimited liability, and because of this reason many credit analysts regard partnership firm as a first class security.

One must, however, be careful to find out the existence of a sleeping partner or a "minor" partner admitted to the benefit of partnership because they are liable only to the extent of their capital in the business; their personal assets are not liable for the debt of the firm. A copy of the *partnership deed* should be called for to find out the existence of these special type of partners. The deed will also enable the credit analyst to find out the manner in which continuance (succession) of the partnership is ensured, because in the absence of any enabling provision in the deed, partnership comes to an end following the death of a partner. Normally, the deed may contain prior agreement among partners to buy out the deceased partner's interest in the firm at a particular mode of valuation. The buy-out agreement does not put any constraints on the cash flow of the firm. The business continues, though without the deceased partner's contribution to the management of the firm. This loss could be a problem, and is something that the firm's creditors would like to monitor.

Although every partner's action binds the other partners in the business, not all partners are found to be 'active' in managing the affairs of the business. It may also be that the partners, among themselves, divide the responsibilities of managing the business. For example, one looks after the production, the other sales while the third may manage the finances of the firm. It is, therefore, important for the credit manager to know whom to contact to monitor the credit sales.

Partnership firms are most prevalent in India in wholesale trade and small scale manufacturing. The former is dominated by family businesses while in the latter, we find both the family and non-family partners having almost equal share. At a later stage many of these partnerships are transformed into private limited companies.

Like sole proprietorship, this segment also suffers from financial opacity to a large extent. It is difficult to obtain financial statements from them, and even if one is obtained, there is often slants in the figures supplied. It is not also unlikely to find many of these firms maintaining more than one sets of books of accounts.

Private Limited Companies

These also include companies which are closely held amongst family members and/or associates. These are general evolution of partnership firms with restriction in the number of shareholders. Liability of the shareholders are limited by their share capital. During recent times we find that many subsidiaries, particularly those of multinational companies, are being registered as private limited companies.

Excepting the subsidiaries, management style of these companies are fairly similar to that of partnership firms. It is, therefore, important for the credit manager to know who is the concerned person (Director) for monitoring of accounts receivable. Legally speaking, these companies do not suffer from succession or continuance problem like partnership firms, but death of a key director can affect the fortunes of such a company.

All the three business entities discussed above pose a challenge to the credit manager in gathering credit information, particularly the financials. It may be a general policy of these enterprises not to disclose financial data to any outside agency (except, perhaps to bank if they have taken loans). The credit manager, however, must always enquire whether this is a long-standing policy of the firm and not a recent introduction. In the latter case, the credit manager should be careful to evaluate the information received from old suppliers of such firms and also from the bank even if it is found on enquiry that recent policy change is due to genuine reasons.

We have already indicated that even when financial statements from the above types of enterprises are available, these often suffer from lack of credibility. This may take two forms. First, the financial results may be understated (obviously for tax purposes). The problem here is not very serious for a credit manager. An enquiry with the market may also reveal that the declared sales or the profit are much lower than the actual. Taking a cue from various studies made on national accounting estimates of underground economy, one can say that incentive level to understate profit operates between 30–50 percent of actual profits made by such enterprises. It is possible for the credit manager to come closer to the actual by using these estimates. However, what is more important, in cases of understatement, is to capture the trend in financial variables than their absolute values. The trend is easily discernible because of consistency in understatement that has to be observed thoroughly by these enterprises year after year, lest they are caught on wrong foot by the tax authorities. As long as the trend is good, the credit manager has reasons to feel comfortable. He need not bother too much about the accuracy of the absolute figures which, in any way, may never be available to him. For a credit analyst, ratios and their trends are better tools to judge the creditworthiness of an applicant, which we shall discuss later.

The second form of misrepresentation takes place when the financial statements are prepared for the purpose of favourably impressing the suppliers or bankers. Here, it is the case of 'overstatement' with the objective of suppressing the instability or downward trend of the business variables. This is a far more dangerous situation than the understatement. A careful and experienced credit manager will be able to capture it by spotting inconsistencies in the supplied data. If there is a slant in accounting information, the business ethics of the credit-applicant can immediately be questioned. The credit manager must always guard against such customers.

Public Limited Companies

These are companies limited by shares. Except the closely-held companies, the shareholding is broad-based, though the promoters and their associates often hold controlling interest. A credit manager feels comfortable in dealing with these companies because of greater amount of transparency in financial and other credit information and the controls exercised by the public and market regulatory authorities like Company Law Board and Securities and Exchange Board of India. But in spite of all these, one cannot hold with conviction that the financial statements prepared by all such companies do reveal the true state of their business, though these might have been certified as such by duly constituted statutory auditors. Hence, it is not always possible for a credit manager to take the financial statements released by these companies on their face value. He may have to subject them to same standard of scrutiny as he does for non-corporate customers, though with lesser rigor. One additional advantage here is that it is easy for the credit manager to know the extent of secured liabilities of these companies as well as the properties/assets by making enquiry with the office of the Registrar of Companies where all such information along with the relevant instruments creating charges are either filed by the company or its creditors. As the accounts payable are generally unsecured in nature, an inspection of these documents is essential to estimate the leverage available to the credit manager for his receivables.

Large firms are invariably incorporated as limited liability companies of the type discussed above. Management of such companies is generally broad-based with hierarchical (vertical) structure. For monitoring receivables, it may begin with a junior accounts payable officer and end at the level of president or director of finance. Payment authority moves along this vertical line depending upon the value of payables. A credit manager must, therefore, know the persons occupying these hierarchical positions so that he can contact the right person depending upon the value of supplies made under a particular invoice.

Parent, Subsidiary, Division

While dealing with companies the credit manager must know whether he is dealing with a parent company, subsidiary or a division of the company.

A parent company stands alone; it is solely responsible for all its liability. It cannot fall back upon any other entity when it faces financial problems and its banker turns away. When this happens, it affects directly all its divisions and subsidiaries. If the parent company becomes bankrupt, all the assets of the divisions, subsidiaries along with that of the parent company become hostage to the creditors.

Looking from opposite angle, when a credit manager deals with a subsidiary or a division, he has reasons to feel more secure because if the subsidiary or the division faces financial problems he can fall back upon the parent company. But one must remember that a subsidiary being a full-fledged legal entity by itself and limited by shares under Companies Act, cannot have any legal access to the assets of the parent company if it fails to honour its commitments. It is an established fact of law that a parent company is not legally obligated to come to the financial aid of a subsidiary; it only has a moral responsibility. Hence, when a credit manager feels uncomfortable with the financials of a subsidiary, he should always try to obtain a guarantee—may be through a letter—from the parent company undertaking payment responsibility for its subsidiary. If the parent company is doing well, such guarantee would ordinarily be available.

The case is different with the 'division' of a company which directly deals with their suppliers. This is becoming increasingly common these days among large corporates who have reorganised themselves into strategic business units

(SBUs). But unlike subsidiaries, Divisions are not separate legal entity even when they are fully autonomous. The parent company is ultimately responsible for all the obligations of its divisions.

When a division that has so long been a good paymaster is suddenly found to be delaying payments, it is a cause for concern for the credit manager. On enquiry it may be found that the parent company is losing on the whole which necessitated syphoning off funds from the division, or there has been a change in management or in corporate policy which resulted into shifting focus from the division. A credit manager would do well if he does his homework in finding out the relationship of the parent company with the division and be vigilant to spot any change in attitude by maintaining constant touch with the market intelligence. While it is essential to know how long the enterprise is in business, it is equally important to know whether there has been any change in ownership of the business, because it might entail a change in attitude towards the payables of the firm.

SOURCES OF CREDIT INFORMATION

The first source of credit information is the application itself. Verification and follow-up is the duty of the credit department. A credit manager must uphold his 'right to know', and under no circumstances and under no amount of pressure he should absolve himself of this right. A prospective customer who is unwilling to give the basic reference data necessary to evaluate the account—whether or not it is a closely-held company or firm—should not be given a credit line.

Bank Checks

Two major sources of credit information are the applicant's bankers and suppliers. Such reference data should be supplied by the prospective customers in the application form.

Bank checks are cost-effective and widely used by the credit managers. But it may not always give a true picture of the creditworthiness of a customer. A very good report from a bank may often mislead a credit manager because a customer's behaviour with a bank may not be similar to that with the supplier. Some customers are found to maintain good records with the bank, but they may be worst with their suppliers.

A bank may not also supply any information without the prior consent of the customer. When the report is likely to be unfavourable, no such consent may be forthcoming. In order to take care of this eventuality, the credit manager would ask the prospective customer to write immediately to his banker permitting him to divulge required information to the supplier. Copy of such letter should accompany the filled-in application form. In India, banks use standard format for giving such information which are often sketchy. It is necessary, therefore, to supplement these by other cross-checks; one such is the checking with the existing suppliers of the applicant enterprise.

Supplier Checks

The credit-applicant is expected to give names of the suppliers with whom he is presently doing business. Suppliers' reference is much better than banks' reference because, unlike banks, they are not legally bound by secrecy code. Supplier firm could be a competitor supplying the same materials to the applicant firm. It need not be that the applicant firm is seeking a switch; it may just want to broad-base its suppliers. But when a firm decides to move over to another supplier from the present one due to strained relationship from either side, the situation becomes rather complex. If the fault is on the applicant's side, such a reference may not be given at all; if it is on the other side then the applicant firm is likely to explain why it is leaving the existing supplier.

Majority of the suppliers' references come from non-competing industry. In cases like these, responses are easy to come by primarily because it is of mutual interest for firms to respond to each other's request. There is a mutual interest existing between a firm and the bank; it is always a one-sided affair. But such is not the case with suppliers. A firm which does not respond to a fellow-firm's request does so at his own peril because some days later he might require the same information. As the businesses in India are being professionalised, such a philosophy is increasingly replacing the secretive stance hitherto taken by them.

While calling for the new supplier's name, the applicant may be asked to give some details of its relationship with the existing suppliers, e.g. number of year's of dealing, maximum credit balance, past-due balances, credit terms, etc. The respondent on the other side, i.e. the accounts payable manager will always have the information readily available with him and there is no reason why he should not supply this information to another credit-giver. The credit manager must not compromise on the information, not because it is he who is taking the risk and not his counterpart, but to facilitate the suppliers' checks in a structured manner. Total effect of this is beneficial to both the parties because it substantially reduces the time for taking credit decisions.

Whether it is a competing firm or a non-competing firm, it is always preferable to gather information over telephone because a respondent is more at ease in verbal response than a written one. Besides this, telephonic information is always cost-effective and much less time-consuming. This mode of information-gathering is, however, not restricted to telephone only. It extends to social gathering, parties, professional meets and ultimately to personal visits. A successful credit manager who wants to make use of informal communication channels for gathering credit information, must develop over a period of time an informal personal relationship also with his counterparts in various other organisations. Checking with suppliers' reference may not always give the conclusive evidence of creditworthiness of the applicant. These have to be cross-checked with other market sources before a definite opinion is formed about the creditworthiness of the applicant. In Exhibit 3.1, a model Credit Application Form is presented incorporating all the aspects discussed above.

Exhibit 3.1 Credit Application Form

Name of the business: .... Articles dealt in ....

Date of establishment: .... Present ownership since ....

Kind of business
(Manufacturing, trading, export, etc.): ....

Constitution
(Proprietorship, partnership, private limited company,
public limited company, etc.) ....

Addresses
a. Registered office: ...... City .... State .... Pincode ...... Phone no. ...... Email Id......

b. Billing office: .... City .... State .... Pincode ...... Phone no. ...... Email Id......

c. Shipping office: .... City .... State .... Pincode ...... Phone no. ...... Email Id......

d. Website
Is this a Division/Subsidiary? .... if yes, Name & Address of Parent Co. ....
....

Person to contact regarding payment: .... Phone no. ....
(Mention designation)

Does your firm borrow against receivables/inventory? ....

if yes, with whom (Mention the credit limit) ....

Annual sales for last three years (Rs.): .... 20 .... 20 20

Annual profit after tax (Rs.): .... 20 .... 20 20

Present number of employees: ....

Bank(s) references with address: 1.

                                             2.

                                             3.

                                           4.

Supplier(s) references

Information Required	Name of supplier (.........................)	Name of supplier (.........................)	Name of supplier (.........................)
a. No. of years of dealing			
b. Types of materials/services			
c. Credit terms			
d. Rate of discount, if any			
e. Present outstanding (Rs.)			
f. Highest amount of outstanding during past 12 months (Rs.)			
g. Past-due balance (Rs.)			

Financial statements enclosed for the years: 20.................; 20...................; 20...............

Name of the person responding with designation: ....

Date: ....   Signature

FINANCIAL STATEMENT ANALYSIS

It is generally held that audited financial statements are more authentic than the unaudited ones. While it is true to a large extent, cases of auditors joining hands with the managers to produce 'manufactured' financial statements are not very rare. The credit analyst should understand that there is 'no absolute guarantee'. But he has to make best use of it keeping the consistency factor in mind as discussed earlier. As long as the financial picture indicates a trend (which is possible to capture through appropriate ratio analysis to which we are coming later), the purpose of financial statement analysis is achieved to a large extent.

Ratio Analysis

It is not important to have a strong accounting background to make intelligent use of financial statements. A credit manager is required to calculate and interpret certain key ratios which will tell him whether his accounts receivables are in danger or not.

Although working capital management, particularly its receivables component, apparently takes on a short-term approach, commitment to a particular receivables policy and the customer-relationship that emanates from it are long-term in nature. Hence, the credit manager must take a long-term as well as short-term view of the business to which he is going to commit himself.

Viability of a firm rests on the strength of its operating structure and financial structure. When both are strong, a credit manager does not have much to worry about, and when both are weak he might as well forget his receivables. But in between, there are several firms who suffer from weaknesses in either of the structures. If the operating structure of a firm is good but its financial structure is poor, there is a chance that the firm would be able to make a turnaround by suitable modification of its financial structure. But if it is the otherway round, i.e. the operating structure is weak but financial structure is strong, then chance of its revival is bleak. The poor operating structure would soon eat into the hitherto good financial structure.

Liquidity

Besides examining the above fundamentals of an enterprise, the credit manager would definitely examine the liquidity of the business of the credit-applicant because payment for receivables would essentially come from the overall liquidity of the business. However, the definition of liquidity has since extended from liquidity *per se* indicated by net liquid assets, to the access to liquidity, i.e. the ability of the business to raise quick finance which includes, besides the goodwill of the business, the availability of un-encumbered assets.

These days, liquidity has almost become synonymous to cash flow. It is being increasingly observed that profit making companies, particularly those which are on an aggressive growth path, suffer from intense liquidity (cash-flow) problem because profit may not often contain cash, and it is by cash alone the bills (payables) of a firm are to be honoured. This is the reason why funds flow analysis is being supplemented or replaced by cash flow analysis.

List of ratios invented so far is quite long and is becoming longer and longer with the invention of new ratios by some scholars at some place of the world every other day. Presently, the list contains more than 330 ratios. A business manager becomes confused in this labyrinth of ratios. This is the reason why ratio analysis as a tool for control and monitoring of business variables, has not been in much use for long at the hands of real-life managers who simply do not have so much time to spend on so many ratios in spite of the advent of desk-top computers. In view of this, what we intend to do here is to select only a few ratios which will be able to capture the different aspects of a business as outlined above.

OPERATING MANAGEMENT

Fixed Assets Turnover Ratio

This ratio is calculated as

$$\frac{\text{Net sales}}{\text{Operating fixed assets}}$$

This is also the ratio used to evaluate the long-term state of the business.

Sales are net of excise duty. Operating fixed assets are net of depreciation and of capital-work-in-progress which has not entered into production. Goodwill and other fictitious assets should also be excluded from calculation of operating fixed assets.

There may be cases where fixed assets of a firm are revalued upwards, particularly the landed properties. Revaluation is merely a book-adjustment; there is neither any cash inflow nor any addition to capacity. Although for a credit manager revaluation indicates the extent of ultimate 'deep pocket' security, for the purpose of understanding the long-term position of a business, it is preferable to ignore the revaluation. Similar adjustment will have to be made against the net worth of the business by deducting therefrom the revaluation reserve.

Fixed assets turnover ratio is also called velocity of fixed assets meaning thereby, the times the fixed assets have turned over during a period in generating sales. Normally, for a manufacturing organisation with high capital intensity the ratio should be around 5. If this ratio is showing a falling trend it is indicative of one or a combination of the following factors:

(a) Technical capacity of the assets are falling due to wear and tear.
(b) Production bottlenecks due to say, faulty line balancing or labour problems.
(c) Failure of marketing function.
(d) Technological or product obsolescence.
(e) Recession in the particular industry or a general recession in the economy.

Credit managers are often found to be complacent with good liquidity ratios (to be discussed later) and ignore the falling trend in fixed assets turnover ratios.

Many do not calculate this ratio at all even when they find that the customer is placing lesser orders. They ignore the fact that when fixed assets are not generating enough sales the problem may be more structural and hence, fundamental to the business. This ratio would put the credit manager on enquiry into these fundamentals and would guide him to determine the appropriate time of pulling himself out from a potential bad-debt case, no matter whether the customer is presently a good paymaster.

On the other hand, if fixed assets turnover ratio is on the rise but the firm is presently suffering from poor liquidity—which may often be the case during the growth phase of a firm—then it would be unwise for the credit manager to deny him credit; he might lose a potentially good customer by being too hamstrong on liquidity ratios.

Return on Investments (ROI)

This ratio is also called *return on assets* (ROA). It is a product of the following two ratios:

$$\frac{\text{Operating profit}}{\text{Sales}} \times \frac{\text{Sales}}{\text{Total operating assets}} = \frac{\text{Operating profit}}{\text{Total operating assets}}$$

The first ratio on the left-hand side of the equation is called *operating profit ratio* and the second one is called total assets turnover ratio. Operating profit is defined here as profit before interest and taxes as this ratio intends to determine the operating strength of the business. Total operating assets include, besides operating fixed assets, all current assets.

The reason behind showing ROI as a product of the above two ratios is to draw attention of the analyst that the ultimate strength of the business lies not only on a consistently good margin on sales (which is only possible with a good cost structure) but also on sales generation capacity of the assets of a firm. In fact, this is the most comprehensive ratio for judging the operating strength of a business, as it translates the financial objective of a firm into such operating terms as selling prices, profit margins, sales turnover, production costs and capital equipments.[21]

It is often argued that ROI should never be below the risk-free rate available in the market. This may not always hold true because with a suitably geared capital structure return on shareholders' fund can be maximised in spite of the firm having a ROI below risk-free rate. While there is strength in this argument, at least on a theoretical plane, one must remember that if the rate of earning of a firm on the total funds employed by it is below the risk-free rate of return, the enterprise might not be employing the resources in the best possible manner. Hence it is advisable for the credit manager to use this rate as the bench-mark and loading it with risk factor he should decide on the required minimum ROI of a business. Considering the present yield on long-term

---

21. Newman, Maurice S., "Return on Investments: An analysis of the concept", *Management Services*, July–August 1966, pp. 15–23.

government securities the desired ROI of a business enterprise should not be less than 12 percent.

Gross Profit Ratio

This ratio is calculated as

$$\frac{\text{Gross profit}}{\text{Net sales}}$$

Gross profit is defined as manufacturing gross profit which excludes all non-manufacturing incomes like that from investments, etc.

This ratio measures the viability of manufacturing function. As gross profit is net of those expenses which are dominantly variable in nature, the ratio would be constant over the years during a given technology period. The ratio may, however, register a moderately upward trend during the initial years of commissioning of the plant, but once the plant parameters get properly tuned, the gross profit ratio is expected to settle down to a constant level. If, however, the ratio is showing a downward trend, then it indicates a serious structural problem of the manufacturing function which, if not corrected well in time, may quickly throw the company out of gear. The primary reason behind a fall in gross profit ratio is that many of the expenses which were supposed to be variable in nature are becoming fixed or disproportionate with sales implying thereby that the productive resources of the enterprise are being wasted at an increasing rate.

In fact, *gross profit ratio* is the single most important ratio to evaluate the strength of the manufacturing function which is fundamental to a business. The trend itself will tell a lot about the strength or weakness of the manufacturing structure of a business. But it is not possible to set a universal standard about the value of this ratio because manufacturing expenses are product/industry-specific. The credit manager should therefore, refer appropriate industry data for setting up a standard gross profit ratio of a given industry.

FINANCIAL MANAGEMENT

Equity Total Debt Ratio

This ratio is calculated in the following manner:

$$\frac{\text{Total outside liabilities}}{\text{Net worth}}$$

This is the reciprocal of *total debt-equity ratio*. This form is used to make it amenable to the scheme of credit scoring discussed later.

Although a financial institution would calculate debt-equity (equity-debt) ratio by taking only long-term debt into account, a receivables manager would consider both short-term and long-term debts for calculating total debt-equity ratio (equity-total debt ratio) because, being unsecured creditors, the ultimate leverage is important to him. This ratio is meant to capture the long-term financial risk of the business.

Networth or equity includes paid-up ordinary share capital, share premium, free reserves, capital subsidies by government and part of any equity type of loans like convertible debentures. Some argue that *preference share capital* should also be included as part of net worth. But a receivables manager would regard preference shares (except irredeemable preference shares which though, are not available in India) as any other loan because they impose on the enterprise fixed obligations both in respect of dividend payment and repayment of principal amount. Since these payments are obligatory cash outflows, it is advisable for the receivables manager to treat it as part of long-term debt.

The next question arises as to the treatment of *revaluation reserve*. We have discussed earlier that revaluation of assets (which is credited to the revaluation reserve on the other side of the balance sheet) does not generate any cash inflow. It is a book entry designed to bring the fixed assets, particularly land and buildings, close to market value. As the equity-debt ratio intends to capture the long-term financial viability and riskiness of a business, a receivables manager would do well to include revaluation reserve as part of net worth. This will give him that 'deep-pocket' confidence.

Equity-debt ratio attempts to measure the efficiency of the applicant-firm in striking a balance between risk and profitability in its capital structure because these two are often inversely related to each other. While a small equity-debt ratio (large debt-equity ratio) might satisfy the shareholders because of high dividend payment (which is possible due to low equity structure and high payout ratio), for a credit manager the situation may appear to be too risky.

A credit manager would always prefer a equity-debt ratio to be more than 1, meaning thereby that net worth of the firm is larger than the total debt. But such a situation is unlikely to be found. Even in developed countries such a ratio is not observable. On one extreme we find Japan boasting of a total debt-equity ratio of 5 (equity-total debt ratio of 0.20) and on the other, we observe that the United States prefers the value of the ratio to be around 1. Considering the fact that industrial development in India is more debt-driven, due to dearth of equity capital, an outer limit of this ratio is generally fixed at a minimum of 0.33 implying thereby that equity capital is expected to provide at least 25 percent of a firm's total capital requirement.

Equity-Short-Term Debt Ratio

This ratio is calculated as

$$\frac{\text{Current liabilities}}{\text{Net worth}}$$

This ratio is also the reciprocal of *short-term debt-equity ratio*. Keeping in mind the minimum value of total equity-total debt ratio of 0.33, as mentioned above, equity-short-term debt ratio should be such as to provide reasonable cushion to current debt holders so that they do not feel nervous. This ratio is equally important, if not more, for receivables managers who happen to be the largest among the current debt-holders of an enterprise.

This ratio, which is also called *credit strength ratio*, indicates the degree of financial prudence of an enterprise which cuts across both small and large firms. There is a tendency among firms to maximise creditors' financing because it is available 'free of cost'. This leads to overtrading on the purchase side. Many well-known companies have been found to fall prey to this allurement particularly because they can use their market command and goodwill to exploit the suppliers' credit. In order to check themselves against such allurement firms with prudent financial management go in for a self-imposed discipline as a part of their financial structure policy. This control is exercised through *equity-short-term debt ratio.*

A receivables manager would be less confident about the financial prudence of a firm whose equity short-term debt ratio is less than 0.60. He will be comfortable if it is around 1. This ratio is also a pointer to the receivables manager when to cut back on further credit to a firm despite the insistence of marketing department to push up sales.

Finished Goods Inventory Turnover Ratio

This ratio, which is also called velocity of finished goods inventory, is calculated in the following manner:

$$\frac{\text{Cost of goods sold}}{\text{Finished goods inventory}}$$

The ratio can also be modified to indicate the number of days of stock holding by the business as:

$$\frac{\text{Finished goods inventory} \times 365}{\text{Cost of goods sold}}$$

This ratio measures the efficiency of the manufacturing function in scheduling the production, and the efficiency of the marketing function in disposal of outputs of an enterprise by constantly feeding the distribution channel. Interpreted properly, this ratio will also indicate the presence of unresolved conflict between the marketing management and financial management; the former trying to keep its distributional channel overstocked for fear of stock-outs and the latter trying to minimise it for fear of high interest cost involved in carrying these inventories. Wider the range of products, greater is the desire for stocking, and larger the demand for funds made on the finance function which often suffers from fund-crunch and increasing cost of financing.

A low (high days) *finished goods inventory turnover ratio* is not only indicative of the presence of the unresolved conflict between the marketing and finance function, on a broader, scale this may also mean that the products of the enterprise are losing in the market, may be due to price competition or a general recession. However, an enquiry may also reveal that the reason behind overstocking is a part of market penetration policy being pursued by the enterprise. In order to push the products of the enterprise and block competition it may deliberately occupy shelf-space of the retailers or distributors by overstocking. But this can only be a temporary phenomenon. After some time the turnover ratio should be back to normal.

On the other hand, if the value of this ratio is large (low days) it indicates that the company's products are being sold fast, or the distribution network of the enterprise is so tuned to the market that it necessitates low level of stocking at distribution points. However, the credit manager considering a credit application must put himself on enquiry if he finds that there has been a sudden and substantial improvement of this ratio over the past. It could be that the enterprise has streamlined its distribution network simultaneously with aggressive selling, but it may as well be that there has been serious bottleneck in production which has forced the firm to reduce its stocking level, or that it may be suffering from acute cash flow problem compelling it to force-sale its products.

Finished goods inventory turnover ratio helps the credit manager to decide on the length of credit that he might allow to the applicant-firm. In case the firm is a trading organisation, the calculation is straightforward. He would not allow him credit for more than one cycle of inventory and receivables turnover. But if the applicant firm is a manufacturing organisation and the vendor-firm supplies material-inputs, the maximum number of days credit that may be allowed will be calculated by extending the chain backward to include turnovers of both the raw materials and work-in-process inventories.

Like gross profit ratio, this ratio is also industry-specific. Attempts were made first by Tandon Committee and then by several other committees appointed by Reserve Bank of India to evolve industry-specific standards of this ratio for purpose of working capital assessment by banks. A credit manager can as well refer to these standards for sanctioning and monitoring of trade credit.[22]

Receivables Turnover Ratio

The derivation of this ratio is made in the following way:

$$\frac{\text{Gross sales}}{\text{Trade receivables}}$$

The ratio can also be transformed to indicate the number of days of holding of debtors.

$$\frac{\text{Trade receivables} \times 365}{\text{Gross sales}}$$

Gross sales are inclusive of excise duty and scrap sales because both may enter into receivables by credit sales. Trade receivables should include bills

---

22. See, Bhattacharya, Hrishikes, *Bank Lending—Principles: Theory: Practice*, Chapter 12, Naya Prokash, Calcutta, 1990.

discounted (which is found not in the main body of the balance sheet but in the list of contingent liabilities appended below it).

Among all the working capital components this one is most important to the vendor-firm because it is from realisation of debtors that the accounts payable of the applicant-firm is met.

This ratio has to be simultaneously interpreted along with finished goods inventory turnover ratio. A very good finished goods inventory turnover ratio (indicating fast sales) may hoodwink the analyst as to the cost at which such sales are made. Marketing department may be very aggressive in making sales, but this may be done by extending longer period of credit, which may as well eat up the profit element by high interest and monitoring costs. Many firms may end up making negative profit out of such sales.

Increasing volume of receivables without a matching increase in sales is reflected by a low (high number of days) *receivables turnover ratio.* It is an indication of slowing down of the collection machinery or an extended line of credit being allowed by the customer organisation. The latter may be due to the fact that the firm is losing out to competition. In such a situation, many enterprises are found to engage themselves in fire-fighting without delving into the real cause behind it. They make frantic efforts to hold on to the market share by giving longer line of credit which swells up the receivables and lowers down the turnover ratio. This may stave off the imminent danger but only temporarily, because the real cause behind losing the market share may be technological or product obsolescence.

A credit manager engaged in the task of granting credit or monitoring receivables should take the hint from a falling receivables turnover ratio and use his market intelligence to find out the reason behind such a falling trend. If the reason turns out to be obsolescence, he is well advised to control further credit and gear up his collection machinery. A temporary fall in this turnover ratio may, however, be not always alarming. This may be the result of market penetration policy of the enterprise. One of the tools employed by the firm is general relaxation of credit policy during the initial period of market thrusts. But once it is over, the turnover ratio should come back to normal level.

Like finished goods inventory turnover ratio, this ratio, specific to a particular industry, has also been evolved by Tandon Committee and subsequently revised by other committees of RBI. The credit manager can refer to these standards. For some industries, combined norm (ratio) for both finished goods and receivables holding is prescribed. The credit manager may bifurcate it suitably between the two.[23]

Creditors Turnover Ratio

The ratio is represented as

$$\frac{\text{Purchases}}{\text{Trade creditors (payables)}}$$

---

23. Bhattacharya, Hrishikes, *Bank Lending, ibid.*

Conversion of this ratio in number of days is done in the following manner:

$$\frac{\text{Trade creditors (payables)} \times 365}{\text{Purchases}}$$

While receivables turnover ratio of the customer-organisation measures the vulnerability of the source from which payables of the vendor-organisation are satisfied, the creditors turnover ratio indicates the actual payment behaviour of the customer-organisation.

In developed countries of the world, large corporations are generally found to be net suppliers of credit (receivables > payables), but in India the situation is predominantly opposite. This is due to the fact that the large corporates operating in India often hold a monopsonic buying position in the market and using that market command, they bully the suppliers in extending longer period of credit. If the receivables manager is dealing with such firms he may not be able to help much, because these firms are otherwise good credit-risks, but he has to protect himself against any lax in the payment behaviour of such firms. Normally, these firms would pay in time but in absence of appropriate monitoring they may also delay payment.

These large enterprises are also prone to 'overtrading' on the buying side as discussed earlier. "Overtrading" by the customer-organisations may also be propelled by the vendor-organisations. When there is glut in the materials (products) market vendors may offer longer line of credit to clear their godowns. When there are too many sellers loaded with large unsold stocks (may be due to recession) competition forces a sellers' market to be transformed to a buyers' market where longer and longer line of credit without cost consideration may play havoc with the finances of the vendor-organisations.

A credit manager would be happy if the *creditors turnover ratio* of a customer is larger (smaller days) than the receivables turnover ratio. If it is the other way round, it could be due to one or more of the reasons mentioned above. If the ratio is registering a falling trend, it is likely that there has been a slowdown in the collection of accounts receivable of the customer which will be reflected by a falling receivables turnover ratio. The time may already be up for the credit manager to pull out from such customers.

No industry-specific standard (norm) has as yet been developed for this ratio. A credit manager may develop a normative standard by referring to the industry specific data and market practices. He should remember that once the market has evolved a particular credit period it is difficult to alter it.

Current Ratio

Derivation of this ratio is as follows:

$$\frac{\text{Current assets}}{\text{Current liabilities}}$$

Some assets, though, are bracketed under current assets in the balance sheet of a firm, they might have lost their 'currentness' in the sense that the firm may not have any access to the funds (blocked in them) as and when it requires. Examples of such assets are: dealer's deposit made with supplier-firms which is available only on termination of supply contracts, fixed deposits with banks and other securities lodged as collaterals for guarantees issued, security deposits with excise authorities, investment in subsidiary companies which are unlikely to be realised by market sale, etc. All these assets do not provide any cushion to the payables of the customer organisation and hence, are to be ignored by the credit manager while calculating the current ratio of the applicant-firm. These assets are better termed as non-current assets. Reserve Bank of India uses this terminology, though their definition also includes non-operating current assets like investment in market securities.

On the other side of the balance sheet, current liabilities may list a few liabilities who are, in reality, not very current. One such examples is dealer's deposit received from buyers. Such current liabilities are ignored while calculating current ratio.

Current ratio is one of the oldest of financial ratios. Its usage dates back to 1891;[24] the primary users were short-term lenders. Even today, this ratio is regarded as a key ratio in the credit appraisal system of banks in India in spite of the fact that current ratio has lost most of its shine in modern-day financial management whose approach is to reduce the value of this ratio rather than increase it. The attention received by current ratio from short-term lenders for such a long time is due to their preoccupation or anxiety over sudden slowing down of realisation of current assets from which they are to receive payment. The 2:1 historical standard was evolved to ensure that even if as high as 50 percent of current assets fail to realise in time, the lenders would not be worse off. The cushion, which is popularly termed as net working capital (current assets – current liabilities), provided a sense of security to the lenders. It had long been regarded as the only measure of liquidity of a business. But over a period of time the notion of liquidity has undergone substantial changes. Modern-day managers consider liquidity as that thing which ensures uninterrupted operations of a business. By this definition, the inventory, which has long been considered as the most illiquid of all the current assets, is now regarded as the most important source of liquidity. To a manufacturing manager, who is charged with ensuring continuous operation of the plant, constant supply of material-inputs is important, no matter how nicely the finance manager has arranged his current assets in ascending or descending order of liquidity. Finance manager may have ample cash and marketable securities and a large volume of paying receivables, but if there is a dearth of supply in the materials market, all his cash would not be able to buy materials needed by the manufacturing manager. Production line would come to a halt for want of materials. Similar is the case with marketing manager whose operation will stop if he does not have ample supply of finished goods at various distribution points.

---

24. Foulke, Roy A., *Practical Financial Statement Analysis*, McGraw-Hill, Heights Town, New Jersey, 1961.

The discussion made above is not to belittle the importance of cash or cash flow from receivables management, because it is by cash alone that the bills of inventory-supplies are paid. We intend to emphasise here the point that the purpose of cash, among other things, is to ensure uninterrupted supply of inventory which, in the final analysis, is the ultimate liquidity of a business. This is possible even with a current ratio of 1 or a zero net working capital.[25]

As the best security of a credit manager (and even other lenders) is the smooth operation of business of the client organisation, he should not be too much bogged down or overclouded by a 'good' current ratio, particularly when it is his firm which supplies materials to the customer. What is important for him is to examine the maturity between receivables and payables of the client-firm in terms of various turnover ratios discussed above. If there is a maturity mismatch, receivables of the vendor will not be paid in time, howsoever large the current ratio might be.

Tandon Committee originally prescribed a minimum current ratio of 1.17 across industries which was to be increased to 1.79 over a period of time. The last one was never adopted as the Chore group subsequently rejected it and recommended 1.33 as the minimum standard under the Second Method of Lending prescribed by Tandon Committee. Presently, banks are made free from observance of this norm. They are allowed to evolve their own norm depending upon the industry performance and the specific need of a customer. However, the general tendency is towards fixing up the standard at 1.5. It is advisable for the receivables manager to adopt this standard.[26]

Debt-Service Coverage Ratio (DSCR)

This ratio, which attempts to determine the ability of an enterprise to discharge its financial obligations, is calculated in the following manner:

$$\frac{\text{Profit after tax} + \text{Depreciation} + \text{Interest}}{\text{Interest} + \text{Repayment obligation} \times [1/(1-\text{Tax rate})]}$$

In the above formula, *repayment obligation* (which includes dominantly term-loan and debenture repayments) is multiplied by a tax factor to bring it in line with the interest payments because the latter gets tax deduction while the former does not.

This ratio, though widely used in a project appraisal, is criticised because *profit after tax* may not always contain cash because of working capital elements (like receivables and inventories) and it is by cash alone that the obligations are required to be serviced. An advancement over this ratio is *priority obligation ratio* which makes adjustment of working capital elements to determine the real cash flow available to meet the debt-service obligations.[27]

---

25. Bhattacharya, Hrishikes, *Banking Strategy, Credit Appraisal and Lending Decisions—A Risk-Return Framework*, Chapter 13, pp. 527–528, Oxford University Press, New Delhi, 1998.
26. *Ibid.*
27. For details, see Bhattacharya, Hrishikes, *Total Management by Ratios*, Chapter 9, Sage Publication, New Delhi, 2007.

Debt-service coverage ratio or its variation, as discussed above, does not directly tell the ability of the enterprise to discharge its short-term obligations, but as it indicates the long-term capability of its operations to sustain its capital structure, it also indirectly tells the ability of the enterprise to repay its trade creditors over and above its priority obligations. If the enterprise does not have a good DSCR nothing may be left to pay up the *trade creditors* who, being unsecured, have only an equitable claim over cash flows (and assets) next to that of secured debt holders.

Term lenders feel comfortable if the DSCR is not less than 1.5. They generally ignore the short-term working capital obligations from the purview of their calculation. But for a credit manager this is most important, and hence he cannot settle the ratio at 1.5. For him, it should be between 1.75 and 2.

APPLICATION

Application of ratio analysis, as discussed above, will now be done with the help of financial statements of a real-life company (name camouflaged for anonymity). Purpose of this analysis is to help the credit manager not only to take credit decisions, but also to monitor receivables once a credit decision is taken. Later, we shall also develop a credit-scoring model based on selected ratios.

Published financial statements or the ones that are supplied by the credit-customer are not always amenable to the decision-formats of a credit manager. It is necessary, therefore, to restructure the *profit and loss account* and *balance sheet* of the customer in the following formats (Exhibits 3.2 and 3.3). Data are taken from the published financial statements of a public limited company engaged in manufacturing electrical machinery. Let us name the company as XYZ Ltd. All the seven ratios discussed above are calculated from these financial statements and presented in Exhibit 3.4.

We have discussed earlier the nature of the seven ratios. A credit manager must keep in mind the nature of each ratio while making interpretation for purpose of determining creditworthiness of a business.

In Exhibit 3.4, we have divided the ratios under two heads: *operating management* and *financial management*. The first contains three ratios and the second has seven ratios. Number of ratios coming under each head is in no way reflective of importance attached to any one of the groups. For a credit manager both the two groups are equally important.

In Exhibit 3.5, these ratios are further analysed against standards (column 3) and trends (columns 7 and 9). Moving averages for three years are used to discern the trend (moving average I compared with moving average II).

Exhibit 3.2 Profit and Loss Accounts of XYZ Ltd.

(Rs. in lakh)

	20X5	20X6	20X7	20X8
Revenue				
Sales	39,671	48,018	56,115	60,607
Less: Excise duty	4073	5044	6389	6185
A. Net sales	35,598	42,974	49,726	54,422
Expenditure				
Purchase of materials	24,005	29,168	34,920	36,566
Manufacturing expenses	4235	5060	5268	5842
Depreciation	553	726	768	780
Sub-total	28,793	34,954	40,956	43,188
Add: Opening stock of				
all inventories	5704	5855	6878	9330
Sub-total	34,497	40,809	47,834	52,518
Less: Closing stock of				
all inventories	5855	6878	9330	10,173
B. Cost of goods sold	28,642	33,931	38,504	42,345
C. Gross profit (A – B)	6956	9043	11,222	12,077
Less: Selling, distribution				
and administrative expenses	4227	5470	7136	7989
D. Operating profit	2729	3573	4086	4088
Add: Other income (interest,				
dividend, sale of assets etc.)	535	600	629	1003
E. Profit before interest and taxes	3264	4173	4715	5091
Less: Interest	1738	2517	3471	3922
F. Profit before taxes	1526	1656	1244	1169
Less: Taxes	540	38	539	366
G. Profit after tax	986	1618	705	803
Less: Dividend	266	296	296	366
H. Retained profit	720	1322	409	437

Exhibit 3.3 Balance Sheets of XYZ Ltd.

(Rs. in lakh)

	20X5	20X6	20X7	20X8
Assets				
A. Fixed assets				
(net of depreciation)	6212	8364	8841	9242
Current assets				
Investments (at market				
rate or cost whichever is less)	206	361	423	1292
Cash and bank balances				
(including fixed deposits)	13	38	186	86
Receivables (trade)	12,524	14,978	18,940	21,588
Loans and advances	3399	3859	4270	5661

(Cont.)

Exhibit 3.3 Balance Sheets of XYZ Ltd. (Cont.)

(Rs. in lakh)

Inventories				
Raw materials	2105	2523	3114	3179
Work-in-process	1958	2288	3550	4223
Finished goods	1792	2067	2666	2771
B. Total current assets	21,997	26,114	33,149	38,800
C. Total operating assets (A + B)	28,209	34,478	41,990	48,042
D. Capital work-in-progress	537	639	554	1328
Non-current assets				
Dealers' deposits	29	32	32	35
Investment in subsidiaries	52	52	52	52
Deposit with excise department	35	41	56	56
E. Total non-current assets	116	125	140	143
F. Miscellaneous expenditure (not written off)	186	516	610	630
G. Total assets (C + D + E + F)	29,048	35,758	43,294	50,143
Liabilities				
Share capital	1480	1480	1480	2250
Revaluation reserve	2141	2094	2048	2006
Other reserves	3039	3127	3638	7744
H. Shareholders' fund	6660	6701	7166	12,000
I. Long-term loans debenture etc. (net of current repayments)	4688	10,749	11,097	8505
Current liabilities				
Creditors (trade)	9870	11,455	14,037	14,355
Advance payments	3108	4029	4183	4226
Expense and other creditors	242	283	447	2741
Bank overdraft	3548	1585	5316	7300
Repayment of term loans	600	620	620	620
J. Total current liabilities	17,368	17,972	24,603	29,242
K. Total outside liabilities (I + J)	22,056	28,721	35,700	37,747
L. Provisions	332	336	428	396
M. Total liabilities (H + K + L)	29,048	35,758	43,294	50,143
Net worth (H – F)	6474	6185	6556	11,370

Exhibit 3.4 Financial Ratios of XYZ Ltd.

	20X5	20X6	20X7	20X8
Operating management				
1. Fixed assets turnover ratio	5.73	5.14	5.62	5.89
2. Return on investment (ROI)	9.67%	10.36%	9.73%	8.51%
3. Gross profit ratio	19.54%	21.04%	22.57%	22.19%
Financial management				
1. Equity-total debt ratio	0.29	0.22	0.18	0.30
2. Equity-short-term debt ratio	0.37	0.35	0.27	0.39
3. Current ratio	1.27	1.45	1.35	1.33
4. Finished goods inventory turnover ratio	15.98	16.41	14.44	15.28
	(23)	(22)	(25)	(24)
5. Debt-service coverage ratio	1.20	1.37	1.10	1.11
6. Receivables turnover ratio	3.17	3.20	2.96	2.80
	(115)	(114)	(123)	(130)
7. Creditors turnover ratio	2.43	2.55	2.49	2.55
	(150)	(143)	(147)	(143)

Note: Figures in bracket represent number of days of holding.

Exhibit 3.5 Analysis of Financial Ratios of XYZ Ltd.

(1)	Name of ratio (2)	Minimum/ Maximum standard (3)	20X5 (4)	20X6 (5)	20X7 (6)	Moving average I (7)	20X8 (8)	Moving average II (9)
Operating management								
1. Fixed assets turnover ratio		5	5.73	5.14	5.62	5.50	5.89	5.55
2. Return on investments		12%	9.67%	10.36%	9.73%	9.92%	8.51%	9.53%
3. Gross profit ratio		20%	19.54%	21.04%	22.57%	21.05%	22.19%	21.93%
Financial management								
1. Equity-total debt ratio		0.33	0.29	0.22	0.18	0.23	0.30	0.23
2. Equity-short-term debt ratio		0.60	0.37	0.35	0.27	0.33	0.39	0.34
3. Current ratio		1.5	1.27	1.45	1.35	1.36	1.33	1.38
4. Finished goods inventory turnover ratio		8	15.98	16.41	14.44	15.61	15.28	15.38
		(45)	(23)	(22)	(25)	(23)	(24)	(24)
5. Debt-service coverage ratio		1.75	1.20	1.37	1.10	1.22	1.11	1.19
6. Receivables turnover ratio		6	3.17	3.20	2.96	3.11	2.80	2.99
		(60)	(115)	(114)	(123)	(117)	(130)	(122)
7. Creditors turnover ratio		4	2.43	2.55	2.49	2.49	2.55	2.53
		(90)	(150)	(143)	(147)	(147)	(143)	(144)

Note: Figures in bracket represent number of days of holding.

Operating Management for XYZ Ltd.

Fixed Assets Turnover Ratio

We have said earlier that this ratio should not be less than 5 for a capital-intensive manufacturing firm like XYZ Ltd. For all the four years under study, the ratio for the company is above this standard. The trend is also upward, though not very high as the difference between *moving averages* I and II would suggest (Exhibit 3.5). It appears, therefore, that the fixed assets of XYZ Ltd. are generating enough sales to sustain its operating structure. However, it has been seen that, at times, many manufacturing firms show high *fixed assets turnover ratio* not because of good performance of the manufacturing function, but due to high trading component of sales. This, on the other hand, means that a substantial part of its sales does not come from selling of goods manufactured by it, but from finished goods directly bought from the market and sold without further processing except putting its brand name on such products. This often happens for products with simpler technology and for firms which are old but have created a brand equity for these products. Being old firms, their overheads are also high, which can no longer be sustained by in-house manufacturing of these products. Although on the face of it, there is nothing wrong for a company to encash its brand equity in this manner, the fixed assets turnover ratio of a manufacturing firm gets vitiated because little fixed assets are necessary to perform a trading function. Hence, existence of substantial trading component in sales would have the effect of pushing up this ratio. In cases like this, it is advisable for the credit analyst to delink trade-sales from the total sales of the company and then calculate this ratio to understand the real strength of its manufacturing function.

Return on Investments (ROI)

Performance of this company against a standard minimum ROI of 12 percent is not encouraging. The trend is also on the decline when we compare moving averages I and II (Exhibit 3.5). When the operating function of the company is doing well, as is revealed by the fixed assets turnover ratio and as will be further substantiated by *gross profit ratio* discussed next, a low ROI indicates that the ills may be lying in its overhead structure. Contribution of its operating function is eaten away by high overheads. The company is old and over a period of time it has expanded its overhead structure which it is unable to reduce now. Although rate of increase in overheads has fallen during recent time, but in absolute term, it is still on the increase and unmatched with the sales the company is generating. When a company suffers from a high-level of unabsorbed overheads, its operating leverage becomes so low as to make it vulnerable to even a moderate downswing in sales.

Gross Profit Ratio

Industry average (electrical machinery) for this ratio is 20 percent. XYZ Ltd. is maintaining this ratio slightly above the standard on an average. More important than this is the stability of this ratio over a period of time which indicates the inherent strength of operating function of the company. We can conclude that the variable expenses of the company do maintain the proportionality with sales.

Analyses of these three ratios indicate good operating structure of XYZ Ltd. but its benefit is eaten away substantially by high unabsorbed overheads as indicated by low ROI. This also makes the company vulnerable to even small downswing in sales. From a credit analyst's point of view the company has already entered into a high-risk zone. It may not be able to absorb shocks of any adverse movement in the economy or the industry to which it belongs.

Financial Management for XYZ Ltd.

Equity-Total Debt Ratio

The company had this ratio closest to the standard in 20X5. But after that it started falling and remained at 0.23 on an average as against the standard of 0.33, though it touched 0.30 in 20X8. This means that the company's debt burden has increased substantially over a period of time. Equity remained at a low-level despite a premium capital issue in 20X8 (included in 'other reserves'). An expansion in capital structure (both equity and debt) was needed to finance capital expenditure during 20X6–20X8. The company being old might have embarked on substantial renewal of its plant and machinery to bring them to the current technology level. This is a step towards the right direction but its financing has been lopsided. Both long-term and short-term debts made quantum jump in 20X6 though, by 20X8, long-term debt appears to have come down (but this is due to conversion of convertible debenture). The high debt-structure has imposed substantial burden on the company both in respect of interest payments and repayment of principal. It is likely that the company has already defaulted on repayments. In situations like this, an enterprise is forced to expand its short-term capital structure, particularly by increasing or defaulting on market credit as we shall be discussing now.

Equity-Short-Term Debt Ratio

As discussed above, this ratio for XYZ Ltd. is substantially lower than the standard—almost half of it on an average. A receivables manager is more concerned here because the credit that he grants belong to this category. The *balance sheet* of the company also reveals that a substantial part of short-term debt belongs to market credits in various forms which are available 'free', but there is a potential danger in this type of overtrading as discussed before. This will be revealed further when we shall discuss *creditors turnover ratio*.

The low *equity-short-term debt ratio* of XYZ Ltd. is indicative of decreased stake of the company in its short-term capital structure which makes the company risky, particularly from the point of view of market creditors, because not much cushion is available to the company when its receivables chain gets expanded due to default or delay.

Current Ratio

XYZ Ltd. is also unable to maintain this traditional liquidity ratio at the standard level of 1.5. It is much lower than that. The company is somehow maintaining this ratio at around 1.33—the minimum required by the banks under the *second method of lending*. Although *current ratio* has lost much of its importance in modern-day financial management and a lower current ratio is the order of the day, this has to be evaluated in terms of other ratios of financial management because a low current ratio might have been achieved not due to an excellent arrangement of current assets and current liabilities, but due to unduly long line of credit taken by the firm from the market, or simply due to non-payment of trade creditors. For XYZ Ltd. the latter is the case as we shall see while discussing creditors turnover ratio. When a company suffers from the problem of slow moving debtors the net working capital cushion becomes very important for a credit manager, which in the present case, is very low.

Debt-Service Coverage Ratio

For a receivables manager, this ratio is very important, though it is not calculated directly for him. When the ratio falls below the required minimum standard as in the present case, a crisis is in the offing. A low and falling ratio indicates that pressure on the company to repay term loans and interest (both on term loan and working capital advance) is very high. In a situation like this, a company would either delay or default payment of its trade payables and use that fund to keep the long-term lenders at bay as long as it can, because the former being unsecured creditors, have less muscle power than the latter. XYZ Ltd. has on an average, a *debt-service coverage ratio* of 1.20. The company might already have started defaulting on payments or gone in for rescheduling the repayment programmes. A persistently low ratio is also indicative of the fact that the enterprise has entered into a debt-trap.

Finished Goods Inventory Turnover Ratio

For XYZ Ltd. this ratio is near-excellent. The norm for maximum holding of stocks for the industry to which it belongs is 45 days. As against this, the company is holding just about 24 days' inventory. There could be three possible reasons for this:

(a) Company's products may be near-monopoly items.

(b) Demand for the products is very high against a supply shortage.

(c) Company has a very efficient marketing department which can sell high in spite of competition.

The first two are not valid for XYZ Ltd. Hence, it can be construed that its sales people are apparently very efficient in selling the company's product. But as mentioned earlier, this ratio cannot tell us about the methods/techniques used in promoting sales and whether they are cost-effective or not. In other words, one has to know at what cost sales are being made. For the receivables manager it is important to find out whether the competition is being beaten by extending unusually longer line of credit. Occasional extension of credit period for new product launching or for increasing the market share may often be imperative for an enterprise for a temporary period, but if it becomes a general feature then the credit manager will have all the anxiety points because it is mainly from the realisation of debtors of the vendee company that his receivables get paid. The receivables turnover ratio will capture this phenomenon to which we are coming now.

Receivables Turnover Ratio

Performance of this ratio for XYZ Ltd. confirms that sales are being made by its marketing department by extending unusually long period of credit. While the industry standard is 60 days of holding, for XYZ Ltd., it is more than double. Worse than this is that the situation is persisting for the last four years. One point that comes out sharply is that trade creditors of this company cannot expect to get paid in less than four months' time, though for XYZ Ltd. it is much worse as we shall see next.

Creditors Turnover Ratio

This is the most important ratio for the receivables manager where the performance of XYZ Ltd. is at its worst. While the industry practice is three months, the company is paying its creditors in not less than five months' time on an average for the last four years. One reason is that the company is unable to collect its debtors in less than four months' time as we have seen above. Another reason is that even if the company collects them in four months' time, the cash flow is eaten up by interest payments and repayment imperatives as indicated earlier.

CREDIT SCORING

We have discussed at length nature of ten ratios—three for operational management and seven for financial management—and also their interpretation with the help of an example. Understanding a ratio is one thing but its usage for taking credit decisions require organising these ratios in some system and formats which will make credit decisions automatic in majority of cases. This leads us to develop a credit-scoring system based on the seven ratios that we have discussed above. But before that, there should be a *caveat emptor* which emanates from the history of the development of credit-scoring models and the difficulties embedded in them.

Lessons from Earlier Studies

Before the Second World War, models used for taking credit decisions were predominantly subjective. These models were highly individualistic as they depended on the experience and 'hind-sights' of an individual credit manager. These subjective decision models had been very successful in the credit department of corporates and banks. The era produced brilliant credit managers and loan officers whose "rules of thumbs" served them very well. But after the Second World War, when the volume of business soared up, the subjective models failed to cope up with the increased volume because of dearth of experienced credit managers down the line. Their experience also could not be handed down effectively to the next line of managers because a large part of the credit decisions was instinctive. The subjective process, while in many cases was sufficient to do an acceptable job, also failed as it did not lend itself to administrative control.[28]

During the post-Second World War period, statistical analysis entered into the domain of credit scoring. First such approach was probably made by Durand.[29] With the advent of computer application for business decisions there had been substantial development in credit-scoring models but with mixed success. Most unsuccessful applications appeared to have failed because of a general lack of credibility or because of their use as a 'black box' that supplanted human judgement.[30]

The credibility question is still valid today. Even in a country like United States, many firms are not found to use a credit-scoring model because of the general perception that such models are not sufficiently accurate. One of the reasons behind this is that most credit-scoring models including the ones using option-pricing methodology were derived not from the experience with commercial credit defaults, rather from experience with the defaults in public bond markets. Even the empirical validation of these models could not be done in most cases, including banks, because of lack of appropriate data base.[31] This is more true for statistical models where credit history and sample size must be sufficiently large to accommodate both analysis and verification.

Credit-scoring models hitherto developed are mostly based on dichotomous classification tests—good credit and bad credit. These models are unable to accommodate shades of difference in loan quality. For example, some slow-paying customers are forced into one category or the other, but in truest sense, they belong somewhere between the two extremes.

Credit-scoring model based on financial ratios was systematically presented first by Beaver[32] by using sophisticated statistical techniques. He made a study of large firms of the United States dividing his sample between

---

28. Hettenhouse, W. George and Jack R. Wentworth, "A New Look for Credit Scoring", *The Journal of Commercial Bank Lending*, September 1971, pp. 26–32.
29. Durand David, "Risk Elements in Consumer Installment Lending", *National Bureau of Economic Research*, Washington, 1941.
30. Hettenhouse, W. George, et. al., *ibid*.
31. McAllister, H. Patrick and John J. Mingo, "Commercial Loan Risk Management: Credit Scoring and Pricing: The Need for a New Shared Database", *The Journal of Commercial Lending*, May 1994, pp. 6–22.
32. Beaver, H.W., "Financial Ratios as Predictors of Failure" *Empirical Research in Accounting: Selected Studies*, University of Chicago, 1967.

79 failing companies and 79 successful companies, for the period 1954–64 by using univariate discriminant analysis. He found that some ratios predicted failure upto five years in advance and of which cash flow to total debt ratio (a close variation of debt-service coverage ratio) was the best predictor.

Altman[33] took the research further and used *multiple discriminant analysis* (MDA) to develop a 'Z Score' that might correctly classify firms which would fail within one year, 95 percent of the time of the initial sample and 79 percent of the time for the validation sample with an expected chance prediction of 50 percent. This, on the other hand, meant that the function derived by Altman had the ability to classify 8 out of 10 firms correctly as compared to 5 out of 10 firms which would have been correctly classified by chance. MDA technique was used by Altman to derive weights for various ratios used by him in the model which, in the final analysis, looked like the following:

$$Z = 0.012X_1 + 0.014X_2 + 0.033X_3 + 0.006X_4 + 0.999X_5$$

where

X_1 = working capital to total assets
X_2 = retained earnings to total assets
X_3 = earning before paying interest and tax to total assets
X_4 = market value of equity to book value of debt
X_5 = sales to total asset
Z = overall index

The least values of cut-off as predicted by Altman are given below:

Predictive status	'Z' score
Bankrupt	1.81 or less
Cannot say	1.81–2.99
Healthy	More than 2.99

It may be seen that Beaver's *cash flow* to *total debt ratio* did not find place in Altman's model. It has also been found by subsequent studies that in the second to fifth year prior to failure, the MDA model of Altman registered more misclassifications than Beaver's dichotomous univariate model using only the cash flow to total debt ratio. The classification error rate was as high as 71 and 64 in Altman's as compared to Beaver's 24 and 22 in the fourth and fifth year respectively before failure.[34] Besides, it has been observed that although some ratios proved themselves to be good predictors in more than one study, no one group of ratios was common to the studies made so far. This implies that discriminant model can be applied reliably only to situations very similar to those from which the function was generated.

---

33. Altman, I.E., "Corporate Bankruptcy Prediction and Its Implications for Commercial Loan Evaluation", *The Journal of Commercial Bank Lending*, January 1970, pp. 8–22.
34. See, Deakin, E.B., "A Discriminant Analysis of Predictors of Business Failures" *Journal of Accounting Research*, Spring 1972, pp. 167–169.

Edmister[35] developed a 'Z' score model by using the MDA technique along the line advocated by Altman, but he used 'industry relatives' instead of direct ratios by dividing borrower's ratios by the industry ratios. He also calculated the trend of a ratio-relative and used it as a variable predicting the health of an enterprise. He noted, for example, that the current ratio might have been high or low without conveying much meaning, but a low and declining current ratio might have portended failure.

Ratios selected for the above study were among those which had been advocated by theorists or had been found to be significant predictors of business failure in previous empirical research. Edmister used a small sample drawn from enterprises who received loans from Small Business Administration of the United States. He, however, could not use a validation sample to test the predictive accuracy of the empirical model developed by him because of lack of sufficient number of loan files with required loan history from which such sample could be drawn. Instead, he used a rather less rigorous method by creating 'synthetic' validation samples which estimated that the function would predict correctly 80 percent of the time on a validation sample.

Edmister's 'Z' score model led him to develop a decision rule as follows:

(a) Grant loan, if the firm scores 53 points or more and reject the applicant if he scores less than 47 points.

(b) The area between 47 and 53 points is the 'grey area' and firms falling within this area be referred, as it is this area which requires the credit analyst's efforts and skills.

(c) Non-financial-statement—information regarding management, markets, plant and equipment and other factors—should be scrutinised to further classify the 'grey area' applicant.

The decision rules laid down by Edmister are the ones that are looked forward by a credit manager in his day-to-day decision making. It indicates the importance of combining both objectivity and subjectivity in credit decisions. But he warns that the ratios, methods of analysis and weights are quite different from one study to another. This implies that credit-scoring models based on ratio analysis are sensitive to either or both the purpose and population studied and that each function is optimal only for firms similar to those used in the specific population. The conclusion is similar to the observation made by us earlier.

Gupta and Sekhar[36] abandoned the pure statistical approach, citing principally the above difficulties, and determined the differentiating power of any particular ratio by arraying their sample companies in ascending or descending order on the basis of individual ratios for each selected year separately. The array is then inspected to find out cut-off point which would

35. Edmister, O. Robert, "Financial Ratios and Credit Scoring for Small Business Loans", *The Journal of Commercial Bank Lending*, September 1971, pp. 10–23.
36. Gupta, L.C. and Archana Sekhar, *Controlling Corporate Sickness*, Oxford University Press, New Delhi, 1988.

divide the array into sick and non-sick zones with the least number of misclassifications. Aggregate of these misclassifications is then converted into percentage which the authors termed as the "percentage classification error" that measures the differentiating power of a ratio. Their findings reveal that profitability ratios are much superior to balance sheet ratios; current ratio suffers from largest classification errors; *debt-service coverage ratio* enjoys the highest discriminating power among all the leverage ratios while the debt-equity ratio has the least forewarning property.

The above review of works done on credit-scoring models based on ratio analysis bring to focus the following major points which a constructor or a user of credit-scoring model must bear in mind:

(a) No credit-scoring model has universal application; it is specific to similar population from which the sample is drawn. Operational aspect of this finding is that a firm must develop its own credit-scoring model and update it periodically with the experience gathered from its usage.

(b) Ratios or sets of ratios that go into developing a credit-scoring model do not also enjoy universality. This finding implies that a firm should begin by using a set of ratios advocated by theorists and or those that are found to have most discriminating power in earlier empirical research. The model so developed should then be put to constant scrutiny and review in order to perfect the ratio set.

(c) Trend of a ratio is more important than its absolute value. It is, therefore, necessary to consider a ratio for at least three years to discern the trend by some statistical method.

(d) It is always desirable to consider industry average of a ratio along with the firm-specific ratio to obtain a better insight into the health of a firm.

(e) Finally, an objective credit-scoring model should be supplemented by subjective analysis, particularly for the firms falling in 'grey area zone'. Complete reliance on objective credit-scoring model may defeat the very purpose of credit-scoring as an instrument of credit-decisions.

Framework of a Credit-scoring Model

We now intend to develop the framework of a ratio-based credit-scoring model taking lessons from the above findings. We shall use the example of XYZ Ltd.

In Exhibit 3.5, we have already rearranged the order of the ratios and calculated moving averages (MA) to discern, the trend of a particular ratio. MA (I) is taken for the first three years as in the Exhibit; MA (II) is then calculated by dropping the first year (20X5) and including the last year (20X8). If MA (I) is greater than MA (II), we can presume a downward trend in the ratio; if it is less than MA (II) the trend is upward; if both are equal, the trend is level. In column 3 we have noted the standard value of the ratios as discussed earlier.

Framework of a credit-scoring model is presented in Exhibit 3.6. The arrangement of the order of ratios is the same as in Exhibit 3.5 represented by serial number in column 1 which is also considered as weight allotted to each ratio. Weights are assigned on the basis of the importance of a particular ratio for receivable management as discussed when we have analysed each ratio from the point of view of a receivables manager. It should be pointed out here that the importance or weight of a particular ratio could be different for the loan officer of a bank than for a corporate manager. For example, *creditors turnover ratio* has received the highest weight (7) in our model, while *equity-total debt ratio* has received the lowest weight (1). The weight-allotment could just be in the opposite direction for a loan officer.

Score of XYZ Ltd. on each ratio given in column 3 of Exhibit 3.6 is calculated by the following formula.[37]

$$\frac{M_t\,(S + M_{t-1})}{SM_{t-1}} - 2$$

where

M_t = moving average for the current period. It is similar to MA (II) as in Exhibit 3.5.

M_{t-1} = moving average for the immediately preceding period. It is similar to MA (I) as in Exhibit 3.5.

S = standard value of a ratio as shown in column 3 of Exhibit 3.5.

One such scoring is done for gross profit ratio by way of an example:

$$\frac{21.93\,(20 + 21.05)}{20 \times 21.05} - 2 = 2.14 - 2 = 0.14$$

Each individual ratio-score is then multiplied by assigned weight as is given in column 1 to derive the weighted score as appearing in column 4 of Exhibit 3.6. *Weighted average scores* for each group—operating management and financial management are calculated in column 5 by dividing the group score with the total of weights of that group as appearing in column 1.

Final credit score of the company is calculated by adding the weighted average scores of the two groups and then dividing it by 2 as shown at the bottom of Exhibit 3.6.

It is clear that with an overall credit score of (–)0.087, XYZ Ltd. is not eligible for obtaining trade credit. If the vendor company has continuing commitment with the vendee company, it has to undertake serious review of the whole situation and take immediate steps to safeguard its interest.

---

37. The formula is derived in the following manner:

$$\frac{M_t - S}{S} + \frac{M_t - M_{t-1}}{M_{t-1}} = \frac{M_t\,(S + M_{t-1}) - 2SM_{t-1}}{SM_{t-1}} = \frac{M_t\,(S + M_{t-1})}{SM_{t-1}} - 2$$

Exhibit 3.6 Credit-Scoring from Financial Ratios of XYZ Ltd.

Sl. no. and weight (1)	Name of ratio (2)	Score (3)	Weighted score (col. 1 × 3) (4)	Weighted average score (5)
	Operating management			
1.	Fixed assets turnover ratio	0.12	0.12	
2.	Return on investments	(–) 0.25	(–) 0.50	
3.	Gross profit ratio	0.14	0.42	
	Total: 6 A. Sub-total		0.04/6 =	0.007
	Financial management			
1.	Equity-total debt ratio	(–) 0.30	(–) 0.30	
2.	Equity-short-term debt ratio	(–) 0.40	(–) 0.80	
3.	Current ratio	(–) 0.07	(–) 0.21	
4.	Finished goods inventory turnover ratio	0.91	3.64	
5.	Debt-service coverage ratio	(–) 0.34	(–) 1.70	
6.	Receivables turnover ratio	(–) 0.54	(–) 3.24	
7.	Creditors turnover ratio	(–) 0.35	(–) 2.45	
Total: 28 B. Sub-total			(–) 5.06/28 =	(–) 0.1807
	Credit score [(A + B)/2]			= (–) 0.087

We now lay down in Table 3.11 the credit-category of trade credit customers on the basis of the *ratio-analytic credit-scoring model* discussed above.

Table 3.11 Categorisation of Trade-Credit Customers (Ratio-based)

Legend/ Category	Excellent 1	Very Good 2	Good 3	Fair 4	Doubtful 5	Poor 6
Credit score	1.00–0.85	0.84–0.74	0.73–0.63	0.62–0.52	0.51–0.41	0.40 and below

Based on the above, the following decision-rules can be framed:

Credit Decision Rules

1. Credit score of 0.63 and above   – Accept
2. Credit score of 0.51 and below   – Reject
3. Credit score between 0.62 – 0.52 – Refer to higher authority for further analysis and probing.

We should point out here that the credit-categorisation model given in Table 3.11 and the decision-rules that followed are normative in nature based on a prior knowledge on the subject. This provides a basis to start with. Every firm should attempt to make it perfect and dynamic by empirical studies of the behaviour of its own customers. Once the process starts, misclassification error can be minimised to a large extent over a period of time.

A company can decide to base its credit-decision solely on *ratio-analytic model* for low value credit applications (say, upto Rs. 1 lakh). For higher value applications, and also those applications which are of low value but have to be referred in terms of Decision Rule 3, subjective considerations need to be taken into account.

Subjective Considerations

Credit-scoring model based on ratio analysis is predominantly objective in nature. But we have already pointed out that credit decisions based solely on objective model may ultimately lead to the failure of the system altogether. We cannot ignore the subjective elements that weigh heavily in the mind of a credit manager, particularly when the applicant for credit is new to the company.

Some writers talk about 4Cs—*character, capacity, capital* and *condition*— as the four determinants of creditworthiness of a customer.[38] Out of these four elements, capacity and capital are amenable to objective analysis.

Capacity is defined as the ability of the enterprise to honour payment commitments which, on the other hand, depends upon its ability to generate cash flows with which the bills are to be paid. Generally, cash flow is defined as profit after tax, plus depreciation and all other non-cash expenditure.[39] Capacity to pay is measured by *debt-service coverage ratio* that we have already discussed and included in our ratio-analytic credit-scoring model.

Capital is defined as the net worth which provides that important cushion to the business to absorb shocks coming from both internal and external environment when regular cash flows are adversely affected. To the credit manager, net worth provides the second defence, the first being the cash flows. However, absolute amount of net worth remains meaningless to an analyst unless it is compared with the debt of an enterprise. This is done by equity-debt ratio or its reciprocal, debt-equity ratio. We have already included this ratio in our credit-scoring model.

Condition relates to the economic, financial and also socio-political environment within which an enterprise operates. These environmental variables are continuously changing resulting into cyclical fluctuations of the business of an enterprise. Modern day analysts also include obsolescence— both product and technology—and the competitive structure of an industry as part of environmental variables which affect the condition of a business. It is possible to capture a substantial part of these environmental variables through statistical analysis which is most essential for a banker, but for a credit manager

---

38. See for example, Smith, K.V., *Guide to Working Capital Management,* McGraw Hill, New York, 1978.
39. At times, this creates problem, particularly for a fast growing company where increasing level of current assets capture a substantial part of cash flows. For detail, see, Bhattacharya, Hrishikes, *Total Management by Ratios,* 2nd ed., Sage Publications, New Delhi, 2007, Chapter 12, pp. 237–269.

such an elaborate exercise may not be necessary because, being the supplier of his own output to the user enterprises, he is always aware about the 'condition' of the business of the vendee company vis-á-vis his own. Cyclical fluctuations may affect both the vendor and vendee company. We therefore, take this variable as given or common, and hence, exclude it for the purpose of credit-scoring, though its influence on the fortunes of a business can never be minimised.

Character of a business (and that of the entrepreneurs) rests on such traits as honour, trustworthiness and commitment. In the final analysis, it is ultimately the character that determines the creditworthiness of a customer. A business may have all the good ratios, regular cash flows and solid capital base, but may still turn out to be a bad customer because it does not keep commitments. On the other hand, an enterprise may not have very good cash flows or capital but its sense of honour is so high that defaulting on commitment is the last thing that it would do. In fact, real test of the character of a business lies when things have gone bad. How a business will react when all other Cs have turned worse, determines its character. The definition sounds good, but the basic problem is that one would never know for certain how a credit-customer will respond in a real emergency. To a large extent this is judgmental, which rests more on hind-sight and the intuition of an experienced credit manager than hard objective data.

Although it is predominantly subjective, the job of a credit manager is made easier when he attends to the following data of the enterprise:

The management: If the board of a company is filled up with entrepreneurs and their relatives, generally the company suffers from lack of transparency and professionalism in the second tier of management. There may be sinecure positions in the organisational structure of the enterprise, but real delegation of power may just be absent. When business situation turns adverse, these are the firms which will default most. On the other hand, if a predominantly professionalised board functions with a properly delegated management structure which honours commitment more than anything else, that is where real professionalism lies. This type of organisation is always more transparent than the former. Even if there are temporary difficulties, straight talks are easily to come by from this kind of enterprise. This goes a long way in putting the credit manager at ease and stave off an impending crisis.

Audit qualifications: Generally, external auditors would not comment on payment practices of a company in their audit report, particularly those relating to supply creditors. Thus, a credit manager may not get anything directly from the audit report about the payment behaviour of a credit-customer. But too many audit qualifications appearing on the body of the audit report indicate that the business is not being conducted in a prudent manner. A business which does not care for adverse audit comments (or is so compelled because it cannot help otherwise owing to its deteriorating condition) may not also care to keep up the commitments.

Market behaviour: Market is an excellent source to estimate the payment behaviour of a customer. Market never fails to give signals about enterprise-behaviour. The problem is that we are either unable to receive or interpret the signals or decide to remain an ostrich. Direct approach is also helpful. A telephone call to the credit manager of other suppliers to the vendee company may produce excellent results. As the counter-part credit managers may require similar information at some future date, they are expected to provide relevant information. Telephone is preferable than writing a letter because a lot of things can be said while talking which may not come by when one is asked to put things in writing.

We have said earlier that a credit manager would make enquiries with the banker(s) of the vendee company as a matter of routine, but the replies that are generally received are guarded. Besides, it has also been found that a customer may maintain very good relation with the banker but is the worst pay master to the suppliers.

Customer Classification

A credit manager having obtained all possible information, as mentioned above, would like to classify a customer by assimilation of these information with his experience and intuitive judgement. He might follow one such classification shown in Table 3.11 like excellent, very good, poor, etc. In order to quantify the subjective categorisation (so that it is amenable to final credit-scoring) the credit manager may take the mid-point of the range noted under each category in Table 3.11. For example, score-value of excellent category would be 0.925 and that for very good category, 0.79 and so on, as are given in Table 3.12.

Table 3.12 Categorisation of Trade Credit Customers by Character

Legend/ Category	Excellent 1	Very good 2	Good 3	Fair 4	Doubtful 5	Poor 6
Score value	0.925	0.79	0.68	0.57	0.46	0.35

We can now follow the rule of simple average while determining the final credit category of a customer. For example, suppose the score of a customer obtained from *ratio-analytic mode* (Table 3.11) is 0.56. This would place him under fair category, and in terms of decision rules, the case has to be referred to the higher authority. On enquiry, character of the customer is found to be very good which has a score-value of 0.79 (Table 3.12). Adding the two scores and dividing it by 2, we obtain the final score of the customer as 0.675. Now, applying the decision rules once again we may accept the application of the credit customer.

It is desirable that the two sets of credit-scoring are done separately by two persons and the final-scoring is given by a third person in order to minimise the effect of individual biases.

COLLECTION AND MONITORING

Marketing department makes the sales, but the collection department has to earn the revenue by realising the sales. While collection and monitoring are activities that are targeted to each individual customer, monitoring at the aggregate level must also be done to understand the movement of receivables in terms of the laid down credit policy of the enterprise and provide information to the collection machinery as to where it is going wrong.

We have mentioned earlier that there is an inherent conflict between marketing department and the collection department. The former in its zest to sell may contract customers with low creditworthiness or may give longer line of credit without taking any responsibility for collecting the sales, while the latter in its desire to see that the receivables are well within the norms of average holding and bad-debts (so that it does not have to look for additional finance which may hit the bottom line) may pester the customers beyond limits of tolerance which may spoil all the endeavours of the marketing department and ultimately affect the goodwill of the firm. XYZ Ltd. is a case in point. We had seen that the marketing department of the company was doing an excellent job as revealed by a very high inventory turnover ratio but the sales remained uncollected for a long time as reflected in a very low receivables turnover ratio. This resulted in high interest cost and delay in creditor's payments. It is very difficult to resolve the conflict, but its effect can be minimised by strict adherence to the credit standards and making the marketing department also responsible partly for failure in collection.

In majority of firms in India, collection and monitoring activities are performed in finance and accounts department. Only in a few large companies under professional management we find a separate department looking after collection and monitoring of sales, though it maintains a reporting relationship with the finance and accounts department.

Collection and monitoring department is the place where experiences of the firm in handling receivables are pooled which, when properly organised, provide important inputs for periodical review of the credit policy and credit-scoring instruments.

Organisation and Procedure

1. Proper organisation of the collection and monitoring activities is essential for the effective functioning of the credit department. We have already mentioned that the department should normally be headed by the credit manager reporting to the controller of finance by whatever designation he is called, e.g. Vice-President (Finance) or General Manager (Finance). For small or mid-size firms the credit manager may report directly to the managing director.

2. For large companies having widespread geographical coverage, credit department, responsible for collection and monitoring, is located close to the point of sales, i.e. either in the zonal or regional organisation with adequate

delegation of authority. The zonal/regional credit manager reports to the zonal vice-president/general manager (finance) who, in turn, reports to corporate controller.

3. Depending upon the volume of receivables, the department should be divided into sections headed by section officers who shall report to the assistant credit manager (in the case of large organisation) or credit manager. Accounts allocated to each section should, as far as possible, be uniform not in terms of monetary value of sales, but in terms of efforts involved. Certain major accounts will, however, be retained by the assistant credit manager or the credit manager for direct dealing.

4. The assistant credit manager will supervise the work of the section officers and take appropriate decisions on matters referred to him within his authority, knowledge and experience. For those beyond, he should refer to the credit manager.

Although the section officers need not be discouraged from having access to the credit manager, it must be seen that line of authority is properly maintained.

5. The credit department must have an appropriate collection policy approved at the corporate level and known to all functionaries of the department. It should preferably be in writing.

The collection policy should, among other things, specify the efforts to be expended on categories of receivables, otherwise, it would not only be unwieldy but it may affect the goodwill of the company as well. For example, one cannot spend same amount of time and efforts and adopt similar steps and techniques for collecting a receivable worth Rs. 5000 and that of Rs. 5 lakh, though nature of delinquency is same in both the cases.

Depending upon the value-range of receivables, one or a particular combination of the measures given in Table 3.13 may be adopted for a given range of past due receivables.

6. All the measures mentioned in Table 3.13 need not be followed in all the cases and also in the order in which they are written. For example, for a large account, the credit department should put in every effort to work with the customer for mutually acceptable payment arrangement, but so much of time and effort cannot be expended on a small account. For this purpose the credit department must define in monetary terms what are small, medium and large accounts and note down appropriate measures thereagainst.

7. Every person in the credit department who makes a collection call or pays a personal visit to the office of the customer shall record in a *call sheet* the facts of conversation in brief but in detail as to the date of call, what the caller said, and what the customer said and promised in response. There should be a 'follow-up' column where the date of the next call—whether emanated from the conversation or caller's own estimate—should be noted. It is always preferable to write the name of the person contacted because next time the call should first be made to him. From the follow-up column of the call sheet a daily

Table 3.13 Measures to be Adopted for Delinquent Accounts Receivable

Days past due	Measure
(a) 10 days	Put a telephone call to the appropriate person in the accounts payable department of the customer. However, before doing so ensure that the monthly outstanding statement has been sent and the same has been received by the customer. Send a duplicate invoice and statement, if required.
(b) 20 days	Put a second telephone call, preferably to the accounts payable manager of the customer followed by a reminder letter quoting the promises made in telephonic conversation. Diarise to remind ten days hence.
(c) 30 days	The situation is serious but still may not be out of control. Examine the past payment records. If it is a regular feature and the company has tolerated this so far, it may decide that no further than a mild warning letter will do. The letter should mention the dates of early telephone calls and the promises made there against and that the company is viewing the matter seriously. If, however, the delay is occurring for the first time a direct contact with the customer is required to know the reasons behind the unusual delay. At this level of exposure, the officer-in-charge of payables should be contacted. A letter shall follow recording the conversation and the promises made therein.
(d) 45 days	The situation may be serious. A strong warning letter should be sent which will mention, *inter alia*, that failure to pay may put the customer on COD basis or the supplies may be stopped till all the overdues are paid.
(e) 90 days	The situation is pretty serious. Further shipment should be stopped for the time being. It is time to contact people at the top, may be Vice-President (Finance) of the customer organisation. The customer may be suffering temporarily from serious cash flow problems. If that be so, the credit manager should hold patience and try to work out a satisfactory paying arrangement and link it with release of further despatches. But if the cash flow problem is going to stay owing to some adverse development in the customer's business, then further despatches should be totally stopped. A workable payment arrangement should be made to liquidate the debt. The account should be closely monitored.
(f) 120 days	All deliveries to stop forthwith. The account may be on the brink of becoming bad-debt. It has to be very closely monitored with a view to collecting as much payment as possible. It is time to consider appropriate legal action depending upon the value of the account and the cost involved.

Note: 'Days past due' means the number of days the bill remains outstanding over the contracted credit period. For example, if credit term is $N/30$ but the bill is not paid in 40 days time, then it is past due 10 days.

follow-up schedule should be prepared (which will act as a diary for the credit officer) so that he does not miss an important follow-up call to be made on a particular date.

PAYMENT PATTERN

A credit department has not done a good job if it does not know payment pattern of each individual customer. Although goods may be sold to all customers on uniform credit terms, the experience of any credit department will reveal that all customers do not adhere to the same credit period despite the penal interest clause. Some pay in time but some others delay by say, 10, 15 or 20 days. Any experienced credit manager will agree that it is difficult to ignore the latter category of customers. Credit budget of a firm often accommodates such 'aberrations'. What is important, however, is to closely monitor this payment pattern of a customer. If suddenly there is a change in payment pattern, particularly of customers who regularly pay within due dates, then it is a cause of concern. But at the same time, it need not always be a disaster in the offing. The deviation simply puts the credit department on enquiry. It may be found that an invoice or the monthly statement of account has not been received by the customer or there is variation in the quantity received/despatched from that mentioned on the invoice and the customer has been waiting for a replacement invoice. A customer may not also make payment on time if the goods received are defective or not the ones that are ordered; he might have made a reference to the marketing department of the company which probably remains unattended.

All the reasons mentioned above are genuine and the responsibility lies with the credit manager to take corrective steps. He must, however, be on guard against a customer using any one of the above, e.g. asking for a duplicate invoice, as a ploy for buying time. These days a credit officer may often hear from the people in customer's payable department that, since payments are all computerised it is not possible to change the sequence once an invoice is missed. This may be more of a ploy to buy time than genuine impossibility of the system. Moreover, howsoever complex is the computerised system, there can never be any problem in handwriting a payment order and the cheque. The call sheet will reveal whether there is a pattern in this.

When, however, deviation from an established payment pattern is occurring regularly, the credit manager must put himself on alert and collect as much information as possible from all formal and informal sources and take a firm hold on the account so that he is not taken by surprise when things really begin to go wrong and he has nothing to do except being an onlooker. The customer may be suffering from a temporary cash flow problem which can be mutually worked out. If, however, the problem is deep-rooted then an alert credit manager would take preemptive action, say by securing his part of the claim before others swarm in.

All said and done, an experienced credit manager knows that collection efforts cannot go beyond a certain point except at the cost of affecting the goodwill of the firm. A tough credit manager is the one who adheres to the credit policy but at the same time helps the customer overcome genuine payment problems. A strict credit manager adheres only to the credit policy and treats the customers as enemies to be fought. No wonder the marketing people also treat him as their enemy and the enemy of the organisation as well. How often it is true!

COLLECTION COSTS

There is always a direct monetary cost involved in running a collection machinery. But there is also an indirect (opportunity) cost associated with collection activities. Due to stricter collection efforts, sales might be lost, and hence the profitability. As against these costs, the benefits of a well-organised collection department are reduction of bad-debt losses and shorter collection period that results into reduction in the average holding of receivables—both adding to the profitability of the enterprise. The goal of a collection policy is therefore, to strike a balance between costs and benefits, or in other words, to search for an optimal solution to the problem.

It has been observed that the level of collection cost does not bear any linear relationship with bad-debt losses, neither such relationship exists when compared with reduction in average collection period. Studies reveal that initial collection expenditure is likely to cause little reduction in bad-debt losses. Additional expenditure begins to have a significant effect up to a point; then it tends to have little effect in reducing further losses. The relationship between the average collection period and the level of collection expenditure is also likely to be similar.[40] The reason behind such a relationship is that initial expenditure for setting up a collection department assures only a minimum maintenance level. Any further reduction of bad-debt losses or of average collection period would entail further expenditure. Beyond a certain point, additional expenditure may not have any impact because, as we have mentioned before, collection efforts cannot also go beyond a certain point for a going concern except at the cost of destroying the goodwill of the organisation to the extent that sales may not altogether be possible.

Sales are never independent of collection effort except at a very moderate level. As the collection machinery becomes stricter and stricter, customers are likely to make a switch except when the firm is a monopoly seller. It is also likely that when the collection effort is intensified, a higher percentage of customers may take the cash discount because the advantage of stretching the payment beyond the credit period may no longer exist.

We shall now evaluate different collection programmes to arrive at an optimal solution with the help of an example.

---

40. Van Horne, James, C., *Financial Management and Policy*, Chapter 15, 12th ed., Prentice-Hall of India, New Delhi, 2004.

Example. A company's present sales are Rs. 7200 lakh. Goods are sold on 45 days credit but the company finds that sales are realised on an average in 90 days. Present bad-debt level is 3.5 percent of sales and the collection expenditure is Rs. 180 lakh.

The company has undertaken a study to evolve a suitable programme of actions that will reduce the average collection period and bad-debt losses.

External customer-survey supported by internal collection experience finally generated three alternative programmes. Previously, the company was not offering any cash discount. The survey revealed that offering of cash discount would contribute positively to the reduction in the average holding period of receivables besides providing immediate cash. Hence, the company has decided to change its selling term to 2/10 net 45. Important elements of the three alternative collection programmes are given in Table 3.14.

It appears from Table 3.14 that as the company intensifies its collection efforts, its sales will be affected negatively for reasons mentioned earlier. At its highest intensity (Programme III), sales will be lost by Rs. 900 lakh.

Table 3.14 Alternative Collection Programmes

(Rs. in lakh)

	Present status	Programme (I)	Programme (II)	Programme (III)
1. Sales	7200	7000	6700	6300
2. Collection expenditure	180	280	400	500
3. Projected bad-debt losses (as % of sales)	3.50	2	1.50	1.00
4. Expected percent of sales taking cash discount	—	10	15	20
5. Expected collection period for customers' not taking cash discount (in number of days)	90	60	50	45

Notes: (a)   Opportunity cost of carrying receivable is 20% p.a.

(b)   Return on sales is 20% before the expenses as mentioned above.

(c)   It is assumed that the intensity of the collection efforts is directly related to the increase in collection expenditure.

Actual holding of receivables under the three programmes is calculated below, assuming uniform monthly sales.

Programme I   (Rs. in lakh)

Monthly sales = 7000/12	=	583.33
Cash discount taken (10%)	=	(–)58.33
Sales remain to be collected in 60 days		525.00

Those taking cash discount pay in 10 days; the remaining in 60 days. Hence, the average holding of receivables will be

$$
\begin{array}{rcl}
58.33 & \times\ 10\ = & 583 \\
525.00 & \times\ 60\ = & 31,500 \\
\hline
583.33 & & 32,083
\end{array}
$$

Dividing 32,083 by 583.33 we obtain average days of collection period = 55 days.

In terms of value or receivables holding, it will be 55(7000/365) = Rs. 1055

Programme II

$$
\begin{array}{lcl}
\text{Monthly sales} = 6700/12 & = & 558.33 \\
\text{Cash discount taken (15\%)} & = & (-)\ 83.75 \\
\hline
\text{Sales remain to be collected in 50 days} & & 474.58
\end{array}
$$

Average holding of receivables:

$$
\begin{array}{rcl}
83.75 & \times\ 10\ = & 837.50 \\
474.58 & \times\ 50\ = & 23,729.00 \\
\hline
558.33 & & 24,566.50
\end{array}
$$

Hence, average days of collection = 24,566.50/558.33 = 44 days or 44 (6700/365) = Rs. 808

Programme III

$$
\begin{array}{lcl}
\text{Monthly sales} = 6300/12 & = & 525 \\
\text{Cash discount taken (20\%)} & = & (-)\ 105 \\
\hline
\text{Sales remain to be collected in 45 days} & & 420
\end{array}
$$

Average holding of receivables:

$$
\begin{array}{rcl}
105 & \times\ 10\ = & 1050 \\
420 & \times\ 45\ = & 18,900 \\
\hline
525 & & 19,950
\end{array}
$$

Hence, average days of collection = 19,950/525 = 38 days or 38 (6300/365) = Rs. 656

Evaluation of alternative collection programmes is given in Table 3.15.

Analysis made in Table 3.15 clearly indicates that Programme I is the optimal solution where the resultant profit is highest.

However, if the company feels that despite the increasing intensity in collection efforts in the three programmes it will be able to hold on to the existing level of sales, Programme I would still be the optimal solution (though not necessarily so in other cases). This is given in Table 3.16.

Table 3.15 Evaluation of Alternative Collection Programmes

(Rs. in lakh)

		Present status	Programme (I)	Programme (II)	Programme (III)
1.	Sales	7200	7000	6700	6300
2.	Revised collection period (number of days)	90	55	44	38
3.	Rupee value of average receivable holdings	1775	1055	808	656
4.	Cost of carrying receivables (@ 20% p.a.)	355	211	162	131
5.	Bad-debt losses	252	140	100	63
6.	Cost of cash discount	—	14	20	25
7.	Collection expenditure	180	280	400	500
	A. Total cost (4 to 7)	787	645	682	719
	B. Return on sales (@ 20%)	1440	1400	1340	1260
	Profit (B − A)	653	755	658	541

Table 3.16 Evaluation of Alternative Collection Programmes (with consistancy of sales)

(Rs. in lakh)

		Present status	Programme (I)	Programme (II)	Programme (III)
1.	Sales	7200	7200	7200	7200
2.	Rupee value of average receivable holding	1775	1085	868	750
3.	Cost of carrying receivables (@ 20% p.a.)	355	217	174	150
4.	Bad-debt losses	252	144	108	72
5.	Cost of cash discount	—	14	22	29
6.	Collection expenditure	180	280	400	500
	A. Total cost (3 to 6)	787	655	704	751
	B. Return on sales (@ 20%)	1440	1440	1440	1440
		653	785	736	689

It may be seen from Tables 3.15 and 3.16 that in both the cases the effective total cost of the alternative programmes rises with the intensity in collection efforts. Optimal solution lies where profit is maximised.

MONITORING AND CONTROL

The collection and monitoring efforts discussed in the previous section will give rise to certain movements in aggregate accounts receivable. Careful scrutiny of these financial aggregates provides excellent management information to the credit manager and the financial controller for evaluation of the functioning of the credit department and pin-point the areas of weaknesses where corrective actions need to be taken before things go out of control. Such an evaluation is not possible for individual credit officers who are bogged down to the routines of collection efforts.

Several methods of monitoring and control of aggregate accounts receivable have been evolved over a period of time. Some methods have limited applicability while some others have inherent difficulties. When sales of an enterprise are more or less uniform every month, there is not much of a problem in choosing an appropriate method, but when the level of sales vary, problem does arise. It follows, therefore, that an enterprise, while choosing a particular method, must see that the control mechanism itself is not faulty, which may give wrong signals to the credit department.

We shall now discuss some of the most widely used methods and their limitations, if any, to enable the credit department to adopt an appropriate method for the enterprise, based particularly upon the temporal sales experience.

Average Age of Receivables

This is a simple and straightforward method which uses a single index to measure the efficiency of receivables management. It is a good method when sales are more or less uniform over the months in a year.

Suppose, a company's sales remain uniform at Rs. 100 per month and the payment pattern is as follows:

- Ninety percent of the sales made remains outstanding in the month of sales, hence 10 percent is paid
- Sixty percent of the sales made remains outstanding in the second month of sales, hence 30 percent is paid
- Twenty percent of the sales made remains outstanding in the third month of sales, hence 40 percent is paid
- Zero percent of the sales made remains outstanding in the fourth month of sales, hence 20 percent is paid

The above payment pattern will give rise to the following cash flows and receivables holding during the two quarters beginning January of a year (Table 3.17).

Table 3.17 Cash Flows and Receivables Outstanding under Uniform Sales

Month (1)	Sales (Rs.) (2)	Cash flow (Rs.) (3)	Receivables outstanding (Rs.) (4)
January	100	10	90
February	100	30 + 10 = 40	60 + 90 = 150
March	100	40 + 30 + 10 = 80	20 + 60 + 90 = 170
April	100	20 + 40 + 30 + 10 = 100	20 + 60 + 90 = 170
May	100	20 + 40 + 30 + 10 = 100	20 + 60 + 90 = 170
June	100	20 + 40 + 30 + 10 = 100	20 + 60 + 90 = 170

Table 3.17 is recast in Table 3.18 to reveal percentage of amount outstanding at the end of quarter for each month's sales.

Table 3.18 Quarter-end Outstanding of Each Month's Sales

Month (1)	Sales (2)	Percent of sales of the month outstanding (3)	Quarter-end amount of sales of the month outstanding (Rs.) (4)
January	100	20	20
February	100	60	60
March	100	90	90
		Total	170
April	100	20	20
May	100	60	60
June	100	90	90
		Total	170

We may observe from Table 3.18 that the total of column 4 of the two quarters tally with the month end figures of column 4 of Table 3.17 beginning March. This is so because barring the first two months, every following month is a complete quarter-end. Henceforwards, this pattern will follow for every month and quarter under the assumption of uniform sales and the given payment pattern. Rupee value of *average sales outstanding* shall continue to be Rs. 170. We can now proceed to calculate average age of receivables. This can be done in two ways assuming uniform months of 30 days or 360 days a year.

Turnover Method

The formula for calculating the average age of receivables is as follows:

$$\frac{\text{Receivables outstanding} \times 360}{\text{Annual sales}}$$

In the present case, the average age will be

$$\frac{170 \times 360}{1200} = 51 \text{ days}$$

Cash Flow Method

As payment pattern is same, we can take cash flows from any month's sales, say January.

Cash inflow

January	February	March	April	Total
10	30	40	20	100

Average receivables collection time or age of receivables will, therefore, be

$$\frac{10 \times 0 + 30 \times 30 + 40 \times 60 + 20 \times 90}{100} = \frac{5100}{100} = 51 \, \text{days}$$

Now suppose that sales do not remain uniform in some quarters, say beginning the month of July and payment pattern also changes, then there is a chance that this method may not be able to capture such a change in payment pattern. The following example which is an extension of earlier example, will make it clear (Tables 3.19 and 3.20).

Table 3.19 Change in Accounts Receivables with Change in Sales (Situation I: Monthly Cash Flow Constant)

(Rs. in crore)

Month	Sales	Cash flows from month's sales									
		April	May	June	July	Aug.	Sept.	Oct.	Nov.	Dec.	Total
July	100	20	40	30	10	—	—	—	—	—	100
August	120	—	20	40	20	20	—	—	—	—	100
September	140	—	—	20	30	30	20	—	—	—	100
October	80	—	—	—	30	25	35	10	—	—	100
November	60	—	—	—	10	25	35	20	10	—	100
December	100	—	—	—	—	20	35	25	10	10	100
Outstanding as on 31st December						15	25	40	90		

	Accounts receivables outstanding from month's sales								
	May	June	July	Aug.	Sept.	Oct.	Nov.	Dec.	Total
July	20	60	90	—	—	—	—	—	170
August	—	20	30	100	—	—	—	—	150
September	—	—	40	70	120	—	—	—	230
October	—	—	10	45	85	70	—	—	210
November	—	—	—	20	50	50	50	—	170
December	—	—	—	—	15	25	40	90	170

Table 3.19 (continued from Table 3.17) reveals that monthly cash flows remain constant at Rs. 100 despite a change in the pattern of sales from August and average sales per month (1200/12) remaining at Rs. 100. The year-end accounts receivable remained at Rs. 170 but their holding for the month of August, September and October rose considerably. The sales of the enterprise went up during August and September and fell during October and November, but the collection department failed to ensure the original payment pattern of receivables. The collection department might have been carried away by

Table 3.20 Change in Cash Flow with Change in Sales
(Situation II: Accounts receivable constant)

(Rs. in crore)

Month	Sales	April	May	June	July	Aug.	Sept.	Oct.	Nov.	Dec.	Total
				Cash flow from month's sales							
July	100	20	40	30	10	—	—	—	—	—	100
August	120	—	20	40	30	30	—	—	—	—	120
September	140	—	—	20	30	50	40	—	—	—	140
October	80	—	—	—	10	20	30	20	—	—	80
November	60	—	—	—	10	10	20	10	10	—	60
December	100	—	—	—	10	10	20	20	20	20	100
Outstanding as on 31st December							30	30	30	80	

May	June	July	Aug.	Sept.	Oct.	Nov.	Dec.	Total
		Accounts receivables outstanding from month's sales						
20	60	90	—	—	—	—	—	170
—	20	60	90	—	—	—	—	170
—	—	30	40	100	—	—	—	170
—	—	20	20	70	60	—	—	170
—	—	10	10	50	50	50	—	170
—	—	—	—	30	30	30	80	170

constancy in monthly cash flows. When the same example is carried to the second situation, we find from Table 3.20 (continued from Table 3.17) that holding of accounts receivable is constant at Rs. 170 throughout the 12-month period despite a change in sales pattern from August as mentioned above. This once again indicates a fall in cash collection, particularly during October and November as revealed in the last column of the table. The average age of receivables, however, remains same at 51 days and hence, it is unable to capture the deviation in payment pattern in between. The collection department might be in euphoria when it finds that cash collections in a given month exactly matches the sales made in the month and during all the months beginning April. The point that is overlooked in this euphoria is that bulk of collections in a given month is from sales made in the earlier periods.

Daily Sales Outstanding (DSO)

In order to circumvent some of the aforementioned problems, DSO method is employed. This is also a popular technique and is in use in a large number of firms both small and large.

DSO is calculated for any point in time (usually at quarter-end) by dividing the total accounts receivable by the average daily credit sales. This is, in fact, a periodic break-up of receivables turnover ratio discussed earlier. The exact formula for calculating DSO is given as:

$$\text{DSO} = \frac{\text{Accounts receivable at period-end}}{\text{Total sales during the period}} \times \text{No. of days in the period}$$

For example, for the June quarter the DSO will be as follows (assuming 30 days in a month):

$$\frac{170}{300} \times 90 = 51\,\text{days}$$

In Table 3.21 we have calculated DSO beginning June quarter under both situations I and II.

Table 3.21 Daily Sales Outstanding

Quarter-end	Calculation	DSO
Situation I (cash flow constant)		
June	(170/300)90	51 days
September	(230/360)90	57.5 days
December	(170/240)90	63.75 days
Situation II (receivables constant)		
June	(170/300)90	51 days
September	(170/360)90	42.5 days
December	(170/240)90	63.75 days

We find from (Table 3.21 that under both the situations, DSO for December quarter is highest (about 64 days). It may give a wrong signal to the credit department. In fact, what has happened is that in December quarter, sales have fallen to Rs. 240 while accounts receivable remained at Rs. 170.

When receivables holding is more or less constant but sales vary over the quarters, then a rise in sales would result in decreasing days of holding. When cash flow is constant, a rise in sales would result in higher amount of accounts receivable and hence, DSO will also be higher, but if in the subsequent quarter sales fall but accounts receivables go back to previous level as has happened in situation I, then DSO rises further.

We get a better insight into the limitation of this technique when DSOs are calculated for moving quarters than standard quarters-end as shown in Table 3.21. These are calculated in Table 3.22 for situation I.

Table 3.22 Calculation of DSOs for Moving Quarters (Situation I)

Month	Sales	Accounts receivable	Quarterly DSO	Percentage growth in sales
April	100	—	—	0
May	100	—	—	0
June	100	170	51 days	0
July	100	170	51 days	0
August	120	190	53.44 days	20
September	140	230	57.50 days	16.66
October	80	210	55.59 days	(–) 42.85
November	60	170	52.76 days	(–) 25
December	100	170	63.75 days	66.67

A scrutiny of Table 3.22 will reveal that if sales during the previous period are rising, then this technique will tend to report a higher DSO as we find for the September quarter-end. The same will also happen when previous sales are lower as we find in the December quarter. It may give confusing and misleading signals to the credit department when aggregate monthly cash flows are constant.

DSO technique is also heavily dependent not only upon the speed with which collections are made, but also upon the past pattern of sales. This technique would report a higher DSO when there is no change in payment pattern but the past period sales are on the increase; if these are decreasing, then it would report a lower DSO. Hence, under constancy of payment pattern also, DSO method gives misleading signals. The following example will further make it clear.

Example

Month	Sales	Collections	Accounts receivable
I	600	240	360
II	800	680	480
III	1200	960	720

Quarter-end DSO(1) = (720/2600) 90 = 24.92 days
(Sales rising)

If we take the sales and collections on the reverse order, then

Quarter-end DSO(2) = (360/2600) 90 = 12.46 days
(Sales falling)

DSO(1) is larger than DSO(2) though in both the cases payment pattern remains at 40 percent in the first month and 60 percent in the second month.

Receivables Aging Schedule

This method is an improvement upon the methods discussed earlier. It is also a commonly used technique, particularly among the small and medium-sized enterprises. Under this method outstanding receivables are grouped against designated time intervals to find out how much of the receivables is away from the 'current'. This schedule is often required by bankers making loan against receivables or the factors deciding the acceptability of receivables and also the commissions. It is preferable to draw the *aging schedule* quarterly. In Tables 3.23 and 3.24 we have drawn up two schedules—one for situation I and the other for situation II—using the same example. Calculations are based on Tables 3.17–3.20.

It would appear from Table 3.23 that under situation I (cash flow constant), the current category (0–30 days) of receivables constitute about 52 percent of the receivables outstanding in all the quarters-end. While holding against 30–60 days has gone down in the last two quarters, the condition has worsened against the next two class intervals during the same periods. In fact, we find that

Table 3.23 Aging Schedules of Accounts Receivables
(Situation I: Cash Flow Constant)

Age group	Amount of receivables outstanding at the quarter-end	Percent of total
Quarter-end March		
0–30 days	90	52.94
30–60 days	60	35.29
60–90 days	20	11.77
90–120 days	—	—
Total	170	100.00
Quarter-end June		
0–30 days	90	52.94
30–60 days	60	35.29
60–90 days	20	11.77
90–120 days	—	—
Total	170	100.00
Quarter-end September		
0–30 days	120	52.17
30–60 days	70	30.43
60–90 days	40	17.40
90–120 days	—	—
Total	230	100.00
Quarter-end December		
0–30 days	90	52.94
30–60 days	40	23.53
60–90 days	25	14.70
90–120 days	15	8.83
Total	170	100.00

in December-quarter, some of the receivables (8.83%) have moved to 90–120 days category which was just not there in the earlier three quarters.

In situation II where holding of accounts receivables is constant at every quarter-end, we find from Table 3.24 that the aging has improved against current category (0–30 days) in September-quarter but worsened against 60–90 days category where receivables holding as percentage of total sales of the quarter has gone up to 17.65 percent as against 11.77 percent in the earlier quarters. December-quarter results are far more worse. Not only that holding in the current category has gone down, we also find some of the receivables (17.65 percent) have slipped down to 90–120 days category.

It is true that aging schedule gives a better insight into the status of receivables holding than what we get by employing the technique of average age of receivables discussed earlier. But it suffers from putting too much emphasis on the current category and is biased more towards sales made in recent months. As a result, when sales of a firm is on the rise the current and recent categories will have more receivables holding which may not speak anything about the efficiency of the collection department, though it may make

Table 3.24 Aging Schedules of Accounts Receivables
(Situation II: Receivables Constant)

Age group	Amount of receivables outstanding at the quarter-end		Percent of total
Quarter-end March			
0–30 days		90	52.94
30–60 days		60	35.29
60–90 days		20	11.77
90–120 days		—	—
	Total	170	100.00
Quarter-end June			
0–30 days		90	52.94
30–60 days		60	35.29
60–90 days		20	11.77
90–120 days		—	—
	Total	170	100.00
Quarter-end September			
0–30 days		100	58.82
30–60 days		40	23.53
60–90 days		30	17.65
90–120 days		—	—
	Total	170	100.00
Quarter-end December			
0–30 days		80	47.06
30–60 days		30	17.64
60–90 days		30	17.65
90–120 days		30	17.65
	Total	170	100.00

them more complacent. On the other end, when sales are falling, receivables holding in current and recent categories will also be falling which once again may not speak anything about the laxity of the collection department. In both the cases the collection department might be doing its job extremely well by holding onto or improving upon the established payment pattern which may not be so reflected under the aging schedule. The improved performance of receivables that we find in September quarter (Table 3.24) may just be due to rise in sales in that quarter, and the worsening performance in the following quarters may be due to a fall in sales in that quarter.

Besides, a substantial fall of receivables holding in say, current category in any quarter need not indicate disaster; it may just be the opposite; some big customers might have paid up faster than their usual time, or that a cash discount is offered during the period which has resulted into large payment (because it is the current category of customers who are most likely to avail themselves of cash discount).

The aging proportions of receivables that we obtain from the aging schedule may not be able to capture any of the phenomena indicated above, but a quarter by quarter comparison would definitely prompt the financial controller to make enquiry about the goings-on at the collection front.

Percentage Collection and Accounts Receivable Matrix

The central problem of the three methods discussed so far rests on aggregation—either of collections or of receivables. Collections of one period may represent sales of different periods, so also the receivables at a particular point in time. Hence, the earlier three methods were attempting to compare with incomparables which resulted in the blinking of wrong signals.

When the problem lies in aggregation, then the solution may be found by disaggregating the relative variables. Collections or receivables have to be traced to the source. Only then it is possible to identify any deviation from established payment pattern. Let us first explain this with the following example (Table 3.25).[41]

Table 3.25 Accounts Receivable as Percentage of Month's Sales

Month (1)	Sales (2)	Outstanding receivables at quarter-end (3)	Percent of receivables outstanding against month's sales (4)
April	100	20	20
May	100	60	60
June	100	90	90
Total	300	170 [DSO = 51 days]	—
July	50	10	20
August	100	60	60
September	150	135	90
Total	300	205 [DSO = 61.5 days]	—
October	150	30	20
November	100	60	60
December	50	45	90
Total	300	135 [DSO = 40.5 days]	—

Note: Column 4 will not add up to 100 because each one represents a different calculation base.

In the above example, the total of quarterly sales remained same at Rs. 300, though intra-quarter sales varied for September and December-quarters, which resulted in different DSOs. But we find from column 4 that the receivables holding pattern (and hence, the collection pattern) had not changed at all for each month's sales.

41. In drawing up this example we have drawn heavily from Lewellen, G. Wilbur and R.W. Johnson, "Better Way to Monitor Accounts Receivable," *Harvard Business Review*, May–June 1972, pp. 101–109.

The receivables pattern presented in Table 3.25 is the one with which we began this section. The pattern envisages a collection pattern of 10%, 30%, 40%, 20% as shown earlier. Now suppose that sales made in February are not collected at 30 percent in the following month but at 20 percent, and sales made in the month of March are collected at 20 percent instead of 10 percent in the first month, then the effect of these changes in payment pattern would be immediately indicated as a deviation from the established pattern, which is shown in Table 3.26.

Table 3.26 Accounts Receivable as Percentage of Sales (Effect of Slow Payment)

Month (1)	Sales (2)	Outstanding receivables at quarter-end (3)	Percent of receivables against month's sales (4)	Deviation from existing pattern (%) (5)
January	100	20	20	NIL
February	100	70	70	(–)10
March	100	80	80	10
Total	300	170 [DSO = 51 days]	—	0

It may be seen that the DSO has remained at 51 days, hence, the credit manager using DSO method need not take any action. But it is clear from column 5 that the 'no change of DSO' is the result of a negative deviation compensated by a positive deviation. A credit manager cannot ignore these deviations except at his own peril. DSO method does not allow these compensating deviations to surface. We should, however, point out here that these deviations may not always toll danger for the enterprise. If these deviations repeat themselves, then it may be likely that payment pattern of some groups of customers is changing, which calls for a credit policy review and change in receivables forecasting. The latter is important for fund planning which depends upon proper assessment of the payment pattern of customers.

We can now draw up collection and receivables matrices under the present method (being discussed) using our original example as elaborated in Table 3.17 through Table 3.20.

First, we present cash flow as percentage of month's sales under situation I (Table 3.27) and situation II (Table 3.28), which are then followed by accounts receivable as percentage of month's sales under both the situations in Tables 3.29 and 3.30.

Percentage Cash Flow Matrix (PCFM)

Cash flow matrices reveal whether collections are slowing down, improving or staying at the same level for appropriate management action.

Under situation I (Table 3.27) where total monthly cash flows from all previous months and the present month are constant, we find that the collection pattern (or customers' payment pattern) is changing from July through

Table 3.27 Percentage Cash Flow Matrix—Cash Flow as Percentage of Month's Sales (Situation I—Monthly Total Cash Flow Constant)

	Jan.	Feb.	March	April	May	June	July	Aug.	Sept.	Oct.	Nov.	Dec.	Total
January	10.00	30.00	40.00	20.00	—	—	—	—	—	—	—	—	100
February	—	10.00	30.00	40.00	20.00	—	—	—	—	—	—	—	100
March	—	—	10.00	30.00	40.00	20.00	—	—	—	—	—	—	100
April	—	—	—	10.00	30.00	40.00	20.00	—	—	—	—	—	100
May	—	—	—	—	10.00	30.00	40.00	20.00	—	—	—	—	100
June	—	—	—	—	—	10.00	30.00	40.00	20.00	—	—	—	100
July	—	—	—	—	—	—	10.00	20.00	30.00	30.00	10.00	—	100
August	—	—	—	—	—	—	—	16.67	25.00	20.83	20.83	16.67	100
September	—	—	—	—	—	—	—	—	14.28	25.00	25.00	25.00	89.28
October	—	—	—	—	—	—	—	—	—	12.50	25.00	31.25	68.75
November	—	—	—	—	—	—	—	—	—	—	16.67	16.67	33.34
December	—	—	—	—	—	—	—	—	—	—	—	10.00	10.00

Table 3.28 Percentage Cash Flow Matrix—Cash Flow as Percentage of Month's Sales (Situation II—Accounts Receivable Constant)

	Jan.	Feb.	March	April	May	June	July	Aug.	Sept.	Oct.	Nov.	Dec.	Total
January	10.00	30.00	40.00	20.00	—	—	—	—	—	—	—	—	100
February	—	10.00	30.00	40.00	20.00	—	—	—	—	—	—	—	100
March	—	—	10.00	30.00	40.00	20.00	—	—	—	—	—	—	100
April	—	—	—	10.00	30.00	40.00	20.00	—	—	—	—	—	100
May	—	—	—	—	10.00	30.00	40.00	20.00	—	—	—	—	100
June	—	—	—	—	—	10.00	30.00	40.00	20.00	—	—	—	100
July	—	—	—	—	—	—	10.00	30.00	30.00	10.00	10.00	10.00	100
August	—	—	—	—	—	—	—	25.00	41.67	16.67	8.33	8.33	100
September	—	—	—	—	—	—	—	—	28.58	21.43	14.28	14.28	78.57
October	—	—	—	—	—	—	—	—	—	25.00	12.50	25.00	62.50
November	—	—	—	—	—	—	—	—	—	—	16.66	33.34	50.00
December	—	—	—	—	—	—	—	—	—	—	—	20.00	20.00

December sales. Although there is a definite improvement in the first month's collection during the period August–November, overall pattern appears to have deteriorated during the entire July–November period. The matrix itself reveals that payments are stretched to five months as against four months earlier, at least for sales during July–September. The pattern is likely to be repeated in the following two months also. From December, it might go back to normal level. Next year's data, when compared with the present year, will confirm whether the change in payment pattern in the second half of the year is going to stay. If this is so, then a major change in credit policy is required, otherwise the payment behaviour may be termed erratic, which calls for management's intervention.

Impact of the change in collection pattern can be better judged by using present value technique. We can calculate present value of cash flows for three months beginning June in the following manner by converting the percentage fraction into rupee value of sales of each month (refer Table 3.19). It is not possible to do it for the remaining months because full data are not available.

Cash Flow from Month's Sales

Month	Sales	June	July	Aug.	Sept.	Oct.	Nov.	Dec.
June	100	10	30	40	20	—	—	—
July	100	—	10	20	30	30	10	—
August	120	—	—	20	30	25	25	20

Present value of collections (assuming opportunity cost at 12 percent per annum or 1 percent per month):

$$\frac{\text{June}}{(\text{Sales Rs. }100)} \quad PV = 10 + \frac{30}{(1.01)} + \frac{40}{(1.01)^2} + \frac{20}{(1.01)^3} = \text{Rs. }98.32$$

$$\frac{\text{July}}{(\text{Sales Rs. }100)} \quad PV = 10 + \frac{20}{(1.01)} + \frac{30}{(1.01)^2} + \frac{30}{(1.01)^3} + \frac{10}{(1.01)^4} = \text{Rs. }97.94$$

$$\frac{\text{August}}{(\text{Sales Rs. }120)} \quad PV = 20 + \frac{30}{(1.01)} + \frac{25}{(1.01)^2} + \frac{25}{(1.01)^3} + \frac{20}{(1.01)^4} = \text{Rs. }117.69$$

Although full payment behaviour of September-quarter would enable us to come to a more precise conclusion, from this limited study we find that for June and July, PVs of collections are 98.32 percent and 97.94 percent respectively of month's sales, and for August, it is 117.69/120 = 98.08 percent. Between June and July the variation is 0.38 percent, and between June and August it is 0.24 percent. Depending upon the volume of monthly sales one enterprise may ignore the variation as being small, while another may consider it substantial warranting management's intervention.

Under situation II (Table 3.28) where monthly receivables holding from all previous and present months' sales is constant, we find, as before, that the collection pattern is changing from July onwards. Although there is a distinct improvement in first month's collection all through, which shall improve the present value of receipts, the collections in subsequent months are erratic and do not show much of a pattern as in the former case. It suggests that collections from second month onwards are not under control of the collection department, which calls for immediate management intervention. The management cannot just sleep over the matter because accounts receivable holding is constant or that the PV is presently good. The danger signal is that some payments have gone into fifth and sixth month. It is from the late payment category that bad-debt losses occur. Entire receivables (credit) planning of the enterprise may go topsy turvy if receivables holding, particularly the average or year-end holding is taken as the basis of planning.

We can now calculate the present values of cash flows. It will be done in the same manner and for same months as before.

Cash Flow from Month's Sales

Month	Sales	June	July	Aug.	Sept.	Oct.	Nov.	Dec.
June	100	10	30	40	20	—	—	—
July	100	—	10	30	30	10	10	10
August	120	—	—	30	50	20	10	10

Present value of collections (assuming opportunity cost at 1 percent per month):

$$\frac{\text{June}}{(\text{Sales Rs. }100)} \quad PV = 10 + \frac{30}{(1.01)} + \frac{40}{(1.01)^2} + \frac{20}{(1.01)^3} = \text{Rs. }98.32$$

$$\frac{\text{July}}{(\text{Sales Rs. }100)} \quad PV = 10 + \frac{30}{(1.01)} + \frac{30}{(1.01)^2} + \frac{10}{(1.01)^3} + \frac{10}{(1.01)^4} + \frac{10}{(1.01)^5} = \text{Rs. }97.94$$

$$\frac{\text{August}}{(\text{Sales Rs. }120)} \quad PV = 30 + \frac{50}{(1.01)} + \frac{20}{(1.01)^2} + \frac{10}{(1.01)^3} + \frac{10}{(1.01)^4} = \text{Rs. }118.41$$

As mentioned above, full payment behaviour of later months would have enabled us to obtain the total picture, but from this limited study we find that PVs of July and August under situation II are similar to that under situation I. What is rather striking is the improvement in PV for August despite some payments having been stretched to fifth month. Between June and July the variation in PV is same at $(-)0.38$ percent while between June and August, it is $+0.35$ percent. This has happened because larger payments for this month's sales have been made in recent months. This should not cloud the mind of the financial controller because despite earlier collections in some months, this is not showing a definite pattern and in some months, payments are being stretched much longer days than usual which may contain seeds of emerging bad-debt losses.

Percentage Accounts Receivable Matrix (PARM)

This matrix is just the counterpart of *percentage cash flow matrix* (PCFM) discussed above. It presents the picture of the percentage of credit sales of a particular month still remaining as receivables at the end of a successive month. When we relate this matrix (PARM) with PCFM we shall find that each month's receivables are reduced by the amount of cash flow coming in from that month's sales. In other words, the percentage remaining in receivables at the end of the month of sale is 100 percent less than the percentage that came in as a cash flow during the month. PARMs are presented in Tables 3.29 and 3.30 under situation I and situation II respectively.

Table 3.29 Percentage Accounts Receivable Matrix (PARM)—Accounts Receivable as Percentage of Month's Sales (Situation I—Monthly Total Cash Flow Constant)

	Jan.	Feb.	March	April	May	June	July	Aug.	Sept.	Oct.	Nov.	Dec.
January	90.00	60.00	20.00	—	—	—	—	—	—	—	—	—
February	—	90.00	60.00	20.00	—	—	—	—	—	—	—	—
March	—	—	90.00	60.00	20.00	—	—	—	—	—	—	—
April	—	—	—	90.00	60.00	20.00	—	—	—	—	—	—
May	—	—	—	—	90.00	60.00	20.00	—	—	—	—	—
June	—	—	—	—	—	90.00	60.00	20.00	—	—	—	—
July	—	—	—	—	—	—	90.00	70.00	40.00	10.00	—	—
August	—	—	—	—	—	—	—	83.33	58.33	37.50	16.67	—
September	—	—	—	—	—	—	—	—	85.72	60.72	35.72	10.72
October	—	—	—	—	—	—	—	—	—	87.50	62.50	31.25
November	—	—	—	—	—	—	—	—	—	—	83.33	66.66
December	—	—	—	—	—	—	—	—	—	—	—	90.00

Table 3.30 Percentage Accounts Receivable Matrix (PARM)—Accounts Receivable as Percentage of Month's Sales (Situation II—Receivables Constant)

	Jan.	Feb.	March	April	May	June	July	Aug.	Sept.	Oct.	Nov.	Dec.
January	90.00	60.00	20.00	—	—	—	—	—	—	—	—	—
February	—	90.00	60.00	20.00	—	—	—	—	—	—	—	—
March	—	—	90.00	60.00	20.00	—	—	—	—	—	—	—
April	—	—	—	90.00	60.00	20.00	—	—	—	—	—	—
May	—	—	—	—	90.00	60.00	20.00	—	—	—	—	—
June	—	—	—	—	—	90.00	60.00	20.00	—	—	—	—
July	—	—	—	—	—	—	90.00	60.00	30.00	20.00	10.00	—
August	—	—	—	—	—	—	—	75.00	33.83	16.66	8.33	—
September	—	—	—	—	—	—	—	—	71.42	49.99	35.71	21.43
October	—	—	—	—	—	—	—	—	—	75.00	62.50	37.50
November	—	—	—	—	—	—	—	—	—	—	83.34	50.00
December	—	—	—	—	—	—	—	—	—	—	—	80.00

The PARM can also be drawn by relating to receivables outstanding at the end of any month to the sales which generated the receivables. Whatever way we proceed, the resultant matrix will be one and the same. If there is a change in receivables holding pattern, the matrix will track it down to the month which originated the sales similar to PCFM. The interpretation of any change of receivables behaviour that we may find from this matrix will also be the same as those which are revealed in PCFM.

For example, let us take up the PARM under situation I and examine the receivables holding pattern for June onward (Table 3.29).

As observed from PCFM, here also we find a distinct change in receivables holding pattern (collection pattern in the earlier matrix) from July. The change is more prominent during August–November. From December, it indicates a likely come back to the original level. Whether it is an erratic behaviour that calls for tightening of control over receivables payment, or it indicates a different trend in payment pattern, has already been discussed while analysing the percentage cash flow matrix.

FORECASTING OF ACCOUNTS RECEIVABLE

Forecasting of receivables holding is very important for funds planning. As receivables claim a major part of working capital, the forecasting becomes important not only for the internal management of funds and for setting up budgetary standards, but also for obtaining working capital finance from commercial banks.

The simplest way to forecast accounts receivable is to assume the latter as being proportional to sales whether directly or via the DSO. The method is dominantly practised in India because of receivables holding norms spearheaded by Tandon Committee in 1975. These norms still influence greatly the minds of bankers as well as corporate financial controllers despite the withdrawal of MPBF system that contained these norms. When firms do not suffer from seasonality and when steady growth in sales is observed, or when the job is the financial evaluation of project requiring long-range forecasting of working capital, this method may serve the purpose moderately well. But when such are not the cases and when monthly or quarterly or yearly forecasts of receivables holding becomes important for day-to-day management of funds and for working capital loan, then this simple method may not be of much help. What comes handy is the percentage accounts receivable matrix (PARM).

The PARMs of an enterprise examined historically for the past two to three years (maximum period should not be more than three years and the minimum two) will reveal an average pattern of holding related not to the aggregate sales but to each month's sales, which when applied to projected sales of every month in the plan period, will give us projected level of accounts receivable at each month-end.

Suppose, such an exercise done for an enterprise, reveals an average receivables holding pattern of 80%, 40% and 10% for every month's sales. The marketing department makes sales projection in the month of November for the following year beginning January. On the basis of these information we can draw up an accounts receivables matrix in Table 3.31 for purpose of projecting monthly receivable holdings of the enterprise.

Table 3.31 Projected Accounts Receivable Matrix

(Rs. in lakh)

	Sales	Jan.	Feb.	March	April	May	June	July	Aug.	Sept.	Oct.	Nov.	Dec.
November	3500	350	—	—	—	—	—	—	—	—	—	—	—
December	2000	800	200	—	—	—	—	—	—	—	—	—	—
January	1200	960	480	120	—	—	—	—	—	—	—	—	—
February	1500	—	1200	600	150	—	—	—	—	—	—	—	—
March	2700	—	—	2160	1080	270	—	—	—	—	—	—	—
April	3800	—	—	—	3040	1520	380	—	—	—	—	—	—
May	3900	—	—	—	—	3120	1560	390	—	—	—	—	—
June	6000	—	—	—	—	—	4800	2400	600	—	—	—	—
July	7500	—	—	—	—	—	—	6000	3000	750	—	—	—
August	9000	—	—	—	—	—	—	—	7200	3600	900	—	—
September	10,500	—	—	—	—	—	—	—	—	8400	4200	1050	—
October	7200	—	—	—	—	—	—	—	—	—	5760	2880	720
November	4500	—	—	—	—	—	—	—	—	—	—	3600	1800
December	3000	—	—	—	—	—	—	—	—	—	—	—	2400
Total	60,800	2110	1880	2880	4270	4910	6740	8790	10,800	12,750	10,860	7530	4920

Note: Total of sales is for January–December.

For firms whose sales are seasonal in nature, like the present one, the projection of receivables holding as a proportion of average sales may give a misleading estimate because, as mentioned before, the two computational bases are different. For example, average monthly sales of the firm is Rs. 60,800/12 = Rs. 5067 lakh whereas average receivables holding is Rs. 78,440/12 = Rs. 6536 lakh; the latter is about 129 percent of average monthly sales. Projecting accounts receivables on the basis of this percentage, say for January and July would give us Rs. 1548 lakh and Rs. 9675 lakh as receivables holding for the respective months, which differ widely from what we have projected in Table 3.31.

Projection for accounts receivable done through accounts receivable matrix not only makes it more accurate, it also enables a credit manager to monitor actual movement of accounts receivable against the budgeted standards. As the receivables are traced to the month's sales, it becomes easier for him to track down the 'erring month' and take appropriate corrective measures.

The financial controller can also draw up the counter part of this matrix, i.e. the projected cash flow matrix for credit sales in the manner discussed before, so that he could know the estimated cash flow for every month and plan the outflows accordingly.

BAD-DEBTS

One of the most important tasks of collection and monitoring is to minimise bad-debt losses. Companies are found to go bankrupt because of bad-debts. When sales cannot be collected, it is not only that the profit remains unrealised but the entire fund invested in the sales is also lost. This phenomenon affects not only the present operation of the business, but also its future operations. Sales made in one year may become bad-debt in the following year, but the profit on such sales might have been booked in the current year on accrual basis, and taxes and dividends were already paid on it. Next year the effect on the enterprise is an erosion of capital. This is the reason why so much importance is given on providing for a bad-debt reserve.

It is often said that a bad-debt is created at the point when the credit decision is taken. While this is true to a very large extent, unusual developments in the customer's business or the industry to which it belongs, cannot often be foretold in spite of the best appraisal system. There cannot be any guarantee against the probability that certain accounts which had performed very well in the past several years might not turn out to be slow or bad. Thus every credit sale is a risky sale. This is also the reason for the existence of a collection and monitoring cell.

We have shown in the earlier sections that a restrictive credit and collection policy has the obvious advantage of minimising or virtually eliminating bad-debt losses. Such policies would definitely create a portfolio of customers of impeccable integrity (though not necessarily inflexible), but such customers are not many, and because they are not many, a company's sales may never grow, so also the profit and capital base. For some period of time the company may remain static before gradually going down to liquidation. An optimal credit and collection policy is the solution to the problem that we have been advocating so far in this chapter. An experienced credit manager lives with the fact that in business bad-debt shall occur. His goal is to keep it at a controlled minimum level.

What is the tolerance level of bad-debt? Internally, it depends upon the capital base and risk-profile of an enterprise, and externally on the industry average. If the bad-debt ratio of a firm is more than the industry average (though not very high) but the company is enjoying a reasonable level of growth with good profits and required capital expansion, then it may be assumed that the company is not following a restrictive policy, but its bad-debt losses, though more than the industry average, are kept under control at a level which is optimal for the enterprise in question. When the bad-debt ratio is lower than the industry average but the company is at the tail-end of the industry, then it is unlikely that it is doing good business. The most welcome situation, of course, is when the enterprise is well within the bad-debt ratio of the industry and is enjoying a good rate of growth with a strong capital base. In future, when the company tries to make a market penetration or increase its market share by relaxing credit standards it will have the power to absorb shocks.

When a receivable account turns bad and is to be written off, the credit and collection department must justify that it has put in all the efforts that are necessary to collect the debt and it is no longer viable to put in more efforts. Rather, the same time and money can be diverted productively to other accounts.

Proper documentation of the efforts put in must be available for all the accounts that are written off. This is necessary not only to convince the Income Tax department (who may not allow it as a deduction from profit unless convinced), but also to build up statistical records which are essential to keep the credit department dynamic by constant review of its policies and credit scoring attributes. When an account becomes uncollectable, not all is lost; the experience gained is invaluable for the survival of the enterprise. This experience will be lost unless properly documented and stored.

A well-documented file also makes it easier for the lawyer to prepare his plaint while filing a suit for the recovery of debt. Many a time, it has been found that an otherwise good case is lost because of improper documentation.

Bad-Debt Reserve

The credit department must prepare a list of accounts which are becoming sticky in terms of time lapsed and also otherwise. The list should contain name and full address of the customer with the name of the contact person, amount of debt outstanding, number of days outstanding, summary and results of efforts made to collect the amount and the considered opinion of the dealing officer about the future prospect of recovery. In some respect it can be treated as a semi-final list because it has been found that often some accounts which have gone over time and hence found their place in this list, have made a come back to current account status. At the year-end the credit manager will prepare two lists for approval of the financial controller. The first list shall contain details of accounts as mentioned above from which chance of recovery is almost nil or further persuation will not be cost-effective. These accounts are written off directly to the debit of profit and loss account. The second list shall contain names of accounts which are not completely lost but chance of recovery is very low. These are termed as doubtful accounts for which adequate provision in the form of bad-dedt reserve has to be made.

There is a tendency amongst some of the credit managers and financial controllers to provide for bad-debt reserve as little as possible. Many a time, almost a battle is fought between the corporate finance officers and the auditors on this issue. The tendency to artificially lower down the bad-debt reserve may often be ruinous for a company. Indian commercial banks, particularly those in the nationalised sector, played this game for a long time which ultimately turned out to be disastrous. A credit manager who has been dealing his company's receivables under a given credit standards is aware of what percentage of sales shall turn out to be bad. A study of the two lists mentioned above for past two to three years also enables him to come to a judgement. A pragmatic financial controller would better agree with him than inventing his own lean figure to present a better view of the profit and loss account.

The estimated bad-debt losses as a percentage of total sales should be continuously provided from monthly sales figure. The continuous accural to bad-debt reserve provides a continuous cushion against probable bad-debts and keeps the financials of an enterprise clean. This is more important for companies which declare quarterly or half-yearly interim dividends. If at the end of the year, or after a period of two years it has been found that the bad-debt reserve has been over-provided, then a company may decide to carry back the over-provision to push up the bottom line. This is much better than providing for lesser amount and eat out of capital later when real bad-debt occurs.

PREDICTING ACCOUNTS RECEIVABLE BEHAVIOUR— THE MARKOV PROCESS APPROACH

When a company has a large portfolio of accounts receivable it is incumbent upon the credit department to record the history of the behaviour of accounts or a group of accounts to enable it to base various receivables-decision on a more objective basis. Reliance on the experiential memory of a credit manager may not work as successful as when the portfolio was small.

We have mentioned before that one of the usages of the historical records of the behaviour of accounts receivable is proper estimation of bad-debt and provision for reserve. Accounts falling in a particular past due category can have four probable outcomes:

    (a) It may be paid up

    (b) It may become current by paying the past due balances

    (c) It may enter into next past due category and finally

    (d) It may turn out to be uncollectable.

An experienced credit manager, who has before him the historical performance of accounts falling under various past due categories, would be able to tell with great precision about the probability of one category of accounts to move from one state to the other as mentioned above. We may call these as transition probabilities and use them in determining what part of the accounts receivable would ultimately end up being paid and what part would become bad through a well-established process called *Markov Analysis*. This is defined as a method of analysing current behaviour of some variable to predict the future of that variable where the probability of occurrence of next event depends upon the outcomes resulting from last event(s).[42]

As a management tool, Markov Analysis has been in wide use in various decision situations, most prominent among them is the prediction of the behaviour of consumers about the extent of their brand loyalty and the probability of their switch from one brand to the other. During the past twenty years, it is being used very successfully in predicting the state of accounts receivable to enable a credit manager to take appropriate corrective actions and also to make provisions for bad-debt.

Let us make use of this robust tool in predicting the behaviour of accounts receivable of an enterprise having a present volume of Rs. 725 lakh divided into two *aging categories*, namely 0–60 days and 61–180 days old. The company has a policy of writing off accounts receivable which are more than 180 days old. The credit department classifies a customer's account in terms of the above categories according to the oldest unpaid invoice. This practice, which is in most prevalent use, allows an account which is presently in say, 61–180 days category to enter into 0–60 days category in the next month by paying the oldest invoices during the current month.

The credit manager of the company informs, from his experience and study of the past records, the various probabilities of occurrence for say, Rs. 100 worth of receivables as given in Table 3.32.[43]

Table 3.32 Probability of Occurrence (in percent)

Category	Paid	Bad-debt	State of movements	
			0–60 days	61–180 days
0–60 days	30%	—	40%	30%
61–180 days	40%	20%	30%	10%

Table 3.32 suggests that the credit manager does not expect an account falling in 0–60 days category in the present month to become bad-debt in the

---

42. This method was developed by Anderi, A. Markov, a Russian mathematician early in this century to describe and predict the behaviour of particles of gas in a closed container. For a more in-depth understanding of Markov Process, see D. Isaacson and R. Madsen, *Markov Chains: Theory and Applications,* John Wiley, New York, 1976.
43. For an approach towards this example and other applications of Markov Process see, R.I. Levin, C.A. Kirkpatrick and D.S. Rubin, *Quantitative Approaches to Management,* 5th ed., McGraw-Hill, Tokyo, 1982.

next month. The table also indicates that eventually all accounts receivable would be either paid or become bad. But the credit manager is interested to know what is the probability of receivables belonging to 0–60 days or 61–180 days category entering into either paid or bad-debt state. This he can estimate by moving along the following steps prescribed in Markov procedure.

The first step is to convert Table 3.32 into the following transition matrix which is given in Table 3.33.

Table 3.33 Transition Probability Matrix

	Paid	Bad-debt	0–60 days	61–180 days
Paid	1	0	0	0
Bad-debt	0	1	0	0
0–60 days	0.3	—	0.4	0.3
61–180 days	0.4	0.2	0.3	0.1

The above matrix indicates the obvious that an account, when paid, cannot be bad-debt, nor can it enter into other categories. Similarly, when an account becomes bad-debt, it can neither be paid nor move to other status.

The transition probability matrix is now partitioned into four matrices and a legend is allotted to each one of them.

$$\begin{matrix} 1 & 0 & 0 & 0 \\ 0 & 1 & 0 & 0 \end{matrix} \qquad I = \begin{matrix} 1 & 0 \\ 0 & 1 \end{matrix} \qquad J = \begin{matrix} 0 & 0 \\ 0 & 0 \end{matrix}$$

OR

$$\begin{matrix} 0.3 & 0 & 0.4 & 0.3 \\ 0.4 & 0.2 & 0.3 & 0.1 \end{matrix} \qquad K = \begin{matrix} 0.3 & 0 \\ 0.4 & 0.2 \end{matrix} \qquad L = \begin{matrix} 0.4 & 0.3 \\ 0.3 & 0.1 \end{matrix}$$

In the next step we shall first pick up matrix L and substract it from an identity matrix[44] of the same size and thereby obtain a new matrix which we may designate as M.

Identity matrix			L matrix			Resultant matrix (M)	
1	0		0.4	0.3		0.6	−0.3
0	1	−	0.3	0.1	=	−0.3	0.9

We shall now find out the Inverse of the resultant matrix M. The procedure is first to place M against an identity matrix as follows:

Resultant matrix (M)		Identity matrix (I)	
0.6	−0.3	1	0
−0.3	0.9	0	1

Our attempt will now be to transform M into an identity matrix by simultaneous operations. When M is thus transformed into an identity matrix,

---

44. An identity matrix (I) is a square matrix whose diagonals are all 1s and remaining terms are zero as shown in the example.

the original identity matrix will become the Inverse. In doing so, we are entitled to use any or all of the following rules:

(a) We can interchange one row with another row
(b) We can multiply a row by a constant
(c) We can add to or subtract from a row a multiple of another row

The step-by-step procedure for transformation is given in Table 3.34.

Table 3.34 Finding an Inverse Matrix

	Original matrix		Identity matrix		Procedure
(a)	0.6	−0.3	1	0	Multiply row 1 by 1/0.6 and
	−0.3	0.9	0	1	obtain (b)
(b)	1	−0.5	1.6667	0	Multiply row 1 by 0.3 and
	−0.3	0.9	0	1	add that figure to row 2 to
					obtain (c)
(c)	1	−0.5	1.6667	0	Multiply row 2 by 1/0.75 and
	0	0.75	0.5	1	obtain (d)
(d)	1	−0.5	1.6667	0	Add 0.5 times of row 2 to
	0	1	0.6667	1.3333	row 1 and obtain (e)
(e)	1	0	2	0.6667	Original matrix is now trans-
	0	1	0.6667	1.3333	formed to identity matrix and
					the original identity matrix is
					now the inverse matrix

It may be observed from Table 3.34 that in doing the transformation we have first picked up row 1, column 1 of the original matrix and converted it to 1 by simultaneous operation within the bounds of the rules laid down before. Next, row 2, column 1 is converted to zero in the same manner and so on, so that ultimately the original matrix is transformed into an identity matrix.

We shall now pick up matrix K and multiply it with the inverse matrix to obtain the probabilistic state of transition of the variables (category-wise receivables).

Inverse matrix   ×   Matrix K = Matrix O (probabilistic estimate)

2	0.6667		0.3	0		0.8667	0.1333
		×			=		
0.6667	1.3333		0.4	0.2		0.7333	0.2667

Note that sum of the elements in both the two rows of the right-hand matrix O, must equal to 1.

In order to interpret the resultant matrix O, we bring back the original category-wise distribution from which we started

Category	Probabilistic state	
	Paid	Bad-debt
0–60 days	0.8667	0.1333
61–120 days	0.7333	0.2667

The above result indicates that there is a 0.8667 (or say, 87 percent) probability that the amount of receivables falling in 0–60 days category will ultimately become paid and that the probability is 0.1333 (or say, 13 percent) that these will ultimately become bad-debt. For the amount of receivables falling in 61–120 days category the probability is 0.7333 (or say, 73 percent) that these will be paid, and 0.2667 (or say, 27 percent) probability that these will turn out to be bad.

What remains now is to find out from the company's books the figures of present outstanding under each category to predict the ultimate behaviour of receivables and provide for bad-debt reserve.

The outstanding accounts receivable of Rs. 725 lakh are found to be falling into the two categories as follows:

Category	Receivables outstanding
0–60 days	Rs. 500 lakh
61–180 days	Rs. 225 lakh

The above information can now be written in the form of a matrix and then multiplied with the matrix O derived before.

$$500 \quad 225 \quad \times \quad \begin{bmatrix} 0.8667 & 0.1333 \\ 0.7333 & 0.2667 \end{bmatrix} = \quad 598.34 \quad 126.66$$

The final result of our operations reveal that out of present outstanding receivables of Rs. 725 lakh it is expected that Rs. 598.34 lakh will ultimately be paid and Rs. 126.66 lakh may turn out to be bad-debt. The company can now set up a bad-debt reserve of Rs. 126.66 lakh.

Notes on Matrix

Definition

A matrix is an array of numbers arranged in rows and columns. If a matrix has, say two rows and three columns, it will be described as 2×3 matrix. Note that while describing the dimension of a matrix, the number of rows will precede the number of columns.

Addition and Subtraction

The addition and subtraction of matrices are only possible if the two matrices have the same number of rows and columns. The process consists of adding or subtracting the corresponding elements of the two matrices.

Example

$$\text{Matrix A} = \begin{bmatrix} 2 & 4 & 5 \\ 1 & 9 & 4 \\ 3 & 0 & 6 \end{bmatrix} \qquad \text{Matrix B} = \begin{bmatrix} 2 & 2 & 6 \\ 5 & 1 & 3 \\ 1 & 2 & 1 \end{bmatrix}$$

$$A + B = \begin{bmatrix} 4 & 6 & 11 \\ 6 & 10 & 7 \\ 4 & 2 & 7 \end{bmatrix}$$

$$A - B = \begin{bmatrix} 0 & 2 & -1 \\ -4 & 8 & 1 \\ 2 & -2 & 5 \end{bmatrix}$$

Multiplication

Two matrices can be multiplied together only when the number of *columns* in the first matrix equals the number of *rows* in the second matrix. Each element of every row of the first matrix shall be multiplied throughout with each element of the columns of the second matrix and the results are added to form the corresponding element in the new matrix. Let us do it with the above example.

$$\text{AB} = \begin{matrix} 2 & 4 & 5 \\ 1 & 9 & 4 \\ 3 & 0 & 6 \end{matrix} \quad \times \quad \begin{matrix} 2 & 2 & 6 \\ 5 & 1 & 3 \\ 1 & 2 & 1 \end{matrix} \quad = \quad \begin{matrix} 29 & 18 & 29 \\ 51 & 19 & 37 \\ 12 & 18 & 24 \end{matrix}$$

Detailed workings for arriving at the resultant matrix are given below.

Row 1 of matrix A = 2 4 5; multiplying the three colums of matrix B with 2, 4, and 5, we get

Row 1 of the resultant matrix as
  (a) $2 \times 2 + 4 \times 5 + 5 \times 1 = 29$
  (b) $2 \times 2 + 4 \times 1 + 5 \times 2 = 18$
  (c) $2 \times 6 + 4 \times 3 + 5 \times 1 = 29$

Row 2 of matrix A = 1   9   4
Row 2 of the resultant matrix will be
  (a) $1 \times 2 + 9 \times 5 + 4 \times 1 = 51$
  (b) $1 \times 2 + 9 \times 1 + 4 \times 2 = 19$
  (c) $1 \times 6 + 9 \times 3 + 4 \times 1 = 37$

Row 3 of matrix A = 3   0   6
Row 3 of the resultant matrix will be
  (a) $3 \times 2 + 0 \times 5 + 6 \times 1 = 12$
  (b) $3 \times 2 + 0 \times 1 + 6 \times 2 = 18$
  (c) $3 \times 6 + 0 \times 3 + 6 \times 1 = 24$

SUMMARY

Accounts receivable is a form of current asset. It occurs when a company has made advance payments in the form of cash or goods to another company or individual. It can, therefore, occur on both sides of the productive system—as cash advances to suppliers and as credit sales to distributors or customers.

The firm may pay advances to suppliers to ensure timely supply, develop a captive supply base, or for pure short-term financial and profitability considerations. On the other hand, the firm may offer credit sales to stimulate demand in the value chain.

The primary goal of receivables management is to maximise the value of the enterprise by striking a balance between liquidity, risk and profitability. The major costs associated with extension of credit facilities are the cost of investigating creditworthiness of parties, cost of collecting receivables, cost of delinquency, opportunity cost of funds locked up in receivables, etc. The management of accounts receivable must, however, match these additional costs with the incremental benefits obtained from increased sales keeping in mind the liquidity problems obtained out of funds being locked away in receivables. The extension of trade credits is limited by marginal cost and tax considerations.

Though accounts receivables are short-term in nature, the policy decisions that create accounts receivables often have a long-term impact on the organisation and its financial structure, because once a policy is decided, it is difficult to come out of it except at the cost of adverse market reactions. It is, therefore, desirable that credit policies be decided by top management and communicated clearly and effectively to all members of the company. The policies should not be subjected to frequent changes.

There are two types of discounts that a firm offers to its customers, namely, trade discount and cash discount. While the former is offered to channel intermediaries, the latter is offered to end customers. The former is used to motivate intermediaries to alter their preferences in favour of the firm's products. And the latter is used to induce buyers to pay up early.

A significant part of receivables management involves the proper selection of customers, because every credit sale involves the risk of delayed payment or non-payment of the value involved. The different customers in increasing order of credit risk include individuals or sole proprietary firms, partnerships, private limited companies and public limited companies.

The receivables manager has a variety of sources for obtaining credit information, namely bank checks, supplier checks and financial statement analysis.

In addition to customer selection, the manager should also effectively monitor and control the firm's receivables with a view to minimising bad-debt losses. The company must have a good documentation of all efforts to be made in the event of a probable default, and the efforts that have already been made in the recovery attempts during the past. Monitoring bad-debt losses should also minimise the incremental costs in retrieving probable bad-debts.

CHAPTER 4

Inventory Strategies and Techniques

In clarity and confusion, imagination and emotion
Creation proceeds towards a perfection
—The unattainable

INTRODUCTION

At the macro-level, inventory constitutes a very small percentage of GNP but its contribution to business fluctuation is great. It has been found that inventory investment typically accounts for about 70 percent of the peak-to-trough decline in real GNP during recessions. But the importance of inventory fluctuation is not limited to cyclical downturns only. In normal conditions also inventory investment has been found to account for 37 percent of the variance of changes in GNP.[1] Predominant types of inventories accounting for this variation are retail inventories, followed by manufacturers' inventories of raw materials and wholesalers' inventories. The inventories of neither the finished goods nor the work-in-process are found to contribute much to the variance.[2]

Impact of inventory behaviour at the macro-level was first forcefully emphasised by Metzler when he pointed out in his seminal study that inventory investment could conceivably destabilise an otherwise stable system.[3] Market clearing models in economics assume that the market will clear outputs at a price where *marginal revenue* (MR) is equal to *marginal cost* (MC). Inventory in such a system does not exist because revenue (sales) always equals production. But the equilibrium will be disturbed when revenue (sales) is not equal to production, and this happens when the system carries inventory. Although it is true that the profit maximising firm would still operate on MR = MC, it is not necessary that output must be equal to sales. When inventory is storable, firms operate on two margins. In order to decide how much of the outputs would be carried to inventory, a firm would equate marginal cost to the shadow value of inventories, and to decide how much to withdraw from inventory, it would similarly equate the marginal revenue with the shadow value of inventory. Under this new equilibrium, output need not be euqal to sales—some portion of the output will be stored by firm.

---

1. Blinder, A.S., "Inventories and the Structure of Macro Models", *American Economic Review*, May 1981, pp. 11–16.
2. *Economic Review*, May 1981, pp. 11–16.
3. Metzler, L.A., "The Nature and Stability of Inventory Cycles", *Review of Economic Statistics*, Vol. 23.

INVENTORY AND PRICE BEHAVIOUR

In an 'inventory-economy', price may not follow the simple demand-supply rule. It may become sticky despite a temporary surge in demand because its effect on the price gets moderated as firms draw down its inventory. Both price and output responses to demand become smaller when the demand shock is viewed as temporary in nature and the output is storable.

An asymmetry in price behaviour due to existence of inventory is observed in quite a few studies. For example, when stock-outs occur, prices respond more strongly to demand shocks than when there are sufficient inventories in store to prevent a stock-out.[4] It may be noted that number of firms experiencing stock-outs is greater at higher level of economic activities. Price response to demand shocks will, therefore, be greater at the high-level of economic activities than at the low-level.

MOTIVES FOR HOLDING INVENTORY

The disequilibrium effect at the macro-level is ironically due to some of the stabilisation strategies followed by firms at the micro-level. Firms hold inventory due to the following motives:

Transaction Motive

Firms may require to hold certain amount of finished products perpetually in stock for display or demonstration purpose. They may also hold inventories to meet a sudden demand, thereby reducing the delivery lags.

Precautionary Motive

Firms may hold inventories for fear of stock-outs and losing its goodwill. A manufacturing firm may carry inventories of both input materials and finished products to ensure smooth production in the face of fluctuating sales. Storage of input materials also act as hedge against future price rises. The work-in-process inventory also helps them in proper scheduling of production.

Some of the precautionary motives give rise to 'safety stock' to deal with uncertainty in supply and demand which we shall discuss in much greater detail at a later stage. However, motives for ensuring smooth production do not necessarily follow from uncertainty. When sales vary with time, even without any randomness, and marginal costs are on the rise, it will be optimal for a firm to smoothen production relative to sales by accumulating inventories when demand is weak, and by drawing down inventories when demand is strong. But when sales vary randomly, firms will be required to hold additional inventory as the buffer-stock against unexpected rise in demand.

---

4. Reagan, P.B., Inventories and Asymmetries in Price Adjustment, *Mimeo*, MIT, Boston, 1980.

Speculative Motive

A firm may also hoard both raw materials and finished products when it expects a price rise in future, thereby realising a stock profit. Inventories held for speculative motive are termed as profit-making inventory by Tandon Group and is positively discouraged by banks in India.[5]

Besides accumulation of inventory due to the three motives mentioned above, inventories also get accumulated because of inefficient management of working capital. This type of inventory is called *flabby inventory*, the accumulation of which is viewed seriously by bankers.[6]

Of the three motives, precautionary motive, in its various manifestations, has received the most attention in inventory literature. We shall also be concentrating on this.

INVENTORY BEHAVIOUR

It should be clear by now that at the firm level production of finished products can hardly be independent of inventory holding. Generally, high-level of inventories would lead to lower prices and low prices would in turn result in a cut-back on production so that in the following period, opening inventories will be much less than in the current period. At times, due to unavoidable circumstances a firm may be required to hold excessive inventories. It may also be the result of inefficient inventory management (flabby inventory). In situations like this, if there is no jump in prices, firms will be drawing down their inventories slowly. They will be selling more than they produce, unlike the situation where inventory holding is at their desired level. The same behaviour is also observed when the economy is in the grip of persistent industrial recession and prices are falling. Production will be low and a part of sales will be met by drawing down on inventories. If, however, there is a sudden rise in prices, an enterprise would definitely like to increase its sales to take advantage of price rises. This, it will do by simultaneously increasing production and withdrawing from inventories. When there is a relative increase in price, it is always advantageous to the firm to sell today rather than tomorrow. At a level of relative price rise incentive to sale could be larger than the incentive to produce more. Hence, on both counts there shall be considerably lower level of opening stock in the next period.

In Indian industries total inventories as percentage of total assets has come down steadily from 6.83 percent in 1997–98 to 4.81 percent in 2005–06, as will be seen from Table 4.1. Coming close on the heels is the aggregate receivables and debtors which have also shown the similar trend that we have seen in the earlier chapter. The fall in inventory holding can be ascribed to the vast technological improvement in the Indian industrial sector during the post-liberalisation period and efficient management of inventory.

---

5. Reserve Bank of India, 'Report of the Study Group to Frame Guidelines for Follow-up of Bank Credit', Bombay, 1975. The Group was headed by P.L. Tandon.
6. *Ibid.*

In India, inventory holding is the largest among all current assets. It is more than 27 percent on an average. Coming close on the heels is the aggregate receivables which constitute about 26 percent of total assets as we have seen in the earlier chapter.

Table 4.1 Movement of Inventories in Indian Industry

(Rs. in crore)

Particulars/Year	1997-98	1998-99	1999-00	2000-01	2001-02	2002-03	2003-04	2004-05	2005-06
Total Assets	2,069,727	2,391,400	2,692,958	3,092,698	3,424,782	3,838,149	4,266,467	5,002,309	5,752,392
Total inventories	141,334	155,592	178,836	179,419	180,312	203,426	207,848	243,894	277,016
	(6.83)	(6.51)	(6.64)	(5.80)	(5.26)	(5.30)	(4.87)	(4.88)	(4.81)
Of which:									
1. Raw material and stores	53,582	54,408	61,546	60,766	60,757	68,461	76,196	99,614	115,439
	(86)	(82)	(95)	(62)	(60)	(57)	(55)	(56)	(55)
2. Work-in-process	16,447	19,615	19,554	18,906	17,531	19,507	20,768	26,985	30,806
	(11)	(12)	(10)	(8)	(7)	(7)	(6)	(7)	(7)
3. Finished goods	43,958	46,706	57,286	64,120	58,020	68,801	70,786	80,126	90,692
	(27)	(25)	(27)	(24)	(22)	(22)	(20)	(19)	(20)
Cost of production	541,810	607,969	738,994	911,675	909,161	1,046,475	1,195,221	1,468,940	1,630,428
Cost of sales	584,070	660,188	782,724	972,195	983,830	1,120,485	1,283,280	1,553,184	1,722,962

Basic data source: Industry: Financial Aggregates and Ratios, Centre for Monitoring Indian Economy (CMIE). Ratios are calculated from the basic data.

Notes; 1. Figures in bracket against Total inventories represent percentage of Total assets.
2. Figures in bracket against Inventories of Raw materials and stores and Work-in-process represent days of Cost of production.
3. Figures in bracket against Inventory of Finished goods represent days of Cost of sales.

MARKET IMPERFECTION

We have seen in Chapter 1 that inventories of different types get built up along the production-distribution line of a business system. Inventories are the largest component of current assets, and like any other current assets, their existence is viewed with distaste by a businessman because he has to carry them at a cost which contributes negatively to the profitability of his business. If the productive-distributive systems were perfectly integrated backward to the input sources and forwardly to an efficient market, and the plant operations ran smoothly and flexibly in response to demand and supply, then perhaps, there would not have been any necessity to hold inventories at different stages of production-distribution line of the enterprise.[7] But neither the productive system nor the market is perfect. The imperfections create fluctuations of various dimensions which transmit shocks to the manufacturing and distribution system of the enterprise. These shocks have the potential to burn

---

7. In fact, from this kind of utopian thought the philosophy of just-in-time manufacturing/inventory has emerged in Japan to which we shall be coming later.

or breakdown the productive-distributive system of the enterprise. Firms, therefore, must take protections against such shocks. Inventories absorb these shocks and thereby keep both the manufacturing and the distribution systems insulated so that they can perform their respective functions smoothly.

In operational terms, it can be said that inventories serve two basic precautionary functions. First, it facilitates smooth functioning of the manufacturing operations and second, it helps avoid losing sales. As for the former, it can be said that it is very difficult and also costly for the manufacturing operations of some industries like petroleum, chemicals, etc. to adjust to fluctuations in sales. In the case of the latter, we can recall the old adage in the market place—if a customer returns from a shop, he may not come back again. The cost of stock-outs which, though not available in the records of a firm, is very real and often enormous, particularly for goods of daily use.

TYPES OF ORGANISATION HOLDING INVENTORIES

We already have some ideas about different types of inventories and their origin while dealing with techno-financial aspects of working capital in Chapter 1. Here we shall briefly describe what types of inventories are held by different types of organisations.

Along the pipeline of the productive-distributive system, retailer is the last organisational unit that holds inventory for sale to the ultimate consumers. A retail organisation receives goods in saleable form from wholesalers/distributor or directly from the manufacturer. Little or no processing is required to be done at this level. As the retail trade generally holds a variety of goods from different and often competing manufacturers, and as it acts as the ultimate outlet to consumers, it simultaneously suffers from the problems associated with quantity holding and regularity of supplies.

A wholesaler or distributor receives large quantity of finished goods from the manufacturer for distribution amongst the retailers. Some processing like labelling and repackaging are done by the wholesalers or distributors. As they generally work for one or more manufacturers, the inventory problems they generally suffer from are associated with demand and supply variation.

A manufacturer is required to hold almost all the three types of inventories, namely raw-materials, work-in-process and finished goods. Inventory problems are most complex here because of the complexity of products (e.g. a project or finished goods), processes (e.g. continuous or intermittent) and distribution (e.g. geographical locations). These problems will be discussed in stages later.

Besides the three major types of inventories, organisations also require an inventory of *supplies* which are not directly a part of the finished goods but are essential for smooth functioning of the organisation. Examples of supply inventories are stationeries, diskettes, bulbs, threads, drill-bits, cutting tools and other non-consumable spares. Although these inventories form only a small part of total inventory holding of an enterprise, these are difficult to control. Problems associated with them are maintenance of records and prevention of wastage.

INVENTORY COSTS

Costs associated with inventories are as follows:

Purchase or Acquisition Cost

Goods may be purchased directly (e.g. raw materials for the manufacturers and finished products for retailers) or manufactured in-house. When it is purchased, the purchase price net of quantity discounts plus freight, insurance, loading, unloading, etc. shall be the acquisition cost. For goods manufactured in-house, the unit cost of production inclusive of factory overheads shall constitute the acquisition cost.

Ordering or Set-up Costs

When goods are outsourced, the costs associated with writing and placing an order, following it up with the vendors, receiving and inspecting the materials and costs of all other jobs necessary for taking the goods to store shall be treated as ordering costs.

The set-up cost shall include items such as preparing the shop order, scheduling the work, pre-production inspection, etc.

Ordering or set-up costs do not vary with the size of the order but with the number of orders or set-ups.

Holding Cost

This cost has two parts: (a) cost of physical carrying of inventories like storage cost, insurance, rates and taxes, handling, shrinkage, deterioration and obsolescence, (b) financial cost of funds engaged in inventories which is generally the opportunity cost of alternative investments.

Holding cost is found to be proportional to the value of the inventories held, and hence it is assumed to be a variable cost in inventory management.

Stock-out Cost

As indicated before, this is an implicit cost of lost sales due to shortage of supplies. It includes such costs as back order costs, lost profit due to loss of present sales, and also cost of losing goodwill of the firm which affects future sales and profit.

Internal shortage cost occurs when the requirement of production department is not fulfilled or it is delayed, resulting in delayed completion, lost production, idle time, etc.

It is difficult to place a monetary value on stock-out cost, though it is clearly understood conceptually by all business managers. The extent of this cost depends upon the reaction of customer who may cancel the order, agree for a substitution or delayed shipment. Last two types of cost can be fairly accurate, but the cost of cancellation of order (goodwill) may be enormous and difficult to estimate.

Similarly, for internal shortage, cost may be very high if the item ordered is critical for production or without which the plant may shut down.

As it is difficult to estimate the stock-out cost, the problem has to be tackled intuitively, which we shall discuss later.

VALUATION OF INVENTORIES

When one looks at a conventional *trial balance* of a firm, one will find that opening inventories appear in the body of trial balance, but closing inventories feature outside it as part of other adjustable entries. Reason behind such an unusual presentation is that except the opening and closing entries, no other transactions take place in inventory accounts. While purchases are separately accounted for, ins and outs of inventories are not passed through the main body of the accounting system of an enterprise but recorded separately in subsidiary books like stock register, issue registers, etc. At the end of the accounting period, inventories at hand are valued, which we find as part of adjustment entries. While opening inventories are charged to the debit of profit and loss account, thereby closing the stock account for the time being, closing inventories are credited to the profit and loss account to the debit of stock account. Thus the debit balance appears in inventories account once again which continues to show the same balance till the end of another accounting period. When closing inventories are credited to the profit and loss account as in sales, a profit or loss is taken to books under accrual system of accounting. If the valuation is wrong the resultant profit or loss shall also be wrong and the enterprise may end up paying more taxes to the government or lesser dividend to its shareholders.

The method of valuation chosen by an enterprise affects the value of period-end inventories. It also affects the cost of goods sold via issuance of materials to the production, and thus the profit or loss of the enterprise. If prices of materials are stable throughout the accounting period and if all materials bought could be charged to production or sale immediately, as in just-in-time (JIT) philosophy of manufacturing management, then the valuation problem could be resolved at one go. But the reality is that the prices vary and in situations where JIT system is not operable, a firm has to buy materials continuously throughout the year at varying quantities and prices. Hence, choice of appropriate method of valuation of inventories becomes important both for charging to production and also for valuing the period-end inventories.

Several methods of valuation of inventories have been evolved over a period; each one has its pluses and minuses and none are absolutely perfect. Selection of a particular method depends also not so much on the concern for accurate costing and valuation but on several other considerations like, size and type of the organisation, the future of the economy, industry practice, tax implications and regulations. Of these considerations tax effects and consequent value of the firm have received greater attention of both managers and researchers. Consistency rule in accounting demands that firms should not change the method of valuation of inventories frequently as it might create confusion in the minds of users of company's financial data: year to year results are not comparable because of changes in the method of valuation. Besides, there may also be unscrupulous motivations to change the method of valuation. Profits may be window-dressed and dividends may be declared in bad years by overvaluation of inventories (though paying higher taxes), or profits can be suppressed and lower taxes paid by undervaluing the inventories. All these manipulations are possible when companies are allowed to change the method of valuation to suit their requirements. This is the reason why regulating bodies and tax authorities restrict indiscriminate changes in valuation methods. For example, the accounting standard (AS-2) issued by the Institute of Chartered Accountants of India requires that any change in accounting policy relating to inventories, which has a material effect in the current period or which is reasonably expected to have a material effect in later periods, should be disclosed in the financial statements. The Company Law Board also requires that a declared system of valuation must be followed for a duration of at least three years. Any change in between is permitted only under extraordinary circumstances.

Valuation Methods

The fundamental basis of major valuation methods is the accounting flow of inventories, not their physical flow. Operationally, this means that when a piece of material is charged to production or taken to inventory it need not necessarily be at a cost at which it is acquired but at a cost determined by a particular accounting mode. This has the advantage of standardising the costing system and the accounting records, though it is always desirable to have a system where the difference between the cost flow and physical flow is minimised. Methods of valuation are now discussed below.

First-in-First-out (FIFO)

This is the most widely used method of valuation. Under this method, it is assumed that materials are issued to production (or cost of goods sold in case of trade) in order of their receipt in store. This implies that inventory cost will be computed on the assumption that goods sold or materials consumed are those which have been on store for the longest period and hence, those remaining in the stock shall represent the latest purchase or production. The latter means that period-end inventory value will be closer to market value. But at the same time, this method will undercharge the production when materials are subject to inflationary price rise or overcharge it when prices are falling. The balance sheet asset may reflect the true value, but the income statement may be distorted under the two price-level situations.

FIFO is a simple, easily understandable system and compatible to a variety of organisations, which made its use so widespread. It is invariably used in organisations which deal in goods which are perishable or prone to quick obsolescence. The following example will make the operation of the system clear (Table 4.2).

Table 4.2 Inventory Recording System under FIFO

		No. of units	Unit cost	Total cost	No. of units	Unit cost	Total cost	No. of units	Unit cost	Total cost
		Receipt			*Issues*			*Balance*		
October	1	—	—	—	—	—	—	300	5.00	1500
	8	—	—	—	200	5.00	1000	100	5.00	500
	15	400	5.10	2040	—	—	—	100	5.00	500
								400	5.10	2040
	18	—	—	—	100	5.00	500	200	5.10	1020
					200	5.10	1020			
	30	600	5.15	3090	—	—	—	200	5.10	1020
								600	5.15	3090
November	2	—	—	—	200	5.10	1020	400	5.15	2060
					200	5.15	1030			
	10	—	—	—	100	5.15	515	300	5.15	1545
	16	400	5.20	2080	—	—	—	300	5.15	1545
								400	5.20	2080
	17	—	—	—	300	5.15	1545	300	5.20	1560
					100	5.20	520			
	30	200	5.30	1060	—	—	—	300	5.20	1560
								200	5.30	1060
December	2	—	—	—	200	5.20	1040	100	5.20	520
								200	5.30	1060
	10	—	—	—	100	5.20	520	200	5.30	1060
	15	400	5.35	2140	—	—	—	200	5.30	1060
								400	5.35	2140
	18	—	—	—	200	5.30	1060	300	5.35	1605
					100	5.35	535			
	29	200	5.40	1080	—	—	—	300	5.35	1605
								200	5.40	1080
Total		2200		11,490	2000		10,305			

We find from Table 4.2 that during the quarter, i.e. Oct.–Dec., production (or cost of goods sold) was charged with 2000 units of goods valued at Rs. 10,305 and the balance at hand was 500 units valued at Rs. 2685. A scrutiny of the table would reveal that while the quarter-end stocks are valued close to the market, the quantities charged to production are more at older prices.

Last-in-First-out (LIFO)

This method is just the opposite of FIFO method. Here, materials are charged to production (or cost of goods sold) in reverse order of their receipts to store. It intends to match current revenues against current costs. The effect of the system is that the production is charged with current cost of materials. Hence, what remains at stock gets valued at older prices.

The LIFO system rests heavily on well-acknowledged matching principle of accounting. Since revenues are realised at current prices, the costs that are to be matched against the revenues should also reflect current prices of acquisition so that the profit taken is real profit and not an illusory one as happens with FIFO under situation of inflationary price rises. During an inflationary period, stocks at hand will be sold at a higher price than what was contemplated when these were first purchased. This will result in a stock profit for the period. However, if the inventory has to be maintained, say at the same level which often is the case, the additional stock profit would have been spent to a large extent in replacement of the inventory. Thus the stock profit remains illusory, but the danger is that once it is taken, taxes and dividend may have to be paid on it. LIFO protects the enterprise against the danger of taking such stock profit. On the other hand, this is precisely the reason why highly profit-oriented corporate managers do not like LIFO, particularly in those organisations where inventory turnover is high. But LIFO should be a preferred system during inflationary rise in prices because of its favourable effect on taxes and real cash flows.

However, despite the fact that income statement under LIFO is much closer to reality, the balance sheet gets distorted because of unrealistic valuation of inventories. Faster the rate of inflation, the more unrealistic is the inventory valuation. As a consequence, not only that the current ratio gets distorted, all other turnover ratios, based on inventory, also become distorted. This makes it difficult to assess the short-term financial position of an enterprise. In Table 4.3 we have presented inventory recording under LIFO system using the same example.

Table 4.3 Inventory Recording System under LIFO

		Receipt			Issues			Balance		
		No. of units	Unit cost	Total cost	No. of units	Unit cost	Total cost	No. of units	Unit cost	Total cost
October	1	—	—	—	—	—	—	300	5.00	1500
	8	—	—	—	200	5.00	1000	100	5.00	500
	15	400	5.10	2040	—	—	—	100	5.00	500
								400	5.10	2040
	18	—	—	—	300	5.10	1530	100	5.00	500
								100	5.10	510
	30	600	5.15	3090	—	—	—	100	5.00	500
								100	5.10	510
								600	5.15	3090
November	2	—	—	—	400	5.15	2060	100	5.00	500
								100	5.10	510
								200	5.15	1030
	10	—	—	—	100	5.15	515	100	5.00	500
								100	5.10	510
								100	5.15	515
	16	400	5.20	2080	—	—	—	100	5.00	500
								100	5.10	510
								100	5.15	515
								400	5.20	2080
	17	—	—	—	400	5.20	2080	100	5.00	500
								100	5.10	510
								100	5.15	515
	30	200	5.30	1060	—	—	—	100	5.00	500
								100	5.10	510
								100	5.15	515
								200	5.30	1060

(Cont.)

Table 4.3 Inventory Recording System under LIFO   (Cont.)

	Receipt			Issues			Balance		
	No. of units	Unit cost	Total cost	No. of units	Unit cost	Total cost	No. of units	Unit cost	Total cost
December 2	—	—	—	200	5.30	1060	100	5.00	500
							100	5.10	510
							100	5.15	515
10	—	—	—	100	5.15	515	100	5.00	500
							100	5.10	510
15	400	5.35	2140	—	—	—	100	5.00	500
							100	5.10	510
							400	5.35	2140
18	—	—	—	300	5.35	1605	100	5.00	500
							100	5.10	510
							100	5.35	535
29	200	5.40	1080	—	—	—	100	5.00	500
							100	5.10	510
							100	5.35	535
							200	5.40	1080
Total	2200		11,490	2000		10,365			

It may be observed from Table 4.3 that under LIFO system cost of goods sold is more by Rs. 10,365 – 10,305 = Rs. 60 than under FIFO while the period-end inventory is lower by the same amount: Rs. 2685 – 2625 = Rs. 60.

Critical review Considerable research has been made on the motivation to use LIFO system of inventory accounting since the system was first approved for usage in the United States in 1934. The research gained momentum when the Revenue Act of 1939 first allowed the use of LIFO for tax accounting in the United States. Butters and Miland[8] observed as early as 1949 that the opportunity to reduce tax liabilities has by far been the most powerful motivation for widespread adoption of LIFO since 1939. But, as we have already indicated, in order to realise the tax benefits under LIFO the firm must also have to report lower profits. Corporate managers declaring lower profit during an inflationary price rise may not be viewed with favour by the shareholders; though it is true that when prices are rising, LIFO always saves present value of cash flow thereby increasing the firm value.

The present tax status of an enterprise may also have a bearing on the motivation to adopt LIFO system. A firm which is not in tax-paying status because it is making losses presently or it has a carry forward of past losses, then LIFO system does not provide any benefit to the firm; on the contrary it increases the losses.

The variability in inventory levels also affects the benefits of LIFO system. If the inventories are non-decreasing, the cost of sales based on LIFO

---

8. Butters, J.K. and P. Miland, *Inventory Accounting and Policy,* Division of Research, Graduate School of Business Administration, Harvard University, Boston, 1949.

accounting will be close to current costs and hence, tax payments will be minimised. But when inventory level decreases, the resultant reduction is charged against income at its original cost which may be very low relative to current costs. As a result, profit will be higher and consequent tax payment will rise. This reduces, though does not eliminate, the benefits of LIFO accounting.

We have seen before that FIFO system is simple to operate and less costly. LIFO is a more elaborate and complex system and therefore more costly. Unless an enterprise is large enough to absorb the high fixed costs associated with the installation of a LIFO system, the unabsorbed overhead will more than eat up the benefits of the system. This may be a likely explanation for many firms not willing to change to LIFO system.[9]

What we find from the above discussion is that for large firms, in general, LIFO system of inventory accounting increases firm's value by minimising the present value of tax payments but it also suppresses the present income which may not be liked by shareholders. In order to by-pass the apparent conflict, firms generally make a switch to LIFO system when the going is good so that the switch may result into merely a lower rate of increase in reported profits.[10]

In conclusion, we may say that LIFO is found to be more useful for internal reporting purpose because it is directed towards the future value of the firm but for external reporting, companies generally adopt FIFO or average cost method (to be discussed next). Only a small number of companies use LIFO for external reporting because it is frowned upon by regulatory and tax authorities. Largest usage of LIFO is found in the United States where AICPA and other regulatory bodies recognise this as an acceptable method of valuation. Such is not the case in Europe and Commonwealth countries.

An extreme variation of LIFO is the *latest purchase price* (LPP) method where issues are made at the last acquisition cost. LPP more accurately values cost of goods sold than LIFO, but the valuation of inventory gets far more distorted than under the LIFO.

Average Cost

This method attempts to smoothen the extremes of FIFO and LIFO with an elusive objective of arriving at a perfect combination of realistic cost of goods sold and period-end inventory. It does not keep any record of what unit is going first or last as under FIFO or LIFO; instead, it averages out the cost of all units purchased at various points in time and at various periods during the accounting year. This rate is used to value the period-end inventory and calculate the cost of acquisition.

---

9. Morse, D. and G. Richardson, "The LIFO/FIFO Decision", *Journal of Accounting Research*, Spring 1983, pp. 106–127.
10. Weil, R.L. and F.W. Lindahl, "Empirical Research in Choice of Inventory Accounting Method", in *The Economics of Inventory Management,* Chikan Attila and M.C. Lovell (Eds.), Elsevier Science Publishers, B.V., Amsterdam, 1988.

Average cost could be of the following three types:

1. Simple Average This is calculated by dividing the total of *unit costs* purchased at different lots during the period by the *number of* such purchases. It ignores the size of purchases in each lot and hence, all the lots receive same weight irrespective of the number of units purchased in each lot.

2. Weighted Average This method corrects the distortion of the simple average by considering the number of units purchased in each lot. It is calculated by first multiplying the unit cost with each lot size, i.e. the number of units in each lot and then dividing the resultant figure by the total number of units purchased. This is superior to simple average method because price fluctuations are evenly distributed and, if the period under consideration is not very lengthy, then both the cost of goods sold and the period-end inventory will be closer to the market.

3. Moving Average Under this method the average unit cost is calculated after every acquisition by taking into account the balance already in hand. This requires a lot of calculations and hence, it is most suited in a computerised environment. Both the simple average and weighted average cannot be calculated until the period is over, but moving average can be calculated on a continuous basis.

With the help of the example given earlier, we calculate below the three types of average cost.

Simple average:

$$= \frac{\text{Total of unit cost of each acquisition}}{\text{No. of acquisitions}}$$

$$= \frac{5 + 5.10 + 5.15 + 5.20 + 5.30 + 5.35 + 5.40}{7} = \frac{36.50}{7} = 5.21$$

Valuation of period-end inventory = No. of units on hand × Average cost
$$= 500 \times 5.21 = \text{Rs. } 2605$$

Weighted average:

$$= \frac{\text{No. of units allotted} \times \text{Total of price per unit}}{\text{Total of units purchased}}$$

$$= \frac{\begin{array}{c} 300 \times 5 + 400 \times 5.10 + 600 \times 5.15 + 400 \times 5.20 \\ + 200 \times 5.30 + 400 \times 5.35 + 200 \times 5.40 \end{array}}{2500}$$

$$= \frac{12,990}{2500} = \text{Rs. } 5.20$$

Valuation of period-end inventory = 500 × 5.20 = Rs. 2600

It may be noted that opening balance has been included while calculating both the above types of averages.

Moving average. Calculations of unit cost, cost of goods sold and valuation of quarter-end inventory are given in Table 4.4.

Table 4.4 Inventory Recording System under Moving Average

		Receipt			Issues			Balance		
		No. of units	Unit cost	Total cost	No. of units	Unit cost	Total cost	No. of units	Unit cost	Total cost
October	1	—	—	—	—	—	—	300	5.00	1500
	8	—	—	—	200	5.00	1000	100	5.00	500
	15	400	5.10	2040	—	—	—	500	5.08	2540
	18	—	—	—	300	5.08	1524	200	5.08	1016
	30	600	5.15	3090	—	—	—	800	5.13	4104*
November	2	—	—	—	400	5.13	2052	400	5.13	2052
	10	—	—	—	100	5.13	513	300	5.13	1539*
	16	400	5.20	2080	—	—	—	700	5.17	3619
	17	—	—	—	400	5.17	2068	300	5.17	1551
	30	200	5.30	1060	—	—	—	500	5.22	2611
December	2	—	—	—	200	5.22	1044	300	5.22	1566*
	10	—	—	—	100	5.22	522	200	5.22	1044
	15	400	5.35	2140	—	—	—	600	5.31	3186*
	18	—	—	—	300	5.31	1593	300	5.31	1593
	29	200	5.40	1080	—	—	—	500	5.35	2674**
Total		2200		11,490	2000		10,316			

* Figures are slightly different due to approximation.
** The approximation error is adjusted.

Cost of goods sold, i.e. Rs. 10,316 is the sum of total costs of issues under moving average. The period-end inventory is valued simply as the balance on hand, i.e. Rs. 2674.

All the three types of average cost methods discussed above are simple to operate, though the last one involves more calculations. When the items are homogeneous in nature, the three methods tend to approximate the physical flow of goods. As against the FIFO and LIFO, income manipulation is less under average methods.

The inventory records exhibited in Tables 4.2–4.4 are the ones that are maintained under *perpetual recording system*, which is predominantly in use in most of the organisations. We have seen that under this recording system all acquisitions and issues are recorded for each transaction immediately after it occurs and hence, one can find the balance of the inventory both by quantity and value at any time.

There is also another accounting system which is called *periodic recording system* where neither the issue records nor the balance are maintained on transaction basis; only records of acquisitions are kept. At the period-end (which is usually a month or a quarter), physical counting of inventories on hand is made and then the total cost of issues and the valuation of inventory are done by applying any of the three methods discussed above. This recording system is prevalent in small enterprises or in those firms that deal in few items that are easily identifiable.

Some differences in the amount of cost of goods sold (total issues) and period-end inventory will arise between a *perpetual* and *periodic recording system* except under FIFO, simple average, and weighted average methods.

Comparative Analysis Comparative analysis of different inventory methods discussed so far and their impact on the profitability of the company can now be made assuming that goods are sold during the quarter at Rs. 10 per unit; other operating expenses are Rs. 2500 and the tax rate of the company is 40 percent (Table 4.5).

Table 4.5 Comparative Statement of Different Inventory Methods

(Amount in Rs.)

			Inventory methods		
	FIFO	*LIFO*	*Simple average*	*Weighted average*	*Moving average*
Opening balance	1500	1500	1500	1500	1500
Addition to inventory	11,490	11,490	11,490	11,490	11,490
Goods available for sales	12,990	12,990	12,990	12,990	12,990
Less: Closing balance	2685	2625	2605	2600	2674
Cost of goods sold (A)	10,305	10,365	10,385	10,390	10,316
Sales (B)	20,000	20,000	20,000	20,000	20,000
Gross profit (B – A)	9695	9635	9615	9610	9684
Less: Operating expenses	2500	2500	2500	2500	2500
Profit before tax	7195	7135	7115	7110	7184
Less: Income tax @ 40%	2878	2854	2846	2844	2874
Profit after tax (PAT)	4317	4281	4269	4266	4310

The comparative statement given in Table 4.5 reveals that compared to FIFO, cost of goods sold is highest under LIFO and profit after tax is the least; hence, the incidence of tax is also the least. This is so because cost of materials is rising. The contrary will happen when cost will fall.

Of the three averages, profit after tax (PAT) is the least under weighted average and highest under moving average. Although there is not much of a difference in PAT between the simple and weighted average, the difference and the methods of calculations should be noted. Under a different range or type of price-level changes, the difference could be significant. Simple and weighted averages dampen the extremes of FIFO and LIFO while moving average is more close to reality, though in this example, the difference in PAT between FIFO and moving average is, incidentally, not found to be large.

Specific Identification

Under this method, specific costs of materials that have been acquired and segregated are charged to identified goods or services. When an item is acquired for a specific purpose it is tagged with a number by reference of which the cost and date of acquisition are easily discernible. As the item is both issued and valued at its specific cost, it provides a more realistic valuation than the methods discussed earlier. The cost flow and physical flow of goods are identical under this method. But the cost of maintaining the system is very high as it entails detail recording both for acquisitions and issues. For purpose of inventory control, this is perhaps the best method, but due to prohibitive cost, it is not adoptable by many organisations. Its usage is limited to custom-made products.

Besides the four methods of valuation discussed above, there are also other methods recognised by the accounting standard (AS-2) which have limited applications for particular types of businesses. Some of these methods as embodied in AS-2 are discussed below.

Base Stock

The minimum quantity of inventory that must be held at all times by certain businesses is called *base stock*. This minimum level of inventory is valued at acquisition cost. Inventories in excess of the base stock are valued by any of the methods discussed above. However, the base stock must not be confused with many companies maintaining a minimum stock level as safety stock. Base stock is embedded in the technical requirement of a business. It should not be mixed up with the safety and other financial requirements.

As only few businesses have the technical requirement of a base stock, its usage is limited. It is commonly found in chemical and petroleum industries.

Adjusted Selling Price

This method has wide applicability in retail business. For this reason, this is also called *retail inventory method*. This method can also be used in industries where inventory comprises items, the individual costs of which are not readily ascertainable.

Under this method, historical cost of inventory is first calculated at the selling price and then an estimated amount of gross margin of profit is deducted from such stock. The gross profit margin may be calculated for individual items or groups of items, or by departments as may be appropriate to a particular type of business. In a manufacturing organisation, this method can be used for valuing the inventory of finished products held against forward sale contracts.

Standard Cost

Standard costs of goods are determined by appropriate forecasting methods, taking into account the price trend, usage rate, storage facilities etc. These standards are then applied to cost the issues and value the inventories. This method enables an enterprise to evaluate the performance of materials management with the tools of variance analysis. Pricing decisions are easily made under this system because of the standard costs of materials.

The use of standard cost for determining the cost of inventories require that the standards are realistic which is possible only when these are periodically reviewed; otherwise this may distort both the valuation of inventories and pricing of the products.

GOAL OF INVENTORY MANAGEMENT

For a long time inventory management remained everybody's concern but nobody's responsibility. Every organisational unit along the productive-distributive channel of an enterprise wants to have full control over the inventory it deals in: the purchasing department for materials inventory; production department for work-in-process, and marketing department for finished goods inventory. Although the distribution appears to be logical, inherent in it is the tendency to maximise individual goals at the cost of organisational goals. Thus the process of suboptimisation begins which leads to disastrous results for the enterprise and put inventory management in disarray.

Worldwide the corporate failures during and after the Second World War and lately during '70s, led the corporate thinkers to redefine the goals of inventory management as a part of overall materials management of the enterprise. *Materials requirement planning* (MRP) which emerged as a new discipline, attempted to define inventory management as an integral part of MRP whose broad goals are: (1) To minimise investment in inventory, (2) To ensure smooth and efficient operation of the plant, and (3) To maximise customer service and satisfaction.

Integrated System

Materials management recognises that in any business organisation, all departmental activities are interdependent. Whenever a department forgets this and tries to operate independently, the result of such action is that the entire organisation is thrown to the web of internal conflicts, which ultimately destroys the very fabric of the organisation. For example, a purchase manager may decide to buy in bulk because it minimises the unit cost due to larger discounts. But this may not at all be beneficial for the organisation as a whole because the cost of carrying the high level of inventory would more than offset the cost saved on discounts.

The integrated system of inventory management holds that inventory problems cannot be handled in isolation. It is unquestionably interrelated with the problems of production, materials handling, and purchasing on the one hand and warehousing, distribution, marketing and finance on the other. A single material, purchased or sold, affects all of them. But it is not always possible for a departmental head to take on such a corporate view and understand the intricacies of coordinated inventory management, busy as he is to discharge his specific function. A modern organisation, therefore, assigns this job to a specialised materials manager. This helps minimise the inter-departmental conflicts and keeps the organisational goal in perspective.

INVENTORY STRATEGIES AND TECHNIQUES

In one of the international conferences on the Economics of Inventory Management,[11] a practising consultant remarked at the end of the day that while inventory can be shown in terms of raw materials, work-in-progress and finished goods, a business perspective of the inventory problem is not about any one of these. Top management must take a total business system perspective which integrates suppliers into business and runs through consumers in a manner that involves the material flow and the two-way information flow. In this perspective, forecasting, order processing, production planning, machine scheduling, vendor engagement, etc. must be handled in a fairly integrated manner rather than aiming to solve any one of the functions individually.

In the foregoing section we have discussed the danger of taking a functional view of inventory management, the problem of suboptimisation and the conflicts that emanate from the functional perspective of the organisation. The remarks, made in the above discussion, attempt to direct our attention to integrate inventory functions into the corporate strategy of a business organisation. Inventories should be managed for purpose of realising the competitive business strategies of an enterprise. In simple terms, it means that inventory strategy must flow from the business strategy of an enterprise. When the latter changes, the former must also change. In other words, inventory management operationalises the competitive strategy of an enterprise. It must do so by integrating itself with other operational strategies of the business like production, marketing and finance. Successful business strategies depend to a very large extent on the right choice of operational strategies.

There are also a number of techniques available for inventory management. The job of the materials manager is to make a choice of such techniques which are appropriate for a particular operational strategy for a given period of time. When the strategy changes, techniques may also change. A particular technique which might have been very successful in pursuing one strategy may be disastrous when the strategy changes. A dynamic materials manager should be prepared to examine the efficacy of a particular technique of inventory management in the light of a change in strategy and be ready to discard the existing technique when it is found to have outlived the strategic purpose. This readiness to change keeps the organisation competitive. If this change does not take place and the inventory manager continues with the old techniques, then not only the operational strategy of inventories will fail, it may ultimately defeat the business strategy itself.

Strategic options of a commercial organisation rest on finding out ways and means by which it can achieve sustainable competitive advantage. Michael Porter argued that there are three fundamental ways in which a firm can achieve competitive advantage.[12] These are cost leadership strategy, differentiation

---

11. Remark of Giridharadas, Shyam in *The Economics of Inventory Management,* Chikan, Attila and M.C. Lovell (Eds.), Elsevier Science, B.V., Amsterdam, 1988, p. 504.

12. Porter, Michael E., *Competitive Strategy,* Free Press, New York, 1980 and *Competitive Advantage,* Free Press, New York, 1985.

strategy and a focus strategy. These generic strategies, proposed by Porter in 1980, have been perfected over the last decade and the process is still going on.[13]

Cost Leadership Strategy

When a firm sets out to become the low-cost producer in its industry, it must find out and exploit all sources of cost advantage. A low-cost producer, typically, sells a standard, or no-frills, product and places considerable emphasis on reaping scale economies or absolute overall cost leadership. It will be an above-average performer in the industry provided it can command prices at or near the industry average.

Although the term 'cost leadership' has run into problems, the direction of the strategy can never be missed. Some writers would rather call it a cost-based strategy which attempts to achieve competitive advantage by reaping benefits from increased margins or surpluses, low prices or efficiency.[14]

As mentioned above, firms which pursue cost-based strategies generally deal in standard products without any special features. These are generally goods of mass consumption, be it products of daily necessity, hardware items, spare parts or industrial intermediates. Demand for these products are stable or amenable to standard forecasting methods. Competition is high in these product markets and consumers are both price- and supply-sensitive. Stock-out cost is also very high. When an order is received the product should immediately be available from stock.

Inventory Strategy

The inventory strategy that should be followed under this business strategy is what may be termed as MARK TO STOCK. Manufacturing or procurement is done on a sufficiently large scale to reap the benefits of economies of scale. When goods are manufactured in-house, large batch size reduces per unit cost by overhead distribution; when these are outsourced, large purchases reduce the per unit cost by quantity discounts. Under this strategy, goods are completely manufactured or acquired and stored in anticipation of demand. The wait-time for customers is very short in MARK TO STOCK inventory strategy.

Differentiation Strategy

Under this strategy the enterprise aims at becoming unique in the industry to which it belongs, along some dimensions that are widely valued by customers. It can charge a premium price for this unique value addition. This strategy requires that a firm chooses the attributes through which it can differentiate,

---

13. See, for example, Hill, C.W.L., "Differentiation vs Low Cost or Differentiation and Low Cost", *Academy of Management Review,* July 1988, pp. 401–412 and Karnani, A., "Generic Competitive Strategies: An analytical approach", *Strategic Management Journal,* April 1984, pp. 367–80.
14. Johnson, G. and Scholes, K., *Exploring Corporate Strategy: Text and Cases,* 3rd ed., Prentice-Hall of India, New Delhi, 1996.

itself from its rivals. A firm that can achieve and sustain differentiation, will be an above-average performer in the industry if its price premium exceeds the extra costs incurred in being unique.

The differentiation need not necessarily be confined to the product; it can also be related to the product. For example, differentiation can be worked out on the selling environment, like location, a different store ambience, delivery types, or even providing a car parking facility and so on.

It is also not necessary to offer differentiation at a premium price. A firm may as well sell at a lower price by cutting down costs in order to enlarge its market share. That is, a firm could simultaneously follow a cost-based strategy as well as differentiation in products. Although Porter did not like the idea and termed it as "stuck in the middle" policy, many firms are found to follow both the two strategies successfully.[15] In order to sustain product differentiation a firm requires continuous investment in R&D which can be handled either through premium pricing or saving on cost. If the firm is not following the former, it has to follow the latter.

Inventory Strategy

Depending upon the type of product and expected volume of sales, the inventory strategy could be *make to stock* or *assemble to order*. In the latter strategy, products or their special features are manufactured in semi-knocked-down condition. When an order is received the product is assembled from the subassemblies already in the inventory. This strategy is suitable for products where differentiation is done by offering a range of optional features requiring a customer to ask for a particular configuration. This inventory strategy is also useful where product differentiation is done regionally according to special requirements of customers belonging to a particular region.

Customer-wait time in *assemble to order strategy* is longer than in *make to stock strategy* but customers are expected to bear it (some even like the waiting time for vanity consideration). However, it is found that in most products, assembly lead time is rather short.

Focus Strategy

This strategy is based on the choice of a narrow competitive scope within an industry. The enterprise selects a segment or a group of segments in the industry and tailors its strategy to serve them to the exclusion of others. The focus could be a *cost focus* where a firm seeks a cost advantage in its target segment or a *differentiation focus* where it seeks differentiation in its target segment.

For example, Maruti Udyog Limited targeted its Maruti 800 standard model to the middle class segment who could never hope to own a car earlier. The car itself was first launched as "People's Car". The segment was hitherto neglected by the then car manufacturers. Maruti was following a cost focus strategy in this segment which is also akin to price-based strategy as some

---

15. Miller, D., "The Generic Strategy Trap", *Journal of Business Strategy,* January 1992.

writers suggest. In other words, a firm which intends to follow a strategy of low price to gain competitive advantage must select a market segment where low price is important and the firm can sustain cost advantage over the competition in that segment. Nirma detergent powder is also a case in point.

A business can also offer higher perceived value to the customers in a particular market segment and charge a premium price for that. The premium range ready-made garments market or the emerging premium car market in India are examples of focussed differentiation. In the premium car market, Esteem, Honda, Opel-Astra are competing in lower premium segment (executive cars) while Mercedes is still unchallenged in the upper echelon of the premium segment (luxury cars).

Focussed differentiation is also practised in high value custom-based products where the consultancy element plays a major role in differentiating a product from the competition. Industrial and electrical engineering products, defense instruments, ships and aircrafts are some of the examples.

Inventory Strategy

Inventory strategies vary with the kind of focus strategy and the product market. For a cost focus strategy, *make to stock* could be ideal. For focussed premium market segment the strategies could partly be *make to stock* and partly *assemble to order*. Focussed differentiation in custom-based products may follow inventory strategies of *make to order* or *engineer to order*. In both the cases production would not start until an order is received. The consultancy element is greater in the latter than in the former strategy, which requires designing and/ or developing a prototype according to customer requirement and then producing it. Customer-wait time is, therefore, longer in *engineer to order* strategy than in *make to order* strategy.

TECHNIQUES OF INVENTORY MANAGEMENT

As mentioned in the foregoing section, techniques of inventory management must observe the inventory strategy employed by a firm. In what follows, we shall discuss a number of inventory management models, each of which has its own assumptions, limitations and applicability. No single model can claim universal application across all the inventory strategies discussed earlier. It is important, therefore, to evaluate the assumptions and limitations of a model from the perspective of an inventory strategy before its final adoption in the inventory control system of the enterprise.

Whichever strategy is employed by a firm, for an inventory manager it ultimately boils down to determining how many quantities to buy and when to place the order, since his ultimate goal is to minimise the total costs—direct and indirect—that are associated with holding inventories.

It is obvious that demand for inventory plays the most important role in determining the inventory requirement. The demand could be independent or dependent. These two terms must be understood from the perspective of internal demand management of an enterprise. For example, the finished goods produced or procured by a firm rests on the demand for the products in the market, but for purpose of inventory management, the demand is considered to be independent because it does not depend upon or result from the demand of any other materials within the organisation. But the demand for finished products, in turn, may demand procurement of input materials for manufacture. Hence, the demand of input materials is dependent upon the demand of finished products. We can, therefore, say that input materials have dependent demand structure.

Demand can also be continuous or discrete. In the former case the demand occurs continuously at a constant rate, i.e. it does not vary from one period to another. In case of discrete demand, time variation of demand is highly pronounced. When demand occurs at discrete intervals rather than continuously, we say that the material has a discrete demand pattern. Both dependent and independent demand structures can have a discrete demand pattern.

The inventory models discussed here belong to two sections: (1) Independent demand structure, and (2) Dependent demand structure. Here, the demand should be understood as demand for consumption. For example, in the case of manufacturing, it could be the raw materials demanded for consumption in various workstations, and in the case of retailers, it could be the quantities demanded by various sales (consumption) counters.

Independent Demand Structure

By now, it should be clear that in order to determine an optimum inventory policy we must know or are capable of estimating the demand of the materials, lead times required for delivery, and the relevant inventory costs.

Let us first make the most simplistic assumption that all the above three parameters are known or estimated with certainty. As the demand and lead time are known stockouts can be avoided.

When the known demand (D) is continuous, what we can have is a fixed-order system where the same number of units is ordered every time. We are, therefore, required to determine the lot size of such order which we denote as (Q). The order size that minimises the total inventory cost is known as *economic order quantity*, popularly called EOQ.

Total annual cost of inventory is composed of purchase cost (P), the ordering cost (C) and the holding cost (H). Purchase cost is the total acquisition cost of a unit of material. Hence, yearly purchase cost will be per unit cost (P) multiplied by the annual demand of units (D), i.e. ($P \times D$). Ordering cost is the cost incurred for placing an order. Generally, it is found that no relationship exists between number of units ordered in a lot and the ordering cost because processing cost of a small order or a large order remains one and the same. But when ordering cost is fixed per order, the per unit ordering cost shall vary with the quantities ordered. The cost behaviour is similar to any other fixed costs. Larger the order smaller is the per unit ordering cost, i.e. (C/Q), while the total annual ordering cost will be $C(D/Q)$.

The holding cost, which is also known as carrying cost as mentioned before, is directly proportional to the average holding of inventory ($Q/2$). We need to explain the quantitative expression of average holding of inventory ($Q/2$) under the given assumption. Suppose, an enterprise consumes 600 units uniformly per month. The opening inventory of the year has been 7200 units and the last item of inventory is consumed on the last day of the year. The monthly stock position will be as given in Table 4.6.

Table 4.6 Monthly Stock Holding under Constant Consumption

Date	Inventory in units	
April 1	7200	
May 1	6600	
June 1	6000	
July 1	5400	
August 1	4800	Average inventory $= \dfrac{46,800}{13}$
September 1	4200	$= 3600$ units
October 1	3600	
November 1	3000	
December 1	2400	
January 1	1800	
February 1	1200	
March 1	600	
March 31	0	
Total	46,800	

Average holding of inventory as calculated in Table 4.6 is 3600 units which is nothing but one-half of the opening inventory ($7200/2 = 3600$). In our model, average holding of inventory can, therefore, be depicted as ($Q/2$). Figure 4.1 captures this phenomenon graphically.

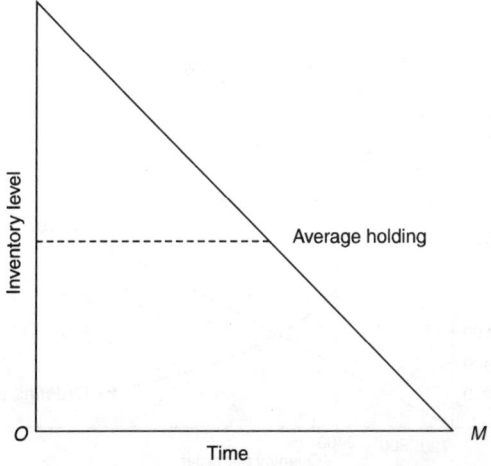

Figure 4.1 Graphical representation of average inventory holding.

Holding cost can be expressed as a percentage annual charge on the value of inventory. Hence, yearly holding cost will be $P \times \dfrac{Q}{2} \times H$. In the above example, if the unit acquisition cost is Rs. 15 and holding cost per annum is 20 percent, then yearly holding cost will be $15 \times \dfrac{7200}{2} \times \dfrac{20}{100} = \text{Rs.}\,10,800$. Holding cost can also be expressed as rupees per unit. In this example it should be Rs. 15 × 0.20 = Rs. 3. This we denote as (H).

We can now find out the economic order quantity (EOQ) first by a process of iteration and then by an algebraic formula. We shall use the above example with an added assumption regarding ordering cost which now is taken at Rs. 1200 per order. The iterative process is shown in Table 4.7.

Table 4.7 Deriving the Optimal Order (Lot) Size by Iterative Process

Quantity per order (1)	No. of orders per year (2)	Ordering cost (Rs.) (3)	Average inventory (units) (4)	Holding cost (Rs.) [col. 4 × 15 × 0.20] (5)	Total cost (Rs.) [col. 3 + col. 5] (6)
7200	1	1200	3600	10,800	12,000
3600	2	2400	1800	5400	7800
2400	3	3600	1200	3600	7200
1800	4	4800	900	2700	7500
1440	5	6000	720	2160	8160
1200	6	7200	600	1800	9000
900	8	9600	450	1350	10,950
720	10	12,000	360	1080	13,080

Note: Annual demand: 7200 units, Ordering cost: Rs. 1200 per order, Holding cost: 20% p.a.

Table 4.7 reveals that optimal solution (EOQ) lies in placing 2400 units per order where total cost is the least. Three such orders shall be placed in a year. The search for optimal solution (EOQ) is done graphically in Figure 4.2.

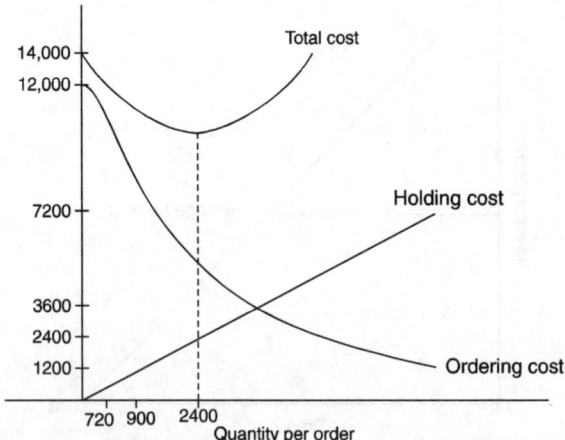

Figure 4.2 Graphical representation of EOQ.

Mathematical Presentation

Both Table 4.7 and Figure 4.2 reveal that at the point where optimal solution (required Q) lies, both the ordering cost and holding cost are equal. Let us approach the problem from this finding.

A. *Economic order quantity (EOQ)*

$$\text{Total ordering cost} = \text{Total holding cost}$$

or

$$\frac{\text{Total demand }(D)}{\text{Quantity per order }(Q)} \times \text{Ordering cost per order }(C)$$

$$= \text{Quantity per order }(Q) \times \frac{1}{2} \times \text{Holding cost per unit }(H)$$

or

$$\frac{D}{Q} \times C = Q \times \frac{1}{2} \times H$$

or

$$\frac{DC}{Q} = \frac{QH}{2}$$

or

$$Q^2 H = 2DC$$

or

$$Q = \sqrt{\frac{2DC}{H}} = EOQ$$

After checking with the above example,

$$Q = \sqrt{\frac{2 \times 7200 \times 1200}{3}} = 2400 \text{ units} = EOQ$$

Let us now calculate optimal number of orders (N), which is given by

$$NC = \frac{DH}{2N}$$

or

$$2N^2 C = DH$$

or

$$N^2 = \frac{DH}{2C}$$

or

$$N = \sqrt{\frac{DH}{2C}} = \text{optimum number of orders}$$

After checking with the example

$$N = \sqrt{\frac{7200 \times 3}{2 \times 1200}}$$

$$= 3, \text{ which is the optimum number of orders}$$

B. *Optimum number of day's supply per order.* We may need to know how many days' supply can be assured by the EOQ. Let us denote this as S. Purchase cost per unit of material is denoted by P as before.

$$\text{Total ordering cost} = \text{Total holding cost}$$

$$\frac{365}{S} \times C = \frac{D}{\frac{365}{S}} \times \frac{1}{2} \times H$$

or

$$\frac{365C}{S} = D \times \frac{S}{365} \times \frac{1}{2} \times H$$

$$\frac{365C}{S} = \frac{DSH}{730}$$

or

$$S^2 DH = 730 \times 365C$$

or

$$S^2 = \frac{730 \times 365C}{DH}$$

$$S = \sqrt{\frac{266,450C}{DH}}$$

Rearranging, we have

$$S = \sqrt{\frac{2(365)^2 C}{DH}}$$

After checking with the example,

$$S = \sqrt{\frac{2(365)^2 C}{DH}}$$

$$= \sqrt{\frac{266,450 \times 1200}{7200 \times 3}}$$

$$= 121.66, \text{ say } 122 \text{ days' supply}$$

C. *Optimum amount per order.* We shall now determine the optimum amount that should be arranged while placing an order. Let us denote this as A. Inventory carrying cost is taken here as a percentage on the amount of inventory holding. Let us denote this as I which, in the present example, is 20% or 0.20 per rupee per annum.

$$\text{Total ordering cost} = \text{Total carrying cost}$$

i.e.

$$\frac{D \times P}{A} \times C = \frac{D \times P}{\frac{D \times P}{A}} \times \frac{1}{2} \times I$$

or

$$\frac{DPC}{A} = \frac{D \times P \times A}{D \times P} \times \frac{1}{2} \times I$$

$$= \frac{AI}{2}$$

$$A^2 I = 2DPC$$

or

$$A^2 = \frac{2DPC}{I}$$

or

$$A = \sqrt{\frac{2DPC}{I}}$$

After checking with the example,

$$A = \sqrt{\frac{2 \times 7200 \times 15 \times 1200}{0.20}}$$

= Rs. 36,000, which is the optimum amount to be arranged.

Results of the above analysis are summarised below:

(i) Optimum number of units per order (EOQ) = 2400 units
(ii) Optimum number of orders per year = 3 Nos.
(iii) Optimum number of days' supply per order = 122 days
(iv) Optimum amount to be arranged per order = Rs. 36,000

All the results can be checked back with Table 3.7 for their accuracy. Mathematical presentation of the models saves much of the time involved in the iterative (trial and error) process.

With the four EOQ answers at hand, it becomes easier for the inventory manager to establish a procurement plan and also for the financial controller to arrange for fund and monitor the inventory levels.

We have already indicated that the EOQ models operate under the following assumptions:

1. Annual total demand for consumption can be estimated with reasonable accuracy,
2. The demand is nearly uniformly spread throughout the year,
3. All goods ordered are received and taken to stock at one time,
4. Estimates of the cost parameters are reasonably accurate.

If any of these assumptions is wrong, EOQ models would not provide the right kind of answers.

The above four assumptions are reasonably valid for articles of daily necessities, e.g. basic food stuffs, which do not suffer from much of seasonality. However, when, the seasonality is too high the EOQ can be calculated for busy season and slack season separately.

Overcoming the Limitations of EOQ Model

EOQ models are often criticised preciously because of the restrictive assumptions mentioned above. It is claimed that in the real world the demand and the constancy of it are hardly predictable with precision, so also is the case with the inventory associated costs. But if we delve deep into the structure of the model, we shall understand its robustness in the sense that it is highly insensitive to variation or errors in prediction. Even if there are wide variations in demand and the cost parameters, EOQ results would not vary that widely. This is primarily due to the mathematical nature of the model. When EOQs are calculated with not so precise estimates, the effect of the errors are blunted to a large extent because of the square root function. A sensitivity analysis of the model function can be made to understand to what extent the EOQ results get influenced by changes or errors in input parameters.

Two inventory costs are associated with EOQ modelling: ordering cost and the holding cost. The former is predominantly fixed, i.e. it does not vary with the quantities ordered while the latter is predominantly variable with the quantities and hence, with the value of the average holding of stock under any ordering scheme. We have seen that the optimum inventory policy is settled at a point where holding cost (variable) equals the ordering cost (fixed). That is also the point where total relevant costs associated with the inventory is at its minimum.[16]

We can now determine the error factors for different parameters as follows:

$$\text{Demands factor} = \frac{\text{Estimated demand}}{\text{Actual demand}} = m$$

$$\text{Ordering cost error factor} = \frac{\text{Estimated ordering cost}}{\text{Actual ordering cost}} = n$$

$$\text{Holding cost error factor} = \frac{\text{Estimated holding cost}}{\text{Actual holding cost}} = k$$

Denote $Q = EOQ$ and $Q^* =$ order quantity with estimation errors.

Hence, percentage variation in order quantity due to estimation error is given by:

$$\frac{Q^* - Q}{Q}$$

where

$$Q = \sqrt{\frac{2DC}{H}}$$

Incorporating the error factors in the model, Q^* becomes:

$$Q^* = \sqrt{\frac{2DCmn}{Hk}}$$

16. It may be noted that we have not considered purchase cost of inventory for purpose of the present analysis because in the absense of any quantity discounts, it ceases to be a relevant cost. Inventory modelling with quantity discounts is considered later.

Hence, impact of the estimation errors on the estimated Q can be calculated as:

$$\frac{Q^* - Q}{Q} = \frac{\sqrt{\dfrac{2DCmn}{Hk}} - \sqrt{\dfrac{2DC}{H}}}{\sqrt{\dfrac{2DC}{H}}}$$

$$= \frac{\sqrt{\dfrac{2DCmn}{Hk}}}{\sqrt{\dfrac{2DC}{H}}} - 1$$

$$= \sqrt{\dfrac{mn}{k}} - 1$$

Let us understand this by varying the parameters of our earlier example.

Parameters	Estimate at EOQ	Actual	Percentage change
Demand (D)	7200 units	10,000 units	+38.9%
Ordering cost (C)	Rs. 1200 per order	Rs. 1000 per order	−16.68%
Holding cost (H)	Rs. 3 per unit	Rs. 4 per unit	+33.33%

Hence

$$m = \frac{\text{Estimated demand}}{\text{Actual demand}} = \frac{7200}{10,000} = 0.72$$

$$n = \frac{\text{Estimated ordering cost}}{\text{Actual ordering cost}} = \frac{1200}{1000} = 1.20$$

$$k = \frac{\text{Estimated holding cost}}{\text{Actual holding cost}} = \frac{3}{4} = 0.75$$

Impact of all the above estimation errors on estimated Q is calculated as below:

$$\frac{Q^* - Q}{Q} = \sqrt{\frac{mn}{K}} - 1 = \sqrt{\frac{0.72 \times 1.20}{0.75}} - 1$$

$$= 1.07 - 1 = 0.07 \text{ or } 7\% \text{ approximately which is not very high.}$$

It is observed that the EOQ inventory model is quite insensitive to changes in parameters wherein lies its strength. Under EOQ model, total cost is found to increase only moderately even when there is a substantial departure from the optimum conditions. As such, the basic models do not require intermittent revisions.

EOQ models tolerate approximation errors without much of loss in economies. Lot sizes can be approximated to round figures, and ordering intervals can be taken to the next convenient interval.

Relaxing the EOQ Assumptions

We have indicated earlier that EOQ models operate perfectly under certain assumptions. We have also shown that if prediction of parameters of EOQ turn out to be inaccurate, the impact of the errors get minimised due to the peculiar mathematical property of the model. However, we shall now be trying to relax these assumptions and modify the EOQ model suitably on the basis of the following assumptions.

Annual demand. EOQ model assumes that annual demand is known with reasonable certainty and it spreads out uniformly throughout the year. But in real life situations, for many firms or products, demand cannot just be predicted because of its erratic occurrences. Or, the product may be totally new in the market for which no market history is available. In situations like this it is neither possible nor advisable to predict annual demand. We must, therefore, find out an alternative approach to EOQ to resolve this problem.

Suppose an enterprise deals in a product for which demand can be estimated only for a few weeks, say six weeks. The inventory manager finds that it already has stocks which can carry the demand for next two weeks, but for the remaining four weeks, i.e. for the 3rd, 4th, 5th and 6th week he would need 150 units, 90 units, 120 units and 120 units respectively. Unit cost of the material is Rs. 62.50; ordering cost is Rs. 60 per order while carrying cost is 20 percent per annum, i.e. $\text{Rs.}\, 62.50 \times \dfrac{20}{100 \times 52} = \text{Rs.}\, 0.24$ per unit per week.

We may now determine the EOQ for this kind of situation through an iterative process.

In the first step we start computing the holding and ordering cost under four alternative buying situations, e.g. for 3, 4, 5 and 6 weeks' consumption. The calculations are given in Table 4.8.

Table 4.8 Cost Calculations under Four Alternative Buying Situations

Sl. no.	Buying alternative	Numbers bought	Holding cost (Rs.)	Ordering cost (Rs.)
1.	3 weeks' requirement	$0 + 0 + 150 = 150$	All units consumed in 4th week = 0	60
2.	4 weeks' requirement	$0 + 0 + 150 + 90 = 240$	90 units held for 1 week = $90 \times 0.24 = 21.60$	60
3.	5 weeks' requirement	$0 + 0 + 150 + 90 + 120 = 360$	120 units held for 2 weeks plus the above = $21.60 + 120 \times 0.24 \times 2 = 79.20$	60
4.	6 weeks' requirement	$0 + 0 + 150 + 90 + 120 + 120 = 480$	120 units held for 3 weeks plus the above = $79.20 + 120 \times 0.24 \times 3 = 165.60$	60

It may be seen from Table 4.8 that as the number of units purchased per order increases, the holding cost rises and crosses the ordering cost at 5 weeks' purchases (360 units). Ordering cost remains same at Rs. 60 per order irrespective of quantities ordered.

We know that the optimal solution or EOQ lies at a point where holding cost equals the ordering cost. An inspection of Table 4.8 will reveal that the point will lie somewhere beyond 4 weeks' purchases (240 units) but less than 5 weeks' purchases (360 units). The question now essentially boils down to finding out how many additional units beyond 240 units will have to be carried to 2 weeks' consumption so that holding cost rises from Rs. 21.60 to the level of ordering cost of Rs. 60. The solution lies in the following simple arithmetic.

$$\text{EOQ} = 240 + \frac{\text{Rs. }60 - \text{Rs. }21.60}{0.24 \times 2 \text{ weeks}} = 320 \text{ units}$$

This EOQ of 320 units will cover the requirement through 80 units of the 6th week. The inventory manager shall begin calculation of another EOQ for the next period sometime during the second week before consuming out the 80 units on hand. Thus EOQs will be different for different periods.

Instantaneous receipt The next assumption made for EOQ modelling is that all the goods which are ordered arrive simultaneously. Under this assumption the inventory level will rise to the maximum level as soon as the goods arrive and these are taken to stock. When the inventory movement and its levels are plotted over a time period under this EOQ assumption, the graph will look like a sawtooth diagram as shown in Figure 4.3.

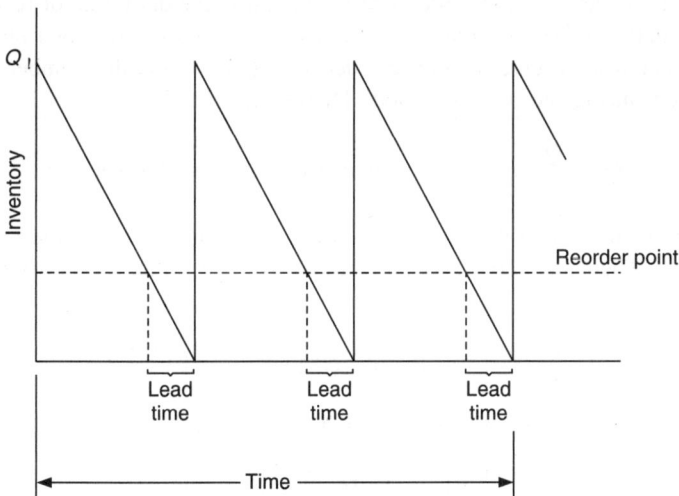

Figure 4.3 Inventory movement under instantaneous receipt.

The instantaneous receipt assumption, however, does not hold good in many cases. The supply pattern depends to a large extent by demand-supply conditions and market practices. In many businesses we find that suppliers deliver order in partial shipments, or portions of order are delivered over a period of time. When such is the case, inventory level does not rise immediately to its maximum point. It is found that inventory continues to get used up while new materials are still being received. As such, the inventory level builds up gradually when materials are received at a rate faster than the rate of consumption; then it falls to its lowest level as the delivery of materials stops while the use of inventory continues. The pattern is captured in Figure 4.4.

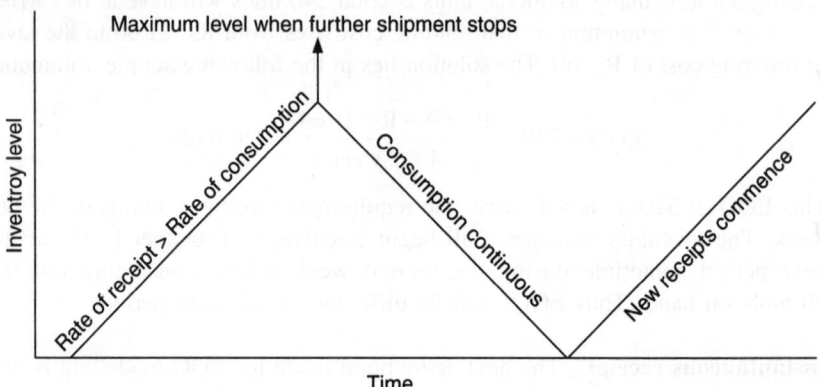

Figure 4.4 Inventory holding and consumption pattern when order is executed over a period.

We can now proceed to eliminate the instantaneous receipt assumption in EOQ models.

Let Q be the optimum order size in units; a is the daily rate of receipt and b is the daily rate of consumption of units. Hence, Q/a is the total number of days required to receive the entire order and $(Q/a) \times b$ is the number of units consumed during the receipt period. Therefore,

$$Q - \left(\frac{Q}{a} \times b\right) = \text{Maximum accumulation of inventory}$$

We already know that average holding of inventory is half the maximum inventory. Then under the above situation, average holding of inventory will be

$$\frac{1}{2}\left[Q - \left(\frac{Q}{a} \times b\right)\right] = \frac{1}{2}Q\left(1 - \frac{b}{a}\right) = \frac{Q}{2}\left(1 - \frac{b}{a}\right)$$

Hence, holding cost of inventory will be

$$\frac{Q}{2}\left(1 - \frac{b}{a}\right) \times H = \frac{QH}{2}\left(1 - \frac{b}{a}\right)$$

where H is the per unit holding cost as before.

Now, total annual demand being D and ordering cost as C per order, total ordering cost shall be

$$\frac{D}{Q} \times C = \frac{DC}{Q}$$

We already know that in EOQ model the total cost is at its minimum when total ordering cost equals total holding cost. Hence,

$$\frac{DC}{Q} = \frac{QH}{2}\left(1 - \frac{b}{a}\right)$$

or

$$Q^2 H\left(1 - \frac{b}{a}\right) = 2DC$$

or

$$Q^2 = \frac{2DC}{H\left(1 - \dfrac{b}{a}\right)}$$

or

$$Q = \sqrt{\frac{2DC}{H\left(1 - \dfrac{b}{a}\right)}}$$

$$= \text{Optimum number of units under}$$
$$\text{gradual receipts of inventory}$$

Cost parameters   It is not difficult to obtain fairly accurate estimates of both the holding cost and ordering cost from organisations who maintain proper inventory recording system. But there are organisations, particularly of the smaller types, which do not have such a formal system of inventory recording, and hence, obtaining the relevant cost data to determine the two cost parameters may always not be possible. There may also be situations where an enterprise would desire to move to formal inventory management system but would not like to wait till adequate cost data are generated. In cases like this, though we may not be able to find out an optimal solution (minimum cost) because cost data are not available, it is possible to reap the benefits of EOQ system of inventory management by suitably working on the model. This can be done in two ways. First, we can minimise the holding cost keeping the purchasing workload (ordering cost) constant and secondly, we can minimise the purchasing work load (ordering cost) keeping the inventory constant.

(a) *Minimising inventory level without increasing the purchasing workload:*   Assuming that the organisation knows or can estimate the annual demand *D* fairly well, we separate the demand parameter from the original EOQ model as follows:

$$Q = \sqrt{\frac{2DC}{H}} = \sqrt{\frac{2C}{H}} \times \sqrt{D}$$

As we cannot estimate either *C* or *H*, we designate the entire first part of the equation as *Z*, then the equation can be represented as

$$Q = Z \times \sqrt{D}$$

Dividing both sides of the equation by D, we obtain

$$\frac{D}{Q} = \frac{D}{Z \times \sqrt{D}}$$

Breaking the numerator of the right-hand side of the equation, we get

$$\frac{D}{Q} = \frac{\sqrt{D} \times \sqrt{D}}{Z \times \sqrt{D}}$$

or

$$\frac{D}{Q} = \frac{\sqrt{D}}{Z}$$

Now, solving for Z, we obtain

$$Z\left(\frac{D}{Q}\right) = \sqrt{D}$$

or

$$Z = \frac{\sqrt{D}}{D/Q}$$

As Z will be constant for any single inventory item, it can be so considered for the entire range of inventories. Hence, the ratio on the right-hand side can be expressed as the summation of both the numerator and the denominator. That is,

$$Z = \frac{\Sigma\sqrt{D}}{\Sigma D/Q}$$

Let us do it with the help of the following example in Table 4.9.

Table 4.9 Limited Inventory Information

Item of inventory (1)	Annual demand in units (2)	No. of times ordered (3)	Quantity per order (4)	Average inventory balance (1/2 of col. 4) (5)
E	5000	5	1000	500
F	4000	5	800	400
G	3000	5	600	300
H	2000	5	400	200
I	1000	5	200	100
Total		25	3000	1500

Now,

$$\Sigma\left(\sqrt{D}\right) = \sqrt{5000} + \sqrt{4000} + \sqrt{3000} + \sqrt{2000} + \sqrt{1000}$$

$$= 70.71 + 63.24 + 54.77 + 44.72 + 31.62 = 265.06$$

and,

$$\sum \frac{D}{Q} = 5 + 5 + 5 + 5 + 5 = 25 \quad \text{as in column 3 of the above table.}$$

This is because number of orders placed for one item shall always be equal to the total number of orders placed.

Incorporating the above two findings, we can now calculate the value of the constant, Z:

$$Z = \frac{\sum \sqrt{D}}{\sum \dfrac{D}{Q}} = \frac{265.06}{25} = 10.60$$

Optimum order quantity for every item of inventory can be calculated by recalling the following formula:

$$Q = Z \times \sqrt{D}$$

For example, optimum order size for item no. E of Table 4.9 will be

$$Q(E) = 10.60\sqrt{5000} = 749.53 \quad \text{or say, 750 units (approx.)}$$

Number of orders per year will be

$$\frac{D}{Q(E)} = \frac{5000}{750} = 6.66$$

Similar calculations are made for all items of inventory in Table 4.10.

Table 4.10 Inventory Holding Pattern (No Change in Purchasing Work-load) under Modified EOQ Model without Cost Information

Item of inventory (1)	Annual demand (2)	Desired order size (3)	No. of orders [col. 2/col. 3] (4)	Average inventory [1/2 × col. 3] (5)
E	5000	749.52	6.66	374.76
F	4000	670.40	5.97	335.20
G	3000	580.58	5.17	290.29
H	2000	474.04	4.22	237.02
I	1000	335.20	2.98	167.60
		Total	25.00	1404.87

Note: Figures in column 4 which are appearing in fractions should first be converted into days and then approximated. For example, item no. E should be ordered every 365/ 6.66 = 54.80 or 55 days. Desired order size (col. 3) may be approximated to nearest unit.

Comparison of column 5 of Table 4.9 and Table 4.10 reveals that as a result of the existing situation, the average holding of inventory is reduced by about 100 units on which the enterprise will save in terms of holding cost. It may also be seen that purchasing workload has not increased; it remains at writing of 25 orders per year.

(b) *Minimising purchasing workload without increasing the average inventory*: So far we have kept purchasing workload as it is and minimised the average inventory holding. We shall now try to minimise the purchasing workload keeping the inventory constant at their original level. As before, we have no information on costs.

Let us recall the equation we have derived above: $Q = Z\sqrt{D}$, where Z is the constant for cost parameters.

As Z is constant for all inventory items we can rewrite the above equation as

$$\sum Q = Z \sum \sqrt{D}$$

or

$$Z = \frac{\sum Q}{\sum \sqrt{D}}$$

From Table 4.9 we can calculate $\Sigma(Q)$ as twice the total of column 5, i.e. 1500 × 2 = 3000 (which is also the sum of column 4). $\sum \sqrt{D}$ is already calculated as 265.06 in the previous section. Hence, Z in the present situation will be

$$Z = \frac{3000}{265.06} = 11.32$$

As, $Q = Z\sqrt{D}$, we can calculate the inventory pattern now by using $Z = 11.32$. For example, quantities per order for item no. E will be

$$Q(E) = 11.32\sqrt{5000} = 800.44$$

Similar calculations are made for all other items in Table 4.11.

Table 4.11 Inventory Holding Pattern under Modified EOQ Model without Cost Informative (No Change in Average Inventory)

Item of inventory (1)	Annual demand (2)	Desired order size (3)	No. of orders [col. 2/col. 3] (4)	Average inventory [1/2 × col. 3] (5)
E	5000	800.44	6.25	400.22
F	4000	715.94	5.59	357.97
G	3000	620.02	4.84	310.01
H	2000	506.24	3.95	253.12
I	1000	357.97	2.79	178.98
		Total	23.42	1500.30

It may be seen from column 4 of Table 4.11 that purchasing workload has been reduced from 25 to 23.42 while the average inventory remained at approximately 1500.

We have now two derived Z value equations for two situations of no cost information.

Situation I

$$Z = \frac{\sum \sqrt{D}}{\sum \dfrac{D}{Q}} = \frac{265.06}{25} \quad \text{Minimising average holding of inventory without changing the purchasing workload}$$

Situation II

$$Z = \frac{\sum Q}{\sum \sqrt{D}} = \frac{3000}{265.06} \quad \text{Minimising purchasing workload without changing average holding of inventory}$$

Now, having derived the Z value under Situation I the inventory manager feels that he has the capacity to increase the purchasing overload to 30 per annum and hence, he desires to know the amount of reduction in purchasing workload that might cause in the average holding of inventory. He would simply pick up the Z value equation under Situation I and recalculate it as follows:

$$Z^* = \frac{265.06}{30} \left[\text{as } \frac{D}{Q} = \text{Number of orders} \right]$$

$$= 8.84$$

With this new Z^* value, the inventory manager can recalculate Table 4.10 and find out the average holding of inventory in the same manner.

Under situation II, the inventory manager may feel that there is a case for reduction in purchasing workload, as the department is now working beyond capacity. As against that he does not mind carrying an average inventory of 500 units. He likes to know to what extent purchasing workload will be reduced if average inventory rises by 500 units.

We can recall the new Z value equation under situation II and recalculate it as follows:

$$Z^{**} = \frac{4000}{265.06} \quad \text{[As } (Q) = 2 \times \text{average holding of inventory,}$$
$$\text{hence } \Sigma Q^{**} = 3000 + 2 \times 500 = 4000]$$

$$= 15.09$$

With this new Z^{**} value, Table 4.11 can be reconstructed to find out the reduction in purchasing load.

The flexibility of the above two models allows the inventory manager to perform many other permutations and combinations with different objectives in mind.

The simplified examples worked out above indicate a moderate savings on average inventory level (6.34 per cent) and purchasing workload (6.32 per cent) under situation I and II respectively. In the example, we have dealt with an inventory consisting of only five items. We have also not considered their value. When the items are large and/or of high value, then this small percentage savings could be very large. Besides, the above analysis also indicates the extent of value-gain over existing system. If it is negligible, the inventory manager may not like to incur additional systems cost for installing the EOQ.

It is not also unusual to find, after all the calculations, that the existing system is more cost-effective than the EOQ. Managerial intuition may often belie mathematical modelling in real-life situation. But it can be known only after we do the comparative calculations.

QUANTITY DISCOUNTS

It is a common practice amongst suppliers to offer quantity discounts as incentives to buy in larger quantity.[17] The advantages that accrue to the sellers are lower order processing cost or set-up costs and lesser carrying cost of inventories. The ploy is also employed by firms to clear a glut in the inventory.

The advantages to the buyers are many. Quantity discounts effectively reduce the unit cost of materials. As the lot sizes are large, the number of orders will be few and hence, the total ordering costs will be reduced. Transportation costs will also be lowered and the chances of stock-outs will be few. Large buying also enables a retailer to take the advantage of mass display of the products sold (which also provides a publicity mileage to the seller).

As against the above, large quantity buying also involves several costs. The first to reckon with is the higher funding requirement and carrying costs. Stock turnover will be lower which may be frowned upon by the bankers. If quantity buying is the general affair, then it is likely that inventory will be replete with older stocks which may suffer from deterioration and depreciation in value.

The purpose of inventory management is to determine the lot size that minimises total costs.

There are two types of discount offer: (1) *All units discount offer,* where a particular fixed rate is available for all units in a lot. That is, if the buyer crosses a particular quantity discount range, the discount will be available for the purchases in a lot. This results in a lower unit price for the entire lot; (2) *incremental discount offer,* where increasing rates of discounts are offered for higher ranges of quantities purchased. Hence, under this discount offer there shall be multiple unit costs for the same item in a lot. The ranges of quantity at which the price changes are called price breakers.

All Units Discount Offer

Let us begin with the following example.

A company's annual demand of a material is 10,000 units. Presently, price of a unit is Rs. 10, but the supplier offers the following quantity discounts for large purchases.

---

17. Quantity discount is also called trade discount. This must be distinguished from cash discount discussed in Chapter 3. Quantity discount is an incentive to buy more; cash discount is an incentive to pay early.

Order size	Discount offer
1–999 units	No discount
1000 units and above	10% discount
	or Rs. 9 per unit

Ordering cost of the company is Rs. 50 per order and the holding cost is 20 percent per annum. Our job is to find out that particular order size where total cost is at its lowest.

We shall first approach the problem in a straightforward manner, i.e. we shall calculate the total cost under various alternatives and then pick up the order size where the total cost is minimum.

In order to keep the number of alternatives at a reasonable level we shall begin with the EOQ, considering that no discount is offered. If the derived EOQ falls within 1–999 units, then only it is acceptable, otherwise it is rejected.

We know that,

$$Q = \sqrt{\frac{2DC}{PH}} \quad \text{where} \quad \begin{array}{l} P = \text{price per unit} \\ H = \text{holding cost in percent p.a.} \\ \quad \text{Presently, it is } 0.20 \end{array}$$

$$= \sqrt{\frac{2 \times 10,000 \times 50}{10 \times 0.20}}$$

$$= 708 \text{ units}$$

The EOQ at 708 units is falling within the first price range (no discount offer) hence, it can form part of our calculation. It should also be obvious that there cannot lie any EOQ at any other point of purchase order upto 999 units since all are priced at Rs. 10. In Table 4.12 we have calculated inventory positions under various alternatives.

Table 4.12 Finding Out the Optimal Solution under Various 'All Units Discount' Offers

Cost	Quantity per order				
	708 (EOQ)	1000	1200	1500	2000
C. Holding cost					
Average inventory	708/2 = 354	500	600	750	1000
Annual holding cost	354 × 10 × 0.20	500 × 9 × 0.20			
	= Rs. 708	= Rs. 900	1080	1350	1800
B. Ordering cost					
Number of orders	10,000/708 = 14.12	10,000/1000 × 50			
		= Rs. 500			
Annual ordering cost	14.12 × 50 = Rs. 706		417	333	250
A. Purchasing cost	10,000 × 10				
	= Rs. 100,000	10,000 × 9			
		= Rs. 90,000	90,000	90,000	90,000
Total cost (A + B + C)	Rs. 101,414	Rs. 91,400	91,497	91,683	92,050

Table 4.12 indicates that the optimum order quantity should be 1000 units per order because total cost is the lowest here among all the alternatives. It may be observed that the optimal solution is occurring at the price-breaker point. Why it is so is explained later.

We now turn to the analytical solution of the problem. We have already calculated EOQ at Rs. 10 per unit as

$$Q = \sqrt{\frac{2\,DC}{PH}} = 708 \text{ units}$$

EOQ at Rs. 9 per unit will be

$$Q* = \sqrt{\frac{2 \times 10,000 \times 50}{9 \times 0.20}} = 745 \text{ units}$$

EOQ at Rs. 9 per unit is not valid because 745 units cannot be available at Rs. 9 per unit. Hence, we are left with only one valid EOQ of 708 units.

We can now compare this with the total cost at the next higher price-break quantity. We know that the total cost is given by total purchase price + total ordering cost + total holding cost, which can be represented as

$$\text{TC}(Q) = P \times D + \frac{DC}{Q} + \frac{HPQ}{2}$$

Therefore, toal cost at 708 units and at 1000 units (where price break occurs) will be

1. $\text{TC}(708) = 10 \times 10,000 + \dfrac{10,000 \times 50}{708} + \dfrac{0.20 \times 10 \times 708}{2}$

$$= 100,000 + 706 + 708$$

$$= \text{Rs. } 101,414$$

2. $\text{TC}(1000) = 9 \times 10,000 + \dfrac{10,000 \times 50}{1000} + \dfrac{0.20 \times 9 \times 1000}{2}$

$$= 90,000 + 500 + 900$$

$$= \text{Rs. } 91,400$$

Hence, desired optimum order size should be 1000 per order. The results tally with that obtained in Table 4.12.

It should be clear from the above analyses that unlike the earlier cases, a separate total cost curve exists for each price range, and hence a separate EOQ. But such EOQs are not necessarily valid. An EOQ is valid only if it falls within the range corresponding to its unit price; lower unit price will result into lower holding costs in aggregate and larger EOQs along the higher range of the discount offer. As each relevant total cost is minimised either at the feasible EOQ or at the point where price-break occurs, searching the overall optimum order size can be narrowed down to the feasible EOQ and the quantity at the price-breaker. This is precisely what we have observed in Table 4.12. Subsequent mathematical formulation is based on this observed phenomenon. It may be noted that since all quantity discounts do not affect demand or the lead time, they do not also affect the reorder point calculations.

Incremental Discount Offer

Here, each quantity discount is limited only to the units purchased in that discount range. As in the earlier case, we proceed here by working out an example which is a modified form of the earlier one. Here all other things remaining same, the purchaser is offered the following price schedule:

Order size	Unit price (Rs.)
1–999	10
1000–2999	9
3000–5999	8.50
6000–9999	8.00
10,000 and above	7.50

Finding out the optimal solution for incremental discount problem is somewhat more complex than the earlier one because of the opportunity cost of not availing of the quantity discount has to be brought in as a new variable. Unlike *all units discount offer* where unit price is same for all units in a lot, under *incremental discount offer,* discount rate varies upward but each rate is available only for a particular quantity range. Hence, if the order quantity is such that full discount available for the total quantities in a given range cannot be availed of, then it is an opportunity loss for the firm to the extent of unavailed quantity discount. This has, therefore, to be brought into the model as an additional cost. This is similar to fixed ordering cost in the sense that whenever an order is placed, the opportunity cost is incurred for the entire quantity range. How much of this cost is absorbed depends upon the quantity ordered similar to ordering cost. Lesser is the order quantity, lower the absorption and higher the opportunity loss. For example, if the discount is Re. 1 per unit for a quantity range of 1000 units and the order quantity is 600 units, then the unabsorbed opportunity cost is (Rs. 1000 × Re 1) – (Rs. 600 × Re. 1) = Rs. 400. In other words, cost per unit will be increased by Re. 1 – (Rs.1000/600) = Re 0.66 per unit due to opportunity loss.

The original EOQ model can now be modified by incorporating the above variable as

$$Q = \sqrt{\frac{2D(C + O)}{PH}}$$ for every discount range, where O is the cumulative

opportunity cost of a given range, P is the price per unit and H is the holding cost in percentage. For the schedule of discount given in our example, cumulative opportunity costs O are calculated for every price-break in Table 4.13.

Table 4.13 Calculation of Cumulative Opportunity Cost under Incremental Discount Offer

Sl. no.	Price per unit (Rs.)	Price-breaker quantity	Opportunity cost (Rs.)
1.	10	1	0
2.	9	1000	$(1000 - 1)(10 - 9) = 999$
3.	8.50	3000	$999 + (3000 - 1)(9 - 8.50) = 2498$
4.	8.00	6000	$2498 + (6000 - 1)(8.50 - 8) = 5498$
5.	7.50	10,000	$5498 + (10,000 - 1)(8 - 7.50) = 10,498$

We can now calculate EOQ at every price-breaker point with the help of the modified EOQ formula.

1. $$Q(10) = \frac{\sqrt{2 \times 10,000(50 + 0)}}{10 \times 0.20} = 707 \text{ (feasible)}$$

2. $$Q(9) = \frac{\sqrt{2 \times 10,000(50 + 999)}}{9 \times 0.20} = 3414 \text{ (not feasible)}$$

3. $$Q(8.50) = \frac{\sqrt{2 \times 10,000(50 + 2498)}}{8.50 \times 0.20} = 5475 \text{ (feasible)}$$

4. $$Q(8) = \frac{\sqrt{2 \times 10,000(50 + 5498)}}{8 \times 0.20} = 8328 \text{ (feasible)}$$

5. $$Q(7.50) = \frac{\sqrt{2 \times 10,000(50 + 10,498)}}{7.50 \times 0.20} = 11,859 \text{ (not feasible)}$$

It may be observed that $Q(9)$ is not feasible because the required order quantity of 3414 do not fall within the relative discount range. $Q(7.50)$ is also not feasible because the order size of 11,859 exceeds the total annual demand of 10,000 units.[18] Of the remaining three feasible solutions we shall decide on the one which has least total cost. Total cost TC (Q) is given as

$$\text{TC}(Q) = \text{Purchase cost} + \text{Ordering cost} + \text{Holding cost}$$

or

$$\text{TC}(Q) = D \times P + \frac{D(C + O)}{Q} + H\left[\frac{(P \times Q) + O}{2}\right]$$

---

18. Except for defence procurement, volume purchase for more than the total annual demand is inadvisable because many of the parameters like, that of demand and costs may undergo substantial changes beyond a year. Inventory norms evolved by banks in India also do not permit inventory holding beyond 3-4 months' consumption except in the case of imported spare parts.

Therefore,

$$TC(707) = 10,000 \times 10 + \frac{10,000(50+0)}{707} + 0.20\left[\frac{(10 \times 707)+0}{2}\right] = Rs.\ 101,414$$

$$TC(5475) = 10,000 \times 8.50 + \frac{10,000(50+2498)}{5475} + 0.20\left[\frac{(8.50 \times 5475)+2498}{2}\right]$$

$$= Rs.\ 94,557$$

$$TC(8328) = 10,000 \times 8 + \frac{10,000(50+5498)}{8328} + 0.20\left[\frac{(8 \times 8328)+5498}{2}\right]$$

$$= Rs.\ 93,874$$

The optimal solution lies at ordering 8328 units per order at a price of Rs. 8 per unit because the total cost is the least among the three alternatives. The firm should place order every $(365 \times 8328)/10,000 = 304$th day of the year.

PRESENT VALUE APPROACH

By now, it should be clear that all the EOQ models have a cost focus. They attempt to minimise period costs of inventory management. A recent criticism of EOQ approach is that it ignores the timing of various cash outflows that result from a particular inventory policy. It is a recognised principle that any alternative inventory policy is acceptable only when it increases the present value (PV) of the firm. But the EOQ system is not amenable to wealth maximisation framework. Although there can be no doubt, at least in theory, that present value approach is superior to cost focus approach embedded in EOQ models, what is important for us is to consider whether it leads to superior decision-making.

Special Features of Wealth Maximisation Framework

1. The timing of making payments (cash outflows) is not explicit in EOQ model while it is the essence of PV approach. The dominant cash outflow is payment for cost of purchases. If payments are immediate, as in the case of cash purchases, there may not be any difference between PV approach and EOQ model. But most often firms enjoy a credit term. Longer the credit term lower will be the present value of cash outflows, hence higher will be the value of the firm. Other cash outflows are due to physical as well as financial carrying cost of inventories. In the absence of specific payment pattern, these costs are assumed to be paid at the end of every quarter.

2. Financial cost of carrying inventory (opportunity cost) is calculated on the average level of inventory holding, i.e. half of optimal order quantity as in EOQ model. As items are gradually released from inventory for sale, funds committed in them are also released. If sales are made in cash, there would be a matching cash inflow as well. Hence, calculation of finance cost on average level of inventory is justified. Even when sales are not made in cash but on credit, then also it is justified because the problem is no longer of the inventory managment

but of accounts receivable department. However, when items are released for production no fund transfer is assumed till the finished goods are sold.

3. Sometimes special credit terms are offered by suppliers depending on the quantity purchased. This may not create much problem because after the initial order, average level of accounts payable will show a steady pattern.

4. Decision criterion under PV approach is straightforward. If net present value of the cash outflows of the proposed policy is lower than that of the existing one, the proposal is acceptable.

5. EOQ modelling for inventory decision is simple and less costly to instal and administer. The PV approach is more accurate, but the system's cost is much larger than the EOQ system. It is also a complex system which requires trained personnel.

Let us first understand the PV approach with the help of an example. We shall critically evaluate the new approach later.

Example   Quarterly demand of a particular item of inventory is 20,000 units. Purchase price is Rs. 10 per unit. Physical carrying cost of the inventory is found to be Re. 0.85 per unit while the financial carrying cost-(opportunity cost) of the firm is 17.20 percent per annum. The ordering cost is Rs. 50 per order on an average. The firm enjoys a credit period of 45 days.

Presently, the firm places 10 orders of 2000 unit each during the quarter. The firm is prepared to consider alternative proposal if it is cost-effective and increases the value of the firm. Assume 360 days a year or 90 days a quarter.

Present value (PV) of an inventory policy is given by the following equation:

$$PV(Q) = \frac{(DC/Q) + hQ/2}{1 + km} + \sum_{i=0}^{(D/Q)-1} \frac{QP(1-d)}{1 + k(n + im\,Q/D)}$$

As given in this example

Q = quantity per order (required)
D = demand of quantity during the period which is 20,000 units
C = order cost per order which is Rs. 50
h = physical carrying cost of inventory which is Re. 0.85 per unit
m = number of days in the period which is 90 days
P = price per unit which is Rs. 10
d = rate of discount in percentage which is 0
k = financial carrying cost (opportunity cost) of inventory per day per rupee which will be $17.20/(360 \times 100)$ = Re. 0.0004778
n = credit period enjoyed by the firm which is 45 days
i = 0, 1, 2, ..., (D/Q) – 1. That is, the number of times the inventory is ordered during the period.

Required order size (Q) of the inventory shall be such where present value (PV) of cash outflows is at its minimum. We shall adopt an iterative process with the assumed order size (Q) of 1000 units, 1250 units, 2000 units and 2500 units and then pick up the one where PV of cash outflows is the least.

Incorporating the figures from the example in the above equation, we get the following:

(a) Order-size (Q) = 1000 units; i = (20,000/1000) − 1 = 19

$$PV(Q) = \frac{\dfrac{20,000 \times 50}{1000} + \dfrac{0.85 \times 1000}{2}}{1 + (0.0004778 \times 90)} + \sum_{i=0}^{19} \frac{1000 \times 10}{1 + 0.0004778 \left(45 + i \times 90 \times \dfrac{1000}{20,000}\right)}$$

$$= \frac{1000 + 425}{1.043} + \sum_{i=0}^{19} \frac{10,000}{1 + 0.0004778(45 + i \times 4.50)}$$

$$= 1366.25 + \sum_{i=0}^{19} \frac{10,000}{1.0215 + i \times 0.00215}$$

$$= 1366.25 + 191,979.56$$

$$= \text{Rs. } 193,345.81$$

(b) Order size (Q) = 1250 units; i = (20,000/1250) − 1 = 15

$$PV(Q) = \frac{\dfrac{20,000 \times 50}{1250} + \dfrac{0.85 \times 1250}{2}}{1 + (0.0004778 \times 90)} + \sum_{i=0}^{15} \frac{1250 \times 10}{1 + 0.0004778 \left(45 + i \times 90 \times \dfrac{1250}{20,000}\right)}$$

$$= \frac{800 + 531.25}{1.043} + \sum_{i=0}^{15} \frac{12,500}{1 + 0.0004778(45 + i \times 5.625)}$$

$$= 1276.36 + \sum_{i=0}^{15} \frac{12,500}{1.0215 + i \times 0.0026876}$$

$$= 1276.36 + 192,028.93$$

$$= \text{Rs. } 193,305.29$$

(c) Order size (Q) = 2000 units; i = (20,000/2000) − 1 = 9

$$PV(Q) = \frac{\dfrac{20,000 \times 50}{2000} + \dfrac{0.85 \times 2000}{2}}{1 + (0.0004778 \times 90)} + \sum_{i=0}^{9} \frac{2000 \times 10}{1 + 0.0004778 \left(45 + i \times 90 \times \dfrac{2000}{20,000}\right)}$$

$$= \frac{500 + 850}{1.043} + \sum_{i=0}^{9} \frac{20,000}{1 + 0.0004778(45 + i \times 9)}$$

$$= 1294.34 + \sum_{i=0}^{9} \frac{20,000}{1.0215 + i \times 0.0043}$$

$$= 1294.34 + 192,177.70$$

$$= \text{Rs. } 193,472.04$$

(d) Order size = 2500 units; $i = (20,000/2500) - 1 = 7$

$$PV(Q) = \frac{\dfrac{2000 \times 50}{2500} + \dfrac{0.85 \times 2500}{2}}{1 + (0.0004778 \times 90)} + \sum_{i=0}^{7} \frac{2500 \times 10}{1 + 0.0004778\left(45 + i \times 90 \times \dfrac{2500}{20,000}\right)}$$

$$= \frac{400 + 1062.50}{1.043} + \sum_{i=0}^{7} \frac{25,000}{1 + 0.0004778(45 + i \times 11.25)}$$

$$= 1402.20 + \sum_{i=0}^{7} \frac{25,000}{1.0215 + i \times 0.005375}$$

$$= 1402.20 + 192,276.87$$

$$= Rs. \ 193,679.07$$

Results of the iterative processes are summarised below:

Order size (Q) units	Present value of total cost (Rs.)
1000	193,345.81
1250	193,305.29
2000	193,472.04
2500	193,679.07

It is clear from above that PV of total costs is at its minimum when $Q = 1250$ units. Hence, the firm should place 16 orders of 1250 each during the quarter at an interval of 90/16 = 5.63 or 6 days.

We have mentioned earlier that PV approach under wealth maximisation framework is superior to cost focus approach of EOQ model. The question is whether it offers superior decision-making. The issue is examined below by finding out the required order quantity with the help of EOQ model.

$$EOQ = \sqrt{\frac{2DC}{h + P \times k \times m}}$$

Incorporating the figures from the example into above model, the equation becomes

$$EOQ = \sqrt{\frac{2 \times 20,000 \times 50}{0.85 + 10 \times 0.0004778 \times 90}}$$

$$= \sqrt{\frac{2,000,000}{1.28}} = 1250 \text{ units}$$

We, therefore, find that the EOQ model offers the same solution as that obtained under PV approach in spite of the fact that the former ignores payment terms (credit period) and other aspects of time value of money.

The issue—whether PV approach should be adopted instead of traditional EOQ model for inventory decisions—is under debate for a long time. Although in theory, the PV approach is always superior, it has been observed from empirical researches that in most instances, the EOQ model recommends order quantities that are quite consistent with the recommendations of the PV approach, and sufficiently accurate for practical applications.[19] Followill et al[20] challenged the findings and critised the traditional EOQ model as it might lead to wealth-decreasing inventory decisions, particularly when quantity discounts are available, i.e. when d in our above model has a positive value. They argued that since quantity discounts alter the size and timing of the purchaser's inventory investment cash flows, the effects of these changes must be weighed against increases in inventory ordering and carrying costs associated with an increased order quantity. The EOQ model by ignoring these aspects may recommend a certain quantity (discounts) that should not be accepted, or reject certain other quantity (discounts) that should be accepted. However, Joglekar and Kelley[21] have found that Followill et al have assumed unreasonable parameter values to base their findings. They asserted that when typical values of relevant parameters prevail, the worst that a traditional EOQ model user can expect is a loss of approximately 8/10th of one percent of the PV of lifetime costs of a product. Hence, they concluded that even in situation of volume discounts, the EOQ model may yield decisions that are sufficiently accurate for practical applications. Of course, in intensely competitive industries, where firms are looking at every penny of the operating costs, the PV approach to quantity discounts could be the desired approach, but in most firms, the costs of implementing the PV approach may be substantial. Hence, it may be counterproductive to the very goal of wealth maximisation.[22]

ORDERING INTERVALS

Fixed Order System

Under this system, the same quantity of goods is always ordered but the timing of the placement of the order varies with fluctuations in usage. The idea is to place an order whenever the inventory on hand is just sufficient to meet a reasonable maximum demand based on usage during both the lead time and order interval.

In cases where lead time is long as compared with the quantity purchased per order in terms of days' consumption, it may be found that some purchase orders are outstanding all the time, which, when filled, will replenish the existing inventory. Reorder points in such cases are to be based upon both

---

19. See for example, McDaniel, W.R., "The Economic Order Quantity Problem and Wealth Maximisation", *The Financial Review*, November 1986, pp. 227–232.
20. Followill, R.A., M. Schellenger and P.H. Marchand, "Economic Order Quantities, Volume Discounts and Wealth Maximisation", *The Financial Review*, February 1990, pp. 143–155.
21. Joglekar, P. and J.M. Kelly, "Volume Discount Decisions: Wealth Maximisation or EOQ Approach?", *Naval Research Logistics*, Vol. 45, 1998, pp. 377–389.
22. *Ibid.*

quantity on hand and on order. On the other hand, when lead time is short as compared to the quantity purchased per order, the quantity on hand and the total balance on that order would all be equivalent at the time of reordering. This system is useful in management of stores, spareparts and input materials in plant, generally known as 'floor stocks' where the inventory consists of items of low unit costs which are purchased in large quantities as compared to their rate of consumption. Generally, these items do not require very tight control, either because these represent a small part of the productive-distributive inventories held by a firm, or because these can be obtained from sources without any strict ordering schedule.

As the order size is fixed under this system, the question essentially boils down to finding out the fixed review period (*T*) and the maximum inventory level (*E*). The fixed order interval system is also known as *T*-system.

Like any other EOQ model, the *economic order interval* (EOI) is derived at a point where the total cost is at its minimum. This point will essentially lie where ordering cost is equal to holding cost. This is presented graphically in Figure 4.5.

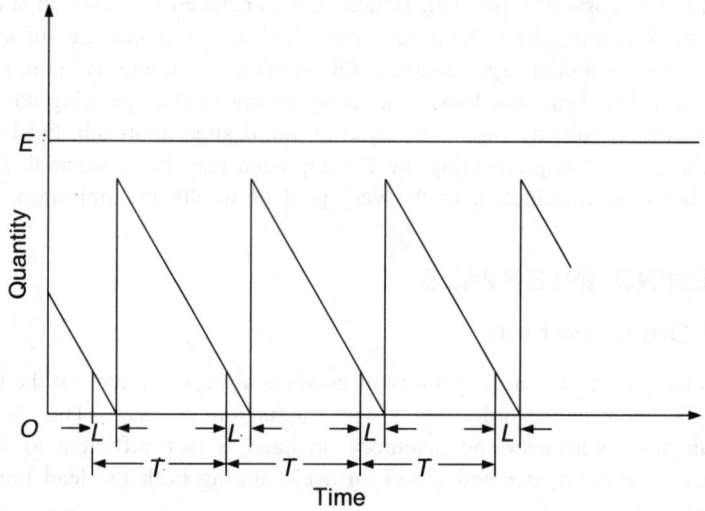

Figure 4.5 Fixed order interval system.

We now define the following parameters:

1. Order interval (years): $T = \dfrac{1}{N}$; where N is number of orders per year

2. Number of orders per year: $N = \dfrac{1}{T}$

3. Average inventory in units: $\dfrac{D}{N} \times \dfrac{1}{2} = \dfrac{D}{N2} = \dfrac{D}{\frac{1}{T} \times 2} = \dfrac{DT}{2}$

Hence,

Total purchase costs = $D \times P$

$$\text{Total ordering costs} = N \times C = \frac{1}{T} \times C = \frac{C}{T}$$

$$\text{Total holding costs} = \frac{DT}{2} \times H$$

where C and H are fixed ordering cost per order and holding cost per unit respectively and P is price per unit.

Now, as economic order interval T lies at a point where total holding costs and ordering costs are equal, we have

$$\frac{DTH}{2} = \frac{C}{T}$$

or

$$DT^2H = 2C$$

or

$$T^2 = \frac{2C}{DH}$$

or

$$T = \sqrt{\frac{2C}{DH}} \text{ (in years)}$$

We have said that maximum inventory level E should be large enough to meet the demand of inventory during both the subsequent order interval and also during the lead time L. Hence, maximum inventory level E is given by

$$E = \frac{D \times T \times Y}{Y} + \frac{D \times L}{Y} = DT + \frac{DL}{Y} = \frac{D(YT + L)}{Y}$$

Where Y is number of working days in a year. Let us explain the models with the help of the following example.

Example Annual demand of a material ordered by a firm is 20,000 units. The purchase price is Rs. 100 per unit. Ordering cost is found to be Rs. 320 per order. Holding cost (both physical and financial) is Rs. 25 per unit per annum. The firm desires to know the economic order interval, the maximum inventory level and the total annual cost. Assume lead time to be 20 days and there are 300 working days in a year.

1. Economic order interval $(T) = \sqrt{\dfrac{2C}{DH}}$

$$= \sqrt{\frac{2 \times 320}{20,000 \times 25}}$$

$$= 0.03578 \text{ years}$$

$$= 0.3578 \times 300$$

$$= 10.73 \text{ days, say 11 days}$$

2. Maximum inventory level $(E) = \dfrac{D(YT + L)}{Y}$

$$= \frac{20,000(300 \times 0.03578 + 20)}{300}$$

$$= 2048.93, \text{ say } 2050 \text{ units}$$

3. Total costs $[\text{TC }(Q)] = DP + \dfrac{C}{T} + \dfrac{DTH}{2}$

$$= 20,000 \times 100 + \frac{320}{0.03578} + \frac{20,000 \times 0.03578 \times 25}{2}$$

$$= 2,000,000 + 8944 + 8944$$

$$= \text{Rs. } 2,017,888$$

As the quantity to be ordered remains fixed at EOQ, i.e. $\sqrt{\dfrac{2 \times 20,000 \times 320}{25}}$

= 715.54 units, the firm should place an order of, say 715 units every 11th day of the year.

Multiple Items

The fixed order interval system discussed above takes care of single item ordering. But in businesses, particularly in retail and wholesale, hardly a single item is ordered at a time. It is also found in this type of businesses that a particular supplier supplies numerous items, e.g. groceries, spare parts etc. and it becomes economical for both the parties when, instead of single item, joint order for a number of items are placed.

When all items, though different products, are ordered from one source by a joint order, it is easy to coordinate stock level review for all these items and keep the inventory maintenance cost at its minimum. Other economies of scale relate to transportation, material handling, inspection, and monitoring activities.

While placing joint orders, the quantity of each item to be ordered would depend upon the time interval between orders for the group of items as a whole. We have, therefore, to determine the time interval T which will minimise the costs of inventory for the entire group. The next problem is to determine the maximum inventory level E and individual order quantity for every item of the group.

As before, economic order interval T is determined by minimising the total costs which have the usual three components:

1. Total purchase costs $= \displaystyle\sum_{i=1}^{m} D_i P_i$

where $i = 1, 2, 3, \ldots, m$ = number of items in a group

2. Total ordering costs $= \dfrac{C}{T} + \dfrac{c \times m}{T} = \dfrac{C + cm}{T}$

where

C = order cost for ordering the entire group of items

c = order preperation cost for individual items in a group

m = number of items in a group

3. Total holding costs = $\dfrac{\left(\displaystyle\sum_{i=1}^{m} D_i P_i\right)}{2} h \times T = \dfrac{Th}{2} \displaystyle\sum_{i=1}^{m} D_i P_i$

where h = holding cost per rupee per annum.

As usual, economic order interval (T) shall lie at a point where ordering costs equal holding costs. Hence,

$$\frac{C + cm}{T} = \frac{Th}{2} \sum_{i=1}^{m} D_i P_i$$

or

$$T^2 h \sum_{i=1}^{m} D_i P_i = 2(C + cm)$$

or

$$T^2 = \frac{2(C + cm)}{h \displaystyle\sum_{i=1}^{m} D_i P_i}$$

or

$$T = \sqrt{\frac{2(C + cm)}{h \displaystyle\sum_{i=1}^{m} D_i P_i}} \quad \text{(in years)}$$

The maximum holding of inventory for each item (E_i) shall be large enough to take care of the requirement during both the subsequent order interval and lead time. Hence, for each item of inventory

$$E_i = D_i T + \frac{D_i L}{Y} = \frac{D_i(YT + L)}{Y}$$

And the total cost is given by

$$TC(Q) = \sum_{i=1}^{m} D_i P_i + \frac{C + cm}{T} + \frac{Th}{2} \sum_{i=1}^{m} D_i P_i$$

$$= \sum_{i=1}^{m} D_i P_i \left[1 + \frac{Th}{2}\right] + \frac{C + cm}{T}$$

Example An enterprise purchases six items from a supplier, the particulars of which are given in Table 4.14.

Table 4.14 Costs and Demand Particulars of Various Items

(Amount in Rs.)

Item code	Annual demand (D_i)	Cost per unit (P_i)	Total purchase cost (D_iP_i)
021	225	50	11,250
052	600	10	6000
067	190	20	3800
074	150	25	3750
082	1200	15	18,000
085	344	50	17,200
			60,000

The ordering cost is Rs. 225 per order while the same for individual item is Rs. 75 per order. The holding cost (both physical and financial) is 20 percent p.a. The ordering lead time is 30 days, assuming working days in a year to be 300.

1. Economic ordering interval (T) = $\sqrt{\dfrac{2(C+cm)}{h\sum\limits_{i=1}^{m} D_iP_i}}$

$$= \sqrt{\dfrac{2(225 + 75 \times 6)}{0.20 \times 60,000}}$$

$$= \sqrt{\dfrac{1350}{12,000}} = 0.3354 \text{ years}$$

or $0.3354 \times 300 = 100$ days

2. Economic order quantity (EOQ) for individual item will be given by $\sqrt{\dfrac{2D_i(C+cm)}{P_ih}}$.

For example, EOQ for item code 021 shall be $\sqrt{\dfrac{2 \times 225(225+75)}{20 \times 0.20}} = 183.71$, or say, 184 units.

3. Maximum inventory level for each item of the purchase order is calculated in Table 4.15 in terms of the formula, $E_i = D_i(YT+L)/Y$.

4. Total costs = $\sum\limits_{i=1}^{m} D_iP_i\left[1+\dfrac{Th}{2}\right] + \dfrac{C+cm}{T}$

$$= 60,000\left(1+\dfrac{0.3354 \times 0.20}{2}\right) + \dfrac{225+75\times 6}{0.3354}$$

$$= 62,012.40 + 2012.52 = \text{Rs. } 64,024.92$$

Table 4.15 EOQ and Maximum Level of Inventory Holding of Different Items

Item code	Annual demand (D_i)	Economic order quantity (EOQ)	Ordering interval (T) (years)	Lead time (L)	No. of working days (Y)	Maximum level $[D_i(YT+L)/Y]$
021	225	183.71	0.3354	30	300	97.96 = 98
052	600	424.26	0.3354	30	300	261.24 = 261
067	190	168.82	0.3354	30	300	82.73 = 83
074	150	134.16	0.3354	30	300	65.31 = 65
082	1200	484.90	0.3354	30	300	522.48 = 523
085	344	143.67	0.3354	30	300	149.78 = 150

Periodic Order System

We have seen that under fixed order system the size of the order does not vary but the ordering time is allowed to vary. Under periodic ordering system, timing of review is fixed, but the order size varies depending upon the quantity on hand at the time of previously determined date of ordering. This system is suitable for firms who have accounting control of inventory and whose types of inventories are such as are capable of being physically examined at periodic intervals. The periodic ordering system is mostly in use where items of inventory are of high value and/or critical to production which requires tight control and monitoring. These items constitute large part of total inventory usage in terms of their value in production and/or distribution. This system is frequently used in warehouses.

Under this system, projection of quantities required during the reorder interval and lead time is made and then the order quantity is determined to bring the total quantity on hand and on order upto the total of the quantities so projected for the lead time and ordering cycle.

The fixed economic order interval is given simply by dividing the EOQ with the average rate of demand during the period, i.e.

$$\text{Fixed economic order interval (FEOI)} = \frac{\text{EOQ}}{\overline{D}} = \sqrt{\frac{2C}{\overline{D}hP}}$$

where $\overline{D}$ is the average demand per period and h is the holding cost fraction per period.

Once the reorder point is determined as above the quantity to be ordered at each interval (lot size) is calculated by adding up the total requirement during the periods falling within each such interval. Let us explain this with the help of the following example.

Example Projected demand of an inventory item during a twelve-monthly period is given in Table 4.16.

The purchase price of the item is Rs. 180 per unit. The ordering cost is Rs. 400 per order and the holding cost is 24 percent p.a.

Table 4.16 Projected Demand of an Inventory Item

Monthly period	Demand (D)
1	30
2	15
3	55
4	180
5	15
6	25
7	140
8	90
9	30
10	40
11	25
12	15
	660

From the above example we find the following:

Average demand $(\overline{D})$ = 660/12 = 55 units

Ordering cost (C) = Rs. 400 per order

Purchase cost (P) = Rs. 180 per unit

Holding cost (h) = 24/(12 × 100) = 0.02

Incorporating the above figures in the model, we obtain:

$$\text{Fixed economic order interval (FEOI)} = \sqrt{\frac{2 \times 400}{55 \times 0.02 \times 180}}$$

$$= 2.01 \text{ say, 2 periods.}$$

Thus a two-period reording cycle would require the following lot sizes (Table 4.17) to be calculated from Table 4.15 given above.

Table 4.17 Periodic Ordering and Lot Sizes

Monthly period	Demand	Lot size
1	30	45
2	15	—
3	55	235
4	180	—
5	15	40
6	25	—
7	140	230
8	90	—
9	30	70
10	40	—
11	25	40
12	15	—
	660	660

Note: If the reordering cycle (FEOI) comes in a fraction, it should be rounded off to the nearest integer before calculating the lot sizes.

It may be seen from Table 4.17 that lot sizes to be ordered vary during the two-period ordering intervals. In this sense, it is considered as an improvement upon the traditional EOQ system. But because of the fixed order interval the FEOI does not allow combining orders for additional periods with low quantity demand, which could be economical for the firm.

BATCH PRODUCTION

In this type of production system products are manufactured in batches or in lots. Generally, multiple products or a family of products are manufactured in the same plant. This gives rise to allocation problems. What is necessary, therefore, is to devise a method by which existing production capacity is allocated among various products in regard to their demands, production rates and the present inventory levels. Planning batch production; requires the determination of optimum batch size in each production run to minimise total annual cost. We shall first discuss the methodology for determining optimum size of a single product manufacturing under a batch system and then move over to multiple products.

Single Product

EOQ model can be modified by redefining the costs in a production system. The acquisition cost is defined as the cost of production when goods are manufactured in-house. Ordering cost is equivalent to set-up costs which include cost of processing the work order and authorising production; engineering cost includes cost of setting up the machines and facilities, and cost of making requisitions of materials and stores for production, etc. It may be noted that the time required for *set-up* or *set-up time* as is known popularly, is a significant constraint to realising full plant capacity. Holding cost is the cost of carrying the finished products from the time these are manufactured to the date these are sold. Assuming no stock-out (cost), the annual inventory cost can be given as

Total annual cost = Cost of production + Set-up cost + Holding cost

Putting this equation within EOI framework we can write

$$TC(Q) = D \times P + \frac{DC}{Q} + \frac{HQ(p-u)}{2p}$$

where

D = annual demand in units
P = cost of production
Q = production order quantity or batch size
C = set-up cost
H = holding cost per unit per year
u = rate of demand
p = rate of production

The difference between the EOQ models discussed earlier and the present one is the inclusion of demand rate u and production rate p in the model. The optimum lot size in the case of production is needed to be determined under a situation where finished products are being sold (consumed) while each lot is being manufactured. Thus, inventory of finished products does not go up immediately to the maximum level, instead it builds up gradually as goods are manufactured faster than they are being sold. It declines then to its lowest point as production of a particular batch stops but sales continue. This phenomenon is captured in Figure 4.6.

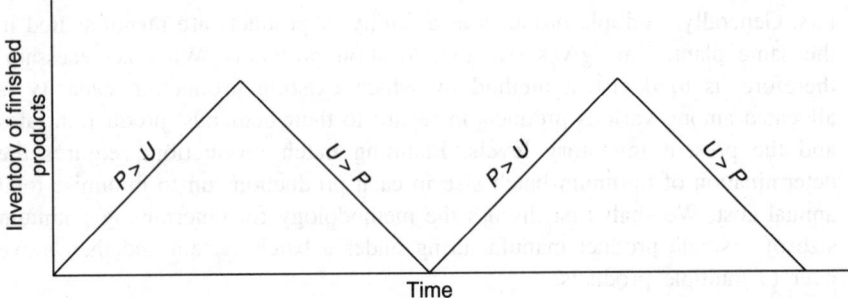

Figure 4.6 Finished products inventory holding pattern under simultaneous production and sales.

We have already seen that EOQ will lie at a point where ordering cost (set-up cost) is equal to holding cost. Thus

$$\frac{DC}{Q} = \frac{HQ(p-u)}{2p}$$

or

$$Q^2 H (p - u) = 2DCp$$

or

$$Q^2 = \frac{2DCp}{H(p-u)}$$

or

$$Q = \sqrt{\frac{2DCp}{H(p-u)}}$$

Having derived the optimum production quantity Q we can proceed to find out the *optimum length of production run* (OLP) simply by dividing Q by the rate of production (p) or Q/p. Production runs (PR) per year will be given by D/Q.

If now we denote N as the number of working days in a year and L as the set-up or lead time in days, then *production reorder point* (PRP) in units will be given by

$$PRP = \frac{D}{N} \times L$$

Let us explain the model with the help of the following example.

Example A firm manufactures an item which has a demand of 18,000 units in a year. It can manufacture 70 such units per day. Cost of production is Rs. 42 per unit and the holding cost is Rs. 10 per unit per year. Set-up cost is Rs. 24 per run and the set-up time is 2 days. Assume there are 360 days in a year.

Applying the above formulae we derive the following:

$$\text{Rate of demand } (u) = \frac{18{,}000}{360} = 50 \text{ units a day}$$

Rate of production (p) = 70 units a day (given)

Thus,

1. Optimum production units (Q) $= \sqrt{\dfrac{2 \times 18{,}000 \times 24 \times 70}{10(70-50)}}$

$$= 549.90, \text{ say } 550 \text{ units per batch}$$

2. Production runs (PR) $= \dfrac{18{,}000}{550} = 32.73$ runs per year

3. Optimum length of production (OLP)

$$= \frac{550}{70} = 7.86 \text{ days}$$

4. Production reorder point (PRP) $= \dfrac{18{,}000 \times 2}{360} = 100$ units

5. Total cost $[TC(Q)] = 18{,}000 \times 42 + \dfrac{18{,}000 \times 24}{550} + \dfrac{10 \times 550(70-50)}{2 \times 70}$

$$= 756{,}000 + 785 + 785$$

$$= \text{Rs. } 757{,}570$$

6. Average inventory holding = 550/2 = 225

It may be noted that when rate of production is same as rate of demand, there shall be no accumulation of inventory. The item must be produced continuously. With the help of the above parameters, production planning, monitoring and control at the plant level and working capital management at the enterprise level become more effective in batch type productive system.

Multiple Products

When a number of products are manufactured in batches on a regular cycle the total length of the production cycle becomes equal to the time to manufacture one full sequence of items. The optimum cycle length should, therefore, be established for the entire family of items rather than for each individual product. In order to resolve the scheduling problems for multiple items of production the model must determine the number of cycles in a period that minimises the total cost of the entire family of products.

The model to be used in a multiple products situation is an extension of the model for single item as discussed before because same arguments hold good in this case also. Assuming no stock-out, cost components for a family of items will be given by

1. Costs of production $= \sum_{i=1}^{n} D_i P_i$

where

D_i = annual demand of individual unit (i)
P_i = cost of production for item (i)

2. Set-up costs $= L \sum_{i=1}^{n} C_i$

where

L = number of cycles in a year
C_i = set-up cost for each cycle

3. Holding costs. Average inventory holding for a given (i) depends upon its rate of demand and production during each cycle run. It will, therefore, be $D_i(p_i - u_i)/2Lp_i$. Holding costs will be incurred on this quantity. Hence, for the entire family of items, total costs payable will be

$$\sum_{i=1}^{n} \frac{D_i(p_i - u_i) \times H_i}{2Lp_i}$$

or

$$\frac{1}{2L} \sum_{i=1}^{n} \frac{D_i H_i(p_i - u_i)}{p_i}$$

where

p_i = rate of production for product (i)
H_i = holding cost per unit
u_i = rate of demand (consumption) for product (i)

As the minimum total cost condition is satisfied where set-up costs equal holding cost, we can write

$$L \sum_{i=1}^{n} C_i = \frac{1}{2L} \sum_{i=1}^{n} \frac{D_i H_i(p_i - u_i)}{p_i}$$

or

$$L^2 \sum_{i=1}^{n} C_i = \frac{1}{2} \sum_{i=1}^{n} \frac{D_i H_i(p_i - u_i)}{p_i}$$

or

$$L^2 = \frac{\dfrac{1}{2} \sum_{i=1}^{n} \dfrac{D_i H_i(p_i - u_i)}{p_i}}{\sum_{i=1}^{n} C_i}$$

or

$$L = \sqrt{\frac{\displaystyle\sum_{i=1}^{n} \frac{D_i H_i (p_i - u_i)}{p_i}}{2 \displaystyle\sum_{i=1}^{n} C_i}}$$

The size of the production Q run for a given cycle, can be given simply by

$$Q_i = \frac{D_i}{L}$$

Example A manufacturer finds that four of his product ranges are manufactured by the same plant and equipment. A study of these four products has revealed the following characteristics (Table 4.18).

Table 4.18 Production Characteristics of Four Products Using Common Facilities

Item code	Yearly demand (D_i)	Unit cost of production (P_i)	Daily production rate (p_i)	Set-up cost (C_i)	Holding cost (H_i)
		(Rs.)		(Rs.)	(Rs.)
01	12,000	60	400	250	15
02	18,000	48	200	340	12
03	8400	36	420	250	5
04	6000	72	150	800	18

The factory has 200 actual working days. We need to formulate minimum cost production cycles.

The capacity of the plant to produce these four items in terms of days is obtained by dividing the annual demand by daily production rate. That is,

$$= \frac{12{,}000}{400} + \frac{18{,}000}{200} + \frac{8400}{420} + \frac{6000}{150}$$

$$= 30 + 90 + 20 + 40$$

$$= 180 \text{ days}$$

The four products can, therefore, be manufactured within the given 200 days capacity of the plant and machinery.

Daily demand (consumption) rate (u_i) of the four products is calculated by dividing the annual demand of each product by the number of working days available. That is,

Product code	Daily demand rate (u_i)
01	12,000/200 = 60
02	18,000/200 = 90
03	8400/200 = 42
04	6000/200 = 30

In Table 4.19, we compute the required figures for incorporating in our model.

Table 4.19

Product code (i)	Annual demand	Daily production rate (p_i)	Daily demand rate (u_i)	$D_i(p_i - u_i)/p_i$	H_i	$D_iH_i[(p_i - u_i)/p_i]$	Set-up cost (C_i)
(1)	(2)	(3)	(4)	(5)	(6)	(7)	(8)
01	12,000	400	60	10,200	15	153,000	250
02	18,000	200	90	9900	12	118,800	340
03	8400	420	42	7560	5	37,800	250
04	6000	150	30	4800	18	86,400	800
						$\Sigma = 396,000$	1640

Hence,

1. $$L = \sqrt{\frac{\displaystyle\sum_{i=1}^{4} \frac{D_i H_i (p_i - u_i)}{p_i}}{2 \displaystyle\sum_{i=1}^{4} C_i}} = \sqrt{\frac{396,000}{2 \times 1640}} = 10.99, \text{ say 11 cycles}$$

2. Total minimum costs will be given by

    Cost of production + Set-up costs + Holding costs

or

$$TC(L) = \sum_{i=1}^{4} D_i P_i + L \sum_{i=1}^{4} C_i + \frac{1}{2L} \sum_{i=1}^{4} \frac{D_i H_i (p_i - u_i)}{p_i}$$

$$= \text{Rs. } 2,318,400 + \text{Rs. } 11 \times 1640 + \text{Rs. } \frac{1}{2 \times 11} \times 396,000$$

$$= \text{Rs. } 2,318,400 + 18,040 + 18,000$$

$$= \text{Rs. } 2,354,440, \text{ say Rs. } 2,354,400, \text{ as second and third terms of the equation should have been equal but for approximation}$$

3. The size of the production run for each product in a given cycle is given by $Q_i = \dfrac{D_i}{L}$.

These are calculated in Table 4.20.

Table 4.20 Production-run Size for the Four Products

Product code (i)	Yearly demand (D_i)	Production-run size $Q_i = (D_i/11)$
01	12,000	1090.90 = 1091
02	18,000	1636.36 = 1636
03	8400	763.63 = 764
04	6000	545.45 = 545

It should be noted that optimum number of cycles (L) per year is independent of capacity considerations. In other words, it assumes that sufficient capacity is available. Hence, before we embark on this model, we have to satisfy ourselves that sufficient capacity is available in the plant to produce the multiple items in terms of their demand and rate of production, as in the present example. If sufficient capacity is not available, the model will not work. In a situation like that, alternative steps like overtime, sub-contracting and ultimately, capacity expansion may have to be undertaken.

BUFFER INVENTORY

We have discussed in Chapter 1 that of the various types of discrete working-capital-assets, buffer inventory of both raw materials and finished products provide safety nets for two major enterprise functions, namely production and distribution, against sudden lengthening of productive-distributive chain.

Buffer inventory can be of two types: *anticipation stock* and *safety stock*, though the two terms are often used interchangeably.

Anticipation Stock

These inventories are predominantly held by enterprises which are highly seasonal in nature. They are meant to provide flexibility to the enterprise against variations in purchasing, production or sales from seasonal factors. However, besides seasonality, anticipation stocks are also held to subserve irregular requirements of inventories like planned shutdowns, promotional campaigns, strikes or breakdowns. As the name suggests, anticipation inventories are procured in advance and allowed to be depleted during peak demand period. These inventories are held in addition to regular safety stock that we shall discuss later. In planning the level of anticipation stock, the combined cost of being out of stock and of carrying inventory are to be minimised.[23]

Whether anticipation stock is required to take care of the seasonality of sales, or a promotional sales campaign, or for other eventualities as mentioned above, the problem ultimately is whether to balance the risk of not having enough stock to fill the demand and thus losing the profit, or of being forced to take urgent steps to buy or produce the goods to fill the demand, vis-á-vis running the risks of having too high an inventory level and hence suffering from risks of wastage and obsolescence.

Magee used the classical 'Newsboy example' to explain the type of 'crash' problem that an inventory manager faces under situations mentioned above.[24]

Example Suppose that a newspaper vendor has, on an average, 10 customers a day. The price of the newspaper is Rs. 5 per copy. The vendor makes a profit of Rs. 3 per copy sold but loses Re. 1 on each copy that remains unsold. The

23. Sishtla, V.S.P., *Working Capital Management in Public Enterprises,* ICPE Monograph Series No. 5, International Centre for Public Enterprises in Developing Countries, Titova, Ljubljana, 1982.
24. Magee, John, F., "Guides to Inventory Policy: Anticipating Future Needs", Harvard Business Review, May–June 1956, Reprinted in *Inventory Policy,* Monograph Series, Harvard University Press, Boston, pp. 184–197.

vendor's records of daily sales reveal that 40 percent of the time he can sell at least 10 papers and 20 percent of the time he can sell at least 12 papers.

Now, every day when the vendor takes out 10 papers, he has a 40 percent chance of selling all the papers and make a profit of Rs. 3 per paper and a 60 percent chance of not selling all papers and incur a loss of Re. 1 per copy not sold. Under the circumstances, the vendor can expect the tenth paper to produce, on the average over time, a *profit* of $3 \times 0.40 - 1 \times 0.60 =$ Re. 0.60.

On the other hand, if the vendor takes out 12 papers every day, he can expect the twelfth paper to produce, on the average over time, a *loss* of $3 \times 0.20 - 1 \times 0.80 =$ Re. (–) 0.20.

Obviously, it would not be profitable for the newspaper vendor to take out twelve papers. But supposing he can sell 11 papers 30 percent of the time, then he would probably make the greatest total profit because he would do slightly better than break-even on the eleventh paper, i.e., $3 \times 0.3 - 1 \times 0.7 =$ Re. 0.20.

It may be clear from the above example that the objective of the newspaper vendor is basically to have enough on hand so that he can expect, on the average, to break-even on the last unit produced, i.e. to carry enough inventory so that on the last unit, the expected risk of loss due to his inability to fulfill the demand equals the expected cost of carrying the unit through the next turn.[25]

The case of the newspaper vendor is similar to that faced by retailers, particularly those dealing in large volume, who are required to place orders for large amount of a great variety of seasonal items like woolens for winter, bathing suits and costumes for summer, toys and festive-items for Christmas, dressing materials for particular festivals etc. Such a retailer may have little information to be able to predict the style of clothes or garments that will be of demand during a particular selling season. But he has to place orders in anticipation of demand because if he places an order in the middle of the season, he may not get the supplies in time. His problem is similar to that of the newspaper vendor in the sense that if he buys too many items of a particular variety, he may be left with unsold stock at the season-end; on the other hand, if he buys too little, he may find his customers returning from the shop, or if he wants to satisfy his customers he may have to buy at a higher cost during the season.

Manufacturers of highly seasonal goods like refrigerators, toys, etc. also face similar problems. So also is the case with hotels and airlines. On the one hand, it would be too much for them to cancel the confirmed bookings of some customers, on the other, if the booking is full, there may be last minute cancellations which just cannot be filled in. The solution to the problems faced by these organisations can be sought, like the newspaper vendor, in balancing the costs and lost profit for lost sales against the costs of carrying or incurring losses due to unsold stock or unused capacity.

Example Suppose, a toy manufacturing company sells fashion dolls at an average price of Rs. 100 each. Total unit cost of the product is Rs. 70 of which

---

25. The example is based on Magee, J.F., *ibid.*

variable cost is Rs. 60. The company always has the problem of estimating its sales-volume during Diwali season. If it produces more than the actual demand, the unsold stocks have to be carried to the next season or sold at a price much lesser than the one obtainable during the season. The carrying cost per unit including repackaging, etc. is Rs. 20 per unit. It is unlikely for the company to sell the toys during off-season at a price more than Rs. 60 per unit. But if it could carry the stocks to the next season it might obtain a better price, though precise estimate of the additional margin cannot be made now.

The market for toys during the peak season is highly competitive and sensitive to children's whims. Hence, the cost of stock-outs (the loss of goodwill) is very high. It is estimated to be Rs. 100 for each customer returning for want of goods (we shall examine the cost of stock-outs and other related problems later).

An approach towards solving the above problem essentially boils down to finding out the probability of selling an amount during the season that maximises profit of the company under the given cost parameters. The following formula can be used to determine the required probability.[26]

$$P(\max) = \frac{p + s - v}{p + s + c}$$

where

p = contribution (profit) per unit sold

s = shortage cost per unit of not fulfilling a demand

v = variable cost per unit which includes cost of production and holding cost during the selling period

c = carrying cost of unit of inventory if remained unsold by the end of period

Putting the figures from the example in the above equation, we obtain

$$P(\max) = \frac{40 + 100 - 60}{40 + 100 + 20} = \frac{80}{160} = 0.50 \quad \text{or} \quad 50\%$$

The result indicates that the company should plan to manufacture enough stock during the initial run which has the chance of fulfilling the demand by 50 percent.

Inventory Built-up

In many seasonal industries, it is possible to predict with reasonable accuracy the peak sales during the season and also the overall sales during the year. But there always remains a chance for products being out-of-stock due to forecast errors. The anxiety thus caused is so high in the minds of entrepreneurs that a very high level of safety stock gets built up in the system resulting in high carrying cost and liquidity problem. This is typical of industries operating in India in seasonal products. In the following example we shall highlight some

---

26. For detailed mathematical derivation of the model see, Magee, J.F., *ibid.*

of these problems faced by a real-life sugar manufacturing company and try to make an approach towards resolving the problems.

Illustration[27]   The case on which the example is based relates to mid '70s, but its relevance to the problems faced by an input-seasonal industry is still valid.

Cane Sweet Mills Ltd. (CSML) is engaged in manufacturing and selling of sugar both under levy and free sales. The company is 30 years old and is closely controlled by a family of entrepreneurs. Performance of the company during the past three years is given in Table 4.21.

Table 4.21 Level of Activity of Cane Sweet Mills Ltd. during the Past Three Years

(Quintals in lakhs)

| Year | Projected figures | | Actual figures | | Recovery yield (Actual) |
	Canes crushed	Sugar production	Canes crushed	Sugar production	
1974–75	14.00	1.19	10.03	0.80	7.98%
1975–76	10.00	0.90	9.43	0.82	8.70%
1976–77	10.00	0.90	10.20	0.90	8.82%

For the year 1977–78, the company has projected crushing of 12.50 lakh quintals of sugar cane with a 9 percent yield, i.e. 1.125 lakh quintals of sugar. Cost of sugar cane is Rs. 13.50 per quintal.

Summaries of *profit and loss account* of the company for the past two years and the projected year are given in Table 4.22.

The company is presently enjoying working capital finance from a bank to the order of Rs. 155 lakh which it intends to increase to Rs. 175 lakh in the projected year. Interest rate (which can also be taken as opportunity cost) is 16 percent per annum. Bank's margin requirement is 15 percent on stocks valued at sale price of both levy and free sugar. Under government's sugar control order, the company sales (holds) 65 percent of production under levy at Rs. 217 per quintal and 35 percent as free sugar at Rs. 275 per quintal.

Production plan, sales and stock position for the projected year are given in Table 4.23.

The company, in its application to the bank for enhancement of working capital loan limits, has explained that, "enhanced cash credit facility is required due to increase in production of sugar from 90,000 quintals to 112,500 quintals in the projected year. Moreover, due to erratic/irregular release order of the union government last year, the closing stock has piled up resulting in large carry-over of stock in the beginning of the crushing season, 1977–78. As such,

---

27. This is based on a case study titled "Cane Sweet Mills Ltd." prepared by Chakraborty, S.K., *Mimeographed,* Indian Institute of Management Calcutta. All the figures and the dates remain unchanged. Only the text has been shortened and paraphrased. Chakraborty, however, does not owe any responsibility to the solution suggested here which is entirely that of the author.

Table 4.22 Profit and Loss Account Summaries

(Rs. in thousand)

Particulars	1975–76	1976–77	1977–78 (projected)
1. Net sales	22,641	20,171	27,963
2. Manufacturing expenses	18,152	19,431	22,862
Add: Opening stocks in process	—	62	146
	18,152	19,493	23,008
Less: Closing stocks in process	62	146	145
3. Cost of production	18,090	19,347	22,863
Add: Opening stock of finished goods	3233	2164	4467
	21,323	21,511	27,330
Less: Closing stocks of finished goods	2164	4467	3596
4. Cost of goods sold	19,159	17,044	23,734
5. Gross profit (item no. 1–4)	3482	3127	4229
6. Selling and general administrative expenses	331	393	403
7. Operating profit (item no. 5–6)	3151	2734	3826
8. *Less*: Interest	1039	1206	1320
9. Profit before tax (PBT)	2112	1528	2506

Notes: 1. Lower level of sales in 1976–77 is due to a fall in price of sugar which has since firmed up due to government's support price.
2. Other incomes and expenses are excluded as these are not relevant for our purpose.
3. Direct labour cost for crushing sugar cane is found to be 15% of the value of canes crushed.

on account of large carry-over of stocks and increased production for the current season the enhanced working capital facility of Rs. 175 lakh is required."

Suggested approach: The company appears to be operationally strong as movement of its gross profit (GP) ratio suggests:

1975–76	1976-77	1977-78 *(projected)*
15.38%	15.50%	15.12%

The GP ratio is stable over the years despite a fall in sales in 1976–77. This indicates the company's ability to maintain proportionality of its manufacturing expenses with sales.[28] But this ratio does not tell us whether the company is manufacturing enough. A comparison with the industry-ratio would have revealed the comparative position, but the data are not available.

---

28. In order to understand the importance of GP ratio in greater depth see, Bhattacharya Hrishikes, *Total Management by Ratio,* 2nd ed. Sage Publications, New Delhi, 2007.

Table 4.23 Operating Plan of CSML for the Projected Year 1977–78

(in quintals)

Month (1)	Sugar canes crushed (2)	Sugars produced (3)	Sales (4)	End-month stock (5)
1977				
September	—	—	—	28,578
October	—	—	9000	19,578
November	94,000 (7.52)	8460	9500	18,538
December	315,000 (25.20)	28,350	9500	37,388
1978				
January	315,000 (25.20)	28,350	10,000	55,738
February	285,000 (22.80)	25,650	10,000	71,388
March	193,000 (15.44)	17,370	10,500	78,258
April	48,000 (3.84)	4320	8000	74,578
May			7500	67,078
June			7500	59,578
July			8500	51,078
August			8500	42,578
September			9500	33,078
Total	1,250,000 (100.00)	112,500	108,000	—

Notes:
1. Sugar canes are produced within the command area of the factory. There is plenty of crops. No crop failure has been observed during recent years. However, sugar canes are to be booked three months in advance by paying an advance amount to growers. The company expects to book sugar canes in about a month's time.
2. Sugar canes are to be crushed as soon as these are procured as otherwise there may be a yield loss.
3. Crushing season begins in mid-November. The factory normally has 150 working days during the season.
4. The factory has a crushing capacity of 10,200 quintals of sugar cane per day.
5. Canes are crushed mainly by agricultural labourers who move to sugar factories after the harvesting/sowing season; often they themselves are the sugar cane cultivators.
6. Figures in column 3 under 'sugar produced' are calculated on the basis of 9% yield.
7. Figures in bracket under column 2 represent monthly percentages of total canes crushed.
8. The company closes its accounts on 30th September.

Selling and other administrative expenses are also under control, but the outgoing on account of interest payment is on the high side; it is about 6 percent of the cost of production. The problem lies in production planning and anticipation of inventory holdings which are typical of seasonal industries, as the following analyses will reveal.

Seasonal industries are mainly of two types: sales-seasonal and inputs-seasonal. The present case belongs to the latter category where principal raw materials, e.g. sugar canes have to be procured and crushed during a particular period of the year only. Variation in the sales of sugar over the year is not very high as Table 4.23 would suggest.

In October of the projected year, the company would start with an opening sugar stock of 28,578 quintals. The company says that this rather high build-up of stock is due to erratic release by the government which has since firmed up. It should necessarily follow, therefore, that in the coming year serious attempts should be made to reduce the stock holdings by streamlining production. But the operational plan as given in Table 4.23 does not reflect such a thinking. On the contrary, we find that end-month stock in the projected year has gone upto 33,078 quintals. The anxiety of being out-of-stock during lean procurement season is responsible for this state of affairs. Let us examine this problem in greater depth.

Although the company has made monthly sales forecast after taking into consideration the expected demand, government policies, etc., it is not unlikely that errors in forecast will emerge in the projected year which may throw the company out of gear. In many businesses the risks and costs of back orders so outweigh the inventory carrying costs that a substantial protection in the form of safety stock is often justified. In case of sugar industry the problem is more acute due to its inability to fulfill back-orders because sugar canes needed to manufacture additional quantity of sugar will just not be available after the harvesting season is over. Another problem faced by the sugar industry in India is that capacity utilisation of a unit may often be frozen by the government to its past performance level (capacity control has since been lifted by the government). All these ultimately lead to overproduction and consequently overstocking.

One approach to resolving the kind of problems mentioned above is to start with a forecast of maximum expected demand or the maximum demand that the company is capable of meeting. Level of safety stock is based on such demand and the production plan is adjusted accordingly.

For CSML, crushing season is over in the month of April. Sufficient sugar stocks should, therefore, be built up by that month so that the company is able to meet the demand for the following months till the beginning of next crushing season in November. That is, it must have enough to carry the demand for six months (May–October), which aggregates to 50,500 quintals (assuming that next year's October sales will remain at 9000 quintals). As there is not much variation in monthly sales during the period, average monthly sales can be taken at 50,500/6 = 8416, say 8500 quintals.

Maximum demand that has been forecasted for the projected year is 10,500 quintals. Allowing that this demand may occur for all these six months, the company will be out of stock to the tune of 2000 quintals per month, i.e. 2000 × 6 = 12,000 quintals in aggregate. It is, therefore, reasonable to plan a safety stock level of 12,000 quintals of sugar in the projected year which will be able to absorb the effects of departure of actual sales from the forecast. As sales occur, the actual level of stocks will fall below or exceed the planned balances which will have to be adjusted fully in the month of November of the year following the projected year, when the new crushing season begins.

Having decided on the level of safety stock, the next step is to formulate a production plan which will gradually reduce the inventory in such a manner that the projected end-month stock of October 1978 comes down to 12,000 quintals (assuming once again that the sales of October of the year following the projected year will remain at 9000 quintals). One has to move gradually because in this particular type of industry, it would be fatal to stop production and draw down on the accumulated inventory and start production once the inventory level reaches the level of safety stock, because by that time harvesting season of sugar cane may just be over. Labourers also may go back or join the competitors and hence, would not be available next time. Keeping these constraints in mind, we may now calculate total production of sugar for the projected year.

Projected sales (13 months):	117,000 quintals (108,000 + 9000)	
Add: Projected closing stock as on October 1978	12,000 quintals	
	129,000 quintals	
Less: Actual opening stock	28,578 quintals	
Projected production for the year 1977–78	100,422 quintals	

Assuming a 9 percent yield, sugar cane required for crushing will be 100,422 × 100/9 = 1,115,800 quintals. Following exactly the pattern of monthly procurement or production as percentage of total procurement/production (given under brackets under column 2 of Table 4.23) the revised operating plan of CSML is drawn up in Table 4.24.

Table 4.24 Revised Operating Plan of CSML for the Projected Year 1977–78

(in quintals)

Month (1)	Sugar canes crushed (2)	Sugars produced (3)	Sales (4)	End-month stock (5)
1977				
September	—	—	—	28,578
October	—	—	9000	19,578
November	83,908	7552	9500	17,630
December	281,182	25,306	9500	33,436
1978				
January	281,182	25,306	10,000	48,742
February	254,402	22,896	10,000	61,638
March	172,279	15,506	10,500	66,644
April	42,847	3856	8000	62,500
May	—	—	7500	55,000
June	—	—	7500	47,500
July	—	—	8500	39,000
August	—	—	8500	30,500
September	—	—	9500	21,000
Subtotal (12 months)	1,115,800	100,422	108,000	—
October	—	—	9000	12,000
Total (13 months)	1,115,800	100,422	117,000	—

It may be seen from Table 4.24 that the end-October 1978 stock of sugar under revised operating plan has come down to projected safety stock level of 12,000 quintals. For the year ended 1977–78, the closing stock would, however, be 21,000 quintals. Any shortfall in the safety stock level of 12,000 quintals will be replenished when production commences in November 1978.[29]

Let us now find out the immediate benefits that would accrue to CSML when they adopt the revised operating plan.

Major Savings

(a) Cane crushing to be reduced by 1,250,000 – 1,115,800 = 134,200 quintals
 Savings on cost @ Rs. 13.50 per quintal = 134,200 × 13.50
              = Rs. 18.12 lakh
 Saving on labour cost @15% on cost of sugar cane = Rs. 2.72 lakh
                   Rs. 20.84 lakh

(b) Average stock holding to be reduced by:
 Yearly total of column 5 of Table 4.23/12 = 50,738 quintals
 Less: Yearly total of column 5 of Table 4.24/12 = 41,930 quintals
   Net reduction in average stock   8808 quintals

 of which 65% levy @ Rs. 217 = 8808 × 0.65 × 217 = Rs. 12.42 lakh
     35% free @ Rs. 275 = 8808 × 0.35 × 275 = Rs. 8.48 lakh
                  Rs. 20.90 lakh
 Savings at opportunity cost of 16% p.a. = 20.90 × 0.16 = Rs. 3.34 lakh
 Total savings (a + b) = 20.84 + 3.34   = Rs. 24.18 lakh

We may recall that the company has projected a PBT of Rs. 25 lakh in 1977–78. The savings made due to revised operating plan will itself double the company's profit.

Calculation of Working Capital Finance[30]

Peak build-up of stock (March 1978)   = 66,644 quintals
 (Revised plan in Table 4.24)

of which 65% levy @ Rs. 217 = 66,644 × 0.65 × 217 = Rs. 94.00 lakh
and 35% free @ Rs. 275 = 66,644 × 0.35 × 275 = Rs. 64.14 lakh
                 Rs. 158.14 lakh
  Less: 15% margin   Rs. 23.72 lakh
  Permissible bank finance   Rs. 134.42 lakh

It may be observed that there is a substantial reduction in working capital limit under the revised operating plan. As against the proposed level of Rs. 175 lakh that the company applied for, it would now require only Rs. 134 lakh. In effect, the company would not actually require this amount because the savings

---

29. Level of safety stock in the following year (1978–79) will, however, depend on projection of sales and production plan for that year.
30. Calculation of working capital finance is made here based on the existing practices of commercial banks. This methodology has, however, undergone substantial changes which we shall discuss in Chapter 7.

of Rs. 24 lakh under the revised operating plan would boost up the net working capital of the company beyond the required margin. The company may not ultimately require more than Rs. 110 lakh on an average in the projected year.

In the earlier example, we have dealt with anticipation problems faced by an enterprise which is subjected to input seasonality. In the following example we shall examine the inventory anticipation problem of a unit which suffers from sales seasonality.

Example[31] Bombay Sports Goods Ltd. (BSGL)—a nationally known manufacturer of sports goods and school items—is facing severe working capital problems. The company's banker had during the recent past, repeatedly expressed its concern about the large amount of debt, and now advised the company that the bank would be compelled to limit the cash credit to 50 percent of the value of inventories and accounts receivable from 20X1 onwards. In a recent letter the bank urged the company to make immediate alternative arrangements of financing the excess portion of cash credit but indicated its willingness to consider any reasonable proposal for converting a part of the existing cash credit into interim term loan.

The company's sales are highly seasonal, the peak of the season being August, September and October. About two-third of the total sales are made directly to schools and the balance to the sports goods dealers. Although the goods are sold on 30 days' credit, the company has never been able to realise the amount within 30 days, particularly from schools whose payments are delayed several months.

On the basis of rate of sales' increase in the past years, the marketing department of the company has projected a sale of Rs. 1400 lakh in 209X1, an increase of Rs. 200 lakh over the last year. Although the sales forecast could not be made for a long period, the marketing department has indicated the following sales level for three years.

Projected year	Projected sales
20X1	Rs. 1400 lakh
20X2	Rs. 1500 lakh
20X3	Rs. 1750 lakh

The marketing department has given monthly break-up of sales and collections. The production department has accordingly planned monthly level of production and also projected the cost of goods sold against each month's sales. These are given in Table 4.25.

The production process of the company is simple and a large part of manufacturing is done through ancilliary cottage industries which are supplied with necessary inputs. The production manager indicates that he normally tries to maintain an inventory level equal to about one third of sales to take care of seasonal fluctuations.

---

31. This example is based on a study (mimeographed) made at Indian Institute of Management Calcutta.

Table 4.25 Monthly Projections for 20X1

(Rs. in lakh)

Month	Projected sales	Projected collections	Projected production	Projected cost of goods sold
January	60	72	65	40
February	70	70	65	48
March	90	80	90	63
April	92	80	88	64
May	94	80	88	65
June	120	80	91	84
July	130	94	68	90
August	208	74	98	140
September	194	180	97	130
October	166	274	89	114
November	108	170	78	74
December	68	140	57	48
Total	1400	1394	974	960

The company purchases raw materials at relatively even rates throughout the year. It does not visualise any change in accounts payable pattern.

In the projected years, selling expenses are expected to increase proportionately with sales. Administrative expenses which are estimated at Rs. 150 lakh for 20X1 are expected to rise by 10 percent p.a. in the next two years.

Other information which are relevant for determining the working capital structure are as follows:

(i) Advance income tax is payable twice a year—June and December.
(ii) The company has been paying regularly a dividend of 10% which it intends to maintain.
(iii) In view of the seasonal nature of the business, the company is desirous of maintaining a minimum cash balance of Rs. 15 lakh during the peak months and Rs. 10 lakh in other months.

Monthly estimates of profit/loss for 20X1 are given in Table 4.26 along with a *proforma income statement* in Table 4.27. The balance sheet of the company as at the close of 20X0 is given in Table 4.28.

Suggested Approach

The following basic calculations are made for making an approach towards development of a comprehensive working capital plan for the enterprise.

Accounts Payable

It is said that there may not be much change in the pattern of accounts payable. Last year's sales was $1400 - 200 = $ Rs. 1200 lakh and the accounts payable balance as on 31st December 20X0 was Rs. 70 lakh. It would have been better if figures for the total purchases were available to determine the turnover ratio of accounts payable. But in the absence of that, we can calculate the ratio in

Table 4.26 Monthly Estimates of Profit/Loss for 20X1

(Rs. in lakh)

Month (1)	Sales (2)	Cost of goods sold (3)	Selling expenses (4)	Administrative expenses (5)	profit/Loss (6)
January	60	40	7	12.5	0.5
February	70	48	8	12.5	1.5
March	90	63	10	12.5	4.5
April	92	64	10	12.5	5.5
May	94	65	11	12.5	5.5
June	120	84	14	12.5	9.5
July	130	90	15	12.5	12.5
August	208	140	24	12.5	31.5
September	194	130	22	12.5	29.5
October	166	114	19	12.5	20.5
November	108	74	12	12.5	9.5
December	68	48	8	12.5	(–) 0.5
Total	1400	960	160	150.0	130.0

Table 4.27 Proforma Income Statement for 20X1

(Rs. in lakh)

Sales	1400
Less: Cost of goods sold	960
Gross profit	440
Less: Selling and administrative expenses	310
	130
Less: Interest on bank finance	30
Income before taxes	100
Provision for taxes @ 40%	40
Net profit	60

Table 4.28 Balance Sheet as at 31st December 20X1

(Rs. in lakh)

Liabilities			Assets		
Share capital	160		Fixed assets		240
Reserves and surplus	145	305	Current assets		
Current liabilities			Inventories	320	
Accounts payable	70		Accounts receivable	150	
Accrued liabilities	8		Loans and advances	10	
Bank loan (cash credit)	357	435	Cash and Bank	20	500
Total		740	Total		740

terms of cost of goods sold (COGS). In the projected year cost of goods sold is found to be (960 × 100)/1400 = 68.57 percent. Assuming that the same ratio prevailed last year also, COGS for last year's sales would have been 1200 ×

0.6857 = Rs. 823 lakh. Hence, turnover ratio of accounts payable was 823/70 = 11.75 or say, one month's COGS.

Inventory Level

BSGL will have an opening stock Rs. 320 lakh (Table 4.28) in 20X1. If we follow the production plan of the company as given in Table 4.25, monthly level of inventories would be as given in Table 4.29.

Table 4.29 Monthly Level of Inventories as per Production Plan of the Company

(Rs. in lakh)

Month (1)	Projected sales (2)	Projected production (3)	Projected cost of goods sold (4)	Level of inventory (col. 5 + col. 3 – col. 4) (5)
December 20X0	—	—	—	320
January 20X1	60	65 (6.67)	40	345
February	70	65 (6.67)	48	362
March	90	90 (9.24)	63	389
April	92	88 (9.03)	64	413
May	94	88 (9.03)	65	436
June	120	91 (9.35)	84	443
July	130	68 (6.98)	90	421
August	208	98 (10.06)	140	379
September	194	97 (9.96)	130	346
October	166	89 (9.14)	114	321
November	108	78 (8.01)	74	325
December	68	57 (5.86)	48·	334
Total	1400	974 (100)	960	4514

Note: Figures in bracket under column 3 indicate percentage of monthly production to total production for the year.

A cursory comparison between column 4 and column 5 of Table 4.29 would reveal that level of inventory is much out of proportion with the level of sales. On an average, the projected average holding of inventories is close to five months (4514/960 = 4.7) of sales (COGs). Even if we take the average of peak months' sales (384/3 = 128) the average holding of inventory is close to (4514 × 3)/(12 × 384) = 2.94 or 3 months of average peak sales. We have mentioned earlier that this is the typical problem faced by seasonal industries, whether it is input-seasonal or output-seasonal. This is the principal reason behind the working capital problems faced by BSGL. It is necessary, therefore, to determine a reasonable level of safety stock which will take care of the company's anxiety of being out of stock.

We shall take recourse to a simple statistical tool, popularly known as *standard deviation* for determining the safety stock of the company. Necessary calculations are made in Table 4.30.

Table 4.30   Computation of Standard Deviation of Projected Cost of Goods Sold for 20X1

(Rs. in lakh)

Projected COGS (X_i)	$X_i - \overline{X}$	$(X_i - \overline{X})^2$	
40	−40	1600	
48	−32	1024	where X_i = monthly sales
63	−17	289	N = Number of observation
64	−16	256	= 12
65	−15	225	Arithmetic mean $(\overline{X}) = \dfrac{\sum X_i}{N} = \dfrac{960}{12} = 80$
84	4	16	
90	10	100	
140	60	3600	
130	50	2500	
114	34	1156	
74	−6	36	
48	−32	1024	
Σ = 960	0	11,826	

Standard deviation (SD) is given by the following formula:

$$SD = \sqrt{\frac{(X_i - \overline{X})^2}{N}}$$

Putting the figures calculated in Table 4.30 in the above equation, we get

$$SD = \sqrt{\frac{11,826}{12}}$$

$$= 31.39$$

The derived standard deviation of 31.39 indicates that sales of BSGL may vary from the mean sales (Rs. 80 lakh) on both sides by Rs. 31.39 lakh. This covers 68 per cent of the probability space. With two SDs the coverage increases to 95 percent and with three SDs, total coverage increases to 99 percent. Depending upon the risk profile of an enterprise, the safety stock can be determined in terms of number of SDs. For example, a high risk-taking firm may settle its safety stock at a single SD level while a low risk-taker may go as far as three SDs. As the risk of being out-of-stock is high in a sales-seasonal industry and the risk profile of BSGL is presently low as reflected in the high level of inventories being carried by the company, it is advisable that its safety stock level be settled at three SDs or 31.39 × 3 = 94.17, say Rs. 94 lakh. Having thus determined the safety stock level we can now proceed to devise an alternative production plan of the company. Annual production of the company for 20X1 is calculated as follows:

Projected yearly sales (COGS)	=	Rs.	960 lakh
Add: Projected closing stock		Rs.	94 lakh
		Rs.	1054 lakh
Less: Opening stock		Rs.	320 lakh
		Rs.	734 lakh

Break-up of monthly sales; production, cost of goods sold and other working capital items are given in Tables 4.31 and 4.32.

Table 4.31 Revised Operating Plan and Resultant Levels of Monthly Inventories

(Rs. in lakh)

Month (1)	Sales (2)	Production (3)	Cost of goods sold (4)	Level of inventory (opening balance Rs. 320) (5)
January	60	49	40	329
February	70	49	48	330
March	90	68	63	335
April	92	66	64	337
May	94	66	65	338
June	120	68	84	322
July	130	52	90	284
August	208	74	140	218
September	194	73	130	161
October	166	67	114	114
November	108	59	74	99
December	68	43	48	94
Total	1400	734	960	2961

Notes: 1. Projected monthly productions as shown in column 3 are calculated by applying the same percentages as are calculated in column 3 of Table 4.29.
2. Level of inventories as shown in column 5 are calculated as: column 5 + column 3 – column 4.

Closing net working capital of the company before bank finance as on 31st December 20X0 is calculated below:

Current assets	(Rs. in lakh)
Inventories	320
Accounts receivable	150
Loans and advances	10
Cash and bank balances	20
	500

Less:

Current liabilities	
Accounts payable	70
Accrued liabilities	8
	78
Net working capital (NWC) before bank finance	422

Table 4.32 Revised Operating Plan and Other Working Capital Items for 20X1

(Rs. in lakh)

Month (1)	Sales (2)	Collections (3)	Level of debtors (Base Rs. 150) [col. 4+2–3] (4)	Level of inventory (5)	Level of cash holding (6)	Level of current assets [col. 4+5+6] (7)	Level of creditor (one month COGs) (8)	Working capital gap (col. 7–8) (9)
January	60	72	138	329	10	477	40	437
February	70	70	138	330	10	478	48	430
March	90	80	148	335	10	493	63	430
April	92	80	160	337	10	507	64	443
May	94	80	174	338	10	522	65	457
June	120	80	214	322	10	546	84	462
July	130	94	250	284	10	544	90	454
August	208	74	384	218	15	617	140	477
September	194	180	398	161	15	574	130	444
October	166	274	290	114	15	419	114	305
November	108	170	228	99	10	337	74	263
December	68	140	156	94	10	260	48	212
Total	1400	1394	2678	2961	135	5774	960	4814

Notes: 1. Level of cash holding is taken as indicated by the company. Opening cash balance of Rs. 20 lakh is ignored here but is considered while calculating the opening net working capital of the company for the projected year 20X1.
2. Other current assets like loans and advances and current liabilities, like accrued liabilities are also ignored here. These have been presumed to be constant in the projected year and are considered while calculating opening net working capital.

Monthly projections of NWC in 20X1 are given in Table 4.33.

Table 4.33 Monthly Projections of Net Working Capital for 20X1 under Revised Plan

(Rs. in lakh)

Month (1)	Profit/Loss (col. 6 of Table 4.26) (2)	Income tax (3)	Dividend (4)	Addition to NWC (5)	Level of NWC (Base Rs. 422) (6)
January	0.5			0.5	422.5
February	1.5			1.5	424.0
March	4.5			4.5	428.5
April	5.5			5.5	434.0
May	5.5			5.5	439.5
June	9.5	20.00		(–) 10.5	429.0
July	12.5			12.5	441.5
August	31.5			31.5	473.0
September	29.5			29.5	502.5
October	20.5			20.5	523.0
November	9.5			9.5	532.5
December	(–) 0.5	20.00	16	(–) 36.5	496.0
Total	130.0	40.00	16	74.0	5546.0

The company's bank has advised that from 20X1 it will limit drawings to 50 percent of the aggregate of inventories and accounts receivable and will consider sanctioning an interim working capital loan to help the company in streamlining its working capital structure. In Table 4.34 we have calculated the working capital requirement of the company for 20X1 keeping in mind the desire of the bank.

Table 4.34 Projection of Working Capital Requirement for 20X1

(Rs. in lakh)

Month (1)	Working capital gap (col. 9 of Table 4.32) (2)	Net working capital (col. 6 of Table 4.33) (3)	Financing gap (col. 2–3) (4)	Cumulative financing gap (opening balance Rs. 357) (5)	50% of inventory + debtors (6)	Difference (col. 5–6) (7)
January	437	422	15	372	233	139
February	430	424	6	378	234	144
March	430	428	2	380	241	139
April	443	434	9	389	248	141
May	457	439	18	407	256	151
June	462	429	33	440	268	172
July	454	441	13	453	267	186
August	477	473	4	457	301	156
September	444	502	(–) 58	399	279	120
October	305	523	(–) 218	181	202	(–) 21
November	263	532	(–) 269	(–) 88	163	(–) 251
December	212	496	(–) 284	(–) 372	125	(–) 497

Column 4 of Table 4.34 reveals that from September 20X1 net working capital of BSGL becomes more than sufficient to finance the working capital gap. But the opening debit balance in *cash credit account* that it is required to carry due to high-level of inventory that was being maintained in previous year has slowed down the process. Column 5 indicates that the company is, in fact, able to repay the entire cash credit in the month of November, and by the year-end it will have excess NWC to the tune of Rs. 372 lakh. But during the interim period (January–October), BSGL requires financing to carry the revised operating plan. As the company has taken positive step towards reducing the inventories (which was the anxiety of the bank), it is likely that the bank would allow the company to draw as per monthly plan given in column 5 of Table 4.34 and get the balance adjusted in full in November. Alternatively, the bank can sanction a working capital loan of Rs. 150 lakh which is the average of financing differences of 9 months as shown in column 7, and accordingly adjust the drawings in cash credit account. Both the loan and cash credit would obviously stand repaid by the end of the year.[32]

---

32. We have limited the workings for the projected year 20X1 only. It would be interesting for the reader to draw up plans for the next two years on the basis of closing balances of 20X1. We have also ignored problems relating to Accounts Receivable and accepted the cash holding figures as given because our purpose here is to focus on the inventory problems. In any case, receivables' collection pattern may not be drastically changed because major buyers being schools who are dependent mostly on grants, there would be erratic lags in payments. Average cash holding in the projected year is (135/12)/1400 = 0.008 or 0.8 percent of sales which is not also on the high side, more particularly when the business is sales-seasonal.

Safety Stock

While an anticipation stock is designed to take care of special type of problems like seasonality etc., general safety stock aims at absorbing shocks from random fluctuations in purchasing, production or sales. It provides a short-term protection to the production department and marketing organisation against uncertainties of customer demand, which is a general phenomenon cutting across all industries and trade whether it is seasonal or not. Even a seasonal industry may have to hold a level of stock beyond the anticipation inventory (though, while deriving the level of anticipation stocks the safety part is implicitly taken care of as we have seen before).

Both the production and marketing departments are ever keen on holding safety stock because of the fear of stock-outs. For the former, it is idle machines and overheads and for the latter, it is the lost sales and consequent loss of goodwill in the market. But this anxiety, which though real, often pushes the enterprise to a culture of playing too safe to eliminate the risk altogether by having a high-level of safety stock, the costs of carrying of which may outweigh the benefits received and erode the bottom line on a continuous basis. It is often forgotton that safety stocks are held not for their usage, but as an insurance against uncertainties, and that the insurance too has a cost. How much insurance one would buy depends upon one's estimation of risks. The same applies to a business enterprise.

The objective of enterprise is to arrive at a reasonable balance between total costs of carrying the safety stock and the protection obtained against stock-outs, remembering at the same time that full protection is never an achievable goal of a business enterprise. Some amount of risk shall always be there and that is why one is in business. But the fundamental problem in determining a safety stock level is to correctly identify and quantify the costs, many of which are not available in accounting records. Costs of customer service failure, varying production rates with the accompanying costs of firing, hiring and training of workers are some of the examples. However, all these costs arise due to forecasting errors which cause variations in demand and lead time. Because certain costs are difficult to estimate, safety stock levels are often determined arbitrarily and almost always at a high-level. In their concern for stock-outs, both the production manager and marketing manager miss the point that each additional unit in safety stock provides a diminishing return (benefit). The question, therefore, boils down to how much additional inventory as safety stock can be economically justified. The commonsense rule is that as the size of the safety stock increases, the probability of a stock-out decreases. Therefore, at some point of safety stock level, the cost of holding additional inventory plus the expected stock-out cost should be minimum. That should be the optimum level.

Estimation of stock-out costs depends upon correctly judging the reaction of customers against stock-outs. There could be two types of reaction: (1) the customer may agree for a late delivery, or (2) he may cancel the order altogether. In the latter case, it is the costs of a lost sale and goodwill and in the former case, it is the backorder costs that need to be estimated. The costs in the latter case (backorder costs) can be estimated with reasonable accuracy.

Backordering

In case of backorder, the time for delivery acceptable to the customer can only be a fraction of the original lead time. Hence, the company may be required to launch an emergency procurement/production drive which will result in incurring additional costs like hiring additional workers, procurement personnel, overtime costs of both manpower and facilities, handling costs and often additional packaging and shipping costs for the particular item(s) which are now out of the line from the mainline of procurement/production. However, all these costs are amenable to fair estimation.

Lost Sales

When the customer refuses to accept backorder, the sale is lost. The first type of cost in such a case is the lost profit. This can be easily calculated. But the cost of the loss of goodwill is difficult to estimate. The unserved customer may go to a competitor who may not only take away the sale of the present items but also of other items which used to be normally bought by the customer from the same establishment. For the production line, the cost of a stock-out could be extremely high if the item in demand is so critical for the output or the manufacturing operation that its non-availability may result in a shut-down of production or the plant as a whole. For a manufacturing organisation such crucial items would have to be segregated for critical attention because no stock-outs may be permitted for such items. As stock-out costs vary considerably for different items depending upon customer reaction and internal usage, it should be possible for an enterprise to prepare a list of items in order of their criticality to customers' demand and production. A stock-out tolerance percentage is then ascribed to each such items in consultation with production/ marketing people.

Stock-out tolerance level   For example, let us assume that there are six items in the inventory: A, B, C, D, E, F. On one extreme, importance of item A in production and/or sales is such that no stock-out is tolerable, and on the other extreme, tolerance level of item number F is as high as 23 percent. Let us further assume that monthly demand for every item is 50,000 units and maximum lead time by which the inventories can be produced/procured is one month. Safety-stock level with 0 percent stock-out tolerance limit will, therefore, be 50,000 units. Monthly demand being 50,000 units, average stock holding for item A will be 50,000 + 50,000/2 = 75,000 units. Item B has a stock-out tolerance limit of 5 percent in a year which, in other words, means that the firm is prepared to be out of stock for (52 × 5)/100 = 2.6 times a year or once in 52/2.6 = 20 weeks. As the firm is ready to tolerate stock-outs for 2.6 times a year, the requirement of safety stock will also be lower than item A as calculated below:

Annual demand: (Item no. B)	50,000 × 12	= 600,000 units
Less: Stock-out tolerance	50,000 × 2.6	= 130,000 units
		470,000 units

Dividing 470,000 by 12 the safety stock for item B comes to 39,167 units. Average stock holding is, therefore, 39,167 + 50,000/2 = 64,167 units.

In Table 4.35 we have calculated the safety-stock and average stock holding of all the six items in terms of their stock-out tolerance limit.

Table 4.35 Safety Stock and Average Stock Holding of Different Items of Inventory under Various Stock-out Tolerance Limits

Item no. (1)	Stock-out tolerance limit (%) (2)	Times stock-out tolerable in a year (52 × col. 2)/100 (3)	Safety stock (4)	Average stock holding (5)
A	0	0	50,000	75,000
B	5	2.60	39,167	64,167
C	10	5.20	28,333	53,333
D	15	7.80	17,500	42,500
E	20	10.40	6667	31,667
F	23	11.96	167	25,167

It may be seen from Table 4.35 that as the stock-out tolerance limit is increasing, safety-stock level is coming down and at 23 percent it is close to zero. The reason behind this is that at that level of tolerance (for item F) the firm is prepared to withstand stock-outs almost every month. The concept is illustrated graphically in Figure 4.7.

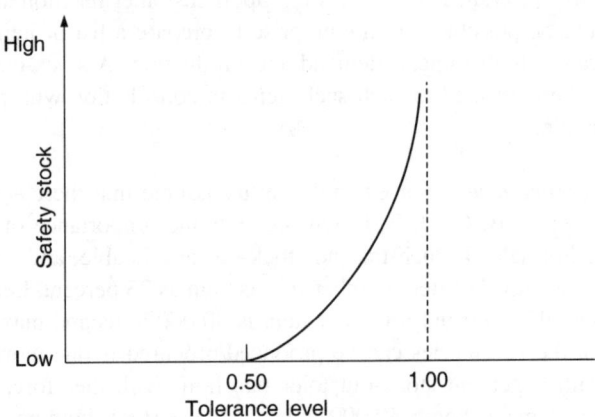

Figure 4.7 Safety stock vs. tolerance level.

The methodology discussed above may appear to be simplistic as it ignores other variables, like costs of stock-outs, but because of its very simplicity and straightforwardness it is useful at the hands of managers who are often vexed with the problem of determining the true costs of stock-outs, though at the conceptual level it is fairly well- understood. However, in what follows now we shall discuss some of the inventory models which regard stock-out cost as an important variable for determining the safety stock.

STOCK-OUT COSTS

It is held that an enterprise needs safety stock because of uncertainty in demand (consumption) or in delivery of goods which give rise to several costs which are grouped as stock-out costs. We have already discussed nature of these costs and the difficulty in estimating them. If there are larger variations in demand or in lead time, the stock-out costs will also be higher, resulting in higher level of safety stock and hence, the reorder point. It will be still larger if holding cost is comparatively low.

The safety stock influences the firm's value in two opposite ways. On one hand, it decreases the total cost of stock-outs (calculated by multiplying the unit cost of stock-out with the number of stock-outs thus prevented by holding the safety stock), but on the other, it increases the carrying costs of safety stock inventory (calculated by multiplying the percentage carrying cost with the safety stocks held). The optimal solution for this apparently conflicting situation must, however, lie in minimising the costs of stock-outs and also minimising the total carrying costs.

Known Stock-out Costs

Stock-out costs are assumed to be known, particularly when the sales are not lost for want of timely delivery; customers wait for a reasonable period of time to make good the order. These costs are also called backorder costs where explicit charges due to procurement, set-ups, etc. are considered. When stock-out costs are thus made finite, the EOQ model must be modified to include such costs in the following manner.[33]

$$Q = \sqrt{\frac{2DCp}{H(p-u)}} \sqrt{\frac{H+E}{E}}$$

where

Q = economic production quantity
D = annual demand
C = set-up costs per production run
p = rate of production
H = holding (carrying) cost per unit per year
u = rate of demand
E = backordering costs per unit per year

The safety stock (S) is determined by

$$S = \frac{HQ(p-u)}{(H+E)p}$$

and the Reorder point in units (R) is given by

$$R = \frac{DL}{N} \frac{HQ(p-u)}{(H+E)p}$$

---

33. For a full derivation of this model see, J. Banks and W.J. Fabrycky, *Procurement and Inventory Systems Analysis,* Prentice-Hall, Inc., Englewoods Cliffs, New Jersey, 1987.

where

  L = lead time in days

  N = number of working days in a year.

Example   The annual demand (D) of an item of inventory is 30,000 units per year. Cost of production (P) per unit is Rs. 60 and the carrying cost (H) is Rs. 15 per unit per year. It costs the company Rs. 25 to set-up the machines for each production run (C).

The daily rate of production (p) is 120 units and the lead time (L) is 5 days. The factory works for 300 days a year.

The customers of the company do not normally cancel an order when delivery is not on time but allow the company to backorder them. The backorder cost (E) in such cases is Rs. 5 per unit.

Daily rate of demand (u) will be 30,000/300 = 100 units. The economic production quantity (Q) with stock-out costs will be

$$Q = \sqrt{\frac{2 \times 30,000 \times 25 \times 120}{15(120 - 100)}} \sqrt{\frac{15 + 5}{5}}$$

$$= 774.60 \times 2 = 1549.20, \text{ say } 1550 \text{ units}$$

Average inventory will, therefore, be 1550/2 = 775 units

Reorder point in units (R) will be

$$R = \frac{30,000 \times 5}{300} + \frac{15 \times 1550(120 - 100)}{(15 + 5)120}$$

  = 500 + 193.75 = 693.75, say 694 units of which 194 units are due to safety stock.

Number of production runs in a year will be

$$\frac{D}{Q} = \frac{30,000}{1550} = 19.35 \text{ runs per year}$$

The annual total cost (TC) under the above arrangement can be calculated as follows.[34]

$$\text{TC} = PD + \frac{HQE(p - u)}{(H + E)p} + \frac{DC}{Q}$$

$$= 60 \times 30,000 + \frac{15 \times 1550 \times 5(120 - 100)}{(15 + 5)120} + \frac{30,000 \times 25}{1550}$$

$$= 1,800,000 + 968.75 + 483.87$$

$$= \text{Rs. } 1,801,452.62$$

---

34. As the objective is to minimise the carrying cost and the costs of stock-out, the *minimum* total relevant cost is often determined by ignoring the last term on the right hand side of the equation, which represents ordering or set-up costs.

Variable Demand

There may be cases where the lead time does not change, but a stock-out may occur due to increased demand (consumption) after the placement of the order to replenish the inventory. Since the order to replenish the inventory is placed only after the reorder point is reached, the stock-outs occur only after this period. If the demand (consumption) has increased before the reorder point is reached, then an order would have to be placed at the time when the inventory level comes down to the reorder point.

In order to take care of such stock-outs the inventory manager has to first examine the past consumption records of the particular item of the inventory during the reorder period mentioned above and then develop a probability distribution at various levels of its usage.

In the above example, average daily usage (demand) is 100 units and the lead time is 5 days. Hence, under normal situation the demand (consumption) during reorder period would be 5 × 100 = 500 units. It is true that most of the time the demand would be 500 units during this period, but at times, the demand might go up or go down from this consumption level giving rise to stock-outs or excess stock respectively. Scrutiny of records of the enterprise during past five years reveals the demands of inventory during reorder periods. These are given in Table 4.36 along with calculation of probability distribution.

Table 4.36 Inventory Demands during the Reorder Period and Their Probability Distribution (Variable Demand)

Quantity demanded during reorder period (1)	Number of times the demand is made (2)	Times demanded as % of total times (3)	Probability of usage (col. 3/100) (4)
350	8	3	0.03
400	11	4	0.04
450	16	6	0.06
500	186	68	0.68
550	24	9	0.09
600	19	7	0.07
650	8	3	0.03
	272	100	1.00

An examination of columns 1 and 2 of Table 4.36 would tell us that if the company reorders when the inventory falls to 500 units, then it will be safe (0.03 + 0.04 + 0.06 + 0.68 = 0.81) 81 percent of time while at the same time, it runs the risk of being out of stock, for (0.09 + 0.07 + 0.03 = 0.19) 19 percent of the time.

Depending upon the risk-profile of the enterprise it may take on a safety stock at any level beyond the normal consumption (demand) level of 500 units. For example, the enterprise may keep a safety stock of 50 units and take the risk of being out of stock, 0.07 + 0.03 = 0.10 or 10 percent of the time or maintain a safety stock of 150 units and take no risk of being out of stock.

Factoring the Costs

The risk-profile approach, though is a very practical one and is often employed by a number of firms, does not take into account various costs of maintaining safety stock, namely, ordering (set-up) costs, holding costs and stock-out costs. When these costs are considered, the safety stock level will be such where total of these costs are at their minimum.

In the earlier example annual demand (D) of the particular item of inventory was 30,000 units. The ordering (set-up) costs (C) and holding costs were Rs. 25 and Rs. 15 per unit respectively. Other things remaining same, economic production quantity before considering stock-outs (and hence, safety stock) will be 775 units as calculated earlier and as repeated below for convenience.

$$Q = \sqrt{\frac{2Dcp}{H(p-u)}}$$

$$= \sqrt{\frac{2 \times 30,000 \times 25 \times 120}{15(120-100)}}$$

$$= 774.60, \text{ say } 775 \text{ units.}$$

Number of orders per year will, therefore, be 30,000/775 = 38.70 or say, 39.

As the danger of being out of stock occurs after the reorder point, i.e. after the order is placed, the company is in danger of being out of stock 39 times during the years.

In Table 4.37 we have recast the probability distribution and calculated the costs of being out of stock.

Table 4.37 Calculation of Stock-out Costs when Lead Time is Constant but Demand is Variable

Safety stock (1)	Probability of stock-out (2)	Shortages (3)	Annual cost (4)	Total stock-out cost (5)
0	0.09 when demand is 550 units	50	$50 \times 0.09 \times 5 \times 39$ = Rs. 877.5	
	0.07 when demand is 600 units	100	$100 \times 0.07 \times 5 \times 39$ = Rs. 1365.0	
	0.03 when demand is 650 units	150	$150 \times 0.03 \times 5 \times 39$ = Rs. 877.5	Rs. 3120
50	0.07 when demand is 600 units	50	$50 \times 0.07 \times 5 \times 39$ = Rs. 682.5	
	0.03 when demand is 650 units	100	$100 \times 0.03 \times 5 \times 39$ = Rs. 585.0	Rs. 1267.5
100	0.03 when demand is 650 units	50	$50 \times 0.03 \times 5 \times 39$ = Rs. 292.5	Rs. 292.5
150	0	0	0	0

Note: Stock-out cost is Rs. 5 per unit as in the earlier example.

In Table 4.38 we have calculated total cost at various levels of safety stock after taking into account the carrying (holding) cost.

Table 4.38 Calculation of Total Costs at Different Levels of Safety Stocks (Variable Lead Time Demand)

Safety stock (units) (1)	Stock-out costs (Rs.) (2)	Annual carrying cost (Rs.) (3)	Total cost (Rs.) (col. 2 + col. 3) (4)
0	3120	0	3120
50	1268	50 × 15 = 750	2018
100	293	100 × 15 = 1500	1793
150	0	150 × 15 = 2250	2250

It may be seen that total cost is lowest (Rs. 1793) at a safety stock level of 100 units. The company should, therefore, maintain a safety stock of 100 units. The reorder point will also change to, $\dfrac{30,000}{300} \times 5 + 100 = 600$ units. That is, when the inventory level falls to 600 units, order for replenishment of stock will have to be placed.

Average inventory holding under this probabilistic model will be, 775/2 + 100 = 488 units, which is much lower than what we have derived in the earlier model. This is because in the present model we have optimised between the risk of being out of stock and the total cost of maintaining a given safety stock level, and picked up the one whose total cost is at the minimum. One should note that at this level of safety stock the enterprise still runs the risk of being out of stock if the lead time demand increases to 650 units, though the probability of such an occurrence is only 3 percent.

Variable Lead Time

In the earlier example we assumed lead time to be constant while the demand (consumption) varied during the lead time. But in real-life situations, suppliers are not always able to conform to the delivery time for reasons which are often out of their control. Records of the procurement section for past periods would reveal a pattern of delays which can be converted into a probabilistic distribution table as we have done before. A simplistic approach, often used by many firms, is to fix up reorder point on the average of lead time. But if there is substantial variation in lead time, it may be necessary to adopt the statistical approach. This is explained below with the help of the above example suitably modified for the purpose at hand. Lead time variations are given in column 1 of Table 4.39 which are subsequently converted to probability distribution as in Table 4.36.

On the basis of information processed in Table 4.39, stock-out costs at various levels of safety stock and final total costs are calculated in Table 4.40 and Table 4.41 respectively.

Column 4 of Table 4.41 reveals that at a safety stock level of 200 units the total cost is at its minimum; hence it is advisable for the enterprise to maintain this level of safety stock when the lead time is variable but the demand is constant.

Table 4.39 Lead Time Variations and Their Probability Distribution

Lead time (days) (1)	Lead time demand (2)	Number of times occurring (3)	Times occurred as % of total times (4)	Probability distribution (5)
2	200	8	3	0.03
3	300	11	4	0.04
4	400	16	6	0.06
5	500	186	68	0.68
6	600	24	9	0.09
7	700	19	7	0.07
8	800	8	3	0.03
Total 35	3500	272	100	1.00

Table 4.40 Calculation of Stock-out Costs when Lead Time Varies

Safety stock (1)	Probability of stock-out (2)	Shortages (3)	Annual cost (4)	Total stock-out cost (5)
0	0.09 when demand is 600 units	100	$0.09 \times 100 \times 5 \times 39$ = 1755	
	0.07 when demand is 700 units	200	$0.07 \times 200 \times 5 \times 39$ = 2730	
	0.03 when demand is 800 units	300	$0.03 \times 300 \times 5 \times 39$ = 1755	6240
100	0.07 when demand is 700 units	100	$0.07 \times 100 \times 5 \times 39$ = 1365	
	0.03 when demand is 800 units	200	$0.03 \times 200 \times 5 \times 39$ = 1170	2535
200	0.03 when demand is 800 units	100	$0.03 \times 100 \times 5 \times 39$ = 585	585
300	0	0	0	0

Table 4.41 Calculation of Total Costs at Different Levels of Safety Stocks (Variable Lead Time)

Safety stock (units) (1)	Stock-out cost (Rs.) (2)	Annual carrying cost (Rs.) (3)	Total cost (Rs.) (col. 2 + col. 3) (4)
0	6240	0	6240
100	2535	100 × 15 = 1500	4035
200	585	200 × 15 = 3000	3585
300	0	300 × 15 = 4500	4500

The *reorder point* will be $\dfrac{30,000 \times 5}{300} + 200 = 700$ units, and the average stock holding under the given situation will increase to 775/2 + 200 = 588 units.

Variable Lead Time and Variable Demand

So far, we have considered situations where one of the above two variables are allowed to vary keeping the other constant. While there may be good number of cases where demand remains constant during the reorder period but constancy of lead time, that is, the suppliers adhering to the agreed delivery time, is hardly to be found. Lead time uncertainty is much more than the demand uncertainty in countries like India, particularly when suppliers are public sector undertakings, who incidentally are the major suppliers of basic raw materials in the country and known for their worse adherence to delivery commitments.

Most of the firms, however, suffer from both demand and lead time uncertainties. There should, therefore, be two sets of probabilities—one for the lead time and the other for the demand. The methodology for dealing with this kind of problem is to develop a joint probability distribution for different combinations of demand and lead time variations. The joint probability distribution will be calculated along a range indicated by the product of the smallest demand and the shortest lead time on one end to the product of highest demand and the longest lead time on the other. The joint probability distribution so arranged will then be used to determine the safety stock level and reorder point.

In the earlier two examples we have used similar probability distributions for both demand and lead time variations. Here we shall use different probability distributions for the two. The example chosen is also of smaller size and of lesser complexity. The purpose here is to demonstrate the method of calculation of joint probability distribution to determine the safety stock level, the reorder point and average stock holding. A number of statistical packages are available to determine the joint probability distribution through computer analysis.

Example The annual demand of an inventory item is 300 units. Cost of production per unit is Rs. 6000 and the carrying cost is Rs. 900 per unit. Set-up cost per production run is Rs. 2500. All stock-outs are backordered at a cost of Rs. 700 per unit. The daily rate of demand and the daily rate of production for the company are 1 unit and 1.2 units respectively. The plant works for 300 days in a year. The past records of the company showed that both the demand during lead time and actual delivery (lead) time had varied during the reorder period. In Table 4.42, daily lead time demand (consumption) of the inventory item and the delivery (lead) time are given with their respective probability of occurrence as determined from past records of the company.

Table 4.42 Probability Distribution of Lead Time Demand

Daily demand in units	Probability of occurrence	Lead time in days	Probability of occurrence
0	0.10	1	0.65
1	0.60	2	0.35
2	0.30		

The above table reveals a pattern where both demand and lead time vary independently of each other. Under the circumstances, possible demands during lead time can be, 0, 1, 2, 3, and 4 units in terms of all possible combinations as the following calculations in Table 4.43 will show. We have also calculated the joint probability distribution against each possible lead time demand.

Table 4.43 Calculation of Joint Probability Distributions

Lead time demand	Possible combinations			Joint probability	
0	1. First day:	Demand = 0		0.10 × 0.65	= 0.065
	2. First day:	Demand = 0			
	Second day:	Demand = 0		0.10 × 0.10 × 0.35	= 0.0035
					0.0685
1	1. First day:	Demand = 1		0.60 × 0.65	= 0.39
	2. First day:	Demand = 1			
	Second day:	Demand = 0		0.60 × 0.10 × 0.35	= 0.021
	3. First day:	Demand = 0			
	Second day:	Demand = 1		0.10 × 0.60 × 0.35	= 0.021
					0.4320
2	1. First day:	Demand = 2		0.30 × 0.65	= 0.1950
	2. First day:	Demand = 0			
	Second day:	Demand = 2		0.10 × 0.30 × 0.35	= 0.0105
	3. First day:	Demand = 1			
	Second day:	Demand = 1		0.60 × 0.60 × 0.35	= 0.1260
	4. First day:	Demand = 2			
	Second day:	Demand = 0		0.30 × 0.10 × 0.35	= 0.0105
					0.3420
3	1. First day:	Demand = 1			
	Second day:	Demand = 2		0.60 × 0.30 × 0.35	= 0.0630
	2. First day:	Demand = 2			
	Second day:	Demand = 1		0.30 × 0.60 × 0.35	= 0.0630
					0.1260
4	1. First day:	Demand = 2			
	Second day:	Demand = 2		0.30 × 0.30 × 0.35	= 0.0315

In Table 4.44, joint probability distribution against the possible lead time demands, as calculated in Table 4.43, is summarised along with the calculation of weighted average demand during lead time.

It is necessary now to calculate *economic production quantity* from the data given in the example.

$$Q(EPQ) = \sqrt{\frac{2 \times 300 \times 2500 \times 1.20}{900(1.20 - 1)}} = 100 \text{ units}$$

Number of production runs per year = 300/100 = 3

The optimum probability of a stock-out is computed by the following formula.[35]

---

35. See Johnson, L.A. and D.C. Montgomery, *Operations Research in Production Planning, Scheduling and Inventory Control*, John Wiley, New York, 1974.

Table 4.44 Probability Distribution of Various Lead Time Demands

Lead time demand	Probability distribution	Weighted average of lead time demand (col. 1 × col. 2)	Moving probability of stock-outs
(1)	(2)	(3)	(4)
0	0.0685	0	0.9315
1	0.4320	0.4320	0.4995
2	0.3420	0.6840	0.1575
3	0.1260	0.3780	0.0315
4	0.0315	0.1260	0.0
Total	1.0000	1.6200	

Figures in column 4 are calculated as 1 minus moving total of column 2. For example, 1 − 0.0685 = 0.9315 or 1 − (0.0685 + 0.4320) = 0.4995 and so on.

$$P(0) = \frac{HQ}{ED}$$

where H, Q, E and D are carrying cost, economic production quantity, stock-out cost and annual demand respectively.

For the given example, the computed probability is

$$P(0) = \frac{900 \times 100}{700 \times 300}$$

$$= 0.4285$$

The reorder point will be indicated by the location of $P(0)$ along the moving stock-out probability calculated in column 4 of Table 4.44. We find that 0.4285 falls between 0.4995 and 0.1575. The lead time demands corresponding to them are 1 and 2 respectively, the lowest point of which, namely 2 will be considered as the reorder point. The safety stock will, therefore, be reorder point in units minus the weighted average of lead time demand calculated in column 3 of Table 4.44. That is, 2 − 1.62 = 0.38 unit.

This fractional unit of safety stock need not appear as unusual because (though the present example is only illustrative) in real-life production system, a full-day production may not always conform to discrete number of units—uncompleted units may often have to be carried over to the next day. However, for purpose of stock holding calculations the figures can be approximated to nearest discrete units as and when necessary, as we have done in several instances before.

Average stock holding will be 100/2 + 0.38 = 50.38 units

The reorder point and safety stock calculated above are optimum under the given production pattern and costs. But an enterprise may decide to take a particular level of the risk of being out of stock depending upon its risk-profile which can be high, medium or low. For example, without bothering for the optimum reorder point, it may straightway prescribe that it can carry a stock-out probability of 20 percent. New reorder point under this prescribed probability of 0.20 can be located between 0.1575 and 0.0315 of column 4 of

Table 4.44 which correspond to 2 units and 3 units respectively in column 1 of the table. Taking the last point between the two, the new reorder point will be 3 units, hence, safety stock will be 3 − 1.62 = 1.38 units and the average stock holding will be 100/2 + 1.38 = 51.38 units.

The methodology prescribed above is applicable for both discrete and continuous probability distributions of lead time demand. But in case of discrete distributions as in the present example, exact location of computed optimum probability of stock-out [$P(0)$] on the moving probability distributions (column 4 of Table 4.44) is not always possible (the same is the case when a particular stock-out probability is prescribed). For example, $P(0)$ of 0.4285 in our present example cannot be located exactly in column 4 of Table 4.44. When such is the case, the next lower attainable stock-out probability is selected as we have done here.

This methodology is straightforward and easy to calculate as it requires only few steps as compared to the elaborate method prescribed in the earlier two examples. Both the methods will give same results because both attempt to optimise between cost of carrying safety stock and the cost of stock-outs. Once the conceptual base is properly understood, the inventory manager can use the latest methodology for ease of computations, resulting in savings in systems cost.

The formula for computed probability of stock-out [$P(0)$] is applicable only in cases where sales are not lost but backordered. In the case where sales are completely lost the formula should be modified as below

$$P(OL) = \frac{HQ}{FD + HQ}$$

where F is cost of lost sales per unit.

Unknown Stock-out Costs

When sales are not lost but backordered, it is possible to calculate with fair level of accuracy the extra charges for a backorder except the cost of impairment of goodwill due to the firm's inability to supply in time. For a trader, direct cost of lost sales could be the markup which is known. If it is back-ordered, then this loss is reduced to markup minus the backorder costs. But in both the cases estimation of goodwill loss is difficult which may at times be much larger than the calculable loss. The assumption of fixed proportionality in calculating stock-out cost is often not valid. That is, being out of stock for 10 units may not be equal to ten times of being out of stock for 1 unit. It can be much more.

For a manufacturing firm the issue is much more complicated. Component parts used in a manufacture are not sold individually and hence, its value is difficult to assess. Moreover, the cost of a production bottleneck due to want of a particular part may vary from idle labour for only a few hours to complete shut down of the plant. Such a wide variation may often make the calculation of stock-out cost difficult, if not impossible.

Service Level Policy

The magnitude of the problems discussed above has led to the development of service level approach by which an organisation first establishes its goal in terms of an acceptable probability of being out of stock. As indicated in the last part of our last example, this is determined mostly by the risk-profile of an enterprise. In some cases, however, industrial practice also determines this level.

Only a few companies can afford to maintain a 100 percent service level because it entails the cost of carrying a very high level of safety stock, which may outweigh the very cost of being out of stock. The enterprise must, therefore, decide at which service level additional investment is justified. For example, in determining a service level policy, the management may have the following three alternatives to choose from:

1. To ensure a 90 percent service level (i.e. the enterprise is prepared to satisfy 90 percent of all demands from out of stock), it may be necessary to carry three weeks' consumption (demand). This will entail an investment of Rs. 69 lakh at a carrying cost of Rs. 13.80 lakh p.a.

2. To increase the service level further to 95 percent, stocks of an additional week's consumption (demand) have to be carried at an additional investment of Rs. 19 lakh with a carrying cost of Rs. 3.80 lakh. That is, the total investment and carrying cost for 95 percent customer satisfaction level would be Rs. 88 lakh and Rs. 17.60 lakh respectively.

3. To push up the service level further to almost 99 percent customer satisfaction, additional investment would increase by Rs. 37 lakh at a carrying cost of Rs. 7.40 lakh. Total investment for 99 percent service level would, therefore, be Rs. 125 lakh at an aggregate carrying cost of Rs. 25 lakh.

[It may be noted that additional investments and carrying costs for increasing levels of customer satisfaction rise more than proportionately, which we shall elaborate later.]

In order to decide an appropriate policy of service level satisfaction, the enterprise must decide whether an extra cost is justified by the improved level of service satisfaction.

The pattern of consumption (demand) during the reorder period determines the safety stock level of an inventory item. For example, if the past records of usage of an item during reorder period has been found to average around 100 units and it has never gone up beyond 110 units at any time during the period, then maintenance of 10 units of safety stock is able to satisfy 100 percent service level. But if the variation is as high as say, 250 units, then 100 percent service satisfaction level would call for maintenance of 150 units as safety stock which may be very costly and hence, may not justify the benefits received by protecting the firm fully against any stock-out. This is more so because inventory investment increases not linearly but exponentially with the increase in service level as we have indicated above. In cases like this, the question arises as to what level of deviation from the average demand is tolerable for the enterprise. In order to arrive at a decision, the manager must know the cost at every point of deviation and choose the one which suits him best.

If we now elaborate the above example, we may find that when the average consumption (demand) is 100 units during the reorder time and the maximum consumption (demand) is 250 units, then there always are some demands which are less than 100 units and some which are more than 100 units, giving rise finally to an average demand of 100 units. Readers may recall that we are ultimately talking about the statistical concepts of mean and standard deviation for a normal distribution which we discussed in the earlier part of this chapter. Here we shall use the standard deviation (SD) as the measurement of the risk of being out of stock.

Example   Recent years' records of an enterprise reveal the following demands (consumption) during the reorder period.

Quantity Demanded

70	90	180	30	180
170	100	190	130	50
90	170	170	50	170
130	90	130	70	200
220	180	100	100	190

Carrying cost of the inventory is Rs. 10 per unit per annum.

In Table 4.45 we have calculated mean $(\overline{X})$ and standard deviation (SD) of the above observations.

Calculations made in Table 4.45 reveal mean lead time demand $(\overline{X})$ of 130 units with a standard deviation (SD) of 53.52 units.

These two parameters suggest that if the enterprise maintains a reorder point at the mean level of 130 units, there is a chance that half of the time it would be able to satisfy the demand during the reorder period, i.e. the demands which fall on the left-hand side of the mean in the normal curve and are lower than 130 units. But at the same time, the enterprise will be out of stock half the time for demands falling on the right-hand side of the mean line, which are more than 130 units. The risk of being out of stock, therefore, lies on the right-hand side of the mean line and is measurable in terms of number of standard deviations. For example, if the enterprise desires to protect itself 95 percent of the time, we have to find out how many standard deviations it represents and, therefore, calculate the safety stocks that it would require to maintain, by multiplying the number of SDs with SD units. This is done by referring to the *standard normal probability distribution table* given as an Annexure to this chapter. If the desired service level is say, 60 percent (0.60) we shall first try to locate 0.60 or its close approximation from the figures given in the columns-rows to the right of the first column of the table. We find that 0.59871 (which is a close approximation of 0.60) is appearing under the column head, 0.05 against the row 0.2. Adding the last two together, we obtain 0.05 + 0.2 = 0.25, as the number of SDs that satisfies the 60 percent service level requirement. That is, the firm should now maintain a safety stock of 53.52 × 0.25 = 13.38, say 13 units to increase its service level to 60 percent. In Table 4.46 we have calculated safety stock requirements at different service levels and their cost assuming a carrying cost of Rs. 10 per unit p.a.

Table 4.45 Calculation of Mean and Standard Deviation of Demand during Reorder Period

Demands (X_i) (1)	($X_i - \overline{X}$) (2)	($X_i - \overline{X}$)² (3)	
70	− 60	3600	
170	40	1600	
90	− 40	1600	Mean $= X = \dfrac{\sum X_i}{N}$
130	0	0	
220	90	8100	$= \dfrac{3250}{25} = 130$
90	− 40	1600	
100	− 30	900	SD $= \sqrt{\dfrac{\sum(X_i - \overline{X})^2}{N}}$
170	40	1600	
90	− 40	1600	
180	50	2500	$= \sqrt{\dfrac{71,600}{25}}$
180	50	2500	
190	60	3600	$= 53.52$
170	40	1600	
130	0	0	
100	− 30	900	
30	− 100	10,000	
130	0	0	
50	− 80	6400	
70	− 60	3600	
100	− 30	900	
180	50	2500	
50	− 80	6400	
170	40	1600	
200	70	4900	
190	60	3600	
3250	0	71,600	

Column 4 of Table 4.46 reveals that the relationship between the service level and the cost is not proportional. The cost rises exponentially with the increase in service level. This fact is sharply revealed in column 5 where we have made a sensitivity analysis of cost with 1 percent rise in service level. To push up the service level from 50 percent to 60 percent additional carrying cost is Rs. 15 while a mere 1 percent rise in service level from 98 percent to 99 percent would entail an additional cost of Rs. 294.

There cannot be any uniform service level policy for all items of inventory. It would be different for different items or groups of items in an inventory. The tabular presentation made in Table 4.46 will help the manager to decide a service level policy for each item of inventory. For some items, which are crucial to production (sales), the service level may go up to 99.9 percent, no

Table 4.46 Calculation of Safety Stocks and their Cost at Various Service Levels

Service level desired (percent of 1) (1)	Number of standard deviations to the right of the mean (2)	Safety stocks required (col. 2 × 53.52) (3)	Annual carrying cost of safety stocks (Rs.) (col. 3 × 10) (4)	Cost of 1% increase in service level (Rs.) (5)
0.50	0.00	0	0	(130 – 0)/10 = 13
0.60	0.25	13	130	(280 – 130)/10 = 15
0.70	0.52	28	280	(450 – 280)/10 = 17
0.80	0.84	45	450	(690 – 450)/10 = 24
0.90	1.28	69	690	(880 – 690)/5 = 38
0.95	1.64	88	880	(940 – 880)/1 = 60
0.96	1.75	94	940	(1010 – 940)/1 = 70
0.97	1.88	101	1010	(1100 – 1010)/1 = 90
0.98	2.05	110	1100	(1250 – 1100)/1 = 150
0.99	2.33	125	1250	(1650 – 1250)/0.9 = 444
0.999	3.09	165	1650	

matter what is the cost, but for some other items which are not so important, the enterprise can take the risk of settling the service level at say, 70 percent.[36]

EXCESS INVENTORY

An organisation which suffers from shortage of inventory, resulting in lost sales, low profitability (and consequent loss of goodwill), may also suffer from an excess inventory and consequent erosion of profitability due to the investments and costs associated with the maintenance of excess inventory. In India, banks discourage holding of excess inventory as recommended by Tandon Committee.[37]

---

36. The statistical techniques used in this section for determination of reorder point, safety stock, etc. assume a normal distribution of various observations used in different examples. For most of business applications assumption of a normal distribution is quite valid. But in some cases, the distribution may not follow the pattern of a normal distribution. It may be a Poisson distribution which, unlike normal distribution, is not symmetrical with respect to the mean; it is skewed to the right. The SD of a Poisson distribution is simply the square root of mean: $SD_P = \sqrt{X}$. For items with low or infrequent demand, a low mean Poisson distribution may be helpful. It is not applicable to distribution with mean values above 20.

   For some retail and wholesale business a *negative exponential distribution* may be observed. This is a single parameter distribution completely defined by its mean. The standard deviation is the same as its mean; $SD_N = \overline{X}$.

37. Reserve Bank of India, *Report of the Study Group to Frame Guidelines for Follow-up of Bank Credit,* Bombay, 1975.

Excess inventory may pile up in the store for reasons mentioned below:

1. Items of inventory might have already become obsolete, but no notice is being taken for their disposal. Obsolescence of an inventory item may be due to any of the following reasons:
   (a) Substantial decrease in the demand for the product.
   (b) Technological change or change in the methods of production which no longer requires the particular items of inventory.
   (c) Introduction of a new product in replacement of the existing one.
   (d) Redesign of the product where the particular inventory item does not have any place.

2. Slow moving items are bought and stored without any regard to their consumption (demand). This may be due to overzealous buying behaviour of the purchase section.

3. Forecasting error may cause surplus inventory even for items which are ordinarily fast moving.

When excess inventory get piled up in the system the accrued carrying costs for extended period of time may gradually erode the bottomline of an enterprise, the total impact of which is often felt when the enterprise suffers a downturn. During this time, materials manager would invariably be asked to reduce excess inventory, which shall always contribute to the profitability of a business. If the return on sales is 5 percent and the opportunity cost of the firm is 25 percent, then a hundred rupees worth of reduction in inventory would be equivalent to making a sales of Rs. 500. This, on the other hand, means that the firm can make the same amount of profit by reducing the inventory by Rs. 100 as it could do by a sale of Rs. 500. But, whatever may be the reason or pressure, a materials manager cannot afford to disrupt the production in his zeal to reduce the excess inventory.

Reduction of inventory can be effected in any of the following ways:

(a) Direct reduction of the surplus items. It may be advantageous to sell or salvage the surplus stocks. This not only saves on the carrying cost of the excess inventory, but also brings in positive cash flows to the enterprise.

(b) By reducing or limiting further purchase/acquisition of the items. For example, safety stock levels can be reduced by decreasing the service level, reducing the lead time, etc.

All the above steps should be taken only after a proper review of the inventory policy and determination of the level of excess stock. The problem is depicted in Figure 4.8.

In order to establish whether there is any excess stock, it is necessary first to determine the *economic time supply* (ETS) for the item of inventory. Any stock above the ETS may be sold. The assumption here is that there is an ongoing demand for the item and the excess stock sold can be replaced at a later date. The economic time supply is calculated by the following formula.[38]

---

38. Tersine, R.J. and R.A. Toelle, "Optimum Stock Levels for Excess Inventory Items", *Journal of Operations Management,* Vol. 4, No. 3, 1984, pp. 245–258.

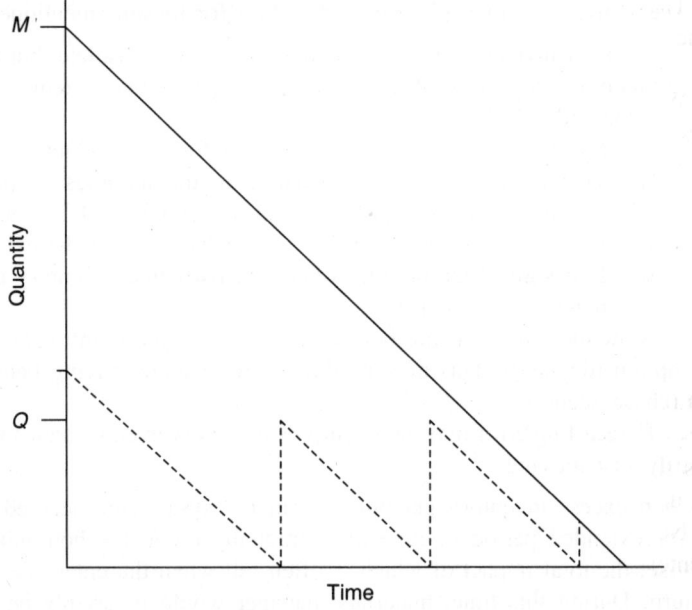

Figure 4.8 Excess inventory levels.

$$\text{ETS} = \frac{V - S + \dfrac{C}{L}}{VH} + \frac{L}{2D}$$

where

V = cost or market value of the item ignoring quantity discounts
S = resale or salvage value of the item
C = ordering cost per order
L = lot size in units
H = carrying cost p.a. as a fraction of Re. 1
D = annual demand in units which is known

The model is suitable for those inventory items which are not perishable and for which there are no constraints on space or fund. No stock-outs are permitted as in any EOQ model.

When lot size (L) equals the economic order quantity (EOQ), the above model will reduce itself to:

$$\text{ETS} = \frac{Q}{D} + \frac{V - S}{VH}$$

Let us explain the model with the help of the following example.

Example As a part of the measure for streamlining inventory management of an enterprise, a thorough investigation of different items of inventory was made. It has been found that the store has been carrying an inventory of 1400 units of an item whose annual demand is 800 units. The lot size is 40.

The unit cost of the material is Rs. 100 on acquisition, but if it is sold back to the market as salvage, the realisable price would be Rs. 75 only. The ordering cost is Rs. 25 per order and the annual carrying cost is 25 percent.

We find that the existing level of inventory represents $1400/800 = 1.75$ years of supply.

The economic time supply will be

$$\text{ETS} = \frac{100 - 75 + \dfrac{25}{40}}{100 \times 0.25} + \frac{40}{2 \times 800}$$

$$= 1.025 + 0.025$$
$$= 1.05 \text{ years.}$$

As 1.05 years' supply is optimal against the existing 1.75 years of supply, 0.70 years supply is in excess which represents $0.70 \times 800 = 560$ units. These units should be sold @ Rs. 75 to reduce the inventory level to $1400 - 560 = 840$ units.

Net benefit accruing to the organisation due to this streamlining of inventory is calculated by the following formula.

$$\text{Net benefit} = t\left(VD - SD + \frac{QVH}{2} + \frac{CD}{Q}\right) + \frac{K^2 VH}{2D}$$

$$+ SK - \frac{DVHt^2}{2} - \frac{KQVH}{2D} - VK - \frac{CK}{Q}$$

where
D = annual demand which is 800 units
V = cost or market value which is Rs. 100 per unit
S = resale or salvage value which is Rs. 75 per unit
Q = lot size which is 40 units
C = ordering cost which is Rs. 25 per order
H = carrying cost fraction which is 0.25
K = available stock which is 1400 units
t = economic time supply which is 1.05 years

Putting the respective figures in the above formula we obtain

$$\text{Net benefit} = \left(100 \times 800 - 75 \times 800 + \frac{40 \times 100 \times 0.25}{2} + \frac{25 \times 800}{40}\right) \times 1.05$$

$$+ \frac{1400^2 \times 100 \times 0.25}{2 \times 800} + 75 \times 1400$$

$$- \frac{800 \times 100 \times 0.25 \times 1.05^2}{2} - \frac{1400 \times 40 \times 100 \times 0.25}{2 \times 800}$$

$$- 100 \times 1400 - \frac{25 \times 1400}{40}$$

$$= \text{Rs. } 4900$$

WORKING CAPITAL RESTRICTIONS

Occasionally banks ration the availability of credit for working capital. This may be due to a general credit squeeze imposed on the banks by the Central Bank of the country to contain expansion during an inflationary situation. A bank may itself also impose a cut in credit due to capital restrictions or for lowering down exposure in a particular industry. It may also be that the bank does not have adequate fund to maintain the credit lines of all their customers at the previous level, and, therefore, it decides to ration the available fund amongst its borrowers at a lower level of availment. From corporates' side, there may also be internal shortage of fund to provide the necessary margin for working capital advance as required by banks, which has the effect of ultimately reducing the availability of fund for maintaining an optimum inventory level.

As with any other constraints, working capital constraint also increases the cost of managing inventory. The goal of inventory management under working capital constraint is to minimise this cost without causing disruption in production (sales). We shall examine this problem with the help of the following example.

Example   The inventory of an enterprise consists of five items. The annual demand and unit cost (P) of the five items are as follows.

Item no.	Annual demand (Units)	Unit cost (Rs.)
A	1500	7.50
B	2250	25.00
C	6000	12.50
D	30,000	15.00
E	45,000	5.00

The ordering cost is Rs. 25 per order and carrying cost is 20 percent per annum.

The bank has imposed restriction which will have the effect of reducing working capital fund against inventories by Rs. 2000.

We shall first calculate EOQ of every item under the condition of unrestricted working capital. For item No. A, the EOQ will be

$$Q_A = \sqrt{\frac{2 \times 1500 \times 25}{7.50 \times 0.20}} = 223.60 \text{ units, say 224 units}$$

Number of orders per year = 1500/224 = 6.70
Average inventory = 224/2 = 112 units

Results of similar calculations for all other items of inventory are presented in Table 4.47.

Column 6 of Table 4.47 indicates that presently the investment in inventories is Rs. 13,937, whose carrying cost is Rs. 13,937 × 0.20 = Rs. 2787.40. Total ordering costs will be 111.47 × Rs. 25 = Rs. 2786.75.[39]

---

39. In fact, both the carrying costs and ordering costs shall be equal because all the items are at EOQ. The small difference is due to approximation.

Table 4.47 EOQ Calculations for All the Five Inventory Items

Item no. (1)	Unit cost (Rs.) (2)	Order size (EOQ units) (3)	No. of orders per year (4)	Average inventory (units) [col. 3/2] (5)	Investment in inventory (Rs.) [col. 5 × col. 2] (6)
A	7.50	224	6.70	112	840
B	25.00	150	15.00	75	1875
C	12.50	346	17.34	173	2162
D	15.00	707	42.43	354	5310
E	5.00	1500	30.00	750	3750
			111.47		13,937

Due to restriction imposed by bank, the enterprise will now be required to work within, Rs. 13,937 – Rs. 2000 = Rs. 11,937. As this restriction is imposed uniformly on all items of inventory, the first step that the firm is required to take is to reduce the order size from the EOQ level by the ratio of restricted fund to the unrestricted fund, i.e. Rs. 11,937/13,937 = Rs. 0.8565. For example, order size for item No. A will now be 224 × 0.8565 = 192 units. This reduction in order size will have the effect of increasing the number of orders per year. For item No. A, it would now be: 1500/192 = 7.81, which in turn will increase the ordering cost to 7.81 × 25 = Rs. 195.25, but reduce the carrying cost to (192/2) × 7.50 × 0.20 = Rs. 144. In Table 4.48 we have presented results of similar calculations for all the inventory items.

Table 4.48 Inventory Positions and Their Costs under Restricted Working Capital

Item no. (1)	Order size (2)	No. of orders (D/col. 2) (3)	Ordering costs (Rs.) (col. 3 × 25) (4)	Average inventory (col. 2/2) (5)	Investment in inventory (Rs.) [P × col. 5] (6)	Carrying cost (Rs.) (col. 6 × 0.20) (7)
A	192	7.81	195.25	96.00	720.00	144.00
B	128	17.58	439.50	64.00	1600.00	320.00
C	296	20.27	506.75	148.00	1850.00	370.00
D	606	49.50	1237.50	303.00	4545.00	909.00
E	1285	35.02	875.50	642.50	3212.50	642.50
		130.18	3254.50		11,927.50	2385.50

Relevant costs before and after the working capital restrictions are calculated and compared below:

Relevant costs = ordering cost + carrying cost
Relevant cost (after) = Rs. 3254.50 + Rs. 2385.50 = Rs. 5640.00
Relevant cost (before) = Rs. 2786.75 + Rs. 2787.40 = Rs. 5574.15
                                                    Rs.   65.85

It may be noticed that restriction on working capital has caused a net increase in cost by Rs. 65.85. The reduction in carrying cost due to lower average level of inventory has been more than offset by a rise in ordering costs.

MATERIAL REQUIREMENTS PLANNING (MRP I)

The basic assumption of EOQ models discussed so far is the constant rate of demand. This is valid, as we have discussed earlier, for large number of business applications. That the demand rate is not always constant in real-life situations does not invalidate the inventory planning under EOQ models. However, these models are particularly valid and suitable for end-items (finished products) whose demand is independent of demands of other items. Being driven by the market, demand for these items customarily exhibits a pattern. But it fluctuates due to random influences of the market place, which we can capture by a probabilistic distribution. Under EOQ systems, demand for independent demand items are forecasted and used to determine the level of replenishment with the objective of making the inventory available all the time.

Demand Characteristics

An independent demand item, e.g. an end-product, creates demand for a number of subordinated items down the line to enable the enterprise to produce the end-item product. Demand for these subordinated items are dependent ultimately upon the independent demand product, but amongst themselves there is also a hierarchy of dependency. For example, demand for a car (independent) will cause demand for manufacturing, among others, four doors which in turn shall create demand for procuring sheet metals of particular sizes. It will follow an output-input staircase from 'highest level' to the 'lowest level' till all items required to produce the end-product are fully covered. It follows, therefore, that unlike independent demand item, the demand for dependent demand items does not require any forecasting as this is derived from the demand of end-items. In other words, the demand for independent items needs to be forecasted, while the demand for dependent items may be directly calculated from the manufacturing requirements of the independent demand items.

It is necessary, therefore, to classify the items of inventory between independent and dependent demands and apply appropriate techniques for their management and control. *Material requirements planning* (MRP I) system has been specifically developed to take care of dependent demand items of the inventory. The primary objective of MRP is to plan the requirement and availability of dependent demand items like, materials, components, etc. for meeting delivery schedules of independent demand items.

Master Production Schedule

MRP, as the name suggests, is a planning tool which takes off after the demand for independent items are settled. A *master production schedule* (MPS) is prepared for all end-items which forms the basic input-document of the MRP system. The MPS outlines the time-phased requirements of products in what is popularly known as *time buckets*. The minimum planning horizon must be long enough to cover the cumulative procurement and production lead times for all materials, components and assemblies comprising the end-product.

Bill of Materials

While the MPS indicates how many of each end-item must be available on given dates, the *bill of materials* (BOM) helps calculate the quantities of dependent demand components required to produce end-items. BOM, which is also called *product structure records,* not only indicates materials needed for end-item for all the levels of production in a structured manner, it also clearly outlines the sequence of steps needed for manufacturing the product—from the conversion of raw materials into sub-assemblies at the lowest level to the subsequent steps involved in building assemblies, and lastly to the final assembly of the end-item at the highest level in the structure. The process is popularly known as 'explosion' because each level in the product structure creates more requirements than the previous one. In other words, aggregate requirements are obtained by exploding the end-item product structure record to its lower level requirements. The explosion process is depicted in Figure 4.9.

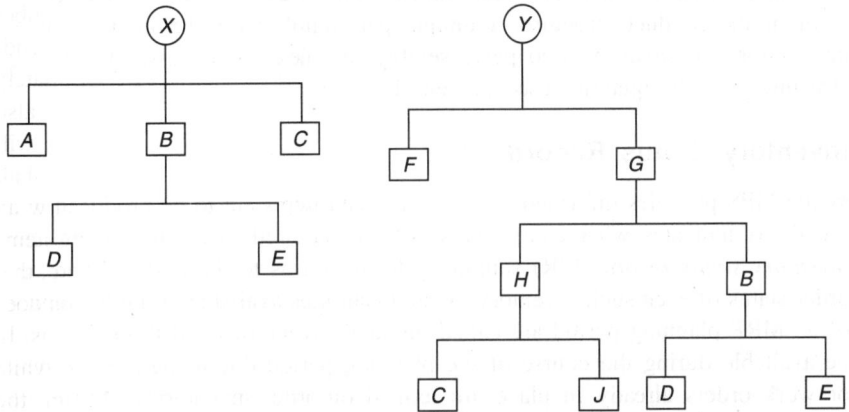

Figure 4.9 Low-level coding for each item of product structures.

The two boxes at the top denoted by *X* and *Y* are two end-items having independent demands. Lower boxes represent subordinated components required for manufacturing *X* and *Y*. A level code is assigned to all boxes to help calculate all requirements of a particular component. For example, both *X* and *Y* being the end-items are assigned O level. *X* has two levels, 1 and 2 while *Y* has three levels, 1, 2 and 3. We now begin by assigning codes to the lowest levels and then move upwards. Thus, components *C, D, E* and *J* are assigned the low-level code 3. Moving upward to level 2 for both *X* and *Y*, we find that there are *B, D, E* and *H* components. As components *D* and *E* are already assigned lower level code 3, we ignore them and assign code 2 to the remaining *B* and *H*. Proceeding further up to level 1 for both the end-products, we find there are *A, B, C, F* and *G* items. *B* and *C* have already been assigned lower level codes 2 and 3, respectively. For the remaining *A, F,* and *G,* we assign code 1. Finally, a table is drawn up as in Table 4.49 indicating different level codes assigned to various items.

Table 4.49 Component Codings at Different Levels

Item	Low-level code	Level code	Items
C	3	0	X, Y
D	3	1	A, F, G
E	3	2	B, H
J	3	3	C, D, E, J
B	2		
H	2		
A	1		
F	1		
G	1		
X	0		
Y	0		

Bill of materials also provides information on every component at every level of the product structure, a unique part number for the item, an item description, the quantity used per assembly; the next higher assembly in the structure, and the quantity used per end-item.[40]

Inventory Status Record

While MPS provides information as to what end-items are to be produced and the BOM indicates what components will be required to produce them, the *inventory status record* (ISR) supplies information as to the on-hand and on-order status of each such inventory items. Quantities available at the beginning of an MRP planning period are called on-hand inventories and those that will be available during the course of the planning period due to purchase orders or work orders already in place are termed on-order inventories. Aggregate requirement of an inventory item as derived from BOM is checked with the ISR; if there is any short fall, MRP will automatically recommend a procurement. Besides providing this main line information, the ISR can also be developed to provide subsidiary information like up-to-date usage and demand pattern of an item, list of vendors, and lead time requirements along with vendor delivery performance.

MRP computation for each component is done through an MRP matrix, a typical example of which is given in Table 4.50.

---

40. Tersine, R.J., *Principles of Inventory and Materials Management*, 4th ed., PTR, Prentice-Hall, Englewood Cliffs, New Jersey, 1994. Chapter 4 of the book can be referred for detailed presentation of Bill of Materials.

Table 4.50 MRP Matrix and Computations of Component

Item	Lot size	Lead time	On hand	Safety stock	Low Allo-cated	Level code	Computations	PD	1	2	3	4	5	6
							Gross requirements		100	150	250	250	300	400
							Scheduled receipts		100	250				
X	250	2	100	0	0	1	Projected on-hand	100	100	200	200	200	150	0
							Net requirements				50	50	100	250
							Planned order receipts				250	250	250	250
							Planned order releases		250	250	250	250		

Notes to Table 4.50

1. Left-hand side of the matrix indicates MRP item characteristics.

2. On the right-hand side, PD represents the *past due period carry over* which has resulted into a present on-hand quantity of 100 units represented as projected on-hand quantity on the right-hand side.

3. In Period 1, against gross requirement of 100 units, we have projected on-hand of 100 units as carry over and scheduled receipts of 100 units due from orders already released before the plan period but expected to be received in Period 1 of the plan period. Netting off the total on-hand from the gross requirement we have projected on-hand of 100 units in Period 1.

4. In Period 2, we have similar scheduled receipts of 250 units and projected on-hand of 100 units from the last period, making a total of 350 units against gross requirement of 150 units. Netting against each other a balance of 200 units will remain projected on-hand in Period 2.

5. In Period 3, against a gross requirement of 250 we have only 200 units as projected on-hand from the last period resulting into a net requirement of 50 units. This in turn will need a planned order receipts by the lot size of 250, the order for whose delivery must have to be placed in Period 1. The replenishment will cause finally a projected on-hand of 200 units in Period 3.

6. In Period 4, the gross requirement is 250 units against only a carry over of 200 units. This results into a net requirement of 50 units for which an order by lot size of 250 units must have been placed in Period 2 to cause a planned receipt during the period. After netting off, the projected on-hand will be 200 units for the period.

7. In Period 5, the gross requirement is 300 units. The carry over of the projected on-hand of 200 units can only partially meet the demand. The net requirement shall, therefore, be 100 units which in turn will necessitate a planned receipt during the period for which a lot size order will have to be placed in Period 3. Netting off, the projected on-hand during the period will be 150 units.

8. In Period 6, the gross requirement has increased to 400 units against which projected on-hand, as carry over from the last period, is 150 units giving rise to a net requirement of 250 units. For a planned order receipt of 250 units, an order must have to be placed in Period 4. As the net requirement is equal to planned order receipts, the projected on-hand quantity will be zero during the period.

It should be remembered that whenever a net requirement occurs during a period, there have to be a planned order receipt during the period. The size of the planned order receipt is determined by the lot size.

The requirement of safety stock can be in-built in the MRP system as indicated in Table 4.50, but the stocks are not available for regular usage. It is preferable to have safety stock at the end-item level and not at the component levels in MRP. However, the need for safety stock for low-level items are greatly minimised because the MRP matrix helps calculate the exact requirement and indicates the correct time of replenishment order.

For dependent demand items, EOQ models are not suitable as they tend to cause excessive inventory investments. Dependent demand items being numerous EOQ modelling also creates operational problems. When demand is dependent, there is no need to forecast. Simple arithmetical calculation by explosion of bill of materials is sufficient to find out the exact requirement. MRP system substantially reduces investment in dependent demand inventories and minimises safety stock requirement while increasing operational efficiency of the production system.

As the number of dependent demand items is numerous in a manufacturing organisation, MRP system is generally computerised. One of the initial difficulties with MRP was that it did not take into consideration the capacity of the plant or process. This created problems for scheduling of manufacturing resources. This led to the development of *manufacturing resource planning,* known popularly as MRP II, which first corrected the capacity problem by introducing a feedback control loop (closed loop MRP) to enable the system to compare the manufacturing workload to the process capacity. MRP II was further developed to link manufacturing with engineering, finance and marketing in order to take a total view of all the major enterprise resources and functions. It now provides an excellent information platform for joint decision-making by all departmental heads to achieve the corporate goal.

JUST-IN-TIME (JIT)

Just-In-Time manufacturing could be regarded as an extension of the original concept of managing the material flow in a production system to reduce the level of inventory. But it is not confined to doing just that. Rather, the reduction of inventory and controlling of costs are the two outcomes of JIT system, which not only encompass the entire manufacturing system, but also go beyond it and bind all the organisational systems under a common philosophy of total quality and no waste.

Under JIT, inventory is regarded as a waste because it does not add value to the product, hence, one of the objectives of JIT system is reduction of inventory to zero level. This way, it appears similar to MRP, at least for the dependent demand items, but the way JIT attempts to do it, is different from the mechanistic approach of the MRP. JIT calls for total commitments of all the levels of the organisation, and of all the suppliers towards total quality and removal of waste. It envisages the philosophy of partnership among various actors in the organisational process like, management, workers and suppliers, who have hitherto been regarded as adversaries having different goals to pursue that are at once conflicting to each other. JIT aims to change this perception by bringing all the parties to a common goal of quality achievement and reduction of waste, which have the ultimate effect of putting all of them in a win-win situation.

If this basic philosophy is not understood properly, JIT shall not work. JIT does not offer a mechanistic solution to the problem. It did not work in the United States during the initial period of its implementation in a number of industries because, they regarded it only as a procedure and not an organisational process which demands total commitment at all levels of organisation. Partial commitment under JIT is no commitment.

Toyota System

Just-In-Time is synonymous with Toyota system. In fact, it is the Toyota system which evolved into the JIT system. During the aftermath of the Second World War, Toyota was close to bankruptcy. The management of the company along with its workers launched a virtual crusade to save the company by improving productivity and the quality of the products. The process gradually embraced all the levels in the organisation and ultimately, Toyota emerged from the nemesis to become one of the most efficient companies of the world. Among the various concepts developed by Toyota, one was to move the materials to work centres along a continuous flow, unlike the batch system. The smallest possible quantity of materials moved only when these were necessary to manufacture the products. This had the effect of reducing both the materials inventory and the work-in-process inventory. Moving away from the traditional push system Toyota followed a pull system for moving materials to the shop floor. The entire process was controlled and monitored by a simple card called *Kanban,* which we shall discuss later.

Customer Focus

Customer is the focal point of a JIT strategy. The importance on quality is the requirement of customer satisfaction. Although at the centre of the quality requirements lies the product quality, the total quality that ensures customer satisfaction demands delivery of the product at the agreed time, and the after-sales service once the product is sold. The JIT system allows no excuse to compensate for quality. The system forces the production line to stop manufacturing whenever there is a quality problem. For example, no buffer stock of materials is supplied on-line; only the exact number of parts are supplied to produce the required quantity. The system has to fix up the quality problems as they occur, as otherwise, the inventories of both usable (safety stock) and defective parts will get built up on the shop floor. This calls for a committed linkage amongst various parties in the organisational process. Figure 4.10 captures such linkages.

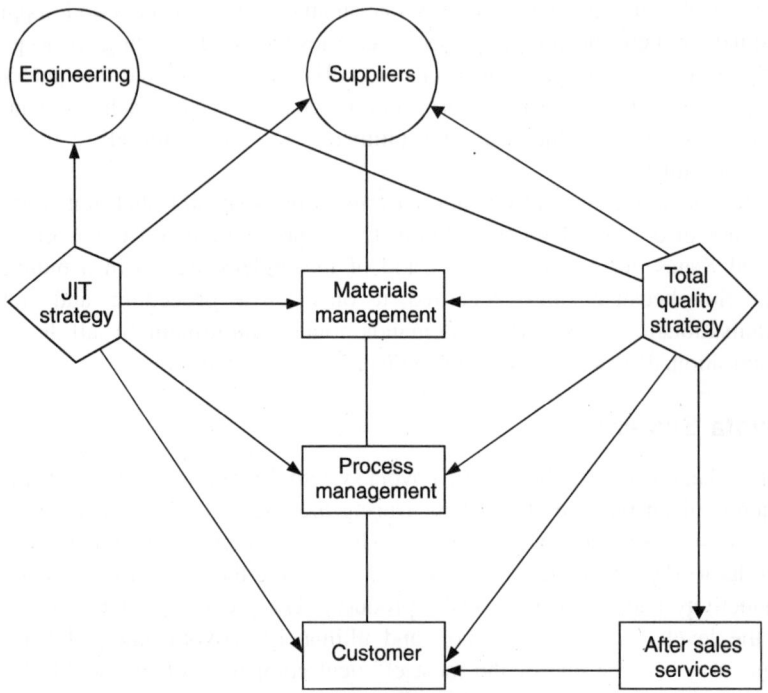

Figure 4.10 Linkages under JIT.

Push vs Pull System

Push System

We have already indicated that MRP is a top-down system which explores the product quantities all the way down to the lowest level. The *inventory status record* takes into consideration all the inventory locations in the plant and then nets off the parts required to manufacture the end-items. In a push system, the MRP triggers a series of workorders required to manufacture the products in designated quantities. A workorder authorises the stores to release the materials to production. (It is also a financial document which records all the inputs spent on the products being manufactured and compares them with the budgeted figures for calculating variances.) The *store kit pulls* all the parts mentioned in the workorder and releases them to the manufacturing along with the workorder document. The workorder then moves from lower level workstation to the higher levels till the products are completed. When the rate of flow of materials from one level to the other level of the product structure is controlled by the *lower levels,* we call it a push system. There are two possibilities in such a system. Materials may be delivered to the manufacturing which are not immediately needed. Even if a workorder is split up, this may happen. For example, suppose a work centre can produce 20 units a day. The workorder is cut to a week and the stores releases a set of 120 parts to the work centre on the first day of the week. But the centre requires only 20 parts on the first day, hence 100 parts are kept on stock for the day. Next day it will produce another 20 and keep 80 parts on stock and so on. Ultimately, on the sixth day of the week, all parts having been consumed, the balance will become zero. Average inventory holding of the system shall, therefore, always be half of 120, i.e. 60 units.

Second possibility is that one work centre having completed its job might deliver the work-in-process to the next higher level which may not be ready to make use of them immediately, not necessarily due to a line balancing problem, but simply because the higher work centre has a quality problem or a breakdown. The problem with the push system of manufacturing is that it is difficult to stop the manufacturing process once the workorder is triggered. As a result, all other workstations which are engaged in manufacturing different portions of the product will continue to produce and deliver them to the work-stations higher to them. But the product cannot be finally manufactured unless the stopped workstation comes to operation and makes its own contribution to the manufacturing process. This will cause work-in-process inventories to be built up along the production lines.

Besides the above, the workorder-based push system is time-consuming and difficult to track. There is a lot of paperwork involved in opening, tracking and closing a workorder. When a workorder is split into small parts which is often done, the paperwork becomes manifold. All these increase overhead costs. Added to this is the cost of carrying inventories which the push system generates. JIT system aims at removing all these costs and the inventories by opting for a pull system.

Pull System

While push system moves materials by *supply,* the pull system moves materials by *demand.* Pull system has one simple rule: move materials to production only when they are needed. Under this system, orders are placed at the end-item level and the work is pulled through the production centres to satisfy the demand of end-item. The order is not moved to the subsequent work centre until it is needed or demanded by it. As the rate of flow of materials from one level to the other of the product structure is controlled or determined by the *higher level,* it is called a pull system. Push is a bottom-up system while pull is a top-down system. As materials are never moved or processed until demanded, there is no excess build-up of stock at any point of the manufacturing system.

However, a pull system can make the MRP work hand in hand with the JIT system. The *master production schedule* (MPS) translates the sales forecast of independent demand items into production schedules and materials requirement chart. Then starting at the last process work centre before the finished goods inventory level, it pulls the materials required to manufacture the products. This pulling activity is done and controlled by a simple system called *Kanban*.

Kanban

Kanban is a Japanese word meaning card. It is a simple, paperless and self-regulatory system for scheduling and controlling shop-floor activities. Under this system, a work centre requests materials from another using a card (Kanban). It is a manual pull system where ordering is triggered by actual usage rather than average planned usage in-built in a MRP push system. As a result, planning errors are avoided and inventory holding is minimised.

A Kanban will always lift materials from preceding processes and send materials to the subsequent processes. If *A, B* and *C* are the three successive processes, *A* sends materials to *B* and hence, it is the preceding process of *B*, the latter in turn is the succeeding process of *A*. Similarly, process *B*, which sends materials to process *C*, is preceding to process *C*, the latter being subsequent to process *B*. A process may at the same time, be a preceding or succeeding process of many other processes.

Types of Kanbans.   Kanbans are of two types: Withdrawal Kanbans and Production Kanbans. The *Withdrawal Kanbans* move between work centres authorising movement of materials from one centre to the other. No withdrawal of materials is permitted unless it is accompanied by a Kanban which must specify the preceding process and the subsequent process with their locations in the plant. When a Withdrawal Kanban fetches parts, it must stay with them till the subsequent process consumes the last piece of materials or parts in the lot. The Kanban will then travel again to the preceding process to fetch new materials.

While Withdrawal Kanbans authorise movement of parts between work centres, *Production Kanbans* authorise the preceding process to manufacture more materials. When an Withdrawal Kanban arrives at a preceding process, it will find containers with the materials to be fetched. A Production Kanban must escort the containers with the Withdrawal Kanban being attached visibly to them. However, before moving the containers the Production Kanban is retrieved which now acts as the authorisation for the work centre to manufacture a new lot. When the work centre completes manufacturing of the lot, the Production Kanban will travel back and wait till a new Withdrawal Kanban starts the cycle all over again.

A Kanban will never transfer defective materials or parts to a subsequent process. This quality requirement is fundamental to the Kanban system operating under JIT.

The number of Kanbans to be issued for a particular item is calculated by the following formula.

$$N = \frac{dL(1+s)}{Q}$$

where

    N = number of Kanbans

    d = daily demand of the item

    L = order cycle time in days or lead time which is equal to (set-up time + process time + queuing time + movement time)

    s = safety stock factor as a fraction

    Q = lot size or quantity held in a container

Example A manufacturing enterprise requires 165 units of a particular item of inventory in a month. The ordering cycle aggregates to 15 days while the process works for 25 days a month. Lot size is 33 units. The process installed is yet to become stable, hence a safety stock factor of 0.3 is proposed.

Daily demand or d in the present example will be 165/25 = 6.60 units per day.

Number of Kanbans will, therefore, be

$$= \frac{6.60 \times 15(1 + 0.30)}{33}$$
$$= 3.90, \text{ say } 4.$$

Over a period of time when the process is settled under the JIT system, there shall not be any need for safety stock. The number of Kanbans at that time will be 3.

Inventory Holding under JIT

One of the principal objectives of JIT is to eliminate inventories at all levels of operations. This is mainly achieved by streamlining purchase procedures, small lot sizes, redesigning of plant lay out and controlling production.

Purchase in Small Lots

As against a large number of suppliers' base under the traditional system, JIT works towards reducing the number of suppliers and developing a close relationship with them for supplying defect-free high quality materials so that cost of inspecting materials before storage is immediately eliminated, and stopping of production line due to defective materials is avoided. This is done by abandoning the concept of adversary relationship and moving towards a long-term partner-relationship. This new orientation requires education programmes for the suppliers to make them appreciate that ultimately it will be beneficial for both the parties. Cost of adherence to quality and commitment to exact delivery time is compensated by long-term contracts and timely settlement of bills. Working towards this orientation, JIT suppliers ultimately also become JIT manufacturers.

JIT aims at synchronising the consumption with the delivery time of the suppliers so that inventory building and safety stock are avoided. This is done by entering into long-term purchase commitment with the suppliers. (This also enables the manufacturer to enjoy quantity discount). The suppliers are then supplied with a monthly forecast covering a period of say, six months to enable them to undertake their own materials planning. The forecast can be changed but only within the agreed lead time specifications. Within this six months the suppliers are given firm release orders of materials for the next month, to be delivered at an agreed rate, e.g. weekly, hourly or daily. The shorter lead time required by a JIT manufacturer also helps the JIT supplier to reduce his own buffer inventory by tuning his production to the consumption rate of the manufacturer.

Vendors Selection

In order to conform to the stringent requirements under JIT, the manufacturer must select the suppliers carefully. This is important because under JIT, the suppliers' base being reduced to a few, the manufacturer may not have alternative source once a default occurs. More important than the prices, it is the suppliers' willingness to conform to the JIT requirements and accept the manufacturer's value analysis to stay competitive on a long-term basis. As the manufacturer is making a long-term commitment, the suppliers should also be sensitive to the issues relating to cost savings for both the parties.

In-plant Storage

Other things being equal, suppliers should be located close to the factory because JIT requires frequent deliveries in small quantities and constant two-way communication and feed-back on quality. An alternative method being tried now is to go in for in-plant stores programme by which a supplier collaborates with the manufacturer in the planning, procuring and storing of materials at the site of the latter. But a sale is concluded only when the supplier delivers the materials to the manufacturer.

A JIT system does not support the concept of buffer-inventory. But during the initial phase of its implementation there may, at times, be the need to hold buffer-inventory. Besides, in some cases, variety of parts and their long lead time may force even a JIT system to store buffer-inventory. In-plant storage system can take care of the buffer requirement of a JIT manufacturer. The contract must specify the supplier's commitment to buffer-inventory and the manufacturer's commitment to lift them. If the materials are off-the-shelf returnable by the supplier, there may not be any compulsion by the manufacturer to lift the buffer-stock, but if they are custom-made as per manufacturer's requirements, there must be a commitment by the manufacturer to lift these materials irrespective of his demand situation.

Pricing Problems

Materials pricing is a sensitive issue that needs to be resolved for in-plant storage system. On one end, the manufacturer may not be willing to pay more than the market price and on the other, the supplier is anxious to recover his overheads of maintaining the in-plant storage and the cost of carrying the buffer-inventory, if any. The conflict can be resolved by both the parties coming to an agreement under which the supplier is willing to accept manufacturer's price based on market quotation of alternative suppliers (who also have to carry buffer-inventories), and in the event the in-plant price is higher than the market price, the manufacturer may opt for purchasing from the market. Although this may, on the face of it, appear to be somewhat coercive, this will act as an incentive for the supplier to reduce his own manufacturing costs to keep himself abreast of market prices. The benefits that accrue to a supplier due to long-term supply contract are many, of which removal of sales uncertainty is one. When we consider this, the demand by the manufacturer to pay by the market price may not appear to be coercive. Besides, being in-plant and having direct communication linkage with the inventory network of the manufacturer, there may also be savings on management costs of in-plant inventory.

The manufacturer may also provide another incentive to the in-plant supplier. The contract may mention that for supply of any new materials the in-plant supplier will have the first option. It should be the aim of the manufacturer to make a conscious effort to buy as many materials from the in-plant store as possible so that a real long-term partnership based on mutual benefits develops over time.

The in-plant store system can create an excellent synergy between the manufacturer and the supplier. By moving the supplier into the manufacture's place the plant can truly operate in a JIT mode.

Moving the Materials

Just-In-Time goes beyond material waste and brings forth the concept of time waste. Conventional manufacturing system pays scant attention to the waiting time of the materials when a machine is being set up. It also ignores the travelling time of materials moving from one location to another. JIT considers waste of time flow as a major factor that only consumes resources without contributing anything.

There is no value addition when materials move from one place to the other, but inventories stay with the movement continuously. JIT adopts several procedures to reduce the moving time with a view to reducing the inventory built-up along the moving line.

The layout of the factory can be redesigned and made process-oriented to minimise the distance the materials have to travel.

Materials handling system can be reoriented to speed up the delivery process. This may depend upon the type of the product, the process of manufacture and the volume handled. But, the material handling system should, as far as possible, be independent from the products the system will transport because when the present products evolve into new ones or new products go into manufacture, there may not be any need to redesign the material handling system which is always a costly affair.

The Kanban system reduces the waiting time of the materials by ensuring that materials only move when the lower-level process consumes all the materials.

Control of Production Line

Under a JIT system production line is controlled by giving the workers as much materials as are exactly required. Under conventional system a worker is normally given full quota of say, a week's consumption. If a piece of material is found to be defective he sets aside that piece and picks up another from his remaining days' quota to complete his day's quota of production. When he continues with this method, at the end of the week, there may lie at hand an inventory of defective materials which had not been attended to at the right time. As against this, a JIT worker receives only the materials for day's (hour's) consumption and if some parts are found to be defective he will not be able to complete his day's quota of production, and hence the supervisor will be forced to attend to the problem immediately by removing the defective material for onward transfer back to the supplier and replacing it by a new one.

Reduction of Wastes

As mentioned before, Just-in-Time manufacturing system launches a crusade against waste which is defined as anything that does not add value to the output. Waste can both be explicit and hidden. Under conventional manufacturing system, the latter is generally ignored and some wastes are regarded as normal. JIT attempts to sensitize people to the fact that all wastes are avoidable and elimination of waste ultimately reduces the cost of the product. We give below (Table 4.51) an assorted list of causes of waste which are eligible for engaging the attention of the management for their removal.[41]

List of wastes given in Table 4.51 is not exhaustive. There may be other wastes in the system which will come to surface gradually during the implementation of JIT.

Performance Criteria and Measurement

An enterprise involved in JIT implementation must draw up a *performance measurement table* (PMT) which shall include all the objectives of JIT including removal of wastes that we have discussed in this section. PMT may look like the one given in Table 4.52.

---

41. Hernandez, Arnoldo, *Just-in-Time Manufacturing: A Practical Approach.* Prentice-Hall, Inc., Englewood Cliffs, New Jersey, 1989. The book is an excellent treatise for practical application of JIT.

Table 4.51   Indicative List of Causes of Wastes in a Manufacturing System

A. Production Line

1. Rework
2. Poor workmanship
3. Low yields
4. Buffer inventories
5. Shutdown due to equipment failure
6. Absenteeism
7. Long breaks
8. Line down due to materials shortage
9. Engineering shortages
10. Poorly designed products
11. Lack of proper tools
12. Unclear assembly instructions
13. Lack of training
14. Poor factory layout
15. Long machine set up times
16. Low quality raw materials
17. Excess paperwork
18. Scrap
19. Worker idle time

B. Materials Management

1. Buffer inventories
2. Excess materials
3. Obsolete materials
4. Inspection of materials
5. Excess freight or duty
6. Inventory loss
7. Too many suppliers
8. Too many purchase orders
9. Early or late shipments
10. Large facilities for storage
11. Travel of materials
12. Count discrepancies with purchase order
13. Expediting shortages
14. Poor forecast and materials planning
15. Too much bidding with suppliers
16. Switching suppliers
17. Poor sales forecast

C. Supplies

1. Poor quality parts
2. Early or late shipments
3. Shipment count discrepancies
4. Large shipments
5. Rework
6. Poor process yield
7. Expediting
8. Invoicing discrepancies
9. Poor product specification
10. Over specification of a product
11. Poor forecasts
12. Changes in production schedules

D. Design Engineering

1. Marginal design
2. Too many parts in design
3. Too many different suppliers for parts used in design
4. Complex design to assemble
5. Complex design to test
6. Complex manufacturing process required
7. Poor testing before releasing to manufacturing
8. Late release
9. Use of unreliable components
10. Too many configurations in product
11. Too many engineering changes and rework
12. Too many bills of materials and levels
13. Low reliability design
14. Not designed for foolproof assembly
15. Use of poor quality parts
16. Design includes features customers do not need

Table 4.52 Performance Measurement Table under JIT

JIT objectives	Target to be achieved	Period achieved	Periodical measurement		
			Short of target	Cumulative achievement	Short of target
1. Turnover of inventories					
(a) Materials					
(b) Work-in-process					
(c) Finished goods					
2. Suppliers base reduction					
3. Lead time reduction					
4. Waste reduction (specify)					
5. Reduction of materials movement time					
6. Percentage reduction of defects					
7. Percentage increase in materials not requiring inspection					
8. Percentage decrease in scrap and rework					
9. Reduction of overheads					
10. Increase in productivity (production/no. of labour hours)					

SUMMARY

At the macro-level, inventory contributes substantially to business fluctuation. In an 'inventory-economy', price may not follow the simple demand-supply rule; it may become sticky in both situations of demand upsurge and demand drawdown. Price response to demand shocks will be greater at higher level of economic activities. The effect on retail inventories is great, followed by manufacturer's inventories of raw materials and wholesaler's inventories. The disequilibrium effect at the macro-level is due to some of the stabilisation strategies followed by firms at the micro-level.

Accumulation of inventory takes place due to transaction motive, precautionary motive, speculative motive and also due to inefficient management. Production of finished goods is a function of the inventory level; generally a high-level of inventories would lead to lower prices, and low prices would in turn result in a cutback on production so that in the following period, opening inventories will be much less than in the current period. Another aspect is that inventories act as a buffer and keep the production and distribution systems insulated from the shocks transmitted by the market-imperfection. It helps avoid loss of sales and protects the frim from the consequences of sending back a dissatisfied customer.

Costs associated with inventories are: purchase/acquisition cost, ordering/ setting-up cost, holding cost and stock-out cost. It is the estimation of these costs compared with the benefits of keeping inventory at specific levels, that gives us the optimum level of inventory. Determination of costs is difficult, and costs like stock-out costs can only be estimated.

Valuation of inventories is another critical area. Due to the fact that prices of acquisition and the work done on inventories vary continuously, valuation becomes difficult. A particular inventory valuation method can change reported loss to profit or vice versa and thus, it has major tax and dividend implications. LIFO, FIFO and average cost are the popularly used methods. Other methods used are: specific identification, bare stock, adjusted selling price, and standard cost. All seven have their positives and negatives; they have different comfort levels depending upon situations.

When a functional perspective of the organisation prevails, as far as inventories are concerned, suboptimisation takes place. Hence, inventory strategies must emanate from the business strategy of the organisation, which might typically be cost leadership, differentiation in product and market focus. Whatever be the inventory strategy it is most important to determine the dependent and independent demand for inventory. Demand can also be continuous or discrete.

The EOQ model is used when the demand is continuous. It is also used to minimise the total inventory cost. This is a very robust model, highly insensitive to errors in prediction. However, for greater accuracy, the assumptions in this model relaxed to incorporate variations can be. For situations when demand can just not be predicted, other methods like interactive process, etc. can be adopted to find optimal solutions. Cases like quantity discounts, multiple products, and ordering pattern are dealt with in a similar fashion.

Since the EOQ model has a cost focus and is not amenable to wealth maximisation, the present value approach has emerged. However, this highly improved accuracy comes at a cost, and the costs may themselves be high enough to outweigh the benefits.

Safety nets are provided by *anticipation stock* and *safety stock*. Calculation for anticipation stocks is typically done by making monthly sales forecast and taking into consideration the expected demand, government policies etc. However, since errors in forecast might emerge in the projected year (and throw the company out of gear), it might be better to start with a forecast of maximum expected demand, bare level of safety stock (calculated on this), and to adjust the production plan accordingly. In this way, we can deal with both input seasonality and sales seasonality. Statistical tools are used in all such calculations.

Whilst an anticipation stock is designed to take care of special type of problems like seasonality, general safety stock aims at absorbing shocks from random fluctuations in purchasing, production or sales.

Safety stock prevents idle machine, hours loss of sales and goodwill, but it comes at a carrying cost for the insurance it provides. The fundamental problem here is to correctly identify and quantify the costs, many of which are not available in accounting records. The optimum level here is the point at which cost of holding additional inventory added to the expected stock-out cost is minimum. Stock-out cost might either be due to back-ordering or lost sales. The latter is very difficult to estimate. The reason for stock-out might be demand variability or lead time variability. Statistical tools are used to estimate stock out costs at various service levels. Besides the usual factors, working capital restrictions might also have an effect on inventory levels.

Lastly, many new models and methods like MRP I, MRP II, JIT and Kanban have gained currency. All of them have as their central theme, a total view of the business. Each aims at resolving the problems in linkages, so that inventory levels are more pull-determined than push-determined.

The Standard Normal Probability Distribution
Areas under the Normal Curve

	00	.01	.02	.03	.04	.05	.06	.07	.08	.09
0.0	.50000	.50399	.50798	.51197	.51595	.51994	.52392	.52790	.53188	.53586
0.1	.53983	.54380	.54776	.55172	.55567	.55962	.56356	.56749	.57142	.57535
0.2	.57926	.58317	.58706	.59095	.59483	.59871	.60257	.60642	.61026	.61409
0.3	.61791	.62172	.62552	.62930	.63307	.63683	.64058	.64431	.64803	.65173
0.4	.65542	.65910	.66276	.66640	.67003	.67364	.67724	.68082	.68439	.68793
0.5	.69146	.69497	.69847	.70194	.70540	.70884	.71226	.71566	.71904	.72240
0.6	.72575	.72907	.73237	.73536	.73891	.74215	.74537	.74857	.75175	.75490
0.7	.75804	.76115	.76424	.76730	.77035	.77337	.77637	.77935	.78230	.78524
0.8	.78814	.79103	.79389	.79673	.79955	.80234	.80511	.80785	.81057	.81327
0.9	.81594	.81859	.82121	.82381	.82639	.82894	.83147	.83398	.83646	.83891
1.0	.84134	.84375	.84614	.84849	.85083	.85314	.85543	.85769	.85993	.86214
1.1	.86433	.86650	.86864	.87076	.87286	.87493	.87698	.87900	.88100	.88298
1.2	.88493	.88686	.88877	.89065	.89251	.89435	.89617	.89796	.89973	.90147
1.3	.90320	.90490	.90658	.90824	.90988	.91149	.91309	.91466	.91621	.91774
1.4	.91924	.92073	.92220	.92364	.92507	.92647	.92785	.92922	.93056	.93189
1.5	.93319	.93448	.93574	.93699	.93822	.93943	.94062	.94179	.94295	.94408
1.6	.94520	.94630	.94738	.94845	.94950	.95053	.95154	.95254	.95352	.95449
1.7	.95543	.95637	.95728	.95818	.95907	.95994	.96080	.96164	.96246	.96327
1.8	.96407	.96485	.96562	.96638	.96712	.96784	.96856	.96926	.96995	.97062
1.9	.97128	.97193	.97257	.97320	.97381	.97441	.97500	.97558	.97615	.97670
2.0	.97725	.97784	.97831	.97882	.97932	.97982	.98030	.98077	.98124	.98169
2.1	.98214	.98257	.98300	.98341	.98382	.98422	.98461	.98500	.98537	.98574
2.2	.98610	.98645	.98679	.98713	.98745	.98778	.98809	.98840	.98870	.98899
2.3	.98928	.98956	.98983	.99010	.99036	.99061	.99086	.99111	.99134	.99158
2.4	.99180	.99202	.99224	.99245	.99266	.99286	.99305	.99324	.99343	.99361
2.5	.99379	.99396	.99413	.99430	.99446	.99461	.99477	.99492	.99506	.99520
2.6	.99534	.99547	.99560	.99573	.99585	.99598	.99609	.99621	.99632	.99643
2.7	.99653	.99664	.99674	.99683	.99693	.99702	.99711	.99720	.99728	.99736
2.8	.99744	.99752	.99760	.99767	.99774	.99781	.99788	.99795	.99801	.99807
2.9	.99813	.99819	.99825	.99831	.99836	.99841	.99846	.99851	.99856	.99861
3.0	.99865	.99869	.99874	.99878	.99882	.99886	.99899	.99893	.99896	.99900
3.1	.99903	.99906	.99910	.99913	.99916	.99918	.99921	.99924	.99926	.99929
3.2	.99931	.99934	.99936	.99938	.99940	.99942	.99944	.99946	.99948	.99950
3.3	.99952	.99953	.99955	.99957	.99958	.99960	.99961	.99962	.99964	.99965
3.4	.99966	.99968	.99969	.99970	.99971	.99972	.99973	.99974	.99975	.99976
3.5	.99977	.99978	.99978	.99979	.99980	.99981	.99981	.99982	.99983	.99983
3.6	.99984	.99985	.99985	.99986	.99986	.99987	.99987	.99988	.99988	.99989
3.7	.99989	.99990	.99990	.99990	.99991	.99991	.99992	.99992	.99992	.99992
3.8	.99993	.99993	.99993	.99994	.99994	.99994	.99994	.99995	.99995	.99995
3.9	.99995	.99995	.99996	.99996	.99996	.99996	.99996	.99996	.99997	.99997

CHAPTER 5

Liquidity and Cash Management

I've crossed three worlds in a single life
I've to cross many, but I may not

INTRODUCTION

Cash does not enter into the *profit and loss account* of an enterprise, hence cash is neither profit nor loss, but without cash, profit (loss) remains meaningless for an enterprise owner. Profit is a liability, and like any other liability it is nominal in nature; cash is the real thing which an enterprise manager learns the hard way in day-to-day payment of obligations. He cannot manage to pay a supplier's bill or salaries and wages by simply making profit; he needs cash to do it. He also cannot pay dividend (share of profit) to the shareholders except through cash alone.

CASH vs PROFIT

This distinction between profit and cash is often not understood clearly. Accountants are used to calculate cash flow from the income statement of an enterprise. Cash flow is believed to be akin to profit before depreciation and other non-cash expenditure. The difficulty is that the income statement does not contain working capital items like receivables and inventories which capture a sizable part of the revenue, giving lesser amount of cash to the system. Enterprise managers often complain that in spite of their companies making good profit they continue to remain in hand-to-mouth condition in discharging their day-to-day obligation.

The problem is more acute for companies which are growing at a fast rate. The rising cash flow (profit) curve gives an euphoric feeling of 'all being well everywhere', which makes the managers to press the growth button faster. What they lose sight of is the real cash position of the company which might be showing a downward trend and hence, pushing the company slowly first and then vigorously towards a severe liquidity crisis despite the company making high profit. Unfortunately, once an enterprise-manager presses the growth buttons, it is difficult for him to retract the steps. The continuous erosion of liquidity ultimately makes a high-growth company sick.[1]

---

1. For a detailed discussion based on empirical investigation, see Bhattacharya, Hrishikes. *Total Management by Ratios,* 2nd ed., Chapter 12, Sage Publications, New Delhi, 2007.

There is nothing wrong in making profit, in fact, that is the purpose of business, but unless there is cash coming through profit, an enterprise will soon be dead. Cash is the lifeline of an organisation. A sustained growth of an enterprise depends upon the cashability of the profit, not the profit *per se* as reflected in the income statement. Although in the long run, all working assets (and for that matter all assets) are cashable (and perhaps, this is the reason why all profit flows in long-term project appraisal are termed as cash flows), a cash shortage in the short run may not allow a company to see out the long-term at all!

CASH FLOW, CASH STOCK AND CASH TO CURRENT ASSETS RATIO

There is a distinction between cash flow and cash stock, which must be understood clearly. Cash is an asset, and like any other asset, it earns only when it is in use. In other words, when cash is in the flow it is earning for the enterprise; when it is idle, not only that it does not earn, it also contributes negatively to the profitability of the enterprise, because the fund that is tied to idle cash has to be carried at a cost. The situation is similar to that of a machine which has been bought but kept idle. An enterprise must, therefore, make its cash work as hard as possible.

Of all the current assets that are found in the balance sheet of an enterprise, cash is most important in terms of its usage, hence its holding in stock form must be the least. With the development of the financial market and rising efficiency in financial management of enterprises, cash (stock) as a percentage of total current assets has been going down significantly in almost all the developed nations of the world. For example, in the United States it was 13.4 percent in 1961, which came down to 8.81 percent in 1970 and to 6.67 percent in 1990.[2] Although the trend of the ratio is on the decline, in absolute percentage the figure is still quite high. This is primarily due to the compensatory balances required to be maintained by the US enterprises with banks from whom they have taken loans. But as against this, in India, cash to current assets ratio went up from 3.1 percent in 1966–67 to 6.67 percent in 1976–77.[3] In Table 5.1 we have calculated this ratio for the period, 1997–98 to 2005–06, by taking into account all cash and bank balances including fixed deposits because all these cash are idle balances earning little or no income.[4] It may be observed that during the recent time cash and bank balances to current assets ratio has stayed at around 30 percent (the ratio is around 16.5 percent when calculated on total current assets, loans and advances), though there is a fall in the ratio of both inventories and debtors to current assets during the same period (1997–98 to 2005–06).

---

2. Calculated from *Quarterly Financial Report for Manufacturing, Mining and Trade Corporations*, Department of Commerce, United States, Various issues.
3. Agrawal, N.K., *Management of Working Capital*, Sterling Publishers, New Delhi, 1983.
4. Some of these fixed deposits are used as margin money or collateral for obtaining bank guarantees, letters of credit etc.

Cash to current assets ratio for Indian enterprises as revealed in Table 5.1 is very much on the high side. From a normative angle the ratio should never have been more than 1.5 to 2 percent under cash credit system of financing. Cash management in India has all along been very inefficient. In fact, there has not been much of cash management in Indian enterprises, thanks to the easy availability of working capital finance from banks under a system which kept the enterprise-managers away from installing a cash management system.

Table 5.1 Movement of Cash and Other Current Assets of Indian Industry

(Rs. in crore)

	1997-98	1998-99	1999-00	2000-01	2001-02	2002-03	2003-04	2004-05	2005-06
Total current assets, loans and advances	1,113,954 [53.82]	1,280,766 [53.56]	1,443,183 [53.59]	1,614,464 [52.20]	1,773,716 [51.79]	1,954,410 [50.92]	2,164,152 [50.72]	2,651,557 [53.01]	3,248,728 [56.48]
Of which:									
Total current assets	671,109 [32.42]	758,605 [31.72]	826,749 [30.70]	906,281 [29.30]	998,722 [29.16]	1,071,736 [27.92]	1,173,941 [27.52]	1,362,327 [27.23]	1,557,360 [27.07]
Of which:									
Inventories	141,335 (21.06) {12.69}	155,592 (20.51) {12.15}	178,836 (21.63) {12.39}	179,419 (19.80) {11.11}	180,313 (18.05) {10.17}	203,426 (18.98) {10.41}	207,849 (17.70) {9.60}	243,895 (17.90) {9.20}	277,054 (17.79) {8.53}
Cash and bank balances	188,384 (28.07) {16.91}	241,372 (31.82) {18.85}	240,524 (29.09) {16.67}	269,752 (29.76) {16.71}	291,644 (29.20) {16.44}	270,524 (25.24) {13.84}	355,766 (30.31) {16.44}	452,350 (33.20) {17.06}	550,557 (35.35) {16.95}
Sundry debtors	139,116 (20.73) {12.49}	144,490 (19.04) {11.28}	158,914 (19.22) {11.01}	179,365 (19.79) {11.11}	193,500 (19.37) {10.91}	204,989 (19.13) {10.49}	199,901 (17.03) {9.24}	229,502 (16.85) {8.66}	240,323 (15.43) {7.40}

Basic data source: Industry: Financial Aggregates and Ratios, Centre for Monitoring Indian Economy (CMIE).

Notes: 1. Figures in bracket [ ] in the first row indicate percentage to total assets.
2. Figures in bracket ( ) in other rows indicate percentage to total current assets.
3. Figures in bracket { } in other rows indicate percentage to total current assets, loans and advances.

There is a saying that large Indian corporate houses are "cash cows". Although liberalisation has opened new investment opportunities, Indian companies still remain conservative. Some years back even the Hindustan Lever Ltd. returned a part of the reserve to the shareholders in the form of redeemable debentures because of lack of investment opportunities. There may also be an agency problem due to which enterprise managers do not want to take risks; they feel safe when cash balances are very high, and they want to keep it that way.

ACCOUNTING STANDARDS—CASH FLOW PRESENTATION

In keeping with the importance being attached to cash these days, the International Accounting Standards Committee has replaced funds flow presentation of *statement of changes in financial position* by *cash flow statement* effective from 1st January 1994. However, in India, the Council of the Institute of Chartered Accountants of India adopted the new cash flow-oriented accounting standards in 1997 with some modifications.

For purpose of presentation to the external world, the new accounting standard has recommended the cash flow statement to be prepared under three main activity-heads of the enterprise.

1. *Operating activities* to cover cash flows relating to all revenue generating activities of the enterprise including those arising from purchase and sale of investments or dealing or trading in securities and derivative instruments, but excluding those generated from sale of any item of fixed assets.

2. *Investing activities* to cover cash flows arising from all investments in fixed assets including cash receipts from sale of fixed assets, cash flows relating to investments in equity or debt of subsidiaries and joint ventures including their disposal and repayments, and all cash advances and loans including their repayments.

3. *Financing activities* to cover cash flows arising out of all capital and debt issues of the enterprise including repayment of loans.

The new accounting standard has put focus on *cash and cash equivalents* which are defined to include cash and bank balances in current account, and investments in short-term highly liquid risk-free instruments. Cash flows are defined as inflows and outflows from these cash and cash equivalents. In annexure to this chapter, cash flow statement with worked out examples under this new accounting standard (AS3) is given. Enterprises are required to present their periodical accounts under this new cash flow standard which, "in conjunction with other financial statements, is expected to provide information that will enable users to evaluate changes in net assets of an enterprise, its financial structure (including its liquidity and solvency) and its ability to affect the amounts and timing of cash flows in order to adapt to changing circumstances and opportunities".

FUNDS FLOW ANALYSIS

The aforementioned quotation from AS3 highlights the importance of cash flow statement, but at the same time it indicates the necessity of supporting it with other financial statements. Emergence of cash flow concept as the guiding principle of accounting presentation and financial analysis should in no way belittle the funds flow concept as some writers and users intended it to be. One should remember that cash flow concept is more useful in short-term than in long-term. It does not tell much about the weakening or strengthening of the financial structure of the business which has a long-term perspective and can be understood only when a funds analysis of business operations is done. A combination of cash flow analysis and funds flow analysis only enables an enterprise manager and other users of the financial statements to take a total and long-term view of the business.

The format of cash flow statement recommended in AS3 is more suitable for external users than for the finance manager who has to manage cash almost on a day-to-day basis. He can neatly divide cash flows among operating, investing and financing activities any time that he desires, but what is more important for him is to plan his cash flows, particularly cash outflows, in terms of options available to him. For example, he simply does not have any option while it comes to payment of taxes, interest or installment of term loans etc. except at the cost of throwing the enterprise on the brink of bankruptcy. But he has the discretion to pay or postpone dividends, incur capital expenditure or acquire a business. We may designate the former type as *priority outflows* and the latter as *discretionary outflows*. The goal of the finance manager is to ensure that priority outflows are met fully out of operating cash inflows. Any balance available after meeting the priority outflows should only be used for meeting *discretionary flows* in conjunction with *financial flows* planned for the budgeted year. If this rule is violated and there is overstepping, then very soon the enterprise may face severe liquidity crisis, and there is every likelihood that the enterprise will enter into a debt-trap.

Example In what follows now we shall outline the above approach with the help of the published final accounts of a real-life company which may be called LMN Ltd., for purpose of anonymity. The company is engaged in manufacturing and marketing of food items and beverages. Balance sheet and profit and loss account of the company for the years 20X0 and 20X1 are given in Exhibit 5.1 through Exhibit 5.4 along with relevant information culled from various schedules annexed to them in the annual reports.

Exhibit 5.1 Balance Sheet of LMN Ltd. as at 31.3.20X0

(Rs. in lakh)

Liabilities			Assets		
Share capital		12,048	Fixed assets	12,489	
Reserve and surplus			Additions	6938	
Capital reserve	347			19,427	
Revenue reserve	22,824	23,171	Disposals	270	
Borrowingws				19,157	
Term loans	3178		Depreciation	1559	
Debentures	15			17,598	
Fixed deposits	2058		Capital work-in-		
Commercial papers	3500		progress	1403	19,001
Bank overdrafts	4537		Investments		
Other short-term loans	5000		Subsidiaries and		
Other borrowings	65	18,353	joint ventures	1289	
Current liabilities			Others	1995	3284
Sundry creditors	19,837		Inventories		
Advance payments	481		Raw materials	19,680	
Interest accrued but			Stores and spares	3058	
not due	332		Work-in-progress	1461	
Other liabilities			Finished goods	9921	34,120
(expenses)	3739		Sundry debtors	5739	

(Cont.)

Exhibit 5.1 Balance Sheet of LMN Ltd. as at 31.3.20X0 (Cont.)

(Rs. in lakh)

Liabilities			Assets		
Unclaimed dividend	1273	25,662	*Less:* Provision for		
Provisions			bad-debts	687	5052
Income tax (net of			Loans and advances	12,254	
advance payments)	412		*Less:* Provision for		
Proposed dividend	3615	4027	bad-debts	380	11,874
			Cash and bank balances		6536
			Misc. expenditure not		
			written off (deferred		
			revenue expenditure)		957
			Other current assets		2437
	Total	83,261		Total	83,261

Exhibit 5.2 Profit and Loss Account of LMN Ltd. for the year ended 31.3.20X0

(Rs. in lakh)

Expenditure			Income		
Opening stocks			Sales (tonnes 531,757)		187,463
Work-in-progress	1359		*Less*: Excise duty		3517
Finished goods	11,283	12,642	Net sales		183,946
Consumption of raw			Other income (net of tax		
materials		103,502	deducted at source)		
Purchase of traded			Dividend from		
goods		8472	subsidiaries	2500	
Salaries and wages		9642	Dividend and interest		
Contribution to			from other investments	628	
provident fund		1576	Profit on sale of fixed		
Staff welfare expenses		1194	assets (net)	13	
Packing materials stores and			Profit on sale of		
spares		17,243	investments	—	
Repairs to machinery		746	Miscellaneous income		
Repairs to buildings		375	accrued (sales tax		
Power and fuel		3280	refund, etc.)	1585	4726
Depreciation		1559	Closing stocks		
Rent		822	Work in-progress	1461	
Rates and taxes		2812	Finished goods	9921	11,382
Insurance		237			
Freight and transport		4340			
Advertising and sales promotion		6068			
Discount and commissions		335			
Brokerage		46			
Postage and stationery		819			
Travelling expenses		2213			
Processing charges		668			
Bank charges		787			
Donations and subscriptions		92			
Audit fees		11			

(Cont.)

Exhibit 5.2 Profit and Loss Account of LMN Ltd. for the year ended 31.3.20X0

(Cont.)

(Rs. in lakh)

Expenditure			Income		
Bad-debts written off		15			
Provision for bad-debt		516			
Miscellaneous expenses		2995			
Profit before interest and					
tax c/d		17,047			
	Total	200,054		Total	200,054
Interest			Profit before interest		
Debentures	12		and tax b/d		17,047
Term loans	552				
Fixed deposits	398				
Bank overdraft and					
others	1674	2636			
Provision for income tax		4500			
Profit after tax c/d		9911			
	Total	17,047		Total	17,047
Dividends			Profit after tax b/d		9911
Interim	2410		Investment allowance		
Final	3615	6025	Reserve written back		94
General reserve		4076	Debenture redemption		
			Reserve written back		96
	Total	10,101		Total	10,101

Exhibit 5.3 Balance Sheet of LMN Ltd. as at 31.3.20X1

(Rs. in lakh)

Liabilities			Assets		
Share capital		12,048	Fixed assets	17,598	
Reserves and surplus			Additions	9496	
Capital reserve	347			27,094	
Revenue reserve	28,844	29,191	Disposals	468	
Borrowings				26,626	
Term loans	2448		Depreciation	1921	
Debentures	4			24,705	
Fixed deposits	1594		Capital work-in-progress	1126	25,831
Commercial papers	4000		Goodwill		638
Bank overdraft	14,125		Investments		
Other short-term			Subsidiaries and		
loans	1700		joint venture	1689	
Other borrowings	52	23,923	Others	2164	3853
Current liabilities			Inventories		
Sundry creditors	27,820		Raw materials	21,929	
Advance payments	443		Stores and spare	4243	
Interest accrued but			Work-in-progress	1303	
not due	329		Finished goods	12,367	39,842
Other liabilities			Sundry debtors	6925	
(expenses)	5493		*Less*: Provision for		
					(Cont.)

Exhibit 5.3   Balance Sheet of LMN Ltd. as at 31.3.20X1 (Cont.)

(Rs. in lakh)

Liabilities			*Assets*		
Unclaimed dividend	1177	35,262	bad-debts	763	6162
Provisions			Loans and advances	11,569	
Income tax (net of			*Less:* Provision for		
advance payments)	1530		bad-debts	506	11,063
Proposed dividend	4216	5746	Other current assets		3366
			Cash and bank balances		6965
			Misc. expenditure not		
			written off (deferred		
			revenue expenditure)		8450
	Total	106,170		Total	106,170

Exhibit 5.4   Profit and Loss Account of LMN Ltd. for the year ended 31.3.20X1

(Rs. in lakh)

Expenditure			*Income*		
Opening stocks			Sales (tonnes 539,779)		210,802
Work-in-progress	1461		*Less*: Excise duty		3404
Finished goods	9921	11,382	Net sales		207,398
Consumption of raw			Other income (net of tax		
materials		116,588	deducted at source)		
Purchase of traded goods		12,886	Dividend from		
Salaries and wages		12,153	subsidiaries	2962	
Contribution to provident			Dividend and interest		
fund		2670	from other		
Staff welfare expenses		1265	investments	803	
Packing materials stores			Profit on sale of fixed		
and spares		19,190	assets (net)	130	
Repairs to machinery		932	Profit on sale of		
Repairs to buildings		438	investments	1435	
Power and fuel		3461	Miscellaneous income		
Depreciation		1921	accrued (sales tax		
Rent		974	refund etc.)	1428	6758
Rates and taxes		2556	Closing stocks		
Insurance		281	Work-in-progress	1303	
Freight and transport		5860	Finished goods	12,367	13,670
Advertising and sales					
promotion		7153			
Discount and commissions		310			
Brokerage		44			
Postage and stationery		952			
Travelling expenses		2522			
Processing charges		766			
Bank charges		905			

(Cont.)

Exhibit 5.4 Profit and Loss Account of LMN Ltd. for the year ended 31.3.20X1

(Cont.)

(Rs. in lakh)

Expenditure					Income
Donations and subscriptions	92				
Audit fees	13				
Bad-debts written off	8				
Provision for bad-debt	202				
Miscellaneous expenses	4097				
Profit before interest and tax c/d	18,205				
	Total	227,826		Total	227,826
Interest			Profit before interest		
Debentures	3		and tax b/d		18,205
Term loans	354				
Fixed deposits	323				
Bank overdraft and others	2179	2859			
Provision for income tax		2700			
Profit after tax c/d		12,646			
	Total	18,205		Total	18,205
Dividends			Profit after tax b/d		12,646
Interim	2410		Investment allowance		
Final	4216	6626	reserve written back		107
General reserve		6127			
	Total	12,753		Total	12,753

RELEVANT INFORMATION FROM THE SCHEDULES ANNEXED TO PROFIT AND LOSS ACCOUNTS AND BALANCE SHEETS OF LMN LIMITED

1. Opening and closing stocks relating to purchase of traded goods being small are included in *finished goods inventory*.

2. Miscellaneous expenditure, to the extent not written off or adjusted, comprises costs which are of deferred revenue in nature, incurred on acquisitions of various businesses dealings in consumer foods and also business restructuring costs such as voluntary retirement schemes, etc. These costs are amortised over a period of 5–10 years as applicable for various items of costs. Balances as appearing in the balance sheets, comprise the following:

(Rs. in lakh)

	20X0	20X1
Business acquisition costs	848	4358
Business restructuring costs	109	4092
Total	957	8450

Above balances are net of amortisation charged to profit and loss account and passed through *miscellaneous income accrued account.*

Miscellaneous expenses debited to profit and loss account for 20X1 include amortisation relating to current year's costs, Rs. 1500 lakh and for the early years' Rs. 92 lakh.

3.   The company had, under appeal, sales tax assessment of Rs. 3943 lakh for earlier years which was not provided for but shown as contingent liability in the year 20X0. The company, however, lost the appeal and the final assessment was done for Rs. 3273 lakh which was paid during the year.

4.   Provision for income tax for the current year (net of advance taxes) was made after considering the full tax benefit arising from business restructuring costs incurred during the year and deferred as mentioned in para 2 of this section. Against a provision of Rs. 4500 lakh in 20X0 the company's final assessment was made at Rs. 4506 lakh. Assessment for 20X1 was pending.

5.   No fresh borrowings under term loans, debentures and other short-term loans and borrowings etc. were contracted during the current year.

However, the following transactions were made during 20X1:

(a)   Fixed deposits amounting to Rs. 1585 lakh were paid on maturity. Fresh deposits amounting to Rs. 1121 lakh were received during the year.

(b)   Commercial papers aggregating Rs. 500 lakh were issued during 20X1.

(c)   Deposits included in 'Other Current Assets':

(i)   Deposits with IDBI amounting to Rs. 391 lakh matured for payment during 20X1.

(ii)   Further deposits of Rs. 179 lakh were made with NABARD during the current year.

(iii) Further deposits of Rs. 947 lakh were made under the category 'other deposits' (NSCs, Government bonds, etc.) during the year.

(d)   Deposits included under 'Loans and Advances':

(i)   Repayment of inter-corporate deposits amounting to Rs. 420 lakh was made during the year. No fresh ICD was made.

(ii)   Further deposit of Rs. 74 lakh was made with Port Trusts during the year.

(iii) Repayment of housing loans to employees received during the year was Rs. 245 lakh. Further housing loans of Rs. 100 lakh were also disbursed during the period.

(iv)   Out of Rs. 903 lakh as loans made to subsidiary companies, an amount of Rs. 552 lakh was received back during the year. There had been no further advance under this head.

(v)   Personal loans of Rs. 358 lakh were paid to directors of the company during the year.

6. Additions to fixed assets disposals and capital work-in-progress during 20X1 are as follows:

(Rs. in lakh)

Items	Additions to fixed assets	Disposals of fixed assets	Additions to capital work-in-progress
(1)	(2)	(3)	(4)
Land	169	37	7
Buildings	1316	3 (1)	86
Plant and machinery	6540	196 (248)	718
Furniture and fixture	963	101 (–18)	187
Vehicles	508	131 (94)	128
Total	9496	468 (325)	1126

Notes:

1. Figures in bracket under column 3 indicate depreciation of the assets under disposal.
2. Capital work-in-progress include capital advance of Rs. 606 lakh in 20X0 and Rs. 416 lakh in 20X1.
3. It is the policy of the company to transfer completed jobs from capital work-in-progress account to fixed assets after these are fully paid.
4. Additions to fixed assets include items acquired under business acquisitions during 20X1. An amount of Rs. 638 lakh was paid in addition to the fair value of the assets acquired which is shown as 'Goodwill' in the balance sheet of the company as at 31.3.20X1.
5. The company made a profit of Rs. 130 lakh on disposal of fixed assets during 20X1.

7. *Investments in quoted instruments*

(Rs. in lakh)

Instruments	20X0		20X1
1. UTI capital gain units (496,860 units @ Rs. 11.36)	56.45	1. UTI capital gain units (29,860 units @ Rs. 11.36)	3.40
2. UTI, other units (9,039,970 units @ Rs. 14.50)	1310.80	2. UTI, other units (3,865,700 units @ 15.69 on an average)	567.93
3. Other quoted shares and debentures (at cost of acquisition)	627.85	3. Other quoted shares and debentures at cost of acquisition	1592.40
Total	1995.10		2163.73

Notes:

1. During 20X1, 467,000 UTI Capital Gain Units were sold at Rs. 11.15 per unit and 5,703,390 other units of UTI were sold at Rs. 15.85 per unit. During the year, 529,120 other units of UTI were also purchased at Rs. 15.90 per unit.

2. The stock market being highly bullish, the company sold its entire holding of quoted shares and debentures of Rs. 627.85 lakh in 20X1 at a profit of Rs. 1358.62 lakh. However, after the market returned to normal the company made further investment in quoted shares and debentures for Rs. 1592.40 lakh. Present market value of these investments is Rs. 2029 lakh.

8. *Investments in subsidiaries and joint ventures*: During 20X1 the company subscribed to the rights issue of 40 lakh shares @ Rs. 10 each of Indian Foods Co. Ltd., a joint venture company.

9. Interest and dividends accrued on investments but not re-ceived were included in the balance sheets under the head 'Other Current Assets' as follows:

20X0	20X1
Rs. 346 lakh	Rs. 540 lakh

10. Miscellaneous income accrued (sales tax refund, etc.) are included in *loans and advances*.

Exhibit 5.5 Cash Flow Statement 20X1

(Rs. in lakh)

Operating cash flow	
Gross sales	210,802
Less: Increase in accounts receivable	(1186)
Less: Decrease in advance payments	(38)
A. Operating cash inflow	209,578
Cash outflow	
Purchase of raw materials	118,837
Purchase of spares, stores and packing materials	20,375
Purchase of traded goods	12,886
Subtotal	152,098
Less: Increase in trade creditors	(7983)
B. Cash paid for materials	144,115
Operating expenditure (cash)	47,444
Excise duty	3404
	50,848
Less: Increase in expense creditors	(1754)
Less: Miscellaneous expenses amortized	(1592)
	47,502
Add: Sales tax liability for earlier years paid this year	3273
C. Cash paid for expenses	50,775
D. Total operating cash outflow (B + C)	194,890
E. Net operating cash inflow (A − D)	14,688
Non-operating cash flow	
Dividend from subsidiaries	2962
Dividend and interests from other investments	803
	3765
Less: Increase in accrued dividends and interests	(194)
Add: Cash inflow from disposal of fixed assets	273
F. Cash inflow from non-operating activities	3844
G. Net cash flow (E + F)	18,532

(Cont.)

Exhibit 5.5 Cash Flow Statement 20X1 (Cont.)

(Rs. in lakh)

Priority outflows	
Interest paid on borrowings	2859
Add: Decrease in interest accrued accounts	3
H. Cash outflow on account of interests	2862
Income tax	
Provision for this year as per P/L account	2700
Add: Closing balance in provision for income	
tax account as per balance sheet of 31.3.20X0	412
	3112
Less: Closing balance in provision for income tax	
account as per balance sheet of 31.3.20X1	1530
	1582
Add: Additional taxes paid on final assessment	6
I. Cash outflow on account of taxes (inclusive	
of advance tax paid during the year)	1588
Repayment of term obligations	
Term loans	730
Debentures	11
Fixed deposits	1585
Others short-term loans and borrowings	3313
J. Cash outflow on account of repayments	5639
K. Total priority cash outflows (H + I + J)	10,089
Discretionary cash flows	
Capital expenditure	
Additions to fixed assets during 20X1	9496
Less: Opening balance of capital work-in-progress transferred	1403
Capital expenditure for the current year	8093
Less: Opening balance of capital advance	606
	7487
Add: Closing balance of capital advance	416
	7903
Add: Cash paid in excess of acquisitions being goodwill	638
L. Cash outflows on account of capital expenditure	8541
Dividends	
Interim dividend	2410
Add: Opening balance of unclaimed dividend account	1273
	3683
Less: Closing balance of unclaimed dividend account	1177
M. Cash outflow on account of dividends	2506
Investments	
Quoted	
467,000 UTI capital gain units sold during the year	52
5,703,390 other UTI units sold during the year	904
Other quoted shares and debentures sold during the year	1987
529,120 other UTI units purchased during the year	(84)
Other quoted shares and debentures purchased during the year	(1592)
N. Cash inflow on account of quoted investments	1267

(Cont.)

Exhibit 5.5   Cash Flow Statement 20X1 (Cont.)

(Rs. in lakh)

Subsidiaries and joint venture	
40 lakh shares at Rs. 10 per share of	
Indian Foods Co. Ltd. acquired on rights basis	(400)
Loan repaid by subsidiaries	552
O. Cash inflow from subsidiary investments	152
Other investments	
Further deposits made with Port Trust	(74)
Further deposits made with NABARD	(179)
Further deposits made in NSC, etc.	(947)
Loans made to directors	(358)
Repayment of intercorporate deposits	420
Encashment of deposits with IDBI	391
Further housing loans made to employees	(100)
Repayment of housing loans by employees	245
P. Cash outflow on account of 'other investments'	602
Business acquisitions and restructuring costs	
Business acquisition costs as per schedule	4358
Restructuring costs as per schedule	4092
	8450
Less: Opening balance	957
	7493
Add: Back amortisation during the year	1500
Q. Cash outflows due to acquisition and restructuring	8993
R. Total discretionary outflows (L + M – N – O + P + Q)	19,223
Financial inflows	
Fixed deposits	1121
Commercial paper	500
Bank overdraft	9588
S. Total financial inflows	11,209
Summary of cash flows (cash abstract)	
Opening cash and bank balance	6536
Add: Net cash inflows during the year (G)	18,532
	25,068
Less: Priority outflows (K)	10,089
Cash available for meeting discretionary outflows	14,979
Add: Financial inflows (S)	11,209
Subtotal	26,188
Less: Discretionary outflows	19,223
Cash and bank balance as on 31.3.20X1	6965

Cash flow statement of the company for the year 20X1 (Exhibit 5.5) is prepared on the basis of profit and loss statement for the year ended 31.3.20X1 where gross sales is the first item of operating cash inflow and purchase of materials is the first item operating cash outflow. These are then treated with relative changes in working capital items obtained from the balance sheets of two years. For example, the company had at the close of year 20X0 Rs. 5739 lakh as accounts receivable (sundry debtors) which increased to Rs. 6925 lakh at the end of 20X1. Therefore, net increase in accounts receivable is Rs. 1186 lakh. In between, there must have been several receipts from and further contracting of accounts receivable (sundry debtors) due to new sales which a full cashbook would reveal, but at the end of 20X1 an incremental amount of Rs. 1186 lakh remained unrealised against the gross sales of Rs. 210,802 lakh. That is, cash realised from sales this year would be Rs. 210,802 lakh – 1186 lakh = Rs. 209,616 lakh which can also be calculated in the following manner:

	(Rs. in lakh)
Opening balance of accounts receivable:	5739
Add: Sales during the year	210,802
Total accounts receivable	216,541
Less: Closing balance of accounts receivable	6925
Cash to be realised during the year (subject to adjustment against advance payment)	209,616

In the absence of any other adjustment, cash receipts from sales would have been Rs. 209,616 lakh as shown above, but the company also received advance payments from customers which got adjusted against the final sales. If we compare balances outstanding under the advance payments for the two years, we shall find that there had been a net reduction of Rs. 481 lakh – Rs. 443 lakh = Rs. 38 lakh under this head. This means that the company did not receive advance payments more than the last year, instead, present sales got adjusted to the tune of Rs. 38 lakh due to payments made earlier. Hence, net cash receipts on account of sales would be further reduced to Rs. 209,616 lakh – Rs. 38 lakh = Rs. 209,578 lakh. This is the operating cash inflow for the year as shown in item (A) of the cash flow statement in Exhibit 5.5. It may be seen that while calculating incremental cash blocked in accounts receivable, we have ignored the figures of provisions for bad-debt, because for the present year these are not cash outflows. When real bad-debts occur, the amount is deductible from the gross sales or included in operating expenses (the resultant effect being same) of the current year.

On the expenditure side we find that purchase of raw materials, spares, stores and packing materials and directly traded goods amount to Rs. 152,098 lakh (see working notes below for calculations). Like selling on credit (accounts receivable) the company also buys on credit (accounts payable). Hence, similar to the treatment of accounts receivable on cash inflows from sales, we can say that the company had not paid for the purchases during the year to the extent of the increase in trade creditors (accounts payable). This can be calculated in the following manner.

	(Rs. in lakh)
Opening balance of accounts payable	19,837
Add: Purchases during the year	152,098
Total accounts payable	171,935
Less: Closing balance of accounts payable	27,820
Cash paid for materials	144,115

This is shown as item no. B in the cash flow statement. Similar will be the treatment of expense creditors on other working expenses of the enterprise during 20X1 as is shown in the cash flow statement. It is important to remember that items involving cash transactions only find place in the cash flow statement. As such, non-cash expenditure items like depreciation, amortized miscellaneous expenditure, etc. are ignored for the purpose of drawing up cash flow statement.

Other calculations, which have formed part of the cash flow statement, are given in the following working notes:

Working notes:	(Rs. in lakh)
1. Purchase of raw materials in 20X1	
Raw materials consumed	116,588
Add: Closing stock	21,929
	138,517
Less: Opening stock	19,680
Purchases	118,837

2. Purchase of stores, spares including packing materials in 20X1	(Rs. in lakh)
Stores, spares, etc. consumed	19,190
Add: Closing stock	4243
	23,433
Less: Opening stock	3058
Purchases	20,375

3. Miscellaneous expenses in the profit and loss account for 20X1 include:	(Rs. in lakh)
Amortisation from current year's amortised cost	1500
Amortisation from earlier years' amortised cost	92
	1592

An amount of Rs. 1592 lakh will, therefore, be excluded while calculating cash operating expenses of the company for 20X1 and an amount of Rs. 1500 lakh will be added back for calculating cash outflows for business acquisitions and restructuring costs (deferred). Cash outflow for business acquisitions and restructuring costs as included in 'miscellaneous expenditure' not written off for 20X1 is calculated below:

Closing balance of miscellaneous:	(Rs. in lakh)
Expenses not written of	8450
Less: Opening balance	957
	7493
Add: Amortisation charged to profit and loss account	1500
Cash outflow during the year	8993

4. Investment activities during 20X1				(Rs. in lakh)
(a) UTI capital gain units				
Opening balance	496,860 units	@ Rs. 11.36 =	56.45
* Sold during the year	467,000 units	@ Rs. 11.15 =	52.01
Loss on sale	467,000 units	@ Rs. 0.21 =	0.98
Balance	29,860 units	@ Rs. 11.36 =	3.40

(b) UTI, other units

Opening balance	9,039,970	units	@ Rs. 14.50	=	1310.80
* Sold during the year	5,703,390	units	@ Rs. 15.85	=	904.00
Profit on sale	5,703,390	units	@ Rs. 1.35	=	77.00
** Purchased during the year	529,120	units	@ Rs. 15.90	=	84.13
Balance	3,865,700	units	@ Rs. 14.69	=	567.93
			(average)		

(c) Other quoted shares and debentures

Opening balance	Rs. 627.85
Profit on sale	Rs. 1358.62
* Cash inflow due to sale	Rs. 1986.47
** New securities purchased during the year, being the closing balance (See p. 283, Note 2 under para 1)	Rs. 1592.40

Summary

	Cash inflow	Cash outflow	Profit/Loss	Closing balance
(a)	52.01	—	(0.98)	3.40
(b)	904.00	84.13	77.00	567.93
(c)	1986.47	1592.40	1358.62	1592.40
Total	2942.48	1676.53	1434.64	2163.73

(d) Investment in subsidiaries and joint ventures

Opening balance	Rs. 1289
**Further investment this year (Rights issue)	Rs. 400
Closing balance (See page 283, Note 8 under para 2)	Rs. 1689

5. Column 4 of item No. 6 of the extract from the schedules indicate that addition to capital work-in-progress was Rs. 1126 lakh which was also the balance appearing in the balance sheet of the company as on 31.03.20X1. This means that the entire balance of Rs. 1403 lakh outstanding in capital work-in-progress account as on 31.03.20X0 was transferred to fixed assets account during 20X1.

6. Since there had not been any fresh term-loans, debentures and other short-term loans and borrowings during 20X1, the difference between their opening balances and closing balances can be taken as repayments.

7. Cash inflow from disposal of fixed assets is calculated as follows:

(Rs. in lakh)

Book value of assets	:	468
Less: Depreciation	:	325
		143
Add: Profit on sale of fixed assets as per profit and loss account, 20X1	:	130
Cash inflow	:	273

8. Financial inflow from bank overdraft is calculated as follows:

(Rs. in lakh)

Balance as on 31.03.20X1	:	14,125
Less: Balance as on 31.03.20X0	:	4537
Cash inflow	:	9588

* Cash inflows
** Cash outflows

9. Other current assets are finally calculated below from the schedules and from cash flows shown earlier for both 20X0 and 20X1.

		(Rs. in lakh)
	20X0	20X1
Interest and dividends accrued on investments	346	540
Deposits with IDBI	679	288
Deposits with NABARD	306	485
Other deposits (NSC, defence certificates, etc.)	1106	2053
Total	2437	3366

10. Only interim dividend for 20X1 has been considered for cash flow purpose. Proposed dividend as appearing in balance sheet would be paid in the following year for which has been made.

NOCF AND PRIORITY OUTFLOWS

It may be seen from the cash flow statement in Exhibit 5.5 that net operating cash inflow (E) of the enterprise is Rs. 14,688 lakh. Principles of cash management requires that *net operating cash inflow* (NOCF) should be sufficient to pay for the entire priority outflows and leave something for discretionary outflows. In the present case, total priority outflows is Rs. 10,089 lakh. Hence, NOCF is sufficient to meet the priority outflows; it also leaves Rs. 14,688 lakh – Rs. 10,089 lakh = Rs. 4599 lakh for meeting a part of discretionary outflows.

Non-operating cash flows are shown separately to emphasise their distinct character. They generally constitute incomes from subsidiary and other investments[5] and unusual incomes like disposal of fixed assets etc. which are generally of non-recurring nature. If these cash flows are combined with the cash flows from the principal operating activity of the enterprise, not only that there will be confusion, but the ability or otherwise of the cash generation capacity of the main line operations will also be suppressed. Many a time it has been found that an enterprise has already lost its competitiveness in main line activities, but the fact is suppressed by non-operating cash flows with which the shareholders are kept satisfied by dividend payments. A business enterprise is not expected to lean heavily on the cash flows from its treasury department for its long-term sustenance unless the enterprise itself is in investment business.

---

5. Cash flow statement prescribed in AS3 include income from investment in securities (other than that in subsidiary and joint venture companies) as part of Operating Activities. But for internal cash management, only the principal activity of the enterprise should be considered for purpose of determining cash flows from operations. Dealing in investments (securities) is a treasury function whose main purpose is to subserve the liquidity need of the enterprise. That the treasury department is now considered as a profit centre, does not in any way affect this goal.

Priority Obligation Ratio

As indicated earlier, at the enterprise-level, priority outflows are the liquidity bugs that sting the finance manager hard after he is able to settle cash flow requirement of operations. He may slowdown production but he can ill-afford to slow down tax payments or defer repayments except at the cost of serious legal complications bordering on bankruptcy. It is advisable that he calculates the following ratio called *priority obligation ratio* and watch its movement periodically.

$$\text{Priority obligation ratio}^6 = \frac{\text{Net operating cash inflow (NOCF)}}{\text{Priority outflows}}$$

For LMN Ltd. the ratio works out to be 14,688/10,089 = 1.46. On the face of it, the ratio appears to be satisfactory, and therefore the company is able to cover its priority obligations by 1.46 times.[7]

Discretionary Outflows

Discretionary outflows generally comprise dividend payments, capital expenditure and portfolio investments including those in subsidiaries and joint ventures. Although theoretically speaking, all these commitments are discretionary in nature, many of them border on essentiality. For example, dividend payments though is discretionary, it is almost impossible for a company management to withhold or skip dividend, particularly when it is making profit except at the cost of their removal and adverse effect on the market value of its shares. (Making profit does not necessarily mean making cash as we have discussed before.) Similarly, a minimum level of capital expenditure must have to be maintained for replacements and/or keeping the technology level up-to-date. It is necessary, therefore, that after discharging priority outflows, the company has sufficient cash to meet these near-priority obligations. Priority obligation ratio of an enterprise must, therefore, reflect, by way of cushion (0.46 in the present case), the ability of the operations to contribute towards meeting these 'discretionary obligations'.

Total discretionary outflows of the company is Rs. 19,223 lakh net of inflows from dealing in investments. Bulk of these outflows are due to capital expenditure on business acquisitions and amortisable expenses on acquisitions and business restructuring. This sizable discretionary outflows were partly financed from cash available after meeting the priority outflows and from

---

6. A financial analyst may calculate this ratio as, net cash flow/priority outflows. But a finance manager is advised to take the NOCF as the numerator by excluding non-operating flows on which he may have to fall back if NOCF is not sufficient to cover the priority outflows. For further discussion see, Hrishikes Bhattacharya, *Total Management by Ratio*, 2nd. ed., Sage Publications, New Delhi, 2007, pp. 184–187.

7. A satisfactory ratio should be 1.5 if we take non-operating flows into consideration. See Hrishikes Bhattacharya, *op. cit.*

financial flows which have registered a steep rise during the year.[8] Particular mention may be made of bank overdraft which with an incremental inflow of Rs. 9588 lakh (more than 200 percent rise) contributed about 50 percent towards the discretionary outflows. Whether it is prudent to use bank overdraft, which is short-term in nature, to finance acquisition of long-term assets, will be discussed later, but for the present, it may be mentioned that resorting to short-term routes to finance acquisitions may have the dangerous potential of triggering a liquidity crisis.

Cash Abstract

Summary of cash flows appended at the bottom of the cash flow statement is, in fact, a cash abstract. It opens with a cash and bank balance of Rs. 6536 lakh and ends with a closing balance of Rs. 6965 lakh as reflected in the balance sheet of the company as at 31.3.20X1. This cash balance will be required to meet the impending payment of income tax and dividends aggregating Rs. 5746 lakh.

The question remains to be answered is, whether the company will be required to pay up in the following year a substantial part of the unusual rise in overdraft in the current year. If it has to, then the company may simply not have enough cash to do it. Under the circumstances, it may have to negotiate with its bankers to convert a part of overdraft to *working capital term loan.*

FUNDS ANALYSIS AND FINANCIAL STRUCTURE

We have already indicated that cash flow statement has a rather short-term perspective; it does not reveal much about where the enterprise is going in terms of its financial structure. A funds analysis enables us to take a total view of the financial structure of an enterprise. The fundamental distinction between funds and cash is that the former is a liability and the latter is an asset, just like any other assets of the enterprise. In the ultimate analysis, fund is nominal in nature; it has no physical existence—it is a pool of promises made by the enterprise to various parties including the shareholders who deliver certain assets including cash to the enterprise. Of course, the promises include agreement to return the assets or their cash equivalents with or without interest (profit) on a specified or unspecified date. A promisee or a group of promisees may supply goods or cash or both. For example, shareholders may directly supply cash or other assets, as in the case of acquisitions. A funds inflow would, therefore, definitely increase the total assets level of the enterprise but need not necessarily increase its cash level. It should also be obvious that funds precede assets. Whenever there is an asset creation in the enterprise,

---

8. It may also be noted that sale of investments has also generated cash inflows of Rs. 1267 lakh. The company utilised the bullish price of the securities in the market and made a large profit by selling off the portfolio. The amount was utilised for part financing the acquisitions/restructuring. The company, however, was careful in building up the portfolio once again, when the market was easy.

whether by production or by acquisition, there must already have been a funds inflow in the system. At the same time, whenever there is diminution of assets, whether it is a piece of furniture or cash, there is also going to be a funds inflow in the enterprise because, it is the funds that get blocked in various assets and on their disposal, the blocked funds get released. To sum up, we may say that there shall be a funds inflow whenever there is an increase in liability or decrease in assets, and a funds outflow whenever there is decrease in liability or increase in assets. This phenomena can be captured in Figure 5.1.

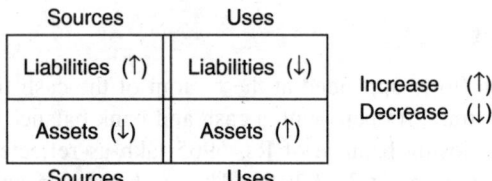

Figure 5.1 Sources and uses of fund.

Funds Flow Presentation

A finance manager, who is concerned with the management of liquidity of the business, would like to see how the funds flow during the year has affected its working capital position. This is prominently focussed by making a funds flow presentation of the balance sheets of the company as we have done for LMN Ltd. in Exhibit 5.6.

One of the principles of financial management is that the long-term funds would not only finance entire long-term assets, it should also contribute reasonably towards financing the working capital requirement of the enterprise. This contribution is located in the funds statement of LMN Ltd. (Exhibit 5.6) as net working capital (E) which is the corresponding part of net current assets (H). While gross current assets constitute the working capital requirement of the firm, net current assets represent that portion which is financed from long-term sources, i.e., the net working capital (NWC). Although arithmetically NWC would always be the difference between current assets and current liabilities, a finance manager would do better by looking at the problem from the upper part of the balance sheet rather than from its bottom, as it would help him in planning the financial structure of the business.

Net Working Capital

Major source of liquidity problem is the mismatch between current payments and current receipts. This mismatch is not unlikely to happen in any business because of sudden lengthening of the pipeline as a result of say, by non-payment of accounts receivable on due date. Net working capital provides that important cushion in the event of such an eventuality. It protects the enterprise against liquidity crisis on an ongoing basis. A decrease in NWC indicates depletion of such protection.

Exhibit 5.6 Balance Sheets of LMN Ltd. (Funds flow concept)

(Rs. in lakh)

	As on 31.3.20X0		As on 31.3.20X1	
Capital and long-term funds				
Share capital	12,048		12,048	
Capital reserve	347		347	
Revenue reserve	22,824		28,844	
A. Shareholders' fund	35,219		41,239	
Debentures	15		4	
Term loans	3178		2448	
Fixed deposits	2058		1594	
B. Long-term loan fund	5251		4046	
C. Total long-term fund (A + B)		40,470		45,285
Application of long-term fund				
Net fixed assets	17,598		24,705	
Capital work-in-progress	1403		1126	
Goodwill	—		638	
Investments in subsidiaries	1289		1689	
Miscellaneous expenditure not written off	957		8450	
D. Total long-term assets		21,247		36,608
E. Net working capital (C – D)		19,223		8677
Short-term assets				
Cash and bank balances	6536		6965	
Investments (others)	1995		2164	
Accounts receivable	5052		6162	
Inventories	34,120		39,842	
Other current assets	2437		3366	
Loans and advances	11,874		11,063	
F. Total short-term assets		62,014		69,562
Short-term resources				
Sundry creditors	19,837		27,820	
Advance payments	481		443	
Interest accrued	332		329	
Expense liabilities	3739		5493	
Commercial papers	3500		4000	
Bank overdraft	4537		14,125	
Unclaimed dividend	1273		1177	
Other short-term loans and borrowings	5065		1752	
Provisions (Income tax and dividend)	4027		5746	
G. Total short-term resources		42,791		60,885
H. Net current assets (F – G)		19,223		8677

When we compare the two years of funds flow statement of LMN Ltd. as shown in Exhibit 5.6, we find that its net working capital has fallen to Rs. 8677 lakh in 20X1 from a high of Rs. 19,223 lakh in the previous year; the reduction is close to 55 percent. While current assets of the company have gone up only by about 12 percent against an almost similar rise in sales, current liabilities have gone up by 42 percent. These two together pushed down the NWC to the present level. Although as long as NWC is positive we cannot say that there is a clear case of diversion of funds, the sharp fall in NWC is a clear indication that the company is utilising its short-term resources for long-term purpose. How far the company is from the liquidity crisis can be judged by making a comparison of the following ratio for the two years under review.

$$\text{Net working capital ratio (NWCR)} = \frac{\text{Net working capital}}{\text{Gross current assets}}$$

For LMN Ltd. NWCR for two years would be as follows:

20X0	20X1

$$\text{NWCR} \quad \frac{19,223}{62,014} = 31\% \qquad \frac{8677}{69,652} = 12.46\%$$

We can see that NWCR, which was providing a 31 percent cushion in 20X0, has gone down to a bare 12.46 percent in 20X1. The situation must be considered serious as it is changing the financial structure of the company for the worse. Major sources of the tightening of the cushion are: rise in accounts payables (sundry creditors) and bank overdraft. As consumption of raw materials including stores and tradeable goods has gone up by only 15 percent during 20X1 (purchases also might be assumed to have risen by the same percentage) there is no case for the trade creditors to rise by 40 percent. There is likelihood that trade creditors are simply not being paid on time. More striking is the case with expense creditors which are much more short-term in nature than the trade creditors. They have gone up by 47 percent during 20X1. As if these were not sufficient, bank overdraft has also registered a rise of more than 200 percent during the year. All these were done to finance business acquisition and restructuring. Unless the company is able to raise sufficient amount of long-term funds in the immediate future, it will face severe liquidity crisis. The company has sizable net worth and its long-term loans are on the lower side as indicated by a low (long-term) debt-equity ratio of about 0.10. The company has a very high cushion in its long-term financial structure but a very low cushion in its short-term structure. It is time that the company removes this lopsidedness in its financial structure.

Cash Gap vs Funds Gap

We have discussed earlier that the *cash abstract* shown at the bottom of cash flow statement (Exhibit 5.5) is the summary of all cash transactions that have taken place during the year under review. At the end of the day, on 31.3.20X1, the company has a positive balance of Rs. 6965 lakh which it had to arrange because of impending tax and dividend payments. In other words, for building up this asset (cash) the company had to contract liabilities (fund) on the other side of the balance sheet. Similarly, all cash transactions during the year would not have taken place had there been no funds flow to support them. However, funds flow need not have to be restricted in cash transactions alone; it encompasses all assets transactions, and its ultimate purpose is to build up (fund) all assets of an enterprise including cash. Now, from all the (funds) transactions of a business if we delete non-cash transactions, the cash flow gap and the funds flow gap must tally. This is how the linkage between funds flow and cash flow is established. This linkage is important for the financial planning of a business.

In Exhibit 5.7 we have presented (incremental) *funds flow statement* of LMN Ltd. for the year 20X1.

Exhibit 5.7 Funds Flow Statement for the Year 20X1 (Incremental)

(Rs. in lakh)

Sources	
Profit after tax	12,646
Add: Depreciation	1921
Add: Decrease in capital work-in-progress	277
A. Total sources	14,844
Uses	
Increase in fixed assets	9028
Goodwill	638
Increase in investment in subsidiaries	400
Increase in miscellaneous expenditure	7493
Decrease in term liabilities	1205
Payment of dividends	6626
B. Total long-term usage	25,390
C. Long-term funds deficit (A − B)	(10,546)
Increase in current assets	7548
Less: Increase in current liabilities	(8506)
(excluding bank overdraft)	
D. Decrease in net-working capital	958
E. Funds flow gap (C − D)	9588
Increase in bank overdraft	9588

Notes:	1. Increase in fixed assets is calculated as below:	
	Opening balance (before depreciation)	19,157
	Additions during the year	9496
		28,653
	Disposals during the year	468
	Closing balance (before depreciation)	28,185
	Less: Opening balance as above	19,157
	Increase during the year	9028
	2. Decrease in net working capital (excluding bank overdraft) is a funds inflow (source), hence it is deducted from long-term funds deficit (*C*) to arrive at the funds gap (*E*)	

We observe from Exhibit 5.7 that funds flow gap for the year has come to be Rs. 9588 lakh. In other words, assuming that the year 20X1 is the projected year and the company has planned to acquire designated assets and discharge specified obligations coming under the head 'USES' during the year, the company would need additional inflow of funds to the tune of Rs. 9588 lakh. The company has decided to fill up this gap by contracting further overdraft with bank.

In Exhibit 5.8 we have calculated cash flow gap of the company for the year 20X1.

Exhibit 5.8 Cash Flow Gap for the Year 20X1

(Rs. in lakh)

Inflows	
Net cash inflow during the year (*G*)	18,532
(As per cash flow statement)	
Add: Opening cash and bank balance	6536
	25,068
Add: Cash inflow from commercial papers	500
Add: Cash inflow from fixed deposits	1121
A. Total inflows	26,689
Outflows	
Priority outflows	10,089
Discretionary outflows	19,223
B. Total outflows	29,312
Net cash flow gap (B – A)	2623
Add: Required closing cash balance	6965
Gross cash flow gap	9588
Increase in bank overdraft	9588

We find from Exhibit 5.8 that the company has a total cash inflow of Rs. 26,689 lakh (A) during the year. Deducting total outflows of Rs. 29,312 lakh constituting *priority outflows* and *discretionary outflows,* we are left with a net cash flow gap of Rs. 2623 lakh. When the company finds that it requires additional cash of Rs. 6965 lakh to pay for impending liabilities, gross cash gap comes to be Rs. 2623 lakh + Rs. 6965 lakh = Rs. 9588 lakh which exactly equals the funds flow gap that we have calculated in Exhibit 5.7.

Before we conclude this section, we want to emphasise that all cash flows are funds flows but all funds flows are not cash flows. Cash flow analysis is a partial concept while funds flow analysis is a total concept, the former gives a short-term view while the latter presents a long-term view of the business. Cash flow analysis concentrates on operations; funds flow analysis concentrates on the financial structure of the business.

MANAGEMENT OF LIQUIDITY

In the preceding section, we have highlighted the importance of liquidity while making the cash flow and funds flow analyses of a business. But to find out a suitable definition of liquidity is a real problem. In fact, economists have long grappled with the problem of defining liquidity, but no universal definition has yet come up. This is because liquidity means different things to different persons.

Shiftability Theory

One of the generally held beliefs is that cash is the most liquid of all assets and hence, liquidity should be understood and calculated in terms of the cashability of all other assets. From this belief, shiftable theory of liquidity management was first developed for financial institutions. According to this theory, which is now also applicable to non-financial corporates, an institution can maintain liquidity if it holds assets that could be shifted or sold for cash quickly with minimum transaction costs and loss in value. Corporate liquidity, according to this theory, depends internally on the fungibility of the assets held, and externally, on the existence of a market sufficiently deep and wide where these assets could be transacted at a short notice and at fine rates. Existence of an efficient market influences the liquidity need of a business to a very large extent.

Liquidity Newly Defined

While a finance manager would readily agree with the shiftable theory based on cashability of assets, for operations managers, this theory is meaningless because to them, liquidity means availability of inventories at the right time and at right places. For a production manager it is the availability of raw materials along the production lines, and for a marketing manager it is the availability of finished goods along the distribution channels. A finance manager may have a very high liquidity in his hands in the form of cash or cash equivalents, but there may be a dearth of raw materials in the market, as a result of which production will stop, distribution channels will dry up and consequently, cash inflow to pay for the maturing liabilities shall also stop throwing the company to the brink of liquidation. If the purpose of liquidity is to keep the operations of a business going, then the inventory, which was hitherto considered to be the most illiquid of all current assets, would turn out to be the first component of the liquidity of a business. This new approach to liquidity has already been discussed at length while highlighting the importance of inventory in the previous chapter.

At the macro level of the firm, however, the test of liquidity is the ability of the firm to meet its cash obligations when they are due and to exploit sudden opportunities in the market, which often come by when a finance manager keeps his eyes and ears open, and maintains sufficient liquidity to seize the opportunities.

Liquidity Crisis and Firm-level Actions

Although the ultimate result of illiquidity is bankruptcy, this does not immediately happen. Corporate managers take several actions one after the other, to stem the process. Some of these actions may arrest the process without much loss of future credibility of the business; some may arrest it only temporarily and some actions may just hasten up the process. When an enterprise first feels a liquidity crunch, the sequence of actions taken by it with their consequent effect on the firm are given in Table 5.2.

Table 5.2 Sequential Actions to Arrest Liquidity Crisis and Their Effects

Action sequence	Action type		Effect
1.	Utilise the unavailed credit limits	(a)	Sudden rise in availment may alert the bankers which may affect future renewals/enhancements.
		(b)	Rise in interest cost will affect profitability.
2.	Sell marketable securities	(a)	Lower price availability.
		(b)	Difficulty to build up a similar portfolio later.
3.	Negotiate spacing of repayment schedule of term liabilities	(a)	Debenture holders may not agree; trustees may crystallize the securities and/or file bankruptcy petition.
		(b)	Even when debenture holders agree, there may be negative signals to the market which will make it difficult for future issues.
		(c)	Financial institutions (FIs) may not agree and may behave like debenture holders.
		(d)	FIs may agree, but may first like to have charges on further assets of the company which may clash with the interests of debenture holders; it may also jeopardise the scope for raising further loans.
		(e)	FIs may like to appoint their own representatives on the board.
		(f)	FIs may charge a premium on the existing interest rate.
4.	Negotiate for enhancement of short-term credit facilities with	(a)	Bankers may get scared for creation of further non-performing assets and keep the enterprise on watch.
		(b)	Bankers may, at best, agree on some ad-hoc increases to be repaid within a given time frame; if this time frame is not observed, bankers may stop further debit operations in the account which may have serious consequences for day-to-day running of the business.
		(c)	Bankers may like to sanction additional facilities but would want additional contribution from owners (equity), which may be of utmost necessity but may not easily come by.
5.	Defer payment of suppliers' bills	(a)	Attempt will be first made to defer long-standing 'friendly' suppliers; if the liquidity crunch persists, there may be total deferment.
		(b)	Supply line may be choked which will seriously affect the production schedules resulting in consequent loss of output/sales. Crisis will thus be further aggravated.
		(c)	Suppliers may be scared and demand payments immediately. This may have a snow-balling effect which will precipitate the crisis.
6.	Advance buyers' payment	(a)	This may be effected by offering large cash discounts which will erode the bottom line.
		(b)	The enterprise may resort to larger cash sales which will affect the future sales of the company.
		(c)	Collection department may be overstretched and buyers pestered for early payment. This will not only affect future sales it may also give signals to the market of impending liquidity crisis.

(Cont.)

Table 5.2 Sequential Actions to Arrest Liquidity Crisis and Their Effects (Cont.)

Action sequence	Action type	Effect
7. Reduce cash outflows		(a) The first axe may fall upon research and development, training and promotional expenses. This will have a long-term effect on the market competitiveness of the enterprise and consequent loss of market share. The effect will be felt even long after the liquidity problem is resolved.
		(b) The next casualty is the plant and machinery whose repairs and maintenance will be postponed, the ultimate cost of which may be tremendously heavy on the enterprise when machines breakdown.
		(c) The third in the line of suffering is the capital expenditure; even the minimum level of expenditure that are necessary to keep the plant going will be postponed. This will affect both the present and future capability of the production system of the enterprise.
8. Sell assets		It is the spare land and buildings which are sold first, followed by pieces of plant and machinery and then inventory of materials. Unfortunately, assets which could be sold immediately are often the prime assets, selling of which may cripple the enterprise. Since assets would be sold under distress, they are unlikely to fetch good prices.
9. Refer to Board for Industrial and Financial Reconstruction (BIFR)		When the company is declared sick, reference can be made to BIFR to examine the possibilities of its revival. BIFR is a quasi-judicial body. After hearing all the parties, it may pass order for a particular package for its revival which generally entails sacrifices from all the parties. If, however, BIFR feels that no revival is possible, it may order winding up of the company.

Although most of the enterprises when faced with a liquidity crunch, follow steps in order of sequences as mentioned in Table 5.2, there are cases where more than one steps are taken simultaneously depending upon the intensity and nature of the crisis.

MEASUREMENT OF LIQUIDITY

A measure of liquidity should be such as to indicate the level of solvency on the one hand and on the other, the financial flexibility of a firm. Corporate managers may like to structure the assets and liabilities of the firm in such a manner as to ensure a desired level of solvency and at the same time, provide enough financial flexibility to attain the strategic goals of the enterprise.

Current Ratio and Quick Ratio

The corporate managers' objectives, which are predominantly long-term in nature, may clash with that of the outside creditors whose main concern is short-term solvency. Faced with this conflicting interests, a finance manager may have to strike a compromise between the two. For example, a *current ratio* of 2 or more is generally regarded by outside lenders and creditors to be a good measure of liquidity, but for a modern finance manager, a high current ratio blocks costly long-term fund and consequently erodes profitability of a firm. In fact, an efficient financial management aims at lowering down the current ratio rather than increasing it. A balance between these two conflicting objectives was struck in India by the banking community with the acceptance of the Chore group recommendation of fixing up current ratio at 1.33.[9]

Window-dressing

Components of current assets are often more important than the current ratio for measuring liquidity of a firm. This has given rise to a variation of current ratio which is called *quick ratio* or *acid test*, as is known popularly. This is calculated by dividing the total of cash, marketable securities and accounts receivable by the current liabilities. Inventory is ignored for calculation of this ratio because it is believed that inventory takes longer time for conversion into cash than marketable securities and accounts receivable. However, both the current ratio and quick ratio are amenable to unethical manipulation or window dressing as the following example will show.

Current account structure:

(Rs. in lakh)

Current liabilities		*Current assets*	
Sundry creditors	65	Cash and bank balance	55
Bank overdraft	60	Marketable securities	15
Expense liability	5	Sundry debtors	60
		Inventories	25
Total	130	Total	155

Suppose the current account financial structure of an enterprise as on 29th March is as shown above. This structure gives a current ratio of 155/130 = 1.19 and a quick ratio of 130/130 = 1. Now, bank will not accept a current ratio less than 1.30 and supply creditors will be scary if quick ratio falls below 1. A finance manager can attain both the objectives by simply paying off the creditors to the tune of Rs. 50 lakh. His action will change the current account structure of the enterprise as follows.

---

9. Reserve Bank of India, *Report of the Working Group to Review the System of Cash Credit*, Bombay, 1979.

Subsequent current account structure: (Rs. in lakh)

Current liabilities		*Current assets*	
Sundry creditors	15	Cash and bank balance	5
Bank overdraft	60	Marketable securities	15
Expense liability	5	Sundry debtors	60
		Inventories	25
Total	80	Total	105

Current ratio of the firm would now be 105/80 = 1.31. Quick ratio remains same at 80/80 = 1.

The action of the finance manager has no doubt improved the current ratio without any deterioration of quick ratio, but can it be said that the liquidity of the firm has improved? It might have worsened in a very practical way with a sizable removal of cash balance which is the most liquid of all current assets.

Due to reasons mentioned above, importance of current ratio and quick ratio has gone down to a large extent, though they have not totally lost their significance. These two ratios are now considered as components of a set of other liquidity measures.

Other Ratio Measurements

Next ratio in the set of liquidity measures is the *net working capital ratio* (NWCR) that we have calculated and discussed earlier. It is a superior measure of liquidity than current or quick ratio.

A finer measure of liquidity is the net liquidity ratio which is calculated as

$$\text{Net liquidity ratio (NLR)} = \frac{\begin{array}{c}(\text{Cash} + \text{Marketables} + \text{Unused creditlines})\\ - \text{Trade and expense creditors}\end{array}}{\text{Total assets}}$$

NLR takes into account the unavailed credit limits enjoyed by the enterprise with banks. This information is not available in the published financial statements of an enterprise and hence, has to be accessed from internal sources. For all practical purposes, unavailed credit lines represent cash because, by simply issuing a cheque, the firm can withdraw the money. When all sales and other receipts are banked through the overdraft account, the reduction in debit balance (and thereby freeing the limit) is nothing but simple transfer of cash from one till to the other.

Net liquidity ratio indicates the ability of the firm to pay up immediately the most 'liquid' liabilities of the firm namely, the trade and expense creditors and consequently, it is one of their preferred ratios.

Turnover Ratios

Other ratios that are generally used as measures for liquidity, which we have already discussed in earlier chapters, are accounts receivable turnover ratio (Chapter 3) and finished goods inventory turnover ratio (Chapter 4). Some writers also include average days of sales outstanding which is a variant of accounts receivable turnover ratio (Chapter 3).

Adjusted Current Ratio

Above turnover ratios can be considered separately or adjusted against the current ratio along with turnover ratios of current liabilities. Under the latter scheme, major current assets and current liabilities are first adjusted by their respective turnover ratios. The adjusted current ratio is then calculated by dividing the aggregate of adjusted current assets with adjusted current liabilities. Adjustment of individual current asset and current liabilities is done in the following manner.

$$\begin{array}{l} \text{Adjusted individual current asset} \\ \text{or current liability} \end{array} = \begin{array}{l} \text{Current asset or} \\ \text{current liability} \end{array} \left[1 - \frac{1}{\begin{array}{c} \text{Turnover of asset} \\ \text{or liability} \end{array}} \right]$$

For example, if the value of accounts receivable is Rs. 1200 and its turnover ratio is 24, adjusted accounts receivable will be

$$= 1200 \times \left[1 - \frac{1}{24} \right]$$

$$= 1200 \times 0.958$$

$$= \text{Rs. } 1150$$

On the other hand, if accounts receivable turnover ratio is 12, the adjusted accounts receivable will be Rs. 1200 × 0.9166 = Rs. 1100. That is, if the turnover ratio of a current asset is low it will have a lower influence on the adjusted current ratio. In the case of current liabilities, the influence will be on the reverse.

Sales Cash Conversion Cycle (SCCC)

This liquidity measurement is drawn from the pipeline theory of working capital that we have discussed in Chapter 1. It is the time taken by sales revenue to convert itself into cash through inventory blockages along the pipeline, cycle and buffer inventories. We have seen in Chapter 1 that the production process manufactures 12 completed units a day, at a cost of production of Rs. 24 per unit, and releases them to the distribution system, at a cost of sales of Rs. 25 per unit, which takes 19 days to reach the consumers who take them on 30 days' credit. True cash cycle of the system is, therefore, 1 + 19 + 30 = 50 days. In other words, we can say that a rupee put to the pipeline would come back in 50 days. Although this cash cycle of 50 days would exactly remain same during a given technology and distributive practices, further cash might get blocked by the cycle and buffer inventory. At the same time, when cash comes in from sales revenue (at 12 × Rs. 25 = Rs. 300 per day) it need not have to pay for a part of purchases (consumption) and expenses. If we convert all these into days we shall find that the pipeline cash cycle will get expanded by cycle and buffer holdings and shortened by the credit period available from trade and expense creditors. Let us calculate this from the example given in Chapter 1. Summary of inventory holdings at different stages are given in Table 5.3.

Table 5.3 Inventory Holding at Different Stages

	Pipeline		Cycle		Buffer		Total	
	Amount (Rs.)	Days	Amount (Rs.)	Days	Amount (Rs.)	Days	Amount (Rs.)	Days
Raw materials	—	—	1260	10.5	900	7.5	2160	18
Work-in-process	288	1	—	—	—	—	288	1
Finished goods	5700	19	4200	14.0	4500	15	14,400	48
Accounts receivable (at cost of sales)	9000	30	—	—	—	—	9000	30
Total	14,988	50	5460	24.5	5400	22.5	25,848	97

Days are calculated for raw materials inventory on raw materials consumption (Rs. 43,200), for work-in-process on cost of production (Rs. 103,680), on finished goods and accounts receivable on cost of sales (Rs. 108,000) assuming 360 days in a year.

Assuming now that accounts payable constitute trade creditors of Rs. 8000 and expense creditors of Rs. 2000, their turnover in terms of days will be

$$\frac{8000 \times 360}{43,200} = 66.66 \text{ or } 67 \text{ days and } \frac{2000 \times 360}{64,800} = 11.11 \text{ or } 11 \text{ days}$$

respectively, where the first denominator, Rs. 43,200 represents materials consumption (taken as equivalent to purchases and the second denominator, Rs. 64,800 represents all other costs except materials consumption (Rs. 108,000 – 43,200 = Rs. 64,800).

Sales cash conversion cycle in terms of days can now be calculated as below:

$$97 - 67 - 11 = 19 \text{ days}$$

In effect, SCCC is nothing but net working capital in days before bank overdraft is taken to finance a part of working capital requirement. For bankers, it is the working capital gap and for corporate managers, it is the days of annual sales revenue getting blocked in the productive-distributive system of the enterprise.

It should be evident that shorter the SCCC, better is the liquidity position of the enterprise and lesser the financing requirement. For two enterprises having equal pipeline length (true cash conversion cycle), their SCCC may be different owing to the difference in their ability to draw trade credits.

Some writers[10] have suggested *weighted cash conversion cycle* (WCCC) as a measure of liquidity. Under this method, total inventory is broken down

---

10. Gentry, J.A., R. Vaidyanathan and H.W. Lee, "A Weighted Cash Conversion Cycle", *Financial Management*, Spring 1990, pp. 90–99.

into materials, working-in-process and finished goods as above and then sales revenue flow time is weighted by the proportion of sales revenue represented by materials cost for materials inventory, cost of production for work-in-process and finished goods inventory, and profit margin for accounts receivable. The weighted accounts payable time is then deducted from it to arrive at WCCC. This methodology is more or less similar to the one that we have discussed above except that its presentation is rather complex and it is difficult for an outside analyst to calculate it because some of the information required to calculate WCCC are purely internal to the company.

UNCERTAINTIES

All the liquidity measures discussed so far do not take into account the uncertainty of future cash flows, though uncertainty is the only certain thing in a business. Emery[11] developed a liquidity measure which he denoted as *Lambda* and defined it by the following formula:

$$\text{Uncertainty factor (Lambda)} = \frac{\text{Liquid resources} + \text{Expected cash flows}}{\text{Uncertainty of cash flows}}$$

Emery includes unused credit lines (as we have done for calculation of net liquidity ratio) in calculating liquid resources besides cash and marketable securities. Expected cash flows comprise net cash flow from operations for the planned period, as in a cash flow statement, plus any expected or planned financial inflows *less* any outflows due to investments. Expected cash flows by their very nature can come out to be negative or positive. Uncertainty is measured by standard deviation (SD) of net cash flow over a period, say three years.

Lambda can be interpreted as a measure of the probability of having insufficient resources to cover operating cash outflows. Denominator of the above equation being standard deviation, Lambda would be given in number of SDs. If the SD is large, Lambda will be fewer SDs and hence, the chance of the firm becoming illiquid will be higher. Reverse will be the case when SD is small.

All the measures of liquidity discussed above are calculated below for LMN Ltd. by making suitable assumption whenever necessary.

1. Current ratio (CR) (before bank overdraft)   (Rs. in lakh)

Current assets	20X0	20X1	Current liabilities	20X0	20X1
Cash and bank balances	6536	6965	Accounts payable:		
Investment-marketables	1995	2164	Trade	19,837	27,820
Accounts receivable	5052	6162	Expenses	3739	5493
Inventories	34,120	39,842	Advance payments	481	443

---

11. Emery, G.W., "Measuring Short-term Liquidity", *Journal of Cash Management*, July/August 1984, pp. 25–32.

Loans and advances	11,874	11,063	Interest accrued	332	329
Other current assets	2437	3366	Unclaimed dividend	1273	1117
			Provisions	4027	5746
Total	62,014	69,562	Total	29,689	40,948

$$
\begin{array}{cc}
 & 20X0 & 20X1 \\
CR = & \dfrac{62,014}{29,689} & \dfrac{69,562}{40,948} \\
 & = 2.00 & = 1.7
\end{array}
$$

2. Quick ratio (QR) (before bank overdraft)

	20X0	20X1		20X0	20X1
Cash and bank balances	6536	6965	Accounts payable—		
Investment-marketables	1995	2164	Trade	19,837	27,820
Accounts receivable	5052	6162	Expenses	3739	5493
			Advance payments	481	443
			Interest accrued	332	329
			Unclaimed dividend	1273	1117
			Provisions	4027	5746
Total	13,583	15,291	Total	29,689	40,948

$$
\begin{array}{cc}
20X0 & 20X1 \\
QR = \dfrac{13,583}{29,689} = 0.46 & \dfrac{15,291}{40,948} = 0.37
\end{array}
$$

3. Net liquidity ratio (NLR)

	20X0	20X1		20X0	20X1
Cash and bank balances	6536	6965	Accounts payable—		
Marketables securities	1995	2164	Trade	19,837	27,820
Unused credit lines	1000	—	Expenses	3739	5493
			Advance payments	481	443
			Interest accrued	332	329
			Provisions (tax and dividends)	4027	5746
Total	9531	9129	Total	28,416	39,831
Total assets	83,261	106,170			

$$
\begin{array}{cc}
20X0 & 20X1 \\
NLR = \dfrac{9531 - 28,416}{83,261} = -0.23 & \dfrac{9129 - 39,831}{106,170} = -0.29
\end{array}
$$

Notes: 1. Unused credit lines in 20X0 have been assumed to be Rs. 1000 lakh. For 20X1 no such assumption is made because bank overdraft must have been utilised upto the maximum for financing acquisition and business restructuring.

2. Normally, provisions for tax and dividend would not be included in liabilities for calculation of NLR except when it is done for the year-end balances.

4. Finished goods inventory turnover ratio (FGITR)

	20X0	20X1
Finished goods inventory	9921	12,367
Cost of sales	171,625	195,951

$$\text{FGITR} = \frac{171,625}{9921} \qquad \frac{195,951}{12,367}$$

$$= 17.30 \qquad\qquad = 15.84$$

5. Accounts receivable turnover ratio (ARTR)

	20X0	20X1
Accounts receivable	5052	6162
Sales	187,463	210,802

$$\text{ARTR} = \frac{187,463}{5052} \qquad \frac{210,802}{6162}$$

$$= 37.11 \qquad\qquad = 34.21$$

6. Adjusted current ratio (ACR) (before bank overdraft)

(a) *Adjusted current assets*

Raw materials, packing materials, stores and spares inventory

20X0

$$\text{Rs. } 22,738 \left(1 - \frac{1}{5.31}\right)$$
$$= \text{Rs. } 22,738 \times 0.812$$
$$= \text{Rs. } 18,463$$

20X1

$$\text{Rs. } 26,172 \left(1 - \frac{1}{5.19}\right)$$
$$= \text{Rs. } 26,172 \times 0.807$$
$$= \text{Rs. } 21,121$$

Note: In the absence of purchases figure for 20X0, turnover ratios for raw materials, stores and spares inventory are calculated on consumption for both 20X0 and 20X1 as follows.

	20X0	20X1
Consumption of raw materials	103,502	116,588
Consumption of stores etc.	17,243	19,190
Total	120,745	135,778
Inventory turnover ratio		
of materials and stores	$\dfrac{120,745}{22,738}$	$\dfrac{135,778}{26,172}$
	= 5.31	= 5.19

(b) *Adjusted work-in-progress inventory*

20X0

$$\text{Rs. } 1461 \left(1 - \frac{1}{98.07}\right)$$
$$= \text{Rs. } 1461 \times 0.9898$$
$$= \text{Rs. } 1446$$

20X1

$$\text{Rs. } 1303 \left(1 - \frac{1}{125.59}\right)$$
$$= \text{Rs. } 1303 \times 0.9920$$
$$= \text{Rs. } 1293$$

Cost of production for determining the turnover ratios is calculated below for two years.

	20X0	20X1
	(Rs.)	(Rs.)
Consumption of raw materials	103,502	116,588
Consumption of packing materials stores etc.	17,243	19,190
Power and fuel	3280	3461
Freight and transport	4340	5860
Salaries and wages (80%)	7714	9722
Contribution to P.F. (80%)	1261	2136
Staff welfare expenses (80%)	955	1012
Repairs to machinery	746	932
Depreciation (80%)	1247	1537
Rent, rates and taxes (80%)	2907	2824
Insurance (80%)	190	225
	143,385	163,487
Add: Opening stock of work-in-progress	1359	1461
	144,744	164,948
Less: Closing stock of work-in-progress	1461	1303
Cost of production	143,283	163,645
	143,283	163,645
Work-in-progress turnover ratio	1461	1303
	= 98.07	= 125.59

(c) *Adjusted finished goods Iiventory*

20X0   20X1

$$\text{Rs. } 9921\left(1-\frac{1}{17.30}\right) \qquad \text{Rs. } 12,367\left(1-\frac{1}{15.84}\right)$$

$$= \text{Rs. } 9921 \times 0.942 \qquad = \text{Rs. } 12,367 \times 0.937$$

$$= \text{Rs. } 9346 \qquad = \text{Rs. } 11,588$$

(d) *Adjusted accounts receivable*

20X0   20X1

$$\text{Rs. } 5052\left(1-\frac{1}{37.11}\right) \qquad \text{Rs. } 6162\left(1-\frac{1}{34.21}\right)$$

$$= 5052 \times 0.973 \qquad = 6162 \times 0.971$$

$$= \text{Rs. } 4916 \qquad = \text{Rs. } 5983$$

Note: Cash and bank balances, marketable securities, loans and advances and other current assets are not adjusted.

(e) *Adjusted current liabilities*
 (a) Adjusted sundry creditors

	20X0	20X1
Purchase of raw materials	105,498	118,837
Purchase of stores and packing materials, etc.	18,308	20,375
Purchase of goods traded	8472	12,886
Total purchases	132,278	152,098

Note: Purchases of raw materials, packing materials, stores, etc. for 20X0 are not available from published accounts. Hence, these are calculated on the basis of percentage of purchases on consumptions for 20X1.

$$\begin{array}{cc} 20X0 & 20X1 \end{array}$$

$$\text{Sundry creditors turnover ratio} = \frac{132,278}{19,837} = 6.67 \qquad \frac{152,098}{27,820} = 5.47$$

$$\begin{aligned} \text{Adjusted sundry creditors} &= \text{Rs.}\,19,837\left(1 - \frac{1}{6.67}\right) \qquad \text{Rs.}\,27,820\left(1 - \frac{1}{5.47}\right) \\ &= \text{Rs. } 19,837 \times 0.85 \qquad\qquad = \text{Rs. } 27,820 \times 0.817 \\ &= \text{Rs. } 16,861 \qquad\qquad\quad\;\; = \text{Rs. } 22,729 \end{aligned}$$

Note: Other current liabilities are not adjusted.

Adjusted Current Assets and Current Liabilities

Adjusted current assets	20X0 (Rs.)	20X1 (Rs.)
Raw materials, packing materials, stores, etc. inventory	18,463	21,121
Work-in-progress inventory	1446	1293
Finished goods inventory	9346	11,588
Accounts receivable	4916	5983
	34,171	39,985
Loans and advances	11,874	11,063
Marketable securities	1995	2164
Cash and bank balances	6536	6965
Other current assets	2437	3366
Total	57,013	63,543

Adjusted current liabilities	20X0 (Rs.)	20X1 (Rs.)
Sundry creditors	16,861	22,729
Advance payments	481	443
Interest accrued but not due	332	329
Expense creditors	3739	5493
Unclaimed dividend	1273	1177
Provisions (tax and dividend)	4027	5746
Total	26,713	35,917
Adjusted current ratio	$\dfrac{57,013}{26,713}$	$\dfrac{63,543}{35,917}$
	= 2.13	= 1.77

7. Sales cash conversions cycle (SCCC)

	Operating current assets			Turnover ratio in days	
	20X0	Days		20X1	Days
Raw materials inventory	365/5.31 =	68.73		365/5.19 =	70.33
Work-in-progress inventory	365/98.07 =	3.72		365/125.59 =	2.91
Finished goods inventory	365/17.30 =	21.10		365/15.84 =	23.04
Accounts receivable	365/37.11 =	9.84		365/34.21 =	10.67
	A. Total days =	103.39			106.95

Operating current liabilities

Sundry creditors	365/6.67 =	54.72		365/5.47 =	66.73
Expense creditors	365/10.42 =	35.03		365/8.35 =	43.71
Advance payments	365/389.74 =	0.94		365/475.85 =	0.77
	B. Total days =	90.69			111.21
SCCC (A – B)	Net days	12.70		(–)	4.26

Note: Turnover ratios for expense creditors are based on cash operating expenditure calculated as below:

	20X0	20X1
	Rs.	Rs.
Salaries and wages	9642	12,153
Contribution to P.F.	1576	2670
Staff welfare expenses	1194	1265
Repairs to machinery	746	932
Repairs to building	375	438
Power and fuel	3280	3461
Rent	822	974
Rates and taxes	2812	2556
Insurance	237	281
Freight and transport	4340	5860
Advertising, etc.	6068	7153
Discount and commission	335	310
Brokerage	46	44
Postage and stationery	819	952
Travelling expenses	2213	2522
Processing charges	668	766
Bank charges	787	905
Donations	92	92
Audit fees	11	13
Miscellaneous expenses (net of amortisation)	2903	2505
Total	38,966	45,852

$$\text{Expenses creditors turnover ratio} = \frac{38,966}{3739} \qquad \frac{45,852}{5493}$$

$$= 10.42 \qquad\qquad = 8.35$$

Note: Turnover ratio for advance payments are calculated on gross sales.

8. Uncertainity factor (Lambda)

For purpose of calculating Lambda we need to have information for prior periods. These are calculated from annual reports of the company for prior periods except unused credit lines. Detailed calculations are now shown.

Liquid resources	19XX	20X0	20X1
Cash and bank balances	5835	6536	6965
Marketable securities	1855	1995	2164
Unused credit lines	800	1000	—
Total	8490	9531	9129
Operating cash flows	13,940	15,934	17,961
Financial inflows	2775	3621	11,209
Discretionary outflows	(1667)	(2689)	(19,223)
Priority outflows	(5742)	(6632)	(10,089)
(Expected) cash flow	9306	10,234	(142)

Notes: 1. Operating cash flows exclude non-operating cash flows and extraordinary items like sales tax liabilities of Rs. 3273 for earlier years paid in 20X1.

2. Actual figures are taken as expected cash flows to illustrate the procedure for calculations.

Standard deviation (SD) for operating cash flows is calculated below. Operating cash flows for the three consecutive years are Rs. 13,940, Rs. 15,934 and Rs. 17,961 respectively.

Year	(x_i)	$(\bar{x})$	$(x_i - \bar{x})$	$(x_i - \bar{x})^2$	S.D.
19XX Rs. 13,940		47,835/3	−2005	4,020,025	$\sqrt{\dfrac{8,084,402}{3}}$
		= Rs. 15,945			
20X0 Rs. 15,934			−11	121	= 1641.58, or
20X1 Rs. 17,961			2016	4,064,256	say Rs. 1642
Total Rs. 47,835			0	8,084,402	

Uncertainty factor (Lambda) for the three years are now calculated below.

	19XX	20X0	20X1
Lambda =	$\dfrac{8490 + 9306}{1642}$	$\dfrac{9531 + 10,234}{1642}$	$\dfrac{9129 - 142}{1642}$
	= 10.84	= 12.04	= 5.47

All the nine liquidity measurement criteria discussed and calculated above are summarised in Table 5.4.

Table 5.4 Summary of Liquidity Measurement Criteria for LMN Ltd.

Sl. no.	Name of measurement criterion	20X0	20X1
1.	Current ratio	2.00	1.70
2.	Quick ratio	0.46	0.37
3.	Net working capital ratio	31.00 (%)	12.46 (%)
4.	Net liquidity ratio	−0.23	−0.29
5.	Finished goods inventory turnover ratio	17.30 (21 days)	15.84 (23 days)
6.	Accounts receivable turnover ratio	37.11 (10 days)	34.21 (11 days)
7.	Adjusted current ratio	2.13	1.77
8.	Sales cash conversion cycle (days)	12.70	−4.26
9.	Uncertainty factor (Lambda)	12.04	5.47

Long-term and Short-term View

All the values of the liquidity measurement criteria of LMN Ltd., as shown in Table 5.4, indicate that the long-term liquidity position of the company is good as indicated by turnover ratios of finished goods (23 days) and accounts receivable (11 days). Both the current ratio and adjusted current ratio (before bank overdraft) have fallen in 20X1, but their values are still good. The fall, however, indicates a definite erosion of liquidity which has to be funded by a very high level of bank overdraft. If we consider bank overdraft and other short-term liabilities including commercial paper, current ratios of the company will be as follows.

	20X0	20X1
Current ratio (including bank overdraft, etc.)	1.39	1.14
Adjusted current ratio (bank overdraft, etc.)	1.43	1.14

The two current ratios indicate that there has been substantial erosion of net working capital and consequent tightening of liquidity cushion. The reason behind such erosion have already been analysed while discussing NWCR.

Quick ratio is much less than 1 and the net liquidity ratio is negative for both the years while uncertainty of cash flows (Lambda) have increased substantially with the reduction in Lambda. All these indicate severe liquidity crisis, which, if not tackled in time by injection of long-term fund, may destroy the long-term viability of the company.

Movement of sales cash conversion cycle (SCCC) from a positive of 13 days to a negative of 4 days presents a tricky situation. If it is considered individually, it may indicate an excellent financial performance of the company where sales revenues get converted into cash extremely fast (even before the sales are made as in 20X1!). But from our discussion above we have seen that with more than proportionate rise in trade creditors the SCCC has come to be negative resulting into severe worsening of NWC. Therefore, SCCC should not be considered in isolation. A low SCCC would ordinarily indicate good liquidity position, but in cases like the present one, it may just be the opposite.

The liquidity measures discussed above are examined by Gentry and Sartoris[12] to find their validity across more than hundred companies belonging to several industries. They found that these measures have the power to differentiate the companies and rank them in terms of their liquidity. The ratio measures, such as current ratio, quick ratio, NWCR and NLR appeared to be consistent across firms within an industry with correlation coefficients falling within a range of 0.8–0.9, all being generally significant at 0.01 level. The cash flow measures like cash conversion cycle or weighted cash conversion cycle were found to be pairwise highly correlated, but usually not so correlated to other measures. Lambda was found to vary greatly in its correlation with the other measures by the industry.

An analyst may use these findings to decide on a particular set of measures to suit his purpose. He may also decide on a weigting scheme in terms of the importance he attaches to various measures and calculate an index of liquidity.

HEALTH RATIO—A SINGLE LIQUIDITY MEASURE

All the liquidity measures discussed above, though useful in a limited way, cannot measure directly the probability of non-payment except the Emery's Lambda. Besides, it becomes problematic for a finance manager to deal with so many measures at a time. The weigting scheme that generates a liquidity index is a superior method, but it is also beset with the vexed question of subjectivity.

In this section, we intend to develop a single liquidity criterion that can measure and predict an impending liquidity crisis. This measure, which we call *health ratio*, is based on a simple definition of liquidity:

$$\text{Funds inflow} \geq \text{Funds outflow}$$

Funds inflow comprises both operating inflows from sales and other income and financial inflows including that from supply creditors. Funds outflow constitutes all operating expenditure including interest, tax and dividend payments, all repayments of term obligations and all incremental assets.

Funds of a business is defined as gross funds or the total liabilities of a firm at any point of time. Gross funds are composed of two parts: (1) *non-revenue generating funds* blocked in current assets and capital work-in-progress and also funds absorbed by accumulated losses, if any, and (2) *revenue generating funds* engaged in operating fixed assets and security investments. It may be mentioned that the former expands the funds base of the business but does not increase revenue while the latter does both.

We now define a ratio called *funds turnover ratio* (FTR) given by

$$\frac{\text{Revenue } (I)}{\text{Funds } (F)}$$

Revenue (I) is defined as all operating inflows comprising sales plus other income.

---

12. Gentry, J.A. and W.L. Sartoris, "Alternative Liquidity Measures: The Good, the Bad and the Indifferent", *Working Paper,* 1991.

When capacity utilisation of existing fixed assets is on the rise, the revenue (sales) will also rise. Hence, the non-revenue generating fund remaining constant, the FTR will be increasing. But if the non-revenue generating fund is also on the rise, it will partly suppress the rise in FTR. The extent to which it does so depends upon the size of the increase in non-revenue generating fund. But it ultimately increases the funds base or the denominator of the above ratio. The resultant effect may even be a fall in FTR from its previous level. The following example will make it clear.

Suppose, the present sales (I) of a firm is Rs. 4800 lakh with a funds base (F) of Rs. 1600 lakh. Next year if sales are increased by 20 percent, its funds turnover ratio may take on five values depending upon changes in total assets (funds). These are given in Table 5.5.

Table 5.5 Changes in Funds Turnover Ratio Consequent upon Changes in Funds Base

Situations	*Funds turnover ratio (FTR)*
1. Present situation	4800/1600 = 3
2. *Sales rises by 20%*	
(a) No change in funds base	5760/1600 = 3.6
(b) Funds base rises by say, 20%	5760/1920 = 3
(c) Funds base decreases by say, 20%	5760/1280 = 4.5
(d) Funds base increases by say, 30%	5760/2080 = 2.8

It may be seen from Table 5.5 that when rise in funds base (assets) exactly matches the rise in revenue, FTR will not change (2(b)). When funds-base does not change with the rise in sales, FTR will obviously rise as in the case of (2(a)). Similar will be the case when funds-base actually falls as in the case of (2(c)), though in this case the turnover will be faster. Both the cases signify good management of current assets. On the contrary, when funds base rises more than proportionately, a fall in FTR may signify slackening of working capital management.

When funds outflow is greater than the operating funds inflow, the firm faces an initial liquidity problem because of the negative funds gap which, now, has to be filled up from financial inflows. This will expand the funds base of the firm, a part of which may be non-revenue generating. If we now evolve a ratio as *funds outflow to funds ratio* (FOFR), impact of this financing decision will be reflected by a fall in this ratio. As long as FTR is greater than FOFR the firm has positive liquidity. When these two are equal, the enterprise is at funds-break-even level, and when FTR is less than FOFR the firm will suffer from negative liquidity. This is illustrated in Figure 5.2 and explained in Table 5.6.

Sl. no.	Sales-funds situation (1)					Funds outflow-funds situation (2)					Effect of FTR (3)	Effect on FOFR (4)
Group A												
1.	↑	Sales;	↔	Funds	↔	FoF;	↔	Funds			↑	↔
2.	↑	Sales;	↓	Funds	↓	FoF;	↓	Funds			↑	↔
3.	↔	Sales;	↓	Funds	↓	FoF;	↓	Funds			↑	↔
Group B												
4.	↓	Sales;	↓	Funds	↓	FoF:	↓	Funds			↑↔↓	↑↔↓
5.	↔	Sales;	↔	Funds	↔	FoF;	↔	Funds			↔	↔
6.	↑	Sales;	↑	Funds	↑	FoF;	↑	Funds			↑↔↓	↑↔↓
Group C												
7.	↓	Sales;	↑	Funds	↑	FoF;	↑	Funds			↓	↔
8.	↓	Sales;	↔	Funds	↔	FoF;	↔	Funds			↓	↔
9.	↔	Sales;	↑	Funds	↑	FoF;	↑	Funds			↓	↔

Legend:

Increasing = ↑

Constant = ↔

Decreasing = ↓

Note: Large (increasing or decreasing) arrows under column 3 indicate more than proportionate rise or fall of FTR against the corresponding FOFR under column 4.

Figure 5.2 Effect of changes in sales revenue and funds outflow on various funds ratios.

Table 5.6 Movement of Funds Ratios with Changes in Revenue

(Rs. in lakh)

Year	Revenue (I)	Operating funds outflow (cost of sales)	Incre-mental current assets	Total funds outflow (col. 3+4)	Funds base (beginning Rs. 1000) (col. 5 – 2)	FTR (col. 2/6)	FOFR (col. 5/6)	HR (col.7/8)
(1)	(2)	(3)	(4)	(5)	(6)	(7)	(8)	(9)
1.	3606	3246	200	3446	840	4.29	4.10	1.05
2.	3967	3570	323	3893	766	5.17	5.08	1.02
3.	4364	3927	437	4364	766	5.70	5.70	1.00
4.	4800	4320	720	5040	1006	4.77	5.00	0.95
5.	5280	4752	1056	5808	1534	3.44	3.78	0.91
6.	5808	5227	1452	6679	2405	2.41	2.78	0.87

Notes:

1. Revenue (*I*) is allowed to increase @ 10% p.a.

2. Operating funds outflow (cost of sales) is taken as 90% of sales.

It may be seen from Table 5.6 that so long as revenue (I) is greater than total funds outflow, there will be a shrinkage of funds base (because of payment of liabilities), hence FTR will become greater than FOFR and consequently, the firm will not suffer from any liquidity problem. The reverse happens when funds outflow becomes larger than the revenue and consequently, the firm has a liquidity shortage. Of course, this shortage will be made good by the firm by contracting outside financial flows (liabilities) which is exactly what has happened in Table 5.6 with the resultant effect of expanding the funds base. This additional funds have gone into fund current assets which are non-revenue generating in nature, and hence they do not contribute towards generating additional sales which continue to rise only at 10 percent p.a. despite the increase in funds base. As matching revenues are not being generated from fourth year onwards to support the expanding funds base, the firm enters into a debt-trap, i.e. the firm is unable to repay the loans except by contracting further loans. The situation will, however, be different when expansion of funds base is due to building-up of additional capacity by purchasing fixed assets like plant and machinery, etc. In this case also, FTR will be less than FOFR (because funds outflow is greater than the revenue), but the situation is expected to continue for a temporary period only, because with the utilisation of additional capacity, revenue will rise more than proportionately and hence, FTR will become greater than FOFR. If, however, the fixed assets are not utilised properly to expand sales base, there may not be any significant improvement in FTR. It is not unlikely for fixed assets to become as non-revenue generating as current assets.

Both FTR and FOFR become equal when revenue matches the total funds outflow, i.e., the firm reaches the funds-break-even level. We can now divide the FTR with FOFR to arrive at the health ratio (HR) as given by:

$$\text{Health ratio (HR)} = \frac{I}{\text{Funds base (F)}} \times \frac{\text{Funds base (F)}}{\text{Funds outflow (FOF)}} = \frac{I}{\text{FOF}}$$

We have calculated the values of health ratio (HR) in column 8 of Table 5.6.

This single ratio is now capable of measuring the liquidity of an enterprise and predict an impending liquidity crisis. So long as the HR is equal to or greater than 1, the firm has no liquidity problem. But even in such a case if the HR is falling through, it is still greater than 1, and it indicates that the firm is losing its liquidity gradually. If the down turn is not arrested in time the firm will soon reach down the funds-break-even level and cross the threshold limit of liquidity when HR becomes less than unity. The health ratio at a value of unity is the last signal for an impending liquidity crisis when it has a downward trend.

On the contrary, when a firm is growing by increasing its capacity utilisation it is likely that the HR will be less than unity, but if the trend is upward, then in spite of the existence of a liquidity problem not much danger is visualised. The upward trend of the HR indicates that the firm is moving towards reaching the funds-break-even level at 1 and then crossing it over to a positive liquidity position.

Absolute value of the health ratio indicates the liquidity position of the enterprise at any point in time; its trend, upward or downward, indicates whether the firm is moving towards strengthening or worsening its liquidity.[13] Figure 5.3 illustrates the movement of health ratio along the life cycle of a firm.

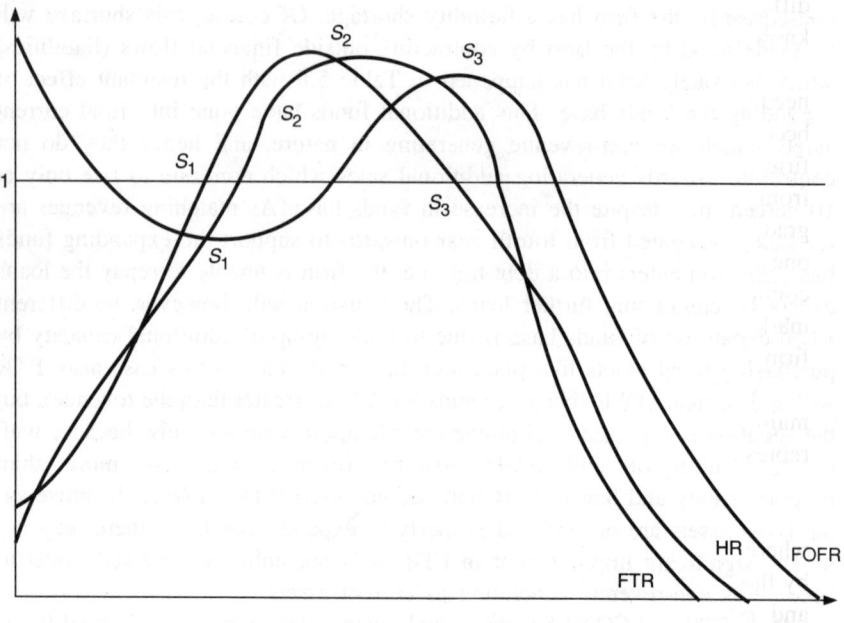

FTR = Funds turnover ratio   FOFR = Funds outflow to funds ratio   HR = Health ratio

Figure 5.3   Life cycle of a firm.

AMOUNT OF LIQUIDITY

All the exercises on measurement of liquidity will remain incomplete till we are able to decide on the amount of liquidity that a firm must maintain at any point in time.

As liquidity is needed to protect a firm against possible illiquid situations that it might face, and as investment in liquidity is always at a cost, the decision to have a particular amount of liquidity must be based on a trade-off between the expected cost of maintaining insufficient liquidity and the cost of carrying liquid sources. It must, however, be remembered that despite the mathematical validity of the liquidity models, that we shall be discussing soon, ultimate decision to hold a particular level of liquidity depends upon the risk-profile of an enterprise. Same is the case when it comes to make a choice of assets to maintain the liquidity which we shall discuss later. For the present, we would like to call all such assets as liquid resources.

13. For an analytical discussion on the Health Ratio, see, Hrishikes Bhattacharya, "Towards the Development of a Single Comprehensive Ratio for Predicting Corporate Failure", *ASCI Journal of Management,* March 1995, pp. 46–68.

Costs of Liquidity

Funds engaged in liquid resources are not available for use in operating activities of a business or for increasing its capacity. Hence, such funds earn a lower rate of return than the operating ROI of the business. Thus, the difference between the ROI of the firm and the return on *liquid resources* is known as a cost of maintaining liquidity.

During modern times, firms need not always have to maintain all the needed liquidity in liquid investments. It is the access to liquidity which has become more important than the liquid assets balances. Liquidity needs of a firm can be handled these days from the liability side of the balance sheet than from its asset side as was being done hitherto. Quick access to the liability is gradually becoming synonymous to having liquidity. This could be done on one end, by maintaining an overdraft limit with the bank (by paying some commitment charges), and on the other, by moving to the forward liability market and picking up appropriate *futures* or *options* instruments to protect the firm against possible illiquidity.[14]

Whichever of the two ways (or a combination of both) the firm adopts to maintain its liquidity, it has to incur an opportunity cost. This can be represented by the following equation:

$$\text{Cost of maintaining liquidity} = CL \qquad (5.1)$$

where C is the opportunity cost per rupee of liquid resources (L) maintained by the firm. C can be taken as the difference between the firms operating ROI and rate of return earned on liquid investments, or it could just be the commitment fee or cost of buying futures or options, both of which increase with the size of the overdraft limit or value of the instruments.

The *expected cost* of not maintaining sufficient liquidity depends upon the probability of the liquid resources turning out to be insufficient and the cost that a firm must incur to remedy the illiquid situation to arrest a crisis. This can be represented by the following equation:

$$\text{Expected cost of illiquidity} = pKL \qquad (5.2)$$

where p is the probability of not having sufficient liquid resources which, in turn, depends upon the amount of liquid resources and the variability of cash flows. K is the cost per rupee that a firm must incur to procure urgently the amount needed to restore the liquidity. This cost will obviously decline with the available liquid resources (L).

Total expected liquidity cost is therefore, the sum total of cost of maintaining liquidity (Eq. 5.1) and expected cost of illiquidity (Eq. 5.2), i.e.

$$\text{Total expected liquidity cost} = CL + pKL \qquad (5.3)$$

---

14. Though in India, futures and options markets are yet to come up in any significant way, in Europe and America growth of these markets has been phenomenal during the past one and a half decade. This has increased the efficiency of the financial markets with the effect of reducing transaction costs. Firms are now able to meet a sizable part of their liquidity need off their balance sheets by accessing these markets.

The optimal level of liquid resources (*L*) that a firm should maintain will lie where total expected liquidity cost is at its minimum. This is the trade-off point.

Let us now explain all these with the help of the following example.

Example The finance manager of a company finds that its net cash flow varies between a negative of Rs. 15 lakh and a positive of Rs. 75 lakh with a uniform distribution pattern.

Operating ROI of the company is 15 percent while income on marketable securities is on an average 9 percent. The finance manager estimates that when the net cash flow ultimately comes down to a negative of Rs. 15 lakh, and he has to procure the entire amount on an urgent basis the cost will be Rs. 3 lakh at 20 percent. He also feels, at the same time, that this cost will decline at the rate of Rs. 0.30 per rupee of additional liquid resources held.

With all these information the finance manager now sets down to calculate the optimal level of liquid resources that he must maintain.

1. *Cost of maintaining liquidity* (Eq. 5.1): Opportunity cost of maintaining liquidity is the difference between operating ROI of the firm and the rate of return on marketable securities, i.e. 15 percent – 9 percent = 6 percent, or Re. 0.06 per rupee invested in liquid resources. The cost of maintaining liquidity will, therefore, be: 0.06 *L*

2. *Expected cost of liquidity* (Eq. 5.2): The probability (*p*) that there will be *insufficient* liquid resources is equal to the *difference* between liquid resources (*L*) and the lowest cash flows *divided* by the entire range of cash flow distribution. That is,

$$p = \frac{|L - \text{Rs.}\,15\,\text{lakh}|}{\text{Rs.}\,15\,\text{lakh} + \text{Rs.}\,75\,\text{lakh}}$$

$$= \frac{|L - 15|}{90},$$

as long as *L* is less than the lowest range of cash flow (– Rs. 15 lakh). If *L* is more than the lowest range of cash flow, then the probability (*p*) of liquid resources being insufficient, will be zero.

The penal cost of arranging liquidity on an urgent basis for the entire negative cash flow of Rs. 15 lakh is Rs. 3 lakh which will be reduced by Re. 0.30 per rupee of liquid resources held. That is,

$$\text{Penal cost} = \text{Rs.}\,3\,\text{lakh} - 0.30L$$

Expected cost of liquidity will, therefore, be

$$= \frac{|L - 15|}{90} \times (3 - 0.30L)$$

and the total expected liquidity cost (Eq. 5.3) will be

$$0.06L + \frac{|L - 15|}{90} \times (3 - 0.30L)$$

We now have to determine at which value of L the total expected liquidity cost is minimum. This can be done in an iterative manner by calculating total expected cost at different levels of liquid resources (L). This has been attempted in Table 5.7.

Table 5.7 Determining Optimal Level of Liquid Resources through Iterative Process

Level of liquid resources (Rs.) (1)	Probability (p) (2)	Cost of maintaining liquid resources (Rs.) (3)	Expected cost of liquidity (Rs.) (4)	Total expected liquidity cost (Rs.) (col. 3 + 4) (5)
8 lakh	0.078	0.480	0.04667 lakh	= Rs. 0.5267 lakh or Rs. 52,670
6 lakh	0.10	0.360	0.12 lakh	= Rs. 0.48 lakh or Rs. 48,000
4 lakh	0.122	0.240	0.22 lakh	= Rs. 0.46 lakh or Rs. 46,000
3 lakh	0.133	0.180	0.28 lakh	= Rs. 0.46 lakh or Rs. 46,000
3.25 lakh	0.13	0.195	0.26437 lakh	= Rs. 0.45937 lakh or Rs. 45,937
3.50 lakh	0.128	0.210	0.2491 lakh	= Rs. 0.4591 lakh or Rs. 45,910
3.60 lakh	0.127	0.216	0.2432 lakh	= Rs. 0.4592 lakh or Rs. 45,920
3.80 lakh	0.124	0.228	0.23146 lakh	= Rs. 0.45947 lakh or Rs. 45,947

It may be observed from Table 5.7 that at a liquid resource level of Rs. 3.50 lakh the total expected liquidity cost is the minimum. At this level the company would have $\dfrac{|3.5 - 15|}{90}$ = 0.1277 or 12.8 percent probability of having a negative cash flow large enough to incur the penalty cost, which is Rs. 24,910. The opportunity cost of maintaining liquid resources of Rs. 3.50 lakh is Rs. 21,000. The two together make up a total expected liquidity cost of Rs. 45,910.[15]

Although the optimal solution obtained from Table 5.7 gives a 12.8 percent probability of being out of liquidity, ultimate decision to hold a particular level of liquid resources finally rests upon the risk-profile of the enterprise (manager). The firm may just feel that it should not go beyond a 10 percent probability and hence, it may desire to know the amount of liquid resources that it must hold under the given probability parameter and the cost thereof. This can be found out simply by locating the row of the desired probability parameter 0.10 from column 2 of Table 5.7. Along this row, level of liquid resources is indicated under column 1 and the total cost is given under column 5, which in the present case are Rs. 6 lakh and Rs. 48,000 respectively.

Forms of Liquidity

The aggregate amount of liquid resources can be maintained in different forms, which once again depends upon the risk-profile of the enterprise. On one end,

---

15. The same result can be obtained by first taking the derivate of the total cost function, setting it to zero and then solving for L. But it is a rather complicated mathematical procedure. The iterative method presented here is easy to calculate.

a highly risk-averse enterprise may decide to hold the entire liquidity amount in cash and bank balances, and on the other, a highly risk-oriented enterprise may decide to hold it entirely in market securities. Between these two extremes a finance manager may like to divide the liquid resources among *primary liquidity* comprising cash and bank balances and very short-term gilt-edged securities, and *secondary liquidity* comprising other marketable securities with terms longer than those comprising *primary liquidity* and unused lines of credit. The latter is also called back-up liquidity. Its primary purpose is to support the liquidity need of the firm, but making some money along the line to support the treasury function is also intended. An active finance manager would first decide, on an average, the expected rate of return on his entire investment in *liquidity* and then build up a portfolio which will ensure such a return. This he does by actively trading in short-term securities. Some important short-term instruments will be discussed in a later chapter.

MAINTAINING CASH BALANCE

Assuming now that the liquidity is maintained in the form of cash and bank balances and a portfolio of marketable securities, it may be necessary for a finance manager to know what should be the optimal cash and bank balances that he must maintain, and for that purpose how often and in what quantity securities should be purchased or sold. We shall be discussing here three models which address these issues. The models are divided in two parts: certainty model and uncertainty model.

Certainty Model—Baumol[16]

This cash model has a portfolio of cash and marketable securities which earn a particular rate of return (i) per period. The marketables are uniformly and infinitely divisible securities, kind of money market mutual fund where deposits and withdrawals can be made in increments of Re. 1. For any transaction into or out of the portfolio of securities, there is a fixed charge (b) per transaction. Total demand for cash (T) of the firm at periodic interval is known. Cash outflows occur continuously and uniformly during the periodic interval. That is, the demand for cash is assumed to be steady. The firm sells securities at fixed intervals to replenish cash. For example, suppose a firm begins with (c) amount of cash. When this amount is spent, it replenishes the cash by selling (c) amount of securities. That is, transfer of funds from securities to cash takes place, when cash balance reaches zero level.

Under the aforementioned conditions, the average cash balance will be $C/2$ during each subperiod. However, if the firm desires a cushion, or there is a lead time to effect securities transaction, the threshold limit for effecting the transfer can be higher, and hence the average cash balance.

---

16. Baumol, W.J., "The Transactions Demand for Cash: An Inventory Theoretic Approach", *Quarterly Journal of Economics,* November 1952, pp. 545–556.

Conditions mentioned above are similar to that of EOQ inventory model under conditions of certainty. This will be evident also from Figure 5.4.

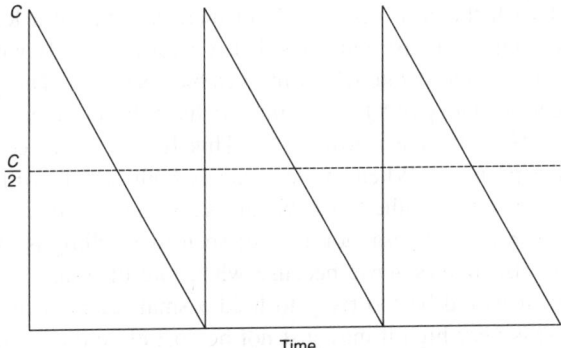

Figure 5.4 Cash management model under conditions of certainty.

Baumol thus extended the EOQ approach to cash management modelling to derive the optimal level of cash replacement (C) that minimises total costs comprising both fixed and variable costs. This cost function is expressed by the following formula:

$$\text{Total costs} = b\left(\frac{T}{C}\right) + i\left(\frac{C}{2}\right) \tag{5.4}$$

where (T/C) is nothing but cash turnover ratio or the number of transactions effected during a period. When this is multiplied by (b)—the fixed charge per unit of transaction, we obtain total transaction cost during the period. ($C/2$) represents the average cash balance which when multiplied by (i) gives the opportunity cost of forgone investment opportunity.

Our purpose now is to find out the value of (C) that minimises the total cost. This we can do by taking the first derivative of the above cost function with respect to (C), and then setting it to zero we obtain the value of (C). But there is also a simpler way. We have found in Chapter 4 while discussing the EOQ model, that the total cost is minimised at a point where two parts of the costs are equal. That is,

$$i\left(\frac{C}{2}\right) = b\left(\frac{T}{C}\right)$$

or
$$iC^2 = 2bT$$

or
$$C^2 = \frac{2bT}{i}$$

or
$$C = \sqrt{\frac{2bT}{i}} \tag{5.5}$$

The equation signifies that cash will be demanded in relation to the square root of the volume of transactions in rupees. It indicates the possibility of the economies of scale because with the increase in the level of cash payments, the amount of cash the firm needs to hold increases, but at a lesser rate.

The derived equation also indicates that (C) varies directly with fixed cost and inversely with interest rate (i) on marketable securities. The phenomenon is similar to any inventory EOQ model that we have discussed earlier. A higher rate of interest (i) will give a lower (C). This fits well into common sense approach to the problem: When interest rate is high, a firm will always like to hold lesser amount of (idle) cash balances. As against this, if the rate of usage of cash is high or transaction cost of securities selling is high, (C) will be larger. This also makes sense because when rate of usage of cash is very high in a firm, it would be too risky to hold a small cash balance, and when transaction cost is very high it may just not be cost-effective to buy securities; it is preferable to hold the liquidity in cash form.

Let us now explain Baumol's model with the help of an example.

Example A firm estimates that it is required to make cash disbursements of Rs. 567 lakh in a year which is spread over uniformly at Rs. 47.25 lakh per month. The firm invests only in treasury bills for cash management purposes. The present yield is 8 percent p.a. It costs the firm Rs. 900 for every transaction in treasury bills.

The optimum level of (C) will be as follows:

$$C = \sqrt{\frac{2 \times 900 \times 56,700,000}{0.08}}$$

$$= 1,129,491 \text{ or say, Rs. } 11.30 \text{ lakh}$$

Cash turnover ratio or the number of times the securities must be sold in a period is given by, (T/C). In the present example, it would be as below:

(i) 56,700,000/1,129,491 = 50.20 or 50 times in a year, or
(ii) 4,725,000/1,129,491 = 4.18 or 4 times a month, i.e. once every week-end.

Problems associated with Baumol's cash-EOQ model are similar to inventory-EOQ model discussed earlier. The first problem is the specification of costs. While rate of interest on marketable securities, particularly treasury bills, is fairly known with accuracy, the fixed costs associated with a security transaction is difficult to estimate because a major part of these costs are overheads which are not directly variable with the number of transactions. Some of these cost items are: recording and placing orders for sale with the security brokers, physical storage costs of securities if these are not with depositories, secretarial costs, etc. While activity-based costing, by converting the treasury department into a pool of activities can capture these costs to a large extent, allocation of unused activities still creates problems.

Another limitation of Baumol's cash management model is the assumption of steady usage of cash during the period under consideration. At times, there may be large collection or payment of cash which may make the model unworkable. One way to tackle the problem is to shorten the period under consideration, say one week, so that both cash inflows and outflows could conform to the steady state assumption of the model.

Baumol's model will not work if the uncertainty in cash flows is very high. If however, the degree of uncertainty is modest, a cushion may be factored into the model like, safety stock as in inventories model.

The model may not be completely foolproof but it provides a benchmark to judge the optimality of cash balance that an enterprise maintains.

Uncertainty Model—Miller and Orr[17]

When uncertainty of cash outflows is very high resulting in random fluctuation in cash balances, EOQ-cash model may not work. One has to find solutions in stochastic models. Miller and Orr applied the concepts of control theory in developing stochastic cash management models under conditions of uncertainity. They set two control limits of cash holding: upper limit and lower limit. When cash balance reaches the upper limit, a transfer of cash to market securities takes place by purchasing of securities, and when it reaches a lower limit, a transfer from market securities to cash takes place by selling of securities. When cash balance stays within these bounds, no transaction takes place in spite of some amount of fluctuations in cash flows. The approach can be visualised from Figure 5.5.

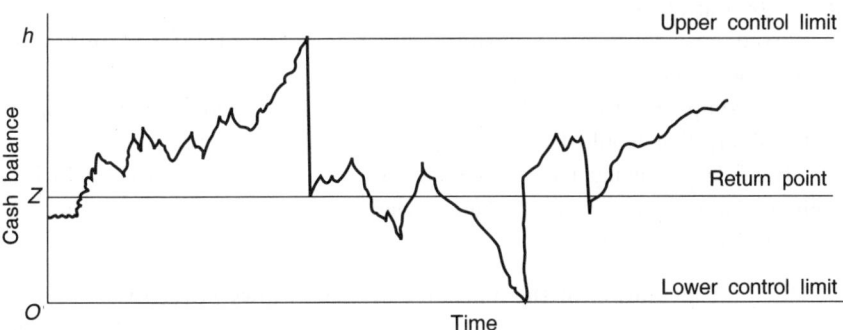

Figure 5.5 Uncertain cash flow pattern and cash control limits.

It may be observed from Figure 5.5 that when cash balance touches the upper control limit, $(h-Z)$ worth of securities are bought to bring down the cash level to (Z) and when it touches the zero level, (Z) amount of securities are sold to bring the cash level back to (Z), which is called the return point. In between there are fluctuations, but no action is taken.

17. Miller, M.H. and Daniel, Orr, "A Model of the Demand for Money by Firms", *Quarterly Journal of Economics,* August 1966, pp. 413–435.

The optimal values of the upper control limit (h) and the return point (Z) depend on one hand, upon the fixed cost associated with securities transaction (b) and the opportunity cost of holding cash balance (i) calculated on daily basis, and on the other, upon the degree of fluctuations in cash balance specified by the variance of daily net cash flows (s^2). Miller and Orr's model specifies the values of (Z) and (h) by the following two equations:

(i) Z (return point) $= 3\sqrt{\dfrac{3bs^2}{4i}}$

(ii) h (upper limit) $= 3Z$

The model assumes lower cash holding limit as depicted in Figure 5.5. But a finance manager may not feel comfortable with a zero cash balance. He may desire to specify a cushion or margin. This may be incorporated on the left side of the above two equations. Let us explain the model with the help of the following example.

Example A company projects the daily net cash flows for the next seven days as follows:

(Rs. in lakh)

Day	1	2	3	4	5	6	7
Cash flow forecast	+ 24	+ 13	− 16	− 12	+ 36	+ 4	− 28

The policy of the company is to maintain a minimum cash balance of Rs. 10,000 at all times.

Fixed cost for every security transaction is Rs. 1600 and return on marketable securities is 10% p.a.

The company desires to know the return point (Z) and the upper limit of cash holding that would trigger a purchase order for securities.

The finance manager first calculates the variance of cash flows (which is nothing but the square of standard deviation) from the cash flow forecasts given in the above table.

Calculation of the Variance of Cash Flows Forecast

(Rs. in lakh)

Daily cash flow forecasts				
(x_i)	($\bar{x}$)	($x_i - \bar{x}$)	($x_i - \bar{x})^2$	s^2(Variance)
24	$\Sigma x_i/n = 21/7$	21	441	$\Sigma(x_i - \bar{x})^2/n$
13	$= $ Rs. 3	10	100	$= 3178/7$
−16		−19	361	$= $ Rs. 454
−12		−15	225	
36		33	1089	
4		1	1	
−28		−31	961	
Total 21		0	3178	

$$\text{Return point } (Z) = \text{Rs. } 10,000 + 3\sqrt{\frac{3 \times 1600 \times 45,400,000}{4 \times (0.10/365)}}$$

$$= \text{Rs. } 10,000 + \text{Rs. } 58,368$$
$$= \text{Rs. } 68,368$$

$$\text{Upper limit } (h) = \text{Rs. } 10,000 + 3 \times 58,368$$
$$= \text{Rs. } 185,104$$

Note: Minimum cash balance (safety stock) is to be maintained at all times.

These two findings signify that the finance manager will allow the daily cash balance to fluctuate till it reaches the upper limit of Rs. 185,104. When the balance becomes greater than this figure, he will purchase sufficient worth of securities to reduce the cash balance to the return point of Rs. 68,368. On the lower side, when the cash balance drops to the minimum balance of Rs. 10,000 (zero in absence of any such stipulation) he will sell adequate amount of securities to raise the cash balance to Rs. 68,368.

The critical assumption of Miller and Orr's model is that the cash flows are random. It is difficult to determine average cash balance in advance, but it will be approximately, $(Z + h)/3$. As this model assumes random fluctuations in cash balances, the average cash balance will be higher than that in cash-EOQ model.

The model indicates that higher the variability of cash flows with the higher fixed cost per security transaction and higher the control limits the firm sets, the further apart they will be. In contrast, the higher the interest rate, lower is the control limits, and the closer they become.[18]

Uncertainty Model—Stone[19]

This model is based on the argument that average cash (bank) balance is determined by bank's requirement of maintaining compensatory bank balance in current account when an overdraft is taken.[20] The objective function, therefore, shifts from *balancing* opportunity cost and security transaction costs to *minimising* transaction costs subject to the constraint that the average balance must always equal the target balance. According to Stone, cash flows can be divided into two parts: one which is random and the other which can be forecasted. He, therefore, uses control-limits similar to that in Miller and Orr model except that he prescribes two sets of limits: outer limits and inner limits. When cash (bank) balance reaches the outer limit, the finance manager does not trigger securities purchase, as in the case of Miller and Orr model, but

18. Van Horne, J.C., *Financial Management and Policy,* 12th ed., Prentice-Hall of India, New Delhi, 2004.

19. Stone, B.K., "The Use of Forecasts and Smoothing in Control-Limit Models for Cash Management", *Financial Management,* Spring 1972, pp. 72–84.

20. As of now, firms in India are not required to maintain any compensatory balance which is a well established practice in the United States. However Stone's model still has practical relevance in India for firms who set up control limits on their own.

checks with the forecasts for the next pre-determined days (which are normally a few days only, say three days). If he finds that the forecasted cash flow is expected to move within the inner limits, i.e. the balance is closer to target balance, he does not order any securities transactions and hence, saves on transaction costs. If, however, the forecasted cash balance is outside the inner limit's, i.e. the closing balance is far away from the target balance, he orders buying or selling of securities to the extent that closing balance at the end of predetermined days become equal to the target balance. Let us explain the model with the help of the following example:

Example A company has the following forecast of cash flows during the next 14 days.

Forecasts

(Rs. in lakh)

Day	1	2	3	4	5	6	7	8	9	10	11	12	13	14
Cash flow forecast	8	4	–5	–4	5	–1	2	0	1	–16	7	–5	2	–5

The finance manager has set up upper outer limits of Rs. 40 lakh and the lower outer limit of Rs. 23 lakh. Inner limits are fixed at Rs. 2 lakh minus or plus respectively from the outer limits. Look out ‘time is 3 days.

The day opened at the target cash (bank) balance of Rs. 30 lakh.

Outer limits are the signals for the finance manager to watch out what are expected to happen in the next 3 days. He takes action of selling or buying securities only when the cash balance crosses the inner limits. Upper inner limit in the present case is Rs. 40 lakh – Rs. 2 lakh = Rs. 38 lakh, and the lower inner limit is Rs. 23 lakh + Rs. 2 lakh = 25 lakh. So long the cash balance is within the inner range, i.e. between Rs. 38 lakh and Rs. 25 lakh, no security transaction takes place.

In the following table, actual cash flows and the result of actions taken by the finance manager in terms of Stone's model and the consequent changes in cash (bank) balances are calculated.

Actuals

(Rs. in lakh)

Day	1	2	3	4	5	6	7	8	9	10	11	12	13	14
Opening cash											(30)	(36)	(30)	(27)
balance (actual)	30	38	41	35	32	38	36	41	37	37	19	25	19	16
Cash flow														
Forecast	8	4	–5	–4	5	–1	2	0	1	–16	7	–5	2	–5
Actual	8	3	–6	–3	6	–2	5	–4	0	–18	6	–6	–3	4
Closing cash balance (before security transactions)	38	41	35	32	38	36	41	37	37	19	25	19	16	20
Security sold/ purchased (+1/–)	—	—	—	—	—	—	—	—	—	11	—	—	—	—
Closing cash balance (after security transaction)	38	41	35	32	38	36	41	37	37	(30)	(36)	(30)	(27)	(31)

It may be seen from the above table that, on the second day the closing cash balance goes upto Rs. 41 lakh. As it crosses the outer upper limit of Rs. 40 lakh, the finance manager looks out for the cash flow *projections* of next three days to find out whether the cash balance is expected to move out or stay within the inner limits. This he calculates as: Rs. 41 lakh – Rs. 5 lakh – Rs. 4 lakh + Rs. 5 lakh = Rs. 37 lakh. As this amount is within the inner limit, he does not order any security transaction.

On the seventh day the cash balance has once again gone upto Rs. 41 lakh. But this time also next three days' forecast (Rs. 41 lakh + 0 + 1 – 16 = Rs. 26 lakh) leaves the balance within the inner limits. Hence, no security transaction takes place.

On the tenth day, however, cash balance has gone down to Rs. 19 lakh crossing the lower outer limit of Rs. 23 lakh set up by the firm. Cash flow projections for the next three days take the cash balance to Rs. (19 + 7 – 5 + 2) lakh = Rs. 23 lakh, which is equal to the lower outer limit but below the inner outer limit of Rs. 25 lakh. This necessitates action in terms of decision rule set out in Stone's model. The finance manager will now sell securities worth Rs. 11 lakh to push up the cash balance to the target level of Rs. 30 lakh. This will now change the actual cash balances from tenth day onwards which are given in brackets inside the above table.

The three models discussed above are based on a range of assumptions—from deterministic (Baumol) to purely random (Miller and Orr) and then a combination of both (Stone). In real-life situations cash flows are expected to fit into any or a combination of these assumptions. This coupled with intuitive judgement of the finance manager may ultimately lead to the development of a cash management model uniquely suitable for a firm. We should point out here that none of the above models have earned unqualified success. Often, simple rules of thumb have been found to be performing just as well.[21] The moral of these findings is that none of these cash management models should be applied mechanistically.

Cash Flow Forecasting

Cash is the language to translate strategic plans of a business. Cash flow forecasting is, therefore, not an independent exercise. A cash manager must keep this important fact in mind, otherwise his actions, while subserving the narrow objective of the treasury department, may subvert the goal of the organisation itself. It is often found that a finance manager, oblivious of the need of the organisation, has invested the surplus cash in a high-yielding security which has just come by, only to discover a week later that cash is needed to purchase materials urgently required by the factory. As the enterprise cannot afford to stop production which is the broad objective of the business, the finance manager may have to sell-out the security, probably at a loss, to

---

21. See for example, Mullins D. and R. Homonoff, "Applications of Inventory Cash Management Models", in *Modern Development in Financial Management*, S.C. Myers (Ed.), Frederick A. Praeger, Inc., New York, 1976.

buy materials. To prevent situations like this, detail cash flow forecasting based on the strategic plan of the business is required to be drawn up.

Different time horizons are used for forecasting with different objectives in mind.

Long-term Forecasts

All forecasts beyond one year come under this head. These are needed for long-range investing and financing of a business in terms of the strategic goals of an enterprise. Purpose of long-range forecasting is to evaluate the ability or otherwise of an enterprise to meet specific cash requirements for say, expansion, modernisation, acquisitions, etc. If there is a cash gap, how the enterprise is going to fill it up, whether by capital issues or by contracting external debt. These are some of the issues that are needed to be resolved in the long-term cash flow forecasts.

It is likely that in the long run, economic and technological environment will undergo changes. Long-term cash flow forecasts are, therefore, made for possible economic and technological scenarios. How the enterprise is strategically positioning itself in each such scenario, becomes an input in the long–range plans.

Medium-term Forecasts

These forecasts, which generally cover a period of 12 months, must fit well within the long-range plan of the enterprise. This enables the business to devise tactical plans to realise its strategic goals. It is also called *cash budgeting* where short-term financing requirement is focussed. The primary variable for this purpose is the sales forecast.

Cash budgets may be divided into quarterly cash flow forecasting with monthly details, say for next three months. Periodical comparison of actual performance with the budgets enables an enterprise-manager to judge whether the business is progressing towards the directions envisaged in the long-range plan adopted by the enterprise.

Several statistical techniques have been developed like Moving Average, Exponential Smoothing, Time Series Analysis, and Regression Analysis to forecast a growth variable like sales. All are based on past data and hence, to an extent, they project past into the future. Some models may work better when more weightages are given to more recent data like that in exponential smoothing; some may be better suited for long-term projections or for capturing cyclical movements as in Time Series models. It is, therefore, necessary for a finance manager to correctly identify a particular statistical model suitable for the type and nature of the industry to which the enterprise belongs, and for the purpose at hand.[22]

---

22. The reader can refer to any good textbook on forecasting techniques to have an introductory understanding of them. See for example, *Statistical Prediction Analysis,* J. Aitchison and I.R. Dunsmore, Cambridge University Press, Cambridge, 1975.

In spite of the availability of all the time-tested statistical models, perhaps the most widely used technique for sales forecasting remain basically 'judgemental'. When sales personnel are asked to forecast sales for, say the next quarter, they often come out with figures which later turn out to be fairly accurate, though they may not be able to tell how they have arrived at the forecasts. Human brains are capable of simultaneously analysing multiple qualitative and quantitative data at a rate much faster than a computer. Hence, their conclusions are truely 'judgemental' in the real sense of the term as these are based on such facts which no statistical technique can assimilate. But at the same time, it is also true that no two persons could always come out with same judgemental figure because they may differ in experience and in analytical mind. What is necessary, therefore, is to gather these judgemental data from informed people and make them useful for forecasting in real business situation by applying some simple statistical techniques which are capable of capturing the variation in their projections and take appropriate steps to develop alternative scenarios. Probability analysis and standard deviations are two such tools which can be used for this purpose. This method is particularly suitable in business situations where a break from the past is clearly visualised.

Short-term Forecasts

This may take the form of weekly or daily forecasts of cash inflows and outflows. This is an elaborate exercise and most difficult to perform. A finance manager may know quite accurately average cash flows during a month or a week but it is difficult for him to determine specific cash flows for the given days of the month or week. It may be difficult but its importance cannot be belittled because, on the basis of daily cash flow forecasts only a finance manager would take decisions about cash transfer from one region to the other, reduction or increase in field balances and short-term investment of surplus cash, etc.

Time-horizon classification of cash flow forecasting that we have done above is not sacrosanct, neither the terminology that we have used. This is based on average practices of firms operating in India. But there are also firms which define long-term as a period comprising more than three years and medium-term, between one to three years. Time-horizon classification depends to some extent on the nature of the business. The term and its periodicity will of course be different for a ship-building firm than for a firm dealing in perishable goods.

As a business must always remain sensitive and alert to changes, cash flow forecasts under each of the above classification should be drawn up in terms of the following scenarios:

(a) *Worst scenario:* The forecast is prepared by putting most conservative parameters to forecasting variables, for example, low or even zero sales growth, high interest on debts, etc. This scenario is drawn up to assist the management to determine the lowest return that it can accept and the most it can borrow under the worst servicing obligations. In other words, the forecast of the worst scenario enables the management to decide on the amount of risk it can undertake.

(b) *Best scenario:* This forecast is obtained by adopting most aggressive assumptions: high sales growth, low interest rates, etc. This scenario is drawn up to assist the management to know what is the maximum return achievable by the firm and under what circumstances. It helps the management to determine the time of purchasing new equipments and contracting new financing arrangement.

(c) *'As is':* This term is a forecasting slang used by managers when they adopt the most likely scenario for forecasting such as continued sales growth, no change in interest rates, existing credit lines, no expansion of market and so forth. This helps the finance manager in planning daily cash needs of a business. From a long-term perspective, the 'As is' forecasts also enable the enterprise-manager to know whether to diversify by new acquisitions, and if so, what is the cash requirement.

The usage of cash flow forecasting as a management tool lies in its flexibility. It must be capable of answering a series of 'what if' questions that a management may ask while practically running a business. Long-term forecasting is beyond the scope of this book. We shall, therefore, concentrate on medium and short-term cash flow forecasting.

OPERATING REVENUE

LMN Ltd., the company we have chosen for analysis in this chapter, is a case in point. In 20X1 the company has acquired another business and has done massive restructuring the result of which will be reflected from 20X2 onwards both on sales and on expenditure. Hence, 20X1 is not a 'normal' year for the company. There is a 'break'. Things are expected to be 'different' from 20X2 according to the management. Projections based on past performance without taking into consideration the 'abnormal' happenings during 20X1 would be faulty. In fact, for statistical business projections it is always preferable to begin with a normal period.

For projecting sales of LMN Ltd., we have to employ a somewhat different statistical technique. This is popularly known as Delphi method under which, first the opinions of informed people are sought on the performance of a particular variable—in the present case it is sales—and then these opinions are subjected to probabilistic estimation to arrive at acceptable levels of sales projection. In order to neutralise the price-effect sales projection should as far as possible, be made in terms of quantity sold, and not in terms of its rupee value.

Sales of the company for the past three years (year ended 31st March) were as follows:

19XX	20X0	20X1	Remarks
522,735	531,757	539,779	Sales and its % growth for 19XX are
(1.82%)	(1.73%)	(1.51%)	taken from annual accounts of the company, not shown in Exhibits.

It may be seen that percentage growth of sales of the company is on the decline. If we project the past rate in the future it is going to be less than 1.51 percent during 20X1–20X2. But the company has acquired similar type of businesses in 20X0–20X1 (market value of which must have been more than their book value as reflected in goodwill payment). It is expected, therefore, that the company will not only be able to stop this falling trend but also register a higher growth rate. How much it should be? This question was asked to the chief of marketing, vice-president, marketing and the managing director of the company. They were asked to indicate on a 100 point scale the chances of the company achieving a particular rate of growth in 20X2. The following probability distribution (Table 5.8) was obtained after averaging their observations. In the same table we have also shown computations required for arriving at the standard deviation (SD) of the observations.

Table 5.8 Probability Distribution of Various Levels of Possible Growth in Sales in 20X2 and Computations of Standard Deviation (year ended 31st March)

Expected growth in sales (%)	Chances of occurring (in decimal points)	Weighted sales (X_i) (col. 1 × 2)			
(R_i) (1)	(P_i) (2)	$\bar{R}$ (3)	($R_i - \bar{R}$) (4)	($R_i - \bar{R}$)^2 (5)	$P_i (R_i - \bar{R})^2$ (6)
2.8	0.05	0.14	0.80	0.64	0.032
2.5	0.10	0.25	0.50	0.25	0.025
2.2	0.20	0.44	0.20	0.04	0.008
2.0	0.30	0.60	0.00	0	0
1.8	0.20	0.36	– 0.20	0.04	0.008
1.5	0.10	0.15	– 0.50	0.25	0.025
1.2	0.05	0.06	– 0.80	0.64	0.032
Total	1.00	Σ = 2.00	Σ = 0.00	Σ = 1.86	Σ = 0.130

Standard deviation for a probabilistic distribution as given in Table 5.8 is calculated by the following formula.

$$SD_P = \sqrt{\sum_{i=1}^{N} P_i (R_i - \bar{R})^2}$$

where

P_i = probability distribution of possible rate of growth in sales
R_i = possible rate of growth in sales as in column 1

$\bar{R}$ = weighted average given by $\sum_{i=1}^{N} R_i P_i$ as shown in column 3

N = number of observations which in the present case is 7

Putting the summation figure arrived at in column 6 of Table 5.8 in the above equation standard deviation of possible growth rate is calculated below:

$$SD_P = \sqrt{0.13} = 0.36$$

Interpretation and usage of standard deviation has been discussed at length in the earlier two chapters. Here, we make use of it in the following way.

Mean sales growth of this probabilistic distribution (R_i) has been found to be 2 percent. With one SD plus/minus we can now evolve possible growth rates in sales as in Table 5.9.[23]

Table 5.9 Sales Projections for LMN Ltd. in 20X2 (year ended 31st March)

Scenario	Growth rate in sales	Sales in tonnes
I. Best scenario	2 + 0.36 = 2.36%	539,779 × 1.0236 = 552,518
II. Most likely scenario	2 (Mean only) = 2%	539,779 × 1.02 = 550,575
III. Worst scenario	2 – 0.36 = 1.64%	539,779 × 1.0164 = 548,631

Pattern of Sales

Having determined the tonnes volume of sales under three scenarios we should now attempt to determine the pattern of sales. An analysis of the monthly sales register and discussion with the marketing people reveal that the sales of the company are subject to seasonal fluctuations. Monthly sales as percentage of total sales are derived from the sales register. Annual projected sales under the three scenarios are then divided accordingly into monthly sales by the same percentage. These are given in Table 5.10.[24]

Table 5.10 Monthly Sales Projections for LMN Ltd. under Three Scenarios (year ended 31st March)

Month	Monthly sales as % of total sales	Sales in tonnes		
		Scenario I (Best)	Scenario II (Most likely)	Scenario III (Worst)
April 20X1	6	33,151	33,035	32,918
May	6	33,151	33,035	32,918
June	5	27,626	27,529	27,431
July	5	27,626	27,529	27,432
August	6	33,151	33,035	32,918
September	8	44,201	44,046	43,890
October	10	55,252	55,058	54,863
November	11	60,777	60,563	60,349
December	12	66,302	66,068	65,836
January 20X2	14	77,353	77,080	76,808
February	9	49,727	49,552	49,378
March	8	44,201	44,045	43,890
Total	100%	552,518	550,575	548,631

---

23. A small SD suggests that there is not a great variation of thinking among the three persons interviewed. Due to small SD, sales variation among the three scenarios will also not be much. But it is always advisable to instal a scenario based cash budgeting system in an enterprise as is being developed here.
24. In case of multi-product companies it is desirable to make projections for each individual product or product-groups.

Realisable Price

Average price realisation per tonne was Rs. 35,255 and Rs. 39,055 during 20X0 and 20X1 respectively. That is, increase in price during 20X1 over 20X0 was around 10.77 percent. Bulk of the price rise was effected during the period October–January. LMN Ltd. is the leader in consumer and beverage products. With recent acquisitions it is able to beat the competition further. However, the marketing department feels that in the projected year the company cannot expect to increase its prices as in the last year owing to consumer resistance. It feels that a 7.84 percent average increase in price realisation will be in order. Plan for effecting price changes and consequent sales value under the three scenarios are given in Table 5.11.

Table 5.11 Price Changes and Consequent Sales Values

(Rs. in lakh)

Month	Price rise (percent)	Price per tonne (Rs.)	Projected sales value		
			Scenario I	Scenario II	Scenario III
April 20X1	—	39,055	12,947	12,902	12,856
May	—	39,055	12,947	12,902	12,856
June	6	41,400	11,437	11,397	11,356
July	—	41,400	11,437	11,397	11,356
August	—	41,400	13,724	13,676	13,628
September	—	41,400	18,300	18,235	18,170
October	10	45,540	25,162	25,073	24,985
November	—	45,540	27,678	27,580	27,483
December	—	45,540	30,194	30,087	29,982
January 20X2	—	45,540	35,227	35,102	34,978
February	—	45,540	22,646	22,566	22,487
March	—	45,540	20,129	20,058	19,988
		Total	241,828	240,975	240,125

Sales Realisation

LMN Ltd. being the market leader follows an aggressive credit/collection policy. Seventy percent of its sales is in cash while the remaining thirty percent is on a month's credit. The company was able to reduce its bad-debts from 0.36 percent of sales in 20X0 to 0.24 percent in 20X1, which it intends to bring down further to 0.15 percent in 20X2. Besides this, the company intends to follow the same credit/collection policy in the projected year. Cash inflows from sales are calculated on this basis in Table 5.12.

Table 5.12 Cash Inflow from Sales

(Rs. in lakh)

Month	Cash realisation		
	Scenario I	Scenario II	Scenario III
April 20X1	15,225 (19)	15,193 (19)	15,161 (19)
May	12,947 (19)	12,902 (19)	12,856 (19)
June	11,890 (17)	11,848 (17)	11,806 (17)
July	11,437 (17)	11,397 (17)	11,356 (17)
August	13,038 (21)	12,992 (21)	12,946 (20)
September	16,927 (28)	16,867 (27)	16,807 (27)
October	23,103 (38)	23,022 (38)	22,940 (37)
November	26,923 (42)	26,828 (41)	26,734 (41)
December	29,439 (45)	29,335 (45)	29,232 (45)
January 20X2	33,717 (53)	33,598 (53)	33,479 (52)
February	26,420 (34)	26,327 (34)	26,234 (34)
March	20,884 (30)	20,810 (30)	20,738 (30)
Total	241,950 (363)	241,119 (361)	240,289 (358)

Notes:

1. Figures in bracket represent probable bad-debt @ 0.15 percent of monthly sales. Actual cash flows will be net of this figures.

2. April cash inflows are calculated by assuming outstanding debtors of Rs. 6162 lakh as on 31.3.20X1 paid in this month.

3. Remaining months' cash inflows are calculated on the basis of 70 percent of the month's sales paid in cash and remaining 30 percent on the following month.

4. Advance payment being small is ignored.

Projected accounts receivable outstanding as on 31.3.20X2 will be as follows:

	Scenario I	Scenario II	Scenario III
Opening balance	6162	6162	6162
Add: Sales for the projected year	241,828	240,975	240,125
	247,990	247,137	246,287
Less: Projected cash realisation	241,587	240,758	239,931
(net of bad-bebt)	6403	6379	6356
Less: Bad-debt	363	361	358
Closing balance	6040	6018	5998

OPERATING EXPENDITURE

Materials

As far as possible, every item of inventory requirement should be forecasted both in respect of consumption, purchases and stock holding in quantitative terms. Smaller items like stores, packing materials, etc. can, however, be grouped together and forecasted in rupee value, as we shall see later.

Considering the past turnover ratios of various types of inventories and the future expectations of the management, the following relationships are projected for 20X2.

(a) Raw materials efficiency ratio = $33^1/_3$ percent, i.e. for every three tonnes of raw materials one tonne of output is produced.

(b) 6 percent of tonnage sold to be held in finished goods inventory.

(c) 1 percent of tonnage sold to be held in work-in-process inventory.

(d) 18 percent of raw materials consumption to be held in raw materials inventory.

(e) Consumption of packing materials, stores, etc. is projected at 16.5 percent of raw materials consumption in rupee value.

(f) 85 days or 22 percent of consumption of packing materials, stores, etc. to be held in inventory.

(g) Price of raw materials was Rs. 6500 per tonne in 19XX–20X0. It rose to Rs. 7200 per tonne in 20X0–20X1, i.e. a 10.76 percent rise. It is expected that it will go up further by about 7 percent in 20X1–20X2. For the projected year, price of raw materials is, therefore, taken at Rs. 7700 per tonne uniformly for all purchases which are also assumed to be uniform throughout the projected year.

(h) Trade creditors rose to 67 days in 20X1 due to delayed payment which had resulted in suppliers' resistance as discussed earlier. In the projected year the company intends to come back to its original policy of 60 days payment schedule.

(i) The new businesses which had been acquired in 20X1 were the major suppliers of tradeable goods that used to be purchased by the company. Hence, from 1st April, 20X2 onwards the company had decided to dispense with direct purchase of tradeable goods from the market.

Salaries and Wages

Hitherto, wages constituted about 7.5 percent of raw materials consumption. Salary bill for 20X1 was Rs. 3400 lakh approximately. With the massive restructuring that had taken place during 20X1 the company calculates that wages would fall to 6.5 percent and the salary bill would be reduced to Rs. 2800 lakh in 20X1–20X2. The company would continue to contribute to employees provident fund @ 16.33 percent and welfare fund @ 10 percent of salaries and wages.

Other Variable Expenses

Excise duty	:	1.60 percent of gross sales
Power and fuel	:	3 percent of raw materials consumption
Freight and transport	:	2.5 percent of gross sales
Discount and commission	:	0.15 percent of gross sales
Processing charges	:	0.60 percent of raw materials consumption

Fixed and Semi-variable Expenses

(a) Following expenses remains *fixed* at the level of 20X1:

Items	Previous year (20X1)	Payment pattern
Rates and taxes	Rs. 2556 lakh	Every following month of the quarter by equal installment
Brokerage	Rs. 44 lakh	June 20X1
Donations, etc.	Rs. 92 lakh	October: Rs. 42; December: Rs. 50
Audit fees	Rs. 13 lakh	April 20X3
Rent	Rs. 974 lakh	Every month following

(b) Following expenses *rise by* 15 percent in the projected year:

- Repairs of buildings
- Postage and stationeries
- Travelling
- Bank charges

All the above expenses are paid uniformly throughout the year.

(c) The following expenses *rise by* 18 percent in the projected year:

Items	Payment pattern
Insurance	Payable in the month of April
Advertising and sales promotion	Incurred uniformly throughout the year but paid on the month following the quarter.

(d) Repairs of machinery *rise by* 20 percent and miscellaneous expenses net of amortisation *rise by* 5 percent in the following year.

All these expenses are paid uniformly throughout the year.

NON-OPERATING REVENUES

After remaining bullish over a considerable period, the stock market is presently experiencing a bearish condition on the border of a crash. The management has, therefore, instructed its treasury department not to enter into any new security deal. It also expects a fall in return on existing investments. On a conservative estimate, the revenues net of taxes that are expected in the following years are calculated as follows.

(Rs. in lakh)

Source	Amount	Month of receipt
(a) Dividend from subsidiaries and joint ventures	2530	June 20X1
Dividend from subsidiaries and joint ventures	320	July 20X1
(b) Dividend and interest from other investments	170	September 20X1
Dividend and interest from other investments	400	April 20X2
Dividend and interest from other investments	200	May 20X3

(c) Last years' accrued dividend and interest
    receivable this year   340   April 20X1
    Last years' accrued dividend and interest
    receivable this year   200   May 20X1
(d) Last years' miscellaneous incomes accrued
    (sales tax refund etc.) are not expected to
    be received during the projected year
    because of some disputes.

FINANCIAL FLOWS

1. While critically analysing the cash flow and funds flow statements of LMN Ltd., we indicated that there had been a more than 200 percent rise in bank overdraft in 20X0–20X1 ostensibly to part-finance business acquisitions and restructuring. The situation was untenable as it disturbed the stability of the company's financial structure; its NWCR came down to a mere 12.46 percent. Besides, bank overdraft was costing the company at 16 percent p.a. It was suggested that the company should go in for raising long-term fund to correct the imbalance. Accordingly, the company decided to issue 116 lakh 12 percent fully secured debenture of Rs. 100 each aggregating Rs. 116 crore redeemable at par after 7 years; interest payable half-yearly. The issue was already placed, to be payable at 50 percent on application and 50 percent on allotment. It was fully subscribed. The company would receive full application money in April 20X1 and expect to receive allotment money in August 20X1.

2. The company intends to repay in full other short-term loans of Rs. 1700 lakh and other borrowings of Rs. 52 lakh in April 20X1. Existing debenture of Rs. 4 lakh will also be redeemed in the same month.

The company desires to repay the excess bank borrowing of Rs. 9600 lakh by equal monthly installments of Rs. 1600 lakh each beginning October 20X1.

3. Interest payment and repayment programme of the term loans during the projected year would be as follows:

(Rs. in lakh)

	June 20X1	*Sept.* 20X1	*Dec.* 20X1	*March* 20X2
Repayment	Rs. 183	Rs. 245	Rs. 125	Rs. 177
Interest	Rs. 62	Rs. 56	Rs. 50	Rs. 45

4. Fixed deposits falling due for repayment during the projected year are as follows:

(Rs. in lakh)

	April 20X1	*May* 20X1	*August* 20X1	*Oct.* 20X1	*Dec.* 20X1
Repayment	Rs. 225	Rs. 315	Rs. 230	Rs. 485	Rs. 345
Interest	100	—	—	120	—

Past experience of the company shows that 75 percent of matured deposits are renewed.

5.   Commercial papers are falling due for repayment at Rs. 2000 lakh each in the month of June and December 20X1. The company, however, intends to issue new commercial papers of Rs. 3500 in the month of September 20X1 at a discount of 14 percent.

FIXED ASSETS

1.   Capital-work-progress as appearing in the balance sheet of the company on 31.3.20X1 is expected to be completed in the month of June 20X1 at a further cost of Rs. 500 lakh. Further capital works are proposed to be undertaken from the month of May which are expected to be completed in June. The company has projected an expenditure of Rs. 745 lakh on this account against which advances to suppliers/fabricators are to be made as per the following programme:

Month	Advance amount (Rs. in lakh)
May 20X1	75
July 20X1	80
October 20X1	100
February 20X2	95
	350

It is the company's policy to account for fixed assets only after full costs have been paid.

2.   The company is under negotiation with a party to dispose of some of its old machinery having book value of Rs. 215 lakh (depreciation, Rs. 90 lakh) at a price of Rs. 160 lakh. The sale is expected to be completed in the month of May 20X1.

OTHER EXPECTED CASH FLOWS

1.   IDBI deposits of Rs. 188 lakh falling due for encashment in April 20X1.
2.   Further deposit with NABARD of Rs. 15 lakh will have to be made during August 20X1.
3.   Inter-corporate deposits (ICDs) will be due for maturity payment during the projected year as follows:

Month of repayment	Rs. in lakh
July 20X1	39
October 20X1	66
January 20X2	48
March 20X2	90
	Total 243

The company does not want to make further investment in ICDs.
4.   Further deposit with Port Trusts amounting to Rs. 25 lakh will have to be made in June 20X1.

5. Repayment of housing loans to employees to be recovered uniformly throughout the year at Rs. 23 lakh per month. Further housing loans of Rs. 25 lakh per quarter are expected to be disbursed.

6. Personal loans given to directors will be repaid at Rs. 6 lakh per month.

7. Subsidiaries are expected to refund Rs. 102 lakh of loan during July 20X1.

8. Income tax. Provision for income tax made in 20X0–20X1 is payable in the month of August 20X1 when final assessment is expected to be over. Advance tax of Rs. 1100 lakh per quarter is estimated to be payable beginning June 20X1.

9. Dividend. Final dividend declared last year is payable in the month of September 20X1. The company desires to increase its dividend payment from Rs. 5.5 per share to Rs. 6 per share (Face value: Rs. 10 each) in the projected year, 40 percent of which will be disbursed as interim dividend in the month of September 20X1.

Drawing Up Cash Flow Statement

All the projections made above will now form the basis for preparing a projected cash flow statement or cash budget with monthly break-ups. We shall do it for the *most likely scenario* (Scenario II) as an illustration. It would be interesting for the readers to do this exercise for the other two scenarios. In doing so, they will feel the sensitivity of different variables on the cash position of the enterprise which we shall discuss later.

Projected sales and cash flows from sales realisation have already been calculated in Table 5.10 through Table 5.12. We have calculated monthly break-up of purchases of raw materials and packing materials, stores, etc. in Table 5.13. Cash outflows due to payment to suppliers are calculated in Table 5.14. Detailed cash flow statement with monthly break-ups is prepared in Table 5.15.

The exercise on drawing up the projected cash flow statement will be incomplete till we prepare projected profit and loss account and projected balance sheet of the company for the year 20X1–20X2. This has been done in Table 5.16 and Table 5.17 respectively. These three documents together form the basis for control and monitoring of the performance of the company during the projected year.

Table 5.13 Projection of Monthly Purchases of Raw Materials and Packing Materials, Stores, etc.

Particulars	April	May	June	July	August	Sept.	Oct.	Nov.	Dec.	Jan.	Feb.	March	Total
A. Sales (tonnes)	33,035	33,035	27,529	27,529	33,035	44,046	55,058	60,563	66,068	77,080	49,552	44,045	550,535
B. Raw materials (A × 3)	99,105	99,105	82,587	82,587	99,105	132,138	165,174	181,689	198,204	231,240	148,656	132,135	1,651,725
C. Requirement for finished goods inventory (60% of B)	5946	5946	4955	4955	5946	7928	9910	10,901	11,892	13,874	8919	7928	99,100
D. Requirement for work-in-process (1% of B)	991	991	829	829	991	1321	1652	1817	1982	2312	1487	1321	16,523
E. Raw materials consumption (B+C+D)	106,042	106,042	88,371	88,371	106,042	141,387	176,736	194,407	212,078	247,426	159,062	141,384	1,767,348
F. Raw materials inventory (18% of E)	19,088	19,088	15,907	15,907	19,088	25,450	31,812	34,993	38,174	44,537	28,631	25,450	318,125
G. Total raw materials requirement (tonnes) (E + F)	125,130	125,130	104,278	104,278	125,130	166,837	208,548	229,400	250,252	291,963	187,693	166,834	2,085,473
H. Purchase of materials (tonnes)	109,431	109,431	91,760	91,760	106,042	141,387	176,736	194,407	212,078	247,426	159,062	141,384	1,780,904
I. Cost of materials purchases (H × 0.077) (Rs. in lakh)	8426	8426	7066	7065	8165	10,887	13,609	14,969	16,330	19,052	12,248	10,886	137,129
J. Stores, etc. consumed (E × 0.077 × 0.165) (Rs. in lakh)	1347	1347	1123	1123	1347	1796	2245	2470	2694	3144	2021	1796	22,453
K. Inventory of stores, etc. (J × 0.22)	296	296	247	247	296	395	494	543	593	692	445	396	4940
L. Purchases of stores etc. (Rs. in lakh)	1521	1521	1297	1298	1347	1796	2245	2470	2694	3144	2021	1796	23,150

Notes for Table 5.13

1. *Purchases of raw materials* (Item no. H) The company has an opening balance of raw materials inventory of Rs. 21,929 lakh in the projected year. Last year, cost of materials was Rs. 7200 per tonne. Hence, Rs. 21,929 lakh/Rs. 7200 = 304,569 tonnes of inventory is on hand at the beginning of the projected year.

Closing balance of inventory at the year-end of the projected year will be 318,125 (Item No. F). Therefore, the company has to procure additional inventory of 318,125 – 304,569 = 13,556 tonnes in addition to monthly consumption. This additional inventory is proposed to be procured over the first four months of the projected year uniformly at 3389 tonnes per month. Hence purchases for the first four months will be the monthly consumption figure plus 3389 tonnes. For example, purchases in April will be 106,042 tonnes + 3389 tonnes = 109,431 tonnes.

2. *Purchases of packing materials, stores etc.* (Item no. L) The company has an opening inventory of Rs. 4243 lakh in the projected year. Required closing balance of this inventory is found to be Rs. 4940 lakh (Item no. K). Hence, the company has to build up additional inventory of these items to the tune of Rs. 4940 lakh – Rs. 4243 lakh = Rs. 697 lakh, which it does by making additional purchases at the rate of Rs. 174 lakh for the first three months and Rs. 175 lakh for the fourth month. Total monthly purchases for first four months will, therefore, be these figures plus monthly consumption figure. For example, purchases for April will be Rs. 1347 lakh + Rs. 174 lakh = Rs. 1521 lakh.

Payment for Purchases

The company has decided to pay the supply creditors in 60 days. Last year there was some delay in payment which made the outstanding creditors jump to 67 days of purchases. Balance outstanding as on 31.3.20X1 was Rs. 27,820 lakh which the company intends to pay up equally at Rs. 13,910 lakh each in the month of April and May of the projected year. Remaining purchases will follow 60 days' payment as usual. Purchases include total purchases of both raw materials and packing materials, stores, etc. (Item no. I + L of Table 5.13). Accordingly, cash disbursement for purchases are calculated in Table 5.14.

Table 5.14   Projected Cash Payment for Purchase of Raw Materials, Packing Materials, Stores, etc.

(Rs. in lakh)

Month	Total purchases	Cash payment
April 20X1	9947	13,910
May	9947	13,910
June	8363	9947
July	8363	9947
August	9512	8363
September	12,683	8363
October	15,854	9512
November	17,439	12,683
December	19,024	15,854
January 20X2	22,196	17,439
February	14,269	19,024
March	12,682	22,196
Total	160,279	161,148

Outstanding trade creditors as on 31.3.20X2 will be the purchases for the month of February and March 20X2., i.e. Rs. 14,269 lakh + Rs. 12,682 lakh = Rs. 26,951 lakh.

Table 5.15 Cash Flow Statement with Monthly Break-ups for the Projected Year 20X1–20X2

(Rs. in lakh)

	April X1	May	June	July	August	Sept.	Oct.	Nov.	Dec.	Jan. X2	Feb.	Mar.	Total
Operating cash inflow													
Sales realisation	15,174	12,883	11,831	11,380	12,971	16,840	22,984	26,787	29,290	33,545	26,293	20,780	240,758
Dividends, etc.													
From subsidiaries	—	—	2530	320	—	—	—	—	—	—	—	—	2850
Others	—	—	—	—	—	170	—	—	—	—	—	—	170
Last year's accrued	340	200	—	—	—	—	—	—	—	—	—	—	540
A. Total	15,514	13,083	14,361	11,700	12,971	17,010	22,984	26,787	29,290	33,545	26,293	20,780	244,318
Operating cash outflow													
Purchases	13,910	13,910	9947	9947	8363	8363	9512	12,683	15,854	17,439	19,024	22,196	161,148
Accrued expenses (last year)	5493	—	—	—	—	—	—	—	—	—	—	—	5493
Wages	531	531	442	442	531	708	885	973	1061	1238	796	708	8846
Salaries	233	233	234	233	233	234	233	233	234	233	233	234	2800
P.F. and welfare	201	201	178	178	201	248	294	318	341	387	271	248	3066
Excise duty	206	206	182	182	218	292	401	441	481	562	361	321	3853
Power and fuel	245	245	204	204	245	327	408	449	490	572	367	327	4083
Processing charges	49	49	41	41	49	65	82	90	98	114	73	65	816
Freight and transport	322	322	285	285	342	456	627	696	752	877	564	501	6029
Discount and commission	19	20	17	17	20	27	38	41	45	53	34	30	361
Rates and taxes	—	—	—	639	—	—	639	—	—	639	—	—	1917
Brokerage	—	—	44	—	—	—	—	—	—	—	—	—	44
Donations, etc.	—	—	—	—	—	—	42	—	—	—	—	50	92
Rent	—	81	81	81	81	81	82	81	81	81	81	81	892
Repairs—Building	42	42	42	42	42	41	42	42	42	42	42	42	503
—Machinery	93	93	93	93	94	93	93	93	93	94	93	93	1118
Postage and stationery	91	91	92	91	91	92	91	91	92	91	91	92	1096
Travelling	242	242	241	242	242	241	242	242	241	242	242	241	2900
Bank charges	87	87	86	87	87	86	87	87	86	87	87	86	1040
Insurance	332	—	—	—	—	—	—	—	—	—	—	—	332

	1	2	3	4	5	6	7	8	9	10	11	12	Total
Advertising, etc.	—	—	—	—	2110	—	—	2110	—	2110	—	—	6330
Miscellaneous expenses	219	219	219	219	219	219	220	219	219	219	220	219	2630
Sub-total	22,315	16,572	12,428	15,133	11,058	11,574	16,127	16,779	20,210	25,080	22,579	25,534	215,389
Interest													
Debentures	—	—	—	—	—	348	—	—	—	—	—	696	1044
Term loans	—	—	62	—	—	56	—	—	50	—	—	45	213
Last year's accrued	329	—	—	—	—	—	—	—	—	—	—	—	329
Fixed deposits	100	—	—	—	—	—	120	—	—	—	—	—	220
Sub-total	22,744	16,572	12,490	15,133	11,058	11,978	16,247	16,779	20,260	25,080	22,579	26,275	217,195
Income tax													
Last year's provision	—	—	—	—	1530	—	—	—	—	—	—	—	1530
Advance tax	—	—	1100	—	—	1100	—	—	1100	—	—	1100	4400
Dividend													
Last year's provision	—	—	—	—	—	4216	—	—	—	—	—	—	4216
Interim	—	—	—	—	—	2892	—	—	—	—	—	—	2892
B. Total	22,744	16,572	13,590	15,133	12,588	20,186	16,247	16,779	21,360	25,080	22,579	27,375	230,233
C. Net cash flow (A – B)	(7230)	(3489)	771	(3433)	383	(3176)	6737	10,008	7930	8465	3714	(6595)	14,085
Other inflows													
Repayments received													
IDBI deposits	188	—	—	—	—	—	—	—	—	—	—	—	188
ICDs	—	—	39	—	—	66	—	—	—	48	—	90	243
Housing loans	23	23	23	23	23	23	23	23	23	23	23	23	276
Subsidiary loans	—	—	102	—	—	—	—	—	—	—	—	—	102
Loan to directors	6	6	6	6	6	6	6	6	6	6	6	6	72
Sale of fixed assets	—	160	—	—	—	—	—	—	—	—	—	—	160
D. Total	217	189	170	29	29	95	29	29	29	77	29	119	1041
Other outflows													
NABARD deposits	—	—	—	15	—	—	—	—	—	—	—	—	15
Port trust deposits	—	25	—	—	—	—	—	—	—	—	—	—	25
Housing loans	—	25	—	—	25	—	—	25	25	—	—	—	100
Capital advance	75	84	80	—	—	100	—	—	—	—	95	—	434
E. Total	75	134	80	15	25	100	—	25	25	—	95	—	574

(Cont.)

Table 5.15 Cash Flow Statement with Monthly Break-ups for the Projected Year 20X1–20X2 (Cont.)

(Rs. in lakh)

	April X1	May	June	July	August	Sept.	Oct.	Nov.	Dec.	Jan. X2	Feb.	Mar.	Total
F. Net other flows (D – E)	217	114	(105)	90	14	4	(5)	29	4	77	(66)	94	467
Financial inflows													
Debentures	5800	—	—	—	5800	—	—	—	—	—	—	—	11,600
Fixed deposits	169	236	—	—	173	—	364	—	259	—	—	—	1201
Commercial papers	—	—	—	—	—	3010	—	—	—	—	—	—	3010
G. Total	5969	236	—	—	5973	3010	364	—	259	—	—	—	15,811
Financial outflows													
Repayments													
Debentures	4	—	—	—	—	—	—	—	—	—	—	—	4
Term loans	—	—	183	—	—	245	—	—	125	—	—	177	730
Fixed deposits	225	315	—	—	230	—	485	—	345	—	—	—	1600
Commercial papers	—	—	2000	—	—	—	—	—	2000	—	—	—	4000
Other short-term loans	1700	—	—	—	—	—	—	—	—	—	—	—	1700
Other borrowings	52	—	—	—	—	—	—	—	—	—	—	—	52
H. Total	1981	315	2183	—	230	245	485	—	2470	—	—	177	8086
I. Net financial flows (G – H)	3988	(79)	(2183)	—	5743	2765	(121)	—	(2211)	—	—	(177)	7725
Cash surplus/Gap (C + F + I)	(3025)	(3454)	(1517)	(3343)	6140	(407)	6611	10,037	5723	8542	3648	(6678)	22,277
Opening cash/Bank balance	6965	—	—	—	—	—	—	—	—	—	—	—	6965
Repayment of bank overdraft	—	—	—	—	—	—	(1600)	(1600)	(1600)	(1600)	(1600)	(1600)	(9600)
Interest on bank overdraft	(188)	(188)	(189)	(188)	(188)	(189)	(167)	(146)	(124)	(103)	(82)	(60)	(1812)
Cumulative cash surplus/Gap	3752	110	(1596)	(5127)	825	229	5073	13,364	17,363	24,202	26,168	17,830	17,830

Table 5.16 Projected Profit and Loss Account for the year ended 31.3.20X2

(Rs. in lakh)

Opening stock						
Work-in-process	1303		Sales	240,975		
Finished goods	12,367	13,670	*Less:* Excise duty	3853	237,122	
Consumption of raw materials		136,086	**Other Income** (net of			
Wages		8846	tax deducted at source)			
Salaries		2800	Dividend from			
Contribution to provident			subsidiaries	2850		
fund and welfare expenses		3066	Dividend and interest			
Consumption of packing			from other investments	770		
materials, stores		22,453	Profit on sale of fixed			
Repairs to machinery		1118	assets	35	3655	
Repairs to buildings		503	**Closing stock**			
Power and fuel		4083	Work-in-process	1490		
Rent		973	Finished goods	14,139	15,629	
Rates and taxes		2556				
Insurance		332				
Freight and transport		6029				
Advertising and sales						
promotion		8440				
Discount and commission		361				
Brokerage		44				
Postage and stationery		1096				
Travelling expenses		2900				
Processing charges		816				
Bank charges		1040				
Donations and subscriptions		92				
Audit fees		13				
Bad debt		361				
Miscellaneous expenses		4222				
Depreciation		2123				
Profit before interest and						
tax, c/d		32,383				
Total		256,406	Total		256,406	
Interest			Profit before interest and tax, c/d		32,383	
Debentures	1044					
Term loans	213					
Fixed deposits	220					
Commercial paper	490					
Bank overdraft	1812	3779				
Provision for income tax		9582				
Profit after tax, c/d		19,022				
		32,383			32,383	
Proposed dividends			Profit after tax, b/d		19,022	
Interim	2892					
Final	4336	7228				
General reserve		11,794				
		19,022			19,022	

Table 5.17 Projected Balance Sheet as at 31.3.20X2

(Rs. in lakh)

Share capital		12,048	Fixed assets	24,705	
Reserves and surplus			Additions	1210	
Capital reserve	347			25,915	
Revenue reserve	40,638	40,985	Disposals	125	
Borrowings				25,790	
Term loans	1718		Depreciation	2123	
Bank overdraft	4525			23,667	
Debentures	11,600		Capital work-in-process	350	24,017
Fixed deposits	1195		Goodwill		638
Commercial papers	3500	22,538	Investments		
Current liabilities			Subsidiaries and		
Sundry creditors	26,951		joint ventures	1689	
Advance payments	443		Others	2164	3853
Other liabilities			Inventories		
(Expenses)	2843		Raw materials	22,972	
Unclaimed dividend	1177	31,414	Stores and spares	4940	
Provisions			Work-in-process	1490	
Income tax (net of			Finished goods	14,139	43,541
advance payments	5182		Sundry debtors		6018
Dividend	4336	9518	(net of bad-debts)		
			Loans and advances		10,495
			(net of bad-debts)		
			Other current assets		3253
			Cash and bank balances		17,830
			Miscellaneous expenses		
			not written off		6858
	Total	116,503		Total	116,503

Notes on projected cash flow statement, profit and loss account and balance sheet

1. Accrued expenses as on 31.3.20X1 are assumed to be payable on the following April. Expenses accrued but not paid as on 31.3.20X2 will comprise the following:

	(Rs. in lakh)
(a) Rates and taxes	639
(b) Rent	81
(c) Advertising and promotional expenses	2110
(d) Audit fees	13
Total	2843

2. Interest accrued but not paid as on 31.3.20X1 will be payable in April 20X1.

3. Interest payable on bank overdraft and balance outstanding are calculated below:

Month	Balance outstanding	Repayment	Interest @16% p.a.
April X1	14,125	—	188
May	14,125	—	188
June	14,125	—	189
July	14,125	—	188
August	14,125	—	188

September	14,125	—	189
October	12,525	1600	167
November	10,925	1600	146
December	9325	1600	124
January X2	7725	1600	103
February	6125	1600	82
March	4525	1600	60
		Total 9600	1812

4. Calculations of closing balances of different items as on 31.3.20X2 are given below:

(a) *Inventory of raw materials*

Opening balance	Rs.	21,929
Add: Purchases	Rs.	137,129
Total materials	Rs.	159,058
Less: Consumption	Rs.	136,086
Closing balance	Rs.	22,972

(b) *Inventory of packing materials, stores, etc.*

Opening balance	Rs.	4243
Add: Purchases	Rs.	23,150
Total materials	Rs.	27,393
Less: Consumption	Rs.	22,453
Closing balance	Rs.	4940

(c) Closing stock of work-in-process and finished goods as on 31.3.20X2 are estimated figures.

(d) *Sundry debtors*

Opening balance	Rs.	6162
Add: Sales	Rs.	240,975
Total debtors	Rs.	247,137
Less: Cash realised	Rs.	240,758
	Rs.	6379
Less: Bed-debt	Rs.	361
Closing balance	Rs.	6018

(e) *Sundry creditors*

Opening balance	Rs.	27,820
Add: Purchases of raw materials	Rs.	137,129
Add: Purchases of packing materials, etc.	Rs.	23,150
	Rs.	188,099
Less: Cash paid	Rs.	161,148
Closing balance	Rs.	26,951

5. *Fixed assets*

(a) Capital work-in-progress as on 31.3.20X1 was Rs. 1126 lakh which included capital advance of Rs. 416 lakh (see cash flow statement for 20X1, Exhibit 5.5). During the projected year an amount of Rs. 500 lakh is proposed to be spent on this capital work-in-progress before it is transferred to fixed assets account. Hence, actual transfer to fixed assets account will be as follows:

Opening balance of capital WIP	Rs.	1126
Less: Capital advance included	Rs.	416

Actual capital work	Rs.	710
Add: Further amount to be spent during the year	Rs.	500
Amount to be transferred to fixed assets account	Rs.	1210

(b) Capital work-in-progress as on 31.3.20X2 will comprise only the capital advance account calculated as follows:

Opening balance	Rs.	416
Further advance during the year	Rs.	434
	Rs.	850
Less: Transferred to fixed assets	Rs.	500
Closing balance	Rs.	350

6. *Loans and advances*

Opening balance			Rs.	11,063
Add: Further port trust deposit	Rs.	25		
Add: Further housing loans	Rs.	100	Rs.	125
			Rs.	11,188
Less: ICDs repaid	Rs.	243		
Housing loans repaid		276		
Loans to directors repaid		72		
Loans repaid by subsidiaries		102	Rs.	693
Closing balance			Rs.	10,495

7. *Other current assets*

Opening balance			Rs.	3366
Add: Further deposit with NABARD	Rs.	15		
Add: Interest accrued but not received	Rs.	600	Rs.	615
			Rs.	3981
Less: Last year's interest accrued received	Rs.	540		
Less: Encashment of IDBI deposit	Rs.	188	Rs.	728
Closing balance			Rs.	3253

SENSITIVITY ANALYSIS

Any exercise on cash flow forecasting will not be complete until sensitivity analysis of important variables is done to assess their impact on cash flows. This is important because cash flow projections are made on the basis of certain assumptions of the behaviour of business variables in the forthcoming year(s), and in real-life situations many such assumptions may go wrong—no matter how careful one has been and howsoever sophisticated forecasting tools one might have used in projecting these variables. This is what we call the uncertainty of a business. Improved methods of forecasting can reduce the zone of uncertainty, but for a business, this zone can never vanish. If there is no uncertainty there is no business. The other name of business, is uncertainty.

Uncertainty being the only certain thing in a business, management of a business is ultimately reduced to the management of uncertainty which, when translated in real terms, means minimisation of the impact of uncertainty. This is possible only when a business is ready to take on a different scenario than the one predicted. Surprise is a word which, in business, implies lack of preparedness.

This preparedness to meet business eventualities stems from a series of 'what if' questions that a manager may ask. These questions may range from projection of sales to the vagaries of tax authorities, but most weighty among them are growth in sales, prices to be realised, materials prices and interest rates.

For LMN Ltd. we have already developed sales projections under three scenarios—best, most likely and worst (Table 5.9). Value of sales, their realisation, purchases and their payments under the three different scenarios are also calculated in subsequent tables and finally a detailed monthly cash flow forecasts or cash budget is prepared in Table 5.15. All these projections are made on the assumption of an average rise in sales price by 7.84 percent and that of materials price by 7 percent during the projected year. Some of the managers participating in the budgetary drill opine that while Scenario II is most likely to occur, the enterprise must be ready for the worst scenario. Even within this scenario they should try to find out what would happen to the business if sales price and materials prices also differ from what are projected. Some of these managers feel that interest rate during the projected year may not undergo much change but with the competition hotting up, the company may not be able to affect any price rise. Another section of the managers declare that assumption of a 7 percent rise in materials price may be too modest; the company may ultimately end up with a rise in cost of materials and other inputs by 10 percent in the projected year. On the basis of these alternative assumptions we can draw up four cash flow statements, by way of illustration, under Scenario III.

Case I: Sales projections are as in worst scenario with no change in projected sales and materials price.

Case II: Sales projections in terms of tonnes are as in worst scenario, but price of output remains at what was obtained in the last year, i.e. at Rs. 39,055 per tonne.

Case III: Sales by tonnes remain the same under worst scenario as in Case I, price of the output also remains at what is projected, but cost of raw materials is increased from 7 percent to 10 percent in the projected year. That is, Rs. 7200 × 1.10 = Rs. 7920 per tonne.

Case IV: Sales by tonnes remain the same under worst scenario but the price of output remains at last year's level as in Case II and cost of materials rises by 10 percent as in Case III.

In Table 5.18 we have drawn up alternative cash flow projections under the above four cases.

Table 5.18 Alternative Cash Flow Projections: Scenario III (Worst)

(Rs. in lakh)

	Case I No change in prices of output and materials	Case II Output price falls	Case III Raw materials price increases	Case IV Output price falls and materials price increases
Operating cash inflow				
Sales realisation (net of bad-debt)	239,931	214,964	239,931	214,964
Dividends				
From subsidiaries 2850				
From others 170				
Last year's accrued 540	3560	3560	3560	3560
A. Total	243,491	218,524	243,491	218,524
Operating cash outflow				
Purchases	160,834	160,834	164,735	164,735
Accrued expenses (last year)	5493	5493	5493	5493
Wages	8814	8814	9066	9066
Salaries	2800	2800	2800	2800
P.F. and welfare	3058	3058	3124	3124
Excise duty	3842	3428	3842	3428
Power and fuel	4068	4068	4184	4184
Processing charges	814	814	837	837
Freight and transport	6003	5357	6003	5357
Discount and commission	360	321	360	321
Rates and taxes	1917	1917	1917	1917
Brokerage	44	44	44	44
Donations	92	92	92	92
Rent	892	892	892	892
Repairs : Building	503	503	503	503
: Machinery	1118	1118	1118	1118
Postage and stationery	1096	1096	1096	1096
Travelling	2900	2900	2900	2900
Bank charges	1040	1040	1040	1040
Insurance	332	332	332	332
Advertising, etc.	6330	6330	6330	6330
Miscellaneous expenses	2630	2630	2630	2630
B. Sub-total	214,980	213,881	219,338	218,239
Net operating cash flow (A – B)	28,511	4643	24,153	285

Working Notes

In all the four cases no change is assumed in income from dividends, etc.
Expenses beginning with 'rates and taxes' in Table 5.18, are fixed in nature
and have been assumed to remain constant in all the four cases. Calculations
of sales and purchases are shown below. Variable and semi-variable expenses
are allowed to vary with sales and raw materials consumption as the case
may be.

Case I (Rs. in lakh)

Sales (tonnes): 548,631
 Sales value (as per Table 5.11, col. 6): Rs. 240,125
 Cash realisation from sales (Table 5.12, col. 6): Rs. 240,289 – Rs. 358
 = Rs. 239,931 (net of bad-debts)

Raw materials

Requirements for output sold: 548,631 × 3 =	1,645,893 tonnes
Requirements for finished goods (6 percent)	98,754 tonnes
Requirements for work-in-process (1 percent)	16,459 tonnes
Consumption of raw materials	1,761,106 tonnes
Raw materials inventory (18 percent of consumption)	317,000 tonnes
	2,078,106 tonnes
Less: Opening stock of raw materials	304,569 tonnes
Purchase of raw materials	1,773,537 tonnes

Consumption of raw materials in rupees: 1,761,106 × Rs. 0.077 lakh =
Rs. 135,605

Purchase of raw materials in rupees: 1,773,537 × Rs. 0.077 lakh = Rs. 136,562

Packing materials, stores, etc.

Consumption of raw materials: 0.165 × 135,605 =	Rs. 22,375
Inventory of stores, etc. (22 percent of above)	4922
Total requirements	27,297
Less: Opening inventory	4243
Purchase of packing materials, stores, etc.	23,054
Total purchases: Rs. 136,562 + 23,054 = Rs. 159,616	
Add: Opening balance of trade creditors	27,820
	187,436
Less: Closing balance of trade creditors	26,602
(being 2 months' purchases)	
Cash paid for purchases	160,834

Case II

Cash Realisation from Sales (at Rs. 39,055 per Tonne)

Month	Sales (Tonnes)	Sales (Rs.)	Cash realisation (Rs.)	
April 20X1	32,918	12,856	15,161	(23)
May	32,918	12,856	12,856	(19)
June	27,431	10,713	11,356	(17)
July	27,432	10,714	10,714	(16)
August	32,918	12,856	12,213	(18)
September	43,890	17,141	15,856	(24)
October	54,863	21,427	20,141	(30)
November	60,349	23,569	22,926	(34)
December	65,836	25,712	25,069	(38)
January 20X2	76,808	29,997	28,712	(43)
February	49,378	19,285	22,499	(34)
March	43,890	17,141	17,784	(27)
Total	548,631	214,267	215,287	(323)

Note: Figures in bracket represent bad-debt.

Net cash realisation = Rs. 215,287 − 323 = Rs. 214,964
Cash paid for purchases remains same as in case I.

Case III

Raw materials

Price of raw materials goes up by 10 percent: Rs. 0.072 lakh × 1.10 = Rs. 0.0792 lakh per tonne
Consumption of raw materials: 1,761,106 × 0.0792 lakh = Rs. 139,480
Purchase of raw materials: 1,773,537 × 0.0792 = Rs. 140,464

Packing materials, stores, etc.

Consumption of packing materials, etc.: 139,480 × 0.165 = Rs. 23,014
(16.5 percent of raw materials consumption)

Inventory (22 percent of consumption)	5063
	28,077
Less: Opening inventory	4243
Purchases of packing materials, stores, etc.	23,834

Total purchases: Rs. 140,464 + 23,834 = Rs. 164,298	
Add: Opening balance of trade creditors	27,820
	192,118
Less: Closing balance of trade creditors	27,383
(being 2 months' purchases)	
Cash paid for purchases	164,735

Cash realisation from sales remains as in Case I.

Case IV

Cash realisation from sales as in Case II	Rs. 214,964
Cash paid for purchases as in Case III	Rs. 164,735
Raw materials consumption as in Case III	Rs. 139,480

Table 5.18 reveals the sensitivity of net operating cash flows to changes in output prices and materials cost under Scenario III (worst). It may be seen that when output prices remain at previous year's level (i.e., when 7.84 percent average price rise is not obtainable in the projected year) NOCF is reduced by 83.72 percent (Case II), and when cost of materials has risen by 10 percent (as against 7 percent originally proposed), NOCF is reduced by 15.28 percent (Case III). Worst is the situation when sales prices remain at the previous year's level but materials cost has gone up by 3 percent more than originally proposed. NOCF is virtually wiped out in such a situation (Case IV).

It is not unusual for eventualities mentioned in the above four cases to occur in real-life situation. If Case IV finally occurs, the company will not be able to pay even interest on borrowings (Rs. 1806 lakh), not to speak of current year's repayment obligations (Rs. 8086 lakh), last year's income tax (Rs. 1530 lakh) and also declared dividends (Rs. 4216 lakh) without the help of substantial financial inflows. The situation will be marginally better if Case III occurs. The company will be able to pay interest and last year's tax, but no other obligations.

This sensitivity analysis suggests that the enterprise should have alternative plans ready to generate additional financial flows to meet these eventualities so that it is not taken by 'surprise'.

Four cases presented above are only illustrative to point out the sensitivity of net operating cash flow (NOCF) to changes in output prices and materials cost. There can be various other combinations; several other items of costs and revenues may also be brought in to test their sensitivity to NOCF. For this purpose, a *spreadsheet* software comes in handy. It can handle changes in several variables at a time in various combinations once the basic relationships (or no relationship, like fixed costs) between variables are defined and fed to the *spreadsheet* programme.

CASH COLLECTION SYSTEMS

One fall out of modern financial system is that you do not 'get paid' though the customer has already made payment. There is a time lag between payment made by the customer and the amount becoming disbursible cash at your hands. This is primarily due to the innovation of cheque as an instrument of payment and its gradual taking over of the cash-economy. Multiple banking and geographical distance have added further complexity leading to further delay in receiving value in disbursible cash.

A cheque-payment may be floating through the mailing system (e.g. post office), waiting for it to be processed at the receiver's office before being put to float once again through the bank's clearing system for its ultimate conversion to cash balance in the receiver's bank account. This entire time-chain holds up cash of a firm and consequently, it loses on its opportunity cost. This time-chain is popularly known as float which is *negative* to the firm when it *receives* payment (as in the present case). The float becomes *positive* when it *makes* payment, which we shall discuss later. It follows, therefore, that the primary objective of a cash collection system is to minimise negative float of the firm.

But a collection system must not only quicken the collection of cash it should also provide relevant information to the firm as to when the payment has become disbursible cash and who made the payment. It is often found that a customer's payment has been duly credited by the bank to the account of the firm, but no such information is available at firm's end, either because the bank statement has not been received in time, or no one cared to find out the fate of an instrument sent for collection. It also happens that a cheque has been received and also duly credited in the bank account but there was no information, or faulty information as to who made the payment. This poses severe problems for the receivables manager who does not know whose account is to be credited. This may result in stoppage of further shipment to a customer and consequent loss of goodwill. The overall objective of a collection system should, therefore, be to minimise the negative float and to ensure a smooth information flow at a cost which maximises firm's value.

Cost of Float

This cost item is not available in the books of accounts of an enterprise and hence, it remains invisible and thus eludes control. But loss of opportunities foregone due to non-availability of cash (tied on float) is always a real cost to the company. The following example is illustrative of what is happening in a large number of firms in India.

Example A company receives per day an average of Rs. 60 lakh in cheques. The practice of the company is to deposit cheques with its bank accounts twice a week: Wednesday and Friday.

The above practice is creating the following float within the organisation:

Time lag	*Float in rupee days*
Monday's receipts deposited on Wednesday	$2 \times 60 = 120$ lakh
Tuesday's receipts deposited on Wednesday	$1 \times 60 = 60$ lakh
Wednesday's receipts deposited on Wednesday	— —
Thursday's receipts deposited on Friday	$1 \times 60 = 60$ lakh
Friday's receipts deposited on Friday	— —
Saturday's receipts deposited on Wednesday	$3 \times 60 = 180$ lakh
	Total 420

Under the given circumstances the firm will continue to run Rs. 420 lakh float-days per week throughout the year. If the opportunity cost of the firm (say, interest on bank overdraft) is 18 percent p.a., then the firm is losing $420 \times (0.18/365)$ = Rs. 0.20712 lakh or Rs. 20,712 per week or Rs. 20,712 $\times$ 52 = Rs. 10.77 lakh per annum.

This is a typical example of internal float generated by a firm. It is generally observable at a time when the firm is cash rich. The hidden losses are overlooked till the time the firm faces a cash crunch. While attempting to make an improvement upon the existing practice of cheque deposit, one should, however, take into account the clerical cost of processing cheques vis-a-vis the cost of insurance and other protection costs of holding receipts in company's till.

External Float

External float evolves outside the organisational system of the firm, particularly in mail and bank clearing. Figure 5.6 captures both external and internal floats of a typical firm.

Despite the introduction of electronic payment system and *automated clearing house* (ACH), payment transactions in Indian businesses continue to be through the mailing system. State-run postal system with its wide network occupies the major part in the mailing system. Privately run courier companies are gaining ground, though by inches, but because of high cost they can cater only to high value remittances and packages in bulk. They do not have network beyond urban and metropolitan areas. Post office has also introduced speed-post to counteract the expansion of the business of private couriers.

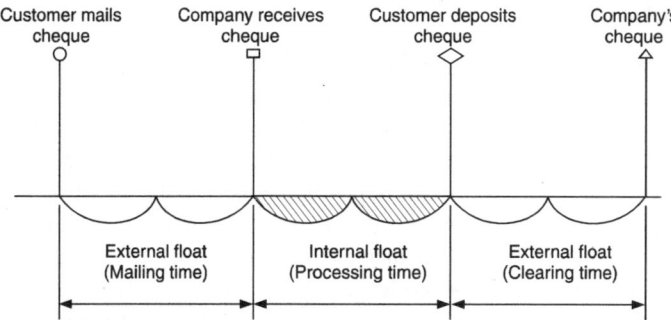

Figure 5.6 Collection float.

Besides, payers are not expected to give in their own float by transmitting the payment through courier or speed-post even when the costs are made reimbursible by the receiving firm. Postal mailing system will therefore be the dominant means for remitting payments and hence, predominantly, a cash collection system will have to be designed around it. Services of couriers or speed-post can be availed of only after receipt of cheques to reduce additional floats between receipts and bank clearing.

A typical mailed payment system for geographically dispersed customer-bases of a firm will consist of several collection centres, each catering to a group of customers; a network of local banks, each designated to take deposits from a particular collection centre, and, an information system that ensures flow of information between the collection centres, banks and central office of the enterprise. In order to optimise the mailed payment system there has obviously to be a trade-off between the reduction of float in the system and costs of operating and administering the collection system.

Wholly-owned Collection System

A firm may desire to operate its own cash collection system without contracting out any part of it. Typically, it may have several collection centres depending upon geographical concentration of customers where its own people will receive the payments, process them, record the transactions in its books of accounts, deposit the cheques with the designated bank and transmit both payment and credit information to the central office. Under this system the firm has total control over the operation, and hence the information flow is smooth. It is easier to make changes in the system as and when needed. There are also other advantages. A firm's own collection centres do not necessarily restrict themselves to receiving payments only. They also monitor and follow-up the receivables originating within the command area of operation. Being close to customers these collection centres also act as valuable source of information about the changing credit-worthiness of a customer. All these have the ultimate effect of preventing bad-debts of the firm. While contracting out the whole or part of the collection function to an outside agent, the firm must weigh the value of these advantages in terms of the savings in cost.

Contracting Out

The administrative costs of maintaining a firm's own collection centres may often be substantial which may have led many a firm to dispense with the collection centres altogether. One way of doing it is to centralise the collection at the central office of the firm or to appoint local agents, namely banks, to do the receiving, processing and depositing jobs for the firm. In the former case, collection float will increase due to two-way mailing distance—one for receiving the cheque from the outstation and the other for sending the same cheque through the bank for collection at its place of origin. However, the administrative cost of managing the system will be greatly reduced. In the latter case, collection float will be reduced, so also the administrative costs net off fees/charges payable to the bank to run the system. In both the cases, however, advantages of customer-monitoring and credit information will be lost.

Bank as Collection Agent

A straightforward version of contracting out a part of collection system is to designate a local bank around a customers-concentration point and instructing the customers to mail their cheques directly to the designated bank who shall send the same to the clearing, and on realisation, credit the proceeds to the current account of the firm. The customer may be additionally instructed to send a copy of the covering letter (accompanied with the cheque sent to the bank) or wire the information to the central office of the firm so that the customer's account is appropriately credited and reconciled with the bank statement when received from the deposit bank.

The wide network of banks in India, particularly that of nationalised banks, may be very helpful for firms in India to switch over to this type of cash collection system which can substantially reduce both the operating and administration costs that are to be incurred in any alternative cash collection system.[25] Generally, the designated local bank will be a branch of the bank where the firm maintains its central account. The bank (or its branch) will charge a processing fee which may be related to each instrument handled or a consolidated charge calculated on the rupee-volume handled per annum and payable monthly or quarterly to the head office of the bank. Arrangement can be made with the bank by which the local deposit branch of the bank will remit every evening the entire credit balance of the account to the central account of the firm maintained with the same bank by wire or other telecommunication or electronic transfer service with all actual costs to the bank. A copy of such transfer advice may also be sent to the central office of the firm. However, though not always officially spelt out, in order to maintain the motivational level of local branch of the bank to deliver efficient service it is desirable for

---

25. Under this system, customers may also be allowed to make payment by cash deposit to the account of the customers and wire the information to the central office of the firm.

the firm to maintain a minimum balance in the deposit account of the local branch of the bank. This will, of course, create a static float in the collection system of the firm with its associated opportunity cost.[26] But even considering the opportunity cost of such a static float, which is often much less than 0.5 percent of the total volume transacted, the benefits accruing to the firm due to virtual elimination of processing float may be substantial.[27] The working of this cash collection system for an individual centre is depicted in Figure 5.7.

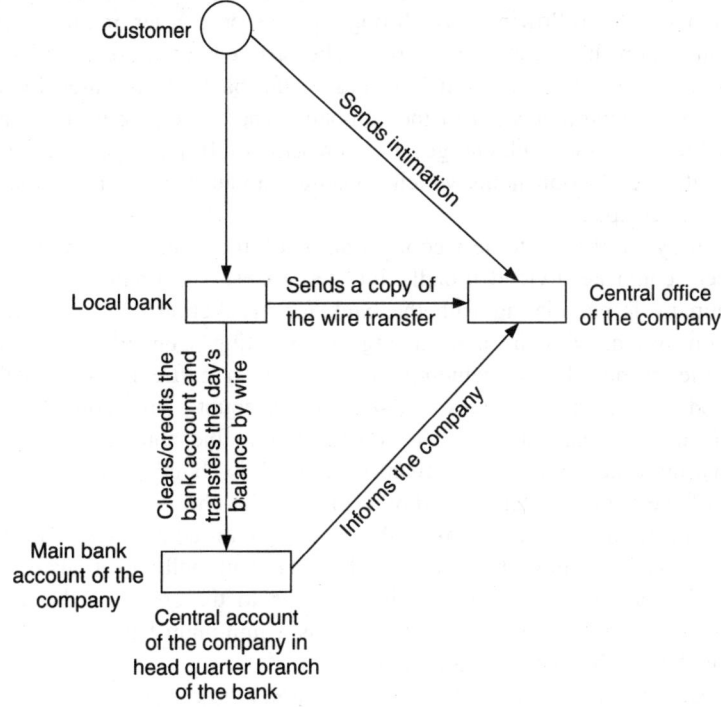

Figure 5.7 Cash collection system through bank.

As indicated before, efficacy of any alternative cash collection system has to be judged by a trade-off between opportunity cost of float saved (reduced) and the additional costs of installing the alternative system. With the help of the following example we intend to find out whether moving from the existing system of cash collection to the one discussed above is cost effective or not.

Example A company, engaged in manufacturing and selling wide range of consumer products, has a centralised cash collection system located at its head

26. In United States and Europe, this may be construed as similar to maintaining compensatory balances with the bank for services rendered.

27. In actual practice, minimum cash balance maintainable at local branches is not calculated as a percentage of volume transacted. It is always a lumpsum amount, hardly exceeding Rs. 10 lakh per branch, negotiable with the bank.

office in Kolkata. Customers all over the country mail their cheques directly to the head office of the company. Average mailing time is six days while the average daily receipt is Rs. 100 lakh. Number of instruments handled per year is 10,000. Average processing time for all cheques at head office is 2 days. Local cheques are directly deposited with the central account(s) of the company maintained with the Kolkata main office of a nationalised bank which sent them for clearing immediately. Clearing time in Kolkata is, on an average, two days. Outstation cheques are sorted by the bank and sent for collection on the following day through postal or courier mailing system depending upon the value of a cheque. The proceeds of these cheques after being collected at the outstation branches of the bank are remitted by wire-transfer to the central account of the company. The entire process takes about 4 days. Presently, the bank charges a commission of 10 paise per Rs. 1000 on all outstation collection items which constitute about 60 percent of the total volume of receipts.

A study of the customers-concentration of the company revealed that customers could be divided broadly into ten zones. The finance manager of the company is negotiating with the bank for installation of a decentralised collection system with the bank acting as collecting agent of the company. Under the proposed arrangement, customers of a particular zone will be instructed to mail their cheques to the current account of the company to be maintained at a designated branch situated within the zone. Average intra-zone mailing time to the local branch of the bank is about one day. The local branch of the bank will take one day to process the cheques and put them on clearing the following day. It takes about one day on an average to clear the proceeds. Every evening, the local branch of the bank will wire-transfer to the company's central account all amount standing to the credit of the account beyond Rs. 10 lakh, which has to be kept as a minimum balance at all such designated local branches of the bank.

Under this arrangement the bank will charge a processing fee of 3.5 paise per Rs. 1000 or Rs. 5 per instrument whichever is higher. Opportunity cost of capital for the company is 15 percent per annum. If the company adopts the alternative proposal, clerical costs of Rs. 5 lakh per annum incurred at head office for processing of cheques can be avoided.

Let us now make a cost-benefit analysis of the alternative proposal.

Existing system

(a)	Average daily receipts	Rs. 100 lakh
(b)	Average mail float	6 days
(c)	Average processing float	2 days
(d)	Average clearing float at Calcutta	2 days
(e)	Average collection float for outstation cheques	4+1 = 5 days
(f)	Bank commission on outstation collections	10 paise per Rs. 1000
(g)	Percentage of outstation cheques to total rupees due	60 percent
(h)	Cost of capital	15 percent

When cheques are processed at Kolkata head office and put to the banking system, two kinds of float emerge: (1) clearing float of two days for cheques drawn on Kolkata, which constitutes 40 percent of total rupee volume of collections, i.e. Rs. 40 lakh, and (2) collection float of six days for 60 percent of collections, i.e. Rs. 60 lakh. Average (weighted) float on the banking system should, therefore, be $(40 \times 2 + 60 \times 5)/100 = 3.8$ or say, 4 days.

Bank commission on outstation cheques which constitute 60 percent of collections is 10 paise per Rs. 1000. Hence, average commission on all collections can be taken as 6 paise per Rs. 1000.

Alternative System

(a) Average daily receipts	Rs. 100 lakh divided amongst 10 zones
(b) Average mail float	1 day in each zone
(c) Average processing float at the local branch of the bank	1 day
(d) Average clearing float at the local branch	1 day
(e) Bank fees on all collections at branches	3.5 paise per Rs. 1000
(f) Minimum balance to be maintained at each local branch	Rs. 10 lakh

(i) *Savings on float under the proposed system:*

Average mail float	$6 - 1 = 5$ days
Average processing float	$2 - 1 = 1$ day
Average float in the banking system	$4 - 1 = 3$ days
Total savings on float	9 days

Opportunity cost savings on float:

$9 \times$ Rs. 100 lakh $\times 0.15$ = Rs. 135 lakh

(ii) *Savings on bank charges:* Average commission payable under the existing system is 6 paise per Rs. 1000. As against this, under the alternative system, commission payable is 3.5 paise per Rs. 1000. Hence, savings on commisssion is, $6 - 3.5 = 2.5$ paise per 1000.

Therefore, total savings = Rs. $10,000,000 \times 365 \times (6 - 3.5)/100,000$
= Rs. 91,250

(iii) *Savings on clerical cost of processing*: Rs. 5 lakh p.a.

(iv) *Total savings* (A + B + C):

A + B + C = Rs. 135 lakh + Rs. 0.91,250 lakh + Rs. 5 lakh
= Rs. 140.91 lakh

(v) *Incremental cost of the proposed system:* Opportunity cost of maintaining cash balance at 10 local branches of the bank,

Rs. 10 lakh $\times 10 \times 0.15$ = Rs. 15 lakh

Net savings in the proposed system will, therefore, be D – E, or Rs. 140.91 lakh – Rs. 15 lakh = Rs. 125.91 lakh, which is quite substantial. Hence, the alternative proposal is acceptable.

Analytical Approach

The entire process described above can be captured analytically for further insights.

General cost function of an alternative cash collection system can be described as follows:

(Opportunity cost savings on float saved) – (Incremental opportunity cost of maintaining minimum balance in local banks + Increased cost of bank charges + Increase in administrative costs)

Above cost function can be put in the algebraic form as:

$$Dki - (DTC + Bni + A)$$

where

D = average daily collection
k = days of float saved
i = opportunity cost of capital
T = number of days in a period
C = incremental cost of bank charges
B = minimum balance to be maintained at the designated local branch of the bank
n = number of designated local branches of the bank
A = increase in administrative cost

The system reaches break-even point when benefits accruing due to cost savings on float saved are equal to the incremental costs of the proposed system, i.e.

$$Dki - (DTC + Bni + A) = 0 \qquad (5.6)$$

or

$$Dki = DTC + Bni + A \qquad (5.7)$$

From Eq. (5.7), we can now find out the minimum level of various variables which can sustain the break-even position. For example, we may find out at which minimum level of daily receipts (D') the system continues to be on the break-even point. This is done by the following algebraic manipulation of Eq. (5.7)

$$Dki = DTC + Bni + A$$

or

$$Dki - DTC = Bni + A$$

or

$$D(ki - TC) = Bni + A$$

or

$$D' = \frac{Bni + A}{ki - TC} \qquad (5.8)$$

For minimum days of float saved (k')

$$Dki = DTC + Bni + A$$

or

$$k' = \frac{DTC + Bni + A}{Di} \qquad (5.9)$$

For minimum level of opportunity cost (i')

$$Dki = DTC + Bni + A$$

or

$$Dki - Bni = DTC + A$$

or

$$i(Dk - Bn) = DTC + A$$

or

$$i' = \frac{DTC + A}{Dk - Bn} \tag{5.10}$$

In the given illustration, some of the incremental costs are positive signifying net savings. For example, there has been a saving in bank charges (C) and in administrative costs (A) under the proposed system. Hence, their signs will have to be reversed in the cost function, i.e.

$$Dki = (-DTC + Bni - A)$$

Break-even point will be

$$Dki = -DTC + Bni - A \tag{5.11}$$

If we now intend to find out the minimum daily receipts (D') that can sustain the break-even level, Eq. (5.11) can be modified as follows:

$$Dki + DTC = Bni - A$$

or

$$D(ki + TC) = Bni - A$$

or

$$D' = \frac{Bni - A}{ki + TC} \tag{5.12}$$

For the present example, D' will be:

$$D' = \frac{1,000,000 \times 10 \times 0.15 - 500,000}{9 \times 0.15 + 365 \times 0.000025}$$

$$= \frac{1,000,000}{1.359125}$$

$$= \text{Rs. } 735,768$$

After checking with the above example, we have

$$D'(ki + TC) = Bni - A$$

or

$$735,768 \ (9 \times 0.15 + 365 \times 0.000025) = 1,000,000 \times 10 \times 0.15 - 500,000$$

or

$$1,000,000.68 = 1,000,000$$

(The difference of 0.68 is due to approximation.)

The asking float days (k) and opportunity cost (i) can also be calculated by using Eq. (5.9) and Eq. (5.10) respectively after appropriate reversing of signs. The former (k') will come to be less than a day (0.61 day) and the latter (i') will be negative (– 0.74 percent) owing to some of the cost items (bank charges and administrative costs) turing out to be positive.

LOCKBOX SYSTEM

This is a variation of the cash collection system discussed above. Under this system, the customers (instead of mailing directly to the local branch of the bank) will mail their cheques to a post office *lockbox* rented by the company at appropriate locations. The designated branch of the local bank will collect the cheques from the lockbox twice or thrice per day as per agreement and put them on clearing directly.

Lockbox system was first introduced in the United States in 1947 and since then it gained its popularity and established itself as the dominant mode of cash collection. As the sorter in the post office directly puts the envelopes containing cheques in the lockbox instead of to the bit-peon, intra-city mailing time is reduced to some extent as compared to the earlier system, though not fully because bank's peon will have to go to the post office to collect cheques.

The system is introduced by the firm after examining its customer-concentration, remittance pattern and volume, and the date the receipts are finally banked after processing. Postal pin codes are used for grouping customers in a particular postal zone, which becomes a candidate for possible lockbox location. However, the cheque mailed by a customer from a particular location may be drawn on a different location in terms of its own disbursement policy. This phenomenon must also be considered while finalising the candidates for lockbox location.[28]

Once a lockbox is rented and a bank is designated to manage it, customers located in the lockbox zone (or whose cheques are drawn on a bank located in the zone) are asked to route their cheques to the post office where the lockbox is rented. As before, customers are requested to mail a copy of the covering letter (or wire-remittance information) to the central office of the company. The designated bank will collect the cheques, put them on clearing and remit the amount standing to the credit of the account beyond the required minimum balance to the central account of the company every evening by wire or electronic transfer with a copy to the head office of the company. Operation of a lockbox system is depicted in Figure 5.8.

Installation of lockboxes in multiple locations generates float savings by reducing the total collection float of a centralised cash collection system. But as mentioned before, unless the benefits derived from float savings is more than the costs of managing lockboxes the new system may not be a feasible proposition. In other words, a firm may continue to add lockboxes till the

---

28. A customer may maintain more than one account in different places and issue cheques on these accounts to maximise its own positive float. He may also choose a particular account on a random basis which makes it difficult for the firm to assign the customer in a particular zone.

opportunity cost of the additional cash generated (float savings) by the new system is offset by the cost of maintaining the last lockbox.[29]

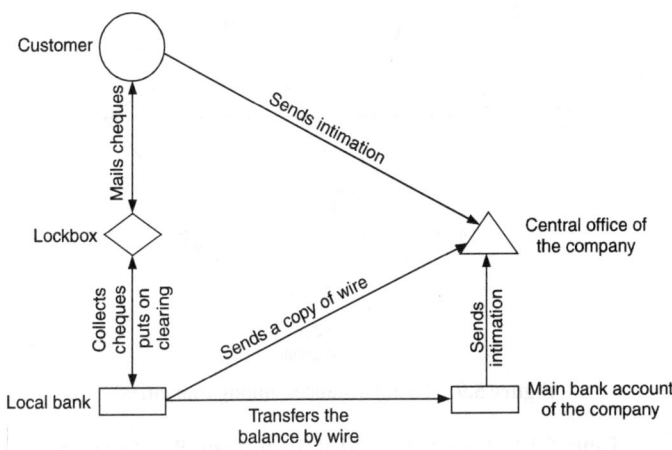

Figure 5.8 Lockbox system.

Example A company having its head office in Kolkata has a centralised cash collection system. A study of the existing system has revealed the following information.

Customer-zone	Number of cheques receipt	Average rupee value of a cheque (Rs.)
Kolkata	1095	100,000
Mumbai	365	200,000
New Delhi	730	80,000
Chennai	500	73,000

Actual postal distance (registered mail) among the four cities is given in Figure 5.9.

Intra–city mailing time is found out to be 1 day. Processing time at head office is also 1 day. Presently, all customers mail their cheques to head office in Kolkata.

The company is desirous of exploring the possibility of replacing the existing centralised cash collection system by a lockbox system. Relevant cost information collected for this purpose are given below (Table 5.19).

29. Bartin, C.A. and Susan Hinko, "Lockbox Management and Value Maximization", *Financial Management,* Winter 1981, pp. 39–44.

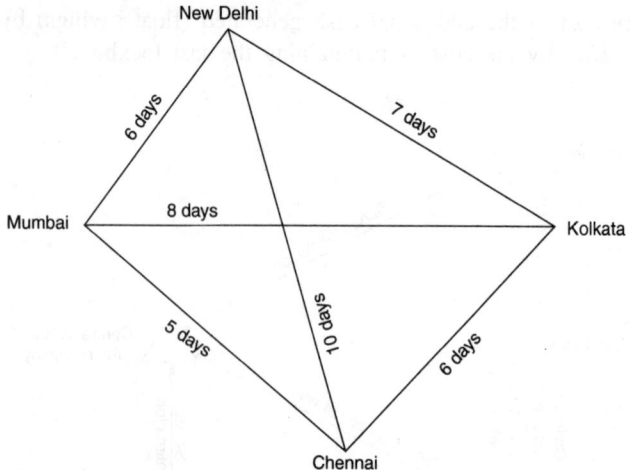

Figure 5.9 Postal distances among four cities.

Table 5.19 Cost–Benifit Analysis of Lock Box Locations

	Kolkata	Mumbai	New Delhi	Chennai
Commission charged by the bank per item processed	Rs. 5.50	5.25	5.60	5.00
Cost of maintaining each lockbox	Rs.10,000	10,000	10,000	10,000
Other fixed costs	Rs. 6000	8000	4000	6000
Opportunity cost of capital	15%	15%	15%	15%
Minimum balance to be maintained at the designated lockbox bank	Rs. 5 lakh	10 lakh	7.5 lakh	5 lakh

Customer-concentration Approach

Under this approach the customers of a zone either mail their remittances to the first lockbox or to the lockbox, (if) located in their zone.

On the basis of the information given in the above problem we first calculate the collection float accruing at central collection system in Kolkata (Table 5.20).

Table 5.20 Collection Float in Kolkata (HO)

	Average collection per day (Rs.) (1)	Present collection time in Kolkata (days) (2)	Total collection float (col. 1 × col. 2) (Rs.) (3)
Kolkata	300,000	1 + 1 = 2	600,000
Mumbai	200,000	8 + 1 = 9	1,800,000
New Delhi	160,000	7 + 1 = 8	1,280,000
Chennai	100,000	6 + 1 = 7	700,000
		Total	4,380,000

Notes: 1. Average collection per day is calculated as:
(Average value of a cheque × Number of such cheques)/365

For example, in New Delhi, average collection per day will be

$$(80,000 \times 730)/365 = \text{Rs. } 160,000$$

2. Intracity mailing time of one day is added to all postal delays amongst cities.
3. Processing delay in Kolkata head office is one day.
   Opportunity cost of the collection floats of the centralised system is Rs. $4,380,000 \times 0.15 = \text{Rs. } 657,000$.

When the company moves to lockbox system, intracity mailing time will be avoided. For city customers, however, one day mailing time to the respective post offices will remain. In Table 5.21 we have calculated floats generated at various lockbox locations.

Table 5.21 Calculation of Floats under Proposed Lockbox System

(Rs. in lakh)

	Average daily collection	Kolkata Days	Kolkata Amount	Mumbai Days	Mumbai Amount	New Delhi Days	New Delhi Amount	Chennai Days	Chennai Amount
Kolkata	3.00	1	3.00	8	24.00	7	21.00	6	18.00
Mumbai	2.00	8	16.00	1	2.00	6	12.00	5	10.00
New Delhi	1.60	7	11.20	6	9.60	1	1.60	10	16.00
Chennai	1.00	6	6.00	5	5.00	10	10.00	1	1.00
Total	7.60	—	36.20	—	40.60	—	44.60	—	45.00

As the total negative float is at its minimum in Kolkata, first lockbox will be located in Kolkata. In order to decide the location of subsequent lockboxes we first go through a process of interaction as follows:

The following chart helps us to decide for the second lockbox when the first lockbox is in Kolkata.

Place	*Negative float*	
Mumbai	36.20 − 16 + 2	= Rs. 22.20 lakh
New Delhi	36.20 − 11.20 + 1.60	= Rs. 26.60 lakh
Chennai	36.20 − 6.00 + 1.00	= Rs. 31.20 lakh

As Mumbai has the least amount of negative float, second lockbox will be located there.

When the first lockbox is in Kolkata, second lockbox in Mumbai, the choice for the third lockbox can be made from the following chart.

Place	*Negative float*	
New Delhi	22.20 − 11.20 + 1.60	= Rs. 12.60 lakh
Chennai	22.20 − 6.00 + 1.00	= Rs. 17.20 lakh

As New Delhi has the minimum float, third lockbox will be located there. If now the fourth lockbox is located in Chennai, we shall find that the float remains in the system will be equal to the total of average daily collection, i.e.

$$\text{Chennai } 12.60 - 6.00 + 1.00 = \text{Rs. } 7.60 \text{ lakh}$$

Having thus calculated the negative float at all possible lockbox locations, we now make a cost-benefit analysis in Table 5.22 to decide appropriate number of lockboxes and places of their location.

Table 5.22   Cost-benefit Analysis of Lockbox Locations

(Rs. in lakh)

No. of lockboxes (1)	Negative float due to time lag (2)	Negative float due to minimum bank balance (3)	Gross negative float (4)	Opportunity cost @ 15% (5)	Cost of managing lockbox (6)	Bank commission (7)	Other fixed costs (8)	Total cost (9)
No. box	4,380,000	500,000	4,880,000	732,000	—	14,795	6000	752,795
1. Box (Kolkata)	3,620,000	500,000	4,120,000	618,000	10,000	14,795	6000	648,795
2. Boxes (Kolkata and Mumbai	2,220,000	1,500,000	3,720,000	558,000	20,000	14,703	14,000	606,703
3. Boxes (Kolkata, Mumbai and New Delhi)	1,260,000	2,250,000	3,510,000	526,500	30,000	14,776	18,000	589,276
4. Boxes (Kolkata, Mumbai, New Delhi, and Chennai)	760,000	2,750,000	3,510,000	526,500	40,000	14,526	24,000	605,026

The optimal solution, as revealed from Table 5.22, is to have three lockboxes (Kolkata, Mumbai and New Delhi) where the total costs are at their minimum.

It has been assumed that even when Kolkata office received and banked cheques, it had to maintain a minimum balance of Rs. 500,000 in the bank account and incur other fixed costs of Rs. 6000.

The principle on which this optimization process has been worked out is that when only one box is located in a particular zone, customers of the remaining zones will mail their cheques to that lockbox. When a second box is located, the customers of that zone, cease to mail their remittance to the first lockbox, instead they send their remittances to the lockbox now located in their zone; the customers of the remaining zones will continue to mail their cheques to the first lockbox. For example, in the present case, Chennai customers will continue to mail their remittances to (Kolkata lockbox only because no box is located in Chennai.

Greedy Approach

Unlike the previous one, customers under this approach are not tied either to the first lockbox or to the one located in their zone only. Here, customers belonging to a particular zone may be asked to mail their cheques to a lockbox located in another zone (which need not be the first lockbox) if that results in cost savings. This approach, popularly known as *Greedy algorithm,* was first proposed by Levy in 1966.[30] The solution to the lockbox location problem under Greedy algorithm is approached by systematically adding new

---

30. Levy, F.K., "An Application of Heuristic Problem Solving to Accounts Receivables Management", *Management Science,* February 1966, pp. B236–244.

collection points to the system only if it reduces the cost of the overall cash collection system of the firm. The experiment continues till an additional lockbox is unable to cause further cost savings.

The first step towards setting up Greedy algorithm is to clearly define and segregate costs into variable and fixed. Examples of variable costs are opportunity cost of collection float, processing charges per instrument handled by the bank etc. Fixed costs include general administrative overheads, cost of maintaining (managing) a lockbox, opportunity cost of maintaining a minimum balance in the local bank which handles the lockbox and so forth. Let us explain this approach by calling back the information which has been processed in Table 5.21 and summarised in Table 5.23.

Table 5.23 Generation of Collection Float in Possible Lockbox Locations

	No. of cheques	Kolkata (Rs.)	Mumbai (Rs.)	New Delhi (Rs.)	Chennai (Rs.)
Kolkata	1095	300,000	2,400,000	2,100,000	1,800,000
Mumbai	365	1,600,000	200,000	1,200,000	1,000,000
New Delhi	730	1,120,000	960,000	160,000	1,600,000
Chennai	500	600,000	500,000	1,000,000	100,000
Total	2690	3,620,000	4,060,000	4,460,000	4,500,000
Processing cost per instrument (Rs.)		5.50	5.25	5.60	5.00

Variable costs:

(a) Processing cost per instrument as given at the bottom of Table 5.23.
(b) Opportunity costs of collection float @ 15 percent p.a.

Fixed costs include the following:

	Kolkata	Mumbai	New Delhi	Chennai
Cost of maintaining a lockbox	Rs. 10,000	10,000	10,000	10,000
Opportunity cost of maintaining minimum balance in bank @15%	Rs. 75,000	150,000	112,500	75,000
Other fixed costs	Rs. 6000	8000	4000	6000
Total	Rs. 91,000	168,000	126,500	91,000

Variable cost calculation for different locations are given in Table 5.24 along with their fixed costs.

Table 5.24 Cost Calculations for Alternative Lockbox Locations

		Kolkata	Mumbai	New Delhi	Chennai
Kolkata	Rs.	51,022.50	365,748.75	321,132.00	275,475.00
Mumbai	Rs.	242,007.50	31,916.25	182,044.00	151,825.00
New Delhi	Rs.	172,015.00	147,832.50	28,088.00	243,650.00
Chennai	Rs.	92,750.00	77,625.00	152,800.00	17,500.00
Total variable costs	Rs.	557,795.00	623,122.50	684,064.00	688,450.00
Fixed costs	Rs.	91,000.00	168,000.00	126,500.00	91,000.00
Total cost	Rs.	648,795.00	791,122.50	810,564.00	779,450.00

As Kolkata has the lowest total cost, it is the best single point location of the lockbox to which customers of all zones will mail their cheques, the total cost of cash collection being Rs. 648,795. Any further addition of lockbox to the system would be feasible only when it reduces this cost. This is examined by reassignment of customer classes through iterative process. The collection zone that generates the highest savings on costs would be the place where next lockbox will be located. The process will continue till the inclusion of an additional collection point is unable to reduce the cost further. The iterative process of customers-reassignment is shown below (Table 5.25).

Table 5.25 Savings from Customers Reassignment: First Iteration

	Kolkata	Mumbai	New Delhi	Chennai
Kolkata	—			
Mumbai	—	210,091.25	59,963.50	90,182.50
New Delhi	—	24,182.50	143,927.00	—
Chennai	—	15,125.00	—	75,250.00
Total savings on variable cost	—	249,398.75	203,890.50	165,432.50
Less: Fixed costs	—	168,000.00	126,500.00	91,000.00
Net savings		81,398.75	77,390.50	74,432.50

Table 5.25 is constructed by comparing the variable costs associated with each possible centre with that of Kolkata centre (where the first lockbox is located). If the variable costs associated with one centre is more than that of Kolkata centre, there is no cost savings and hence, that centre is ignored. For example, variable costs at Mumbai, New Delhi and Chennai (first row of Table 5.24) are all more than that of Kolkata and hence, ignored. But variable costs at Mumbai–Mumbai is less than that in Kolkata–Mumbai (second row of Table 5.24), hence it is included. As Mumbai centre is registering highest cost savings, customers of Mumbai, New Delhi and Chennai will be directed to mail their remittances to Mumbai lockbox instead of to Kolkata.

In the second iteration we examine the possibility of a third lockbox centre by comparing the cost savings at other two centres with that of the Mumbai centre. This is done in Table 5.26.

Table 5.26 Savings from Customers Reassignment: Second Iteration

	Kolkata	Mumbai	New Delhi	Chennai
Kolkata	—	—	—	—
Mumbai	—	—	—	—
New Delhi	—	—	119,744.50	—
Chennai	—	—	—	60,125.00
Total savings on variable cost			119,744.50	60,125.00
Less: Fixed costs			126,500.00	91,000.00
			(−) 6,755.00	(−) 30,875.00

Table 5.26 reveals that although there will be savings on variable costs at New Delhi and Chennai centres, fixed costs associated with these two

centres outweigh savings on variable costs. When reassignment of customer classes are considered, as in Greedy algorithm, we find that it is most cost-effective to have lockboxes situated at Kolkata and Mumbai only. Total cost of collection under this system will be Rs. 648,795 – 81,398.75 = Rs. 567,396.25.

We have seen that under customer-concentration approach total costs of the collection system is Rs. 589,276 with three lockboxes. If we follow the Greedy algorithm, the net cost savings will be Rs. 589,276 – 567,396.25 = Rs. 21,879.75 with only two lockbox centres.[31]

Although in our example, the two-centre lockbox system has been found to be most cost effective, the Greedy algorithm does not always guarantee an optimal solution. It has been found that the collection centre that is best single-point system might not be in the best two-point system. However, the algorithm is simple and straightforward and is readily programmable in a computer which has increased its popularity in real-life applications.

Once a cash collection system is installed in a firm it would be necessary to put it under periodical review to incorporate changes in the system. Necessity for such changes may come from changes in interest rate, bank charges, sales volume and, customers moving from one place to the other. At times, the changes may be so overwhelming that a review of their long-term effect may suggest adding or dropping some collection centres to or from the system.

OTHER INSTRUMENTS FOR CASH COLLECTION

We are discussing below a few instruments or methods which are gaining popularity in Western countries particularly due to development of electronic payment system. In India some of the methods/instruments are already in use and for some, a beginning has already been made by the corporate sector.

Preauthorised Cheques

Under this system a customer deposits with the supplier firm pre-signed cheques. The date of the cheque corresponds to the date payment is due. The

---

31. The Greedy algorithm articulated by N.C. Hill and W.L. Sartoris in *Short-term Financial Management: Text and Cases,* Prentice Hall, Englewood Cliffs, New Jersey, 1992 is as follows: The total cost function (TC) is defined as

$$TC = \sum_{k=1}^{k} F_k Y_k + \sum_{k=1}^{k} \sum_{c=1}^{c} N_c (iA_c T_{ck} + h_k) X_{ck},$$

where

c = number of customer groups
k = number of collection centres
i = daily opportunity cost
N_c = number of items from collection group c
A_c = average size of an item in group c
T_{ck} = average total time for an item in group c to be sent through collection site k
h_k = variable cost per item at collection point k
F_k = fixed cost of collection point k
Y_k = 1 if collection point k is in the system, 0 otherwise
X_{ck} = 1 if group c is assigned to collection point k, 0 otherwise.

payee-firm deposits this cheque on the appointed date with its banker who initiates fund transfer through normal clearing. Under this system entire mail float is avoided. Monopoly sellers like Hindustan Unilever is practising a variation of this system for a long time. Customers keep with the company pre-signed bank cheque book. The company having despatched the goods to the customer's destination will put the date on a cheque, fill up the amount column corresponding to the value despatched and send it to the bank for clearing/collection. In many cases, Hindustan Unilever gets the payment even before the customer actually received the goods!

The system of payment is also widely used in installment or deferred payment arrangements.

When preauthorised payment system is linked through automated clearing house (ACH) not only that the payment is received faster, it also reduces lot of paper work and administrative costs.

Electronic Funds Transfer

With the development of electronic transfer media, corporate to corporate payments are made through the banking/ACH system across the globe in seconds. The savings of float and administrative overheads and certainity of cash flows are quite significant.

Several variations of this payment system are observed; several other variations are also emerging very fast with the establishment of direct computer linkage with the receiving firm (payee), the bank and the customer (payer). Under one such system the customer may send an electronic payment through the banking/ACH system to the firm's (payee's) collection bank which immediately credits the firm's account and sends the remittance advice electronically through computer terminal. As the format used is the one that has passed through the banking/ACH system the payee has no need to match payment and remittance data.

In another system a company (payee) may send an electronic debit through the banking/ACH system by which the customer's (payer's) account is debited simultaneously with the credit of the company's account, provided of course the payee has sufficient balance in his account. The last point has made the system somewhat less popular to both the payer and the payee. For the former he has to part with the control over his cash balance partly to the payee and for the latter, the chance that when the electronic debit is being effected the customer may not have balance in the account.

A variation of the above system has been developed by which the customer sends electronically coded advice to the payee authorising him to debit his account electronically for a specified amount. This takes care of the anxiety of both the payer and the payee as in the above method.

Electronic payment media though has tremendous potential, it needs a lot of change in the attitude of both the payer and the payee. A paperless situation is slow to gain acceptance. There are situations when some customers might have switched over to electronic payment media but some other may continue to pay by cheques which may make the electronic payment media less cost-effective because capital cost of installation of electronic payment system is quite high. Another problem originates from the customers' side who may not be willing to forego the float they enjoy under the cheque system of payment through mail.

Settlement Payments

Where a company is both a payer and a payee, like airlines, oil companies, electricity, coal companies etc. receivables and payables between two companies may be netted off periodically on agreed dates, say monthly or quarterly. This arrangement eliminates all the collection floats between the two companies and saves on administrative costs. Specific benefits or losses will occur to a company periodically depending upon whether on the settlement date it is a payee company or a payer company.

In conclusion, we may say that in designing a cash collection system and making a choice of instruments for collection, a totally selfish approach may not always pay. Pushing the customers too much to drastically reduce the collection float may quicken the cash flow but destroy the relationship with the customer. Similar may be the case when a numerical cost-benefit analysis of the existing collection system suggests closing down of some of the collection points, but considering the long-term relationship with the customers in a particular zone and that with the collecting bank it may not always be desirable for a firm to close down these collection points.

SUMMARY

Cash is the lifeline of an organisation. A sustained growth of an organisation depends on the cashability of the profit, not the profit per se as reflected in the income statement. The rising profit curve of an organisation may mislead managers to pursue high rates of growth, which are unsustainable due to the actual cash position of the company. This leads to continuous erosion of liquidity, and may even make a company sick.

There has not been much of cash management in Indian enterprises due to the easy availability of working capital finance from banks. However, recently, cash management as a discipline is emerging in the country.

Three main activities contribute to the cash flow:

- *Operating activities* cover cash flows relating to all revenue generating activities of the organisation.
- *Investing activities* cover cash flows arising from investments.
- *Financing activities* cover cash flows arising out of all capital and debt issues of the organisation.

For a finance manager faced with the task of planning the cash flows, the goal must be that all *priority outflows* be met fully out of operating cash flows (OCF) while all *discretionary outflows* be met with the remaining balance of in conjunction with the financial flows. If this rule is violated, there is a danger for the enterprise getting into a debt-trap.

The cash flow concept is more useful in the short-term, but does not tell much about the state of the financial structure of the business over a long-term. It is only a combination of cash flow analysis and funds flow analysis that gives the total view.

The fundamental difference between funds and cash is that the former is a liability and the latter is an asset. A funds inflow would definitely increase the total assets level of the enterprise but may not necessarily increase its cash level. Funds thus precede assets, and encompass all assets transactions of an enterprise.

One of the major sources of liquidity problems in an enterprise is the mismatch between current payments and current receipts. This may happen due to a lengthening of the pipeline of cash. The net working capital provides an important cushion against this. Moreover, this also serves as an index for impending liquidity crises. The *net working capital ratio* (NWCR) is used as a measure in this regard.

At the macro-level of the firm, the test of liquidity is the ability of the firm to meet its cash obligations when they are due and to exploit sudden opportunities in the market.

The ultimate result of illiquidity is bankruptcy. However, corporate managers take several actions to stem the process. This series of actions may be:

1. Utilise unavailed credit limits
2. Sell marketable securities
3. Negotiate spacing of repayment schedules of term liabilities
4. Negotiate for enhancement of short-term credit facilities with the bank
5. Defer payment of suppliers' bills
6. Advance buyers' payment
7. Reduce cash outflows
8. Sell assets
9. Refer to the Board for Industrial and Financial Reconstruction

A measure of liquidity should indicate the level of solvency and the financial flexibility of a firm. For outside creditors, the *current ratio* is a good measure of liquidity, but a high current ratio blocks costly long-term fund. The *quick ratio* or *acid test* is also used for measurement. However, both these ratios may be manipulated, such as by removing part of the cash balance to offset some current liabilities. Turnover ratios are also used as liquidity measures, but the net working capital ratio is a superior liquidity measure.

A finer measure is the *net liquidity ratio* (NLR), which takes into account the unavailed credit limits enjoyed by the enterprise with banks. It indicates the ability of the firm to pay up immediately the most liquid liabilities.

Another liquidity measure is the *sales cash conversion cycle* (SCCC). The shorter the SCCC the better is the liquidity position of the enterprise and lesser is the financing requirement.

Yet another liquidity measure, which takes into account uncertainty of future cash flows, is the uncertainty factor, or Lambda, developed by GW Emery.

The *health ratio* is a single liquidity measure that can measure and predict an impending liquidity crisis. It is based on a simple definition of liquidity: Funds Inflow ≥ Funds Outflow. So long as it is greater than 1, the firm has no liquidity problem.

The decision to have a particular amount of liquidity is a tradeoff between the expected cost of maintaining insufficient liquidity and the cost of carrying liquid resources. The ultimate decision depends on the risk profile of an organization. The risk profile also determines the various forms in which liquidity is held. A highly risk-averse enterprise may hold the entire liquidity amount in cash and bank balances whereas a risk-oriented one may hold the amount in market securities. Between these extremes, the finance manager may like to divide the liquid resources between primary liquidity and secondary liquidity.

In order to know what should be the optimal cash and bank balances that must be maintained, or what quantity of securities be sold, two types of models may be used:

Certainty models

- **Baumol's cash-EOQ model:** This model has a portfolio of cash and marketable securities. The EOQ approach is extended to derive the optimal level of cash replacement that minimises the total costs.

Uncertainty models

- **Miller and Orr model:** When uncertainty in cash outflows is very high, stochastic methods must be used to find solutions. In this model, two control limits of cash holding are set. When cash balance reaches the upper limit, a transfer from cash to marketable securities takes place and when it reaches the lower limit, the opposite happens.

- **Stone model:** Here, outer and inner control limits are set. When the outer limit is triggered, the finance manager checks with the forecasts for the next pre-determined days. If these are now outside the inner limits, he orders buying or selling of securities.

Cash flow forecasting is not an isolated exercise; it must be aligned with the goal of the organisation itself, based on the strategic plan. Different time-horizons like long-term, medium-term and short-term are used for forecasting.

As a business must always remain sensitive and alert to changes, cash flow forecasts should be drawn up for the worst case, best case and as-is scenarios. Several statistical techniques are used in forecasting growth variables, but human judgement always plays an important role in this respect.

A sensitivity analysis of important variables is also important to assess the impact of such variables on the cash flows.

There is a time-lag between the customer's making the payment to amount becoming disbursible cash. The primary objective of a cash system is to minimise this time chain, or float. The collection sys' provide relevant information to the firm as to when the payment has become disbursible, and who made the payment. Float may be internal, or generated by a firm, or external, which evolves outside the organizational system.

Since the postal mailing system is the dominant means for remitting payments, a cash collection system will have to be designed around it. A typical system will consist of several collection centres, a network of local banks and an information system. A firm may desire to operate its own cash collection system, or it may appoint local agents say banks, to contract out the receiving, processing and depositing cheques.

The firm may also opt for a *lockbox system* wherein the customers, instead of mailing directly to the local branch of the bank, will mail their cheques to a post office lockbox rented by the company at appropriate locations. The designated branch of the local bank will collect the cheques at frequent intervals and put them on clearing. In this way, the firm can reduce the total collection float for the cost of managing the lockboxes. Two approaches are used in this regard:

- *Customer-concentration approach,* where the customers of a zone mail their remittances to the lockbox of their zone.
- *Greedy approach,* in which the customers are not tied to a single lockbox, but mail their cheques to the one that results in the greatest cost savings.

Other instruments for cash collection include:

- *Preauthorised cheques* where a customer deposits with the supplier pre-signed cheques, with the date corresponding to the due date.
- Electronic funds transfer.
- *Settlement payment,* when receivables and payables between two companies are netted off periodically.

CHAPTER 6

Management of Accounts Payable

> *Their Lordships disperse in a single file*
> *With three Judgements on a single life*

INTRODUCTION

Accounts payable includes *trade credit* and *accrued expenses* which together provide finance to the operations of a business on an ongoing basis. This is the reason why these are often called 'Spontaneous', self-adjusting sources of financing. As long as a business remains a *going concern*, this financing is available more or less in proportion to the level of operation, under given *terms of trade* and practices of a particular industry to which a firm belongs. These practices, over a period of time, attain some rigidity which is difficult to change except, when the industry is dominated by *monopoly suppliers*.

TRADE CREDIT

Accounts payable is the opposite face of *accounts receivable*. The former exists because of the existence of the latter. If in an industry, there is no accounts receivable, there shall never be accounts payable. The dominant part of accounts payable is *trade credit* which is first offered by the seller of goods which, when accepted by the buyer, creates accounts payable in the books of accounts of the latter. Hence, accounts payable policy of an enterprise depends, to a very large extent, on the accounts receivable policy of the supplier. There is not much scope for manoeuvering when an enterprise is a taker of trade credit.

In Chapter 3, we have discussed at length why trade credit is a viable option over institutional financing in many cases, and why in the first place, trade credit is offered by a supplier. The dominant reasons behind the origination of trade credit are summarised below to clear the ground for this Chapter.

Trade credit provides a firm access to fund that it is unable to raise through normal institutional channels because of its inability to meet the given standards of *creditworthiness*. Or, even if it could raise such finance, the *risk premium* that will be levied on the firm by the institutional system, because of dilution of standard, will be uneconomical to the firm. Suppliers being close to the buyers have better *information* about the creditworthiness of a buyer and also greater control over him than the institutional financing agencies and hence, they can offer better terms to the buyers in extending trade credit. By doing so, both the seller who has a better access to capital and the buyer who lacks such access, share the financial market tariff. Unlike institutional financing, credit terms are generally found to be invariant to the credit quality of the buyer because, when a decision to grant credit has been taken, the credit terms tend to follow the market or industry practice. Hence, trade credit effectively reduces the price to the low credit-quality buyers.[1]

Even when a supplier does not enjoy financing advantage over the financial institutions, he may still use trade credit as a means of price discrimination particularly, in a product market segment which is highly price-elastic. A natural reason why this segment's demand may be more price-elastic is because it is typically credit-rationed. If it is so, trade credit both lowers the effective price of the goods and permits this segment to express its demand.[2]

We find that under both the circumstances mentioned above, it is the sellers who supply the trade credit, determine the terms and hence, influence the accounts payable policy of the recipient of trade credit.[3]

In many countries of the developed world, like the United States, trade credit is the single most important source of finance.[4] Large firms are found to be net suppliers of credit. It is also found that in many US firms, aggregate accounts payable often exceeds aggregate of inventories. This may be partly due to LIFO method of inventory valuation prevalent in the United States, but mostly it may be due to liberal trade credit policies of large firms on the face of rather stringent credit standards of banks and financial institutions.

Implicit Credit to Large Companies

In India, separate data on small firms are not available. However, we can get some idea of the status of trade credit from the financial data of Indian industries given in Table 6.1.

We may notice from Table 6.1, that in Indian industry though debtors turnover ratio has come down sharply, such is not the case with creditors turnover ratio. Unlike matured economies where corporate sector has been net suppliers of trade credit (sundry debtors > sundry creditors), in case of Indian industry which, though has been so till about 2001–2002, has now become net takers of trade credit, and the trend is increasing (Compare Table 3.1 with Table 6.1). Table 6.1 also reveals that sundry creditors exceed raw materials inventory by a considerable margin. When we consider the total inventories we find that creditors are covering almost 1.5 times the total inventories. The margin of difference is also increasing at a fast rate. The trend suggests that resort to trade credit is on the rise in Indian manufacturing sector. We have

---

1. Peterson, M. and R.G. Rajan, "The Effect of Credit Market Competition on Lending Relationships", *Quarterly Journal of Economics*, Vol. 60, pp. 407–444, 1995.
2. Peterson, M.A. and R.G. Rajan, "Trade Credit: Theories and Evidence", *The Reviews of Financial Studies,* Fall 1997, pp. 661–691.
3. The situation will, however, be different when a buyer holds a monopsonic position in the market.
4. Peterson, M.A., et al., *ibid.*

Table 6.1 Movement of Accounts Payables (Sundry Creditors) in Indian Industry

(Rupees in crore)

Particulars/Year	1997–98	1998–99	1999–00	2000–01	2001–02	2002–03	2003–04	2004–05	2005–06
Inventories									
1. Raw material and stores	53,582	54,408	61,546	60,766	60,757	68,461	76,196	99,614	115,439
2. Work-in-process	16,447	19,615	19,554	18,906	17,531	19,507	20,768	26,985	30,806
3. Finished goods	43,958	46,706	57,286	64,120	58,020	68,801	70,786	80,126	90,692
Total	113,987	120,729	138,386	143,792	136,308	156,769	167,750	206,725	236,937
Sundry creditors	121,850	137,594	157,495	175,261	189,342	210,971	253,878	295,806	325,405
Sundry creditors as percentage of:									
1. Raw materials and stores inventory	227.41	252.89	255.90	288.41	311.63	308.16	333.19	296.95	281.88
2. Total inventories as above	106.89	113.97	113.80	121.88	138.91	134.57	151.34	143.09	137.34
Debtors turnover ratio (days)	61	56	53	50	52	48	42	40	38
Creditors turnover ratio (days)	82	83	78	70	76	74	78	74	73

Basic data source: Industry: Financial Aggregates and Ratios, Centre for Monitoring Indian Economy. All the ratios are calculated from the basic data.

shown in Chapter 3 that this is due to rising market power of Indian corporate sector which unlike matured economies, exercise this leverage to squeeze both the customers and suppliers.

Bulk of the suppliers credit the large corporate is enjoying comes from unorganised sector. In India, despite low creditworthiness, small scale sector has been enjoying for long, preferential (differential) rate of interest from banks as they belong to the priority sector. In fact, in India till recently, cost of credit to large companies has been higher than that of small scale firms. The large firms implicitly enjoy this cheaper finance by resorting to long line of credit from their suppliers. Priority sector lending might have benefited the large sector more than the small sector and hence, the former does not have much of an incentive to reverse the process and become net supplier of trade credit. During the post-liberalisation period this interest rate differential is gradually being withdrawn and it is hoped that once the interest rate is fully decontrolled, trade credit practices will evolve around market-determined interest rate. The regulation-determined tariff will be replaced by market tariff.

MANAGING ACCOUNTS PAYABLE

Accounts payable originates from the production budget of an enterprise but enters into the books of accounts when materials are delivered and taken to stores. While timing of purchases or placing an order is the domain of materials procurement manager, he will be able to increase the value to the firm if he works in close collaboration with the finance manager. While discussing inventory management in Chapter 4, we have shown that quantity discount for large purchases acts as a powerful incentive for a purchase manager, even to the point of allurement, to place large orders. But cost-benefit analysis may only suggest an optimal size of the purchase order under a given range of discount offers and cost of capital. It is not only for the optimum trade-off that the purchase manager needs to collaborate with the finance manager, it is also the arrangement of fund to finance the purchases in a capital scarce economy like India, that the role of finance manager often becomes more important than the procurement manager, because a good buy may just not be possible for want of fund. Seeking appropriate credit line from the supplier is the first job towards this direction wherefrom the accounts payable management begins.

While the goal of accounts payable management is to provide as much spontaneous financing as possible at zero cost, a firm has to operate within a given terms of purchase (which is mostly dependent upon market practice). This determines the cost to the firm of financing obtained from the suppliers.

Terms of Purchase

Terms of purchase generally consists of a credit period and a cash discount for early payment. If the term is quoted as 2/10 net 30, it means that a 2 percent discount on the billed amount will be available, if paid within 10 days; otherwise normal credit period of 30 days will be applicable. There may or may not be any penal clause attached to the terms. Penalty comes in the form of upfront payment on the bill amount, if it is not paid by the due date.

We have said earlier that cash discount has great attraction to the buyer because it effectively reduces the price of the materials, as the true price of a material is ultimately the cash paid for it. It follows, therefore, that if the cash discount is not availed of, the buyer imposes a penalty upon himself, or in other words, he sets upon to pay interest equivalent to the cash discount foregone. We have discussed later the effect of cash discount with the help of an example.

Stretching Accounts Payable

Cost-benefit analysis of an accounts payable policy will invariably rest on minimising the net present value (NPV) of disbursement. The model will obviously include cash discount as a benefit-variable. But minimisation of NPV of an accounts payable disbursement provides an incentive to the finance manager to stretch the payment beyond the due date, i.e. to increase the float. Longer the time for payment, lower is the net present value of such payment and higher the value to the firm. However, the policy of *stretching accounts payable* has some limitations. First limitation is obviously the provision of penal interest. If the supplier is holding a commanding position in the market, he would enforce the penal provision even when the payment is delayed only by a few days. But generally, most of the suppliers do not resort to such an action if the delay is within a reasonable level of tolerance (or, if they belong to the lot of small suppliers) because of anxiety to maintain the goodwill of a customer-base. We have mentioned earlier that the market does not take lightly a harsh treatment meted out to a member of the community, and they might retaliate by switching to other suppliers, particularly when there is glut in supply. A finance manager should keep a note of this market behaviour and, stretch payment but only to a reasonable extent.[5]

Next comes the ethical question. Whatever may be the market command of the buyer, the fact remains that he has taken to stock materials supplied by a supplier under agreed terms and conditions. The supplier not only has supplied the materials, he has also agreed, at the same time, to provide finance for purchases. Now having received the materials, if he does not honour the commitments he cannot be regarded as an honest businessman. This practice may not take him a long way. Besides, by not paying in time he would upset the financial planning of the supplier, which might have the effect of delaying the supply of the next lot. The symbiosis is disturbed to the disadvantage of both. Any long-term business relationship can be developed only when the two parties in a transaction consider each other as trading partner.

An attempt is often made to moderate the ethical standard by arguing that as long as the supplier does not demand or press for payment, he does not have the need and hence, the payment could be delayed till he demands, without breaching the ethical boundary. Although there may be some argument which most of the firms do resort to while delaying payment, it cannot pass the ethical standard. If a firm truly wants to be within the ethical boundary of the business, which is ultimately beneficial in the long run, it should remain satisfied with taking the cash discount only and forget about delaying payment beyond the agreed date.

Small firms in the United Kingdom have been complaining of delayed payment by large companies for a long time. The problem was debated nationwide, and in July 1992 the Confederation of British Industries introduced a code of practice: 'Prompt Payers—In Good Company'. More than 700 British companies have signed up the code agreeing to pay within the agreed payment terms. The code runs as follows:

A responsible company should

- *have a clear, consistent policy that it pays bills in accordance with the contract;*
- *ensure that the finance and purchasing departments are both aware of this policy and adhere to it;*
- *agree payment terms at the outset of a deal and stick to them;*
- *not extend or alter payment terms without prior agreement;*
- *provide suppliers with clear guidance on payment procedures;*
- *ensure that there is a system for dealing quickly with complaints and disputes and advise suppliers without delay when invoices or parts of invoices are contested.*

Problems of small scale suppliers in India is more acute. It is time that

---

5. At the same time we must recognise that the supplier is not so naive as to ignore the possibility of delayed payment. He would obviously try to build in, the cost of delay in the price. This aspect will be elaborated later.

Confederation of Indian Industries address these problems and come out with similar codes.

Cost of Stretching

The economic benefit of stretching is, of course, the value of the positive float enjoyed by the firm. It is a function of the amount of payment, the opportunity cost of the firm, and the float days due to stretching. There is no explicit cost in absence of penalty for delayed payment. But there may be indirect economic costs due to stretching. One such cost is gradual erosion of goodwill leading to poor credit rating in the market. This will be reflected in decreasing level of credit available from the market, not necessarily restricted to the suppliers whose payment has been stretched.

Delayed payment also sours the relationship with the supplier. Flexibility and mutual accommodation, at times of special need, are the two important outcomes of this relationship. When this is hampered by the practice of stretching, supplier's behaviour will be reflected in unfulfilled or delayed supplies at times of tightening of the materials market.

While the above indirect economic costs are true, in general, the magnitude of these costs depends upon the bargaining power subsisting between the customer and the supplier. It is also difficult to quantify these costs, but a finance manager has to keep them in mind while pursuing a policy of stretching payment.

THE MODEL

We can now develop a model to evaluate the economics of stretching accounts payable.

$$C = V\left[\frac{1 + D}{1 + t_s k} + I\right]$$

where
C = cost to the firm for making delayed payment
V = value of the order
D = direct costs of delayed payment calculated on Re. 1
t_s = number of days payment is stretched
k = daily opportunity cost of the firm on Re. 1
I = indirect costs of stretching payment

Example A seller offers credit term of 30 days. He generally does not mind if payment is delayed by say, 10 days, but beyond that he imposes a penalty of 1.5 percent on the invoice value for every month of delay. The finance manager of the buyer-firm is required to evaluate the alternatives of stretching payment. The firm's opportunity cost of capital is 15 percent p.a.

The daily opportunity cost of the firm (k) is $15/36,500 = 0.000411$. Assuming average invoice value of the order (V) is Rs. 10,000, cost (c) to the firm for 10 days' stretching will be

$$C = 10,000 \left[\frac{1+0}{1+40\,(0.000411)} \right] = \text{Rs.}\,9838.26$$

If he delays payment by 30 days, the permissible float of 10 days may not be available. In addition, he shall be required to pay a penal interest of 1.5 percent. Cost to the firm in such a situation will be

$$C = 10,000 \left[\frac{1+0.015}{1+60\,(0.000411)} \right] = \text{Rs.}\,9905.72$$

It is obvious that under the given circumstances, it is preferable to stretch payment only to 40 days where cost to the firm is lowest. It must be clear by now that (C) is nothing but net present value of a payment option which, as the objective function of accounts payable policy, is found to be minimised only in the first case.

Second option will be viable only when opportunity cost of the firm is very high, say 30 percent p.a., other things remaining same, as the following calculation will show:

$$\textit{Option}\ 1:\ \ C = 10,000 \left[\frac{1+0}{1+40\,(0.000822)} \right] = \text{Rs.}\,9681.67$$

$$\textit{Option}\ 2:\ \ C = 10,000 \left[\frac{1+0.015}{1+60\,(0.000822)} \right] = \text{Rs.}\,9672.93$$

Although the cost to the firm under the second option is lower than the first option, the benefit accruing to the firm is very small, only Rs. 10 per Rs. 10,000 order. It is unlikely that the firm will resort to delaying payment by 20 days for such a small benefit.

Similar calculations can be made for varying percentages of penal interest rates, keeping other things constant.

Effect of Cash Discount

In the above example, cash discount is not considered. Suppose, now the sellar offers a 2 percent cash discount if the payment is made within 10 days, otherwise normal credit period of 30 days is available (2/10 net 30). Other terms and conditions shall remain unchanged.

As we have indicated earlier, cash discount effectively reduces the price of the material. In the present situation the price is reduced to Rs. 9800 when the discount is availed of. If the payment is made in 30 days no discount is available, and hence cost to the firm will be $\dfrac{200}{9800} \times \dfrac{365}{30} = 0.2483$ or 24.83%.

Option 1: If the buyer makes payment on the 10th day, present value cost of the payment will be Rs. 9800 against which other options will be evaluated.

Option 2: If payment is made on the 40th day (assuming no penalty), the payer will lose the discount; full payment of Rs. 10,000 will have to be made, but the firm will enjoy 10 days stretch float. Hence, present value cost will be Rs. 9838.26 at an opportunity cost of 15 percent p.a. as calculated before. The present value cost will be Rs. 9681.69 at an opportunity cost of 30 percent p.a.

Option 3: If payment is made on 60th day, the payer will be required to pay a penal interest rate of 1.50 percent on the invoice value of the bill. Present value cost of exercising such option at 15 percent opportunity cost, is Rs. 9905.72. The amount will be Rs. 9672.93 at an opportunity cost of 30 percent p.a. as shown before.

Analysis of the three options indicate that at an opportunity cost of 15 percent p.a., option 2 is marginally superior to option 1, i.e. Rs. 38.26 per Rs. 10,000 order. The buyer may not exercise option 2 for such a small benefit. option 3 is clearly ruled out because the negative differential is quite substantial.

When the opportunity cost is 30 percent p.a., both options 2 and 3 are clearly better than option 1. But between option 2 and option 3 the payer may go in for option 2 despite a positive differential which is just about Rs. 10 per Rs. 10,000 order for reasons discussed earlier.

We should point out here that even though the arithmetic of cost-benefit analysis might favour one option against the other, it is ultimately not the cost or net benefit but the availability fund at the right time that weighs heavily in the mind of the finance manager. In a capital-scarce economy like India, funds, even if at the market rate of interest, may not always come by. This is more true for a small supplier whose access to institutional credit is limited. Any small supplier will testify this fact of business in a real-life situation.

DISBURSEMENT FLOAT MANAGEMENT

While discussing cash management practices in Chapter 5, we have indicated that careful management of disbursement float enables a firm to enjoy additional financing without officially stretching the payment date. But on the other side of the market, the receivables manager would also attempt to minimise the collection float by employing various techniques including installation of lockbox system as we have discussed in Chapters 3 and 5. Hence, it is a game of systems efficiency between buyer and the seller in the matter of disbursement and collection. As long as there exists a systems difference between the two parties, one would always win over the other.[6]

Besides normal clearing and mailing time float (available locally) that a payer enjoys by making disbursement by cheques (which may not, however, be available if the seller insists on payment by bank draft), the float time can be

---

6. We should point out here that with the emergence of electronic payment facility and issuance of multicity cheques the benefit from float managemtnt is getting narrower.

increased by making payment from different locations. The methodology is just the opposite to what the collection department of the seller will do when customers are concentrated in different parts of the country.

Example Suppose a firm located in Kolkata gets its supplies of different inputs from Guwahati, Ahmedabad and Nagpur. Average monthly payments to suppliers in these cities are given below:

City	Amount of monthly payment (Rs.)
Kolkata	409,600
Guwahati	972,800
Ahmedabad	563,200
Nagpur	655,400

The firm maintains current accounts in all these cities, which can also be used for making payment to suppliers, if necessary. The suppliers will obviously have their accounts in the cities of their locations. A study of the bank reconciliation statements of disbursement accounts in various cities reveal the following mailing and clearing times between different cities.

Mailing and Clearing Time (Days)

City	Kolkata	Guwahati	Ahmedabad	Nagpur
Kolkata	0	4	5	6
Guwahati	3	0	7	8
Ahmedabad	2	5	0	3
Nagpur	4	6	3	0

Maintenance of current account and its usage for disbursements in each city would cost the firm additionally Rs. 1600 per month including cost of maintaining minimum balance. Cost of capital of the firm is 15 percent p.a.

In Table 6.2 we have made disbursement float analysis of the firm under different locations of bank accounts.

Positive float due to mailing and clearing time in each city is calculated in Table 6.2 by multiplying the payment amount for the city with the maximum of mailing and clearing distance from the city. The principle behind it is that payment to a particular supplier is made from the city with the longest mailing and clearing time. For example, under *two bank accounts* system it is proposed to have a combination of one account in Kolkata and the other in Guwahati. The company will mail cheques for Ahmedabad suppliers from Guwahati rather than from Kolkata because mailing and clearing time between Guwahati and Ahmedabad is highest (7 days), as appearing under the column for Ahmedabad against para 1 (Kolkata) and para 2 (Guwahati). Positive float from Ahmedabad suppliers will, therefore, be Rs. 563,200 × 7 = Rs. 3,942,400.

Maximum positive float under each of the four systems as appearing in Table 6.2 along with cost benefit analysis are summarised in Table 6.3.

Table 6.2 Disbursement Float Analysis under Different Locations of Bank Accounts

(Amount in Rupees)

City/Type	Disbursement float				Total float
	Kolkata	Guwahati	Ahmedabad	Nagpur	
A. Only one bank account in Kolkata					
1. Kolkata	0	3,891,200	2,816,000	3,932,400	10,639,600
2. Guwahati	1,228,800	0	3,942,400	5,243,200	10,414,400
3. Ahmedabad	819,200	4,864,000	0	1,966,200	7,649,400
4. Nagpur	1,638,400	5,836,800	1,689,600	0	9,164,800
B. Two bank accounts					
1. Kolkata and Guwahati	1,228,800	3,891,200	3,942,400	5,243,200	14,305,600
2. Kolkata and Ahmedabad	819,200	4,864,000	2,816,000	3,932,400	12,431,600
3. Kolkata and Nagpur	1,638,400	5,836,800	2,816,000	3,932,400	14,223,600
4. Guwahati and Ahmedabad	1,228,800	4,864,000	3,942,400	5,243,200	15,278,400
5. Guwahati and Nagpur	1,638,400	5,836,800	3,942,400	5,243,200	16,660,800
6. Ahmedabad and Nagpur	1,638,400	5,836,800	1,689,600	1,966,200	11,131,000
C. Three bank accounts					
1. Kolkata, Guwahati and Ahmedabad	1,228,800	4,864,000	3,942,400	5,243,200	15,278,400
2. Kolkata, Guwahati and Nagpur	1,638,400	5,836,800	3,942,400	5,243,200	16,660,800
3. Guwahati, Ahmedabad and Nagpur	1,638,400	5,836,800	3,942,400	5,243,200	16,660,800
4. Ahmedabad, Nagpur, and Kolkata	1,638,400	5,836,800	2,816,000	3,932,400	14,223,600
D. Four bank accounts					
1. Calcutta, Guwahati, Ahmedabad and Nagpur	1,638,400	5,836,800	3,942,400	5,243,200	16,660,800

For Table 6.3 opportunity savings or value of positive float per month under each system is calculated as below.

Say, for system *A* with a daily opportunity cost of 0.000411 @ 15 percent p.a., the value will be:

Rs. 10,639,600 × 0.000411 = Rs. 4372

Cost for each system as appearing under column 4 Table 6.3 is calculated at Rs. 1600 per disbursement account.

We observe that except under system *A*, maximum positive floats under all the other systems are same. But the net benefit is highest under system *B*. Hence, the firm should have two disbursement accounts, one in Guwahati and the other in Nagpur. This optimal solution suggests that suppliers from Kolkata and Guwahati will be paid from Nagpur and Ahmedabad respectively, and Nagpur suppliers will be paid from Guwahati.

Table 6.3 Maximum Positive Floats under Different Systems of Disbursement and their Cost-benefit Analysis

Disbursement systems	Positive float (Rs.)	Opportunity savings @ 15% p.a.	Cost	Net benefit
(1)	(2)	(3)	(4)	(5)
A. One bank account in Kolkata only	10,639,600	4372	1600	2772
B. Two bank accounts in Guwahati and Nagpur	16,660,800	6847	3200	3647
C. Three bank accounts in				
(a) Kolkata, Guwahati, Nagpur	16,660,800	6847	4800	2047
(b) Guwahati, Ahmedabad, Nagpur	16,660,800	6847	4800	2047
D. Four bank accounts in Kolkata, Guwahati, Ahmedabad and Nagpur	16,660,800	6847	6400	447

Supplier-relationship

While it is legitimate to locate disbursement centres at different places and an optimal solution might indicate an appropriate combination of centres under a cost-benefit framework, in practical business situations the borderline consideration is supplier-relationship. A Kolkata supplier may not mind being paid from Nagpur under ordinary circumstances when his cash position is good, but if the situation is otherwise, he might feel let down and this may ultimately affect the buyer's business because no enterprise can sustain itself for long with disgruntled suppliers. Short-term economic benefits should not outweigh the indirect economic costs. All the optimal solutions suggested in this chapter should be subjected to these considerations before adoption.

OTHER ACCRUALS

Many employees of the firm, particularly the salaried ones, do not often realise that they provide credit to the firm on a continuous basis because they receive their salaries and wages only after a period, say a month, or a fortnight, or a week, while they add value to the firm daily by their work. They also supply this credit free of cost. A Rs. 10 lakh wage bill paid at the end of the month is no different from raising a loan from the bank. But in the latter case, it is at an interest cost while in the former case, there is no such charge. When the disbursement of emoluments are paid by account payee cheques, another one to two days' clearing float could be enjoyed by the firm due to bank clearings.

Like trade credit, this is regarded as a spontaneous and flexible source of financing on the assumption that during the busy season, when more employees are needed to increase in production, higher wage bill provides higher level of financing, while during the slack season, the opposite happens. But in India, except in purely seasonal industries like sugar, such flexibility is not generally available due to rather rigid wage and employment structure.

Variable and Fixed Expenses

Other accruals are variable and fixed operating expenses of the firm. These are power, water, municipal rates and taxes, contract maintenance, etc. The variable ones among them increase or decrease with the scale of operations while the fixed expenses do not so much vary with the level of outputs. The fixed expenses are mostly paid after expiry of a period and hence, are similar to salaries and wages in providing finance to the enterprise.

Taxes

In some countries of the developed world income taxes are payable in the period following their accrual. Due to this, the funds stay with the enterprise as payables for quite some time. But under Indian Income Tax Act, estimated tax is required to be paid by a firm as advance tax, hence the scope for using this as a source of financing is rather limited.

Dividends

Dividends to shareholders accrue on the date of closing of the accounts but the amounts are finally disbursed not before three months at the minimum. As such, this is also considered as any other accrual that provides short-period finance to an enterprise.

Limited Flexibility

Although accruals do provide a stable source of finance, the amount is small as compared to trade credit. When we analyse various types of accruals we find that these are much less manoeuvrable than the trade credit because of severe penalty involved in stretching their payments. If, for example, payment of wages and salaries are delayed, it may cause severe disruption in production; if taxes are not paid in time, the Revenue Department may even cause arrest and seizure which would affect the market standing of the enterprise.

OVERTRADING AND THE NEED FOR A GOOD INFORMATION SYSTEM

Although accounts payables are good sources of financing of working capital and available almost free of cost, these are also risk prone, and at times, more risky than even bank finance. Even accepting that stretching is a tolerable practice in the market, payment in time rules the trade. A default in loan repayment may take a longer time to impact upon the enterprise, but a default on creditors' payment have such a snowballing effect on the firm that it may not even allow the minimum time necessary to recover the position. As trade credit provides free financing, there is a tendency among firms to do over-trading, particularly when there is a glut in the market and the suppliers offer longer credit period just to get the stocks out of their godowns. This not only creates problems for inventory management that we have seen in Chapter 4, it also disrupts the cash budget as many payments may fall due at a time while the stocks so bought might not have moved from the stores to production, not to speak of sales that could have created matching cash inflows to meet the payments due. Many firms are found to go bankrupt just because of overtrading.

In order to protect the firm against the situations described above, an enterprise must have a good information and accounting system linked to purchase and cash budgets. In the absence of a good information system, materials may be overbought; several early payment cash discounts may be lost while the cash remains idle. Undue delay in creditors' payment may create market resentment and invite legal actions (particularly for accrued expenses), which may ultimately jeopardise cash forecasting.

Validation

When an invoice is received from a supplier, the first job of the information system is to validate it. The validation is to be done first against the purchase order. Many a time, goods are despatched by the supplier as a matter of routine, which may not have any use for the present. If the order is verbal it must be validated by the purchase manager on the basis of approved purchase budget. The next step in validation is to scrutinise the transport and other related documents to establish the title of the goods despatched. Lastly, it has to be checked with the stores department to find out whether the goods have been received as per the order in undamaged condition and taken to store. Often it is found that the validation process itself takes a very long time. Even in many large companies in India it is found that it takes about two weeks to validate an invoice. The reason behind such a delay is primarily due to lack or absence of synchronisation between various departments which are responsible for validation. The delay may often result in missing the deadline for taking cash discounts, as we have discussed above.

Scheduling of Payment

After the validation, the date for writing the cheque should be scheduled in accordance with the credit terms. Simultaneously, the cash forecast is to be updated. Some companies schedule the cheque writing and update the cash forecast as soon as an invoice enters into validation process. If an invoice is ultimately found to be invalid, the schedule for cheque writing is cancelled and cash forecast is adjusted. The latter system can work for companies when only few invoices are found to be invalid, as otherwise the system's cost may outweigh the benefits derived. While installing an MIS for payables we should see that the system provides a smooth flow of information with minimum reentry of data.

Outsourcing

In countries of the developed world many specialised agencies have come up to take over and manage a part of accounts payable, particularly the disbursement system. In India, only a slow beginning has been made with the advent of computerised information technology. Under this system, the validation and scheduling of payment are done in-house. After that, the file is sent to the disbursing agency who verifies the file, generates payment and remittance information and remit the invoice value to the supplier by debiting the account of the customer. A reconciliation statement is sent to the customer either after making the payment, or periodically.

SUMMARY

Accounts payable is the opposite face of accounts receivable. It includes trade credit and accrued expenses which provide spontaneous, self-adjusting source of finance.

Accounts payable policy of an enterprise depends mostly on the accounts receivable policies of the supplier.

Trade credit provides an access to fund for enterprises with low creditworthiness. A supplier is in a position to provide finance to these firms because of his proximity and control over them as compared to institutional agencies. Trade credit is also used by the supplier for price discrimination.

In the developed world like the United States, large companies are net suppliers of trade credit, but in India, large firms are found to implicitly enjoy the cheaper institutional credits available to the small supplier.

While the goal of accounts payable management is to provide as much spontaneous financing as possible, a firm has to operate within the given terms of purchase which ultimately determine the cost of trade credit of the firm.

Terms of purchase generally consist of a credit period and a cash discount for early payment and also a penalty for delayed payment. Firms are often motivated to stretch accounts payable to enjoy additional float. But it involves also the economic costs of loss of goodwill. Serious ethical questions are also raised against stretching of payments. All these factors are combined in a model to determine the effective costs of various accounts payable policies.

Firms can also enjoy additional float without officially stretching the payment date by locating disbursement centres at places, which optimises enjoyment of disbursement float. A model for arriving at such solution is discussed with examples. But an optimal solution may not always be desirable because it may negatively affect supplier-relationship.

Other accruals include outstanding salaries and wages, overheads, taxes, dividend payments, etc. They do provide spontaneous short-term financing, but a firm has limited flexibility on these sources due to severe organisational and legal implications.

A good information system for accounts payable is necessary not only to protect the firm against overtrading and missed-out discount opportunities, but also for cash forecasting and budgeting. One such MIS is suggested in this chapter. Outsourcing as a part of such MIS has also been discussed.

CHAPTER 7

Financing Working Capital Gap

You protect yourself against the shadows you never see
But the shadows elongate

INTRODUCTION

In the earlier Chapter we have shown that accounts payable provide a stable source of finance for working capital. Although this finance is directly related to inventories, once the funding is done it enters into the general pool of working capital. We have seen in Chapter 1, how current assets are generated along the pipeline of productive-distributive system of an enterprise. These *gross current assets* (GCA) capture fund, or in other words, they need financing. The first dose of financing comes from accounts payables (AP). When such credits are deducted from GCA, what is left is popularly called, *working capital gap* (WCG) in Indian banking parlance. Funding of this gap comes from three sources, viz. bank finance (BF), short-term financial instruments (SFI) and long-term fund sources of the enterprise, known as margin or net working capital (NWC). In algebraic equations these look like the following:

$$\text{GCA} = \text{AP} + \text{BF} + \text{NWC} \qquad (7.1)$$
$$\text{WCG} = \text{GCA} - \text{AP} \qquad (7.2)$$
$$\text{NWC} = \text{GCA} - \text{AP} - \text{BF} \qquad (7.3)$$

FINANCIAL STRUCTURE

In India, banks would not like NWC to become zero or negative. They insist that the current ratio, which is an expression of NWC level of the enterprise, should not be less than one. Even a slip-back in current ratio is viewed unfavourably by a banker. This ratio which was invented by bankers as far back as 1890[1] continues to occupy the centre stage in the credit appraisal system of any commercial bank in India. Liquidity of any business enterprise is still determined by current ratio, though notion of liquidity has undergone substantial changes in modern-day financial management.

Hitherto, current assets are considered in the descending order of their liquidity or shiftability. These are:

(i) Cash
(ii) Marketable securities

---

1. Horrigan, J.O., "A Short History of Financial Ratio Analysis", *The Accounting Review*, April 1968, pp. 284–294. Current Ratio is calculated as Current Assets/Current Liabilities.

389

(iii) Accounts receivable

(iv) Inventories

Quick ratio, which is the more refined form of current ratio, is calculated on the first three current assets which, according to the ruling notion, provide most liquidity to a business.[2] Inventories are considered to be the least liquid among them.

NEW NOTION OF LIQUIDITY

The aforementioned concept of liquidity is found to be narrow, because it does not take into consideration the total operations of a business. Generally speaking, the purpose of liquidity is to ensure smooth operation of a business. As discussed in Chapter 5, functional managers view liquidity as something that could remove the bottlenecks in their respective functions. The manufacturing managers on the shop floor and the marketing managers at various distribution points do not have much use for cash or for that matter, any other current assets, except inventories, to maintain continuity of their respective operations. A firm may have plenty of cash in its till or in the bank, but if there is a shortage of materials in the market, then any amount of cash will not be able to provide liquidity to the manufacturing managers. Production will stop and consequently, the line of distribution will also come to a halt for want of finished goods. The firm as a whole will suffer from a dearth of liquidity, which incidentally, is not due to the absence of cash, but of inventories.

Since the focus of liquidity management is maintenance of a smooth flow of inventories, a finance manager faces a financial bottleneck when he does not have money to acquire inventories. There may be large quantities of materials available in the market, but if the firm does not have enough cash, then in the ultimate analysis, the problem lies in the financial structure or more particularly in the working capital structure of the business, not necessarily in poor current ratio or net working capital. A good working capital structure can do without the two as the following example will clarify.

Suppose, a trader buys uniformly at Rs. 1000 per month on three months' credit and sells uniformly the same amount every month at one month's credit. The policy of the company is to maintain an inventory level of one month's sales. The working capital structure of the firm from the third month onwards will be as below.

Working Capital Structure of the Hypothetical Firm after Three Months

Liabilities	Rs.	Assets	Rs.
Trade creditors	3000	Inventory	1000
		Accounts receivable	1000
		Cash	1000
Total	3000	Total	3000

---

2. Quick Ratio is calculated as (Cash + Marketable Securities + Accounts Receivable)/ Current Liabilities.

It may be noted that the firm has a zero NWC and the current ratio is just one. That is, the firm has financed all the current assets from trade creditors. The policy which has given rise to such a working capital structure of the firm is neither unusual nor unreasonable. The important requirements of such a policy are high creditworthiness maintained with the suppliers, moderate command over them, and strict collection and monitoring systems for receivables.

An examination of the working capital structure shown above will reveal that the firm has built up inventory of one month's consumption and cash of one month's cost of sales. Even if the debtors' realisation is lengthened due to some unforeseen circumstances, the firm can first fall back upon its inventory and then on its cash to maintain continuity of operations, and still pay its creditors without resorting to NWC or any other source of finance.[3]

BANK FINANCE

But in India, such a balance sheet would not be acceptable by a commercial bank at the first instance even if the firm desires to seek bank loan for any expansion or diversification, where similar working capital structure may not continue. The reasons ascribed by banks are that the borrower must have its own stake in all assets that are financed. Besides, all the firms which come for bank finance do not have the kind of market command envisaged in the above example, hence they must have some elbow-room in the form of NWC to fall back upon to pay the creditors in time, including the bank. The kind of balance sheet they look for is given in Figure 7.1.

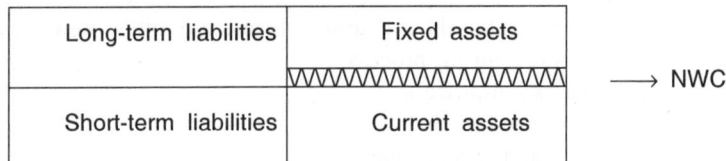

Figure 7.1 Balance sheet.

The principle behind the balance sheet depicted in Figure 7.1 is that, long-term fund of an enterprise should not only finance the whole of fixed assets, but leave something towards financing current assets also, which is nothing but NWC or margin as indicated by the dotted box on the right hand side of the balance sheet. If we look at the balance sheet from the bottom we would find that NWC is nothing but the positive difference between current assets and current liabilities including bank finance as shown in Equation (7.3).

PRINCIPLES OF LENDING

Till mid-1970s the principle of commercial bank lending in India was predominantly security-oriented. It was more or less networth-based,

---

3. Bhattacharya, Hrishikes, *Total Management by Ratios,* 2nd ed., Sage Publications, New Delhi, 2007.

collateralised financing. Major banks were nationalised in 1969 and with that, approach to lending also changed. In 1974, a study group under the chairmanship of P.L. Tandon was formed to examine the existing methods of lending and suggest changes. The group submitted its report in August 1975, which came to be popularly known as Tandon Committee's Report.[4] It was a landmark in the history of bank lending in India. With the acceptance of major recommendations by Reserve Bank of India a new era of lending began in India.

Tandon Committee's Recommendations

Breaking away from the traditional methods of security-oriented lending, the committee enjoined upon the banks to move towards need-based lending. The committee pointed out that the best security of bank loan is a well-functioning business enterprise, not the collaterals. Major recommendations of the committee were as follows:

(a) Assessment of the need-based credit of the borrower on a rational basis on the basis of their business plans.

(b) Bank credit would only be supplementary to the borrower's resources and not a replacement of them, i.e. banks would not finance one hundred percent of borrower's working capital requirement.

(c) Banks should ensure proper end-use of bank credit by keeping a closer watch on the borrower's business, and impose financial discipline on them.

(d) Working capital finance would be available to the borrowers on the basis of industry-wise norms (prescribed first by the Tandon Committee and then by Reserve Bank of India) for holding different current assets, viz.

    (i) Raw materials including stores and other items used in the manufacturing process

    (ii) Stocks-in-process

    (iii) Finished goods

    (iv) Accounts receivable

    (v) Spares

(e) Credit would be made available to the borrowers in different components like cash credit, bills purchased and discounted, working capital term loan, etc., depending upon the nature of holding of various current assets.

(f) In order to facilitate a close watch on the operations of the borrowers, banks would require them to submit, at regular intervals, data regarding their business and financial operations, for both the past and the future periods.

THE NORMS

Tandon Committee had initially suggested norms for holding various current assets for fifteen different industries. Many of these norms were revised and the list extended to cover almost all major industries of the country. These norms,

---

4. Reserve Bank of India, *Report of the Study Group to Frame Guidelines for Follow-up of Bank Credit*, Bombay, 1975.

which are now only indicative in nature (reasons discussed later) are given in Annexure 1 to this chapter.

Expression of Norms

The norms for holding different current assets were expressed as follows:

(a) Raw materials, as so many months' consumption. They include stores and other items used in the process of manufacture.

(b) Stocks-in-process, as so many months' cost of production.

(c) Finished goods and accounts receivable, as so many months' cost of sales and sales respectively.

(d) Stocks of spares were not included in the norms. In financial terms, these were considered to be small part of total operational expenditure and hence, did not merit the development of a general norm for them. Banks were expected to ascertain the requirement of spares on case-by-case basis. However, they should keep a watchful eye if spares exceed 5 percent of total inventories.

The norms were based on average level of holding of a particular current asset, not on the individual items of the group. For example, if the receivables holding norm of an industry was two months and a unit had satisfied this norm, (calculated by dividing annual sales with the average receivables), then the unit would not be asked to delete some of the accounts receivable, which were being held for more than two months.

The Tandon Committee while laying down the norms for holding various current assets made it very clear that it was against any rigidity and straight-jacketing. On the one hand, the committee said that norms were to be regarded as the outer limits for holding different current assets, but these were not to be considered as entitlements to hold current assets upto this level. If a borrower had managed with less in the past, he should continue to do so. On the other hand, the committee held that allowance must be made for some flexibility under circumstances justifying a need for re-examination. The committee itself visualised that there might be deviations from norms in the following circumstances:

(a) Bunched receipt of raw materials including imports.

(b) Interruption of production due to power-cuts, strikes or other unavoidable circumstances.

(c) Transport delays or bottlenecks.

(d) Accumulation of finished goods due to non-availability of shipping space for exports, or other disruptions in sales.

(e) Building up of stocks of finished goods, such as machinery, due to failure on the part of the purchasers for whom these were specifically designed and manufactured.

(f) Need to cover full or substantial requirement of raw materials for specific export contract of short duration.

While allowing the above exceptions, the committee observed that the deviations should be for known and specific circumstances and situations, and allowed only for a limited period to tide over the temporary difficulty of a borrowing unit. Return to norms would be automatic when conditions returned to normal.

METHODS OF LENDING

The lending framework proposed by the Tandon Committee dominated commercial bank lending in India for more than 20 years and it continues to do so despite withdrawal of mandatory provisions by Reserve Bank of India in 1997.

As indicated before, the essence of Tandon Committee's recommendations was to finance only a portion of the borrower's working capital need, not the whole of it. It was envisaged that gradually, the borrower should depend less and less on banks to fund his working capital need. From this point of view the committee proposed three graduated methods of lending which came to be popularly known as *maximum permissible bank finance* system of lending, or in short, MPBF system.

For purpose of calculating MPBF of a borrowing unit, all the three methods adopted Equation (7.2) (shown earlier) as the basis which is translated arithmetically as follows:

Gross current assets	Rs. . . . .
Less: Current liabilities	
other than bank borrowings[5]	Rs. . . . .
Working capital gap	Rs.

Under the First Method, 75 percent of this *working capital gap* (WCG) would be financed by the bank, and the remaining 25 percent would be financed by the borrowing unit form its long-term sources.

Under the Second Method, the borrowing unit would be required to finance, from its long-term sources, 25 percent of *gross current assets* (GCA). A certain level of trade credit and other accounts payable will then be adjusted against it, and the bank would finance the balance. However, total current liabilities inclusive of bank finance would never exceed 75 percent of GCA.

In the Third Method, permissible bank finance would be calculated in the same manner as in the Second Method, but only after deducting *core current assets* (CCA) from the gross current assets. It was envisaged that CCA would be financed by the borrower from long-term sources.

Core portion of current assets was presumed to be that permanent level which would not generally vary with the level of operations of a business. For example, in the case of stocks of materials, the core line goes horizontally below the ordering level, so that when stocks are ordered, materials are consumed down the ordering level during the lead time and touch the core

---

5. The Tandon Committee had not prescribed any norm for holding of current liabilities other than bank borrowing.

level, but are not allowed to go down further. While discussing inventory management in Chapter 4, we have said that this core level provides a safety cushion against any sudden shortage of materials in the market, or lengthening of delivery time. This core level was considered to be equivalent to fixed assets and hence, was recommended to be financed from long-term sources.

The committee had illustrated the three methods of lending with the help of the following example of a borrower's financial position projected at the end of the next year.

Current liabilities	Rs.	*Current assets*		Rs.
Trade credit	100	*Inventories*		
Other current liabilities	50	Raw materials		200
	150	Work-in-process		20
Bank borrowing, including		Finished goods		90
bills discounted	200			310
		Accounts receivables		
		(including bills discounted)		50
		Other current assets		10
Total	350		Total	370

First method		*Second method*		*Third method*	
Gross current assets	370	Gross current assets	370	Gross current assets	370
Less: Current liabilities		25% of GCA from		*Less*: Core current	
other than bank		long-term sources	92	assets (assumed)	95
borrowing	150		278	Real current assets	275
Working capital gap	220	*Less*: Current		25% of above from	
25% of above from		liabilities other		long-term sources	69
long-term sources	55	than bank borrowing	150		206
Maximum permissible		Maximum permissible		*Less*: Current liabilities	
bank finance	165	bank finance	128	other than bank	
Actual bank borrowing	200	Actual bank borrowing	200	borrowing	150
Excess borrowing	35	Excess borrowing	72	Maximum permissible	
Current ratio	1.17	Current ratio	1.33	bank finance	56
				Actual bank borrowing	200
				Excess borrowing	144
				Current ratio	1.79

It would appear from the above illustration that there is a gradual decrease in MPBF from one method to the other, which is also reflected by the gradual rise in the required current ratio. The committee proposed that excess borrowing over the MPBF, shown above, should be segregated and placed on a repayment basis to be adjusted over a period of time.

The level of current ratio prescribed under the three methods of lending should be considered as the minimum threshold level. Units whose existing current ratio is higher than the minimum prescribed, would not be allowed any 'slip back' except under special circumstances. Reserve Bank of India allowed such 'slip back' for the following purposes only if, a current ratio of at least 1.33 was maintained:

(a) For undertaking either an expansion of existing capacity or for diversification, which would also include setting up of new units.

(b) For fuller utilisation of existing capacity; for meeting a substantial increase in the unit's working capital requirements on account of abnormal price rise.

(c) For investment in allied concerns with the concurrence of the bank.

(d) For bringing about a reduction in the level of deposits accepted from public in order to comply with statutory requirements.

(e) For repayment by installments foreign currency loans and other term–loans.

(f) For rehabilitation/reviving weaker units in the 'Group' by allowing flow of funds from cash rich companies, provided that by such transfers the current ratio of the transferor companies would not fall below 1.33.

Under the liberalised lending regime (discussed later) the RBI has allowed the banks to decide on their own 'slip back'. But the circumstances mentioned above, being exhaustive, continue to act as guidelines.

From an analysis of the operations of cash credit accounts of many non-seasonal industries, Tandon Committee observed that the outstandings in a cash credit account did not fall below a certain level, which represented the stable fund requirement during the year. The committee, therefore, suggested that permissible bank finance be made available to the borrower in the form of a demand loan for that minimum level which constituted the stable fund requirement, and the fluctuating portion, by cash credit. But neither this segregation nor the concept of core current assets found favour with banks because of difficulties in calculating them. This was later abandoned by the Chore Group.

Michel Fleuriet,[6] a Brazilian economist who popularised a 'new concept' of working capital in Brazil, basically held the same view as that of Tandon Committee, though in a different way. He segregated current assets between operating current assets and financial current assets, and current liabilities between operating current liabilities and financial current liabilities. He held that rather than treating all liabilities as financing debt, only those liabilities that raise cash for operations (like bank loans, short-term commercial papers and bonds) should be classified as operating current liabilities and those liabilities (like term debt, short-term portion of long-term debt, bills discounting, etc.) that are due to financing and should be treated as such. Similarly, some current assets are deemed to be financial in nature (such as cash and bank balances, short-term financial investments that absorb excess cash, etc.) while those that are linked to the operating cycle should be designated as operating current assets.

From working capital point of view Fleuriet defined treasury balances as the difference between financial liabilities and financial assets. This treasury balance is the amount of liquid resources available to finance a firm's working

---

6. Fleuriet, M., *Questioning Fleuriet's Model of Working Capital Management on Empirical Grounds—A Rebuttal,* Working Paper, SSRN, 2005.

capital requirements. If working capital requirements are financed only by the net working capital, treasury balance is positive and as a consequence, the current financial assets exceed short-term financial debt. If the net working capital does not cover the total requirement of working capital, the gap is financed by short-term financial indebtedness and hence, the treasury balance is negative.

CHORE GROUP

Although Tandon Committee made a significant contribution towards modernising lending system of Indian commercial banks, both the banking community and the industry were slow to implement the system in true spirit. The Reserve Bank of India became anxious and wanted to make a further in-depth study of the working of the lending system and constituted a working group under the chairmanship of K.B. Chore in April 1979. The group submitted its report in August 1979.[7]

Shortcomings of Cash Credit System

While reviewing cash credit system of lending, Chore Group observed that under this system, limits were fixed according to the maximum requirement of individual borrowers and drawals were allowed according to the needs of the borrowers at any point of time. This resulted in the existence of unutilised cash credit limits which often frustrated any attempt of monetary authorities to contain creation of credit by banks: the unutilised portion of the cash credit limits, which was found to be about one third of the sanctioned limits, acted as a source of liquidity which could be drawn upon in full the moment a credit restriction was imposed, thus defeating its very purpose.

This gap, however, was not unique in India. It was found in all the countries where the cash credit or overdraft system was prevalent. For example, the group observed that in the United Kingdom, the gap was around 60 percent. Some of the reasons behind the existence of this gap, which are still valid today, are given below.

(a) As the peak level borrowing requirement of individual borrowers occurs at different points in time, borrowers as a whole would not utilise all their facilities at the same time.

(b) Historically, the mind-set of Indian bankers is such that they prefer large fluctuations in the cash credit account of a borrower. If the account comes to credit many times during the year, it is considered to be a good sign. On the contrary, full utilisation of the limit throughout the year is viewed with disapproval by the bankers, as it is considered to be indicative of financial unsoundness of the borrower.

(c) At the time of submitting their credit proposals, most of the borrowers prefer to inflate their requirement because of the delay involved in getting the

---

7. Reserve Bank of India, *Report of the Working Group to Review the System of Cash Credit,* Bombay, August 1979.

proposal sanctioned. The fear is that by the time the proposal is sanctioned, the price level may increase, requiring additional funds which may once again take long time to get sanctioned.

(d) Larger limits are also asked for to insure against imponderables like power cuts, flood, transport bottlenecks, changes in import policies and budgetary uncertainties of the government.

(e) Under the cash credit system, the bankers desire that all receipts of the borrower should be routed through the cash credit account. These receipts include sales (which also include profit), public deposits, unutilised portion of term loans, debentures, etc. As a result, the balance in the cash credit account may often come to a credit.

(f) The imperfections in the movement of economic variables make the projections of business parameters difficult. As a result, both the borrowers and bankers play safe in setting up limits.

The Tandon Committee tried to control the gap by prescribing a quarterly information system, but the Chore Group observed that the system could not find proper roots, and hence the gap continued.

The Chore Group argued that under the cash credit system, management of cash resources is shifted to the bank by the borrowers. There is no problem of managing investment of surplus cash, as is prevalent where loan system is in vogue, because all the surplus cash is deposited in cash credit account where it can earn (save) at the highest rate of the economy.

The cash credit system is not conducive to the efficiency in working capital management. On the contrary, it encourages inefficiency. For example, an efficient unit will get less finance because its inventories and receivables are less due to high turnover of both. As against this, a borrower may withhold release of outputs to take advantage of rising prices. The high inventory level will enable him to obtain more finance from bank than the borrower who sells output faster and thus reduces the inventories.

The group also observed that one year review generally practiced for cash credit account is too long a period for short-term finance. More often than not, even the annual reviews are delayed. As such, it is difficult for bankers to track the end-use of credit. When reviews are made (generally, at the time of renewal or enhancement of credit limits), it might be observed that number of assumptions have gone wrong, which, if timely measures were taken, could have saved the borrower's as well as the bank's money.

Against the disadvantages of cash credit system cited above, the group also noted the arguments in favour of it. It was argued that the cash credit system was in vogue for a long time in India, mainly because of its flexibility which could take care of temporary requirement of funds.

The system also enabled recycling of funds into the bank. The funds remained with the bank as the borrowers were not forced to invest surplus cash outside the cash credit system. Due to this recycling arrangement, the borrower's drawal was always limited to the minimum requirement of fund at all the time. This enabled him to save on interest, which would otherwise have been payable under a loan system.

LOAN SYSTEM

In other developed countries like, the United States and Japan, working capital finance and other short-term finances are available in the form of term loans. Under this system, loan is sanctioned for definite purpose and period. This is usually accompanied by maintenance of compensatory cash balance in the current account (as a percentage of loan sanctioned) which involves an additional cost to the firm. Unlike cash credit system, this system forces the borrower to plan his cash budget, which ensures a degree of self-discipline.

Under loan system of financing, management of funds in banks would be easy as they can plan their credit portfolio rationally. This, in turn, would enable the monetary authorities to regulate credit expansion effectively. At the same time, the borrower would also not face any problem as there would not be any cut in the finance already made available to him.

Automatic review is built into the loan system as every loan has to be negotiated afresh. This gives an opportunity to the bank to deny loan if the performance of the borrower is not found to be satisfactory.

Loan system is also easy to operate as compared to cash credit which is rather cumbersome with limits, sub-limits, documentation, maintenance of drawing power, and so forth. Leakage of income, which is common in cash credit system, is virtually absent in loan system.

There are also certain disadvantages in loan system, emanating particularly from its inflexibility. A borrower is expected to repay the existing loan before negotiating further loan. But in the meantime, if the borrower needs additional fund due to some adverse economic and financial conditions, it is not generally available under loan system. This inflexibility might often lead to dilution of the loan system. In many cases it is found that ad hoc loans are given, and new loans are sanctioned just to repay the earlier loans. In such situations, loan system becomes similar to cash credit system.

As every loan has to be negotiated afresh, there may be a tendency among the borrowers to inflate the requirement to make provision for contingencies, similar to cash credit system when approval takes a long time. The excess fund, if kept in the deposit account of the bank or in outside investments, ultimately increases the money supply of the economy.

It is also claimed that under loan system, monitoring of the end-use of the fund is difficult as the banker does not have much of a control over the operations of the borrower's business after the loan is disbursed.

Chore Group came closer to grasping the problems of the cash credit system but stopped short of recommending its replacement by loan system. The demerits of the loan system, as generally claimed, are results of maladministration of the system, not its inherent weaknesses. Cash credit system lost its efficacy long time back. It retards the development of a financial system where securitisation of balance sheet loan is the order of the day, and this is not possible under cash credit system of bank finance.[8] It has taken

---

8. Cash credit system is also open to the risk of maturity mismatch which makes the task of proper assets-liability management difficult in a commercial bank.

rather a long time for Reserve Bank of India to come to terms with reality, and only during the past few years the RBI gradually replaced the cash credit system by loan system. Presently, the ratio between cash credit and loan is 20:80 for large loans.

BILLS SYSTEM

Financing of working capital through purchase or discounting of trade bills is prevalent in India concomitantly with cash credit system, though its usage is much lower than cash credit. Bills are direct securitisation of book debt or trade credit.

Date of retiring a bill is pre-fixed. This enables a supplier to plan his cash budget more accurately. As bills are market instruments, the suppliers can discount them in the bill market or with banks directly, as a part of working capital finance. For banks also, bills are a good mode of financing not only because of their self-liquidating nature, but also the rediscounting facilities available with Reserve Bank of India and other financial institutions.

A well developed bill market is the part of a good financial system of a country. Corporates, banks and other financial agencies can invest their surplus fund, in bills of different maturities to suit their requirements which, in turn, provide finances to those who need them for short-term.

Unfortunately in India, despite their distinct advantages and, encourage-ment from monetary authorities, bill market has not developed fully. It continues to be at its nascent stage for the last twenty years. Primary reason behind this can be ascribed to the general absence of financial discipline among the business enterprises in India, which cuts across both large and small scale operators. Under the bill system, drawee becomes committed to a definite payment date with associated legal stricture. This makes them reluctant to accept bills as a mode of payment. Moreover, where part payment of a bill is an accepted business practice, particularly in government departments, the bill system cannot operate satisfactorily.

In India, all-out efforts are being made by the Reserve Bank of India and Discount and Finance House of India to instill a bill culture in the economy to bring it in line with well-developed financial systems of the world. Chore Group also advocated progressive use of bill system of financing. The increased use of bills could have smoothened some of the undesirable features of cash credit system. But the financial discipline, which is the basis of the development of a bill culture, is yet to be ingrained in Indian business practices.

CHORE GROUP'S RECOMMENDATIONS

Chore Group worked within the framework of lending system proposed by Tandon Committee. After reviewing various systems of lending, the Group came to the conclusion that even if increasing use of bills and loans are made in working capital finance, a borrower would still require cash credit limits mainly for holding of stocks. The group proposed a *drawee bill system* to ease payment to small suppliers and also to make increasing use of bill. In Annexure 2 to this chapter we have given a summarised version of the drawee bill system.

As mentioned before, Chore Group, perhaps thought that the time was not yet ripe to progressively replace the cash credit system by loan system of which bill is a part. The group's approach at that time was to improve upon the use and administration of the cash credit system, and to supplement it with other forms of finance. We should mention here that gradual replacement of the cash credit system is restricted to borrowing limits of Rs. 10 crore and above from the banking system. Majority of loan accounts falls below this limit for whom cash credit system is still the dominant mode of financing. Mechanics of lending system, proposed by the Tandon Committee and modified by the Chore Group, is still relevant for these borrowers despite withdrawal of mandatory provisions of MPBF system by Reserve Bank of India.

Abandoning the 'Core' Concept

Chore Group found that despite the lapse of a considerable period, the system of bifurcation of current assets into 'core' and 'variable' portions had not found acceptance either by the banks or by borrowers. The group observed that bifurcation might not serve the purpose of better credit planning by narrowing the gap in sanctioned limits to the extent of their utilisation. Unless the 'core' portion was fixed at a fairly high level, say about 80 to 85 percent of total cash credit, the disadvantage of underutilisation would remain, even after bifurcation. Besides, the 'core' idea would not apply to seasonal industries. In view of all these, the group abandoned the idea of core current assets and hence, the Third Method of Lending.

The group examined the First and Second Methods of Lending proposed by the Tandon Committee and came to the conclusion that the borrower's own contribution to working capital finance under the first method was very low, with a current ratio of only 1.17. Although Tandon Committee desired that borrowers would on their own move to the Second Method by increasing their stake, it did not happen. The group, therefore, desired that the borrowers be placed directly under the Second Method immediately. If due to this changeover there happened to occur any excess borrowing, the amount should be segregated and placed as *working capital term loan* (WCTL) repayable over a period of time.

In order to reduce the gap between sanctioned limits and their availability the group recommended bifurcation of the limits between 'normal non-peak level' requirement and 'peak-level requirement'. While fixing such limits, banks should examine the borrower's utilisation of credit limits in the past. Within such limits, drawings would be allowed on the basis of quarterly projections submitted by the borrower.

Quarterly Information System

For this purpose the group recommended a *quarterly information system* (QIS) comprising Forms I, II and III. Borrowers would submit Form I within a week preceding the commencement of the quarter to which it relates, and mention therein, among other things, the requirement of his fund for the quarter. The requirement, as indicated in the form, would be the operative limit within the overall sanctioned limits subject to the availability of drawing power calculated on monthly stock statements submitted by the borrower.

Within six weeks from the end of the relevant quarter, borrowers would submit Form II giving comparative statement of projected availability and the actual availability of the credit limits with proper explanation of variations, if any. Information available from this form should also act as the basis for determining the operative limit of the quarter. Banks would examine whether projected level of production and sales, current assets and current liabilities of the ensuing quarter were realistic, by comparing past performance data as available in Form II.

In the case of consortium advance, these QIS statements would be submitted by the borrower to all the consortium members. Non-submission of these quarterly statements within the prescribed time would attract penal rate of interest, and in case of consistent irregularity, freezing of accounts.

In addition to submission of the above quarterly statements, borrowers should also submit half-yearly operating statements and funds flow statements in Form III, along with a half-yearly balance sheet within two months from the close of the half-year to enable the bank to undertake a review of the borrowal account.

The QIS statements along with half-yearly statement in Form III were well designed for off-site monitoring of borrowal accounts, and they still form part of information system of a lending banker. But unfortunately, the QIS were not taken as seriously as it was envisaged by the Chore group. In many instances, these were simply filed; no scrutiny was made; no follow-up action was taken. If proper attention was given to this information system and corrective actions were taken in time, many of the large borrowal accounts would not have turned non-performing.

LENDING POLICIES OF COMMERCIAL BANKS DURING POST-LIBERALISATION PERIOD

In the credit policy announcements of 1997–98 Reserve Bank of India gave freedom to the banks and the borrowers in respect of sanction/availability of working capital facilities. Banks would henceforth make their own assessment of credit requirement of borrowers based on a total study of the borrowers' business operations. RBI would no longer prescribe detailed industry-wise norms for holding of various current assets as in MPBF system, except that it may provide broad indicative levels for the guidance of banks. Accordingly, banks can decide the levels of holding of each item of current assets which, in their view, would represent a reasonable build-up of current assets for being supported by banks. Banks are encouraged to evolve suitable internal guidelines for evaluating various projections made by the borrowers, including level of trade credits available to them, and also to install appropriate risk analysis mechanism in view of changing risk perceptions under a liberalised regime.

Small-scale Borrowers

Earlier, the RBI recommended a special credit dispension methodology based on turnover method for borrowers upto a credit limit of Rs. 2 crore. Under this method, 25 percent of the projected turnover of a borrowing unit was to be considered straightaway as the working capital requirement, of which four-fifths would be provided by bank and the balance one-fifth would come by way of promoter's contribution towards the margin money. The method is simple and easy to implement. It is based on an expected working capital turnover ratio of four. Many banks are found to have adopted this methodology for assessment and dispension of working capital requirement upto Rs. 2 crore. Some banks have also indicated their desire to raise the limit gradually to Rs. 5 crore. As long as the system remains flexible to take care of the special requirements of an industry/unit (where working capital turnover ratio could as well be less than four or more than that), it can take away a lot of hassles both of the borrower and of the banker and quicken the credit delivery.

Export Credit

In order to help boost up foreign exchange reserve and ease balance of payment position of the country, Reserve Bank of India desires that banks should extend 12 percent of their net credit to export sector. Further, to make available maximum finance to the exporters the RBI has indicated that there should be no margin requirement on current assets, as are represented by export receivables. Additional credit needs of the exporters arising out of the firm orders/confirmed *letters of credit* should be met in full.

For those borrowing units which are engaged in marketing/trading the products manufactured by village, tiny and SSI units, the RBI originally proposed application of the First Method of Lending (to make available higher quantum of finance) provided dues of units belonging to such sectors are settled by the borrower within 30 days from the date of supply. Commercial banks presently are found to continue this socio-financial policy.

Loan Component

As indicated before, Reserve Bank of India gradually raised the loan component of working capital finance to 80 percent for borrowers having aggregate limits of Rs. 10 crore and above from the banking system. Although RBI intended that banks would gradually lower down the threshold limit of Rs. 10 crore and increase the loan component to 100 percent, banks are reluctant to increase the pace. Most of the Indian commercial banks continue to maintain the threshold limit of Rs. 10 crore arguing that borrowers below this threshold limit generally draw funds close to their credit limits throughout the year. Although no statistical evidence has been put forward to justify the argument, one can say that this argument itself should be the ground to introduce loan system in such accounts. It appears that having lived in directed lending regime for a long time, banks are hesitant to move on their own. Credit policy documents of many a bank contain provisions for selective exemption from loan system even if their borrowal limits are over Rs. 10 crore.

CONSORTIUM AND SYNDICATION

In order to spread the lending risk and also to provide a forum for 'learning by experience' for banks who did not have desired level of expertise in handling large credit proposals, Reserve Bank of India directed compulsory formation of consortium of banks if the aggregate credit limits of a borrower from the banking system was beyond a particular threshold level. During 1993–94 the RBI raised the threshold level from Rs. 5 crore to Rs. 50 crore.

Under the obligatory consortium arrangement the members of consortium were chosen by the lead bank. The members were also allowed to walk out of consortium under certain conditions. Borrowers did not have any say in the matter of formation of consortium, nor they could stop any bank from walking out. The industry in general was not happy with the arrangement. The stronger banks having enough funds and expertise at their disposal were also expressing their reluctance to share a good account with other banks, particularly because management of the account virtually became the sole responsibility of the lead bank. Other banks' responsibilities were virtually limited to attending periodical consortium meetings.

In view of the above, Reserve Bank of India first increased the threshold limit, as mentioned above, and then went in for replacing the obligatory consortium by voluntary formation, multiple banking arrangement and loan syndication.

Loan syndication and multiple banking arrangements are in line with modern financial economy where customers are allowed more and more freedom of choice. Keeping this in mind Reserve Bank of India mooted the idea of Syndication of credit as far back as 1993, though at that time it was limited to raising long-term funds by borrowers.[9]

A syndicated credit is an arrangement between two or more banks or financial institutions to provide a credit facility using common loan documentation. A prospective borrower desiring to raise resources by this method would award a mandate to a bank, generally called the 'Lead Manager', to arrange credit on his behalf. The mandate would spell out the commercial terms of the credit and prerogatives of the lead manager in resolving contentious issues in the course of transactions.

The lead manager would prepare an information memorandum about the prospective borrower in consultation with the latter, and distribute it amongst the prospective lenders, soliciting their participation in the loan. The mandated bank does not sell the credit risk, but presents an opportunity to lend. The information memorandum provides the basis for each lending bank

---

9. Reserve Bank of India, Circular No. IECD/20/08.13.08/93–94, dated 28th October 1993, Mumbai.

to make its own evaluation of the borrower and the proposal, if necessary, by seeking additional supporting information from other sources as well.

The lead manager then convenes a meeting of the willing banks to discuss the syndication strategy relating to coordination, communication and control within the syndication process, and finalises the deal timing, charges towards management expenses, cost of credit, share of each participating bank in the loan, etc. The loan agreement is signed by all the participating banks.

The borrower would give prior notice to the lead manager or his agent for drawing the loan amount to enable the latter to tie up disbursements with the other lending banks.

It would appear from the above discussion that syndication is very similar to consortium lending in terms of dispersal of risk, but the freedom the borrower has in terms of competitive pricing makes it different from consortium lending.

Finance under multiple banking arrangement are preferred for concerns having multiple divisions or concerns engaged in hire purchase or leasing where neither the consortium arrangement nor the sole banking arrangement is acceptable to the bank or the borrower. Under this arrangement it is necessary that the primary securities are easily identifiable for being charged separately by each financing bank.

EXPOSURE LIMITS

Commercial banks in India tend to follow the exposure norms for individual and group borrower as laid down by Reserve Bank of India from time to time. Presently, aggregate loan to individual borrower would not exceed 25 percent of the capital fund of the bank while aggregate loan to a group of companies should not exceed 50 percent of the capital fund of the bank. For this purpose, capital fund has been defined as paid-up capital plus free reserves (excluding Revaluation reserve) while exposure is defined to include funded (100 percent), non-funded credit limits (50 percent) or outstanding whichever is higher.

In addition, or within the above exposure limit, individual banks can fix up industry-wise exposure considering the demand-supply position and also the overall performance of the industry, or any of its segments. Generally, banks would not like to increase their exposure to a particular industry by more than 10 percent of bank credit.

Priority Sectors

Directed lending to priority sectors continue to be 40 percent for Indian banks despite Narasimham Committee's recommendations in 1991 to reduce it to 10 percent. Within the priority sector the RBI fixes up minimum deployments of bank credit which banks are required to adhere to.

WORKING CAPITAL REQUIREMENT AND ASSESSMENT METHODOLOGY OF COMMERCIAL BANKS

For purpose of assessment of working capital requirement of a borrowing unit, Indian commercial banks have adopted formats originally proposed in the *credit authorisation scheme* (later termed as credit monitoring arrangement) of Reserve Bank of India. These formats, as they stand today, are the result of many revisions done to conform to the changing requirements of banks and industries. In the process, what has evolved is an excellent instrument for credit appraisal and lending decision, which is widely used not only by banks but other financial agencies as well with some modifications.

These formats restructure the balance sheet and profit and loss account of an enterprise (which are drawn up either in terms of the provisions of *Companies Act* or *Income Tax Act*) to suit the requirements of a credit appraiser. Several assets and liabilities and also operating variables are reclassified in these formats. For example, a distinction is made between current assets and non-current assets, gross working capital and net working capital, or between gross profit and operating profit. A borrower is required to submit both past and projected financial data of his business in these formats only for raising working capital finance from banks.

We shall explain presentation of financial data in these formats with the help of a real-life case of a company engaged in manufacturing consumer durables The company has made application to the bank for enhancement of credit limits. Working capital problems of this company will be analysed thereafter in order to evolve a plan for financial restructuring. Assessment of working capital requirement of the company will be made in the light of this plan. Let the company be called OSB Ltd. for purpose of anonymity.

Classifications of current assets and current liabilities and instructions for filling up these forms are given in Annexure 3 to this chapter.

Form I

OSB LIMITED

ASSESSMENT OF WORKING CAPITAL REQUIREMENT

Particulars of the existing/proposed limits from the banking system

(Limits from all banks and financial institutions as on the date of application)

(Rs. in lakh)

A. Working capital limits

Sl. no.	Name of bank/ financial institution	Nature of facility	Existing limits	Extent to which limits were utilised during the last 12 months Max.	Min.	Balance O/S as on 31.3.20X2	Limits now requested
(1)	(2)	(3)	(4)	(5)	(6)	(7)	(8)
1.	ABC Bank	Cash credit	8750	8846	8520	8846	12,040
2.	ABC Bank	Bills purchased and discounted	1750	1860	1630	1860	2410
3.	—	—	—	—	—	—	—
		Total	10,500	10,706	10,150	10,706	14,450

B. Term loans/DPGs (excluding working capital term loans)

Sl. no.	Name of bank/ financial institution	Sanctioned limit	Outstanding as on 31.3.20X2	Overdues, if any	Remarks
(1)	(2)	(3)	(4)	(5)	(6)
1.	AFI	7000	5000	400	Under negotiation for rescheduling
2.	BFI	2400	1908	308	Under negotiation for rescheduling
3.	CFI (DPG)	500	170	—	—
4.	NBFC	118	118	—	Bridge loan

Form II
OSB LIMITED

(Rs. in lakh)

Operating statement

		20X0	20X1	20X2	20X3 (Projected)
1.	Gross sales				
	(i) Domestic sales	61,188	74,065	86,436	89,934
	(ii) Export sales	4243	5133	6118	10,028
	Total	65,431	79,198	92,554	99,962
2.	*Less:* Excise duty	6717	8320	10,537	10,200
3.	Net sales (1 – 2)	58,714	70,878	82,017	89,762
4.	% rise (+) or fall (–) in net sales as compared to previous year	—	+20.72	+15.72	+9.44
5.	Cost of sales				
	(i) Raw materials (including stores and other items used in the process)				
	(a) Imported	5160	6634	7433	7442
	(b) Indigenous	19,591	21,365	28,575	33,164
	(ii) Other spares				
	(a) Imported	11	80	60	161
	(b) Indigenous	41	47	111	154
	(iii) Power and fuel	418	710	608	813
	(iv) Direct labour (factory wages and salaries)	5241	6518	7534	8284
	(v) Other manufacturing expenses	512	584	664	773
	(vi) Depreciation on plant and machinery	721	977	1006	906
	(vii) Sub-total (i to vi)	31,695	36,915	45,991	51,697
	(viii) Add opening stocks-in-process	3190	3405	3776	5855
	Sub-total	34,885	40,320	49,767	57,552
	(ix) Deduct: Closing stocks-in-process	3230	3774	5855	6965
	(x) Cost of production	31,655	36,546	43,912	50,587
	(xi) Add opening stock of finished goods	3449	2964	3409	4398
	(xii) Add finished goods purchased	14,271	19,108	20,443	19,282
	Sub-total	49,375	58,618	67,764	74,267

(xiii) Deduct closing stock of finished goods	2957	3409	4398	4571
Sub-total (Total cost of sales)	46,418	55,209	63,366	69,696
6. Selling, general and administrative expenses	7797	9775	11,770	13,308
7. Sub-total (5 + 6)	54,215	64,984	75,136	83,004
8. Operating profit before interest (3–7)	4499	5894	6881	6758
9. Interest	2866	4152	5725	6468
10. Operating profit after interest (8–9)	1633	1742	1156	290
11. (i) Add other non-operating income	883	991	1038	1655
Sub-total	883	991	1038	1655
(ii) Deduct other non-operating expenses	—	—	—	—
Sub-total	—	—	—	—
(iii) Net of other non-operating income/ expenses [Net of 11(i) and 11(ii)]	883	991	1038	1655
12. Profit before tax/loss [10 + 11(iii)]	2516	2733	2194	1945
13. Provision for taxes	890	64	889	603
14. Net profit/loss (12 – 13)	1626	2669	1305	1342
15. (a) Equity dividend paid	440	488	488	605
(b) Dividend rate (%)	18	20	20	16.30
16. Retained profit (14 – 15)	1186	2181	817	737
17. Retained profit/net profit (%)	72.94	81.72	62.61	54.92

Notes:

Item no. 5(v) : "Other manufacturing expenses" comprise service charges, repairs of plant and machinery and insurance.

Item no. 5(xii) : "The company purchases finished goods from approved small-scale manufacturers and sells them directly with company's brand name.

Item no. 6 : "Selling general and administrative expenses" include depreciation on buildings, etc. and miscellaneous expenditure written off as follows:

	20X0	20X1	20X2	20X3
Depreciation of building, etc.	191	201	260	381
Miscellaneous expenditure written off	100	101	124	170

Form III
ANALYSIS OF BALANCE SHEET

(Rs. in lakh)

Liabilities

Current liabilities	20X0	20X1	20X2	20X3
1. Short-term borrowings from banks (including bills purchased, discounted and excess borrowings placed on repayment basis)				
(i) From applicant bank	7023	3138	10,522	14,450
(ii) From other banks	—	—	—	—
(of which BP and BD)	(1171)	(523)	(1754)	(2408)
Sub-total (A)	7023	3138	10,522	14,450
2. Short-term borrowings from others	46	—	118	3178
3. Sundry creditors (trade)	16,279	18,894	23,152	23,677

4. Advance payment from customers/ depositors and dealers	5126	6646	6899	6971
5. Provision for taxation	—	—	193	—
6. Dividend payable	439	488	488	605
7. Other statutory liabilities (due within one year)	—	—	—	—
8. Deposits/installments of term loans/ DPGs/debentures, etc. (due within one year)	538	1650	1411	1380
9. Other current liabilities and provisions (due within one year)				
(i) Expense creditors	352	464	616	298
(ii) Premium on redemption of debentures	108	67	25	48
Sub-total (B)	22,888	28,209	32,902	36,157
10. Total current liabilities (Total of 1 to 9)	29,911	31,347	43,424	50,607
11. Debentures (not maturing within one year)	3143	6920	6920	2866
12. Preference shares (redeemable after one year)	—	—	—	—
13. Term loans (excluding installments payable within one year	944	6043	6208	6070
14. Deferred payments (excluding installments due within one year)	300	304	170	81
15. Term deposits (repayable after one year)	1422	1768	1737	1873
16. Other term liabilities	2276	2070	2885	3825
17. Total term liabilities (Total of 11 to 16)	8085	17,105	17,920	14,715
18. Total outside liabilities (10 + 17)	37,996	48,452	61,344	65,322
Net worth				
19. Ordinary share capital	2440	2440	2440	3710
20. General reserve	3670	3242	4008	4639
21. Revaluation reserve	3532	3454	3378	3309
22. Other reserves (excluding provisions)	1030	1334	1368	7522
23. Surplus (+) or deficit (−) in profit and loss A/c	+231	+583	+626	+612
24. Total net worth	10,903	11,053	11,820	19,792
25. Total liabilities (18 + 24)	48,899	59,505	73,164	85,114

Assets

Current assets

26. Cash and bank balances	3	9	41	99
27. Investments (other than long-term investments)				
(i) Government and other trustee securities	44	55	55	107
(ii) Fixed deposit with banks	20	55	265	43

28. (i) Receivables other than deferred and exports (including bills purchased and discounted by banks)	20,526	23,622	30,898	34,428
(ii) Export receivables (including bills purchased and discounted by banks)	1302	1605	2096	3586
29. Installments of deferred receivables (due within one year)	—	—	—	—
30. Inventory				
(i) Raw materials (including stores and other items used in the process)				
(a) Imported	683	951	1048	941
(b) Indigenous	2521	2990	3912	4100
(ii) Stock-in-process	3230	3774	5855	6965
(iii) Finished goods	2957	3409	4398	4571
(iv) Other consumable spares				
(a) Imported	18	140	62	104
(b) Indigenous	66	81	114	99
31. Advance to suppliers of raw materials and stores/spares	4446	4742	4846	6847
32. Advance payment of taxes	191	127	—	95
33. Other current assets	48	103	170	236
34. Total current assets (Total of 26 to 33)	36,055	41,663	53,760	62,221

Fixed assets

35. Gross block (land and building, machinery, work-in-progress)	17,805	22,803	24,840	27,258
36. Depreciation to date	6674	7953	9343	9823
37. Net block (35 – 36)	11,131	14,850	15,497	17,435

Non-current assets

38. Investments/book debts/advances/ deposits which are not current assets				
(i) (a) Investments in subsidiary companies/affiliates	198	64	64	1416
(b) Others	288	683	810	845
(ii) Advances to suppliers of capital goods and contractors	—	—	—	—
(iii) Deferred receivables (maturity exceeding one year)	—	—	—	—
(iv) Others (security deposits)	89	241	318	381
39. Non-consumable stores and spares	—	—	—	—
40. Other non-current assets including dues from directors	832	1152	1709	1778
41. Total of other non-current assets (Total of 38 to 40)	1407	2140	2901	4420
42. Intangible assets (patents, goodwill, preliminary expenses, bad and doubtful debts not provided for, etc.) Misc. expenditure not written off	306	852	1006	1038

43. Total assets (Total of 34, 37, 41 and 42)	48,899	59,505	73,164	85,114
44. Tangible net worth (24 – 42)	10,597	10,201	10,814	18,754
45. Net working capital [(17 + 24) – (37 + 41 + 42)] to tally with items (34 – 10)	6144	10,316	10,336	11,614
46. Current ratio (34/10)	1.21	1.33	1.24	1.23
47. Total outside liabilities/tangible net worth (18/44)	3.59	4.75	5.67	3.48

Additional information

A. Arrears of depreciation	—	—	—	—
B. Contingent liabilities				
(i) Arrears of cumulative dividends	—	—	—	—
(ii) Gratuity liability not provided for	—	—	—	—
(iii) Disputed excise/customs/tax liabilities	85	312	277	669
(iv) Other liabilities not provided for	19,690	20,023	22,515	28,183

Notes:

Item no. 1(ii) : Figures for 'bills purchased and discounted' do not appear in the main body of the balance sheet because of accounting entries which remove them from the books of accounts. These figures are picked up from under the head 'contingent liabilities' appearing at the bottom of the balance sheet.

Item no. 16 : 'Other term liabilities' comprise, security deposits, incentive loans from government and unclaimed dividends.

Item no. 19 : Increase in 'ordinary share capital' in the year 20X3 is due to conversion of fully convertible debentures issued in the year 20X1 after adjusting for premiums.

Item no. 20 : Under a settlement awarded by Board for Industrial and Financial Reconstruction, the company is slated to take over an associate company in the year 20X3. The excess of liabilities over assets of the merged company being Rs. 977 lakh is treated as goodwill and written off against general reserves.

Item no. 22 : 'Other reserves' include share premium, capital reserve, capital subsidy, etc.

Item no. 33 : 'Other current assets' include deposits with excise and customs departments in current accounts.

Item no. 40 : 'Other non-current assets' are never defined by Reserve Bank of India. But from the examples cited by them we can summarise that these are such assets which, though look to be current assets on the face of them and hence appear in the balance sheet as such, have lost their currentness or are not engaged directly in the operations. For example, fixed deposits or other securities lodged with bank as collaterals against a facility, deposits with landlord, security deposits with suppliers of materials or with excise or customs authorities, etc. These assets are not realisable in short-term. Similar is the case with staff advances.

Investments in subsidiary companies are not intended to be realised in short-term. Investments, other than in government and approved securities, are presumed to be outside the main operations of the business. All these investments are, therefore, treated as non-current assets. Because of their rather fixed nature, funding of these assets should be made from long-term sources of the enterprise.

Form IV

COMPARATIVE STATEMENT OF CURRENT ASSETS

(Rs. in lakh)

	20X0	20X1	20X2	20X3 (Projected)
A. Current assets				
1. Raw materials (including stores and other items used in the process)				
(a) Imported	683	951	1048	941
(months' consumption,	(1.60)	(1.70)	(1.70)	(1.50)
(b) Indigenous	2521	2990	3912	4100
(months' consumption)	(1.55)	(1.70)	(1.65)	(1.50)
2. Other consumable spares excluding those included in 1 above)				
(a) Imported	18	140	62	104
(months' consumption)	(18.67)	(20.95)	(12.51)	(7.75)
(b) Indigenous	66	81	114	99
(months' consumption)	(19.50)	(20.75)	(12.41)	(7.73)
3. Stocks-in-process	3230	3774	5855	6965
(months' cost of production)	(1.20)	(1.25)	(1.60)	(1.65)
4. Finished goods	2957	3409	4398	4571
(months' cost of sales)	(0.75)	(0.75)	(0.85)	(0.80)
5. Receivables other than export and deferred receivables (including bills purchased and discounted by bankers)	20,526	23,622	30,898	34,428
(months' domestic sales excluding deferred payments sales)	(4.00)	(3.85)	(4.35)	(4.65)
6. Export receivables (including bills purchased and discounted	1302	1605	2096	3586
(months' export sales)	(3.70)	(3.75)	(4.10)	(4.30)
7. Advances to suppliers of raw materials and stores/spares/consumables	4446	4742	4846	6847
8. Other current assets including cash and bank balances and deferred receivables due within one year (specify major items) [Advance payment of taxes, investments, fixed deposits, cash and bank, etc.]	306	349	531	580
9. Total current assets (To agree with item 34 in Form III)	36,055	41,663	53,760	62,221
B. Current liabilities (other than bank borrowings for working capital)				
10. Creditors for purchase of raw materials, stores and consumable spares	16,279	18,894	23,152	23,677
(months' purchases)	(7.75)	(7.90)	(7.50)	(7.00)

11. Advances from customers	5126	6646	6899	6971
12. Statutory liabilities (income tax)	—	—	193	—
13. Other current liabilities (specify major items): [Short-term borrowings, unsecured loans, dividend payable, installments of term loan, deferred payment, guarantee, public deposits, debentures, etc.]	1483	2669	2658	5509
14. Total of current liabilities (To agree with sub-total B of Form III)	22,888	28,209	32,902	36,157

Form V

COMPUTATION OF MAXIMUM PERMISSIBLE BANK FINANCE FOR WORKING CAPITAL

(Rs. in lakh)

	20X0	20X1	20X2	20X3 (Projected)
1. Total current assets (Item no. 9 of Form IV)	36,055	41,663	53,760	62,221
2. Other current liabilities (other than bank borrowings and repayments) [Item no. 14 of Form IV minus Item no. 8 of Form III]	22,350	26,559	31,491	34,777
3. Working capital gap (WCG) [1 – 2]	13,705	15,104	22,269	27,444
4. Minimum stipulated net working capital (NWC) i.e., 25% of total current assets as per second method of lending [export receivables to be excluded, i.e. item no. 6 of Form IV]	8688	10,015	12,916	14,659
5. Actual/projected net working capital (Item no. 45 + Item no. 8 of Form III)	6682	11,966	11,747	12,994
6. Item no. 3 – Item no. 4	5017	5089	9353	12,785
7. Item no. 3 – Item no. 5	7023	3138	10,522	14,450
8. Maximum permissible bank finance (Item no. 6 or 7 whichever is lower)	5017	3138	9353	12,785
9. Excess borrowing representing short fall in NWC (4 – 5)	2006	(1951)	1169	1665

Form VI
FUNDS FLOW STATEMENT

(Rs. in lakh)

	20X1	20X2	20X3
1. Sources			
(i) Net profit (after tax)	2669	1305	1342
(ii) Depreciation	1178	1266	1287
(iii) Increase/decrease in capital and reserves	(2031)	(50)	7235
(iv) Increase in term liabilities			
(including public deposits)	9020	815	—
(v) Decrease in:			
(a) Fixed assets (gross)	—	—	—
(b) Other non-current assets	—	—	—
(vi) Others (misc. expenditure written off)	101	124	170
(vii) Total	10,937	3460	10,034
2. Uses			
(i) Net loss	—	—	—
(ii) Decrease in term liabilities			
(including public deposits)	—	—	3205
(iii) Increase in:			
(a) Fixed assets (gross)	4998	2037	2418
(b) Other non-current assets	733	761	1519
(iv) Dividend payments	488	488	605
(v) Others (Increase in intangible assets, etc.)	546	154	1009
(vi) Total	6765	3440	8756
3. Long-term surplus (+) Deficit (−) [1 − 2]	+4172	+20	+1278
4. Increase/decrease in current assets			
(as per details given below)	5608	12,097	8461
5. Increase/decrease in current liabilities other			
than bank borrowings	5321	4693	3255
6. Increase/decrease in working capital gap (4 − 5)	287	7404	5206
7. Net surplus (+)/Deficit (−)			
(difference of 3 and 6)	+3885	−7384	−3928
8. Increase/decrease in bank borrowings	(3885)	7384	3928
9. Increase/decrease in net sales	12,164	11,139	7745
Break-up of increase/decrease in current assets			
(i) Increase/decrease in stock of raw materials	737	1019	81
(ii) Increase/decrease in stock of work-in-process	544	2081	1110
(iii) Increase/decrease in stock of finished goods	452	989	173
(iv) Increase/decrease in receivables			
(a) Domestic	3096	7276	3530
(b) Export	303	491	1490
(v) Increase/decrease in stock of stores/spares	137	(45)	27
(vi) Increase/decrease in other current assets	339	286	2050
Total	5608	12,097	8461

Notes:

Item no. 1(ii) : 'Depreciation' include total depreciation, namely on plant and machinery as appearing in item no. 5(vi) of Form II and on buildings, etc. shown separately under *Notes* appended below Form II (Item no. 6).

Item no. 1(iii) : 'Increase/decrease in capital and reserves' is calculated first by adding 'retained profit' of current year (Item no. 16 of Form II) with outstanding net worth of last year (Item no. 24 of Form III), and then deducting it from the current year's closing balance.

Item no. 2(v) : 'Others' in the year 20X3 include adjustment of goodwill amounting to Rs. 977 lakh due to merger. See, *Notes* appended to Form III (Item no. 20).

ASSESSMENT OF WORKING CAPITAL REQUIREMENT OF OSB LTD.

The company is an old enterprise which was, at one time a leader in consumer durables market. As is normally with the case in such companies, its fixed overheads expanded unmatched with the growth in sales. With the liberalisation of the economy some of the company's product failed to match the competition because of high cost. The company sought out an alternative strategy by dismantling the production-structure of such products, outsourcing them from small manufacturers at a cheaper cost and selling them with its own brand-names, which were well established in the market. The strategy has paid off. Presently, these outsourced products constitute about 20 percent of sales.

The company has embarked on substantial renewal/replacement during the last three years, as the growth in fixed assets during the period will indicate. A major part of these investments was financed through fully convertible debenture issues made in 20X1, which were finally converted to share capital with a substantial premium.

The company is in the process of consolidation and restructuring which will take some more years to yield full results. Net sales of the company grew at the rate of 20.72 and 15.72 percent during the last two years, but for the projected year the rate of growth has been estimated to be around 9.45 percent. The company has taken a conservative stance in view of the fact that it is yet to implement the full consolidation and restructuring plan, and many of the plants, where new technology has been installed, are yet to pass the teething problems and go over full stream.

The major strength of the company is its operating structure, but its financial structure is very weak as the following ratios will reveal:

	20X0	20X1	20X2	20X3
1. Gross profit ratio (% on net sales)	20.94	22.10	22.74	22.35
2. Operating profit ratio (before interest) [Item no. 8 divided by Item no. 3 of Form II]	7.66	8.32	8.39	7.52
3. Operating profit ratio (after interest) [Item no. 10 divided by Item no. 3 of Form II]	2.78	2.46	1.41	0.32

Note: Gross profit is calculated as net sales minus cost of sales, i.e., Item no. 3 – Item no. 5 of Form II.

Let us recall from Chapter 3 (p. 98) that stability in gross profit ratio (G.P. Ratio) indicates stability in the production structure of the business. We may notice from the operating statement in Form II that the expenses or cost of sales, that are netted from sales to derive the gross profit, are predominantly variable in nature. If this variability is maintained, then the G.P. ratio would obviously be constant over a period of time. During the initial years of the installation of a new technology the ratio may show a rising trend, but once the technology is stabilised the ratio will remain constant during the given technology period.

On the other hand, a falling G.P. ratio indicates weakening of the production structure. This is reflective of the fact that many of the expenses, which were supposed to vary with sales, are becoming fixed or unrelated to sales. If such a situation is allowed to continue, the enterprise will soon become sick.

For OSB Ltd. the G.P. ratio appears to be stable, which the company is able to maintain even after the technology-renewal.

The only group of expense items that comes between G.P. ratio and operating profit ratio (O.P. ratio) is selling, general and administrative expenses. While selling expenses, to a large extent, vary with sales, other expenses remain predominantly fixed. Hence, O.P. ratio should rise slowly with the rise in sales due to higher absorption of fixed costs.

We find that O.P. ratio (before interest) has been rising slowly from 20X0 to 20X2 but, has fallen to touch the level of 20X0 in the projected year. This may be due to low sales growth projected by the company. If we further analyse this Group of expense items for OSB Ltd., we may find that these overheads grew at around 25.40 percent between 20X0 and 20X1 but the growth rate fell to 20.40 percent in the following year. In 20X3 the company has projected a moderate rise of about 13 percent.

All the above discussions indicate that the company's operating structure is strengthening.

But all the strengths and gains of the operating structure of the enterprise are eaten away by its weak and high cost financial structure, as will be revealed from a small and continuously falling O.P. ratio (after interest). In the projected year the ratio has come down to a mere 0.32 percent from 2.78 percent in 20X0. The situation is serious which calls for major financial restructuring of the company, particularly its working capital structure, as we shall see later.

In the projected year the company is supposed to pay an average rate of interest of 20 percent p.a. on the aggregate of term liabilities, short-term borrowings and working capital finance from bank. Further enquiry has revealed that average cost of financing from long-term sources is about 22.6 percent p.a.

This rate is simply unsustainable. It is necessary for the company to explore cheaper sources of finance to repay the high cost loans. We have seen that the company was able to successfully market its share issue at a premium (through convertible debentures). This indicates that the company still carries considerable goodwill among investors, which would enable it to explore the possibility of funding through debentures and public deposits which are cheaper sources, and presently underexploited.

It is necessary for the company to set a target of bringing down the average cost of long-term financing from the present 22.6 percent to 17 percent p.a. which will lower down the interest burden by about Rs. 635 lakh in the projected year. Over the next four years the company should aim at bringing it down further to 15 percent p.a.

Form I reveals that the company has already defaulted on repayment of term loans. It has opened dialogue with the financial institutions to reschedule the repayments. This initiative should be pursued, as longer repayment period will ease the cash position due to low installment payment.

The total debt-equity ratio of the company is very high. It was 5.67 percent in the concluding year, though in the projected year the company has planned to bring it down to 3.48. Reason behind this high debt-equity ratio is primarily due to high-level of current liabilities reflected in lowcurrent ratio (Item no. 46 of Form III).

When we examine various turnover ratios of current assets (given in brackets against Item nos. 1 to 3 of Form IV), we may find that while finished good stock turnover ratio is small (about 3 weeks' stock) the receivables turnover ratio is very high (more than four and a half month). Comparison of these two ratios indicate that though the company's marketing people are highly aggressive in making sales, they are not equally adept in collections. Or due to competition, they may be forced to sell with longer line of credit. This, in fact, is eating into the working capital structure of the business, and creating severe liquidity problem, which has resulted in non-payment or delayed payment of trade creditors. Presently, creditors are not being paid in less than 7 months' time (Item no. 10 of Form IV). The suppliers are still tolerating this delay in payment because they are old-suppliers who do not want to break the relationship at a time when the company is in crisis. But they cannot be pushed further. If these problems are not resolved quickly, they may stop supplies or file bankruptcy petition which may destroy the firm.

What the company needs now is immediate cash to stave off the impending crisis, and long-term restructuring of working capital.

The company must bring down its receivables holding, where most of the working fund is tied up. In the short run the company should bring down its receivables holding to 3 months, and during the next four years the holding should come down to 2 months. The marketing people must be made to realise that uncollected sales not only needs funding, it also eats up the profit expected to be earned on such sales. It is necessary to review the credit and collection policies of the company to bring it in line with its financial objective. The company should place the responsibility of collecting sales on the marketing department also. It can no longer be the responsibility of the accounts department alone.

As an immediate step, the company should explore the possibility of offering cash discount for immediate realisation of debtors. We have shown earlier that cash discount is very attractive to the buyers because it reduces the effective cost of the product. The offer is virtually unresistable. The company should, therefore, immediately undertake a cost-benefit analysis of various levels of discount offer in the light of what we have discussed in Chapters 3 and 6, and come out to the market with an appropriate offer. This will ease the cash position of the company and thus keep the suppliers at bay for some time.

The company must start immediate dialogue with the supply creditors, in consultation with the banker. They should explore the possibility of making the creditors agree to a 4 months' payment period with a definite plan to reduce it further to three months during the next 2–3 years. Considering the long-term relationship and definite assurances from the company/banker, the creditors are likely to agree to such proposal. In order to bring further assurance to the creditors the company and its banker may curve out a drawee bill limit from the cash credit limit of the company, as given in Annexure 2 to this chapter. During the restructuring period the company should stop paying dividend to prevent further cash outflow at the time of cash crisis.

In view of the restructuring plan of working capital discussed above, the requirement of working capital finance should be recast as follows:

Measures	*Revised level* (Rs. in lakh)
1. Domestic receivables to be reduced to 3 months of domestic sales	22,485
2. Export receivables to be reduced to 3 months of exports sales	2507
	24,992
3. All other current assets—no change	24,207
Gross current assets (revised)	49,199
4. Less trade creditors to be reduced to 4 months of purchases	13,530
	35,669
5. Less other current liabilities (other than bank borrowings and repayment liabilities)—no change	11,110
Revised working capital gap	24,559

The company has projected a net working capital of Rs. 12,994 lakh (excluding repayment of term loans). We should add to this Rs. 635 lakh being interest saved on long term loans and Rs. 605 lakh due to postponement of dividend payment as mentioned before. Net working capital in the projected year should therefore, be Rs. 14,234 lakh.

But we should remember, at the same time, that this revised NWC includes profit which the company will not be able to generate unless full finance is available to the company to make the sales as projected. Savings on interest on long-term loans may not also come by the beginning of the projected year. A realistic view would be to take half of the projected profit and interest savings for purpose of NWC calculation. That is, Rs. 14,234 lakh – Rs. 0.5 (1342 + 635) lakh = Rs. 13,246 lakh. Deducting this from revised working capital gap, projected requirement of working capital comes to be Rs. 24,559 lakh – Rs. 13,246 lakh = Rs. 11,313 lakh or say, Rs. 11,315 lakh as against Rs. 14,450 lakh originally intended.

The company should revise the application for working capital finance from the bank and along with it submit full financial restructuring plan as discussed above. The bifurcation of the working capital finance should be as follows keeping in line with the existing guidelines, but not exactly following it, because the company is in a turnaround stage.

	Rs. in lakh	
Cash credit	4565	(40.35%)
Bills purchased and discounted	2400	(21.21%)
Working capital loan	4350	(38.44%)
Total	11,315	(100.00%)

While concluding this section we want to reemphasise that mere obtaining of finance from the bank would not solve the problem unless the restructuring plan is implemented simultaneously. Bank finance should be considered only as a part of the total financial restructuring of the company.

CASH BUDGETING APPROACH

Over the past decade, cash budgeting approach to working capital is gaining ground over the funds flow approach because of the need of cash as means of discharging obligations. Funds are nominal in nature. Unlike cash, they have no physical existence except in the books of accounts of a firm. Profit is one such fund element which may not always contain cash, and one cannot pay bills by profit but by cash only.

In the ultimate analysis, cash gap always equals funds gap, i.e. the working capital gap. The net surplus or deficit [as revealed in Item no. 7 of the funds flow statement (Form VI)] will also be matched with the cash gap in a cash budgeting system. But the latter, being far more detail, provides a better tool for monitoring and control of working capital than the fund's flow statement.[10]

With the adoption of cash flow statement by the International Accounting Standard Committee for financial reporting from 1st January 1994, and its subsequent adoption in modified form in 1996 by the Accounting Standards Board of the Institute of Chartered Accountants of India, as an alternative form of presentation, many corporates have moved towards cash budgeting as a tool of funds management. This was voiced by the Governor of Reserve Bank of India in his policy announcement on 16th April 1997 when he said that in view of such a move by the corporate sector, banks may follow cash budget system for assessing the working capital requirement in respect of large borrowers.

In Chapter 5, we have made detailed analysis of cash flow presentation with worked out examples, and calculated cash gap for purpose of estimating working capital requirement of a business.

OTHER SHORT-TERM SOURCES OF FINANCING

Besides banks, financial market offers several other sources of financing working capital requirement of a firm. With the increase in the spread and

---

10. Bhattacharya, Hrishikes, *Banking Strategy, Credit Appraisal and Lending Decisions*, *ibid.*, See, Chapter 11 for fuller exposition of the concept along with examples.

depth of financial markets all around the world, newer and newer financial instruments are emerging in the advanced financial markets. Developing countries, like India, are adopting these instruments with some modifications during different stages of their development.

Commercial Paper (CP)

One such instrument is commercial paper which is one of the oldest instruments of short-term finance. It originated in the United States in early nineteenth century and soon gained popularity. It first spread itself to Canada and then to other financial markets of the developed world.

Although CP markets at most of the places got developed by US model, some differences still exist in different markets due to varying local conditions. For example, in Canada, Australia, the Netherlands, and Norway, no distinction is made between banking and non-banking companies for issuance of CP. But in many other countries, including India, CPs cannot be issued by banking companies. However, in India, an exception has been made recently whereby primary dealers and all-India Financial Institutions are made eligible to issue CPs to enable them to meet their short-term funding requirements. In the United Kingdom, companies listed on stock exchanges only are entitled to issue CPs. Such was the case in India until recently but now the restriction has been withdrawn. Although in most countries the average maturity of CPs is about 30 days, in Canada, CPs are issued for periods as short as seven days, and in France, CPs can be issued for a period upto seven years. In India, CPs can now be issued for maturities between a minimum of seven days and a maximum upto one year.

Virtually, there does not exist much of a secondary market for commercial paper in the United States, but the tremendous growth of the primary CP market in that country is due primarily to banks standing guarantors either through a back-up line of credit or a letter of credit. In India, though secondary market transaction in CPs existed, the market did not expand, as it should because of prohibition imposed on banks over issuing any standby guarantee. This had really restricted the market among the blue chip companies only. The withdrawal of listing requirement was not of much help. However, the rules were gradually relaxed. Although no issue of CP could be underwritten or co-accepted, presently, banks and financial institutions have the flexibility to provide credit enhancement by way of standby assistance/credit, back-stop facility etc. based on their commercial judgement. Non-bank entities including corporates may also provide unconditional and irrevocable guarantee for credit enhancement provided the guarantor has a credit rating at least one notch higher than the issuer.

The growth in CP issues remained erratic during the initial years of its introduction. The first batch of CPs was issued in India on 27th January, 1990 aggregating Rs. 51 crore. Total amount of issues during 1990 was of the order of Rs. 343 crore. The size of the issue was Rs. 577 crore in 1993 which rose to a high of Rs. 3264 crore in the following year but fell to Rs. 604 crore in 1995, plummeted further to a low of Rs. 76 crore in 1996 and then again rose to Rs. 646 crore in the following year. But from 1998 there has been a steady growth in the issues of CPs which, by the end of 2005, came to be Rs. 13,419 crore. During recent years many companies renewed their CPs, and there are companies which have more than one issues. Some have even made issues varying between 8 and 14, though the number of such companies is small.

In India, the working group on money market under the chairmanship of N. Vaghul recommended introduction of commercial paper in its report of January 1987. The group defined a commercial paper as an *unsecured* promissory note negotiable by endorsement and delivery and sold directly by the issuer to investors or placed through merchant banks and security houses. It is a privately placed money market instrument to enable highly rated corporate borrowers to diversify their sources of short-term borrowings. The important feature of CP is that unlike a trade bill, there is no self-liquidating trade transaction behind it. However, this is not a 'Kite' or accommodation bill which generally records a fictitious commercial transaction and hence, is not overboard.

On the basis of the Vaghul Group's recommendations, the RBI issued detailed guidelines in January 1990. These guidelines were subsequently modified to a great extent to conform to the market requirements. Summary of present guidelines are given below.

1. All non-banking companies, both financial and non-financial, including companies under Foreign Exchange Management Act, are eligible to issue commercial papers. Primary dealers and all-India financial institutions are also eligible to issue CPs within the overall umbrella limit fixed by the Reserve Bank of India. However for these institutions, issue of CPs together with term money borrowings, term deposits, Certificate of Deposits and inter-corporate deposits should not exceed 100 percent of its net owned funds.

2. Commercial papers will be issued in the form of usance promissory notes negotiable by endorsement and delivery at such discount to face value as may be determined by the company issuing them. CP will also be subject to payment of stamp duty as applicable.

3. Tangible net worth of a company desiring to issue CP should not be less than Rs. 4 crore as per latest audited balance sheet, and the company must have been sanctioned working capital limit by bank(s) or all-India financial institution(s).[11]

4. The issuing company must have a minimum prescribed credit rating from approved rating agencies of India. Presently, the approved rating agencies are (a) Credit Rating Information Services of India Limited (CRISIL), (b) Investment Information and Credit Rating Agency of India Limited (ICRA), (c) Credit Analysis and Research Limited (CARE), and (d) Fitch Ratings India (P) Limited. The rating should be current and equivalent to the minimum

---

11. Presently the RBI is considering to allow the banks to offer *revolving underwriting facility* (RUF) to their customers. RUF is a medium term commitment (which may go up to 5 years) by a bank to underwrite continuous issue of short-term notes like CP, by corporates.

P-2 of CRISIL, and it has not fallen due for review at the time of issuance of the CP. The credit rating agency shall indicate the date when the rating is due for review. While credit rating agency can decide the validity period of the rating, they would have to closely monitor the rating assigned to the issuers vis-à-vis their track record at regular intervals and make their revision in rating public through their publications, and the Website.

5.   The borrowing accounts of the company must have been classified as standard assets by the financing bank(s)/institutions(s).

6.   Commercial papers can be issued for maturity between seven days and a maximum upto one year. The maturity date of the CP should not go beyond the date up to which the credit rating is valid. There is no grace period available for making payment on maturity.

7.   Commercial papers can be issued on a single date, or in parts on different dates within a period of two weeks from the date on which the issuer opens the issue for subscription. The issue must be through a scheduled bank acting as Issuing and Paying Agent (IPA). Although CPs may be issued in parts on different dates, maturity date of all such CPs will be the same. Every issue of CP including renewal should be treated as a fresh issue.

8.   CPs may be issued in multiples of Rs. 5 lakh, and the minimum amount to be invested by a single investor in the primary market shall also be Rs. 5 lakh.

9.   All issuing expenses of commercial papers such as, dealers' fees, rating agency's fees and other charges, should be borne by the issuing company.

10.   Commercial papers may be issued to any person or corporate body registered or incorporated in India, including banks, and also to unincorporated bodies.

CPs can also be issued to Non-resident Indians (NRIs) and Foreign Institutional Investors (FIIs).

Procedure for Issue of Commercial Paper

1.   As mentioned before, a company desiring to issue CP must appoint an Issuing and Paying Agent (IPA). Only a scheduled bank can act as an IPA. The IPA should verify all the required documents, viz. copy of board resolution, signatures of authorised executants, and certify that the documents are in order and that it has a valid agreement with the issuer. The IPA would also ensure that the issue of CP is well within the prescribed credit rating.

2.   The issuer should disclose to the potential investors its financial position as per the standard market practice and will give copies of IPA certificates as mentioned above to the investor(s).

3.   After the exchange of deal confirmation between the investor and the issuer, the issuing company shall issue physical certificates to the investor or arrange for crediting the CP to the investor's account with a depository approved by SEBI. Every CP issue should be reported to the Reserve Bank of India through the IPA within three days from the date of completion of the issue.

4. The initial investor in the CP shall pay the discounted value of the CP by means of an *account payee* cheque to the issuing company's account through the IPA.

5. Total CPs issued by a company should not exceed working capital fund-based limit (WCFBL).

6. Once the issue is placed in the market, the fund-based working capital limit will be correspondingly reduced.

7. As mentioned before, the issue of CP cannot be underwritten or co-accepted in any manner though banks/FIs can now provide standby assistance/credit backstop facility for credit enhancement of a CP. If the issuing company wants an enhanced working capital limit, it has to apply for the same afresh. Restoration of working capital limit is no longer automatic.

8. The IPA should immediately report to the Reserve Bank of India whenever a default occurs in the repayment of CP on due date.

The Central Government has granted exemption with respect to the issuance of CP from the purview of Section 58A of the *Companies Act* relating to public deposits.

The primary investors in CPs are generally banks and mutual funds. Other financial institutions, public sector undertakings and DFHI also buy CPs to park their surplus funds. In order to develop secondary market in CPs the DFHI provides a forum for buying and selling CPs. They offer a two-way quotes on a daily basis. But as yet, not much turnover is visible in the secondary CP market, which is retarding its growth. The reason behind this is that major buyers of CPs hold them till maturity.

In India, default in repayment of CPs is few and far between.

Pricing of Commercial Paper

The Vaghul Group observed that on the one hand, the CP market could provide highly rated corporate borrowers with cheaper funds as compared to bank finance, and on the other, it would allow other corporates or institutional investors to get better interest rate than they could obtain from bank deposits. This suggests that pricing of CP should be such that it could maintain this competitive position with bank deposits.

Besides bank deposits, CP will also have to compete with other short-term financial instruments in the market like certificate of deposit (CD), inter-bank call money, treasury bills, bills rediscounting and of course, the emerging money market mutual funds units.

The pricing of CP must take into consideration various expenses connected with the launching and issuing of CP. The Vaghul Group estimated in 1987 that these issue expenses could be 1 percent of the amount issued, which included the management fees of merchant bankers (0.50 percent), commitment charges for standby arrangement (0.25 percent), fees for credit rating (0.10 percent) and stamp duty, etc. (0.15 percent). Presently, with the rise in volume and competition the issue expenses have come down. Now, major expenses are as follows:

Stamp duty	0.20 percent, if placed through banks and 1 percent, if placed through merchant banks
Rating fees	0.10 percent subject to a minimum of Rs. 1 lakh
IPA's fee	0.10 percent
Stand-by fee	0.15 percent
Management fee	0.20–0.25 percent

The aggregate issue expenses is between 0.75 percent and 0.80 percent. Keeping this in mind we can now examine the rates offered by major competing instruments in the market.

1. *Bank deposits:* Average rate offered by banks during 2007 for a period of 14 days, 30 days, 3 months, 6 months and 1 year are 4 percent, 5 percent, 5.5 percent, 7 percent and 9 percent respectively.

2. *Inter-bank call money:* When ceiling on the inter-bank call rates was removed by the RBI, the call money market became highly volatile, and often turned out to be outrageous. The rates were anywhere between 5 percent and more than 100 percent. However, with the removal of inter-bank deposits from the calculation of net demand and time liabilities for the purpose of cash reserve ratio and statutory liquidity ratio, the call market is showing signs of stabilisation. Presently (January 2008) the average rates move around 6 percent.

3. *Bank's certificate of deposits:* These are offered at different rates depending upon the need of funds of the bank issuing it. The rate is on the decline during the past few years owing to substantial liquidity in the banking system. Presently (January 2008) the average rates vary between 6.85 and 10 percent p.a. for a period of 3 months to 1 year.

4. *Treasury bills:* Average ruling rates (January 2008) for 91 days, 182 days and 364 days treasury bills are 7.02 percent, 7.23 percent and 7.39 percent p.a. respectively. Weighted average rate (market-non-standard) in Repo transactions in treasury bills is 6.05 percent and the rates for Reverse Repo transactions vary between 5.75 percent and 6 percent.

5. *Bills re-discounting:* Presently (January 2008), the ruling rate is about 12.5 percent p.a.

6. *Bank's PLR:* The average rate presently (January 2008), varies between 12.75 percent and 13.25 percent p.a.

7. *Bank rate:* Presently (2007), it is 6 percent.

Commercial paper has to find a place among these competing instruments keeping in mind, that it should be aligned to the market rates and, at the same time, the rate must be lower than or close to PLR at which rate a first class corporate can raise working capital loan from banks.

We should, however, remember that in India, rates of interest on various financial instruments are yet to be properly aligned owing to existence of some administrative element in the interest rate structure. An effective reference rate in the economy is yet to emerged. So far RBI's attempt to resurrect bank rate for this purpose has not been successful. As the indication goes, perhaps the Repo rate is likely to emerge as a reference rate. When the rates are closely aligned, the rate on commercial paper should find a place certainly below the PLR, but above the treasury bill rate.

Effective Interest Rate

Effective rate on CP is influenced by methods of placement,—whether it is purchased directly or through a dealer—interest rate (discount) and commitment charges for back-up/guarantee/LC, if any. The formula for calculation of *effective interest rate* (EIR) is given by

$$EIR = \frac{\text{Total financing costs}}{\text{Net cash from CP}} \times \frac{365}{\text{Maturity period of CP}}$$

Total issue expenses can be taken as 0.75 percent of the face value of CP. By way of example, assume that a company plans to issue commercial papers for Rs. 100 lakh at a discount rate of 7 percent p.a. The effective interest rate (EIR) to the issuer for 30 days and 180 days maturity will be as follows:

Thirty days' maturity:
Total financing cost
Discount cost: $(0.07 \times 100)/12$ = Rs. 0.5833 lakh
Issue expenses: $(0.75 \times 100)/100$ = Rs. 0.7500 lakh

| Total | Rs. 1.3333 lakh |

Cash received: Rs. $100 - 0.5833$ = Rs. 99.4167 lakh
Hence,
$(1.333/99.4167) \times (365/30) = 0.1632$ or 16.32 percent

One hundred eighty days maturity:
Total financing cost
Discount cost: $(0.07 \times 100 \times 6)/12$ = Rs. 3.50 lakh
Issue expenses: $(0.75 \times 100)/100$ = Rs. 0.75 lakh
Total Rs. 4.25 lakh
Cash received: Rs. $100 - 4.25$ = Rs. 95.75 lakh
Hence,
$(4.25/95.75) \times (365/180) = 0.0900$ or 9 percent

It would appear that under the given conditions, 30 days' maturity is cost-prohibitive because the EIR is much above the PLR, while it is feasible for 180 days' maturity, as it is lower than PLR. The reason behind this is that the issue expenses are spread over a longer period in the latter case. During 2007 the average rate for CPs has been 7.6 percent. There is a case for reduction of issue expenses to align the rate further with the market. Cost of stamp duty in India is very high, around 0.20 percent, which calls for substantial reduction or total withdrawal. There is no stamp duty on CP in the US, France or UK.

Securitised Commercial Paper

Although CPs were originally conceived to be unsecured in nature, in several countries of Europe and America, collateralised commercial papers have already emerged. First movers in this CP market are large finance companies, which created specific pools of automobile loans to be tied to a particular issue of *securitised commercial paper.*

During the recent times, small and less creditworthy firms have also been able to raise funds through securitised CPs. For example, a small firm could be the supplier to highly rated companies, and thus may have a pool of high quality receivables. But given the status of the firm, it may not be able to get the required credit rating from a rating agency. In such a situation, the firm may form a financial subsidiary and transfer these receivables to this new company. Because of the high quality receivables this new company will be able to obtain a good rating of CPs collateralised by such high quality receivables. Due to this credit enhancement, the not-so-creditworthy firms often get a better rate in the CP market.

FACTORING

Factoring may appear to be similar to obtaining bank loan against receivables (through cash credit or bills purchased and discounted), but it is much more than that. Factoring is a value-added service that goes much beyond providing finance.

Factoring is among the oldest of financial services for facilitating trade transactions. Originally, it evolved as a means of financing trade between England and Colonial America. It was very popular in textiles and apparel business, but others regarded it as an omen of financial distress. Although such a stigma is no longer there, and factoring has spread all over the world, in the United States factoring continues to be mostly prevalent in textiles and apparels; not so much in other industries.

When it comes to financing small and medium enterprises (SMEs) banks continues to be conservative (even where credit guarantee is available, as in India, from specialised institutions). They ask for collateral as a condition for financing. For a start-up enterprise all available collaterals are mortgaged/ pledged with the bank to secure the first doze of finance. When it comes to short-term financing it may not have any further collateral to offer. This forces the enterprise to seek alternative sources of financing. One such source is suppliers' credit. This has become an important source of working capital finance than bank loans. But suppliers' credit is more costly than bank loans as the rate of discount on bills is very high. Unfortunately, the SMEs with liquidity constraints have no choice but to go for more costly solutions.

Late payment of sales invoice is the major source of liquidity problem of SMEs. The problem is almost universal. In United States and EU countries it varies between 45 days and 60 days. In developing nations, like India, it is anywhere between 60 days and 180 days. Factoring services typically address this problem.

A factor's approach to client's risk assessment is significantly different from that of banks. Banks are primarily concerned about the ability of the borrower to use the bank loan to ensure a sufficient return to service the debt. As they do not have enough confidence in SMEs, they mitigate the risk of non-payment by obtaining collateral. For banks it is a lending operation. But factors do not lend money to the client in the typical sense; they in fact take over the client's invoice or in effect, purchase the client's bills for a discount. Hence, a factor's risk assessment revolves around the ability of the buyers of the client to make payment of supplier's bills on due date. As SMEs typically supply to large corporates, the risk assessment becomes easy and less costly for the factor. Therefore, factors generally do not ask for collaterals from a client except, in some extreme cases, as security against fraudulent practice by the client. However, factors would invariably take personal guarantees from the owners of the client organisation. A factor would generally look for the performance of the sales ledger of the client, the profile and creditworthiness of the principal debtors of the client and the integrity of sales invoices.

As against bank lending, factoring offers a mix of finance, credit insurance and financial management services. It is a composite financial product for management and financing of accounts receivable. It enables businesses access to finance based on their growth in sales rather than on growth of assets, which is the typical concern of banks. As small but growing businesses typically needs investment in sales rather than in fixed assets, factoring services would be of immense help to them.

In spite of great advantages that factoring offers it suffers from some image problems, which retards its growth. Due to lack of concentrated marketing efforts the factoring product is not properly understood by the prospective client organisations. When a factor is a non-banking finance company clients feel uneasy to hand over the management of the sales ledger. Even in advanced countries, factoring is often perceived to be a distress financing. It often gives wrong message to the buyer-organisations: they feel that the supplier must have been refused bank financing because of lowering of creditworthiness, and hence he can no longer be considered as a reliable supplier. With banks and well-established financial institutions entering the factoring market the negative image will be mitigated to a large extent. Banks have reasons to enter this market because they have the resources and skills of debt-management. Factoring is a viable alternative to overdraft/loan financing. It would enable banks to effectively service their clients, particularly in SME segments, in line with their sales-related growth. Although the factoring business would get tremendous boost as more and more banks join in, there is a downside to it as pointed out by Soufani[12]. He demonstrated that as banks are used to standardised approach in risk assessment, factoring services offered by banks would tend to be limited to more established business.

---

12 Soufani, K., "The Role of Factoring in Financing UK SMEs: A Supply Side Analysis", *Journal of Small Business and Enterprise Development,* Vol. 8(1), 2001.

In advanced financial markets, factoring has evolved as a 'without recourse financing'. This is popularly called *maturity factoring without recource.* Under this type, accounts receivables are sold directly to the factor but only on the approval of the trade credit by the latter. When a client desires to sell to a party on credit, he notifies his intention to the factor who undertakes a credit analysis of the prospective buyer, and if satisfied, he approves of the sale and assumes full responsibility of collection and bad-debt. The (client) seller on his part informs the customer to pay directly to the factor on the expiry of the credit period, and sends a copy of the invoice to the factor. On receipt of the invoice the factor remits cash to the client-supplier after deducting his commission. This arrangement, however, does not preclude the supplier to make sale to a customer not approved by the factor. But in cases of such sales, the factor would assume no responsibility for collection.

In underdeveloped financial markets like India, factoring is predominantly done on recourse basis. The most general type is *maturity factoring with recourse.* This closely resembles bank finance against pledge of book debt or bills discounting. In this case, the factor does not purchase the receivables straightaway, but gives loans upto a certain percentage, say 80 percent, of invoice value. After the factor approves a trade credit, the book debt is assigned to the factor by the seller under a general agreement to that effect which entitles the factor to invoice and collect the debt in his own name. As and when the payment is received, it is first adjusted against the loan and then the balance amount is passed over to the seller. The factor here does provide all collection and credit services, which are not available when the finance is taken from the bank. But the factor does not assume the responsibility of bad-debt which remains with the seller.

There is also a third type of factoring which is called *Invoice Discounting.* It is much more about providing finance than the two types of factoring discussed above, which provide finance as well as professional services relating to management of sales ledger. Invoice discounting follows almost exactly the same process as with other two types of factoring but in this case there is a confidentiality clause incorporated in the agreement whereby the buyers of the client are not aware of the engagement of the factor. The client direcly obtains payment from the buyers to the credit of a trust account controlled by the factor.

In India, the working group on the money market (Vaghul Group), referred to earlier, first recommended that the banks and private non-bank financial institutions should be encouraged to provide factoring services. The group observed that introduction of factoring services could solve the financial problems of small-scale suppliers to a large extent. In fact, in India, factoring has been conceived to primarily help out small suppliers both in obtaining finance and managing their accounts receivables. Vaghul Group's recommendations were followed up by Reserve Bank of India by the appointment of another committee headed by C.S. Kalyanasundaram to examine the scope and need for factoring services in India. The committee submitted its report in 1988 where it observed that problem of timely realisation of the bills by the small scale industrial (SSI) sector was causing liquidity crunch and retarding their growth. To solve this problem, the committee recommended introduction of factoring services in India. Accordingly, the RBI advised banks to introduce factoring through creation of a subsidiary. Later, the Central Government also declared factoring as a permitted activity under *Banking Regulation Act, 1949.*

Among the first of such factoring companies to come up in India was SBI Factors and Commercial Services Ltd. It was jointly promoted in 1991 by (i) State Bank of India: its two subsidiaries State Bank of Indore and State Bank of Saurashtra, (ii) Union Bank of India and (iii) Small Industries Development Bank of India. Presently, it has five branches at Delhi, Baroda, Mumbai, Pune and Coimbatore. But the company has not been able to make much headway towards the objectives for which it was set up. During the first eight years of its existence, it was able to develop a portfolio of only about 300 clients out of which only 40 percent were from small-scale sector. Primary reasons behind the slow growth of factoring services in India could be attributed to the absence of systematic credit information in SSI sector and general risk aversion of the bankers who man the factoring arms. One must understand that factoring is different from banking both in respect of the attitude towards risk and the scope of financial services.

As discussed above, factoring should be viewed more as a provider of financial services than a mere lending operation. The range of financial services provided by a factor, besides financing, are discussed in the following sections in greater detail.

Administration of Sales Ledger and Collection

A factor has specialisation in administration of sales ledger of the client organisations. The latter, after concluding the credit sales, sends a copy of the invoice to the factor who makes necessary entries in the sales ledger of the client organisation. Similarly, payment advices are also marked to the factor. Periodical reports on the status of the receivables are sent by the factor to the client organisation along with an accounting statement. This is a pure book-keeping and accounting service provided by the factor. In view of large clientele base, it is easy for the factoring organisation to computerise the operations which reduces the transaction costs and distributes overheads. As a result, the fees charged by the factoring organisation is often much below the in-house cost of the client organisation.

In addition to administration of sales ledger, a factor may also undertake collection of receivables. This enables the client organisation to reduce the cost of collection substantially. In fact, the collection department of the client organisation could be totally dismantled under this factoring arrangement. Besides this, the client being freed from the worries of collection can concentrate on sales.

The factor with specialised and skilled manpower and sophisticated information system is often in a better position to monitor and collect receivables. This is more suitable to SSI sector which generally lacks which such sophisticated infrastructure. It is also found that debtors are more responsive to a factor than to the client organisation because of the single-purposeness and distance maintained by the factor.

Credit Information and Other Advisory Services

As a factor deals with a large number of clients and their debtors, he has access to wide-ranging information on the financial standing, track record of payments and general creditworthiness of the buying or selling organisations. The factor can pass over these information at a fee to a client enabling the latter to have better control over trade credit. The same network of information also enables a factor to locate good customer for the products of the client organisation.

Besides providing credit information services, many factors, particularly in the developed world, provide advisory services on economic trends, implication of fiscal policies for a particular industry, global scenario affecting a domestic industry and so forth. At their advanced stages, many factors are found to advise their clients on work-load analysis, machinery replacement programmes, technology identification and import, etc. Some also provide information as to the availability of suitable marketing and technical personnel for hiring by a client organisation.

Cost of Factoring Services

The cost calculations for using factoring services have two main elements: (i) the fee or commission charged by the factor and (ii) the interest cost for providing finance against receivables. At times, the factor combines these two charges and quote a comprehensive rate.

The economics of the cost of factoring services should be viewed against the cost of operating the accounting ledgers and/or the collection department plus the interest cost of financing receivables against the effective rate of interest to the factor-user vis-á-vis the cost of finance available from banks.

Example A company's sales average around Rs. 25 lakh per month with credit period of one and a half month. The company is negotiating with a factor who has quoted a fee of 1 percent for administration and collection of receivables, and 12 percent interest p.a. on money advanced, which may be 100 percent of the invoice value. The amount is remittable after 10 days of the invoice date. Presently, the variable cost of running the collection department is Rs. 20,000 per month. Financing cost for engaging the factor is calculated as follows:

Total financing cost includes:	*Rs. in lakh*
Factor's commission: Rs. 25×0.01	$= 0.25$
Interest cost: Rs. $25 \times 0.12 \times 35/365$	$= 0.29$
	$= 0.54$
Less: Savings on the cost of collection department	$= 0.20$
Total	$= 0.34$

We can now calculate the *effective interest rate* (EIR) of the firm for availing of factoring service as below:

$$EIR = \frac{Rs.\ 0.34}{25} \times \frac{365}{35} = 0.1418 \text{ or } 14.18\%$$

The EIR should now be compared with the lending rate of the bank to arrive at a decision.

Existence of a factor in the sales function of an enterprise not only smoothens the distribution process but also improves the quality of the receivables, because it acts as a deterrent to the firm against contracting receivables of questionable creditworthiness.

Forfaiting

Forfaiting is an extension of factoring services in international trade. It enables an exporter to discount his export receivables with an agency called forfaiter. It also frees the exporter from the commercial and political risks inherent in international trade, as forfaiting is mostly done on 'without recourse' basis.

In India, EXIM Bank acts as the nodal agency for forfaiting contracts. Generally, the following steps are followed in a forfaiting arrangement:

1. The exporter finalises the contract with the importer with regard to order quantity, price, currency of payment, credit terms, delivery period, nature of documentation, etc.

2. The exporter then approaches the EXIM Bank or the Indian arm of an international forfaiter. The exporter shall provide the forfaiter all the relevant details of the transactions to enable the forfaiter to evaluate the credit risk and political risk involved in the transaction. This evaluation is generally done by the international correspondent of the Indian forfaiting firm in view of their expertise and knowledge of the rules and regulations prevalent in the countries concerned.

3. After completion of the appraisal, the forfaiting agency will indicate the discount rate, which has a bearing upon the extent of risk undertaken. Having obtained the discount rate quotation from the forfaiter, the exporter would approach the EXIM Bank for its approval. If the EXIM Bank feels that the rate is not competitive, it might ask the forfaiter to reduce the rate or advise the exporter to contact another forfaiter for a better rate.

4. After finalisation of the discount rate, the exporter will quote the final contract price to the overseas importer by loading the discount charges on the sale price. On finalisation of the deal the exporter will simultaneously sign a commercial contract with the importer and a forfaiting contract with the forfaiter through EXIM Bank. The latter will have to issue two certificates: one on the commitment fees and the other on the discount rate.

5. The forfaiter would now discount the bills of the exporter drawn on the importer. It would present the bills on due date to the importer for payment, or it may sell them in the secondary market.

In India, exporters are generally not able to negotiate a sale contract beyond 180 days because of the restriction imposed by the RBI on export bills financing beyond that period. For deferred credit beyond 180 days the exporter will have to obtain special permission from the RBI which is beset with several procedural hassles. Forfaiting enables the exporter to bypass all such problems because forfaiting contract has much longer duration. It can go upto even 5–7 years.

Forfaiting also enables an exporter to make exports to countries where *export credit guarantee coverage* is not available.

Cost of forfaiting is a combination of the financing charge, commitment charge and the EXIM Bank fee.

Financing charges are dependent on the tenor, the country risk and the counter party (bank) risk. Presently, it varies between 50 and 1400 basis points over LIBOR. The financing charge is payable from the date of providing finance.

The commitment charge depends on the usance period and the country of destination. It is the opportunity cost of the forfaiter, which he does not want to lose out in case the exporter ultimately does not utilise the designated credit line. Presently, the commitment charge varies between 13 and 15 basis points.

As a normal practice, a forfaiter sets out exposure limit for a portfolio of countries depending on the extent of credit and political risks.

INTER-CORPORATE DEPOSIT (ICD)

ICD market has been in existence much before the emergence of commercial paper. It was an informal market to begin with and then gradually it acquired the formal character of inter-corporate funds clearance mechanism. The market provides both an inlet and outlet of short-term corporate funds.

The *Indian Companies Act* does not make any distinction between public fixed deposits and inter-corporate deposits. Hence, the provisions that limit the quantum of deposits to 10 percent of the paid-up capital and free reserves of the company are also applicable to ICDs. Besides, Sub-section (9) of Section 58 (A) of Indian Companies Act which debars companies from raising further deposits if they default in payment of interest or repayment of the principal amount, is also applicable to inter-corporate deposits.

ICDs are predominantly unsecured in nature. But some companies making investments in ICDs are often found to ask for collaterals if the amount is very large, or if the borrowing company has a low credit standing.

The rate of interest on ICDs depends primarily upon the demand and supply of fund in the market and the risk perception of the lender.

Inter-corporate deposit market is highly sensitive to default. As number of players is small, default-information spreads very fast. During the last few years, the market has become subdued owing to a few renowned companies defaulting on repayment of ICDs.

INTEREST RATE SWAPS AND FORWARD RATE AGREEMENT

In 1999, Reserve Bank of India permitted banks, financial institutions and primarily dealers to undertake *forward rate agreement* (FRA) and *interest rate swaps* (IRS). They could offer these two products to corporates and also use them for their own assets-liability management. However, the RBI has advised the participants that before undertaking any activity in these instruments, they should ensure that appropriate infrastructure and risk management systems are put in place.

Both IRS and FRA, being derivative financial products, do not by themselves provide funds, but they protect the firm from erosion of value due to interest rate variation.

Interest Rate Swaps (IRS)

The most popular definition of interest rate swaps is that it is an agreement between two parties to exchange cash flow streams for a specified period to reap mutual advantage of interest rate differentials faced by them and also to protect themselves against adverse movement of interest rates. IRS exists because of imperfections in financial markets. These imperfections result in differences in rates faced by two parties. They may be located in two different financial markets, which having grown differently also react with differing speed to a market stimulus giving rise to difference in rates at a given point in time. This is the reason why a large number of IRS occurs between firms in the United States, Europe and Asia.

Interest rate swaps may occur in the domestic market also when two parties face different types of interest rate obligations (fixed rate or floating rate) or different levels of creditworthiness in the financial market. IRS can be carried out directly between two parties or through an intermediary, generally a bank. In the latter case, the bank may also act as a counterparty to both the parties, and thus bear the risk of default by either party which eliminates the need for both the parties to investigate the creditworthiness of each other. This is of particular advantage to the borrower with low creditworthiness. Under this arrangement, anonymity of the parties could be maintained.

We shall first discuss IRS between two parties in two different financial markets.

Example A financial company in the United States with high creditworthiness desires to obtain a loan of $ 75 million. The company could raise this fund by selling fixed-rate bonds @ 9 percent p.a. It can also borrow in the Euromarket at a variable rate of LIBOR plus 0.5 percent. But the company is more inclined towards raising the finance at variable rate.

A manufacturing company in Sweden has plans to buy new plants and machinery, the cost of which is equivalent of US $ 75 million. As the investments are going to be in fixed assets, the Swedish company prefers fixed rate loans. The company can raise this amount by selling bonds at 11 percent p.a. It can also obtain the finance at a variable rate of LIBOR plus 0.5 percent but it would rather prefer fixed rate financing.

Both the US company and the Swedish company can be brought together by a bank to undertake an IRS transaction. The modalities of the operation will be as follows:

First, the US company agrees to raise $ 75 million by 10-year fixed rate bonds @ 9 percent p.a. and the Swedish company agrees to raise the equivalent amount at LIBOR plus 0.5 percent. The two companies now agree to swap interest payments for the next 10 years, which, in effect, means that the US company will remit to the Swedish company the variable LIBOR rate, and the Swedish company agrees to make fixed-rate interest payments to the US company at a rate of 9.50 percent p.a. This swap arrangement is explained in Figure 7.2.

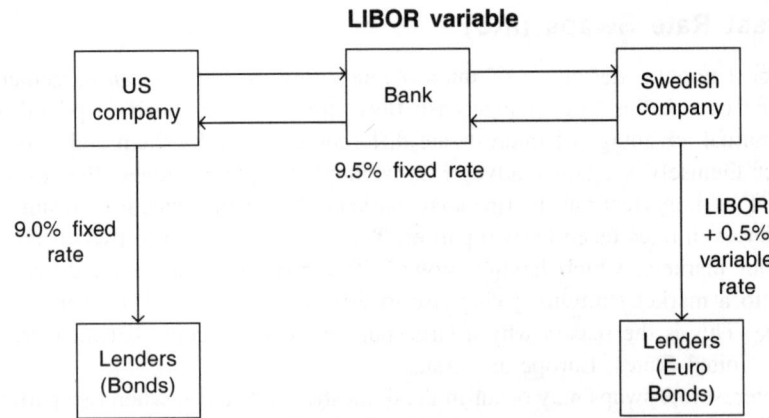

Figure 7.2 Interest rate swap.

The above swap arrangement will benefit both the US and the Swedish companies as the following calculations will show.

US company
Option 1: Without swap arrangement
      Pays Euro lenders   (–) $ 75 million × (LIBOR + 0.5%)
Option 2: With swap arrangement
      Pays the Swedish company   (–) $ 75 million × (LIBOR)
      Receives from the
      Swedish company $ 75 million × 9.5%
      Pays bond subscribers   (–) $ 75 million × 9%
      Net yearly benefit $ 75 million × 1% = $ 750,000

We may observe that the US company saves 0.5 percent on its variable rate borrowing in addition to the 0.5 percent it makes from the difference between the rate paid to the bond holders and the rate paid by the Swedish company. Total benefit, therefore, comes to be 1 percent p.a. This, in effect, means that the US company obtains financing at an effective rate of LIBOR minus 0.5 percent.

Swedish company
Option 1: Without swap arrangement
      Pays bond subscribers   (–) $ 75 million × 0.11

Option 2: With swap arrangement

Pays the US company	(–) $ 75 million × 9.5%
Receives from the US company	$ 75 million × LIBOR
Pays variable rate lenders	(–) $ 75 million × (LIBOR + 0.5%)
Net yearly benefit	$ 75 million × 1% = $ 750,000

Under this swap arrangement the Swedish company also enjoys the benefit equal to the US company. The effective rate paid by the Swedish company is $11 - 1 = 10$ percent p.a.

It would appear from the above calculations that the figure $ 75 million is common to all transactions and hence, can be bracketed out as *notional amount* which is used as a base for calculating interest. This may or may not be the actual face value of the transaction, but the sum agreed between two parties on which interest rate will be calculated for swapping. In the ultimate analysis it is only the interest payments that are swapped. Generally, only the *net amount* is remitted by one party to the other on the *payment exchange date.*

Suppose the average of LIBOR is 6 percent p.a. during the past six months to the *payment exchange date.* The US company would owe the Swedish firm;

$$\$ 75 \text{ million} \times 0.06 \times 0.5 = \$ 2,250,000$$

and the Swedish company would owe the US company;

$$\$ 75 \text{ million} \times 0.0950 \times 0.5 = \$ 3,562,500$$

Hence, the Swedish company would remit the *net amount* of $ 3,562,500 – 2,250,000 = $ 1,312,500 to the US company.

IRS in the Domestic Market

In the domestic market, opportunities for interest rate swap exist due to variation in interest rates at which two parties could raise the similar amount of loan. This variation is due to the difference in the creditworthiness of two borrowers. The risk premium makes the difference in rates. IRS can also be used to protect a bank or corporate against interest rate fluctuations in future. The operation is similar to the one discussed above.

We have indicated earlier that in India, a true reference rate like LIBOR is yet to emerge. Till the time such a rate is developed, one can use average of treasury bills rate for a specified period as the rate on which swap transactions can be based.

Example Company X Ltd. and Company Z Ltd. both desire to raise a loan of Rs. 100 lakh.

X Ltd. having good rating in the market can raise the loan either at a fixed rate of 10.55 percent p.a., or at a variable rate of TBR 6 months plus 0.30 percent, but the company prefers to borrow at a floating rate. Z Ltd., being not so creditworthy, could raise the same amount but at a higher fixed rate of 11.75 percent p.a. or 6 months TBR plus 1 percent p.a., but it prefers to borrow at fixed rate.

An analysis of the rates available to the two companies will reveal that difference in rates in the variable rate market is lower than in the fixed rate market. This difference could set the motion of a swap agreement between the two parties whereby X Ltd. would borrow at a fixed rate and Z Ltd. at a floating rate and exchange their cash flows in the following manner:

X Ltd.

Option 1: Without swap arrangement

Pays the lender	(–) Rs. 100 lakh × TBR + 0.3

Option 2: With swap arrangement

Pays to Z Ltd.	(–) Rs. 100 lakh × TBR
Receives from Z Ltd.	Rs. 100 lakh × 10.5%
Pays to the lender	(–) Rs. 100 lakh × 10.55%
Net yearly benefit	Rs. 100 lakh × 0.25% = Rs. 25,000

Z Ltd.

Option 1: Without swap arrangement

Pays the lender	(–) Rs. 100 lakh × 11.75%

Option 2: With swap arrangement

Pays to X Ltd.	(–) Rs. 100 lakh × 10.5%
Receives from X Ltd.	Rs. 100 lakh × TBR
Pays to the lender	(–) Rs. 100 lakh × TBR + 1%
Net yearly benefit	Rs. 100 lakh × 0.25% = Rs. 25,000

Swap is an arrangement similar to sharing financial market tariff between two parties. In the above example, the tariff appears to be 0.50 percent which is shared equally by the two parties.

Characteristics of Interest Rate Swaps

1. IRS can be based on new or existing loan. Firms may often desire to *swap out* their existing fixed rate loans for variable-rate loans or vice versa.

2. Swap can also be undertaken without any underlying loan amount as it is only an agreement to pay a defined cash flow stream for a specified period.

3. Transaction costs and legal expenses in swap transactions are high which make transaction in small amount uneconomical. International swap transactions are often conducted for a sum of US $ 25 million.

4. Swaps can be employed by firms which do not want to sell underlying assets or liabilities but desire to replace unwanted assets or liabilities at better rates.

5. Swaps can be contracted many years in advance to protect a firm from adverse interest rate movements.

6. Swap is an off-balance sheet transaction. A balance sheet may show a high level of fixed-rate loans, but the firm might have swapped them for variable-rate loans. This may create problems for the user of balance sheet unless the fact is disclosed in the balance sheet.

Risk Element

The risk element in swap agreement emanate from the default by either party to honour the commitment. In our first example, the US company originally wanted variable-rate financing but had agreed to go in for fixed-rate under swap arrangement. If now the Swedish company failed to remit the agreed cash flows, the US company would not also make any payment to the Swedish company, but it is now stuck with a fixed-rate loan which it never wanted. The contrary will happen if the US firm defaults.

The guidelines issued by Reserve Bank of India on interest rate swaps require the banks to disclose in their balance sheets any concentration of credit risks arising out of IRS deals. Concentration would mean exposures to particular industries or swaps with highly geared companies.

Banks will also have to disclose the 'fair' value of swap book. If swaps are linked to specific assets, liabilities or commitments, the 'fair' value would be the estimated amounts receivable or payable to terminate the swaps. For trading swaps, the 'fair' value would be the marked-to-market value.

Banks will be required to quantify losses which would be incurred in the event of counterparties failing to fulfil their obligations. The nature and terms of swaps including information on credit and market risk, and the accounting policies adopted for recording swap transactions will also have to be disclosed.

The income and expenditure relating to trading swaps can be recognised only on the settlement date whereas fees could be recognised as an immediate income or expenditure.

The RBI guidelines also stipulate separate capital adequacy norms for banks, financial institutions and primary dealers for undertaking IRS, or forward rate agreements.

FORWARD RATE AGREEMENT

A *forward rate agreement* (FRA) is a forward contract where the parties agree to lend or borrow at a certain interest rate in future. This is also called *future rate agreement*. By this instrument, future short-term interest rate could be locked-in.

In the advanced financial market FRAs are available over the counter. A set of bid-offer spreads is published there indicating rates of interest for different future periods. FRA's are entered into between say, a bank and the customer on a *notional amount* on which such rates will be calculated. Both the parties agree that compensation amount would pass between them if there is any deviation of interest rate (as published at the time of the agreement) from the rate available on the date the loan was agreed to be made.

For example, a company may have a loan of £ 10 million in its books at a floating rate of interest payable three months hence. The company fears that if the rate of interest goes up it will be required to pay more amount which will make its projections topsy-turvy. Hence, the company desires to protect itself against such a situation. The company finds that bid-offer spreads for three months' sterling pound contracted today are 10.82500–10.70000. The company may now buy an FRA for a notional amount of £ 10 million deliverable three months hence at 10.825 percent rate of interest.

Suppose now that the interest rate spread has moved up to 11.82500–11.70000 on the contracted date of delivery. Under the FRA the bank will be required to pay to the customer a sum equal to 1 percent on £ 10 million for three months, which is £ 25,000. By this time the floating rate payable by the company on its original loan has also gone up by 1 percent. But the company does not lose out on such a rise because it has already received that 1 percent equivalent from the bank under the FRA.

On the contrary, if the rate of interest, instead of rising, has fallen, then the compensation amount would have been payable by the customer to the bank. The customer would lose on its FRA but gain on the original floating rate loan.

We should mention here that the actual compensation would be slightly less than £ 25,000 because this amount will be discounted at the settlement rate as the compensation is paid at the beginning of the interest period, whereas the interest on the original loan is payable at the end of the interest period. In other words, the compensation plus interest receivable on it during the interest period would equal to £ 25,000.

SUMMARY

Accounts payable provides the first dose of financing towards gross working capital requirement of an enterprise. The remaining part, popularly known as *working capital gap* (WCG), is financed by banks, other short-term lenders and finally, by the promoters from long-term sources i.e., net working capital (NWC).

In India, banks would not like the NWC to be zero or negative (or, current ratio to be one or less than that) because NWC provides liquidity cushion against sudden lengthening of cash cycle of an enterprise. The notion of liquidity has, however, undergone considerable change from cash, marketable securities and receivables to functional liquidity like, providing inventories along the production-distribution line of an enterprise. By suitable structuring of working capital, a firm can do business with zero or even negative NWC.

Principles of lending for working capital by commercial banks have undergone considerable changes during the last 25 years. Tandon Committee's recommendations in 1975 replaced security-oriented lending by need-based lending. The committee observed that bank credit would be only supplementary to borrowers' resources who should gradually lessen their dependence on bank finance. The working capital finance would be available to the borrowers on the basis of industry-wise norms for holding different current assets. Maximum permissible bank finance (MPBF) would be calculated under three methods of lending which would increase borrowers' contribution to working capital finance in a graduated manner. The committee, however, was against any rigidity in the application of norms and held that allowance must be made for some flexibility under circumstances justifying a need for reexamination. Several such examples were also cited by the committee where norms could be relaxed.

The Chore group, constituted by Reserve Bank of India in 1979, made an in-depth study of cash credit system of lending in India vis-á-vis loan system prevalent elsewhere. The group observed that the huge gap between the sanctioned limits and their actual availment was creating problems for monetary planning at the macro-level of the country, and funds planning at the bank-level. It was also found that cash credit system encouraged inefficiency in working capital management, and the practice of annual review, being too long, perpetuated this inefficiency.

Loan system, mostly prevalent in developed countries, could take care of many of the problems of cash credit system. It could also force the borrowers to plan their cash budget and thus make working capital management more efficient. But the inflexibility apparent in a loan system might dilute the system if proper care was not taken.

Bill system of financing, inspite of its several advantages and encouragements by the RBI and the government, has not developed in India as it should, primarily because of the reluctance of the business community to adhere to payment discipline embedded in the system and, the part payment of the bill being a prevalent practice.

The Chore group having reviewed the three systems of lending, though recognised the superiority of loan and bills system of financing, stopped short of replacing cash credit system by them. It might have thought that time was not yet ripe to do so. The group advocated revamping the cash credit system and bringing in financial disciplines among borrowers. It abandoned the *third method of lending* since the 'core current assets' concept embedded in it was found to be difficult to become operational. But the group directly placed the borrowers under the *second method of lending* with a minimum current ratio of 1.33. The group also recommended a new *quarterly information system* (QIS) for monitoring and control of working capital finance by banks.

The MPBF system prevalent in India since 1975 earned rigidity in some aspects of bank finance and it was felt that during the post-liberalisation era it was falling short of meeting the changing requirements of the business, particularly the large corporates. In accordance with this, the RBI in 1997–98 withdrew mandatory provisions of MPBF system and associated current assets' holding norms. Banks were made free to develop their own system of lending and norms. In the mean time, RBI had also gradually replaced cash credit system by loan system. Presently, the ratio is 20:80 between cash credit and loan for borrowers who have working capital limits of Rs. 10 crore and above.

Although the MPBF system is no longer mandatory, it still acts as the basic framework within which banks have formulated their credit policies. For loans below Rs. 10 crore, MPBF system is mostly followed.

The RBI has also replaced mandatory requirement of formation of consortium beyond a threshold limit by voluntary consortium, multiple banking arrangement and loan syndication. The exposures of a commercial bank to an individual borrower or a 'Group' are limited respectively to 25 percent and 20 percent of the capital fund of the bank. Directed lending to various priority sectors at 40 percent of total credit still continues despite the recommendation of the Narasimhan Committee to bring down the exposure to 10 percent.

Profit and loss account and balance sheet drawn up by enterprises to conform to the requirements of *Companies Act* or *Income Tax Act* do not suit the need of a credit appraiser. Reserve Bank of India devised special formats, originally under Credit Authorisation Scheme, to suit banks' requirement, which, over a period of time, have come to be established as excellent instruments for assessing working capital need of an enterprise. These formats are explained with the help of a real-life company. Working capital requirement of this company has been assessed along with proposal for working capital restructuring by taking a total view of the business.

Among other short-term financial instruments, commercial paper (CP) has come to be established as a viable instrument to finance working capital requirement of well-rated companies. CP can now be issued for a period between seven days and a maximum upto one year. Minimum net worth requirement of a company issuing CPs has been reduced to Rs. 4 crore and the listing requirement has been removed to allow smaller companies to come to the market. However, the stand-by arrangement and automatic restoration of working capital limits by banks have been removed. This is retarding the growth of CP market in India.

Factoring for domestic receivables and forfaiting for export receivables, have already emerged in the Indian financial market, particularly to aid small scale business enterprises. But they are growing only slowly due to difficulty in obtaining credit information. Besides, providing finance, the factors, by providing specialised accounting and collection services at a cheaper cost, take away several worries of an entrepreneur who can now concentrate more on production and sales—the prime activities of an enterprise.

Inter-corporate deposits (ICDs) market provides opportunities to the companies having temporarily excess fund to invest in ICDs of companies who need short-term fund. The market, though easily accessible at market-determined rate of interest, is highly sensitive to failure by one or a few companies, as information passes very quickly in this market. Indian ICD market is a recent example. All regulations that govern the raising of public deposits by companies, apply to ICDs.

In 1999, Reserve Bank of India allowed banks, primary dealers and financial institutions to undertake *interest rate swaps* (IRS) and *forward rate agreements* (FRA) for their own balance sheet management and also for the benefit of corporates. These two financial instruments do not directly provide working capital finance to corporates, but they are useful tools to aid in working capital planning of the corporates. While IRSs allow a borrower with low creditworthiness to reduce the cost of credit by sharing the market tariff with a party of high market standing, forward rate agreements allow firms in general to hedge against the interest rate risks. Operational aspects of these new instruments and the RBI guidelines towards risk exposure have been discussed in this chapter.

ANNEXURE 1

Norms for Inventories and Receivables

(In months of holding)

Industry		Raw-materials (including stores and other items used in the process of manufacture)	Stock-in-process/Semi-finished goods	Finished goods	Receivables
1		2	3	4	5
1. Textiles (a) Cotton/ blended textile mills	(i)	Raw cotton 2.00 (Bombay and Ahmedabad areas) 3.00 (Eastern areas) 2.50 (Other than the above areas)	1.5 (Composite mills) 0.50 (Spinning mills) 0.75 (Processing mills for non-job work)	— 3.00 — (Combined for composite mills) — 2.50 — (Combined for processing mills for non-job work)	
	(ii)	Synthetic fibre/ yarn 1.50	0.50 (Processing mills for job work)	— 2.25 — (Combined for processing mills for job work)	
	(iii)	Cloth 0.50 (for processing mills and composite mills using grey cloth as raw material)			
	(iv)	Other raw materials 2.00			
(b) Silk and art silk mills	(i)	Synthetic yarn 1.00	0.50 (Weaving mills)	— 2.50 — (Combined for weaving mills)	
	(ii)	Cloth 0.50 (for processing mills)	0.75 (Processing/ composite mills for non-job-work)	— 2.50 — (Combined for processing/ composite mills)	
	(iii)	Other raw materials 2.00	0.50 (Processing/composite mills for job work)		

(Cont.)

1	2	3	4	5
(c) Woollen (i) Raw wool	1.25		— 4.00 —	
mills	3.00	(Weaving mills)	(Combined off-season: April-Sept.)	
(ii) Rags and waste	3.00		— 3.00 —	
			(Combined busy season: Oct.-March)	
(iii) Synthetic fibre/yarn	1.00			
(iv) Other raw materials	2.00			
(d) Man-made/	1.50	0.50	— 2.00 —	
synthetic fibre			(Combined)	
(e) Jute textiles	2.50	0.33	1.00 (for domestic sales)	
			1.50 (for exports)	
2. Rubber	2.00	0.50	— 2.00 —	
(a) Tyres	(Combined for imported and indigenous) 1.25 (additional for peak season only)			
(b) Other rubber	2.00	0.25	— 1.75 —	
products			(Combined)	
3. Fertilisers[1]				
(a) Nitrogenous	0.75 (Units near refinery)	Negligible	1.75 (Busy season: Oct.-Feb.)	1.50
	1.50 (Units away from refinery)		2.25 (Off-season March-Sept.)	1.75
(b) Single super-	2.00 (Units in	Negligible	1.50 (Busy season:	1.25
phosphate	(port areas)		Oct.-Feb.)	
	3.00 (Units away from port areas)		2.25 (Off-season: March-Sept.)	1.50
(c) Complex	2.00 (Units in	Negligible	1.75 (Busy season:	1.25
fertilisers	port areas)		Oct.-Feb.)	
	3.00 (Units away from port areas)		2.50 (Off-season: March-Sept.)	1.75

(Cont.)

1. In addition to the above norms, spares holding for 12 months consumption for all the three types of fertilizer industry were permitted.

1	2	3	4	5
4. Chemicals (other than fertilisers)				
(a) Drugs and pharma- ceuticals	2.75	0.75	1.50	1.50
(b) Pesticides, weedicides, etc.	2.75	0.75	2.00	1.50
(c) Paints and varnishes	2.25	0.50	1.50	2.00
(d) Petro chemicals	1.50	0.50	1.00	1.50
(e) Speciality chemicals[2]	1.50	0.75	1.50	2.00
(f) Inorganic chemicals (other than fertilisers)	2.00	0.50	1.00	2.00
(g) Dyes and dye inter- mediates (a) Imported/ canalised 2.50 (b) Indigenous/ non-canalised 2.25		1.00	— 3.50 — (Combined)	
(h) Basic industrial chemicals	2.75	0.25	1.00	1.75
(i) Essential oil- based	1.50	0.25	1.75	1.50
5. Paper				
(a) Imported				
(i) Pulp, waste paper, paper cutting, etc.	4.00	7 days	— 1.00 — 2.00 — (Combined level: 2 months)	
(ii) Felts and wires	6.00			
(b) Indigenous				
(i) Bamboo, wood bagasse, straw, etc.	6.00			(Cont.)

2. Speciality chemicals include (i) Adhesives, (ii) Rubber chemicals, (iii) Textile auxiliaries and miscellaneous speciality processing chemicals, (iv) Leather chemicals, (v) Foundry and smelting chemicals, (vi) Surface finishing and electroplating chemicals, (vii) Industrial explosives.

1	2	3	4	5
(ii) Waste paper, rags leads, etc.	3.00			
(iii) Chemicals	2.00			
(iv) Coal	2.00			
+ 2 months for mills using bagasse as raw material				
(v) Felts and wires	3.00			
6. Cement				
(a) Gypsum	2.25	0.50		— 2.50 — (Combined)
(b) Limestone	1.25			
(c) Coal	2.00			
(d) Packing materials	1.50			
7. Engineering				
(a) Four-wheelers and commercial vehicles	2.25	0.75		— 2.50 — (Combined)
(b) Two-wheelers and auto-rickshaws	2.25	0.75		— 2.50 — (Combined)
(c) Agricultural machinery	2.25	0.75		— 2.50 — (Combined)
(d) Ancillary industry	2.25	0.75		— 2.50 — (Combined)
(e) Machinery other than electrical machinery	2.75	1.50		— 3.50 — (Combined)
(f) Electrical machinery	2.75	1.25		— 3.50 — (Combined)
(g) Machine tools	2.75	1.25		— 3.50 — (Combined)
(h) Electrical cables, wires, etc.	2.00	0.75		— 2.75 — (Combined)
(i) Steel, tubes, pipes, nuts, bolts, bars, etc.	2.00	0.75		— 2.50 — (Combined)
(j) Bearings	3.00	1.00		— 3.00 — (Combined)
(k) Consumer durables	2.00	0.75		— 2.50 — (Combined)

(Cont.)

1	2	3	4	5
(l) Bulbs, fluorescent tubes and dry cell batteries	4.00 (imported)			
	2.50 (Indigenous)	0.50	— 3.00 — (Combined)	
(m) Storage batteries	4.00 (Imported)		— 3.00 — (Combined)	
	2.50 (Indigenous)	1.00		
(n) Fans	3.00 (Imported)	0.50	— 4.00 — (Combined: Off-season)	
	1.00 (Indigenous)		— 2.50 — (Combined: Busy season)	
(o) Other (excluding heavy engg. industries)[3]	2.25	0.75	— 2.50 —	
8. Glass	2.50	Nil	— 3.25 — (Combined)	
9. Ceramics				
(i) Insulators	3.00	1.00	— 3.50 — (Combined)	
(ii) Others	3.00	0.50	1.00	1.00
10. Breweries				
(a) Hops	3.00			
(b) Malt and others	2.00	0.50	0.75	1.00
11. Distillaries[4]	3.00	0.25	1.00	1.00
12. Leather manufacturers (processing of raw hides and skins into finished leather and leather products)	— 3.50 — (Combined)		— 2.00 — (Combined)	

(Cont.)

3. Heavy engineering would include supply of whole or substantial plants involving a long manufacturing period, e.g. sugar, cement, steel and textile plants. Inventories and receivables for heavy engineering industry would be assessed on the basis of past actuals.
4. If the allotment of molasses is on a monthly basis, the norms should be suitably reduced, say, to one month.

1	2	3	4	5
13. Food and food products:				
(a) Flour mills	2.00	—	0.25	2.00
(b) Biscuits and bakery products	1.00	0.10 (3 days)	0.50	0.50
(c) Vegetable and hydrogenated oils	1.00	Negligible	— 0.75 — (Combined)	
14. Diamond exporters[5]	— 2.5 — (Combined)		1.00	3.00
15. Power generation/ distribution industry	Coal 1.50 Fuel oil 2.00 Consumable spares (i) Indigenous 9.00 (ii) Imported 12.00	—	—	2.50
16. Bicycle tyres	1.75	0.50	— 3.00 — (Combined)	
17. Consumer electronics (e.g. radio receivers, tape recorders, television sets, etc.)	Imported 4.00 Indigenous 2.00	0.75	— 2.50 — (Combined)	
18. Communication equipments (e.g. telephones, tele-printers, railway signalling equipment, etc.)	Imported 4.00 Indigenous 3.00	1.50	— 3.50 — (Combined)	
19. Computers (including calculators)	Imported 4.00 Indigenous 3.00	1.25	— 4.00 — (Combined)	

(Cont.)

5. The combined norm for raw materials include work-in-process (to be computed based on so many months consumption of raw materials). Further, the combined norm of 3.5 months in respect of raw materials, work-in-process and finished goods is inclusive of the transit period of 15 days for receipt of rough diamond in the case of sight-holder; in the case of non-sight holders, the norm applicable should be reduced to 3 months (combined), within which normal processing cycle should be completed.

1	2	3	4	5
20. Control instruments and industrial electronics (e.g. electronic meters, oscilloscopes, testers, measuring instruments, etc.)	Imported 4.00 Indigenous 3.00	1.25	— 3.50 — (Combined)	
21. Electronic components, (e.g. resistors, capacitors, connectors, relays, etc.)	Imported 4 Indigenous 2	1.00	— 2.50 — (Combined)	
22. Aerospace and defence	Imported 4 Indigenous 3	1.25	— 3.50 — (Combined)	

Notes:

1. Raw materials are expressed as so many months' 'consumption'. They include stores and other items used in the process of manufacture.
2. (a) Stocks-in-process are expressed as so many months' 'cost of production'.
   (b) In individual cases, banks may deviate from the norm for stocks-in-process if they are satisfied that the actual process time involved in any particular unit, say, in view of the nature of production, past experience and technology employed, is more than the norm suggested.
3. (a) Finished goods and receivables are expressed as so many months' 'cost of sales', and 'sales', respectively. These figures represent only the average levels. Individual items of finished goods and receivables could exceed the indicated norms so long as the overall average level of finished goods and receivables does not exceed the amounts as determined in terms of the norm.
   (b) The norm prescribed for receivables relates only to inland sales on short-term basis (i.e. excluding receivables arising out of deferred payment sales and exports).
4. Stocks of spares should be classified as non-current assets. However, the projected levels of spares on the basis of past experience but not exceeding 12 months' consumption for imported items and 9 months' consumption for indigenous items, may be treated as current assets for the assessment of working capital requirements.

Drawee Bill System

The Chore group paid great emphasis on bill finance. The purchase and discount of bills by banks is already quite well known in the country for financing receivables, though its usage is still limited. For a long time, the RBI had been advising banks to replace cash credit against book debts by bill finance. As a part of this endeavour, the Chore group proposed a *drawees' bill system,* in addition to the existing *drawers' bill system* of financing.

The System Mechanics

The group recommended that, to begin with, banks must extend at least 50 percent of the cash credit limit against *raw materials* by way of drawee bills in case of units (both in the public and private sectors) whose aggregate working capital limits from the banking system was Rs. 50 lakh and above.

It is probable that for operational convenience, bills of large amounts could only be taken under the drawee bills system, and hence the system may tend to favour large suppliers only. Bills of small units which are generally of small amounts may not be taken under this system, and as a result, these units would suffer. This was against the objective of the group. It, therefore, suggested that large borrowers should maintain control accounts of sundry creditors in respect of small-scale industries and others separately, and report them in their quarterly information statement. A portion of the drawee bill limit should be utilised only for small-scale industries.

It was hoped that the drawee bill system would automatically ensure better inventory control of raw material purchases, and better discipline and planning consciousness among borrowers.

Under this system, the seller is assured of payment on a definite date. This would benefit small-scale industries, in particular, because they do not get payment of their bills from large and medium units promptly. Besides, when they obtain the acceptance of a bank, they can get the bill discounted promptly, and at a better rate.

The buyer also gets advantages from the system. As his bills are accepted by a bank, he can obtain purchases at a better rate of discount. Procurement of additional stocks also becomes easy for him for the same reason. He would also have no difficulty in satisfying the bank of the amount of unpaid goods with him, to the extent such goods are covered by bills.

The buyer's bank also runs no risk in accepting a drawee bill, as the goods covered by such a bill would form part of the stock charged to it in the cash credit account. The bank will also have ready information regarding paid or unpaid stocks of the borrower which form the security of the advance made to him at any time. The banker may not, therefore, depend solely on the borrower for this information.

For a seller's bank, its investment is safe because the bills are accepted by other banks. The bank can also discount such bills with other institutions as and when necessary.

Let us now see how a drawee bill system operates.

The system may operate in two ways: viz. Acceptance System and Bill Discounting System.

Acceptance System

In this system, a supplier (S), draws a bill on a buyer (B), which is accepted by the buyer's banker (BB). S may now discount this bill with his banker and get funds promptly. On the due date, BB debits the amount of the bill to B's account, and remits the proceeds to S's banker. The goods covered under the bill may be taken as security from the date the bill is accepted by BB, if an alternative arrangement is not made.

Under this system, B would give authority to his banker BB to accept bills drawn under this scheme. It is also possible for B to have an arrangement by which S may draw bills on BB directly, as 'BB-A/c B', upto a certain amount. BB, who is also maintaining the cash credit account of the buyer, will maintain an *indirect liability ledger* for bills accepted. In the stock statements submitted by the borrower, the amount of goods purchased on credit under the acceptance limit will be shown separately. While calculating the drawing power in the cash credit account of the borrower, the outstanding liability in respect of acceptance of bills (as available from the indirect liability ledger) will be excluded, and earmarked for making payment of the bills accepted by the bank on their due dates. This earmarking can be done under two different methods illustrated below.

(Rs. in lakh)

Limit sanctioned against raw materials	200
50% of the limit earmarked for drawee bill	100
Amount available for drawings against raw materials	100

Assuming that there are no other limits, and also no other current assets, the above limit might have been fixed on the basis of the following calculations:

(Rs. in lakh)

Gross working capital represented by stock	400
Less: Trade creditors	100
Working capital gap	300
Less: 25% of current assets as NWC (margin)	100
Permissible bank finance or limit sanctioned	200

Hence, classification of the stock will be as under:

Stock paid for	300	
Stock unpaid for	100	(represented by creditors)
Total stock	400	

Normally, when the party submits stock statements, effective stock for calculation of drawing power will be only Rs. 300 lakh. Assuming the margin on stock being 33.33 percent, the drawing power available will be Rs. 200 lakh which is equal to the limit. If the drawee bill limit is carved out of the total limit, this margin on stock for calculation of drawing power will have to be increased, as we shall see now.

Method I

Suppose 50 percent of the limit, i.e. Rs. 100 lakh (which cannot exceed the amount of sundry creditors for raw materials) is granted by way of a drawee bill limit, and all bills aggregating Rs. 100 lakh are accepted by the bank, drawing power will be calculated and earmarked in the following manner:

	(Rs. in lakh)
Stock paid for	300
Stocks represented by accepted bills	100
Total stocks available	400
Less: 50% margin	200
Drawing power available	200
Less: Drawing power earmarked for accepted bill	100
Drawing power available for cash credit	100

Now if the cash credit limit is drawn in full, the bank's books of records will show Rs. 100 lakh in the indirect liability ledger as bills accepted, and Rs. 100 lakh in the cash credit account of the party. When all bills are paid on the due dates, and assuming no other creditors are contracted, the indirect liability ledger will show a nil balance, and the debit balance in the cash credit account will go up to Rs. 200 lakh; the paid-up stocks now being Rs. 400 lakh, drawing power will be Rs. 200 lakh. There will, therefore, be no irregularity in the account. This is Method I proposed by the Chore group.

Criticism

It may be seen that if the drawee bill limit had not been there, the borrower would have been able to draw upto Rs. 200 lakh against paid-up stocks of Rs. 300 lakh with 33.33 percent margin as shown earlier. But because of the drawee bill limit being carved out of the total limit, he is able to draw only Rs. 100 lakh against the same stock, which means that for the time being, at least, he is asked to provide for a higher margin, i.e. 66.67 percent in this case. It is likely that the borrower may resist it on the ground that even if the bank had not accepted the bills of his creditors, he would have commanded the same length of credit from his suppliers. Moreover, his bargaining power over the creditors is to some extent impaired. Against this, it can be argued that when the bills drawn on the borrower are accepted by his banker, or discounted (as we shall see later), it is done on the full value without keeping any margin. This counterbalances his higher margin on paid-up stocks. Moreover, because a bank is accepting the bills, the borrower's goodwill with the creditors increases, which enables him to contract more creditors at a bargain price. After all, he has to pay his creditors from realisation of his current assets or from his cash credit account only. What the bank is doing is just entering as an agent with its full financial weight for the benefit of both, with a little more emphasis on creditors, who may be small.

Method II

Under Method II, drawing power will be calculated as below:

Paid-up stocks	Rs. 300 lakh
Drawing power at the rate of 50%	Rs. 150 lakh

This method may be liked by the borrower for reasons mentioned earlier. But assuming now that the bank has accepted bills for Rs. 100 lakh represented by unpaid stocks/creditors, the account will become irregular when these bills are paid by the bank on their due dates by debiting the cash credit account of the borrower, because the debit balance in the cash credit account will now become Rs. 250 lakh against a drawing power of Rs. 200 lakh (50 percent of Rs. 400 lakh). The irregularity is to the extent of drawing power of Rs. 100 lakh worth of goods now taken into stock after payment of the bills. This is due to the fact that bills are debited to the account with their full value. In order to regularise the account, the borrower must now be asked to bring in the amount of margin money on bills. In order to avoid this difficulty, the banker would obviously prefer the first method.

Bill Discounting System

Under this system, the buyer's banker (BB) will discount the bill and remit the proceeds to the creditors of the buyer. The goods covered under the bill are straightaway taken as security by the banker as cover against bills discounted, which appear separately in the *drawee bill discounting ledger.* The rate of interest will be the same as that applicable in case of cash credit against hypothecation/pledge of stocks. Fixation of limits and calculation of drawing power will be the same as in the Acceptance System. The bank should suitably earmark the drawing power available against stocks after providing the prescribed margin. On the due dates, discounted bills are debited to the borrower's cash credit account, and the drawing power recalculated in the same manner as in the Acceptance System.

In this system, creditors of the borrower are most favoured, but the borrower may object to this system on the ground that he is called upon to pay interest and discounting charges for the unexpired period of the credit otherwise available to him free of cost from his creditors.

The drawee bill system has the excellent potential of infusing a bill culture among both the upper and lower ends of the market. It can also solve to a large extent the perennial problem of delayed payment suffered by small- and medium-scale enterprises, and hence, of banks, because these small borrowers would approach the banks only with intermittent requests for higher limits, which, in effect, are implicitly enjoyed by large enterprises. But unfortunately, the system is yet to be implemented with as much vigour as is expected of bankers. There has been initial resistance from large borrowers, but it could have been overcome by willing bankers. The system is straightforward, and it can be implemented with little effort.

Classifications of Current Assets and Liabilities

Tandon Committee had made a departure from the norms for the classification of current assets and current liabilities prescribed by the Companies Act, and recommended that this be made as per the usually accepted approach of bankers. The committee had asked bankers to follow the method prescribed by the Reserve Bank of India under the Credit Authorisation Scheme (since replaced by the Credit Monitoring Arrangement). The recommended classifications, as amended by the RBI from time to time are given below.

CURRENT ASSETS

   (i)   Cash and bank balances.
   (ii) Investments: (see Note 1 below).
         (a)   Government and other Trustee Securities (other than for long-term purposes, such as Sinking Fund and Gratuity Fund).
         (b)   Fixed deposits with banks.
   (iii) Receivables arising out of sales other than deferred receivables (including bills purchased and discounted by bankers (see Note 2 below).
   (iv) Installments of deferred receivables due within one year.
   (v)   Raw materials and components used in the process of manufacture, including those in transit (see Note 3 below).
   (vi) Stock-in-process, including semi-finished goods (see Note 4 below).
   (vii) Finished goods, including goods in transit.
  (viii) Other consumable spares (see Note 3 below).
   (ix) Advance payment of tax.
   (x)   Pre-paid expenses.
   (xi) Advances for purchase of raw materials, components and consumable stores.
   (xii) Amount receivable from contracted sales of fixed assets during the next 12 months.

[Deposits kept with public bodies for normal business operations, i.e. security deposits, earnest deposits kept by construction companies, tender deposits, etc. whether maturing within the normal operating cycle of one year or not, be classified as non-current assets.]

Notes:

   1.   Investments in shares and advances to other firms/companies, not connected with the business of the borrowing enterprise be excluded from current assets.

   2.   Export receivables may be included in the total current assets for arriving at the maximum permissible bank finance, but the minimum stipulated

net working capital (i.e. 25 percent of total current assets under the second method of lending) may be reckoned after excluding the quantum of export receivables from the total current assets. Within the MPBF thus arrived at, banks may continue the existing practice of fixing suitable need-based post-shipment/ pre-shipment credit facilities, taking into account the borrower's export performance, export orders and other relevant factors where necessary.

3. 'Dead Inventory', i.e. slow moving or obsolete items, should not be classified as current assets. Projected level of spares on the basis of past experience but not exceeding 12 months consumption for imported items and 9 months consumption for indigenous items, be treated as current assets for the purpose of assessment of working capital requirements.

4. While analysing the current assets and current liabilities of construction companies and turnkey projects for purpose of determining the borrower's contribution under the second method, the net work-in-progress, i.e. gross work-in-progress less advance/progress payments outstanding, be taken into consideration.

CURRENT LIABILITIES

(i) Short-term borrowings, including bills purchased and discounted from:
   (a) Banks.
   (b) Others.
(ii) Unsecured loans.
(iii) Public deposits maturing within one year.
(iv) Sundry creditors (trade) for raw materials and consumable stores and spares.
(v) Interest and other charges accrued but not due for payment.
(vi) Advance/progress payment from customers (see Note 4 under current assets, and also Note 3 below).
(vii) Deposits from dealers, selling agents, etc. (see Note 2 below).
(viii) Installments of term loans, deferred payment credits, debentures, redeemable preference shares and long-term deposits, payable within one year. (The Reserve Bank of India has since advised that installments of term loans falling due within one year shall not form part of current liabilities.)
(ix) Statutory liabilities:
   (a) Provident funds dues.
   (b) Provision for taxation (see Note 1 below).
   (c) Sales tax, excise, etc. (see Note 4 below).
   (d) Obligations towards workers considered as statutory.
   (e) Others (to be specified).
(x) Miscellaneous current liabilities:
   (a) Dividends (see Note 1 below).
   (b) Liabilities for expenses.
   (c) Gratuity payable within one year.
   (d) Other provisions.
   (e) Any other payments due within 12 months.

Notes:

1. In cases where specific provisions have not been made for these liabilities, and the liabilities will eventually be paid out of general reserves, estimated amounts should be shown as current liabilities.

2. These deposits may be treated as term liabilities irrespective of their tenure, if such deposits are accepted to be repayable only when the dealership/agency is terminated. Banks should satisfy themselves about the fulfilment of this condition before treating them as term liabilities. If necessary, they should verify the terms of agreement between the concerned borrower and the dealers/selling agents. The deposits which do not satisfy the above condition should continue to be classified as current liabilities.

3. These advances should continue to be classified as current liabilities. However, in case of certain enterprises, e.g. manufacturers of automobiles, and two-wheelers who accept deposits while booking orders for new vehicles and are required, in terms of regulations framed by the Government, to earmark a part of such amount for investment in certain approved securities, etc., the benefit of netting is allowed to the extent of such investment, and only the balance amount is to be classified as a current liability.

4. Previously, disputed liabilities for payment of excise duty, income tax, sales tax, customs duty and electricity charges were treated as current liabilities even where the liability for payment of these was shown as a contingent liability in the balance sheet, and no provision was made therefore in the final accounts. As this method of treatment of disputed liabilities (not provided for and shown as contingent liabilities) as part of current liabilities resulted in reduced levels of permissible bank finance, the RBI reviewed the position in the light of representations made by the industry, and since advised that the above disputed liabilities shown as contingent liabilities, or by way of notes to the balance sheet, would not now be treated as part of current liabilities for calculating the permissible bank finance, unless they had been collected or provided for in the account of the borrower, and certified as such by the statutory auditor of the company.

ASSESSMENT OF WORKING CAPITAL REQUIREMENTS: INSTRUCTIONS FOR FILLING UP THE APPRAISAL FORMS

Form I

(i) Information should be given separately in respect of each of the working capital credit facilities, viz. cash credit/overdrafts, export packing credit, working capital team loan, bills purchased and discounted, both inland and exports, etc. Details of quasi-credit facilities, viz. letters of credit, co-acceptances, guarantees, etc. should also be indicated. Data relating to term loans/DPGs including foreign currency loans as also foreign currency loans not backed by DPGs issued by banks in India should be shown separately under subhead 'B'. The exchange rate applied to arrive at the outstanding under existing foreign currency loans should be indicated.

(ii) In the case of a multidivision company, if separate credit limits are sanctioned for the different divisions, the data should be shown division-wise. Division-wise sub-totals should also be indicated.

(iii) Details of credit facilities, if any, availed of by the borrower from non-consortium banks should be indicated separately. Details of deposit accounts, if any, maintained with other non-consortium banks should also be indicated.

(iv) Maximum and minimum utilisation of the limits during the past 12 months and outstanding balances as on a recent date should only be given—month-wise figures need not be indicated.

(v) In case the existing sanctioned limits have remained or are largely unutilised, the reasons for the same should be given.

Forms II, III and IV

(i) In case the audited balance sheet and profit and loss account for the previous accounting year are not available, estimated/provisional data for that year may be indicated in Forms II, III and IV.

(ii) The assumptions on which the projections, viz. sales turnover, profitability, build-up of inventory and receivables, other current assets, current liabilities, etc. have been based, should be indicated.

(iii) In the case of a multidivision company, division-wise data should be indicated separately for each division, on Forms II and IV. In such cases, Form III/(analysis of balance sheet) should encompass data for the company as a whole. Wherever possible, separate data for each division may also be indicated in Form III.

(iv) The valuation of sales-projections should be based on the current ruling prices. Similarly, the valuation of various inputs of cost of sales in the projections should also be based on current costs. It should be ensured that price escalations are not built into the projections. Where the projections relating to production show wide variations in comparison with the past trend, information in regard to the physical quantity of goods produced/to be produced, their unit price, etc. should also be furnished. Where the number of items manufactured is large, the information may be classified under three or four broad categories.

(v) The projected inventory and receivables shown in Form IV should normally be in conformity with the norms and/or the past trends/levels usually maintained by the borrower, whichever are lower. In case the level of projected inventory/receivables is higher than the norms/past levels, the reasons thereof should be explained. In such cases, a definite programme for conforming to the stipulated norms as prescribed by the bank should also be indicated.

(vi) Spares should be classified as non-current assets. However, the projected levels of spares on the basis of past experience but not exceeding 12 months consumption for imported items and 9 months consumption for indigenous items may be treated as current assets for purpose of assessment of working capital requirements.

(vii) The projected level of current assets other than inventory and receivables, and that of current liabilities should also compare with the past trends and prevailing market conditions. In case there are significant/abnormal variations, the position should be explained in respect of each item of variation.

(viii) The basis of valuation of current assets should be in accordance with that adopted for a statutory balance sheet. The estimates of current liabilities and recording of income and expenses should also be on the same basis as that adopted for the statutory financial statements.

(ix) The classification of current assets and current liabilities should be done as per the usually accepted approach of banks, and not as per definitions in the *Companies Act*. The guidelines indicated in this regard by the RBI should also be kept in view.

(x) In case, specific provisions have not been made for known liabilities like dividend payable, tax payable, etc., estimates thereof should be made for eventual payment during the year, and the amount, though not provided for, should be shown as current liabilities.

(xi) Details of term liabilities raised during the year (debentures, term loans, deferred payment credits, long-term deposits etc.) should be furnished separately.

(xii) Bills purchased and discounted (though shown as contingent liability in the balance sheet) should be included under items 28(i) and (ii) of Form III and 5 and 6 of Form IV.

(xiii) Outstanding liabilities in respect of credit purchases under *usance letter of credit/co-acceptance* facility from the banks should be shown under item 3/Form III (Sundry creditors (trade)).

(xiv) In case of borrowers having seasonal activity where the working capital limits are required to be sanctioned based on peak level requirements (not coinciding with the balance sheet date) the corresponding data for the previous/preceding year(s) should also be indicated separately on Form IV. In such cases, the corresponding build-up of the balance sheet position as on the date of peak requirement should also be indicated.

(xv) If the canalized items form a significant part of the raw material inventory, this may be shown separately.

(xvi) Income received from and the expenses paid to or in respect of, subsidiary companies/affiliates in respect of sales/purchases, should be indicated separately by way of footnote(s) to Form II.

(xvii) If the company is a subsidiary, the extent and nature of interest the holding company is having, and also its name, should be furnished as a footnote to Form III.

(xviii) If the company is a holding company, the extent and nature of its interest in subsidiary companies and their names should be furnished as a footnote to Form III.

(xix) Three copies of the last audited balance sheet should be submitted along with the appraisal data.

Form V

(i) In all cases other than sick/weak units, the computation of permissible bank finance should be done as per the Second Method of Lending.

(ii) In other cases where appraisal of working capital requirements is sought to be done under the First Method of Lending, specific reasons thereof should be furnished.

Form VI

(i) Increase of various items of inventory which is disproportionate to percentage rise in sales turnover should be explained in detail separately.

(ii) Similarly, a decrease in current liabilities which is not commensurate with the percentage rise or fall in sales turnover should be explained in detail separately.

(iii) In case the increase in working capital gap is not commensurate with the increase in net sales, the position should be explained in detail separately.

(iv) Item 7 (net surplus/deficit) and item 8 (increase/decrease in bank borrowings) would be algebraically opposite figures, and these should agree with each other.

CHAPTER 8

Channel System, Logistics and Channel Financing

Slowly, He entered in them and they in Him
The three became One and One three

INTRODUCTION

In Chapter 1, we have presented pipeline theory of working capital as a system of integrating productive and distributive functions of an enterprise. Although the concept evolved in the early 1980s, it took its time to dislodge the Accountant's static concept of working capital embedded in net working capital or net operating cycle theory. With the emergence of supply chain management greater attention is now given to pipeline theory of working capital. The pipeline perspective has now shifted the attention of managers towards viewing the production and distribution functions not as independent units but as participants in a coordinated system for maximising efficiency of the channel to optimise (maximise) customer satisfaction.

THE CHANNEL SYSTEM

In order to understand channel arrangement as it has evolved now, let us recall the pipeline depicted in Chapter 1 in a somewhat modified form as in Figure 8.1.

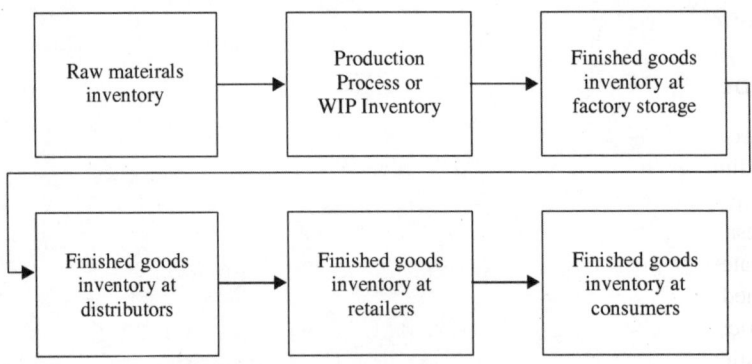

Figure 8.1 Pipeline movement of inventories.

The boxes in Figure 8.1 represent functional units and the lines between the boxes indicate the movement of inventory from one place to the other (some of the boxes or the lines may be owned by the enterprise). Earlier, different functional units were viewed as loosely linked distinct entities with different objectives and strategies, which were often at variance with each other. Specific activities of these units were managed as end in themselves, rather than as contributing to the overall performance of the channel. The logistical operations represented by long arrows in Figure 8.1 were similarly performed purely on functional basis. As against this, channel management takes a holistic view of the entire channel by integrating the channel partners to a common objective of customer satisfaction. The concept of partnership has changed the entire dimension of working capital management. In place of loosely joined units in the pipeline we now have partners having clearly defined stakes in the successful operation of the entire channel. The stakes of the channel members may not be equal, but it is understood that though they are independent units, the efficiency of the channel depends upon cooperation among them.

LOGISTICS

In fact, channel management is a combination of logistical management and relationship management. Logistics involves integration of information about inventory position at different strategic locations, transportation of goods, warehousing arrangement, material handling, packaging and packing of goods in accordance with customers' requirements. Operating responsibility of logistics is the geographical positioning of raw materials, work-in-progress and finished goods at the lowest cost possible.[1] The performance cycle of logistical operation integrates temporal and spatial aspects of logistical operations linking procurement, manufacturing, support and physical distribution. Logistics add value only when inventory is correctly positioned to facilitate manufacturing and sales. When inventories are misplaced or do not reach in time, logistics instead of adding value eats into the vitals of the enterprise. In other words, when costs are incurred without realising the purposes (manufacturing and sales) for which these were originally intended, the costs do not enter into value but are wasted.

In-bound and Out-bound Logistics

In case of manufacturing, logistics starts from in-bound movement of materials including parts and spares from suppliers to the point of production. For a trading organisation like wholesaler or retailer, it is the movement of products for resale to respective warehouse(s). In-bound logistics ends after adding value to material-inputs at different stages of manufacturing process ending with finished goods (or, products ready for delivery in case of traders) to out-bound logistics, which is popularly known as supply chain or marketing channel. Logistical management aims at integrating the in-bound logistics with the out-

---

1. Bowersox, Donald. J. and Closs, David. J., *Logistical Management: The Integrated Supply Chain Process,* Tata McGraw-Hill Publishing Company Ltd., New Delhi, 2000.

bound logistics. The common objective that runs through the entire chain is customer satisfaction. In fact, with the market becoming more and more competitive the need for logistical integration has arisen to satisfy customers' need.

Interdependence

In-bound logistics deals in procuring materials on the basis of purchase orders and moving them to designated places. Three parties are involved in this exercise namely, vendors, transporters and the manufacturing organisation. One would say that the manufacturing organisation is central to this as the process is triggered with the manufacturing unit generating the purchase orders. But under integrated logistics management all the parties are of equal importance. Logistics is a cross-functional activity both within and outside the enterprise; all the functionaries are part of the planning process. The ruling philosophy behind it is the recognition of interdependence among channel functionaries.

Normally, generation of a purchase order is triggered by the requirement of finished goods at the end of the pipeline, as in Figure 8.1, which in turn depends on the marketing plan of the enterprise. When the raw materials supplier participates in evolving the marketing strategy of the enterprise both the parties would try to fit into each other's strategy. The resultant effect is the evolvement of a common strategy. Thus the materials supplier would know in advance the exact time and types of materials to be supplied to different locations, which in turn will require him to engage in similar exercise with his own suppliers. As the process is repeated for all other industries, the entire economy ultimately comes under an integrated supply chain management, where generation of purchase orders ultimately becomes redundant; only variations, if any, are informed well in advance to enable parties involved to take appropriate steps to maintain the integrity of the channel arrangement.

Transportation of materials from the sourcing points to the different locations operationalises the procurement plan. Hence, integration of the transport function is of utmost importance. This is ensured similarly by making the transport organisation, whether within the enterprise or outside it, involved in the planning process along with materials vendors as described above.

In-bound logistics does not end with placing the input materials at different locations; it is also responsible for carriage of materials from stores to the points of production, and moving work-in-progress inventories from one process to the other which may be stationed at different locations within the factory premises or outside it; the objective being to cut down idle time between processes.

Out-bound logistics takes over from the point finished goods are delivered to factory storage. It is responsible for smooth functioning of the distribution channel, which also includes after-sales service and reverse logistics like return and recalls. Logistical objectives of output management are to minimize, (1) cost of transportation, and (2) cost of carrying inventory without being out of stock.

Economics of Transportation

Railways

Different modes of transportation namely, railways, roadways, river and seaways, pipeline, airways, have now become highly competitive and customer-oriented. The railways, which used to hold almost monopolistic position before World War II due to wide network connecting almost all cities, are facing stiff competition from road transportation as road systems expanded vastly during the post-World War II period. In developing countries like India, roads, highways and bridge construction, though started somewhat late, have gained tremendous momentum during the past three decades. Improvement in automobile technology has also added to this momentum by reducing cost of operations and increasing fuel efficiency. Although railway systems in these countries are predominantly government-controlled, these are also found to be aggressively reorienting themselves on commercial lines with a customer-face due to increasing competition from road transportation. These days, railways are providing intermodal transport by acquiring or entering alliance with motor carriers that provide removable container-service. Goods are now picked up from consignor's doorstep, put on railway wagons and delivered at the consignee's end. Several other transportation technology and innovations like double-decker, unit train (an entire train carrying only one product) etc. have increased the ability of railways to satisfy needs of diverse customer-segments. Increasing electrification of railway tracks and advanced train engines are also reducing the variable costs of operations. But fixed costs of railways are still very high. Hence, on long-haul transport total cost is lowest as compared to short distance haulage.

Roadways

As indicated above, road transportation by motor carriers has expanded tremendously during the recent decades. The strength of this mode lies in its door-to-door operating flexibility and manoeuvrability to ply on almost all types of roadways. Also, a truckload could carry much smaller quantity of goods than a wagonload. In contrast to railways, motor transportation has low fixed overheads (as maintenance and upkeep of roads are State's responsibility) but high variable costs (owing to high, fuel costs, wages, safety measures, wear and tear, etc.). Hence, on long haul total cost of motor carriers is higher than that of railways.

Waterways

While railways and road transports are primarily national, and in some cases, intercontinental, so also the internal riverways. Seaways are truly international. Import and export trades take place mostly through seaways. This is the oldest mode of transport in international trade and it continues to hold the dominant position even today. Water transport is supplemented by railway and road transport on both ends. Despite improvement in engine and shipbuilding technology, the water transportation, continues to be slowest among all modes of transportation, but it is compensated by its capacity to move very large shipments and the low cost of operations, both fixed and variable.

Airways

Air transport is gaining ground slowly as a mode of cargo transport; particularly in high value segment where speed is of essence. Parcel and courier service operators, many of whom have dedicated aircrafts for this purpose, also extensively use this mode of transport. During recent times, the service is extended to comparatively large parcels. Highly perishable commodities both in respect of its physical characteristics like, ornamental fish and high value live or fresh fish, and of market characteristics like high fashion items or gift items during festival seasons, are most suitable for air transportation. However, cost of air transport is highest among all the modes of transport due to high-variable cost of operations but it can be traded off with high speed, and increasing cost of warehousing and inventory storage, as in other modes.

Pipelines

Pipeline is a specialised mode of transport for bulk liquids like, petroleum and natural gas. This is also being used for transporting liquid chemicals and coal and non-coal slurry. A line is dedicated to carrying only a particular item for which it is laid out and hence, it lacks flexibility. Pipelines are operated on 24-hour basis at high speed. Operating variable cost of pipelines is very low, though fixed cost is very high.

Choice of Appropriate Modes of Transport

It is clear from the above discussion that a logistical manager needs to consider both the physical and market characteristics of the materials to be moved, which shall determine the choice of appropriate set of transport modes. A cost-benefit analysis will then follow to finally arrive at the right kind of mode(s) from among the initial set. He should recognise that a particular mode of transport for movement of raw materials and other inputs might not be suitable for movement of finished products made out of it. In Table 8.1, we have differentiated different modes of transport in terms of several parameters.

Different attributes, as mentioned in Table 8.1, are explained below:[2]

Table 8.1 Characteristics of Different Modes of Transport

Mode	Flexibility	Speed	Connectivity	Reliability	Capacity	Frequency	Cost
Railways	Medium	Medium	Medium	Medium	High	Low	Low
Roadways	High	Medium	High	Medium	Medium	High	Medium
Waterways/ seaways	High	Low	Low	Medium	High	Medium	Low
Airways	Low	High	Medium	Low	Low	Medium	High
Pipelines	Low	Low	Medium	High	Low	High	Medium

2. Some of these characteristics and attributes are taken from Bowersox and Closs, *ibid.*

Attribute of a carrier	Definition
Speed	Time taken between the time goods are handed over to the carrier and their delivery to the consignee. In a logistical sense one should consider total time taken and not necessarily the absolute speed of the carrier. For example, in some cases of inter-city transfers, road transport, particularly by contract carrier, is superior to even air transport as the time taken, in processing, scheduling and loading while goods remain in the terminal, is much less for the former.
Customer connectivity	This refers to the ability of the carrier to reach the place of origin of the shipment and the destination desired by the consignee. Apparently, motor carriers may have the highest customer-connectivity but railroad can equally match it by owning a fleet of its own or making an alliance with road transport operators.
Reliability	This refers to the discipline of a transport mode to adhere to the agreed or scheduled loading and delivery time of cargo. This is, perhaps the most important logistical requirements of channel management that is focused on customer satisfaction, the important aspect of which is timely delivery. However, reliability of a carrier is often affected by conditions, which are beyond its control like weather in case of water transport, worsening of road conditions for motor transport etc. Alternative arrangement should be in place to take care of such eventuality and the cost should be factored in.
Capacity	Generally, this refers to the ability of a transport mode to handle different kinds of cargo and load. For example, railways and seaways take almost any kind of cargo; their load capacity is also among the highest.
Frequency	This refers to the number of movements offered by a transport mode. Frequency of pipelines is highest—virtually continuous—among all the modes of transport followed by road transport.
Cost	Total cost of a transport operator includes fixed and variable costs. For some operators fixed cost is high but variable cost is low, e.g. pipelines. Opposite is true for road transport operators. It follows, therefore, that cheaper rate is available for long haulage, e.g. railways and pipelines though, shippers or road transport operators may not be able to offer significant discount on long distance despatch because their variable cost is high.

Quality of different attributes ascribed to a particular mode of transport, as shown in Table 8.1, are subjective in nature. One is often tempted to put them on a scale of say, 1–5 and calculate total scores of individual modes of transport. We have avoided such scoring, as we fear that it might lead to wrong decision because despite a high total score, a particular mode may not be suitable for a particular cargo. An example is road transport, which may have a high composite score, but it is not suitable for international trade. Even domestically, road transport may not be suitable for transport of minerals because of limited space and high cost. What we have done in Table 8.1 is to give an idea as to the relative merit of a transport mode in terms of various attributes. We should mention at the same time that any of these transport modes, which has weakness in one or two attributes, could improve upon its total performance by combining with another mode which is strong in those attributes. A logistic manager needs to consider a transport system in its totality. Different modes can be connected to form an integrated system of transport. An integrated channel system works best with an integrated transport system. For example, seaway transport which is low on customer connectivity (due to the fact that it can pick up and deliver cargos only from docks) can enhance its performance by combining with road transport whether by owning a fleet or by entering into an alliance with other road transport operators. Presently, various transport operators are found to be moving along these lines. They are realising that earning by way of demurrage charges is in fact a disservice to the users of the transport services. Part of this endeavour is coming from the needs of enterprise channel logistics to bring down the costs of logistical operations and carrying cost of inventories. The latter is possible only when inventories stay for the minimum time in transport lines, and at different locations.

Safety Stocks

Manufacturing managers face increasing pressure to reduce inventories across the supply chain. However, in complex supply chains, it is not always obvious where to hold safety stocks to minimise inventory-holding costs while at the same time provide a high level of service to the consumer.[3] A least cost logistical design should, therefore, emanate from locational proximity of warehouses both to the production (raw materials) and customers (finished products), and safety stock policies at both ends. A certain level of safety stock calculated on the basis of combined probability of demand and lead-time uncertainty as discussed in Chapter 3, should be capable of ensuring full satisfaction. However, it is found that incremental service resulting from additional locations diminishes and the cost associated with each new location increases. Thus, the service pay-off for each new facility is incrementally less. Besides, as service is increased the safety stock required to achieve each equal increment of service availability will also increase. It has been observed that

---

3. Grares, S.C. and S.P., Willems, "Optimizing Strategic Safety Stock Placement in Supply Chains,". *Manufacturing and Service Operations Management,* Vol. 2(1), pp. 68–83, 2000.

safety stock inventories of the total enterprise system increases with the addition of warehouses. This results from the inability to aggregate the uncertainty across a large market area. Hence, separate safety stocks must accommodate all local variations.[4] These important facts are often forgotten by enterprises in their overoptimistic service commitments, which results in a vicious circle of meeting high customer satisfaction at high cost followed by erratic performance resulting in still higher cost.

Least Cost Warehousing Network

It is necessary, therefore, to focus on a trade-off between the number of locations and the total costs associated with it. Designing of a least cost logistical system is based on the following hypotheses:[5]

1. So long as the combined cost of warehousing and local delivery is equal to or less than the combined cost of shipping direct to consumers, setting up of additional warehouses is economically justified provided sufficient shipment volume is available to cover the fixed cost of each warehouse facility.

2. Total transportation cost decreases as consolidation locations are added to the logistical network. But if facilities are expanded beyond the maximum consolidation point, the total cost increases. Maximum consolidation point is reached at the lowest point of the transportation cost curve vis-à-vis number of warehouse facilities.

3. The base level stock within a logistical system is determined by the manufacturing and transportation lot sizes, which do not change with the increase in the number of warehouses. That is, the base stock determination is independent of the number of warehouses included in the logistical system.

4. The average in-transit inventory for the total system drops as new warehouses are added because of reduction in days required to service customers

5. Average safety stock of the system as a whole increases as warehouses are added. This increase in safety stock emanates from an inability to aggregate the uncertainty across a large market area. Separate safety stocks must take care of all variations in local demand. However, given the same demand and customer service goals, average inventory for the entire system increases at a decreasing rate as the average inventory is the safety stock plus half of the order quantity plus transit inventory, the latter diminishing with the increase in the number of warehouses as in (4) above.

On the basis of the above hypotheses Bowersox and Closs[6] captured the interactions of relevant logistical costs of a warehouse-network in graphical

---

4. Bowersox and Closs (2000), *ibid.*
5. *Ibid.*
6. *Ibid.*

form and showed that the least cost solution lies not in the least transportation cost nor in the least inventory cost but in the least total cost of the network. It is important to note here that the least cost solution ignores additional revenues generated from each new location. As each additional location increases the level of customer satisfaction, there is a likelihood of additional sales generation from each such location and hence, the sales of the enterprise as a whole will rise. So long as the revenue curve remains above the total cost curve, an enterprise may add additional locations beyond the least cost point, other things remaining the same. One cannot also ignore the 'delighting effect' on customers (by providing whatever services necessary and at whatever time), and the rise of premium customer-base by 'word of mouth'[7]. Additional sales from increased warehousing support and profitability thereof can, therefore, be both in the general and premium segments. An acceptable logistical strategy must generate adequate sales at least to break even with the additional cost of warehousing.

Conflict Resolution under Channel Management

There often arises a conflict between number of warehouses and the desired level of customer service. The following example highlights such a conflict and offers a resolution under channel management.

Suppose, the existing least cost logistical system of an enterprise with seven warehouses is capable of providing service to at least 85 percent of its customers at 90 percent inventory availability within 60 hours of receiving an order. The marketing department has proposed that if service capability is increased to the point where 90 percent of customers are serviced by 95 percent of inventory availability, delivered within twenty-four hours of order receipt, it is possible to generate additional sales of Rs. 50 lakh of which premium category sales will be at least 20 percent.

Previously, when channel system was not installed, such a proposal could have led to a conflict situation between marketing department and finance department. If the finance department was to reject the proposal on the basis of sound logic, the marketing department would pick up the issue and highlight that it was the finance department which always throws a spanner whenever they sought support to make a breakthrough in sales, even when records might show that in 90 percent of cases the finance department had accepted the marketing department's recommendations! But when the philosophy of channel management is ingrained in an enterprise the situation would be handled differently. Under the channel system the channel members concerned with it will examine the proposal; they shall also be responsible for implementing the decision. The channel members are, departments of marketing, logistical design and analysis, cost management and finance from within the enterprise, and transport operators from outside the enterprise. Each one has the common

---

7. Schlesinger, Leonard. A. and Heskett, James. L, "The Service-driven Service Company", *Harvard Business Review*, Vol. 69(5), September–October, 1991.

objective of increasing the profitability of the enterprise, which shall ultimately be beneficial for all of them.

Suppose now, the logistical design and analysis department and cost management department provide an estimate that the least cost network capable of achieving the new service standards would be eleven warehouses. This will increase logistical cost by Rs. 7.5 lakh p.a. Finance department estimates that premium category sales will give a PBT return of 25 percent on sales. For non-premium segment standard PBT of 10 percent will apply. The following calculations are now made:

Additional sales: Rs. 50 lakh of which 20% or Rs. 10 lakh from premium category

Profitability (PBT):		*Rs. in lakh*
(a) 10% on Rs. 40 lakh	=	4.00
(b) 25% on Rs. 10 lakh	=	2.50
Additional return	=	6.50
Additional expenses	=	7.50
Net loss	=	1.00

It is clear that the proposal, if implemented, would not add any value to the channel. In fact, break-even point of sales is Rs. 57.69 lakh as shown below:

$$0.10 \times 0.80x + 0.25 \times 0.20 x = \text{Rs. } 7.5 \text{ lakh,}$$

where x is the required break-even sales.

or, $\qquad 0.08x + 0.05x = \text{Rs. } 7.5 \text{ lakh}$

or, $\qquad x = 7.5/0.13 = \text{Rs. } 57.69 \text{ lakh}$

The proposal, as it stands, results in less than break-even sales. However, if the marketing department can convince the other participating members of channel that it can increase additional sales by say, Rs. 60 lakh, the proposal can still be acceptable.

RELATIONSHIP MANAGEMENT

The next pillar of a successful channel arrangement is the relationship management. It is not that the relationship management was not there before the advent of channel concept. No enterprise could have existed without managing its relations with different stakeholders like, suppliers, buyers, transport operators, financial institutions etc. But such relationship was managed not as an organised effort; it was considered part of the responsibility of functional managers. The new thrust behind relationship management, in the context of successful functioning of channel operation, is the realisation that no matter how well a system is designed, it may not work unless all the participating units/organisations cooperate in planning and executing channel objectives. The emphasis on cooperation and participation has changed the adversarial and power-driven approach of the earlier years. The underlying philosophy is that all parties engaged in the channel will be better off if they participate in the enterprise planning process, share information and engage in joint problem solving for improving the overall efficiency of the channel system. In order for that to happen several critical attributes must be present.[8]

1. All the partners of the channel must be strong and positive towards developing the channel relationship. Strength lies in the capability of execution and the positive attitude refers to the desire and commitment to perform.
2. Interdependence among the members of the channel is a key to the success of channel system. The members must realise that they need each other to achieve each other's goals. None of them can accomplish alone what both together can.
3. The partners must be prepared to devote financial and other resources in each other to demonstrate their respective stakes in the channel system. This is the ultimate test of commitment.
4. Communication among channel members must be reasonably open to make the relationship work. Information sharing relating to objective and goals, possible conflict situations, technical data, identification of emerging trouble spots and changing market conditions should be done in an open environment, but with the assurance that none of the channel members would abuse such information for selfish advantage or for undermining each other. This is the test of trust among the channel members.
5. The channel system must allow the partners to develop linkages and find ways of operating with people at different levels of the organisation.
6. Finally, channel partnership should be institutionalised with clear responsibilities and the decision process, as if it is a single organisation.

Adjustment and Sacrifice

It is a well-established fact that for any relationship to work—be it at individual level or at organisational level—it must be based on trust, communication, and the faith that it will work. But what is not so openly talked about is the preparedness of the members to adjust and sacrifice for the long-term success of the relationship. Adjustment calls for accommodating each other's point of view to build a consensus, while sacrifice calls for taking on a real loss unto oneself to pull out another from a difficult situation. For example, when a road transport organisation in a channel system faces a wildcat strike, the easier alternative is to switch to other transporters, but a channel relationship demands that the enterprise stands by its member knowing fully well that it might cause temporary dislocations in the market and a consequent loss to the enterprise. One approach is to give the responsibility to the same transport organisation to find alternative mode(s) of transport, both the parties sharing the additional

---

8. Kanter, Rosabeth, Moss, "Collaborative Advantage: The Art of Alliance", *Harvard Business Review,* Vol. 72(4), pp. 100, July–August, 1994.

cost so incurred. This is how solidarity is built among channel members. If the enterprise does not stand by another member in times of crisis, it creates a disgruntled member in the channel. A channel system cannot function effectively with a disgruntled member, as the negative feeling soon spreads among other members. We must emphasise here that though the objective of the channel relationship is mutual benefit, it calls for mutual sacrifice as well to reap the benefits in the long run. Kumar[9] gives an example of how the concept of mutual benefit and mutual sacrifice work in real-life situation:

A manufacturer of kitchen products in supply chain relationship with a large retail chain had introduced a product with innovative features. After a few months the manufacturer-supplier realised that the cost of the product exceeded the price at which it made deliveries to the retail chain. In the meantime, the product had picked up good sales owing to the new features and low price at buyers' hands. The manufacturer brought the problem before the retail chain. The managers of the retail chain and that of the supplier got together and evolved a value engineering that reduced the cost of the product. Not only this, the retail chain also reduced its margin on this product to leave sufficient profit to the manufacturer. In the long run both the participants benefited.

CHANNEL MEMBERSHIP

Membership of a channel can be broadly divided into three groups:

Primary members:
(i) Manufacturing, extracting and producing (agriculture)
(ii) Wholesalers or distributors
(iii) Retailers

Functional members:
(i) Assembly
(ii) Warehousing
(iii) Transportation
(iv) Merchandising

Support members:
(i) Informational
(ii) Financial
(iii) Publicity and advertising
(iv) Insurance
(v) Research, consulting and advisory services

Specialisation

The above list is only indicative. One member may combine more than one function. For example, warehousing may be done by the manufacturing enterprise or by the distributors/retailers in the area of their operations. But over the years specialisation has become fundamental driver of distribution

---

9. Kumar, N., "The Power of Trust in Manufacturer-retailer Relationships", Harvard Business Review, November–December, 1996, pp. 92–106.

efficiency. More and more services, which were once integral to the manufacturing organisation, are being handed over to specialised agencies and then integrated back to the enterprise under channel management. The economic basis of the growth of specialised service organisations is the economies of scale, which lowers down the cost and increases the service efficiency. It is now well recognised that when a firm specialises in the performance of a specific function and, for a number of organisations, it develops the scale and efficiency to achieve operational economies. This also reduces the risk of the operating organisation through diversification. For example, a wholesaler/distributor or even retailer can minimise the risk by being members of several channels. This diversification helps the organisation not only to hedge risk by working for many but also to offer the final consumers a wide range of manufacturers of the same product.

Rising Power of Retailers

On the other side, a manufacturer with limited product lines may run the risk of finding himself captive to the capabilities of a limited number of supply chain members. The diversification advantage may not be available to him. Therefore, he has to be very choosey about selecting channel members. Commonality of organisation culture among the channel participants becomes very important in such a situation. The channel members having most at stake (here, the manufacturer) has to take more active roles and responsibilities in channel management. But the power of a channel member may not be commensurate with the stake he has with the channel management. Over the years (and more so, in this particular case) there has been a general shift of power to retailers. Principal reasons behind this shift are:

1. Increasing difficulties and high cost of brand building by a manufacturer, particularly in small and medium scale (SME) segment have increased the dependence on retailers. Despite the general shift towards 'pull' situation, there always exists a 'push' situation in retail outlets—whether large or small—as customers seek information from and give information to the retailers on various product lines of different manufacturers. The old adage that a retailer acts more as an agent of his customers than that of the manufacturer still holds. Though the process is rather slow, retailers can successfully build a brand virtually at no cost to the manufacturer.

2. As the retailers are always in face-to-face contact with the customers, they are the first to know about the performance of a product, changing habits, tastes etc. of customers. In the absence of a feedback mechanism these vital information may not be available to the manufacturer as fast as it should be to enable him to adjust production to the demand of the market. Under a channel structure this feedback mechanism is fully exploited.

3. Retailers are generally consolidated within a region. They know the peculiarities of the market in the region in which they operate. These

peculiarities range from cultural and religious variations to food habits and 'ideas and beliefs' about what is healthy and not healthy. Retailers are in the most advantageous position to identify the peculiarities, which may be at variance with the 'average' behaviour of consumers at the national or international level.

4. Retailers being in close contact with the consumers can not only identify problems of a particular product but can also come out with innovative solutions. In many cases, the retailers first articulate the innovations that are spearheaded by the manufacturing and marketing later.

It is necessary here to put a cautionary note that the rising power of the retail organisation during the past two and a half decades in Europe and the United States is a backlash of over exploitation of retailers by the manufacturing organisations. Channel management must recognise that the exploiting power by one stage is always at the expense of other stage(s) of the channel. The disgruntled participants also find out ways to resist such exploitation. This is already happening. Well-known manufacturers, unable to get along with exploitative power play by retail organisations, have opened shops of their own to access customers directly. Sony Corporation is one such example. Internet has also opened vast possibilities for manufacturers to sell directly to the customers. Exploitive power play is against the philosophy of channel system. The economic objective behind a channel arrangement is to increase the profit of the entire channel and, it is possible only when the profit is equitably distributed among the channel members. Equity demands commitments, coordinated efforts, sharing of strategic information and finally, faith and mutual trusts among the channel members.

CHANNEL FINANCING

The outline of channel arrangement presented above makes it clear that it seeks high-level of functional integration. In an integrated system transmission effect is very fast, which is also the major objective of the system. But it also holds both for a good event and a bad event. A re-look at the basic channel system presented in Figure 8.1 will make it clear. Suppose, debtors realisation at the end of the channel is delayed beyond the probabilistic estimate, as agreed by all channel members, then the retailer may not be able to place further order. This will dislocate all other functions integrated with it affecting ultimately the production of the manufacturing organisation. The difficulty with the channel system is that though it is designed to serve consumers more efficiently, final consumers themselves are mostly outside the channel system. They are independent units having financial problems of their own. In order to see that the basic channel system works, channel financing should be designed to provide solutions to financial problems faced at any stage of the channel arrangement. Channel financing attempts to relate to the channel system to ensure its smooth functioning

Conventional Financing vs Channel Financing

Channel financing differs from conventional financing in the sense that under the latter the financing banks provide working capital finance to different units of the pipeline independent of each other. For example, when a bank finances the manufacturer it is not generally concerned with the financials of the suppliers or of the distributors except examining the behaviour of certain turnover ratios as discussed in the last chapter. In the absence of channel arrangement manufacturers are also not overtly concerned about the finances of the suppliers or the distributors; they rather try to squeeze out as much credit as possible from the suppliers and provide as low credit as possible to the distributors. But under a channel arrangement the channel members as well as the channel financiers take a total view of the channel and its financial flows to ensure that commercial transactions are not held up due to financial bottlenecks. A channel financier recognises the fact that when the financial position of say, the suppliers or distributors deteriorates, the production which is the life blood of the channel, is hampered due to delayed or non-supply of materials by the suppliers on the one hand and the delayed or non-placement of orders by the dealers on the other. When that happens, liquidity of the entire channel is affected very quickly. Snowballing effect on a highly integrated system is very fast. Ultimately, the financing bank suffers as the accounts turns from doubtful to bad.

It is not that the methods and instruments that are being used today under the head channel financing are very new. These have been in existence for quite sometime. What has changed during the recent time is to treat them as a package to solve financial problems of different stages of the channel arrangement in a unified manner.

Buyer's Credit

Financing of inventories for manufacturers or traders is as old as banking. Book-debt financing came later and became very popular when its instrumentalised form, bills of exchange, came to be statutorily recognised during the middle of the nineteenth century. Subsequent innovation came up in the twentieth century. Industrial Finance Corporation of the United Kingdom introduced Buyer's credit immediately after the World War II with the objective of rebuilding the war-ravaged industries by providing credit to buyers of machinery and instruments of British origin. This form of credit is still very popular among EXIM banks of different countries.

Buyer's credit, however, is no longer limited to financing purchase of machinery and instruments. It is now used to finance purchase of bulk raw materials including petroleum products through what is known as Drawee Bills Financing. Advantages of buyer's credit are two-fold:

1. It makes available cash to the seller immediately.

2. It shifts the risk of non-payment by the buyer to the financing institution. The financing institution assesses the creditworthiness of the buyer. As these institutions are specialised agencies with proper

appraisal system in place and having offices across the world, these are in a better position to assess the creditworthiness of prospective buyers at a much lower cost.

Large manufacturing companies, particularly in automobile sector, have created financing arms of their own or in collaboration with banks or financial institutions to provide finance for purchase of products manufactured by the parent company. Financing is done either in the form of direct buyer's credit or discounting of receivables of the authorised dealers. Mahendra Finance, Maruti Citicorp Finance fall in the first category and L & T Finance comes in the second category. As compared to banks, which also extend similar credit, delivery of finance by these agencies is more efficient primarily because it is just a single portfolio for the latter whereas, it is one of many portfolios for the former. However, to take on competition banks have also set up separate departments or subsidiaries dedicated to provide what they claim, 'integrated commercial and financial solutions to the supply and distribution channel of their client by providing short-term lending against qualified receivables'.[10] These banks also discount payables to support suppliers' relationship with their clients. Citibank and Bank of India are two such examples.

During the recent time a number of private financing agencies have come up in the arena of channel financing that provide finance ranging from buyer's credit to discounting of receivables. Some of them are also engaged in factoring and forfaiting as discussed in Chapters 3 and 7.

Despite the development of specialised agencies for providing finance to different stages of supply and distribution channel, channel financing is yet to be integrated with it. Efforts are still disjointed and restricted to certain stages of the channel only. Hardly, a 'channel financier' is found to take a total view of the channel's financial requirement, make commitments towards it and put in coordinated efforts for smooth flow of finance through the channel.

Problems of SMEs and the Credit Channel Effect

Despite so much development in lending technology banks continue to be conventional. This is truer for SMEs who, unlike large corporates, do not have easy access to debt market. In the absence of an integrated channel financing, these bank-dependent borrowers suffer most due to 'credit crunch effect'; which is defined as scaling back of loans by banks in the event of monetary tightening. As monetary squeeze [for example, raising the cash reserve ratio (CRR)] increases the level of interest even for risk-free assets, and banks are unable to increase deposit rates proportionately owing to pressure for building-up low cost reserves, there occurs a deposit drain due to depositors reshuffling their portfolio for high yielding assets. This reduces the loan supply by banks.[11]

---

10. Taken from Citibank's brochure on Channel Financing.
11. Gertler, M. and S. Gilchrist, "Monetary Policy, Business Cycles and the Behaviour of Small Manufacturing Firms". *Quarterly Journal of Economics*, Vol. 109, pp. 309–340, 1994.

The SMEs are disproportionately affected in such a situation as the squeeze triggers a flight to quality in bank lending. More specifically, banks may respond to monetary restriction not only by generally restricting credit but also by adopting more stringent lending policies for those customers who are perceived to be less creditworthy.[12] This is also called *credit channel effect.*

It has been found that there is a strong correlation between relative size of the lending bank and that of the borrowing firm. That is, small (or financially weak) firms tend to borrow from small banks and large firms from large banks.[13] It has also been observed that small banks, rather than large ones, are more likely to be hit in the event of a monetary squeeze due to small capital base and thus, the ability of small banks to extend loans is reduced substantially during the crisis.[14] Hence, in the ultimate analysis, the credit channel effect affects the SMEs disproportionately. The impact is larger because these firms have low- level of tolerance owing to low net worth.

The 'credit channel effect' also increases the cost of borrowing for SME sector when negative shocks hit an economy. Ding et al.[15], while examining the 'credit channel effect' in East Asian crisis found that in Korea the crisis caused sharp increases in the spread between corporate and government bond yields spearheading a worsening of general risk premium (the balance sheet effect) particularly, for bank-dependent borrowers (SMEs). The impact of the interest rate spread was much larger for SMEs as these are generally over-leveraged and suffer from information opacity from bank's point of view. Due to rationing of credit and substantial rise in the cost of borrowing, the operation ratio (output/ productive capacity) of SMEs of Korea fell sharply below the threshold level of 80 percent during the crisis.[16]

The findings of various studies discussed above indicate that although credit crunch (which has now become a regular occurrence in any economy) or external shocks lowers down the availability of credit in general, the impact is disproportionately high for small and medium scale businesses. The 'credit channel effect' on an integrated channel system becomes severe for industries where majority of suppliers and/or dealers come from SME segment. And this is the case with most industries.

12. Bernake, B.S., M. Gertler, and S. Gilchrist, "The Flight to Quality and the Financial Accelerator", *Review of Economics and Statistics*, Vol. 78, pp. 1–15, 1998.
13. Berger, A.N., A.K., Kashyap, and J.M. Scalise, "The Transformation of US Banking Industry: What a Long, Strange Trip Its been". *Bookings Papers on Economic Activity*, Vol. 2, pp. 205–239, 1995.
14. Kashyap, A.K. and J.C. Stein, *What Do a Million Banks Have to Say About Transmission Mechanism of Monetary Policy*? NBER Working Paper No. 6056, 1997.
15. Ding, W.,J. Domac, and G. Ferri, *Is There a Credit Crunch Effect in East Asia?* Policy Research Working Paper No. 1959, World Bank, Washington D.C., 1998.
16. Goldstein, M., *The Asian Financial Crisis: Causes, Cures and Systemic Implications*, Policy Analysis in International Economics, Institute for International Economics, Washington D.C., 1998.

Inventory Flow—The Ultimate Liquidity of the Channel

The operational objective of the channel system is to ensure uninterrupted movement of inventory through the channel. This is the ultimate liquidity of the system. An examination of the pipeline discussed earlier will reveal that it is the inventory that moves through different stages. While logistics ensure physical movement of inventory from one stage to the other, channel financing makes it possible to happen by ensuring payment for inventory along the stages, as without this the former will not take place. Besides pipeline inventories that flow through the system, we also have discrete inventories that gather up alongside every stage to take care of fluctuations in demand and production. These are safety stocks, as discussed in Chapter 4. As average level of safety stock never leaves the system, it should be treated as permanent investment of the channel. Which stage of the channel would be responsible for making this investment? One suggestion could be that as the safety stocks are accrued at different stages, the investment should be decentralised to these stages. The other suggestion is that the channel participant who has the most stakes say, for example, the manufacturer of the principal product or the large retail chain organisation, should finance this. It is important that the channel participants should join together to decide on this issue before the channel arrangement is put in place. It is not relevant where the safety stocks are held; it may be at warehouses strategically located at different places, but the ownership and control of safety stocks shall vest in the party financing it, though the possession may be with other parties. Such an arrangement is not difficult to achieve within a channel framework, which is based on mutual trusts and commitments. There should, however, be explicit agreement to this effect among the concerned participants.

Financial Integration of the Channel System

Financial prudence demands that as safety stocks are permanent in nature, these should be financed from long-term resources of the channel participants. In fact, banks ensure it by insisting on a margin on current assets before deciding permissible bank finance for working capital. For financing the flow of inventories through the channel we need to determine the point(s) of financing that integrate the channel financially. It is necessary here to take a total view of the channel and track the movement of inventories through different stages as shown in Table 8.2.

In Figure 8.2, we have captured the movement of financial assets and liabilities as inventories move from one stage to the other.

It may be seen from Figure 8.2 that inventory moves from one stage to the other after adding value. For example, inventory acquired in stage 2 (manufacturer) at a cost of Rs. 20 is transferred to stage 3 after adding value of Rs. 5. After successive addition of value in stages the inventory reaches the consumer at Rs. 35. While the cost of inventory received by a stage is reflected in its payables (financial liability), value addition is reflected in its receivables (financial assets).

Table 8.2 Movement of Inventories Through the Channel System

Participants	Receipt and disposal	Relevant financial assets/ liabilities
Materials/component suppliers (manufacturers of intermediate goods, minerals and farm products)	(a) Receives from raw materials supplier (miners, farmers etc.) (b) Manufactures and/or makes despatches to principal manufacturer	(a) Raw materials Inventories—payables (b) Materials inventories— receivables
Principal manufacturer	(a) Receives from materials supplier (b) Manufactures and makes despatches to dealers	(a) Materials inventories— payables (b) Finished goods inventories—receivables
Dealer (wholesaler, distributor)	(a) Receives finished goods from principal manufacturer (b) Processes the goods and makes despatches to retailers	(a) Finished goods inventories—payables (b) Finished goods inventories (processed) —receivables
Retailer	(a) Receives finished goods from dealer (b) Makes despatches to final consumers	(a) Inventories—payables (b) Inventories—receivables
Final consumer[17]	Receives finished goods from retailer	Inventories—payables

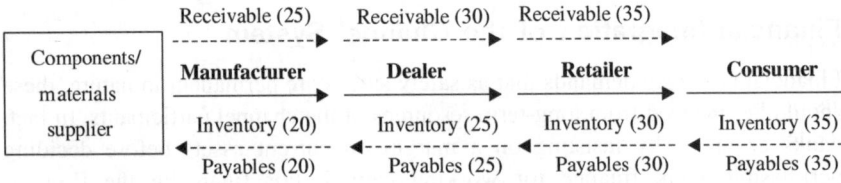

Figure 8.2 Channel movement of inventories and creation of financial liabilities and assets.

Receivables Financing vs Payables Financing

The prevalent approach of lending organisations generally rests on financing receivables of the transferor (seller). The assumption is that once the receivables of the transferor are financed the payables will be paid off from the proceeds. While conceptually the assumption is not untrue, what happens in real-life situation is that when cash comes in payables are not immediately paid off, particularly when suppliers are small enterprises. Payable-period is much longer than the receivable-period, which usually is the case with SMEs. The

---

17. Final consumer may or may not be an official channel participant.

delay in making payment to suppliers is one of the principal reasons for delay or default in making deliveries by the suppliers. As SMEs are mostly bank-dependent borrowers, who may not always get extended credit from banks, the situation worsens during the period of credit rationing or other external shocks that we have discussed earlier. The lower the economic power of an enterprise, the higher the credit period demanded of it and the lower is the availability of bank finance.

A channel management initiative aimed at ensuring uninterrupted movement of inventories through the channel should, therefore, concentrate on payables financing rather than receivables financing. It is not the chicken-egg problem. Payables come first; receivables are created only thereafter. When payables are financed directly chances of default or delay in supplies would be less. A look at Table 8.2 and Figure 8.2 would show that payable of one stage is the receivable of the earlier stage. The mechanism through which the financial instrument is created to support this transaction is by the former stage (drawer) drawing bills on the latter stage (drawee) on despatch of inventories, which when accepted by the latter becomes a Bill of Exchange. The bill contains, among other things, the credit terms agreed between the seller and the buyer. Conventionally, bank finances the drawer (seller/supplier) of the earlier stage by discounting the bills receivable and demand payment from the drawee (buyer in the latter stage) on expiry of the credit terms but, as mentioned earlier, it does not automatically ensure payment of drawer's own payables (suppliers), that is, where he is the drawee. A true channel financer oriented to the philosophy of the channel system would rather finance the drawees than the drawers to ensure uninterrupted supply of inventories through the channel. This arrangement also benefits the SME suppliers who now get immediate cash through discounting of bills without depending on the buying enterprise for payment. There is a credit enhancement of the suppliers' bills when these are accepted by a large corporate buyer (which mostly is the case). Banks should also feel comfortable to discount such bills, more so because they can rediscount these bills or sell these as securitised assets in the Bill Market. Banks can also offer a better rate on such bills the benefit of which is enjoyed by the suppliers.

Drawee Bills Scheme

The genesis of the above arrangement is contained in Chore Group's recommendations, though not exactly in the context of channel financing[18]. The group was concerned with growing complaints of small suppliers about inordinate delay in getting payment of their supplies, particularly from large companies. In order to ease their problems the group recommended that banks should earmark a part of the credit limit of the borrower to be utilised for discounting small suppliers' bills. The mechanics of the scheme, which came to be known as Drawee Bill system, are discussed in Chapter 7 and its Annexure 2. The scheme could not be operationalised fully owing to some operational

---

18. Reserve Bank of India, *Report of the Working Group to Review the System of Cash Credit,* headed by K.B. Chore, Bombay, August 1979.

problems but mostly due to the resistance of large companies who 'feared impairment of control over the suppliers'. However, in the present context Drawee Bill Scheme has the potential of integrating the channel system with channel financing, as we shall see now.

We take the example of the principal product manufacturer and dealer as in stages 2 and 3 of Figure 8.2 to explain the scheme. Assuming that all supplies and sales are on credit the scheme can be simplified to work as in Table 8.3 which depicts the inventory flow, and the actions of the principal manufacturer and the channel banker.

Corresponding journal entries in the books of account of the Manufacturer and the Dealer are shown below:

BOOKS OF ACCOUNTS OF THE MANUFACTURER

1. Materials purchase a/c   Dr.   Rs. 20
   To
       Bills payable a/c   Rs. 20
   (Being materials purchased on credit
   from sundry suppliers)
2. Bills payable a/c   Dr.   Rs. 20
   To
       Drawee bills discounted a/c   Rs. 20
   [Being the bills receivables of the
   suppliers (bills payable by us) discounted
   by bank on our account]
3. Bills receivable a/c   Dr.   Rs. 25
   To
       Sales a/c   Rs. 25
   (Being goods sold on credit to sundry buyers)
4. Bills receivable discounted a/c   Dr.   Rs. 25
   To
       Bills receivable a/c   Rs. 25
   [Being bills payable by the dealers
   (bills receivable by us) discounted by bank]
5. Bank (SD) a/c   Dr.   Rs. 25
   To
       Bills receivable discounted a/c   Rs. 25
   [Being the proceeds received in the
   specially designated (SD) a/c]
6. Drawee bills discounted a/c   Dr.   Rs. 20
   Main bank a/c   Dr.   Rs. 5
   To
       Bank (SD) a/c   Rs. 25
   (Being adjusting entries on receipt of proceeds
   in the specially designated a/c)

Table 8.3 Inventory Flow, Conversion and Financial Actions of Channel Member and Channel Banker under Drawee Bill Scheme

Inventory flow at manufacturer	Amount (Rs.)	Financial actions of manufacturer	Financial instruments	Bank's action (financing)	Bank's action (adjusting)
Materials inventory from suppliers (payable in one month)	20	A. Accepts bills drawn by materials suppliers	A. Bills payable by the manufacturer Rs. 20	A. Bank sets up drawee bill limit of Rs. 20 for the manufacturer —discounts the bills receivable of the supplier (bills payable by the manufacturer) by debiting the drawee bill account of the manufacturer and credits the proceeds to a specially designated account of the supplier. The bank now takes materials inventory of the manufacturer as security.	A. On due date of the discounted bills, bank debits Rs. 20 to the specially designated account of the manufacturer (where an amount of Rs. 25 has already come in as in (B) of the earlier column) and credits the drawee bill account of the manufacturer which will now show a nil balance. The balance remaining in the specially designated account (Rs. 5) is now transferred to the main account of the manufacturer.
Manufacturing expenses	2				
Finished goods	22				
Profit	3				
Receivables from dealer (one month)	25	B. Draws bill on the dealer	B. Bills payable by the dealer Rs. 25	B. Bank sets up drawee bill limit of Rs. 25 for the dealer—discounts the bills receivable of the manufacturer (bills payables by the dealer) by debiting the drawee bill account of the dealer and credits the proceeds to a specially designated account of the manufacturer. The bank now takes finished goods inventory of the dealer as security.	B. On due date of the discounted bills, bank debits Rs. 25 to the specially designated account of the dealer (where an amount of Rs. 30 has already come similarly from the retailer) and credits the drawee bill account of the dealer which will now show nil balance. The balance remaining in the specially designated account (Rs. 5) is now transferred to the main account of the dealer.

BOOKS OF ACCOUNTS OF THE DEALER

1. Finished goods purchase a/c   Dr.   Rs. 25
   To
       Bills payable a/c   Rs. 25
       (Being goods purchased on credit
       from manufacturer)
2. Bills payable a/c   Dr.   Rs. 25
   To
       Drawee bills discounted a/c   Rs. 25
       [Being the bills receivables of the
       manufacturer (bills payable by us) discounted
       by bank on our account]
3. Bills receivable a/c   Dr.   Rs. 30
   To
       Sales a/c   Rs. 30
       (Being goods sold on credit to sundry retailers)
4. Bills receivable discounted a/c   Dr.   Rs. 30
   To
       Bills receivable a/c   Rs. 30
       [Being bills payable by the retailers
       (bills receivable by us) discounted by bank]
5. Bank (SD) a/c   Dr.   Rs. 30
   To
       Bills receivable discounted a/c   Rs. 30
       [Being the proceeds received in the
       specially designated (SD) a/c]
6. Drawee bills discounted a/c   Dr.   Rs. 25
      Main bank a/c   Dr.   Rs. 5
   To
       Bank (SD) a/c   Rs. 30
       (Being adjusting entries on receipt of proceeds
       in the specially designated a/c)

     The scheme presented in Table 8.3 reveals that the channel banker, in fact, takes over the responsibility of ensuring that the suppliers of the earlier stage always receive cash on delivery of materials to the next stage so as to enable them to make uninterrupted supply of materials through every stage of channel system. The specially designated account at each stage also ensures automatic adjustment of outstanding in the drawee bill account on due date without any interference. Suitable agreement to that effect should be formalised between the channel participants and the channel banker. Although all through it is the bills receivables that are discounted, in fact, it is the holder of bills payables who gets the financing. Under conventional system bills receivables financing is forward moving; under the drawee bills scheme of channel financing it is backward financing, the instrument remaining same.

SUMMARY

During the past two decades channel management has evolved as a new discipline. This is the operational side of the pipeline theory of working capital discussed in Chapter 1. Earlier, different functional units of a pipeline were viewed as loosely linked distinct entities with different objectives and strategies, which were often, at variance with each other. As against this, channel management takes a total view of the pipeline as an integrated system with the common objectives of customer satisfaction and raising the profitability of the entire channel. The basic philosophy of the channel system is complete faith and commitment among the channel partners.

Channel management is a combination of logistics and relationship management. Operational objectives of logistics are minimisation of cost of transport and holding of inventories without being out of stock. The performance cycle of logistical operation integrates temporal and spatial aspects of logistics linking procurement, manufacturing, support functions and physical distribution. Logistics add value only when inventories are correctly placed to facilitate manufacturing and marketing.

The logistical manager while making a choice of a set of different modes of transport should try to match the physical and market characteristics of products to be moved with the attributes of different modes of transport as are shown in Table 8.1.

There often arises a conflict between number of warehouses and the desired level of customer service. It is generally observed that while safety stocks (and their carrying costs) increase with the number of warehouses, the service pay-off for each new facility is incrementally less. The least cost logistical design aims at resolving this conflict by providing an optimal solution between total costs and number of warehouses. However, if revenues generated from additional facilities are more than the total costs, setting up of new facilities can still be considered.

The next pillar of channel system is relationship management, which is based on the realisation that no matter how well a system is designed it may not work unless all channel members cooperate in planning and executing the channel objectives. The underlying philosophy is that all parties will be better off if they participate in the enterprise planning process, share information and engage in joint problem solving, as in a group. For channel relationship to work it must be based on trust, open communication, and readiness for mutual sacrifice. No channel member shall make profit at the expense of other(s). Exploitive power play is against the philosophy of relationship management.

Despite the advent of a number of specialised agencies to provide finance to different stages of a channel system, channel financing is yet to be fully integrated with the channel system. Banks still prefer to operate independently with individual units of a channel rather than take a total view of the credit requirement of the entire channel. As a result, suppliers are often squeezed and not paid on time, which dislocates supply of inventories to the channel system. The credit channel effect of a credit crunch is also severe on a channel system because it is highly integrated. Worst suffers are the SMEs, which happen to be the dominant suppliers to industries but having limited economic strength to withstand a crisis. In situations like this inventory flow, which is the true liquidity of the channel, is disturbed slowing down the channel movement or stopping it altogether. A channel financier should, therefore, focus on ensuring availability of quick cash to the suppliers of materials to enable them to maintain the inventory flow to the channel. Drawee bills scheme tuned towards channel financing has the potential to integrate the channel system with the channel banker. Operational aspects of such a scheme are discussed at the end of the chapter.

Author Index

Subject Index